Several Selections from the S...  ... Referencing)

Baker, Susan W. "Biological Influences on Human Sex and Gender." Stimson and Person 175-91.

Leifer, Myra. "Pregnancy." Stimson and Person 212-23.

Stimpson, Catherine R., and Ethel Spector Person, eds. <u>Women: Sex and Sexuality</u>. Chicago: U of Chicago P, 1980.

An Article in an Encyclopedia or Other Reference

A well-known reference work:

Harmon, Mamie. "Folk Arts." <u>The New Encyclopaedia Britannica: Macropaedia</u>. 15th ed. 2002.

"Morrison, Toni." <u>Who's Who in America</u>. 57th ed. 2003.

"Yodel." <u>The Shorter Oxford English Dictionary</u>. 1973.

A lesser-known reference work:

Hames, Raymond. "Yanomamö." <u>South America</u>. Vol. 7 of <u>Encyclopedia of World Cultures</u>. Boston: Hall, 1994.

A Preface, Introduction, Foreword, or Afterword

Bradford, Barbara Taylor. Foreword. <u>Forever Amber</u>. By Kathleen Winsor. 1944. Chicago: Chicago Review, 2000.

PERIODICALS AND NEWSPAPERS

An Article in a Magazine

Block, Toddi Gutner. "Riding the Waves." <u>Forbes</u> 11 Sept. 1995: 182+.

Jellinek, George. "Record Collecting: Hobby or Obsession?" <u>Opera News</u> Feb. 2003: 85.

Van Zile, Susan. "Grammar That'll Move You!" <u>Instructor</u> Jan./Feb. 2003: 32-34.

An Article in a Journal

Pages numbered continuously throughout the volume:

Larter, Raima. "Understanding Complexity in Biophysical Chemistry." <u>Journal of Physical Chemistry</u> 107 (2003): 415-29.

Each issue begins on page 1:

Mitchell, W. J. T. "The Surplus Value of Images." <u>Mosaic</u> 35.3 (2002): 1-23.

An Article in a Newspaper

Argetsinger, Amy. "Lobbying Gets Old College Try." <u>Washington Post</u> 13 Jan. 2003: B2.

Leonhardt, David. "Defining the Rich in the World's Wealthiest Nation." <u>New York Times</u> 12 Jan. 2003, natl. ed.: sec. 4: 1+.

Ranii, David. "New AIDS Drug Is Step Closer to Approval." <u>News and Observer</u> [Raleigh] 7 Nov. 1995: 1D+.

An Editorial

"Six Sigma Schools." Editorial. <u>Wall Street Journal</u> 15 Jan. 2003: A10.

A Letter to the Editor

Rothschild, Michelle. Letter. <u>Kiplinger's</u> Jan. 2003: 14.

A Review

Flanagan, Caitlin. "Get a Job." Rev. of <u>What Should I Do with My Life?</u>, by Po Bronson. <u>New York Times Book Review</u> 12 Jan. 2003: 4.

Glenn, Kenny. Rev. of <u>Man on the Moon</u> [film]. <u>Premiere</u> Jan. 2000: 20.

Rev. of <u>Going to the Territory</u>, by Ralph Ellison. <u>Atlantic</u> Aug. 1986: 91.

Stearns, David Patrick. Rev. of <u>The Well-Tempered Clavier</u>, by J. S. Bach [CD]. Angela Hewitt, piano. <u>Stereophile</u> Dec. 1999: 173+.

OTHER SOURCES

An Audio Recording

Dickinson, Dee. <u>Creating the Future: Perspectives on Educational Change</u>. Audiocassette. Minneapolis: Accelerated Learning Systems, 1991.

Mahler, Gustav. Symphony No. 7. Michael Tilson Thomas, cond. London Symphony Orch. CD. RCA Victor, 1999.

Shuster, George N. Jacket notes. <u>The Poetry of Gerard Manley Hopkins</u>. LP. Caedmon, n.d.

A Film, DVD, or Video Recording

A theatrical video:

<u>25th Hour</u>. Dir. Spike Lee. Screenplay by David Benioff. Touchstone, 2003.

<u>All About Eve</u>. Dir. Joseph L. Mankiewicz. Perf. Bette Davis, Anne Baxter, and George Sanders. Fox, 1950. DVD. Studio Classics, 2003.

A nontheatrical video:

<u>The Classical Hollywood Style</u>. Program 1 of <u>The American Cinema</u>. Prod. New York Center for Visual History. Videocassette. Annenberg/CPB, 1995.

A Lecture

Granetta, Stephanie. Class lecture. English 315. Richardson College. 7 Apr. 2003.

Kamenish, Eleanor. "A Tale of Two Countries: Mores in France and Scotland." Public lecture. Friends of the Public Library. Louisville, 16 Apr. 2003.

A Pamphlet

Golden Retriever Club of America. <u>Prevention of Heartworm</u>. N.p.: GRCA, 2004.

<u>Who Are the Amish?</u> Aylmer, Ont.: Pathway, n.d.

An Interview

Barefoot, Blake. Personal interview. 18 Sept. 2002.

(continued on next page)

Spacey, Kevin. Interview with Terry Gross. _Fresh Air_. Natl. Public Radio. WHQR, Wilmington, NC. 21 Jan. 2003.

Trump, Donald. "Trump Speaks." Interview with Aravind Adiga. _Money_ Feb. 2003: 28.

A Television or Radio Program

The Crossing. Dir. Robert Harmon. Screenplay by Sherry Jones and Peter Jennings. History Channel. 1 Jan. 2000.

Stone, Susan. Report on Japanese comic books. _All Things Considered_. Natl. Public Radio. 9 Jan. 2003.

An Unpublished Essay

Gould, Emily. "Fast Food Comes at a High Price for Workers." Essay written for Prof. Katherine Humel's English 12 class. Fall semester 2002.

An Unpublished Letter

Cilano, Cara. Letter to author. 5 Mar. 2003.

An Unpublished Questionnaire

Questionnaire conducted by Prof. Barbara Waxman's English 103 class. Feb. 2003.

INTERNET AND ELECTRONIC SOURCES

An Online Book

Irving, David. _Hitler's War_. New York: Viking, 1977. 19 Jan. 2003 <http://www.fpp.co.uk/books/Hitler/>.

Richards, Hank. _The Sacrifice_. 1996. 3 Mar. 2003 <http://www.geocities.com/Area51/Vault/8101/>.

Wollstonecraft, Mary. _Vindication of the Rights of Women_. 1792. Bartleby.com, 1999. 13 Feb. 2003 <http://www.bartleby.com/144/>.

A Part of an Online Book

Coyle, Edward R. Spies and Their Work. _Ambulancing on the French Front_. 1918. 30 Apr. 2003. <http://www.ku.edu/carrie/specoll/medical/Coyle/Coyle04.htm#18>.

A Print Periodical (Newspaper, Magazine, or Journal) Accessed on the Publication's Web Site

Falsani, Cathleen. "Did Respect for Religion Cloud 'Clone' Coverage?" _Chicago Sun-Times_ 10 Jan. 2003. 19 Jan. 2003 <http://www.suntimes.com/output/falsani/cst-nws-fals10.html>.

Fineman, Howard, and Tamara Lipper. "Spinning Race." _Newsweek_ 27 Jan. 2003. 19 Jan. 2003 <http://www.msnbc.com/news/861383.asp?>.

Young, A. J., A. S. Wilson, and C. G. Mundell. "Chandra Imaging of the X-Ray Core of the Virgo Cluster." _Astrophysical Journal_ 579.2 (2002): 560-570. 19 Jan. 2003 <http://www.journals.uchicago.edu/ApJ/journal/issues/ApJ/v579n2/54935/54935.html>.

A Nonprint Periodical Accessed on the Publication's Web Site

Clinton, Bill. "The Path to Peace." 10 Sept. 2002. _Salon.com_ 20 Jan. 2003 <http://www.salon.com/news/feature/2002/09/10/clinton/>.

A Work Accessed in an Online Database

Jovanovic, Rozalia. "Snowmobilers Tied to Rules of the Road." _National Law Journal_ Aug. 5, 2002: B1. _InfoTrac OneFile_. 20 Jan. 2003 <http://infotrac.galegroup.com/>.

Parks, Noreen. "Dolphins in Danger." _Science Now_, 17 Dec. 2002: 2-3. _Academic Search Elite_. EBSCOhost. 20 Jan. 2003 <http://web3.epnet.com/>.

"Political Inclination of the States." _Associated Press_. 9 Jan. 2003. _LexisNexis Academic Universe_. 20 Jan 2003 <http://web.lexis-nexis.com/universe>.

An Online Encyclopedia Article

"Humpback Whale." _Encyclopaedia Britannica_ 2003. Encyclopaedia Britannica Online. 28 Jan, 2003 <http://0-search.eb.com.uncclc.coast.uncwil.edu/eb/>.

An Online Review

Ebert, Roger. Rev. of _Identity_, dir. James Mangold. _Chicago Sun-Times Online_ 25 Apr. 2003. 29 May 2003. <http://www.suntimes.com/output/ebert1/wkp-news-identity25f.html>.

An Organization's Web Site

The Coral Reef Alliance. "Coral Friendly Guidelines." 21 Jan. 2003 <http://www.coralreefalliance.org/parks/guidelines.html>.

A Course Web Page

Reilly, Colleen. English 204: Introduction to Technical Writing. Course home page. U of North Carolina at Wilmington. Spring 2003. 29 Apr. 2003 <http://people.uncw.edu/reillyc/204/>.

An Academic Department Page

Dept. of English home page. U of North Carolina at Wilmington. 10 Mar. 2003 <http://www.uncwil.edu/english/>.

A Personal Web Page

Hemming, Sally. Home page. 4 Feb. 2003 <http://www.sallyhemming.com>.

Computer Software

Atoms, Symbols and Equations. Vers. 3.0. Software. 2002 <http://ourworld.compuserve.com/homepages/RayLec/atoms.htm>.

Twain's World. CD-ROM. Parsippany, NJ: Bureau Development, 1993.

E-Mail

Wilkes, Paul. E-mail to author. 29 Dec. 2002.

WRITING, READING, AND RESEARCH

WRITING, READING, AND RESEARCH

SIXTH EDITION

Richard Veit

Christopher Gould

University of North Carolina at Wilmington

PEARSON

Longman

New York Boston San Francisco
London Toronto Sydney Tokyo Singapore Madrid
Mexico City Munich Paris Cape Town Hong Kong Montreal

Senior Vice President and Publisher: Joseph Opiela
Vice President and Publisher: Eben W. Ludlow
Development Manager: Janet Lanphier
Associate Development Editor: Lai T. Moy
Executive Marketing Manager: Ann Stypuloski
Senior Supplements Editor: Donna Campion/Teresa Ward
Production Manager: Ellen MacElree
Project Coordination, Text Design, and Electronic Page Makeup: Nesbitt Graphics, Inc.
Cover Designer/Manager: Wendy Ann Fredericks
Cover Art: Copyright © 2003 by Celia Johnson/c/o theispot.com
Photo Researcher: Photosearch Inc.
Manufacturing Buyer: Mary Fischer
Printer and Binder: R. R. Donnelley & Sons, Inc.
Cover Printer: Coral Graphic Services

Library of Congress Cataloging-in-Publication Data

Veit, Richard.
    Writing, reading, and research / Richard Veit, Christopher Gould.—6th ed.
        p. cm.
    Includes bibliographical references and index.
    ISBN 0-321-19832-8 (pbk.)
        1. English language—Rhetoric. 2. Research—Methodology. 3. Academic writing.
    4. College readers. I. Gould, Christopher, 1947-II. Title.
    PE1408.V45 2003
    808'.042—dc21

                                                                    2003047606

Please visit our Web site at http://www.ablongman.com

ISBN 0-321-19832-8

1 2 3 4 5 6 7 8 9 10—DOH—06 05 04 03

To Jeanne Gould, Frances Noble,
and Mary Bryan McCotter

Freshman Class of 1938,
Woman's College of the
University of North Carolina

Contents

To the Instructor

Writing, Reading, and Research, Sixth Edition, reflects the assumption that the three activities in its title are central to a college education. Every college student must be able to access information and ideas, analyze and synthesize them, and communicate the resulting knowledge to others.

What is more, writing, reading, and research are so closely and symbiotically related that they should be studied together. We believe that the research paper should not be seen (though it often is) as one among many isolated writing tasks, distinguished chiefly by its intricate search protocols and citation formats. Research, in the broader sense that we envision, includes activities both large and small. Every task involving sources is a research activity, whether it be reading a textbook, using a library, searching the Internet, asking questions, taking notes, or writing a summary analysis in response to an essay-exam question. A textbook, as we see it, should reflect this inclusive definition, engaging students in the rewards and excitement of research writing while preparing them to do it well.

It follows that students need to develop and refine the many skills involved in college research. Writing an essay based on library sources, for example, employs a wide range of skills that, in our experience, many first-year college students have not yet mastered. Most basic of all is active critical reading. Students need to employ efficient strategies to read with perception and understanding, to analyze and critique what they read, and to make productive use of the information and ideas that arise from their reading.

For these reasons, we believe that writing, reading, and research skills should be taught and practiced together. A composition course that prepares students for the tasks they will actually face during their college and professional careers can and should be a unified whole. That unity is the principle that informs this book.

Developing the skills of writing, reading, and research is a process that can be divided into successive stages. We have attempted to take a common-sense approach to this process by introducing concepts sequentially. Although each chapter has its own integrity, each also builds on the concepts developed in preceding chapters.

In general, our book moves from simpler to more complex tasks—from working with a single source to connecting multiple sources, from comprehension to analysis and critique, from paraphrase and summary to synthesis, before presenting the more advanced and creative aspects of writing, reading, and research.

We have pursued several specific goals in writing this book:

- Broadening the traditional notion of undergraduate research
- Presenting the processes of research in a practical sequence
- Blending the best features of a theoretically informed rhetoric, an interdisciplinary reading anthology, and a research guide
- Creating a text that instructors will find serviceable as a teaching resource and that students will find lively, readable, and instructive as a guide to research writing
- Supplementing assignments with student responses, illustrating the processes that lead to a finished product
- Providing helpful and engaging exercises, frequent opportunities to write, and many occasions for discussion and critical response.

Changes in the Sixth Edition

The sixth edition of *Writing, Reading, and Research* has undergone an exciting revision. The most outstanding change can be seen in our Table of Contents. All of the readings have been clearly labeled so that our readers can more easily distinguish between student and professional readings. For the sake of clarifying the purposes of each reading, we've also indicated whether it is for in-text practice, that is, for applying a particular concept discussed within a chapter, or whether it is an end-of-chapter reading for practicing and applying the concepts discussed in the chapter overall.

In Chapter 2, "Strategies for Reading," we provide a more detailed discussion of critical reading with a focus on inference. In Chapter 9, "Tools for Finding Sources," we have expanded and updated our discussion of electronic sources, as well as provided all new screenshots of actual Web-based research sites. We've also updated our sections on avoiding plagiarism (Chapter 11) to reflect the increasing trend of Internet research and the tendency of students to rely on unevaluated electronic sources. Chapter 14, "Argument: Reading, Writing, and Research," has been completely revised. We open the chapter with a discussion of emotional persuasion, followed by an expanded section on logical argument, which includes in-depth coverage of its structure, as well as varieties of evidence and types of emotional and ethical appeals used in logical arguments. The MLA documentation sections found in Part II have been updated and expanded to conform with the new sixth edition of the *MLA Handbook for Writers of Research Papers*. Finally, all the exercises from Chapters 1–14 on have been revised to engage our students, responding to their interests, and reflecting the trends of research writing today.

New to the Sixth Edition

- **The Readings.** In the fifth edition of *Writing, Reading, and Research,* we included nine major readings. In this edition we've replaced these nine with all *new* readings, and also offer *eighteen* additional readings. Each chapter's set of Additional Readings is thematically arranged, covering topics from the September 11 tragedy to great discoveries and inventions. We have also replaced more than three-fourths of our Practice Readings with new selections, all thematically connected to the major readings found at the end of each chapter. Furthermore, while in the last edition we offered a sample student paper at the beginning of the book, in this edition, we have added three more in the middle and near the end of the text: two appear in Chapter 8, "Beginning a Research Project," and one appears in Chapter 14, "Argument." All sample student research papers are *new.*

- **Mini-Internet Research Projects.** In order to emphasize the "three-in-one" concept of writing, reading, and research, as well as to acknowledge the increased use of the Internet in all aspects of research, we've added a new feature to this sixth edition. At the end of each chapter's major reading, students will find a Web-based exercise entitled, "Write, Read, and Research the Net." These small Internet projects are intended to encourage students to consider, select, evaluate, and use the Web and other related sources in their own research.

Supplements

The instructor's manual offers suggestions for using *Writing, Reading, and Research* in the classroom. It provides an overview of each chapter and suggested assignments, along with responses to exercises and the questions that follow end-of-chapter readings.

Acknowledgments

Our greatest debt is to our students, from whom we have learned most of what we know about teaching composition. In particular, we wish to thank the student writers who shared their notes and drafts with us and allowed us to use their papers and experiences in this edition: Mark Craig, Justin Stafford, Jane Carlton, and Emily Gould (who, in case you're wondering, is the daughter of one coauthor).

We also thank the following reviewers, whose wise and thoughtful suggestions made an immeasurable contribution to the sixth edition: Tom Amorose, Seattle Pacific University; Shirley Hart Berry, Cape Fear Community College; Deborah K. Chappel, Arkansas State University; Lu Ellen Huntley, University of North Carolina, Wilmington; Bryan Moore, Arkansas State University; Gregory J.

Pulliam, Illinois Institute of Technology; and George T. Vaughn, Maysville Community College.

Finally, we acknowledge Eben Ludlow, vice president and publisher, and Lai Moy, associate development editor at Longman, and our friends and colleagues at the University of North Carolina at Wilmington.

Richard Veit
Christopher Gould

PART I

Writing, Reading, and Research

1 Introduction to Writing, Reading, and Research

A college education does more than just introduce you to current information about a field of study. It also teaches you how to find that information, how to analyze and evaluate it, and how to place it in specific contexts alongside other, sometimes conflicting, information. In short, a college education invites you to learn and think on your own. The sum of knowledge in any field is too vast and the world is changing too rapidly for an education that merely imparts facts and statistics. Instead, an education worthy of the name helps you develop skill and confidence in finding, interpreting, assessing, and synthesizing what you are expected to know, both now and after you graduate. Professionals, technicians, executives, and other educated adults who have developed and refined these skills are more likely to contribute new ideas and to communicate discoveries within their fields.

Nearly all the courses you take, whether in biology, accounting, theology, or forestry, presuppose certain skills and knowledge. The most important of these—the ones most vital to success in college as well as your career—involve writing, reading, and research. As a fluent writer, an alert reader, and a resourceful researcher, you enjoy enormous advantages. This book is designed to help you assume these roles.

Writing, reading, and research are not mysterious or unusually difficult. You have been reading and writing for years, and whether you realize it or not, you perform certain kinds of research all the time, both in and out of school. For example, when you were deciding which college to attend, you probably conducted research by examining college catalogs, visiting Web sites, consulting with your guidance counselor, talking with friends, or traveling to several campuses. In fact, if you found and read a catalog and then wrote an application essay, you used all three skills.

Since writing, reading, and research are interrelated activities, it makes sense to study them together. Research often involves finding what others have written, reading it, and then writing in response. Even as you write, you frequently read what you have written, deciding whether further research, organizational changes, or further editing is needed. And finally, what you have written about your research becomes someone else's reading.

■ WRITING

Writing is a complex process that includes various subskills, from the basics of handwriting and spelling to the subtler nuances of tone and organization. Unlike the ability to speak, acquired in early childhood without formal instruction, writing skills are developed later, usually in school. Time and practice gradually lead to competence, and although most of us master the fundamentals easily enough, no one ever *completely* perfects the craft of writing. Even the most admired authors, after years of accomplishment, continue to learn from experience and refine their craft. Although a course in composition or a book like this can help you improve your writing, repeated practice remains the best teacher.

The essence of writing is *options;* writers continually make choices. Even on those rare occasions when you know exactly what to say, you still confront a vast array of options. You must choose an organizational plan, gauge the level of formality that best suits the occasion, determine the most effective strategies for opening and closing your text, and decide which facts, arguments, or supporting details are most appropriate. Even the selection of individual words often involves considering a number of synonyms.

In one sense, choice makes writing difficult. Too many options can be overwhelming. Even accomplished authors are familiar with writer's block: staring at the blank page or computer screen, agonizing over what to say next. And while there are compensating periods when words seem to flow, the text that "writes itself" is a fiction. Nevertheless, experienced writers persevere through moments of frustration, confident in the strategies they have developed for generating ideas and overcoming obstacles.

Fortunately, choice brings opportunities as well as difficulties. Creative opportunities are, after all, what make writing an art, rather than just a competency. As writers, we are not word mechanics churning out assembly-line products. We are artisans, using our imagination, experience, and talent to create, from the unlimited options available to us, texts that are both functional and original. Writing allows us to communicate ideas and information in ways that are profound, funny, provocative, or highly persuasive. Despite, or perhaps because of, the demanding work and hard choices that writing involves, the sense of achievement we derive from creating a work uniquely our own can be great, even exhilarating.

Writing Habits and Strategies

Skilled writers devote considerable time to the preliminary stages of composing before they try to produce a complete, polished draft. They do not, however, all follow the same routine, nor do they, as individuals, pursue a uniform approach to every writing task. In fact, one of your goals in this course should be to discover which procedures bring the best results in specific situations: a timed essay exam vs. an informal response to assigned reading vs. a research paper due at the end of an academic term. In the following passage, Nancy Sommers, a scholar who has studied writing processes for more than twenty years, discusses her experiences as a writer and a teacher of writing:

I stand in my kitchen, wiping the cardamom, coriander, and cayenne off my fingers. My head is abuzz with words, with bits and pieces of conversation. I hear a phrase I have read recently, something about "a radical loss of certainty." But, I wonder, how did the sentence begin? I search the air for the rest of the sentence, can't find it, shake some more cardamom, and a bit of coriander. Then, by some play of mind, I am back home again in Indiana with my family, sitting around the kitchen table. Two people are talking, and there are three opinions; three people are talking, and there are six opinions. Opinions grow exponentially. I fight my way back to that sentence. Writing, that's how it begins: "Writing is a radical loss of certainty." (Or is it uncertainty?) It isn't so great for the chicken when all these voices start showing up, with all these sentences hanging in mid-air, but the voices keep me company. I am a writer, not a cook, and the truth is I don't care much about the chicken. Stories beget stories. Writing emerges from writing. . . .

If I could teach my students one lesson about writing it would be to see themselves as sources, as places from which ideas originate, . . . all that they have read and experienced—the dictionaries of their lives—circulating through them. I want them to learn how sources thicken, complicate, enlarge writing, but I want them to know too how it is always the writer's voice, vision, and argument that create the new source. I want my students to see that nothing reveals itself straight out, especially the sources all around them. But I know enough by now that this . . . ideal can't be passed on in one lesson or even a semester of lessons.

Many of the students who come to my classes have been trained to collect facts; they act as if their primary job is to accumulate enough authorities so that there is no doubt about the "truth" of their thesis. They most often disappear behind the weight and permanence of their borrowed words, moving their pens, mouthing the words of others, allowing sources to speak through them unquestioned, unexamined.

At the outset, many of my students think that personal writing is writing about the death of their grandmother. Academic writing is [from their point of view] reporting what Elizabeth Kübler-Ross has written about death and dying. Being personal, I want to show my students, does not mean being autobiographical. Being academic does not mean being remote, distant, imponderable. Being personal means bringing their judgments and interpretations to bear on what they read and write, learning that they never leave themselves behind even when they write academic essays. . . .

With writing and with teaching, as well as with love, we don't know how the sentence will begin and, rarely ever, how it will end. Having the courage to live with uncertainty, ambiguity, even doubt, we can walk into all those fields of writing, knowing that we will find volumes upon volumes bidding *us* enter. We need only be inventors, we need only give freely and abundantly to the texts, imagining even as we write that we too will be a source from which other readers can draw sustenance.

Notice how Sommers, a published scholar, grapples with the same self-doubts and frustrations that beset less experienced writers. But, after years of practice and reflection, she has come to view these distractions as an inevitable stage in a process that almost always produces an acceptable draft. In fact, she has learned to exploit the potential of distractions. For example, Sommers understands that ideas and isolated bits of language come to mind at unexpected, sometimes inconvenient moments—while you cook, exercise, shower, or try to go to sleep. Proficient writers do not disregard or try to postpone these moments of invention and discovery, which more typically result from deliberate contrivance rather than spontaneous inspiration. Notice how Sommers, recalling an experience evoked by the perplexing phrase, "Writing is a radical loss of certainty," has to "fight [her] way back" to the topic at hand. She understands that personal associations and experiences are not irrelevant distractions during the early stages of composing. Sommers therefore embraces "uncertainty, ambiguity, even doubt," confident that insightful ideas and fluent language will eventually emerge.

The chief difference between experienced writers and most first-year college students is that the former, like Sommers, have learned to break down the complexity of writing by approaching it in manageable stages, so that what starts out as an awkward exploration ends up, several stages later, as a polished essay or a crafted report. Writers who strive for early perfection are usually doomed to frustration. Polish and clarity evolve over time through patient drafting and redrafting. Although composing is seldom easy for anyone, skillful writers rely on the routines they have developed over time. They know that with patience and persistence, good ideas, graceful sentences, and appropriate vocabulary will come. Like these writers, you too can learn to settle down to the hardest part of writing—getting started.

EXERCISES · Writing Habits and Strategies

1. In each of the following passages, a published author talks about the craft of writing. As you read each passage, take note of anything that relates to your own writing processes.

   a. With a blank [Microsoft] Word document before me, I waited for the right words to come. I had always found that getting started was one of the hardest parts of technical writing, and that was certainly holding true now. I decided to skip the introductory matter for the time being and jump right into documenting the software's functions. This material didn't seem to require as much creativity, and it was something I could tackle bit by bit.

      Over the next few months I slowly, and sometimes painfully, documented each function of the program. Half the battle was simply trying to understand what I was writing about. The program's interface certainly left something to be desired, and my lack of building knowledge was a definite obstacle. Oddly enough, even the programmers didn't have a complete grasp of their creation. To top things off, I had to learn RoboHelp and attempt to produce a written and online document simultaneously. Until now there had been no online help, so this was another blank slate I had to fill all on my own.

      —Alina Rutten, "How I Became a Goddess"

   b. Only the very young and the very old may recount their dreams at breakfast, dwell upon self, interrupt with memories of beach picnics and favorite Liberty lawn dresses and the rainbow trout in a creek near Colorado Springs. The rest of us are expected, rightly, to affect absorption in other people's favorite dresses, other people's trout.

And so we do. But our notebooks give us away, for however dutifully we record what we see around us, the common denominator of all we see is always, transparently, shamelessly, the implacable "I." We are not talking here about the kind of notebook that is patently for public consumption . . .; we are talking about something private, about bits of the mind's string too short to use, an indiscriminate and erratic assemblage with meaning only for its maker.

—Joan Didion, "On Keeping a Notebook"

c. Writing isn't hard; no harder than ditch-digging.

—Patrick Dennis

After reading all three passages, write for approximately twenty minutes about one or more stages in a composing routine that you have developed, deliberately or otherwise, to carry out academic writing tasks. You may want to relate what you do to the ideas presented in one or more of the above passages.

2. Exchange your writing in small groups and discuss similarities and differences.

In this book we assume that you have completed a course in college or high school that introduced you to stages of the writing process. Nevertheless, we think it useful to review a sequence of composing strategies that many seasoned writers have adapted to their own individual needs and preferences. Remember that since occasions for writing differ, this is not a rigidly uniform sequence of "steps"; those who use it productively make adjustments. The main thing to keep in mind is that there are no shortcuts to effective writing.

Several times in this book, we present papers that college students have written in response to assignments in their composition classes. In this chapter, you will read a paper by Mark Craig, a first-year college student who addressed the assignment detailed below. In addition, to illustrate the composing processes that led to his polished draft, we have recorded the evolution of Mark's paper from his first encounter with the assignment through the proofreading of his final draft. (Also, we have provided several other examples of this type of essay, sometimes referred to as a *profile*, at the end of this chapter.)

Writing from Observation   ASSIGNMENT

Research involves deciding what you want to know, focusing your investigation, and then making discoveries about a topic. Later in this course you will engage in *secondary research,* finding out what other researchers have already learned and reported. Library research is an example. The paper you write in response to this assignment, on the other hand, involves *primary research,* gathering information first-hand, through direct observation.

Here is the assignment in brief: *Investigate a place or activity, discovering as much as you can through careful, persistent observation; then report your discoveries in an engaging, informative paper.*

The following suggestions and guidelines should be helpful:

- Choose an organization, office, building, or outdoor locale where a particular activity takes place. Examples include a health-food cooperative, art gallery, community festival or pageant, hospice, auction, or farmer's market.

- Select a place or activity that is relatively unfamiliar to you. If you describe something you know well, you may be influenced by unconscious preconceptions and thus take for granted or overlook details that an outsider would find unusual and interesting. For this assignment, it is important that you observe and write as an *objective reporter,* not as a participant or insider.

- Take careful note of what goes on, particularly anything that might not be obvious to the casual observer. Notice how people act, how they respond to each other, their behavior, and the unspoken rules that operate within the context.

- Adopt one of two methods of gathering data: Be an unobstrusive "fly on the wall," listening and watching others who are generally unaware of your presence; or be an inquiring reporter, talking to people and asking questions.

- Return to the site as often as necessary until you understand your subject thoroughly. Take copious notes during or immediately after each visit.

- Write about the institution/activity and about your personal experiences during your visit(s). Report what *you* see and feel free to use the word *I* in your report. You can state what you expected or intended to find, what you actually discovered, and how your views were changed or reinforced by the observation.

- Do not devote much space to obvious or surface details about the place or activity you describe. Try not to tell readers things they may already know. Get behind the obvious and describe what *really* is going on.

- Describe what you witnessed during your observation(s) rather than generalizing about what happens on typical occasions. Use specific details.

Submit prewriting, notes, and preliminary drafts along with the final version of your paper.

After you have read Mark Craig's polished essay and followed his progress through the several stages that led to it, the nature and requirements of this assignment should become clearer to you. Notice that the assignment calls for something beyond purely personal writing. That is, the instructor asked members of the class to draw on sources outside their own opinions and past experiences; they were expected to rely on direct observation and, possibly, to conduct an interview or informal survey. This procedure might involve visits to several sites or repeated observations of a single site.

To be a fair, open-minded observer is not necessarily to assume a completely detached, impersonal stance toward a topic. In fact, when you read Mark's essay, you will find that he became personally involved with what he was writing about, his observation of the Cape Fear Literacy Council. The assignment on pages 7–8 calls for a type of writing not completely different from the personal essays that Mark had written in high school, nor from the more formal research-based writing he would do later in his composition course. Although the assignment does not call for a traditional research paper—the kind that cites library sources and uses formal documentation—it does involve a particular type of research. (Later chapters of this book explain other methods of research in greater detail.)

Audience and Purpose

Whenever we engage in discourse—that is, whenever we converse, write a letter, give a speech, compose an essay, or participate in any other type of transaction involving language—we adapt our words and style of delivery to our intentions. Imagine, for example, overhearing a dialogue between a male and a female college student who meet at a party. The conversation might begin with little more than customary phrases of introduction, followed by routine questions about hometowns, majors, interests, and tastes in music. Nevertheless, an astute observer would recognize in this dialogue certain subtle attempts to manipulate a familiar ritual for complex purposes. Each speaker may be trying to gauge the degree of his or her attraction to the other, to make an impression, and to advance (or perhaps to slow down or even to end) the progress of a relationship. Like these speakers, all of us, since early childhood, have become skilled at adapting language behavior to specific situations. So it is when we write.

Effective writers carefully consider their reason *(purpose)* for writing and the persons *(audience)* that they hope to inform, persuade, entertain, or otherwise influence. These considerations affect a wide range of decisions involving language, because there is no multipurpose style or structure that suits every writing task. To illustrate, consider the following excerpt from the Declaration of Independence:

We hold these truths to be self-evident, that all men are created equal. . . .

Now contrast it with this excerpt from H. L. Mencken's comic paraphrase, "The Declaration of Independence in American":

All we got to say on this proposition is this: first, me and you is as good as anybody else, and maybe a damn sight better. . . .

Both passages are widely admired, but since they address different audiences and purposes, they exemplify vastly different styles. In the original version, Thomas Jefferson hoped to justify American independence to the world and to persuade fellow colonists of the necessity of armed rebellion. In contrast, Mencken wanted to amuse readers while making a point about language; therefore, his writing is informal and humorous. Each style suits the writer's goals, but neither would have been appropriate in the opposite situation, nor for the assignment that Mark Craig received from his instructor.

Mark's purpose and audience were defined by the assignment on pages 7–8. He was expected to report, from a personal point of view, information and impressions that would engage the interests of a particular audience of readers. He understood that his instructor wanted to simplify the task by defining that audience as readers like himself. However, he could not entirely ignore the fact that his instructor—who would be reading and responding to his paper—was an important part of his audience as well.

With these considerations in mind, Mark began his research and writing, the stages of which are traced in the following pages. As you read these pages, you can judge how effectively he took into account the demands of his purpose and audience. The final draft of Mark's paper appears on the following pages.

Craig 1

Mark Craig

English 201

Mr. William DiNome

Illiteracy: America's Secret

A freight train thunders by outside, its whistle
blaring stridently a few yards away from the window sill
where I sit. Billie Granger, executive director of the
Cape Fear Literacy Council, sits at her desk, unfazed.
Over piles of books and paper I see her mouth moving, but
I can't hear a word. As the train clears the crossing, she
describes in her gravelly drawl the frustration that
parents feel when they cannot read bedtime stories to
their children because they can't make out the words--
because they are "functionally illiterate."

"It's America's secret," Billie says. "Twenty-four
percent of the population is functionally illiterate."
They can sign their names, perhaps total a bank deposit,
but they can't read the newspaper, a job manual, or a road
map.

Since the 1970s Billie has promoted literacy through
an agency that began as a mission project for her church
and, by the mid-1980s, had grown into one of the area's
most recognized nonprofit organizations. The council's
annual spelling bee, cosponsored by the daily newspaper,
is both a public event and a major fund-raiser. Although I

Craig 2

have attended this event twice, I was not aware of ever
having met a functional illiterate. "Come back on a Monday
or Wednesday night," Billie suggests. "Maybe I'll get you
interested in volunteering."

Returning later the same week, I cross an unpaved
parking lot and enter the council's headquarters, a
building that once housed a construction company. Inside,
I notice a plastic tub full of donated books sitting
beside the door. Except for the tutor-training room, every
space in the building is tiny. In the computer room, a
volunteer assists an adult student in a wheelchair. Ten
donated computers range in vintage from old to ancient.
The hallway, adorned with an array of photographic
collages and a three-foot-wide facsimile of a check for
$1,000 from Wal-Mart, is so narrow that people have to turn
sideways to pass each other. On one wall hangs an
autographed photo of Clint Eastwood, inscribed "Go ahead,
make my day--keep reading."

Students arrive, and volunteers escort them to the
"tutoring units," rooms measuring about five by six and
furnished with only a table and two chairs. Because
tutoring sessions are private, I remain in the resource
room beside Billie's office.

Here it is quiet but for the swoosh of cars down
Oleander Drive and the drumming of tires across the

Craig 3

railroad tracks. The walls are lined with white shelves filled with colorful books and games--Teaching Adults: An ESL Resource Book, Patterns in Spelling: Book 4, Essential Words for the GED, Laubach Way to Reading, Voyager: Reading and Writing for Today's Adults. Billie introduces me to Chris Turner, the council's assessment specialist, an energetic woman with short hair and spectacles who seems to be in perpetual motion. Chris explains her role to me, all the while glancing over her shoulder. She shows me two forms that she uses to assess students' reading and math skills. Her assessments allow her to prescribe appropriate course work, after which she consults with tutors, then retests each student after each fifty hours of tutoring.

As we talk, a student wishes Chris a good night, and she gives him a warm hug. "He's so determined," she tells me, explaining that his math tutor gives him five problems each night, three nights a week, and that his weekly sessions will soon increase to four. The tutoring process she describes--gradually introducing new material, building upon previously developed skills--is painstaking. Progress can be excruciatingly slow. She has known students and tutors to work one-on-one for forty-five minutes a day, five days a week, for years on end. Her proudest achievement is helping a stroke victim, father of six, who had lost all reading ability and some spelling skills. After working three days a week for many months, Chris reports, he is doing well and recovering some proficiency. "It's intensive work," she says, "and the school system can't afford it." She should know. A teacher for twenty-five years, now retired, she raised a son who is deaf and learning disabled. "But that's how it's got to be done: a little at a time over a long period of time."

The job of pairing students and tutors falls to Billie Granger, who according to Chris, demonstrates uncanny insight. Billie has a knack not just for matching teaching skills with learning needs, but also for finding compatible personalities. Many of the tutoring relationships develop into something more gratifying for both partners, often reaching beyond boundaries of race, creed, or social class. According to Chris, most volunteers expect to provide help but don't anticipate the help they get in return.

Suddenly Chris interrupts herself. "I'm giving a test right now, and I don't want the student to be looking for me." She hurries off to check. Soon she is hurrying down the hallway to greet another student at the entrance.

I hear Billie speaking on the telephone in her office: "I hate asking people on short notice. I've approached everybody I can think of, and several people

Craig 5

mentioned your name." It is nearly six o'clock the evening before the spelling bee, and Billie needs a replacement for one of the two emcees. I gather that she's trying to recruit the associate publisher of the newspaper. "Tell them to let you off early tomorrow," she says with a hoarse giggle.

When Chris returns, she introduces me to Joe Carpenter, a veteran tutor-trainer. Soon a student appears in the hall, and she's off again. Now it's Joe's turn to carry me. It's like a relay race, and I'm the baton.

Meanwhile, Billie hangs up the phone after agreeing to call back in the morning; then she claps her hands loudly and exclaims, "Got him!"

"You can't say no to Billie," Joe quips. He glares at me expressively. "She'll rope you in too before long. You watch!"

Another tutor stops by to tell Joe how pleased she is to have been paired with a student who shares her interest in photography. "Billie does it again!" cries Joe. This particular student, a videographer who owns a small business, is a high-school graduate who cannot decipher technical manuals for the equipment he operates. Joe remarks that this is a prime example of what is often labeled <u>functional illiteracy</u>, a fairly subjective term. For some, it means the inability to compute ratios; for others, the inability to write work reports. Each year an increasing number of Americans try to learn English as a second language. Most of the 450 students that the council helps each year read below the fifth-grade level, which Billie considers a minimum level for survival. Among them are mechanics who aspire to supervisory positions, factory workers who must learn how to operate new equipment, and parents who want to help their children with homework. Technology constantly raises the bar in the workplace: maintenance workers must often use computers to log hours and carry out work orders. Weak readers stand at a crossroad between getting the necessary training and falling by the wayside. Their self-esteem is constantly on the line. Although many people assume that illiteracy is caused by insufficient access to education, as many as 80 percent of the council's students have never learned to read because they have disabilities that public schools are not equipped to address, disabilities like dyslexia, neurological dysfunction, cerebral palsy, and even schizophrenia.

According to Joe Carpenter, the literacy council is often a "last-ditch effort" for adults who are highly intelligent but who feel they aren't because they've had to depend so much on other people throughout their lives. "You see a fifty-year-old who thinks, 'I'm just stupid.'

Craig 7

Others are scared they might be recognized by an employer or coworker. Others want to get a driver's license or read Mark Twain, the Bible, or the newspaper."

Joe takes me into the training room, where a retired engineer is writing an equation on the white board. His student, a high-school dropout now in his twenties, stands beside him. Sensitive to the need to protect students' privacy, Joe tells me that these two won't mind a brief visit. He introduces me, then asks the student how it's going. I'm suddenly aware of the pen and notepad I'm holding; I keep them at my side. The student answers "Good," but his tutor says he's doing great: "We're going to tackle the GED in a few weeks and we're going to be ready."

A few days later, I sit with Joe at a picnic table. He smokes while awaiting his next student, whom he refers to as his "guinea pig." Severely dyslexic, this student has supported a family at minimum wage during the six years he has studied with Joe. "He's religious about attendance," Joe says. Soon a pickup truck pulls up and three people emerge, a middle-aged couple and their young daughter. The student is a tall, quiet man carrying a large book bag. They greet Joe like old friends, and Joe asks if his student is ready to do some writing. The man groans. Joe turns to his wife and says, "I'm going to kill him with writing, you know that." The woman laughs, "He sure hates that writing."

"Six years!" I think to myself as I follow them into the building. The six years I spent acquiring most of my language skills are too remote to retrieve from memory. And although my reading today is sometimes labored and inefficient, I love words; writing is part of my everyday routine. I take for granted the ability to understand newspaper articles, books, advertisements, bank statements, and insurance policies. Just by knowing how to read a want ad, to apply for automobile registration, or to balance my checking account, I enjoy a form of independence that not every American shares. I had to cross the railroad tracks to become aware of this.

Later that evening, as I carefully roll out of the literacy council's rough-surfaced parking lot, I am quietly aware that the independence I enjoy is largely the result of good fortune, not to have been born with a disability, not to have suffered a stroke. My independence is not so much earned as granted, a gift I had long mistaken for achievement.

Mark's paper is one of a wide variety of possible responses to the assignment on pages 7–8. It is a polished piece of writing, but it did not start that way. The following pages trace the stages of his research and writing, which culminated in the essay you have just read. These stages include *prewriting, composing a first draft, peer review, revision,* and *editing.*

Prewriting

Drafting a paper is easier when you have an idea of what you want to say. Before you begin a first draft, it makes sense to pursue strategies that can help you generate or discover ideas and put them in writing. These strategies include *brainstorming, mapping, freewriting, collecting data,* and *outlining.* Mark used all five in a sequence that helped him get started.

Brainstorming

Writers, business people, and scientists often unlock their thinking through *brainstorming,* a way of bringing to mind as many ideas about a topic as possible. Brainstorming not only provides raw material to work with, it also arouses creativity. You can brainstorm out loud or on paper. One way is to write down all the words or phrases about a topic that come to mind, listing them on the page, one after the other as they occur to you. Don't evaluate them or worry about whether they're consistent with each other. Sometimes, you must pass over three or four— or even a dozen—useless ideas before a good one comes along. The purpose is to bring associations together in your mind, like rubbing sticks to create a spark.

When Mark's instructor presented the assignment on pages 7–8, he asked the class to brainstorm possible topics. Here is an excerpt from the list that Mark produced:

```
University
  —campus visits
    parents and high school students
      How many come each year? What do they ask?
    information session by Admissions Office
    student guides
      How are they selected? What do they get paid?
  —non-academic functions
    grounds and maintenance
    housekeeping
    campus police
      Hours, pay, working conditions
      What kind of employer is the university?
Work
  —campus jobs (Lindsay)
  —paid internships
    professional writing/journalism (Margo)
    museum work
```

—tutoring (Jasper)
—non-traditional students
  How many hold jobs and have families?

Mark jotted down ideas as they came to mind, without rejecting anything as inappropriate, unworkable, or silly. He wrote quickly, not worrying about punctuation or spelling. He wrote entirely for his own benefit, and some of the names and items on his list made sense only to him. But you can see his mind at work—and the way brainstorming helped his thought processes gather momentum, with one idea provoking another. The list shows his train of thought, moving from campus visits by prospective students to types of nonacademic employment on campus, then to paid internships, and finally to tutoring, the eventual focus of his paper.

EXERCISE | **Brainstorming**

Choose a friend or classmate as a writing partner. While you generate a list of *the most creative or effective* television commercials, ask your partner to brainstorm a list of *all* television commercials. After ten minutes, compare lists to see which one contains more interesting or promising items for an essay on television advertising. Can you draw any inferences about effective brainstorming—what contributes to it and what may impede it?

Mapping or Clustering

Mapping involves making ideas concrete, putting them in black and white so you can look at them and see their relationships. Basically, you want to make patterns of words and phrases that radiate out from a central concept. When they do this, writers are often surprised how the linking process generates new ideas. Sometimes, the visual pattern itself can suggest an essay's basic organization. As in brainstorming, it is better to jot down ideas quickly, without trying to evaluate them.

From his brainstorming notes, Mark found that he was focusing on tutoring, which he further explored in the map shown in Figure 1.1. Each of the types of tutoring that he listed led to a variety of ideas, and, in the process of filling out the map, Mark came up with several interesting ideas for his paper. Some of the paths his mind took turned out to be dead ends ("For $$," e.g.), but others were promising leads. He considered volunteer work coordinated through church groups and high schools, as well as online tutoring. Also on his map was the idea of adult illiteracy, which for Mark proved to be the most promising of all.

Freewriting

After an unfocused invention activity such as brainstorming or mapping, the best way to arrive at more focused ideas is to *freewrite.* Begin writing about your topic at a steady, comfortable pace, jotting down whatever comes to mind; then continue, without stopping, for a particular length of time, perhaps ten or fifteen

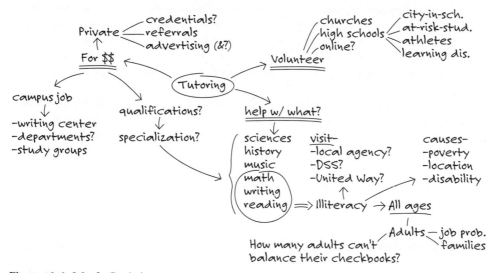

Figure 1.1 Mark Craig's map.

minutes. Don't reject any ideas; simply let them flow. Don't worry about spelling, punctuation, or even coherence. Freewriting is not for others to read; its purpose is to allow you to explore your topic and come up with ideas to use later. Mark's ten-minute freewriting looked like this:

Illiteracy—inability to read. Various levels of inability—poor comprehension in terms of grade level. Can't do math. How to follow directions when you can't read? I've heard of functional illiteracy. What is it, though? What does it look like? How common is it? Never known anyone who was illiterate, though I've known slow readers. Which comes first—inability to read or dropping out of school?

Newspaper article—Literacy Council Spelling Bee. Contestants are mostly adults—librarians, teachers, media, business people. Are there still people in America who can't read? Where? How do they earn a living? Do they have kids in school who can read? I learned to read very young, always have read, something anyone can do. What makes a person illiterate? Can't afford school?—doubtful. Can't get to school? Rural areas? Can't learn? Poor teachers, ineffective schools, learning disability? Falling through the cracks, maybe. Schools can't give all students what they need.

Literacy Council—at the crossroads (in more ways than one). Busy street crossed by railroad tracks, across from the newspaper.

Me: take reading for granted—newspapers, want ads, applications, checkbook, bank statements, phone bills, insurance information. No disabilities that required treatment; always a "good student," never "at risk." But I haven't always taken literacy for granted—always been a slow reader, struggled. But yet I love writing, words, processing thoughts on paper and computer screen; enjoy reading for pleasure and study. Good facility with computers, largely self-taught, relied on manuals, online help. Familiar with feelings of inadequacy when confronted by more talented writers/readers. Always felt I should read better.

This is typical freewriting—rambling, conversational, uncensored. If it were clearly organized and carefully edited, it would not be authentic. Beginning with several possibilities in mind, Mark used freewriting to focus his thinking. As he freewrote, Mark considered talking with his friend Jasper, whose internship involved literacy training. Later, when Jasper suggested that he observe a tutoring session at the Cape Fear Literacy Council, Mark arrived at a tentative topic for his paper.

Collecting Data

Mark called his friend, who arranged an interview with Billie Granger, Executive Director of the Cape Fear Literacy Council. At the end of this interview, Granger urged Mark to visit again another evening, when he could observe the council's routine operations. When he returned several days later, Mark was not sure whether he should introduce himself to any of the students and staff members or explain his purpose in being there. Deciding to play it by ear, he was surprised to find that all his time would be occupied by conversations with staff members. Although disappointed to learn that he could not interview any of its clients, Mark discovered a great deal about the council itself, its mission and daily operations. Finally, when Mark was allowed to visit a tutoring session briefly, he immediately sensed that a pen and notepad were awkward and inappropriate in that context. Consequently, Mark's notes consisted of information recorded during interviews with staff members, supplemented with a few details written hastily right after his visit. Following are some excerpts from those notes:

> Students/"clients"
>   —350–450 students annually
>   —c. 200 at any time
>   —targets adults, age 16+
>   —some h.s. students in need
>   —Average student: 4th–5th grade reader ("survival level")
>   —disproportionate # of men
>   —Most come by word-of-mouth, all voluntary
>   —Math students, prepare for var. tests
>   —Assisted-care students: wide range (CP, mentally disabled, schiz)
>   —privacy, confidentiality
>   —At points in their lives when hard decisions must be made
>   —Not only material success, but also self-esteem is on the line
> Staff (2 FT; 3 FTE total)
>   —Billie Granger, exec Dir.
>   —short, gravelly voice; southern accent
>   —involved since 1970s; knowledgeable

—matches tutors, students
—describes illiteracy as "America's secret"
—Katie Morrow, program coordinator
—Chris Turner, assessment specialist
 —25-yr teacher; left system
 —son: deaf, learning disabled
 —energetic, busy, outgoing, committed
 —short hair, spectacles
 —"how it's got to be done: little at a time over a long period"
 —works with stroke survivor (her "acid test")
  —father of six: lost all reading, some spelling
 —hugs student as he leaves
 —dashes off, remembering a tutor needs to speak with her
—Joe Carpenter, tutor/tutor-trainer
 —Billie has "uncanny ability" to match tutors and students
 —sees Council as "last-ditch effort"
 —student ("guinea pig") is "religious about attendance"
Literacy
 —"Functional illiteracy"—subjective
 —Pre- & post-tests
 —Reading/writing, language skills, math, ESL
 —Common assumption: literacy due to lack of access to education
  —Reality: most due to disability (inadequate education)
 —ESL, big shift in local need = 1/3 of all students

These excerpts—a small portion of Mark's notes—illustrate several kinds of note-taking:

- **Listing details.** Knowing that his essay would benefit from concrete descriptive details, Mark took careful notes about everything he observed. His second cluster of notes, for example, includes information about the appearance and mannerisms of several members of the council's staff.

- **Recording events.** A subcluster of notes records some of Chris Turner's interactions with students and tutors. Here, as elsewhere, Mark used a form of shorthand, omitting details that he knew he could fill in later.

- **Interviewing.** Although Mark was unable to interview tutoring partners as he had hoped, he found that staff members were well informed and generous with their time. He paraphrased many of their remarks and managed to record a few short quotations. Knowing that he had to get as much information and as many ideas into writing as quickly as possible, he occasionally relied on a phrase that made a particularly strong impression (e.g., "acid test," "last-ditch effort"). Nonetheless, he usually contented himself with conscientious efforts to paraphrase what people said. If, however, he had quoted anyone at length about specific facts, controversial opinions, historical context, or anything else demanding strict accuracy, thoroughness, and objectivity, Mark would not have been justified in taking this approach. As it is, he used direct quotations sparingly, only when a speaker's words were memorable and more telling than a paraphrase was likely to be.

• **Analysis and interpretation.** At several points during his visit, Mark formed interpretations of what he was observing. At one point he wrote, "self-esteem is on the line" and later, "functional illiteracy—subjective." Interpretive details like these are often the most valuable part of note-taking, since they highlight what you have learned. They also may help you find a focus for your paper.

Outlining

Good notes furnish raw material for your paper, but at this stage that material is very raw. Later, when you compose a draft, you must *select* which parts to use (good notes typically contain two or three times as much material as the writer ultimately includes) and decide how to *organize* them. For some writers, selecting and organizing result in an **outline.** However, since they are not separate, distinct "steps" in a sequence, and since many decisions about selecting and organizing are best made while composing a draft, few writers try to produce a detailed outline at this point. Some, however, may sketch a brief, informal outline before drafting—if only to arrive at a very general notion about how to select and organize material. Regardless of whether you adopt this approach, you should feel free, as you compose, to alter organizational plans whenever you encounter new ideas or recognize a better way to structure your emerging draft. Mark Craig drew up this brief outline before beginning his first draft:

Cape Fear Literacy Council

First Visit
    Facts about illiteracy
    History of the council
Second Visit
    Appearance of CFLC offices
    Chris Turner
    Joe Carpenter
    No interviewing of students!
Third Visit
    Joe's "guinea pig"
Conclusion: What I learned?

This outline helped Mark get started on a first draft—a valuable impetus. But he was not a slave to it, and as you will see, he had already refined and elaborated on it when he wrote the draft reprinted in the following pages.

Composing a First Draft

If you have explored a topic in your mind and on paper through prewriting and have taken good notes, you have a head start. You are now ready to begin a first draft. As you compose this draft, keep your prewriting plans in mind, but remain flexible. Since you are still discovering ideas in this preliminary version, try not to worry about spelling, punctuation, or usage. The time to make these corrections comes later, when you edit a revised draft. Pausing at this stage to check punctuation or spelling is counterproductive because it often interrupts composing. Unlike freewriting, however, a first draft should be arranged in paragraphs, and the ideas should be supported with examples, reasons, or illustrations.

Mark polished his draft and brought the following revision to class. His instructor paired students and asked them to respond to each other's drafts following detailed guidelines.

GUIDELINES for Peer Review

Read your partner's draft from beginning to end as you might read an article in a magazine or newspaper—to understand what the writer has to say, engaging with ideas and information presented. Don't look for problems in content, organization, or usage. After this first reading, describe in one or two sentences the draft's impact on you as a reader—what it makes you think about, how it makes you feel, what questions it raises. Then briefly state the writer's purpose as you see it—how you think the writer wants to influence readers. If you recognize some general way that the draft's organization or content doesn't suit that purpose, call attention to it constructively. The important thing is to offer helpful, supportive comments without being insincere or patronizing. After this initial response, reread analytically, examining content and organization. Comment briefly in the margins on whatever arouses your interest or attention. Often, the most useful comments point to details that arouse questions or cause confusion. Consider in particular how various parts of the paper advance or digress from what you consider to be the author's purpose. When both you and your partner are finished, return the drafts, read each other's review, and discuss both for as long as necessary.

As you read Mark's draft on the following pages, notice his classmate's brief marginal notes and the longer comment written at the end.

Craig 1

Mark Craig

English 201

Mr. Bill DiNome

Title?

Like approaching thunder, a freight train rumbled by outside and blared its strident horn just as it passed the window where I sat. Billie Granger, the executive director of the Cape Fear Literacy Council, sat behind her desk, unfazed. I peered over the pile of books and paper on her desk, to see her mouth moving, but I couldn't hear a word. As the train noise faded beyond the crossing, Billie continued in her gravelly voice to explain the frustration some parents feel when they cannot read bedtime stories to their children because they can't make out many of the words on the page--because they are "functionally illiterate."

"It's America's secret," Billie says in a drawl from North Carolina's warm interior. ("Twenty-four percent of the   *Really?!* population are functionally illiterate.") They can sign their names, she explains, and maybe make a bank deposit, but they can't read the newspaper or a job manual or a road map. Since the 1970s Billie Granger has worked to fight illiteracy with an organization that started as a mission project for her church and which, by the mid 1980s, had grown into one of the area's most recognized

Craig 2

nonprofit agencies. The annual spelling bee, sponsored by the daily newspaper headquartered right across the street, is the literacy council's most popular fund-raiser, and although I had attended two "bees" in previous years, I had, to my knowledge, never seen a functional illiterate. "Come back on Monday or Wednesday night," Billie suggests. "Maybe I'll get you interested in volunteering."

When I return the following Wednesday, (my first concern is finding a safe place to park my motorcycle in the uneven, unpaved parking lot.) *You felt unsafe? Why?* The building, a compact, stuccoed box, once housed offices of a construction company. On the floor just inside the entrance lies a plastic tub full of donated books. In the computer room, a volunteer tutor assists an adult student in a wheelchair. The ten computers available there are a mixed collection ranging from old to ancient; beige, faded-looking, but functional. Except for the tutor-training room, every space is tiny. The hallway, adorned with collaged photographs, is so narrow that I must turn sideways to pass people. On the wall hangs a three-foot-wide facsimile of a bank check, a donation of $1,000 from Wal-Mart. Opposite that hangs an autographed photo of (actor) *Necessary?* Clint Eastwood pictured running alongside a presidential limousine. In bold marker it is inscribed, "Go ahead, make my day--Keep reading."

Craig 3

As students arrive, their tutors escort them to a
work space, typically one of the miniscule "tutoring
units," each measuring about five feet wide by six feet
deep and furnished with little more than a table, two
chairs, and a white board. I seat myself in the resource
room beside Billie Granger's office.

minuscule

The resource room, barely large enough for a small
glass-top table and four chairs, is quiet but for the
smooth swoosh of cars on Oleander and the (drumming of
tires across the railroad tracks). The walls are lined with
white shelves filled with books and games in colorful,
well-ordered array--Teaching Adults: An ESL Resource Book,
I Love Holidays, Patterns in Spelling: Book 4, Essential
Words for the GED, Laubach Way to Reading, Voyager:
Reading and Writing for Today's Adults. There, Billie
Granger introduces me to Chris Turner, the council's
assessment specialist, an energetic woman with short hair
and spectacles who seems to be in perpetual motion. Chris
begins to describe for me her role in assessing students'
skills, (all the while looking over her shoulder). She sets
on the table before me some complicated test forms she
uses to assess students' skills. Based on her assessments,
she prescribes course work appropriate to the students'
needs, consults with the tutors, and retests each student
after fifty hours of tutoring.

*Great
description*

*You're showing
this instead
of just telling—
vivid image!*

Craig 4

As we talk, a student, finished with class for the evening, wishes Chris a good night. She hugs him as he leaves. "He is so determined," she tells me, explaining that his math tutor gives him five problems each night, three or four nights each week, ("and he just hits it. He even added an additional session per week.") The process she describes of introducing new material gradually and building upon older skills seems painstaking. Often progress is excruciatingly slow. She has known students to work one-on-one for forty-five days, five days a week, for two solid years. "It's intensive work," Chris says. "The school system can't afford it." She should know. A school teacher for twenty-five years, now retired, she also raised a son who is deaf and learning disabled. "But that's how we do it; that's how it's got to be done: a little at a time over a long period of time."

The job of matching volunteers to students falls to Billie Granger, something Chris says she does with uncanny insight. Billie has a knack for matching not only skills but personalities too, permitting the frequent transformation of the tutoring relationship into one of mentoring, mutual support and friendship, regardless of race, creed, and social class. According to Chris, a lot of people volunteer expecting to help someone in need.

Is the quote necessary?

Craig 5

(What they don't expect is how much they get out of it in *Can you give an example?*
return. Opportunities for boundary-crossing abound.)

Suddenly Chris interrupts herself. "I'm giving a test right now and I don't want the student looking for me." She hurries off to check on the student. In a few moments I see her hurrying down the hallway to greet someone at the entrance.

I can hear Billie speaking on the telephone in her office. "I hate asking people on short notice, and several people brought up your name." It is nearly six o'clock the night before the all-important spelling bee, but Billie is trying to find a replacement for one of the two masters of ceremonies who is down with a bad back. I gather that the person on the other end of the conversation is the associate publisher of the daily newspaper. "Tell them to let you off tomorrow," she says with (a hoarse giggle). *This helps me see a familiar type of person.*

When Chris returns, she introduces me to Joe Carpenter, one of the council's veteran tutor-trainers; then she sees her student in the hall. "All right," she says, "let me get you one more test," and she's off again. Now Joe will carry me. It's a relay race, and I'm the baton.

Billie hangs up the phone after agreeing to call back first thing in the morning, then claps her hands loudly and exclaims, "Got him!"

Craig 6

Joe quips, "You can't say no to Billie." He glares at me and adds, "She'll rope you in too, before long. You watch!"

Functional illiteracy, Billie tells me, is a subjective term, ~~defined by~~ individual ~~based on~~ what she or he ~~is called on to~~ do. For some that means being able to figure percentages or ratios; for others it may be writing job-related reports. An increasing number of literate adults need to learn English as a second language. Most students read below a fifth-grade level, what Billie calls "survival level." And they're typically not uneducated people. Among the 450 people receiving help from the council each year are mechanics aspiring to become supervisors, small business owners hoping to stay abreast ~~with~~ new technologies, factory workers needing to learn how to operate new machinery, mothers wanting to help their children with homework. Computers have raised the bar at the workplace: janitors and mechanics are increasingly expected to use them for logging hours and fulfilling work orders. Weak readers must choose between getting the necessary training or risk falling by the wayside. Their self-esteem is always on the line. "The literacy council is for people who want to improve their literacy skills," says Billie Granger, "not for people who can't read." We often assume that people can't read

Craig 7

because they lacked access to education. Not so. Possibly
as many as eighty percent of the council's students can't
read because of a disability that schools are not equipped
to address, disabilities including dyslexia, neurological
dysfunction, cerebral palsy, and schizophrenia.

Joe Carpenter says the literacy council is often a
"last-ditch effort" for adults who are highly intelligent,
but they (think differently) because they've depended so
much on other people all their lives. "You see a fifty-
year-old who thinks, 'I'm just stupid!' Others are scared
they might be recognized by their employers or coworkers
when they can't read the job manual; others want to learn
to drive, or read Mark Twain, the Bible, the newspaper."

I think this phrase may confuse readers. My first thought was that you mean a different style of thinking.

At this point, I begin to wonder whether I'm ever
going to get what I came for--an opportunity to observe
and interview a pair of tutoring partners. Startled by my
request, Joe explains that the council's strict observance
of confidentiality prevents this. More embarrassed than
disappointed, I realize that, having seen the purpose of
my visit as self-evident, I've never stated it explicitly.
Alert to my disappointment, Joe proposes a brief visit to
the training room, just long enough to say hello to a
tutor and his student, who he knows will not object to our
presence. The tutor, a retired engineer, is writing a
simple equation on the white board. His student, a high-

school dropout now in his twenties, stands ready to solve it. Joe introduces me and asks the student how he's doing. Suddenly I'm terribly aware of the pen and notepad I'm holding. I keep them at my side. The student shrugs and answers, "Good." His tutor says he's doing great: "We're going to tackle the GED in a few weeks, and we're going to be ready."

By the end of my visit, I've learned a lot about the Cape Fear Literacy Council. Most of what I know, however, involves the council's organizational structure, guiding principles, and daily operations. Nearly all of my information has come from the top down--from the point of view of administrators. Sensing the rapport that Joe and I have established, I express my frustration. "Come back again, next week," he replies cheerfully. "I'll introduce you to my guinea pig." I can tell he isn't going to elaborate on this cryptic remark. But it's my only hope, and my curiosity has been piqued anyway.

A week later, I wait with Joe outside the council offices at a picnic table with an umbrella. Smoking a cigarette, he tells me about his "guinea pig." Severely dyslexic, this student has been supporting a family on minimum wage while studying with Joe for the past six years. "He's religious about attendance," Joe says. Soon a pickup truck pulls into the lot and three people emerge, a

Craig 9

middle-aged couple and their young daughter. The student is a tall, quiet man who smiles as he approaches. He carries a weighty-looking book bag. All three greet Joe like old friends, and Joe asks his student if he's ready to do some writing. The man groans. Joe turns to his wife and says, "I'm going to kill him with writing, you know that." The woman laughs, "He sure hates that writing."

And that's it. I realize that I'm not going to get any closer. I feel like someone who's almost beguiled a stray kitten into being touched and petted, yet at the last second the animal panics and flees. At the very moment of formulating this thought, I recognize something faulty about my assumptions. I thought I'd come here only to understand, but maybe I'd come also to stare. What was I thinking when I thought to myself that I'd never <u>seen</u> a functional illiterate. And so, although I learned a lot about <u>illiteracy</u> and somewhat less about <u>illiterates</u>, (I ended up learning much more about myself and my unexamined attitudes and beliefs).

I want to know more about this!

Mark,

I feel like I've learned a lot just by reading your paper! I'm not sure whether or not you intended to influence readers like this, but I come away from this draft with lots of questions about how many different ways people define literacy. Billie Granger says that the CFLC is not for people who can't read.

Craig 10

(Are there many such people, and if so, who does help them?) It all seems to revolve around "functional illiteracy," and it sounds like no one agrees on what that is. But I guess if it weren't for these contradictions and gray areas, illiteracy wouldn't be so much of a social problem.

What I think you're trying to show in this paper is how the literacy council operates, and you do an awfully good job of it. So I'm surprised by the tone of defeat, if not failure, that I hear in your last paragraph. You seem to be saying that a certain human interest is missing from your paper because you couldn't interview a student. On the other hand, you end this draft on a tantalizing note when you say you've learned something about yourself. Is that maybe what this paper is (at least partly) about? Would telling what you've learned maybe compensate for whatever you feel is missing because you couldn't get the students' point of view about literacy education?

Peer Review

As you can see by comparing Mark's editing draft with his final paper, he benefited from the careful *peer review* of his classmate Phoebe. Most experienced writers are eager, even greedy, for this kind of feedback. By the time you complete a draft for others to read, you should have read it and reread it so often that you no longer view it objectively. A fellow student can help you see this draft through her or his eyes, enabling you to gain a fresh perception of it.

A peer reviewer's principal task is to give you a sense of how a detached reader might respond to your draft. When you read and comment on another person's writing, you should not think of yourself as a teacher or judge. Instead, be yourself and respond as honestly and helpfully as you can. Notice several important features of Phoebe's response to Mark's paper:

- **Holistic response.** The longest comment is a final *holistic* response, reflecting on the entire draft—the intentions of the writer and how the text makes an impact on one reader—rather than addressing isolated details. Phoebe carefully provides two indispensable kinds of feedback in a few sentences: telling the writer, truthfully but tactfully, what took place in her mind as she read the draft ("I come away from this draft with lots of questions about how many different ways people define literacy") and suggesting only one or two possibilities for revision (e.g., "Would telling what you've learned maybe compensate for whatever you feel is missing because you couldn't get the students' point of view about literacy education?").

- **Respect for the writer's ownership.** The respondent respects the writer's ownership of the draft: Her comments are tentative, not directive. When she thinks a particular revision might be called for, she asks questions rather than dictates how to change the draft (e.g., "Is the quote necessary?").

- **Attention to positive features.** The respondent notes positive features of the text without being insincere or patronizing. She is supportive ("Great description") while letting the writer know where she has difficulties ("I think this phrase may confuse readers").

- **Little concern for mechanical errors.** The respondent gives scant attention to lapses in style or mechanics. Occasionally, a reviewer will point out an error that may escape the writer's attention (e.g., *minuscule,* a word often misspelled by experienced writers), but that is far less relevant now than providing other kinds of help. (Proofreading for awkward sentences and mechanical correctness is important later, when you can enlist the assistance of an alert editor.) Notice, however, that Phoebe does call Mark's attention to an awkward phrase ("defined by") and suggests an alternative ("assigned to").

- **A range of comments.** Comments fall into several different categories: *proposals for revision* (e.g., the suggested alteration of the opening sentence of paragraph 13), *responses to the writer's strategies* (e.g., "You're showing this instead of just telling"), *descriptions of the reader's response* (e.g., "My first thought was that you mean a different style of thinking"), and *requests for clarification or amplification* (e.g., "You felt unsafe? Why?"). Although each type of comment may provide valuable help, those closer to the end of this list tend to be more useful in "opening up" a draft for the writer by allowing him to remain in charge of revising his own draft.

By far the most useful of Phoebe's comments were those that encouraged Mark to reconsider his overall aims:

> You seem to be saying that a certain human element is missing from your paper because you couldn't interview a student. On the other hand, you end this draft on a tantalizing note when you say you've learned something about yourself. Is that maybe what this paper is (at least partly) about?

These comments helped resolve a dilemma revealed in the final sentence of Mark's draft: when he began thinking about his topic, Mark had intended to learn about illiterate individuals—persons he assumed to be different from anyone he had ever known. While visiting the Cape Fear Literacy Council, however, he discovered that illiteracy is both widespread and often invisible. Furthermore, during the brief interval when he was able to observe a tutoring session, Mark recognized that interviewing a student would have been awkward and inappropriate. As a result, the final paragraph of Mark's draft expresses frustration, embarrassment, and disappointment about the näiveté of his original goals and his failure to accomplish them. Phoebe, however, viewing Mark's draft from a more detached perspective, suggested that he alter the focus of his paper. By communicating sincere curiosity about his self-discovery and new understanding of illiteracy, Phoebe encouraged Mark to consider other possibilities for his essay. Consequently, his final draft includes additional paragraphs that examine the preconceptions he brought into his initial observations.

Revision, however, involves more than just adding new material at the end of a first draft. Mark now reconsidered his entire paper in light of his altered intentions. For instance, the first sentence of his third paragraph reveals his initial misconceptions about the council's clientele—the stereotypic assumption that adult illiterates are often criminals. Likewise, his final draft omits any mention of his original plan to interview a tutor and student. Instead, he discreetly imbeds information about council policies in one short phrase: "*Sensitive to the need to protect students' privacy,* Joe tells me that these two won't mind a brief visit."

Revising

Careful, deliberate revision distinguishes accomplished writers from novices. Experienced writers devote time to rereading, changing words, rearranging sentences and paragraphs, adding new material, and rewriting. Some drafts require more revision than others.

A few things about revision hold true for almost any successful writer. First, you need feedback from an alert, objective respondent. You yourself may be that respondent, provided that you can step back and view your work as a detached reader. After you have completed a draft, let it sit (for a few days if possible, but at least overnight) so you can see it from a fresh perspective. Many writers like to read their work aloud, either for themselves or for someone else. Some discover ideas as they recopy or retype what they have written, since this allows them to read their work slowly and attentively. Frequently, however, the most valuable help comes from a trusted friend or classmate who reads your draft and offers suggestions. This is the kind of help Mark Craig received from his classmate Phoebe during a peer-review session.

Of course, not all writers are alike, and different writers prefer different strategies for revision. Some prefer all-at-once revisions. They write a draft all the way through and then compose a revised second draft, followed by a third, and so on. Others engage in ongoing revision, altering one sentence or paragraph again and again before moving on to the next. Mark Craig falls somewhere in between. He composed his drafts on a word processor and made frequent changes as he proceeded. But he printed out complete drafts several times and marked changes in pencil before entering them into his word processor. Here, for example, is a revision of his opening paragraph:

~~Like approaching thunder, a~~ freight train *A* ~~rumbled~~ *thunders* by outside ~~and blared its~~ strident *, its whistle blaring* ~~horn just as it passed~~ *ly a few yards away from* the window *sill* where I s~~a~~*i*t. Billie Granger, the executive director of the Cape Fear Literacy Council, ~~sat behind~~ *sits at* her desk, unfazed. I ~~peered over the pile of books and paper on her desk, to~~ see her mouth moving, but I ~~couldn't~~ *can't* hear a word. As the train ~~noise fades beyond~~ *clears* the crossing, ~~Billie continued~~ *She describes* in her gravelly voice ~~to explain~~ the frustration some parents feel when they cannot read bedtime stories to their children because they can't make out ~~many of~~ the words ~~on the page~~ --because they are "functionally illiterate."

As you can see by comparing Mark's two drafts, this type of rephrasing was only part of his revision process. He also deleted some parts entirely (e.g., the final paragraph of his first draft), while adding a few details elsewhere (like his description of the stroke victim who receives intensive tutoring from Chris Turner).

Writers often reassess their basic goals during revision. They consider the readers they are addressing, how they want those readers to respond, and how they can provide more and better evidence to support their aims. Revision means *seeing again,* and often the best way to accomplish this is to look at your concluding paragraphs to see whether they reflect the same purpose as earlier parts of your draft. Writers often discover or revise their purpose as they compose a first draft, and it is not unusual for the last parts of that draft to reflect an emerging aim that the opening paragraphs do not anticipate. This was the case for Mark.

Before completing a final draft, Mark sketched another brief outline—one that reflects the aims of that draft:

> Illiteracy: America's Secret
> Introduction
>   Extent of adult illiteracy in the U.S.
>   Background and history of Cape Fear Literacy Council
> Description of council headquarters
> Administrative roles
>   Chris Turner—assessment
>   Billie Granger—pairing tutors and students
>   Joe Carpenter—tutor-training
> "Functional illiteracy"
>   Various definitions
>   Practical implications
> Descriptions of students
>   Tutoring session—student preparing for GED
>   Joe's "guinea pig"
> My new understanding of (il)literacy

Editing and Proofreading

Finally, you need to edit and proofread your revised draft. This involves deleting imprecise or inappropriate words and ambiguous phrases as well as carefully checking punctuation and spelling. After editing and proofreading, you are ready to print another copy of your paper and give it a final review for errors. Though the spell-check feature of your word-processing program identifies many mistakes, it overlooks others (e.g., word substitutions like *then* used for *than*). Therefore, you should give your paper a careful proofreading as well.

Developing Your Own Writing Routines

Writing is sometimes compared to swimming, woodworking, and other such skills. Basically, these comparisons are valid and reassuring; college students *can* indeed develop their writing abilities to the point of proficiency. However, writing differs from certain other skills—long division, for instance—in that it involves hardly any rigid rules, all of which are mastered at an early age (e.g., beginning every declarative sentence with a capital letter and closing it with a period).

Well-meaning teachers sometimes try to reduce writing to a set of "rules," which includes such admonitions as "Never open a sentence with a conjunction" and "Never use the words *you* and *I* in an essay." However, most experienced writers not only have found these dictates unreliable (frequently disregarding those just mentioned) but also have learned that writing is seldom systematic, orderly, or predictable. This is not to say that their approach is haphazard. Knowing that trial and error is inefficient, experienced writers rely instead on a repertoire of procedures, which may include brainstorming, mapping, freewriting, and other techniques described in earlier parts of this chapter.

Throughout this book you will be introduced to procedures for approaching each stage of a writing process. Keep in mind that this process does not work in the same predictable fashion for every individual. It will not result in a single correct response to each of the writing tasks introduced in this book, nor to those assigned by your instructor. What it should do is encourage you to experiment with some techniques that experienced writers use to get past the moments of writer's block that everyone encounters from time to time. The best way to find out which procedures help you under which circumstances is to engage in as many of them as possible, merely going through the motions at first if necessary. Over time, however, you may come to rely on a few standbys that minimize anxieties brought on by the interplay of complex skills involved in writing for academic purposes.

■ READING

Reading demands active participation. Without the alert engagement of a reader, words on a page have no meaning. Only you can bring them to life. Your ability to interpret words, your knowledge of how sentences and paragraphs are put together, your past experiences with reading and with life, your current mood—all these work together to make your reading of an essay, a poem, or even a recipe different from those of other readers.

Reading Habits and Strategies

No one else reads exactly as you do. In some ways, reading is a very personal activity. No matter what you read—even a textbook like this one—it is unlikely that anyone else will interpret it exactly as you do. Even among classmates with similar backgrounds, responses are not often the same. Since no one is an exact duplicate of anyone else, each person's reading experience is unique. Furthermore, even the same reader may experience the same text very differently on separate occasions. In the following passage, Wendy Lesser, editor of the literary journal *Threepenny Review*, illustrates this point in a description of her reading habits:

> Nothing demonstrates how personal reading is more clearly than rereading does. The first time you read a book, you might imagine that what you are getting out of it is precisely what the author put into it. And you would be right, at least in part. There is some element of every aesthetic experience, every *human* experience, that is generalizable and communicable and belongs to all of us. If this

were not true, art would be pointless. The common ground of our response is terrifically important. But there is also the individual response, and that too is important. I get annoyed at literary theorists who try to make us choose one over the other, as if *either* reading is an objective experience, providing everyone with access to the author's intentions, *or* it is a subjective experience, revealing to us only the thoughts in our own minds. Why? Why must it be one or the other, when every sensible piece of evidence indicates that it is both?

Rereading is certainly both, as I was to discover. You cannot reread a book . . . without perceiving it as, among other things, a mirror. Wherever you look in that novel or poem or essay, you will find a little reflected face peering out at you—the face of . . . the original reader, the person you were when you first read the book. So the material that wells up out of this rereading feels very private, very specific to you. But as you engage in this rereading, you can sense that there are at least two readers, the older one and the younger one. You know there are two of you because you can feel them responding differently to the book. Differently, but not entirely differently: there is a core of experience shared by your two selves (perhaps there are even more than two, if you include all the people you were in the years between the two readings). And this awareness of the separate readers within you makes you appreciate the essential constancy of the literary work, even in the face of your own alterations over time, so that you begin to realize how all the different readings by different people might nonetheless have a great deal in common.

You may note some similarities between Lesser's characterization of reading and Nancy Sommers's description of writing (page 5). Both Lesser and Sommers examine literate acts that engage both individual creativity and interaction with others. Both talk about mediating between free associations of recollected experience and the completion of a task (publishing an essay or getting to the end of a story). Most important, though, both Lesser and Sommers stress the *active* nature of reading and writing: readers do much more than retrieve information, and writers do not simply transcribe facts and ideas from useful sources.

Interpreting Texts

We have seen that writing practices differ among individuals and vary according to purpose and audience. The same is true of reading; there is no single best way to read. When we encounter the short, precise sentences in a set of directions, we want to find out how to do something quickly and efficiently, like programming a VCR. When we pick up a poem or a short story, however, we have other aims and expectations. Instead of looking for information or instruction, we want to derive pleasure from the way words and images are used, to engage with sympathetic characters, or to enjoy a suspenseful plot. To participate fully and actively in this type of reading, we must connect our values and experiences with an imaginative text.

Audience

What you get out of reading depends on what you bring into it. For example, if you bring an extensive background in music to the following passage, you will get much more from it than the average reader:

Passage written for an audience of musical experts

Although Schoenberg sometimes dreamed of serialism as a reassertion of German musical hegemony, he more commonly thought of it as a purely formalistic ordering device, and most American serialists share that view. So [did] the Soviets, with their crude denunciations of "formalism." But just as with psychoanalysis, dismissed by its opponents as a web of metaphors conditioned by time and place, serialism can be considered narrowly Viennese and, by now, dated. And not just dated and extraneous to an American sensibility, but out of fashion.

—John Rockwell, *All-American Music*

Even if all the names and terminology were explained, most readers would still find this passage obscure. Actually, though, its level of difficulty depends on the reader. To thousands of music experts, the meaning is clear, but to those who do not bring musical expertise to the reading, not much emerges. Evidently, the passage is aimed at a small, informed **audience** of readers. If you were reporting on musical trends for a wider audience, you would not quote this passage from John Rockwell's book, at least not without clarification.

Consider now another passage that addresses a somewhat wider audience, readers of the *Chronicle of Higher Education,* most of whom are university professors and administrators with backgrounds in a variety of academic fields:

Passage written for a highly educated audience without musical expertise

About three years ago, I tried an experiment with a group of scholars and artists. . . . "As you know," I said, "I write about classical music. Suppose I named the main styles in musical composition since serialism. Would any of you understand what I was talking about?" "No," said everybody, and I can't say I was surprised.

Something odd has happened to classical music. Somehow, it—and most notably its advanced, contemporary wing—has unhitched itself from the wider world of art and culture. Readers of the *Chronicle* might know about contemporary painting, or films or novels, or (the younger readers, anyway) ambient music or alternative rock. But I'd be surprised if they were familiar with current classical composers. . . .

Serial music—conventionally thought to be the high-water mark of musical modernism—may have been, at least in America, both a cause and a symptom of this breach. It was pioneered in Europe in the 1920s, by Arnold Schoenberg, the composer who (very loosely speaking) did for music what abstract painters did for painting, and who is defended in a recent book, *Arnold Schoenberg's Journey* . . . , by Allen Shawn. Just as abstract painters gave up painting faces, objects, and scenes, Schoenberg began by writing music without familiar chords and melodies. More crucially, he gave up repetition and regular rhythms, and instead wrote complex pieces with unexpected contours and an irregular pace.

—Greg Sandow, "Serialism as a Museum Piece"

The author of this passage, who also writes for the *Wall Street Journal* and *Village Voice,* starts by reassuring readers that many well-educated people don't know much about recent classical music. Then, before trying to explain serialism, he provides some historical context and draws an analogy to modern painting, which probably is more familiar to most educated adults. Unlike John Rockwell, who addresses a musically sophisticated audience, Greg Sandow targets readers who know less about music in particular, but are generally conversant with history and the arts.

Many other writers adapt language and content to a still wider audience of readers with varied backgrounds. For example, the following passage describes a collection of unconventional musical instruments designed and built by visionary composer Harry Partch. The author of the passage, Allan Ulrich, is the classical music and dance critic for the *San Francisco Examiner,* a daily newspaper with a large circulation. Ulrich is reviewing an exhibition of Partch's work for readers of the *Examiner's* Sunday supplement:

> There are the visionaries and then there are the cranks. Somewhere in that wispy zone of shadow separating the two, in that spiritual limbo for which we lack a precise word, posterity has deposited Harry Partch (1901–74)—composer, instrument builder, philosopher, multiculturalist, great California-born creative maverick.
>
> The twenty-five instruments devised and constructed by Partch . . . reflect his obsession with the ancients, not merely in their names—Kithara I and Kithara II, Chromelodeon—but in his belief that they should affect an area beyond human consciousness. The enormous Marimba Eroica, individually hung Sitka spruce blocks laid over cave-like resonators the size of the piano, emits four low tones, the lowest of which is not audible to the human ear. That you can also feel Partch's music has no doubt endeared him to a younger generation; vibes and all that. . . .
>
> What the "Sounds like Art" Festival should accomplish is to place Partch in some kind of context. He may have been one of the greatest American individualists; still, he has spawned a generation of composer-instrument makers who feel free to journey down their own paths. The Bay Area's Beth Custer and Matt Heckert, Los Angeles' Marina Rosenfeld and the German-born, Seattle-based artist who goes by the sole name of Trimpin, will all add their distinctive constructions to this project.
>
> Here, perhaps, is where the Harry Partch legacy truly resides. Idiosyncrasy may have ventured, ever so timorously, into the mainstream of American music, but the current remains as unpredictable as ever.
>
> —Allan Ulrich, "American Visionary"

Passage written for a general audience

Even readers without much musical knowledge or interest can derive something from this passage. Although Ulrich introduces information unfamiliar to most of us, he uses informal language and relies on concepts (e.g., vibes) that most adults can readily understand.

Tacit Knowledge

Interpretation is influenced by more than just the vocabulary of a particular text, the length of its sentences, or the educational credentials of the reader. It also depends on the amount of ***tacit knowledge*** that writers and readers share—that is, how much a writer can safely assume that readers understand without explanation. For example, almost any reader knows what a DVD is without a parenthetical decoding of the abbreviation. On the other hand, few people other than public-school teachers and administrators in North Carolina can be expected to know that an LEA is a local educational agency or school district. However, educators who frequently use the term LEA in their professional discourse would be distracted by a memo that continually refers to "local educational agencies," just as most newspaper readers would be distracted by a column that repeatedly refers to "digital video discs."

Context

Interpretation is also affected by context. Removed from the sports page of a newspaper in the Southeast, the headline "Yellow Jackets Overcome by Green Wave" is ambiguous at best. Similarly, the headline "High Budget Hopes Give Footsie a Fillip" may seem clear to a reader of the financial pages of the London *Daily Mail,* but outside that context, it would perplex most educated Americans, including many experienced investors.

Successful reading, then, depends not only on knowledge and skill, but also on the reader's familiarity with context and the writer's ability to assess the needs and expectations of a particular audience. It depends on what the writer and the reader bring to a text. Good readers are alert and flexible. For them, reading is as creative a process as writing—and as varied.

Efferent and Aesthetic Approaches to Reading

Louise Rosenblatt, a pioneer in the study of reading processes, draws a distinction between *efferent reading* and *aesthetic reading.* When readers need information, they adopt an efferent stance: they just try to grasp what a text is saying. When they adopt an aesthetic stance, readers pursue unique personal engagement with a text (usually a work of literature). When the first edition of this book appeared, in 1985, many English teachers assumed that nearly all students enter college already proficient at efferent reading. As a result, reading assignments in first-year English courses were often confined to literary texts. Reading, to the extent that it was taught at all, involved mastery of the aesthetic stance described in the final paragraph of the excerpt from Wendy Lesser's essay (page 41).

As teachers and textbook authors, we remain skeptical of these assumptions. Therefore, in Chapter 2, as well as in various other parts of this book, we explain and illustrate strategies that facilitate efferent reading. Nevertheless, as enthusiastic, life-long readers of literature, we do not discount the value of aesthetic reading in the daily lives of educated adults. Nor do we approach these two types of reading as totally distinct, let alone incompatible. In fact, your response to most of the selections in this book will be enriched by your ability to move smoothly and productively between both types of reading.

Problems arise when students restrict themselves to one type of reading or adopt a stance unsuited to the situation at hand. When you read a textbook to acquire information, for example, you overlook style, tone, and figurative language. If a friend accidentally swallowed a poison, you would search the back of the bottle for an antidote and read rapidly, perhaps aloud: "Do not induce vomiting. Have the victim drink two quarts of fresh water." Needless to say, you would not comment to the victim about the author's prose style: "Hey, Phil, listen to these short, precise sentences!" Under these circumstances you want only information.

At the opposite extreme, if you were asked to respond to the following poem, a haiku by Bashō , a seventeenth-century Japanese poet, gathering information would not be your aim:

> *The ancient lagoon*
> *A frog jumps*
> *The splash of the water.*

These lines invite you to respond to images. You do not read them to increase your knowledge of amphibian behavior or marine ecology. And though experienced readers of poetry may respond differently than novices, each reader's aesthetic response is personal and unique. One reader may recall a childhood experience. Another may simply derive a sense of peace and beauty. A third reader, familiar with Zen Buddhism, may have a more philosophical response. This reader may note a contrast between the poem's first line (an image of eternal stillness) and the second (a momentary action), finding in the last line, where the two contrasting images merge, an insight into timeless truth. Someone unused to reading such an open-ended text may find it puzzling and ultimately useless.

Interpreting Texts   **EXERCISE**

To test the validity of what we have said about interpretation, see how your responses to two very different passages compare with those of other readers. Reread the passage about Harry Partch on page 43 and state in a sentence or two what you consider its main idea to be.

Now read the following haiku by another Japanese poet, Buson, and write an equally brief interpretation of it:

> *On the bell of the temple*
> *rests a butterfly,*
> *asleep.*

Express your personal response to the poem, even if you feel it is not very insightful. (Keep in mind that a single "correct" interpretation of such a poem probably does not exist.)

Compare your responses with those of classmates. Do they differ? Is there more agreement about interpreting the prose passage as opposed to the poem? How do you account for any differences? Even with the passage about Harry Partch, is there room for difference?

Responding to Reading

Most of the reading you will do in this book lies somewhere between the objective prose of how-to instructions and the subjective language of poetry. It requires active, alert participation. When you conduct research, you cannot read a source without being critically aware of both the information it presents and the author's attitude, purpose, and reliability.

In addition to exercises that engage writing, reading, and research, most chapters in this book conclude with several longer texts, followed by questions about ideas and interpretations that the readings may arouse. Deliberate response to these texts demands care and persistence because, just as good writing involves revision, good reading entails rereading.

When you discuss the reading selections in this book, you will find that your responses often coincide with those of classmates, but there also will be legitimate differences. You may form interpretations that others do not share or understand, and readers often resist interpretations that diverge from their own. Nevertheless, this is inevitable; reading affirms both the connectedness of communities and the differences that distinguish us as individuals.

The best way to respond to reading is to write about it. Writing stretches our thoughts by encouraging us to connect one idea with another. And because it is visible, writing helps us see what we mean. It also helps us become clearer, more logical, and more concrete. As you learned earlier in this chapter, freewriting is a method of open-ended response that invites us to jot down whatever comes to mind through focused (or unfocused) thought. Freewritten responses to reading may evoke personal associations, observations about style, restatements of what the author is saying, or any other thought or feeling that comes to the tip of the pen.

EXERCISES — Responding to Reading

1. Each of the following short reading selections presents difficulties in interpretation for at least some readers. Read each one carefully, then freewrite about it for five minutes. Remember, you create the rules for freewriting as you write (except for the basic rule that you keep writing at a steady pace for a designated period of time.)

   a. A sign posted in a clothing store reads:

      Kindly spare us the discomfort of refusing requests for refunds.

   b. These personal ads appeared in a community newspaper:

      • M, 44, clean, sporty, original equipment, runs great, seeks F that needs a lift.
      • F, 28, black and glossy, seeks confidential WM, very giving, who's bound for whatever.
      • Mistress Marcy seeks playmate.
      • Ornery, self-sufficient, prof SWF, mid 40s, seeks man with integrity. If you're not honest, don't bother.

   c. The following advertisement appeared among "Help Wanted" ads in an issue of the *Nassau Guardian,* the most widely circulated daily newspaper in the Bahamas:

      The Firm Masterminds Historians, Scientists, Financiers, Philosophers, Senior Pastors, Bankers, Solicitors, Doctors (1998) Inc.
      Wisdom / Reversals / Expulsions / Nulls & voids available via discernments laws & sciences/disengagements laws & sciences to discern / Expel / Call out / Shutdown / Reverse / Null & void / Secret or suspected child molesters/incestors / False pastors/mistressings / Homosexuality / Wife beaters & spousal batterers etc IF you can establish just cause which is Mandatory! We cleanse homes / Marriages / Businesses / Churches. Rates are $750 to $2,500 per hour.

   d. Following is an entry from the *New York Times* column "Metropolitan Diary":

      Dorothy Loudon was on a bus when a homeless woman entered with what Ms. Loudon described as "the whole business—layers of clothing, multiple hats, a cart full of old newspapers and odd items." The woman seated herself across the aisle from Ms. Loudon and after settling in, stood up and addressed the stunned passengers in a voice that carried. "Well, if you want to know the truth, blame it all on Woody Allen," the woman said. Then she sat down. That was it.

e. The following tale opens a magazine article, "When Evil Is 'Cool,'" preceded by this headnote: "Our culture, in particular the institution of the university, has contrived . . . to transform sin into a positive: *transgression,* a term that, as used by postmodern critics, refers to an implied form of greatness":

> Living alone in a Paris garret, an idle young bohemian meditated on the sudden, perverse spurts of energy that can interrupt a life of laziness and boredom. Such urges lead one to unthinkable acts—such as starting a forest fire or lighting a cigar next to a powder keg—just to see what will happen, to tempt fate.
>
> One morning the young man awoke in a mood to perform such an outrageous act. Seeing below in the street a window-glass vendor, *un vitrier,* with his stock of panes in a pack on his back, he summoned the vendor to climb up the six stories to his garret. He asked for tinted glass, which the vendor did not have. In a rage the young man kicked the vendor back out into the staircase, where the tradesman almost stumbled under his heavy load. Then, watching from the balcony, the young man dropped a flower pot just as the vendor reappeared in the street, and thus broke his stock of glass to smithereens. This vicious prank might damn him, the young bohemian said to himself, but it also brought a moment of infinite bliss.

2. Exchange freewrites in groups of four. Are there differences? If so, how can you explain them? Have one member of your group list the types of difficulty that these selections present—for example, ambiguities (perhaps intentional), assumptions about the tacit knowledge of readers, unfamiliar or unclear context.

Reading Response Groups

Thus far, we have presented reading as a process that engages individual, independent thought as well as literal understanding. Specifically, we have stressed the idea that readers often *create* meaning rather than passively *receive* it from a "determinate" text—one that supposedly elicits a single accurate interpretation that coincides with the author's intentions. In order to dispel the notion that reading amounts to little more than *retrieving* information and ideas that writers have *put* into their texts, we have emphasized the autonomy of individual readers—their privilege to interpret what they read.

Granted that autonomy, one might plausibly interpret the passage by Allan Ulrich on page 43 as a satirical jab at avant-garde music. To go a step further, another person might view it as a parody of museum reviews—a mischievous hoax at the expense of literal-minded readers. While most of us would consider that a peculiar response, a carefully selected group of like-minded readers might accept it as an inventive, possibly useful, interpretation—though one that the author probably did not anticipate. But most reasonable people will agree that there are limits. It is unlikely, for example, that any community of readers would entertain the possibility that Ulrich is denouncing avant-garde music as an elitist conspiracy launched by multinational corporations. Such an interpretation is too eccentric to be plausible.

The autonomy of individual readers, then, can be exaggerated. Reading, like writing, is not a completely solitary activity. It is, instead, a *social* process, and readers often benefit from the responses of peers just as Mark Craig did when he revised his essay.

The following transaction among three experienced readers demonstrates the collaboration of a **reading group,** two or more individuals who share, often in writing, their personal responses to a text. Although they vary in size, most groups consist of three to six members. Your instructor may place you in a reading group and assign specific tasks, often called **prompts,** for you and your partners to address. (On the other hand, students in the same class may create reading groups of their own, and collaboration is sometimes spontaneous and unfocused.)

The following assignment is designed to initiate discussion and collaborative response to a short magazine article. Take a moment now to read it, along with the article itself, which follows.

ASSIGNMENT   **Freewriting Prompt**

Read "A Short History of Love," an article from *Harper's,* a magazine of opinion concerned with political and cultural issues. (Before publication, the article was delivered as a paper at an academic conference cosponsored by the Columbia University Psychoanalytic Center and the Association for Psychiatric Medicine.) As you read, use your pencil to mark important or noteworthy ideas and to record any reactions or personal associations that come to mind. Keep your writing brief, using shorthand as much as possible, and try not to pause for more than a few seconds in perhaps three or four places at most. Then read the article again, this time looking more closely at how Lawrence Stone presents the history of romantic love and draws conclusions about it. After this second reading, freewrite for twenty minutes in response to the article's ideas. In particular, consider whether you agree with the author's suggestion that there is something dangerous or unhealthy in contemporary attitudes about love. Bring this freewriting to class next time, prepared to share it with other members of your reading group.

PRACTICE READING

A Short History of Love

Lawrence Stone

Historians and anthropologists are in general agreement that romantic love—that usually brief but intensely felt and all-consuming attraction toward another person—is culturally conditioned. Love has a history. It is common only in certain societies at certain times, or even in certain social groups within those societies, usually the elite, which have the leisure to cultivate such feelings. Scholars are, however, less certain whether romantic love is merely a culturally induced psychological overlay on top of the biological drive for sex, or whether it has biochemical roots that operate quite independently from the libido. Would anyone in fact "fall in love" if they had not read about it or heard it talked about? Did poetry invent love, or love poetry?

Some things can be said with certainty about the history of the phenomenon. The first is that cases of romantic love can be found in all times and places and have often been the subject of powerful poetic expression, from the Song of Solomon to Shakespeare. On the other hand, as anthropologists have discovered, neither social approbation nor the actual experience of romantic love is common to all societies. Second, historical evidence for romantic love before the age of printing is largely confined to elite groups, which of course does not mean that it may not have occurred lower on the social scale. As a socially approved cultural artifact, romantic love began in Europe in the southern French aristocratic courts of the twelfth century, and was made fashionable by a group of poets, the troubadours. In this case the culture dictated that it should occur between an unmarried male and a married woman, and that it either should go sexually unconsummated or should be adulterous.

By the sixteenth and seventeenth centuries, our evidence becomes quite extensive, thanks to the spread of literacy and the printing press. We now have love poems, such as Shakespeare's sonnets, love letters, and autobiographies by women concerned primarily with their love lives. The courts of Europe were evidently hotbeds of passionate intrigues and liaisons, some romantic, some sexual. The printing press also began to spread pornography to a wider public, thus stimulating the libido, while the plays of Shakespeare indicate that romantic love was a concept familiar to society at large, which composed his audience.

Whether this romantic love was approved of, however, is another question. We simply do not know how Shakespearean audiences reacted to *Romeo and Juliet*. Did they, like us (and as Shakespeare clearly intended), fully identify with the young lovers? Or, when they left the theater, did they continue to act like the Montague and Capulet parents, who were trying to stop these irresponsible adolescents from allowing an ephemeral and irrational passion to interfere with the serious business of politics and patronage?

What is certain is that every advice book, every medical treatise, every sermon and religious homily of the sixteenth and seventeenth centuries firmly rejected both romantic passion and lust as suitable bases for marriage. In the sixteenth century, marriage was thought to be best arranged by parents, who could be relied upon to choose socially and economically suitable partners. People believed that the sexual bond would automatically create the necessary harmony between the two strangers in order to maintain the stability of the new family unit. This assumption is not, it seems, unreasonable, since recent investigations in Japan have shown that there is no difference in the rate of divorce between couples whose marriages were arranged by their parents and couples whose marriages were made by individual choice based on romantic love.

In the eighteenth century, orthodox opinion about marriage began to shift from subordinating the individual will to the interests of the group, and from economic or political considerations, toward those of well-tried personal affection. The ideal marriage was one preceded by three to six months of intensive courting by a couple from families roughly equal in social status and economic wealth; that courtship, however, took place only with the prior consent of parents on both sides. But it was not until the Romantic movement and the rise of the novel, especially the pulp novel of the nineteenth century, that society accepted a new idea—that it is normal and indeed praiseworthy for young men and women to fall passionately in love, and that there must be something wrong with those who fail to have such an overwhelming experience sometime in late adolescence or early adulthood. Once this new idea was publicly accepted, the arrangement of marriage by parents came to be regarded as intolerable and immoral.

Today, the role of passionate attachments between adults is obscured by a new development: the saturation of the whole culture—through every medium of communication—with the belief that sexuality is the predominant and overriding human drive, a doctrine whose theoretical foundations were provided by Freud. In no past society known to me has sex been given so prominent a role in the culture at large, nor has sexual fulfillment been elevated to such preeminence in the list of human aspirations—in a vain attempt to relieve civilization of its discontents. We find it scarcely credible today that in most of Western Europe in the seventeenth century, in a society in which people usually married in their late twenties, a degree of chastity was practiced that kept the illegitimacy rate—without contraceptives—as low as two or three percent. Today, individualism is given such absolute priority in most Western societies that people are virtually free to act as they please, to sleep with whom they please, and to marry and divorce when and whom they please. The psychic (and, more recently, the physical) costs of such behavior are now becoming clear, however, and how long this situation will last is anybody's guess.

Here I should point out that the present-day family—I exclude the poor black family in America from this generalization—is not, as is generally supposed, disintegrating because of the very high divorce rate—up to fifty percent. It has to be remembered that the median duration of marriage today is almost exactly the same as it was a hundred years ago. Divorce, in short, now acts as a functional substitute for death: both are means of terminating marriage at a premature stage. The psychological effects on the survivor may well be very different, although in most cases the catastrophic economic consequences for women remain the same. But the point to be emphasized is that broken marriages, stepchildren, and single-parent households were as common in the past as they are today.

The most difficult historical problem regarding romantic love concerns its role among the propertyless poor. Since they were propertyless, their loves and marriages were of little concern to their kin, and they were therefore more or less free to choose their own mates. By the eighteenth century, and probably before, court records make it clear that the poor often married for love, combined with a confused set of motives including lust and the economic necessity to have a strong and healthy assistant to run the farm or the shop. It was generally expected that they would behave "lovingly" toward each other, but this often did not happen. In many a peasant marriage, the husband seems to have valued his cow more than his wife. Passionate attachments among the poor certainly occurred, but how often they took priority over material interests we may never know for certain

Finally, we know that in the eighteenth century—unlike the seventeenth—at least half of all brides in England and America were pregnant on their wedding day. But this fact tells us more about sexual customs than about passionate attachments: sex began at the moment of engagement, and marriage in church came later, often triggered by the pregnancy. We also know that if a poor servant girl was impregnated by her master, which often happened, the latter usually had no trouble finding a poor man who would marry her, in return for payment of ten pounds or so. Not much passion there.

Passionate attachments between young people can and do happen in any society as a byproduct of biological sexual attraction, but the social acceptability of the emotion has varied enormously over time and class and space, determined primarily by cultural norms and property arrangements. We are in a unique position today in that our culture is dominated by romantic notions of passionate love as the only socially admissible reason for marriage; sexual fulfillment is accepted as the dominant human drive and a natural right for both sexes; and contraception is normal and efficient. Behind all this lies a frenetic individualism, a restless search for a sexual and emotional ideal in human relationships, and a demand for instant ego gratification.

Most of this is new and unique to our culture. It is, therefore, quite impossible to assume that people in the past thought about and experienced passionate attachments the way we do. Historical others—even our own forefathers and mothers—were indeed other.

The responses of the reading group, which appear below, have been edited to remove crossed-out phrases, spelling errors, and other distractions that appear in the original versions.

Janet's freewriting

The author wants us to think more critically about romantic love, perhaps even to view it as unnecessary. Too many of us assume that living without romantic love is to be deprived. Stone wants us to examine and question that assumption. He addresses readers familiar with Shakespeare and Freud and comfortable with terms like orthodox opinion and ego gratification. He assumes an audience already a bit cynical about romance and passionate love. I think the reader most receptive to Stone's ideas has lost any idealism about such matters and is willing to believe that passion is not necessary, maybe unhealthy, in long-term relationships. The essay is for people more likely to sneer at Valentine's Day than to search for just the right greeting card.

Stone's point is that passion, romance, and sexual fulfillment are less crucial to happiness than our culture conditions us to believe. He argues that poets and playwrights created romantic love and that Freud added the notion that sex is an overriding drive. The presumed need for passionate attachments has been constructed by a culture in

which the individual comes first and the needs of the group
are relegated to a distant second. Stone warns that addiction
to romance places us at peril, and he lists the increase of
sexually transmitted diseases, divorce, depression, and even
mental illness among the results.

Stone supports his ideas with evidence from history, with
particular attention to the mass distribution of novels, the
Romantic movement, and the influence of Freud. There's a
gradual change in tone as the reading progresses. After the
first few paragraphs, I expected a scholarly, informative
piece with no earth-shaking point to it. But by the time I
was finished, I realized that Stone was on a soapbox. As the
essay develops, I get the picture of an embittered prude
manipulating history to argue against something he either
doesn't want or can't have.

Alex's freewriting

Stone asks readers to consider a cultural norm in an
unfamiliar and unconventional way. The trappings of romantic
love so permeate our daily lives that we assume there's
something wrong with an adolescent or young adult who doesn't
experience the feeling. So Stone asks us to set aside this
conditioning for a moment and to entertain the idea that a
thing we all "know" to be natural and proper really isn't.
Also he wants us to see that there's something at stake. I'm
not sure he wants to alarm us and alter patterns of behavior,
but he does want us to think about the consequences of our
beliefs and to get a debate going. I think he makes two
important points. First, love may be a form of learned
behavior. Second, because of historical developments
(democracy and individualism, invention of mass media,

Freudian psychology), romantic love has run rampant and poses certain dangers.

I think Stone is addressing a well-educated, broad-minded audience--the sort of people who subscribe to <u>Psychology Today</u>. Ironically, that type of reader, like the people who perpetuated the concept of romantic love prior to the eighteenth century, are an elite. An essay like this is probably leisure reading for such persons. I think Stone envisions a reader who prides herself on being an independent, tough-minded skeptic--someone who isn't taken in by bunk just because it's popular or "nice." An iconoclast, I guess you could say. I'm not sure whether Stone is <u>addressing</u> this type of audience so much as he is <u>conjuring it up</u>.

I see a contradiction. In paragraph one, Stone mentions the uncertainty of "scholars" (psychologists?) about whether love is "culturally induced" or "has biochemical roots." If it's biochemical, aren't historians and anthropologists mistaken in the view that Stone attributes to them? Or are psychologists less certain about this than scholars in other fields? Does Stone express himself poorly, or am I reading carelessly? Stone introduces more specific support in paragraph five, referring to the divorce rate in Japan. It's interesting, though, that he relies on emotionally charged language in his next-to-last paragraph: words like <u>frenetic</u>, <u>restless</u>, and <u>demand</u>. This seems out of keeping with the rest of the essay, which sounds more scholarly.

The essay is chronologically ordered, tracing the history of romantic love. But beneath that, I see a question-answer approach. Stone opens with a problem or dilemma, and the first paragraph ends with two questions. The next paragraph opens with "Some things can be said with certainty," and Stone lists those things. Paragraph four then opens with "another question," and that question leads to two more. Paragraph five goes back to certainty, beginning with "What is certain is that. . . ."

Agnes's freewriting

Stone reminds an audience of psychoanalysts of the history of romantic love. He assesses where we stand today, with tremendous pressures to seek and insist upon sexual fulfillment. For me, it's not clear whether Stone sees romantic love and sexual love as the same thing. Stone fails, probably on purpose, to give a detailed explanation of how "love" took the place of arranged marriage and how, through "saturation of the whole culture," sexual gratification was encouraged, even idealized. The chips seem to go down when he examines the influences of Freud. Is he trying to discredit the Freudian theory of human sexuality, now taken for granted in some circles? Is that the reason for the sly allusion to Freud's justification of neurosis, Civilization and Its Discontents? Stone seems to say that we pay a heavy price for license and excess. Is he trying to upset the Freudians? To urge therapists to stress social values rather than individual desires as they guide their patients out of a self-induced wilderness?

Stone is speaking to a group of professionals interested in new ways of thinking about mental illness and its treatment. The allusion to Romeo and Juliet isn't so important, since every high schooler has read the play. The troubadours are less familiar, but anyone who's heard of Bing Crosby or Perry Como has heard the term. So I think Stone is

flattering his audience without really demanding much of
them. It seems scholarly, but is it really? His tone is
earnest, though bias slips in near the end. There's not a
great deal of hard evidence. Frankly, I think this essay
could be adapted for the <u>Parade</u> section of the Sunday paper
with only minimal editing. After all, we're all interested in
what makes us tick, and all the emphasis on the demons of
instant gratification, license, and unfettered individualism
would hit home with people trying to figure out what's gone
wrong with their relationships. Why not say something about
the psychic toll taken by adulterous liaisons or arranged
marriages?

"A Short History of Love" is not an obscure or difficult text, yet each of these readers responds to it a bit differently. One difference involves their interpretations of the author's purpose. Janet sees Stone as "an embittered prude manipulating history to argue against something he either doesn't want or can't have." Alex seems more inclined to take the article at face value, simply as an attempt to provoke thought and debate. Agnes seems annoyed, believing that Stone wants to display knowledge and flatter the self-image of his readers.

Other differences emerge. Alex is analytical, examining the structure and language of the article—down to the author's choice of specific words. Agnes refers to things outside the text (from the title of a book by Freud to the names of popular singers during the 1940s). Janet falls somewhere in between: She records personal associations, such as the reference to greeting cards, while noting Stone's ideas and the order in which he presents them. Both Alex and Agnes pose questions, interrogating the text as well as their own responses to it.

Although other differences can be found, an important point emerges: The personality, interests, and thinking style of each individual affect his or her reading of "A Short History of Love." None of the readings is inherently better than the others; on the contrary, the best reading would be informed and enriched by all three perspectives. It would benefit from Janet's speculations about the author, Alex's analysis of language and structure, and Agnes's skepticism. This formidable array of skill and perspective is something that no single member of the group possessed as an individual.

The sharing of freewritten responses is not always an end in itself. Instructors may ask groups to address an issue or problem introduced by a reading. For example, reading groups might receive the following guidelines after having freewritten in response to "A Short History of Love."

GUIDELINES for Group Work

Read your freewriting aloud to members of your group. As you listen to others read, take note of any interesting observations, but be particularly alert to the following:

- Do group members feel that the origins of romantic love are mainly cultural or biological?
- Do they see any unhealthy obsession with romance, sex, or individualism in modern society? Do they share Stone's sense of alarm or urgency?
- Did anyone in your group connect what Stone calls "frenetic individualism" and the desire for immediate self-gratification with other areas of life?

After all group members have read their freewriting aloud, try to reach some consensus regarding these questions:

- Has Stone identified a serious social problem that needs to be addressed?
- What is the most plausible way to resolve the tensions that Stone outlines?
- Does extreme individualism and the desire for self-gratification contribute to other social problems? If so, which ones?

Reading groups strive for consensus—or at least mutual understanding—rather than a single authoritative interpretation. After Janet, Alex, and Agnes had read their freewritten responses aloud, they discussed each other's ideas and observations. For example, Alex remarked on Janet's belief that as Stone gets further into his topic, he sounds more like a soapbox orator than a scholar. Alex connected that idea with something he had noted about the tone of the article—that "emotionally charged language" appears in the next-to-last paragraph. Janet's point thus helped Alex see the language of one paragraph as part of a broader pattern. Janet, on the other hand, benefited from Alex's narrower focus on words in a specific segment of the text. Not only was her perception reinforced by what Alex noted, but also she found supporting evidence for what had been only a vague impression about the author's tone.

As Janet, Alex, and Agnes proceeded to discuss each other's responses, a number of similar transactions ensued. Agnes took issue with Janet's and Alex's notion that Stone wishes to alter public behavior. She reminded her partners that Stone's article was delivered as a paper at an academic conference and that his primary audience was psychoanalysts rather than a randomly selected group of single men and women. Acknowledging that they had overlooked that fact, Janet and Alex modified their interpretation of Stone's purpose. Later, influenced by her partners' doubts about Stone's authority in fields other than history, Janet grew skeptical herself. All continued their discussion for about fifteen minutes.

At the end of this and many of the following chapters, you will be invited to work in reading groups, engaging in a similar process of collaborative response and inquiry. When you do so, try to adopt the constructive approach exemplified by these three readers.

■ RESEARCH

Many students expect research to be an excruciating ordeal, and the idea of THE RESEARCH PAPER looms in student mythology as the academic equivalent of a root canal.

Fortunately, the myth is wrong. Research needn't be a tedious ordeal, though it can be for those who begin without knowing what they are doing or why. *Research* is nothing more than finding out what you need to know. If you are good at it—if you have learned a few elementary skills—it can be useful and satisfying; it can even be fun.

You are already skilled in certain kinds of research. Right now, for example, if you wanted to find your dentist's telephone number, you could easily do so, even though your phone book contains thousands of names. Your research skills enable you to find out what movies are showing on television tonight and the current price of Raleigh mountain bikes. Research in college involves additional skills that are equally useful and not any more difficult to acquire. These skills not only help you become a competent college researcher, but also prove useful after you graduate.

Research takes many forms, from looking up the definition of a word to conducting an opinion poll. Depending on what you want to find out, you may ask the opinions of experts, undertake fieldwork or laboratory experiments, interview eyewitnesses, analyze photographs, or observe the behavior of people who don't know they're being watched. This more observational type of research is the kind that Mark Craig conducted for his essay. Other research methods—those explained and illustrated in this book—involve written sources. You can discover general information in reference works such as encyclopedias and almanacs. More specific information and ideas can be found in magazines, newspapers, journals, pamphlets, books, and Web sites. Your college library and computer databases are two valuable resources for conducting this type of research.

The skills you develop as a researcher provide personal benefits outside of college. For example, knowing how to use the library can help a pharmacy major locate a summer job. Or it can help consumers find out which videorecorders are most reliable. Unlike these more private kinds of inquiry, the research you perform as a college student has a more public purpose. It may be part of a larger project in which you share your findings with other scholars, communicating what you have learned through *research writing.*

In short, any organized investigation can be called research, and any writing you do as a result—from poetry to scientific reports—may be called research writing. Research is an important academic skill because college students rarely begin a major assignment with all the information they need. When you write about personal feelings, research is unnecessary; no one is likely to challenge expressions of feeling. However, if you write about dating customs of the early twentieth century, you must rely on more than feelings or casual conversation. Since readers expect your writing to be dependable and accurate, research is indispensable.

Not all good writing, of course, is research writing. Your responses to the readings on pages 46–47, for example, are probably based on personal reflection and opinion rather than research. For the same reason, the following passage would not qualify as research writing:

> Since I decided to marry at the age of twenty-three, I've been made to feel as if a career is no longer a viable option. . . .
>
> I've been accused of misrepresenting myself during college as someone trying to earn an MRS degree rather than an education. When "feminist" friends hear that I am taking my husband's name, they act as if I'm forsaking "our" cause. One Saturday afternoon, a friend phoned and I admitted I was spending the day doing laundry—mine and his. Her voice resonated with such pity that I hung up.
>
> New York City, where we live, breeds much of this antagonism . . . but I've also experienced prejudice in my hometown in Colorado. At a local store's bridal registry, I walked in wearing a Columbia University sweatshirt and the consultant asked if I'd gone to school there. On hearing that I'd graduated ten months earlier, she explained that she had a daughter my age. "But she is very involved in her career," she added, presuming that I, selecting a silver pattern, was not.
>
> —Katherine Davis, "I'm Not Sick, I'm Just in Love"

Though this personal account is well written and honest, it does not report research. Instead, it is a personal reflection that is not based on sources or systematic inquiry. If, however, the author had cited quotations and facts gathered from formal interviews with experts or friends, had found and reported published scholarship relating to marriage and family, or had cited the opinions of feminist scholars, then her essay would have been based on research rather than personal reflection. This is what we mean by research writing—locating and citing sources.

EXERCISE | **Distinguishing Features of Research Writing**

Would you call Mark Craig's essay "Illiteracy: America's Secret" an example of research writing? Explain. Are any parts of that essay based on research? Could the essay be made more convincing through additional research? If Mark wished to incorporate more research into his essay, what kinds of research would you recommend?

◼ READING SELECTION

Following is an excerpt from a recently published book, *Reading Don't Fix No Chevys: Literacy in the Lives of Young Men.* The authors, both university professors of English education, report the findings of their study of forty-nine adolescent males from a variety of ethnic, socioeconomic, and geographical backgrounds. Included in the excerpt are references to *Flow: The Psychology of Optimal Experience,* a book by adolescent psychologist Mihaly Csikszentmihalyi. Numbers cited in parentheses designate pages in Csikszentmihalyi's book.

Going with the Flow

What Boys Like to Do and Why They Like to Do It

MICHAEL W. SMITH AND JEFFREY D. WILHELM

Csikszentmihalyi (1990a) begins his book with a simple premise: that "more than anything else, men and women seek happiness" (p. 1). Everything else for which we strive, he argues—money, prestige, *everything*—is only valued because we expect (sometimes wrongly) that it will bring us happiness. Csikszentmihalyi has spent his professional life studying what makes people happy, more specifically by examining the nature of flow, "the state in which people are so involved in an activity that nothing else seems to matter" (p. 4). — 1

He offers eight characteristics of flow experience that we think can be usefully collapsed into four main principles: — 2

- A sense of control and competence
- A challenge that requires an appropriate level of skill
- Clear goals and feedback
- A focus on the immediate experience

These principles resounded throughout all of our data.

What we found in our study is that all of the young men with whom we worked were passionate about some activity. They experienced flow. But, unfortunately, most of them did not experience it in their literate activity, at least not in school. . . . — 3

A SENSE OF COMPETENCE AND CONTROL

According to Csikszentmihalyi (1990a), when people describe flow experiences, they typically talk about a sense of competence and the feeling of control that stems from having developed sufficient skills so that they are able to achieve their goals. . . . — 4

Again and again we heard boys talk about how a feeling of competence kept them involved in an activity. Again and again we heard boys exclaim that they would quickly give things up if they did not gain that competence. That's why it was so striking that only two boys made a link between accomplishment and reading. . . . — 5

The boys also discussed the importance of feeling control. This came out clearly in their discussion of school. Csikszentmihalyi (1990a) notes that "knowledge that is seen to be controlled from the outside is acquired with reluctance and it brings no joy" (p. 134). The boys in our study seemed to concur . . . in their discussions of reading and of writing. — 6

Here's Chris talking about writing: — 7

A lot of times with writing I get excited, especially when the teacher doesn't give you a limitation. Like with _____, we did a lot of writing assignments with poems and whatnot and that really caught my interest because you could write about whatever you wanted to write about.

Guy echoed his point: — 8

I like writing without having any guidelines to follow, just where you have to do your own thing. I might not mind having a guideline as [to] how long it has to be, but I don't like having a topic to write about, just to make up my own story.

9   According to some of the boys, what was true for writing was also true for reading. Joe noted the importance of control over his reading:

> I don't like it if I have to read it, but if I read it on my own then it would probably seem a little better. . . .

A CHALLENGE THAT REQUIRES AN APPROPRIATE LEVEL OF SKILL

10   As Csikszentmihalyi (1990a) notes, "By far the overwhelming proportion of optimal experiences are reported to occur within sequences of activities that are goal directed and bounded by rules—activities that require the investment of psychic energy, and that could not be done without the appropriate skills" (p. 49). He explains: "Enjoyment comes at a very specific point: whenever the opportunities for action perceived by the individual are equal to his or her capabilities" (p. 52). We found that the young men in our study gravitated to activities that provided the appropriate level of challenge. . . .

11   The emphasis on an appropriate level of challenge . . . marked their discussions of reading in interesting ways. Some of the boys wistfully recalled reading *Goosebumps* books that they had found interesting but that were now too easy. But more often the boys talked about feeling overmatched by reading. Haywood put it this way:

> Ah, well I like a book that isn't, isn't easy but not so difficult that you don't understand what is going on. Ah, because if you are reading a book that doesn't make sense to you then you just, you know, "Well I don't know how to read this" and then you have [a] negative attitude and you don't concentrate and you don't really gain anything from the experience.

12   Ricardo provided a specific example:

> Ah, I don't like reading plays because it's hard, it's just everything is talking and . . . when you've done a page you have to look back and say OK, this person is talking to that person.

13   The potential impact of feeling "overmatched" is clear as we recall the comments in our discussions with the boys about the importance of competence and control. The young men in our study wanted to be challenged, but they wanted to be challenged in contexts in which they felt confident of improvement, if not success. If the challenge seemed too great, they tended to avoid it, instead returning to a domain in which they felt more competent. . . .

CLEAR GOALS AND FEEDBACK

14   The importance of clear goals and feedback is intimately associated with the two characteristics of flow experiences that we have discussed so far. First, without a clear sense of a goal, it seems impossible to have a sense of competence. Second, it is impossible to identify an appropriate level of challenge. As Csikszentmihalyi (1990a) points out, sports and games provide goals and feedback by their very nature: a tennis player wins or loses a point, a lacrosse player scores a goal or is scored upon, a video game player moves up to a new level or loses the game. . . .

15   This emphasis on immediate feedback has important consequences for reading. Reading extended texts such as novels is not likely to provide quick and clean feedback, but reading short informational texts, such as magazines and newspapers, does.

16   For example, in the activity interviews, when boys spoke of their enjoyment of reading, most spoke about how they valued it as a tool they used to address an immediate interest or need. Here's Timmy talking about what he reads on the Internet:

Well, I like to go to the sports and stuff [']cause I like to see, I like sports a lot . . . I like to see what is going on and what's, like, who won the games and . . . I like to go to NASCAR and I like NASCAR a lot so. I like to see what is happening and they are like [mumble] it is just fun to ah, find out.

And Mark talking about reading a golfing magazine:

'Cause ah, it's probably the best golf magazine out there and it, I mean it just tells you ways and shows you pictures on how you can improve your swing, and if you slice the ball, it teaches you how to hook the ball so it goes straight, and it ah shows you what new balls come out that are fit for you and new clubs that would fit you and just different things like that.

And Bam on reading the newspaper:

Like, if you find something that happened around your neighborhood, "Oh, I didn't know that happened. I should read it." Stuff like that. I didn't know my friend went to jail because he tried to rob somebody. I didn't know that until I read the paper. They put his name there in the paper.

And Maurice on reading his driver's education book:

That was something that I thought was interesting because it helps me. It helps me to put my seat belt on because before, if they see me without a seat belt on, they couldn't do anything about it unless you were actually stopped and they saw you without a seat belt on. But now, if they see you, they can just stop you like that. So that's helping me put my seat belt on at all times, and it's keeping me out of ticket trouble, keeping points off my license.

And Barnabas on reading about video games:

Some of the stuff be frustrating. All the magazines I read, they say how they made the game too hard. It's true. They made the game too hard. And, sometimes, I beat the game already and I want to see what all the secret stuff was. I mean, it tells you where all the secret stuff is, but I still got to find them myself. That's all. I'm just asking for a little map.

The boys we cite here could be described as taking an efferent (Rosenblatt, 1978) **17** stance in their reading. Or perhaps it's more accurate to say that they choose texts that reward an efferent reading. Csikszentmihalyi (1990a) provides a lens through which to understand that choice. Efferent reading by its nature provides an opportunity for clear and immediate feedback that aesthetic reading does not. If you're looking for information and you find it, you know that your reading is successful: You can beat the game, fix the electrical problem, or hit the ball straighter. . . .

A FOCUS ON THE IMMEDIATE EXPERIENCE

The implications of the way that boys valued reading become even clearer in light of **18** the final characteristic of flow experiences. The *sine qua non* of flow experiences is that people are so focused on what they are doing they lose awareness of anything outside the activity. Csikszentmihalyi (1990a) speaks of this quality in a number of ways: the merging of action and awareness, concentration on the task at hand, the loss of self-consciousness, and the transformation of time. In his study, a young basketball player provides testimony: "Kids my age, they think a lot . . . but when you are playing basketball, that's all there is on your mind—just basketball. . . . Everything seems to follow right along" (p. 58).

The young men in our study spoke in ways that resonate with the words of this **19** basketball player. They valued their favorite activities for the enjoyment they took from the immediate engagement in those activities, not for their instrumental value. The boys played sports because they enjoyed them, not to win a scholarship or to impress others. They played music or rapped because they enjoyed being engaged in that way. And when they engaged with other media, they did so because it made them laugh or kept them on the edge of their seats. Unlike their experience with reading, their focus was on the moment, not on the instrumental value of the activity. . . .

THE IMPORTANCE OF THE SOCIAL

20   Although Csikszentmihalyi's (1990a) work helped us understand our boys' activity ratings, it wasn't fully explanatory. Csikszentmihalyi notes that "Another universally enjoyable activity is being with other people" (p. 50), yet as he admits, socializing appears to be an exception to the rules for flow that he posits. What wasn't an exception was how important socializing was to the young men in our study. . . .

21   The boys talked about how their friendships allowed them to be themselves. What they seemed to mean was that they could talk more intimately with friends. Only two of them alluded to friends as a protection against the pressure of being male in a specified way. Both of those who did were very involved with the arts, and they seemed to see girls as more accepting of their artistic inclinations. Pablo put it this way:

> I guess boys are more—they judge you. They think you have to be a big macho man in order for you to hang out with them. I mean, not all boys, but a lot of 'em, and I guess girls accept you more, for who you are, and I guess it depends on person to person, but that's what I've found.

22   But this was decidedly a minority opinion. . . .

23   The friendships occasionally affected the boys' literate lives. Gohan had two friends with whom he shared poetry. Mark checked the Internet or the newspaper to keep up with the hockey scores not because of his interest but because his friends would expect him to know. Neil's friendship circle was characterized by long discussions of movies by favorite directors. . . .

24   Their friendships also affected their attitudes toward school. Of the twenty-one who talked about liking school, nineteen said they did so because of the social dimension of schooling. Buster's sentiments provide a summary of this viewpoint:

> Probably my favorite part of going to school is the social aspect. I don't know, I guess I just like interacting with my friends and stuff. I mean, that's probably my favorite part about school. As far as classes go, there's certain classes I really don't like and some that are OK, but . . . probably my favorite part of school is seeing my friends.

25   In contrast, only two boys talked about valuing school because they loved to learn. . . .

SIGNIFICANT DEPARTURES

26   As we noted previously, virtually all of the boys noted that reading played a part in their lives outside school, but only seven spoke of the enjoyment they received from reading extended text[s] outside of school, which seems to us to be the conventional understanding of what it means to be a reader. Of these seven, two were primarily readers of history and five of novels, though two of the novel readers talked especially of their interest in historical fiction

27   These seven boys provided a number of reasons for their enjoyment of books. Stan worked the hardest to articulate his feelings:

> I like reading books because they let you think about certain things that have happened, or they . . . I wouldn't say I want to get away from the world, but it's kind of

an escape, like watching TV but it's better than TV. You can't really—like reading a book is—watching TV is, like, no comparison to reading a book because reading a book you can get right into it and all that stuff, and I'm not quite sure what makes a book good, just it has to be sort of interesting, I mean it's different for, you know, certain people. Certain people like certain things. I like a lot of books, I like books that sort of keep you on your toes, books that make you think, controversial books, just a little bit of everything I think.

Stan's last statement resonates with previous ones we've cited on the importance of challenge. Suspense and the drive to figure out the "puzzle" a book provides were important. He raises other key points as well, including the need to be able to enter a book. We took this to mean that he was able both to visualize the story world and to see things from the perspectives of others. Like Stan, the [other] boys who were readers spoke of a desire to be engaged in the big ideas they encountered in reading. . . .

Our attention to students' likes and dislikes . . . doesn't mean that we are simply   28
saying, "Just give them reading that relates to their interests." The boys' interests were sufficiently different that doing so would mean a class could never read a common text. Rather, we are saying that if we understand why they like what they like, we can work to create the conditions that will make students more inclined to engage in learning what they need to know. These conditions are those of "flow" experiences: a sense of control and competence, an appropriate challenge, clear goals and feedback, and a focus on the immediate.

Freewriting

Freewriting helps you focus your thoughts about what you read. Write a full page in your journal or notebook, recording your reactions to "Going with the Flow," along with any thoughts that the passage arouses. Write at your normal pace about whatever comes to mind. Because this writing is not for others to read, try to put your ideas on paper without stopping to polish your writing or to correct errors. Though free to record any thoughts that relate to the reading, you may wish to respond to some of the following questions: Do the authors' findings accord with your experience as a high-school student? Do they confirm, contradict, or alter your perceptions of adolescent males? What findings do you suppose a similar study of adolescent girls might produce? Do you think the attitudes and literate behaviors of previous generations of adolescent boys would have been different from those that Michael W. Smith and Jeffrey D. Wilhelm report? Do their findings have any social implications?

Review Questions

1. What four principles do Smith and Wilhelm cite as characteristic of flow experiences?

2. How do efferent and aesthetic responses to reading differ? How does the distinction between these two responses relate to the boys that Smith and Wilhelm interviewed?

3. In what respects do the seven boys who read longer texts outside of school differ from others?

Discussion Questions

1. Which of the quoted comments about reading or writing experiences do you most identify with? Which do you least identify with?

2. In another part of the article from which the excerpt on page 5 was drawn, Nancy Sommers quotes Ralph Waldo Emerson: "One must be an inventor to read well." What evidence for that assertion do you find in "Going with the Flow"?

3. Do you think that Smith and Wilhelm overvalue aesthetic reading or undervalue efferent reading? If so, how and why?

Writing

1. In a dictionary, look up any of the following words with which you are unfamiliar:

premise (paragraph 1)   optimal (paragraph 10)   *sine qua non* (paragraph 18)

2. Interview four or five classmates or friends about how they use literacy in their daily lives (school, work, leisure) and how they feel about reading and writing. Use the information you gather to confirm or modify Smith and Wilhelm's conclusions.

WRITE, READ, and RESEARCH the NET

1. *Write:* Using one or more of the prewriting strategies discussed and illustrated on pages 19–24, record your thoughts, observations, or personal experiences regarding the empowerment that comes with reading and writing well or the disempowerment that often accompanies illiteracy.

2. *Read:* Review the following Web site:
http://dana.ucc.nau.edu/~krb42/cultures_and_ politics_of_literacy.htm.

3. *Research:* Using the Internet, find articles and other sources that relate to changing definitions of literacy and the political and social implications of how we define this term. Draft an outline and summary of your findings.

■ ADDITIONAL READINGS

The following articles and essays illustrate a type of writing that the assignment on pages 7–8 (the one to which Mark Craig responded) is designed to elicit.

The first two readings address the theme of literacy, introduced in "Going with the Flow" and in several shorter passages imbedded within this chapter. "The Best" by Stefan Fatsis is a passage from *Word Freak: Heartbreak, Triumph,*

Genius, and Obsession in the World of Competitive Scrabble Players. It is followed by an article from the *New York Times* concerning an unusual reading program for prison inmates.

The last two readings, "Just Showing Off" and "The Holly Pageant," detail the customs and conventions surrounding two events that are commonly governed by rigidly enforced, yet sometimes unspoken, rules of behavior.

The Best

STEFAN FATSIS

Matt Graham is popping pills. **1**

It's unclear which ones he's downing at precisely this moment, but the possibili- **2** ties seem endless. Plastic containers are scattered on the end tables, on the desk, next to the television, inside drawers. Zinc. Caffeine. Glucose. Glycine. L-phenylalanine. Pyroglutanic acid. Taurine. Tyrosine. Next to the sink, atop the toilet tank, spread across the bed. On a five-by-seven index card, Graham has written in one column the names of twenty pills to be taken in the morning on an empty stomach; in another column, he has listed seventeen more to be downed with breakfast. NADH. Gluta- mine. Herb for men. Mega Mind. Gotu kola. Potassium.

Graham squeezes a few drops of DMAE-H3 into a glass of cranberry-orange- **3** flavored Blast Off II, a powdered amino-acid concoction containing twenty-one vitamins and minerals—and, more to the point, eighty milligrams of caffeine—per serving. The label reads: "Excessive consumption of tyrosine or phenylalanine may cause symptoms of excessive stimulation such as tremors, rapid heartbeat, irritability, or insomnia."

"This stuff," Graham announces, "turned me around more than anything else." **4**

We are in Washington, D.C., in Room 611 of the gilt- and marble-adorned **5** Mayflower Hotel, where every president since Herbert Hoover has held an inaugural party. It's 7:55 a.m. on a cold Monday in late November, and the tyrosine is kicking in. In precisely sixty-five minutes Graham will play a best-of-five-games match against Joel Sherman to determine the world Scrabble champion. Six feet tall, with a buzz cut on a long, narrow head that is dominated by wide, energetic eyes, Graham is a thirty- two-year-old standup comedian who wears unbuttoned flannel shirts over old T- shirts; droopy, tattered jeans; and high-top Nike basketball sneakers. He talks rapidly, his mind racing ahead of his thoughts. He refuses to see an orthopedist about a dam- aged knee that sometimes leaves him hobbling in pain. He doesn't sleep much, does- n't eat much, and doesn't relax much, certainly not on this morning. The pills, of course, have something to do with it; if they drug-tested in Scrabble, Matt Graham would be banned for life.

The hotel room reflects the man. Housekeeping has left a voice-mail message **6** apologizing for not making the bed or cleaning the bathroom, but the maid was afraid to touch anything. There are copies of *Sports Illustrated* and *Playboy's Nudes.* Myriad cassette tapes are scattered across the bed: Indigo Girls. Bad Religion. R.E.M. The Pro- claimers. *Super Hits of the 70s, Volume 10.* There's a fading photograph of Graham's grandmother, a computer mouse pad in the shape of a Shar-Pei ("It's a lucky charm," he says), a red and white stocking cap, and pens with smiley faces on one end. More bottles: Ginseng. Lipoic acid. Ashwagandha. Healthy Greens. Coenzyme Q. Pygeum, a prostate drug promising "Natural Health Care for Men Over 50." Sulphedrine. Herbal Formula for Men. ("The reason I take this is it's got ma huang, which is ephedrine, which is a stimulant," Graham says, as if there were any doubt.)

7   There are index cards plastered with obscure words. A Cookie Monster doll. A copy of the December 1993 issue of a Scrabble newsletter called *Medleys* which includes an article about that year's world championships titled "On Crowns and Clowns." The piece takes a potshot at Graham, who was then just emerging on the Scrabble scene but qualified for the event in New York nonetheless. "We sent a few of our best—and a few comedians," the article notes. "I brought it for inspiration," Graham says. "A lot of petty fuckers in this game." And there are the stuffed animals: the bear, the gorilla, the lucky manatee. Graham won't play without the lucky manatee.

8   All of it—the junk, the souvenirs, the "smart drugs" he ingests like a bird pecking from a feeder—has one purpose: to help Matt Graham win, to beat not only Joel Sherman but everyone who resents the fact that he doesn't study as obsessively as they do, that he is an outsider in an insider's game, that he doesn't join in the rabid on-line discussion groups or perform in the annual talent show at the Atlantic City Tournament or show up for the Thursday-night sessions at the Manhattan club.

9   "Different breed of cat," says Marlon Hill, one of Graham's few friends on the competitive Scrabble circuit, an African-American guy from inner-city Baltimore and an expert himself, who is helping Graham prepare for the championship match. ". . . alien."

10   Might as well be a UFO convention. The Scrabble tournament scene, it turns out—and I'm shocked, *shocked*—isn't the most highly functional subculture around. "We're dealing with some borderline pathology here," Charlie Southwell, a former highly ranked player who is directing the World Scrabble Championship, says as he surveys the hotel ballroom where eighty top players are competing.

11   My limited exposure [at a previous tournament] in Washington Square Park has prepared me well. I arrive on the third day of the four-day tournament and, as a journalist, am given free roaming rights on the playing-room floor. Southwell and John Williams, who has invited me to attend, point out the exotic mammals in their natural habitats. There's Adam Logan, a red-bearded mathematics doctoral student at Harvard, padding around in short pants and holey socks, his hands pulled inside his shirtsleeves like a sky schoolgirl. There's Bob Felt, a former national champion, notorious for his rambling monologues about long-forgotten games and his slovenly appearance; at this moment his fly is open. There's Joel Sherman, who calls himself a professional Scrabble player. He lives in the Bronx with his brother and father and hasn't worked in years, ostensibly because of a *Merck Manual's* worth of physical disorders; his most notorious is a volcanic gut that has earned him the nickname G.I. Joel, as in gastrointestinal. There's Joe Edley, who in addition to being a two-time national champion is associate director of the National Scrabble Association and perceived as arrogant by his peers. When I first encounter Edley, he is lecturing Felt for messing up the score of their game, a fact that went uncorrected and has affected the pairings for the next round of play. Overhearing the exchange, an expert-level American woman not participating in the event mutters about Edley, "Busy, busy, busy. He plays. He administers. Prick."

12   Graham started the tournament with a 2-4 record, but by the time I arrive he has reeled off ten straight wins, a feat unmatched in the history of the Worlds, and one of the greatest pressure-packed streaks ever. When I first glimpse Matt, he is wearing a

Walkman, inhaling nose spray, and swallowing a handful of unidentified pills. Then he sits down to play Joel, who extracts a piece of pita bread from a mug of water and eats it. Matt whips him by a score of 576-327 to improve to 13-4. "He might run the table," says Marlon Hill, who seems to be president of the Matt Graham Fan Club. "It's like DiMaggio's fifty-six."

Joel has a different perspective. "Matt just got every . . . thing in the world," he **13** says. "That game probably cost me twenty-five thousand. Somehow it always goes this way. I always get blown out in the key game. He just played EGOTISE in the last game on the second play. This time he did it for twenty points more." Joel belches. It's his stomach talking. He can't control it.

Matt wins his next game, and the one after that. Thirteen straight wins. Two to **14** go. The top two finishers will play in the finals. Matt, Joel, and Edley are in the strongest position to advance. First prize is $25,000. Second prize is $10,000. It's not the World Series of Poker, where the winner takes home $1 million, but to these players it's not small change, either. "I owe my mom ten thousand or she's going to throw me out of my apartment," Matt says. "I'm maxed on one of her credit cards for twenty thousand." Standup comedy, which Matt does part-time when he isn't studying words or playing games, is not a lucrative vocation, and neither is Scrabble.

In the hallway between rounds, the players and spectators—which include a **15** number of top American experts who didn't qualify for the event—gather to pore over the results and swap stories about great plays or tricky board positions. I listen attentively, struggling to understand the Scrabble argot. Even more than I was in [Washington Square] park, I'm amazed by the words I'm seeing played, and there's a reason: British Scrabble has a more expansive word source than does Scrabble in North America, an additional thirty thousand or so two through eight-letter words above the hundred thousand in the *O[fficial] S[crabble] P[layers] D[ictionary]*. At the Worlds, words found in both the *OSPD* and the British word source, *Official Scrabble Words*, or *OSW*, are acceptable. (Play using both word sources is known as *SOWPODS*, a pronounceable combination of *OSPD* and *OSW*.) "Ours or theirs?" is a commonly asked question, meaning, Is that word in our (the North American) or their (the British) dictionary?

I came looking for a story, and I found one. I came wondering whether this world **16** was interesting enough to write about, and I wasn't disappointed. But I didn't expect to get so absorbed so quickly. I'm blown away by the plays—HAFTAROT, NITCHIE, OXTERING, RATICIDE, ANGIOMAS. I'm drawn to the intense concentration and complex banter. After losing to Matt, Joel, a balding, sunken-eyed thirty-five-year-old, is kneeling on his chair hovering over the board. "Oh, shit. OUTEDGES is good," he says. "I could have bingoed instead of playing UDO. I could have been in the game, darn it. I could have bingoed right through the G." "Oh, Jesus Christ," he says a bit later. "I missed FILARIID. That's bad. That's disgraceful. There's no reason I shouldn't have spotted that. I was just making incredibly stupid plays." He's suffering, I think, he's really suffering.

By the time I observe my third game in the room, I'm running scores to a woman **17** who is posting the results on a Web site. I'm hanging on the results. The [previous tournament in Washington Square] park felt casual, an intellectual challenge more than a competitive one. But this—the money, the tension, the pressure, the egos, the pride, the prestige. This isn't just about playing a board game. This is about skill and achievement and self-worth.

Standing at the front of the playing room, rapt with wonder, I think: I want to be able to do what they do. I want to be one of these people. **18**

Making Fairy Tales into Learning Tools

RICHARD ROTHSTEIN

1   Most people recognize the importance of reading stories to toddlers, who can then learn how books work (for example, that a line of text proceeds from left to right), how letters form words, and how narrative flows.

2   But literacy is only one benefit of storytelling. Another is the chance for children to identify with fanciful characters who try to work out conflicts with others and within themselves. If very young children can't do this in the safety of an adult's lap, the later costs to them and to society can be greater than poor reading skills.

3   Can any of this loss be made up later? A storybook program at a San Antonio juvenile prison suggests that it may never be too late.

4   Three people came together to create the program. Celeste Guzman works for Gemini Ink, a group that seeks opportunities for creative writers to give workshops in schools, seniors' centers, shelters for battered women, and prisons. Glenn Faulk, a prison officer at the Cyndi Taylor Krier Juvenile Correctional Treatment Center, designs activities for violent youths while they serve their sentences. Grady Hillman, a poet, trains artists and writers to teach in community settings.

5   Their plan evolved slowly, with few of its possibilities apparent at first. Youths at the Krier juvenile prison are expected to perform public service. Mr. Faulk proposed to several that rather than mow lawns at the courthouse or pick up trash on the highway, they write children's books that could be donated to a library at a battered-women's shelter. He thought the idea might be particularly attractive to youths who had themselves fathered children before being imprisoned. He also knew that in writing children's stories, the youths would be forced to abandon their tough-guy street language.

6   Ms. Guzman then recruited Mr. Hillman to run a writing workshop for seven juvenile offenders who volunteered. He began each session by reading a children's book aloud, expecting to teach story structure and character development. But it soon became apparent that the storytelling had another, unanticipated effect: the six young men and one young woman, none of whom had lived healthy childhoods that included adults' reading stories, were enjoying the tales themselves.

7   Their favorite, Mr. Hillman said, was *Millions of Cats,* by Wanda Gag. It is an "ugly duckling" kind of story in which an old woman wants to pick a single cat as a pet, from millions of cats who hope to be selected. Her choice is unexpected, a cat who has been least aggressive in seeking her favor.

8   Mr. Hillman surmised that the story was popular because the youths had spent their adolescence driven toward arrogance and feigning toughness. The notion that humility might have a reward was surprisingly attractive to them.

9   Mr. Hillman's own favorite was *The Tale of Peter Rabbit,* by Beatrix Potter. Because Peter disobeys his mother's rules, he is trapped in Mr. McGregor's garden. Peter's predicament becomes progressively worse, but he ultimately resolves it and escapes to the security of home. This, Mr. Hillman thought, might be a parable for the young offenders' own lives.

10 The workshop's explicit goal was the youths' contribution of their work to the community. Each of them wrote a story. Some were fanciful, like a tale about a wizard who can't spell and whose wishes are therefore fulfilled improperly: when he wants a bath, he spells *bat,* and so instead of getting a bath, he gets a bat that chases him around his cave. Some stories were more realistic, like one about a girl who has to accept that she is shorter than others.

Ms. Guzman had the storybooks printed, and in May the youths read their stories aloud at a prison meeting to which their parents were invited. Now, as the young offenders earn behavior points that make them eligible for supervised trips away from the center, they will be permitted to perform readings for children on the outside.   **11**

Thirty years ago, literacy programs were more common in adult and juvenile prisons alike, because reading and writing skills were thought important for future employment. Some adult programs included "bibliotherapy," using literature to explore psychological problems as a step to rehabilitation.   **12**

But today, prisons give more emphasis to punishment, protection of the community, and restitution. The San Antonio program is an exception to that trend, though not the only one. Mr. Hillman now hopes to train writers around the country to use storybooks with youthful offenders. If all children heard fairy tales when they were small enough to sit on laps, though, perhaps fewer would have to do so in prison.   **13**

Just Showing Off

MILLARD K. IVES

It's three o'clock Sunday morning.   **1**

Hundreds of young adults engaged in conversation line both sides of the 900 block of Castle Street as . . . police officers watch from a nearby parking lot.   **2**

To the unfamiliar approaching the area, it may appear something serious is going on.   **3**

But it's just like any other weekend in the early morning hours—young people pack the streets, talking, and police watch them.   **4**

It's eleven o'clock Wednesday evening.   **5**

More than a hundred people are gathered in the parking lot at Parrish Caine Motorsports on Oleander Drive while police officers walk through the crowds, shining flashlights into cars.   **6**

The young adults are just comparing rims, custom-made spoilers, and other vehicle accessories as police try to make sure the displays of their sound systems aren't pumping too loud. In fact, the management of Parrish Caine actually condones the gathering.   **7**

"There's a lot worse things we can be doing, so I don't see why police think we need supervision," said Jack Hilton, showing off the DVD screen in his purple 2002 Expedition.   **8**

Both social spots are receiving increased police attention after complaints from surrounding residents about the large crowds. Complaints include loud noise, litter left in yards, and public urination.   **9**

Police officials say they can patrol for illegal activity, but there's little they can do about people just "hanging out."   **10**

"We can't just throw people off the sidewalk for standing there," said Randy Pait, patrol division commander.   **11**

Wilmington has its share of spots where large crowds gather at night, even after the bars close. Early this year, dozens of police had to be called downtown when a crowd of hundreds got out of hand and attacked police and punched a police horse, said Linda Rawley, public information officer for the Wilmington Police.   **12**

Residents and businesses downtown also complain about loud noise and public urination as well as open alcohol containers, Ms. Rawley said.   **13**

14   Most people on Front Street after nightspots close said they are looking to socialize.

15   "I just come here to meet new women, ask them how they are doing," said Vaughn McDuffie of Cary, sitting near the Pulse nightclub one Sunday morning.

16   The many bars and nightclubs attract people downtown on the weekend, whether they patronize the businesses or not, Ms. Rawley said.

17   Two Wilmington City Council members introduced a resolution earlier this month that calls for a twelve-month moratorium on new bars, hoping to cut down on rowdy crowds and scuffles with police.

18   "It seems that we never have enough police to control the crowds," said Lt. Daniel Bullard, patrolling downtown one recent Saturday night.

19   Complaints from Castle Street residents concerning the crowds prompted police to conduct two massive patrols in that area last month. Police covered the area surrounding the 900 block on foot, in squad cars, and on horseback.

20   Most arrests and tickets were for driving offenses such as operating a vehicle without a license, said Lt. J. J. Lightner. One man was picked up on a warrant charging statutory rape. The patrols, however, did little to decrease the crowd's numbers.

21   "The vast majority of them aren't interested in doing anything illegal, so regardless of residents' complaints, we have to leave them alone," Ms. Rawley said.

22   Police also frequently stand nearby to observe the crowd. But many young adults [argue] they are doing nothing wrong.

23   "There's a lot of us hanging out here, and I've never seen one fight," said Joey Long, sitting on top of a 1985 Fleetwood Cadillac in the 1000 block of Castle Street early one Saturday morning.

24   Mustangs, Spyders, Corvettes, and other vehicles with glossy chrome rims, neon lights shining underneath, and thousands of dollars in sound equipment are parked beside their owners in the Parrish Caine parking lot as crowds tour through, comparing the machines.

25   Because residents have complained about loud music in the parking lot of Parrish Caine, salesman Matt Ramsey said the business is working with police to quiet the noise.

26   "We told [the police] we don't mind them coming out here at night to make sure no one is violating the law," Mr. Ramsey said. "But it's not much they can do when they get out here because everyone is just hanging out having good, clean fun."

27   The police presence does seem to lower the decibels, but patrols can be a drain on police resources. Ms. Rawley said the department tries to use innovative solutions.

28   "We ask property owners to get involved and post no-trespassing signs on their property. That way violators can be charged with trespassing, or towing can be enforced," Ms. Rawley said.

29   Webster Johnson, who rents business space in the 800 block of Castle Street, posted no-trespassing signs and regularly comes out to his property in the wee hours of the morning to ask crowd members to remove their vehicles from his parking space.

30   Ms. Rawley said the Police Department may help him put chains around the parking lot.

31   Kmart officials got police to start diverting crowds from its parking lot on South College Road after car owners began coming there to compare vehicle accessories. That's when the crowd moved a couple of miles to the Parrish Caine parking lot.

32   When downtown bars close at two o'clock, some business operators try to help clear the streets.

"We try to encourage our patrons to go straight home, although we don't have   33
rowdy customers," said Paleo Sun doorman Thurman Burgess, showing people out after a recent Justin Fox show.

The only law the city has in reference to loitering is related to drug activity and   34
prostitution.

Officials said it is difficult to make loitering arrests in other events.   35

"Loitering statutes may raise the question of the federal constitutional right to   36
freely assemble," said Delores Williams, assistant city attorney.

Not everyone is complaining about the large crowds. Booty's Soul Food Restau-   37
rant, at 918 Castle Street, opens only late at night on the weekend. Employees there
said people in the crowd are its biggest supporters.

The late-night crowd at Parrish Caine is welcomed by its staff.   38

"We don't discourage them coming out here," Mr. Ramsey said. "Many of them   39
support our business."

The Holly Pageant

LAVONNE ADAMS

Everything is ready. The fire trucks and ambulances have been moved outside, floors   1
have been swept, chairs have been placed in orderly rows. At seven o'clock, the Holly
Pageant is scheduled to begin.

Armed with a green metal cash box and a rubber stamp for the patrons' hands, I   2
take my seat behind the folding table to the left of the front door. I watch as the girls
and their parents arrive, chattering excitedly, arms laden with garment bags, shoe
boxes, makeup cases, curling irons. The mothers greet each other, size up the competition, push compliments from their tongues—"Oh, you look so pretty tonight!"—
"What a beautiful dress!"—"I love what you've done to your hair!"

Barbara, one of the pageant organizers, arrives. She is in charge of acquiring the   3
judges from the "Certified Judges List," a product of the judging seminars held every
year in Raleigh. Each year, she assiduously sets the judge's table with a white tablecloth, glasses of water, and bowls of snack foods. Once the judges arrive, she ushers
them into the radio room, where they remain sequestered until the pageant com-
mences. She stands at that door, as anxious as a presidential body guard.

I have heard rumors of corrupt judges, bribed by overanxious mothers at other   4
pageants, yet have been assured that these judges are not told the names of the contestants until they are handed the programs.

Barbara's four-year-old son runs up to her, yanks impatiently on her arm, whis-   5
pers something in her ear. She glances around anxiously, frowns as she takes his hand,
then disappears in the direction of the bathroom. The inner sanctum has been left un-
guarded. I take advantage of the opportunity. Unobtrusively, I walk toward the radio
room, cautiously turn the knob, ease open the door, and slip inside. The judges look
up, startled . . . perturbed. Once I explain why I am interested in talking to them, they
smile, settle back in their chairs, obviously relieved. They agree to let me interview
them after the pageant. I slip back outside.

The Holly Pageant is a tradition in this small North Carolina town, a social event   6
rivaled only by the yearly parish "reunion" at the town's largest Baptist church. The
Holly Ridge Volunteer Fire Department and Rescue Squad officially adopted the
pageant a few years ago, after a group of local citizens abandoned it. There was much

debate that night. Since I was a new member, I felt unsure of my local standing, so I kept my mouth firmly closed. The other female members had stars in their eyes; the men had dollar signs. "This," one of them declared, "could be financially rewarding." He saw it as a means of breaking the endless cycle of barbecue dinners and bake sales. He was proven right: the department cleared approximately $1,400 that first year.

7   The theme for this year's program is "Rock around the Clock." Mounted on the wall directly opposite the front door is a large black and white poster featuring a caricature of two "jitter-buggers," the male sporting a fashionable crew cut, the pony-tailed female wearing a poodle skirt, bobbie socks, and saddle oxfords. The stage is done in a 1950s motif, a reminder of an age of American innocence. Black 45-rpm records and oversized red musical notes are plastered on the white walls. All the props are surrounded with a gold tinsel garland, the kind used to decorate Christmas trees. Everything is supposed to shine in the harsh white glare of the spotlights.

8   I hear music, applause, the introduction of this year's emcee, a popular local disc jockey. The entertainment is beginning.

9   "Notice how carefully she walks—so ladylike," says the emcee. She is referring to Tiny Miss contestant number two, who is carefully placing one patent-leather clad foot in front of the other. With every step, her fluffy pink iridescent party dress shimmers.

10   The Tiny Miss contestants are three to five years old—there are four of them this year. Glenda, another of the pageant organizers, told me that there was no contestant number one; she dropped out after the third night of practice—simply refused to continue.

11   "It's time for our former Tiny Miss to present her portrait to Chief Duane Longo. Duane?" calls out the emcee.

12   Traditionally, each of the outgoing queens presents the department with a framed photograph—twinkling eyes, smile, and crown preserved for posterity. Duane walks toward the stage, bouquet of roses lying awkwardly across his left arm. Each footstep resounds from the plywood platform that functions as the stage. The Tiny Miss Holly is staring at his knee caps. He kneels. They look at each other uncertainly for just a moment, then swap the flowers for the photo. The little girl wraps her free arm around his neck, briefly buries her face against his shoulder.

13   "Awww," I hear from a woman in the audience, "isn't that sweet!"

14   Duane leaves the stage a flattering shade of crimson.

15   The four Tiny Miss contestants return to the stage. One is hiding behind the emcee; the rest are waiting expectantly, anxious smiles frozen on their faces.

16   "And your new Tiny Miss Holly is contestant number . . . three!"

17   The audience cheers, screams, whistles. A crown is placed upon a small head.

18   "When she grows up," the emcee tells the audience, "she wants to be a cheerleader."

19   I remember when they crowned last year's Tiny Miss Holly. One contestant, who stood to the winner's right, folded her arms across her chest, stamped her foot, eyebrows lowered over a fierce angry glare, bottom lip stuck out petulantly. For just an instant, I feared for the physical safety of the new little queen, afraid the other girl was going to hit her. As the twinkling crown was placed carefully upon the winner's blonde curls, her competitor burst into tears.

20   "How embarrassing for her mother," whispered a voice in the crowd.

21   There is a brief intermission. I see one of the defeated contestants standing next to the stage. She's surrounded by friends and family. Her father is talking softly to her as she hangs her head dejectedly. I move closer, catch the funereal terms of the adult

voices as her parents pat her shoulder consolingly. "You looked real pretty, honey"—"You did a good job"—"You'll be ready for them next year."

The pageant continues with the introduction of the Little Miss contestants, ages **22** six to nine, a bit older than the Tiny Miss contestants. These young girls appear on stage one at a time wearing incredible concoctions of satin, lace, taffeta, beads, and rhinestones: fairy-tale visions from our youth. The women in the audience gasp, sigh, exclaim enthusiastically over the beauty of each dress. Contestant number one steps onto the stage wearing a stunning teal-green party dress, appliquéd with a combination of rhinestones, pearls, and sequins.

"Contestant number one," reads the emcee, "enjoys shrimping with her daddy." **23**

I sit down in a chair recently vacated by one of the covey of visiting queens, win- **24** ners of other local pageants. To my left sits a stately, composed woman who is scrutinizing the proceedings. I ask her if she is the mother of the queen whose seat I just appropriated. "No," she answers, pointing to yet another queen who is getting ready to entertain the crowd. "That's my daughter."

As we discuss pageants in general, I ask her about the cost of the clothing. **25**

"You can't wear a sack, you know. This is based on more than talent and poise. **26** You can put the most talented, beautiful girl up there, but if her dress is not competitive . . . well . . . ." She leaves the sentence unfinished, raises her eyebrows, looks at me knowingly. She then describes a dress she saw at another pageant: floor-length black velvet with white satin flowers, spaghetti straps, $15-a-yard rhinestone trim. Total cost, $2,500.

She points to the owner of that dress, who later entertains the crowd with a **27** "Dixie/Battle Hymn of the Republic" medley. Tonight she is wearing a royal-blue sequined cocktail dress. I am disappointed that she has not worn the black gown, as I've never seen a dress that cost $2,500.

My curiosity piqued, I head backstage to track down the owner of the blue party **28** dress. I walk into the combination meeting room and kitchen, now transformed into a massive dressing room, the smell of makeup, hair spray, perfume, and hot bodies hanging thick in the air. One teen contestant is in the kitchen area, practicing her tap routine on a sheet of plywood meant to protect the new linoleum floor, purchased with proceeds from last year's pageant. I look around the room, searching for that particular child, or rather that particular dress, in the confusion. I spot her on the far side of the room. As I work my way toward her, I dodge the hyperactive contestants and the tense chaperons who dress the girls and have them on stage at all the appropriate times. Once I catch up to her, I ask the woman I assume to be her mother, "If it's not too personal, would you mind telling me how much you spent on that dress?" I pause to gauge her reaction, then add encouragingly, "It's absolutely gorgeous."

To the mother's right stands a woman who has been acknowledged periodically **29** throughout the evening as being instrumental in helping several contestants with both their dance routines and their hairdos. She is dressed in a pink lace, pearl-studded tea gown, blonde hair and makeup flawless. The mother pauses uncertainly, looks to this woman for support.

"Why do you want to know?" the woman growls. A feral look comes into her **30** eyes; her demeanor becomes aggressive, yet with an oddly defensive undertone.

I catch myself taking a step backward, totally unprepared for the hostility in her **31** voice. I straighten my back, refuse to be intimidated, wonder if she thinks I'm a spy for a competitor. I explain, "I'm a writer. I'm working on a story."

I wait as she stares me up and down, then nods to the mother before once again **32** turning her back on me.

33   "Three hundred and fifty dollars," states the mother.

34   While Glenda stressed that this year's parents have not been as competitive as those in years past, by the time you figure in the costumes and the dance lessons, it's about a $2,000 investment for each contestant. This year the pageant has a total of fifteen contestants.

35   Before the crowning of the new Little Miss, the former Little Miss makes her final appearance on stage. Tradition. With tears in her eyes, she waves farewell to her admirers. Well-wishers step forward with balloons and bouquets of flowers as a pre-taped message plays, "I want to thank God for giving me the opportunity to be Little Miss Holly . . . and Uncle Roger for letting me use his Corvette to ride in the parades."

36   My daughter says that several years ago the winner of the Little Miss competition wore her full-length dress to school the day after the pageant.

37   "And she wore her crown, too!" she adds emphatically.

38   "The sash?" I ask.

39   "Yep," she says. "Her daddy stayed with her all day. He even spread out napkins across her lap at lunch. And her friends had to hold up her skirts during recess because the playground was muddy and the grass was all wet. But she still climbed on the monkey bars."

40   We have another brief intermission, then the visiting queens go up on stage one by one to introduce themselves. Our newly crowned Tiny Miss and Little Miss are allowed to join the throng. When the Tiny Miss steps up to the microphone, she says, "Hi. I'm . . . ." She panics, has obviously forgotten what to say, looks around like a cornered mouse. "Mommy!" she calls out in a frightened voice. Her mother steps up to the stage with an indulgent smile and prompts her daughter. The little girl returns to the microphone and announces her name.

41   Glenda chuckles, "If that wasn't precious!"

42   Most of the older girls, the Pre-teens and the Teens, have been in pageants before. They're familiar with the routine, know all the ins and outs, understand how to play up to the judges, an art in itself.

43   Teen contestant number one, for instance, seems to be a house favorite. She does a clogging routine entitled "Texas Tap" that brings down the house. Her talent is undeniable, her exuberance contagious. I find myself smiling and clapping in time to the music along with the rest of the audience. Unfortunately, when it comes time for her prepared speech, this contestant forgets what she was going to say, stumbles verbally. She mumbles, "Oh God," then continues the best she can.

44   A young woman to my right shakes her head, turns to me and says with resignation, "She would have had a hard time, anyway. Her gown is red."

45   My face must reflect my bewilderment.

46   "With red hair?" she adds with implied significance.

47   Obviously, the contestant is unenlightened. Redheads don't wear red. Faux pas. One just doesn't do these things.

48   Some rules in the pageant circle are even more specific. Wearing black shoes with an evening gown is forbidden, as are hats, parasols, and elbow-length gloves. Rules are rules. I have heard that one mother, in another pageant, tried to add an extra row of lace to her daughter's socks. It was specified that only two rows of lace would be allowed. The pageant's organizers solemnly handed this mother a seam-ripper.

49   According to Glenda, this pageant has done away with collective judging, the commonly accepted practice of simultaneously lining up the girls on stage, having them turn, pose in front of the judges. "We don't want them compared to one another. They stand on their own merit."

Teen contestant number one does not win.   **50**

The pageant over, I weave through the departing crowd toward the radio room,   **51**
anxious to talk to the judges. There is a long line. Accompanied by their mothers,
each contestant is given the opportunity to discuss her performance with the judges,
find out what cost her the competition, where she lost those valuable points. It is a
quiet cluster.

To my left stands one of the winners. Her mother is not waiting with her, not   **52**
monitoring her behavior. One of her friends walks by, teases, "Hey, you won this year.
Why are *you* waiting to see the judges?"

The victor smiles, puffs out her chest with pride, swings her right hand up to her   **53**
forehead. She nods toward the closed door. "I just want to tell them . . . (with a saucy
salute) . . . thanks!"

A mother and her daughter, one of the defeated contestants, try to slip past unno-   **54**
ticed. Another mother looks up, asks, "Aren't you going to conference with the
judges?"

"No, I'm afraid I might start crying," the first mother answers. Her daughter says   **55**
nothing, but her eyes are red.

After a thirty-five minute wait, I am finally able to talk to one of the judges, a man   **56**
named John. He's wearing a black tuxedo, sports a diamond stud in his ear, has a red
carnation pinned on his lapel. He's a hairdresser, has done hair for lots of the
pageants—that's how he got "hooked." Most of the judges, he explains, become involved when either friends or their own children enter a pageant. These judges don't
get paid for their work; instead, they receive a small gift.

"Why do you do it, then?" I ask.   **57**

"I like to see the girls have a good time," he answers.   **58**

Every year I'm asked if I'm going to enter my two little girls in the pageant. Every   **59**
year I say no.

"Mommy," asks my youngest, "don't you think I'm pretty enough to win?"   **60**

■ ABOUT THE REST OF THIS BOOK

The chapters that follow in the first part of this book present an orderly progression for developing your skills as a college writer, reader, and researcher. A number
of chapters are concerned with reading, since an essential first step is to become a
careful, perceptive reader. The early chapters are devoted to techniques and skills
in reading for understanding. Later we introduce skills in reading critically and in
writing analytically about a text. One area that receives special attention is reading
argumentative writing and then writing to persuade others.

Our approach to research is systematic and incorporates several stages. We
first introduce important skills that involve single sources, including paraphrase
and summary. Those skills are then applied to working with multiple sources. The
next step is to synthesize paraphrases and summaries of several readings.

We introduce you to various kinds of research, with particular attention to locating and using sources in the library. Our aim is to enable you to find almost
any available information you are looking for. We show you how to compile

information, select it, arrange and present it, and document it. In short, you will learn how to write research papers with skill and confidence.

The second part of this book, the Research Paper Reference Handbook, explains the formal conventions of research writing, including lists of works cited, parenthetical notes and footnotes, outlines, and typing conventions. In addition to the MLA style used in most composition classes, two alternative formats are also explained.

We believe you will find this course rewarding and interesting. The activities you will engage in and the skills you will acquire are all eminently practical, and you will have ample opportunity to use them in the years to come. Being able to find the sources you are seeking, to read them perceptively, and to write clearly and articulately about what you have found can give you both a sense of power and a lasting satisfaction.

2 *Strategies for Reading*

Reading is one of the most useful abilities that college students can develop and improve. Of course, you already read well, since you are processing the words on this page. However, being an alert critical reader involves complex skills that we all should refine continually.

INFERENCES

As you learned in Chapter 1, reading is more than just recognizing words on a printed page. It involves the ability to interpret texts by drawing *inferences*—recognizing a writer's intentions, perceiving what is implied but not stated, making connections between the ideas you read and other ideas that you bring from outside the text, and drawing conclusions. You already exercise sophisticated interpretive skills when you read, as the following hypothetical example demonstrates.

Imagine that after having missed three meetings of your psychology class, you receive the following communication from the Dean of Students' office:

> This is to inform you that this office has been notified that you have reached the maximum number of absences permitted by the instructor of _Psychology 207_. In accordance with University Academic Policy, further absence will cause a lowering of your course grade and may result in your failing the course. This office will continue to monitor your academic progress. Do not hesitate to contact us if we can be of any help to you.

You might form this interpretation: First, the fact that you received a formal notification from the office of a campus administrator, rather than a friendly verbal comment from your instructor, indicates a problem. The formality of the language ("This is to inform you") and the impersonal style ("This office has been notified," rather than "your teacher has told me") give you a sense that a formidable bureaucracy has its eye on you. You conclude somewhat uncomfortably that the university takes attendance seriously. In addition to the actual warning about lower grades, you also note the more vague, implied threat ("This office will continue to monitor your academic progress"), which is only partially eased by the more benevolent final sentence. Upon reading this notice, you understand that it would be unwise for you to miss any more classes if you can possibly help it.

Prior knowledge allows you to interpret the notice in this way. Your previous experience with schools and school officials, with policies and grades, and with the way people use language all lead you to a particular understanding of the notice. Of course, not every reader will respond precisely as you do to such a message, but the point is clear—your mind is actively at work whenever you read. Good readers remain alert—recognizing, understanding, comparing, and evaluating the information they encounter.

EXERCISE | **Drawing Inferences**

Imagine the following scenario. Two weeks before Election Day, Mr. and Mrs. Davis, both in their late thirties, are walking with their five-year-old daughter through a shopping mall. Suddenly a man, smiling broadly, grabs Mr. Davis's hand and shakes it vigorously. On the lapel of his suit jacket is a large button that reads, "Bob Inskip for State Senate." He says:

> Hi, folks, I'm Bob Inskip. Hope you're havin' a great day. My what a beautiful little girl! [*To the girl:*] Hello, sweetheart, do you know how much you look like your mama? [*To Mrs. Davis:*] But, wait a minute, you're too young. This has to be your little sister. [*To both Mr. and Mrs. Davis:*] You know, I'm running for State Senate, and I need the support of honest, hard-working family folks like you. I'm not one of those professional politicians, and you won't find a lot of fancy degrees tacked onto my name. But then you won't find any drug charges on my record either. Now I'm not saying anything against my opponent, who's probably a well-meaning young fella. But anybody who compares our records can see I'm a local taxpayer, businessman, and property owner who grew up the hard way without any handouts. And that's the kind of senator we need keeping an eye on those government bureaucrats. I think smart folks like you will understand the issues and vote for me, Bob Inskip. Have a good one.

In a flash, he's off grabbing another shopper's hand and introducing himself.

1. Take a few minutes to write your interpretation of what you have read. What do you learn about Bob Inskip, outside of the explicit content of his remarks to the Davises? What kind of an impression does he make on you? Is that the impression he wishes to make? Specifically, what qualities do you find in him, and what alerts you to them? Why do you think he says what he does?
2. Now think about why you were able to read the passage as you did. What previous knowledge and experiences allowed you to interpret it in that way? Would a visitor from a country with a different political tradition, say, Libya or China, interpret Bob Inskip's behavior and intentions as you have?

■ CONTEXT

Introduced briefly in Chapter 1, *context* refers to the often complex web of circumstances surrounding almost every text or utterance. Suppose someone were to lead you blindfolded through the stacks of your college library, asking you at some arbitrary point to reach out and remove any book from one of the shelves. Still blindfolded, you flip the book open and point your finger at the open page; then, when your blindfold is removed, you begin reading. In all probability, it will take some time before the words begin to make sense—if indeed they ever do. With no idea of why or when or by whom the book was written, without any inkling of what preceded the passage you turned to, it is likely that you will misconstrue what you read. (This helps to explain why *quoting out of context* is so misleading and is therefore discouraged in all types of discourse, but especially in research writing and argument.)

When good readers approach any type of text, from a comic strip to a technical report, they form expectations about what it will say. Otherwise, even the simplest language would make little or no sense. We have all participated in or witnessed conversations similar to this: Two friends, Phoebe and Reuben, are discussing the rain clouds that loom threateningly in the western sky. Phoebe's mind then turns to an upcoming softball game and she says, "I hope they'll be able to come." Reuben, still thinking about the clouds, stares at her with a puzzled look. He cannot understand Phoebe because he is unable to place her words in the appropriate context. She is addressing one topic while he is trying to relate her words to another.

Like conversation, reading requires you to fit words into a context, which includes background information, tacit knowledge, and prior experience. For example, if you are reading the directions on the box of a frozen dinner, your familiarity with context allows you to anticipate a particular type of information, style, structure, and language. Consequently, the statement "Preheat conventional oven to 375°" makes sense.

Several elements contribute to the context of any passage you read. Imagine, for example, that you are reading the final chapter of a detective novel. In this case, context includes the following:

1. Recognition of the defining features of a particular type of text (e.g., knowing that detective novels end by solving a crime)

2. Familiarity with terms such as *homicide* and *motive*

3. Knowledge of what happened in previous chapters

All these elements allow you to anticipate what you are likely to encounter as you read. Without this context, reading is virtually impossible.

| **Analyzing Context** | EXERCISES |

1. To test our claim that it is nearly impossible to read without a context, see if you can draw meaning from the following passage:

. . . As the tellers passed along our lowest row on the left-hand side, the interest was insupportable—two hundred and ninety-one, two hundred and ninety-two—we were all standing up and stretching forward, telling with the tellers. At three hundred there was a short cry of joy, at three hundred and two another—suppressed however in a moment. For we did not yet know what the hostile force might be. We knew however that we could not be severely beaten. The doors were thrown open, and in they came. Each of them as he entered brought some different report of their numbers. It must have been impossible, as you may conceive, in the lobby, crowded as they must have been, to form any exact estimate. . . .

a. Are there any words in the passage that you do not know? Can you tell what the passage is describing? What guesses did you make as you read it?

b. Although its language is not especially difficult, it is likely that the passage did not make much sense to you, since you were deprived of the context that a reader would normally have. Had you encountered the passage in its original context, you would have had the following information: It is an excerpt from a letter written in 1831 by British historian Thomas Babington Macaulay. As a Member of Parliament, Macaulay had voted in favor of the important Reform Bill, which liberalized voting privileges. Along with other supporters of this legislation, he had had little hope that the bill would gain the more than three hundred votes needed for passage. Excitement grew as the tellers (clerks who counted and certified individual votes) announced their tallies.

Provided with this context, would it be easier to read the passage a second time? If so, why?

2. Imagine you have been asked to read the following process description as a test of your powers of recall. Here are the directions: Read it once, put it aside, and then write down as many specific facts as you can remember.

The procedure is actually quite simple. First you arrange things into different groups. Of course, one pile may be sufficient depending on how much there is to do. If you have to go somewhere else due to lack of facilities, that is the next step; otherwise you are pretty well set. It is important not to overdo things. That is, it is better to do too few things at once than too many. In the short run this may not seem important but complications can easily arise. A mistake can be expensive as well. At first the whole procedure will seem complicated. Soon, however, it will become just another facet of life. It is difficult to foresee any end to the necessity for this task in the immediate future, but then one can never tell. After the procedure is completed, one arranges the materials into different groups again. Then they can be put into their appropriate places. Eventually they will be used once more, and the whole cycle will then have to be repeated. However, that is part of life.

—John D. Bransford and Marcia K. Johnson, "Cognitive Prerequisites for Understanding"

Although the vocabulary and sentence structure of this passage are simple, you probably had difficulty recalling details. But suppose you had been provided the title "Doing the Laundry." Do you think you could have recalled more specific facts?

3. Now read the following narrative paragraph:

The Prisoner
Rocky slowly got up from the mat, planning his escape. He hesitated a moment and thought. Things were not going well. What bothered him the most was being held, especially since the charge against him had been weak. He considered his present situ-

ation. The lock that held him was strong, but he thought he could break it. He knew, however, that his timing would have to be perfect. Rocky was aware that it was because of his early roughness that he had been penalized so severely—much too severely from his point of view. The situation was becoming frustrating; the pressure had been grinding on him for too long. He was being ridden unmercifully. Rocky was getting angry now. He felt that he was ready to make his move. He knew that his success or failure would depend on what he did in the next few seconds.

—John D. Bransford, *Human Cognition: Learning, Understanding, and Remembering*

Now reread the paragraph, replacing the title with "The Wrestler." Does this alter your response? Why is it possible to play with the meaning of this paragraph by changing its title? What if the paragraph opened with a summarizing sentence? From a reader's perspective, what is the value of a title and summarizing sentence?

■ STRATEGIES FOR UNDERSTANDING ✳ *study guide*

As the preceding exercises demonstrate, familiarity with context makes it easier to interpret a passage. Since the context in which you place a passage depends on your knowledge, experiences, values, opinions, and interests, another reader may place the same passage in a somewhat different context and, as a result, interpret it differently.

There are skills, however, that all good readers share. They are observant of context and seek clues to enrich their understanding of it, thus refining their interpretation. In large part, readers develop this ability through practice. The more you read, the better reader you become. But it also helps to be familiar with some of the principles and strategies of good reading. You can become a better reader quickly with a little training and lots of practice.

Good readers routinely adopt various *reading strategies.* These strategies take time—and, at first, may seem counterproductive—but they save time in the long run, since they make your reading more alert, thorough, and efficient. Choosing the most appropriate and effective strategies depends on your purposes for reading. Sometimes you read for entertainment, at other times, for information or ideas. Often you read for several different purposes at the same time. Sometimes you accept the writer's authority and strive to understand and absorb what you read. At other times, you approach a text more critically, assessing the writer's authority and the validity of her ideas. Chapter 7 presents strategies for critical reading. The focus of this chapter, on the other hand, is reading for understanding and information. The strategies that experienced readers use to understand a text include the following:

- Looking for clues in a text before starting to read it
- Responding to clues provided by the author
- Reading with a pencil
- Rereading as necessary

Surveying a Text

To understand even the simplest passage, you must first place it in an appropriate context so as to anticipate what it is likely to contain. The more you know about context, the more reliably you can anticipate and the more efficiently you will read. It is therefore useful to discover in advance as much about a text as you can. The technique is simple: *Look over what you intend to read—quickly but alertly—before you begin to read it.*

Specifically, there are several clues to look for before you begin your actual reading, as the following situation demonstrates. Suppose you are reading an issue of *Newsweek* and you come upon the essay shown on the facing page. What might you do before reading it (or even as you decide whether you want to read it)?

EXERCISE | ### Surveying a Text

Look now at the *Newsweek* essay on the facing page and see how much you can gather about it *without actually reading its text.* What do you expect the topic of the essay to be? What do you guess is the writer's point of view? What allowed you to make these guesses?

Prereading

Good readers search for clues when they first encounter a text. Following are some of the sources of information that can improve your understanding of a text and enrich your interpretation of it. These sources of information can improve your understanding of most of the reading you do in college.

Title

It may seem obvious to begin reading a text by taking note of its title, but a surprising number of students read assigned chapters and articles without doing so. Consequently, they miss an important source of information.

Article titles, chapter headings, and newspaper headlines usually identify topics discussed in the text, helping you anticipate content. For example, the title of this chapter, "Strategies for Reading," led you to expect an explanation of how to get more from your reading. The *Newsweek* essay provides both a title, "Pay Your Own Way! (Then Thank Mom)," and a subtitle indicating an argument that college students should finance their own education.

Highlighted Quotations

Important passages are often highlighted, providing clues to the central idea of a text. In the *Newsweek* essay, for instance, a quotation appears beneath the author's photograph in italic type: "I didn't eat out every weekend or own a car. I

Pay Your Own Way! (Then Thank Mom)

Working my way through college taught me how to manage time and money. Why don't more kids do it?

By AUDREY ROCK-RICHARDSON

IS IT ME, OR ARE STUDENTS THESE days lazy? I'm not talking about tweens who don't want to do their homework or make their bed. I'm referring to people in legal adulthood who are in the process of making hugely consequential life decisions. And collectively, their attitude is that they simply cannot pay for college.

Don't get me wrong. I realize that there are people out there who pay their own tuition. I know that some cannot put themselves through school because of disabilities or extenuating circumstances. But I have to say: the notion that parents must finance their children's education is ridiculous.

During college I consistently endured comments from peers with scholarships and loans, peers who had new Jeeps and expensive apartments, all who would say to me, eyes bulging, "You mean your parents didn't help you at *all?*"

I resented my fellow students for asking this, first because they made it sound like my parents were demons, and second because they were insinuating that I wasn't capable of paying my own way. "How did you pay tuition?" they'd ask. My response was simple: "I worked." They would look at me blankly, as though I had told them I'd gone to the moon.

As an undergrad (University of Utah, 1998), I put myself through two solid years of full-tuition college by working as a daycare provider for $4.75 an hour. I then married and finished out seven more quarters by working as an interpreter for the deaf and a tutor in a private school.

I didn't work during high school or save for years. I simply got a job the summer following graduation and worked 40 hours a week. I didn't eat out every weekend, shop a lot or own a car. I sacrificed. I was striving for something bigger and longer-lasting than the next kegger.

Looking at the numbers now, I'm not sure how I managed to cover all the costs of my education. But I did. And I bought every single textbook and pencil myself, too.

I remember sitting in a classroom one afternoon during my senior year, listening to

I didn't eat out every weekend or own a car. I was striving for something bigger than the next kegger.

everyone introduce themselves. Many students mentioned their part-time jobs. There were several members of a sorority in the class. When it came to the first girl, she told us her name and that she was a sophomore. "Oh," she added, "I major in communications." After an awkward silence, the teacher asked, "Do you work?"

"Oh, no," she said emphatically, "I go to school full time." (As if those of us who were employed weren't really serious about our classes.)

The girl went on to explain that her parents were paying tuition and for her to live in a sorority house (complete with a cook, I later found out). She was taking roughly 13 credit hours. And she was too busy to work.

I, on the other hand, was taking 18, count 'em, 18 credit hours so I could graduate within four years. I worked 25 hours a week so my husband and I could pay tuition without future loan debt. And here's the kicker: I pulled straight A's.

I caught a glimpse of that same girl's report card at the end of the quarter, and she pulled C's and a few B's, which didn't surprise me. Having to juggle tasks forces you to prioritize, a skill she hadn't learned.

I'm weary of hearing kids talk about getting financial help from their parents as though they're entitled to it. I am equally tired of hearing stressed-out parents groaning, "How are we going to pay for his/her college?" Why do they feel obligated?

I do not feel responsible for my daughter's education. She'll find a way to put herself through if she wants to go badly enough. And (I'm risking sounding like my mom here), she'll thank me later. I can say this because I honestly, wholeheartedly thank my parents for giving me that experience.

I'm not saying that it's fun. It's not. I spent the first two years of school cleaning up after 4-year-olds for the aforementioned $4.75 an hour and taking a public bus to campus. My husband and I spent the second two struggling to pay out our tuition. We lived in a cinder-block apartment with little privacy and no dishwasher.

Lest I sound like a hypocrite, yes, I would have taken free college money had the opportunity presented itself. However, because my parents put themselves through school they expected me to do the same. And, frankly, I'm proud of myself. I feel a sense of accomplishment that I believe I couldn't have gained from 50 college degrees all paid for by someone else.

Getting through school on our own paid off in every way. My husband runs his own business, a demanding but profitable job. I write part time and work as a mother full time. I believe the fact that we are happy and financially stable is a direct result of our learning how to manage time and money in college.

So, kids, give your parents a break. Contrary to popular belief, you can pay tuition by yourself. And you might just thank your mother for it, too.

ROCK-RICHARDSON *lives in Stansbury Park, Utah.*

was striving for something bigger than the next kegger." This allows an alert reader to infer that the author bases her argument on personal experience and that she believes college students should assume more of the responsibilities of financing their own education.

The Author

Information about an author can enrich your reading of a text. Recognizing an author's name often allows you to make predictions. The title "Teenagers and Sex" would arouse different expectations if the author were evangelist Pat Robertson as opposed to Hugh Hefner, the publisher of *Playboy*. Professional titles, academic degrees, titles of other publications, or information about an author's occupation and accomplishments may provide clues about her expertise or bias. Often a book will introduce its author on the flap of a dust jacket. Articles may do this in an introductory headnote, in a footnote to the first page, or on the last page.

The *Newsweek* article includes a photograph of the author while identifying her only as a resident of Stansbury Park, Utah. Since neither her name nor her face is familiar, you may infer that the article presents the opinions of a recent college graduate who is neither a professional writer nor a celebrity.

Past Experience

Sometimes prior reading provides clues about what to expect. A regular reader of *Newsweek* will recognize the "My Turn" column as a recurring feature of that magazine. Articles in this series typically relate the personal experiences or express the opinions of individual readers. This provides further confirmation that this is a personal essay about the benefits of paying for one's own college education.

Section Headings

Headings and subheadings are especially useful in longer passages. One effective strategy is to leaf through a text to distinguish the parts that compose it. Before reading a book, examine its table of contents; before reading an article or chapter, look for headings. Accurately predicting a text's major ideas and organization makes reading more efficient. Although the *Newsweek* article has no subject headings, a text that does can be found on pages 59–63.

Date of Publication

Knowing when a text was published can help you to evaluate it. If you need information about international terrorism, for instance, it makes an enormous difference whether a source was published in 2000 or 2003. Date of publication may also put an author's ideas and claims into perspective. Some readers might respond differently to an article on the same topic as Rock-Richardson's if it had been written three years earlier, before federal law allowed parents to deduct tuition payments from their taxable income.

Length

Noting the length of a text can give you an indication of how thoroughly the author's point is developed. It also helps to know where you stand within that development as you read.

Bold Type, Illustrations, and Captions

You can find additional clues to the contents of a book chapter by briefly examining it before you read. Key words that name central concepts are often printed in bold typeface. (Look for examples in this chapter.) Other major ideas are often illustrated in drawings and photographs and explained in their captions. Open a textbook that has illustrations and see what you can learn about any given chapter from looking at them.

With an article like the one we have examined, it takes only a few seconds of prereading to gather most of this information. Prereading strategies amply repay the small investment of time you make in carrying them out: Your mind is receptive as you begin to read, your reading is made easier, and you can read more alertly and profitably.

Prereading

EXERCISES

1. Read "Pay Your Own Way! (Then Thank Mom)" and determine the accuracy of the predictions you made using prereading strategies. Did these strategies enable you to read more efficiently?

2. Using as many prereading strategies as possible, explain what predictions you can make about the rest of this chapter and about the reading that appears on pages 90–92.

Responding to Textual Clues

Good writers help their readers in several ways. They anticipate who their readers are likely to be, and then they write to be understood by them. They write clear sentences, using a vocabulary and style appropriate to their audience. They provide punctuation to signal when a pause in reading should occur or when one idea ends and another one begins. Good readers, for their part, recognize and profit from the signals that writers give them.

It is always easier for us to read a passage if we have a reasonably clear notion of what it is likely to be about. In a variety of ways, authors allow us to anticipate their ideas. Even inexperienced writers provide readers with various signposts to help them, as the following paragraph from a student's paper on teenage drinking demonstrates:

Another cause of drinking among teenagers is peer pressure. They are told, "If you don't join in with everyone else, you're going to feel left out." Before you know it, they are drinking along with the rest of the crowd. Soon they are even drinking before class, at lunch, and after school. They now have a serious drinking problem.

This paragraph, taken from a rough draft, would benefit from additional development and other kinds of revision. Even so, it demonstrates some of the signposts that writers provide for readers. Previous paragraphs in the paper discuss other factors contributing to teenage drinking. The opening words of this paragraph, *Another cause,* are a ***signal phrase,*** indicating that a further reason is about to be introduced. The first sentence is a ***topic sentence*** summarizing the general point of the paragraph. Upon reading it, we can predict that the rest of the paragraph will explain how peer pressure works. The writer does just that, detailing the process of how teenagers develop a drinking problem through peer pressure, and she uses transition words or phrases like *before you know it, soon,* and *now* to show that she is describing a sequence of stages.

Notice also how your mind works as you read the following passage with numbered sentences:

1 Scarfe was always a tyrant in his household.   **2** The servants lived in constant terror of his fierce diatribes, which he would deliver whenever he was displeased. **3** One of the most frequent causes of his displeasure was the food they served him.   **4** His tea, for example, was either too hot or too cold.   **5** The soup had either too much or too little seasoning.   **6** Another pet peeve was the servants' manner of address.   **7** God help the butler who forgot to add *sir* to every sentence he spoke to Scarfe, or the chauffeur whose tone was deemed not properly deferential.   **8** On the other hand, when one of the most timid parlor maids would hesitate in speaking so as to be certain her words did not give offense, he would thunder at her, "Out with it, you stupid girl!"
  9 Scarfe's wife and children were equally the victims of his tyranny. . . .

Observe how each sentence in the passage creates a context for sentences to come and so allows you to anticipate them. In the analysis that follows, we have made some assumptions about how you, or any typical reader, might respond to the passage. Take some time to examine the analysis carefully and see if you agree with it.

As you read the Scarfe passage, your mind follows a fairly predictable path. First, since sentence 1 makes a general statement, you recognize it as a topic sentence. In other words, you guess that Scarfe's tyranny is the ***main idea*** of the paragraph. It comes as no surprise that sentence 2 provides a specific detail about his tyranny—he terrorized servants. After sentence 2, you might expect either to learn which other members of the household Scarfe terrorized or to get more specific information about his treatment of the servants. The latter turns out to be the case. The signal phrase "one of the most frequent causes of his displeasure" in sentence 3 shows where the paragraph is heading: "one of" indicates that food is among several causes of Scarfe's anger and suggests that you may learn about others. The author makes the relationship between 2 and 3 clear by ***repeating key words and phrases:*** "his displeasure" in 3 recalls "he was displeased" in 2, and "they" in 3 refers to "the servants" in 2. Sentence 4 also provides a signal phrase, "for example," helping you anticipate an instance of Scarfe's displeasure. Although sentence 5 offers no explicit signal, it is phrased like sentence 4 and contains the words "either too . . . or too . . . ," suggesting a parallel purpose. In sentence 6, "another pet peeve" refers back to sentence 3, which describes the first pet peeve. Since 3 is followed by examples, you can expect the same of 6, and in fact both 7 and 8 also give specific instances of the servants' manner of address. Sentence 8 begins with the signal phrase, "on the other hand," which indicates a change in direction; that is, the sentence offers an example different from the one in 7. It says that servants could be criticized for being too deferential, as well as for not being deferential enough.

Through *topic sentences, repeated key words,* and *signal phrases,* writers give readers clues to make reading easier. Without having to think about it, experienced readers respond to these clues, make predictions, and read with greater ease and effectiveness as a result. Chapter 4 pays special attention to topic sentences. The remaining sections of the chapter are concerned with other reading clues.

Responding to Textual Clues

1. Only the first sentence (sentence 9) of the second paragraph is given in the passage about Scarfe. Make some predictions about the rest of the paragraph. Do you think sentence 9 is likely to be the paragraph's topic sentence? What would you expect the rest of the paragraph to be about? How does sentence 9 relate to the preceding paragraph? Does it contain any signal words or phrases linking it to that paragraph?

2. By inventing details, complete the second paragraph, illustrating how Scarfe mistreated his wife and children. When finished, see what clues you have provided your readers.

Recognizing Transitions ✗

Just as it is important for readers to recognize clues, it is also important for writers to provide them. Signal words and phrases make reading easier because they clarify the relationship between one sentence and another. For this reason they are also called *transitions.* They help the reader see in which direction the ideas in a passage are moving. Relationships between sentences can be classified into several general categories. The following are four of the most important relationships, together with commonly used transition words for each.

And *Signals*

And words signal movement in the same direction. They tell you that the new idea or fact will in some way be like the previous one. Here are the most common *and* signals:

and	first	similarly	furthermore
too	second	finally	what's more
also	another	indeed	moreover
then	in fact	likewise	in addition

Example: Pilbeam's wisecracks got on his classmates' nerves. He *also* angered the teacher by snoring during the metaphysics lecture.

But *Signals*

But words signal a change in direction. They tell you that the new fact or idea will be different or opposite from the previous one.

but	however	conversely	unfortunately
still	the fact is	nonetheless	notwithstanding
instead	in contrast	nevertheless	on the other hand

Example: The doctor ordered Gerstenslager to give up all spicy foods. *Nonetheless,* he could still be found most nights by the TV set, munching happily on jalapeños and pickled sausages.

For Example *Signals*

For example words signal a movement from the general to the specific. They tell you that the new fact or idea will be a specific illustration of the previous general one.

for example	for instance	specifically	to begin with

Example: Mopworth is a splendid athlete. At a high-school track meet, *for example,* she took firsts in both the low hurdles and the ten-kilometer race.

Therefore *Signals*

Therefore words signal a cause-and-effect relationship. They tell you that the new fact or idea will be the result of the previous one.

thus	therefore	accordingly	consequently
so	hence	as a result	thereupon

Example: The Godolphin twins never remembered to set their alarm clocks. *As a result,* they were always late for their eight o'clock statistics class.

EXERCISES | **Transitions**

1. The following passages are made difficult to read because signal words have been removed. Supply signal words where you feel they would be useful to clarify relationships between sentences or to make the flow of the passage smoother.

a. The open-source movement traces its roots to 1984, when MIT computer scientist Richard Stallman quit his job in academia to start the Free Software Foundation. In the 1960s and early 1970s, virtually all software was in the public domain [i.e., uncopyrighted and marketable], and thus open for constant revision and review. By the early 1980s, nearly all new software was proprietary, or "closed-source"— its underlying code copyrighted and guarded as closely as the Coke recipe. Stallman felt that this approach hampered the free flow of ideas and ultimately delivered bad software. He devised a clever legal device known as a General Public License (GPL), or "copyleft." Software that is licensed under a copyleft is in the public domain. Any derivative works that use a piece of copylefted code must be in the public domain. The copyleft is like a virus, passing itself on to its descendants.

—Leif Utne, "Free at Last!"

b. What is Benford's Law and why is it weird? Think of a large and random set of numbers that is somehow derived from other numbers. Closing stock prices are essentially derived from a host of other numbers. Growth, cost of labor, prevailing interest rates, and so on [affect stock prices]. [There is an] amazingly large volume of numbers in [economic data]. You'd think those numbers, which are basically assembled randomly, would be spread out randomly. There'd be just as many numbers beginning with nine or four or one. That's where you'd be wrong. Some unseen and unknown universal force . . . bunches these kinds of random numbers into very predictable patterns.

—Kevin Maney, "Baffled by Math?"

Nearly every sentence in these paragraphs has an *and, but, for example,* or *therefore* relationship to the sentence before it and, presumably, could carry a signal word or phrase. But since so many signals would clutter the paragraph, you must decide where to include and where to omit them. For each signal you add, explain why it seems necessary or desirable.

2. Reread the passages above and identify other cohesive techniques (repeated words and phrases, topic sentences) that the writers have provided to help readers.

3. What transition words and phrases can you find in the article on page 83?

4. Find a passage from another of your textbooks—one that uses a variety of transitional signals. Write a brief commentary on how those signals alert readers to connections among ideas.

5. Look at the paragraph you wrote in response to exercise 2 on page 87. What transitional words and phrases did you provide? Add any others that seem necessary.

Reading with a Pencil

Students confront two basic tasks when reading for academic purposes: remaining alertly engaged and facilitating later review. Almost everyone has had the disconcerting experience of struggling to remain alert only to drift into a trance, as the eyes continue to plod across the page after the mind has wandered elsewhere. When concentration is a struggle, reading is slow, unpleasant, and ineffective. Fortunately, there is a way to read more efficiently while maintaining concentration: You can read better if you use a pencil.

Reading with a pencil involves two activities—**underlining** and **note-taking.** If a book is yours, you may do both. When underlining, you highlight main ideas and significant information. When writing marginal notes, you summarize the author's ideas in your own words or jot down your own ideas and responses.

Reading with a pencil keeps the mind alert and active. When you combine writing with reading, you bring a larger area of your brain into play. Reading with a pencil also forces you to respond more actively. When you search for an author's main ideas and connect them with personal experiences or with other texts, you become more involved with what you read. When you are thinking in this manner, you are more likely to understand what you read.

Besides increasing alertness, reading with a pencil creates a useful record that provides ready access to what you have read. For example, if you have marked a textbook chapter with underlining and marginal notes, you can review the material quickly and effectively before an exam. You won't have to reread everything, since you have marked what seems most important. Moreover, by reviewing the highlighted passages, you stimulate memory and thereby recollect most of what you learned and thought about the first time through.

Just as no two people interpret or respond to a book in exactly the same way, no two readers will mark a book in the same way either. In general, people's diverse experiences provoke a multitude of associations and reactions to the same text. Likewise, even the same reader may respond differently to the same text, when her purposes for reading change.

Annotating and Underlining for Recall

Let us assume that a student in developmental psychology is about to be tested on a textbook chapter that analyzes relationships between adolescents and their parents. Seeking literal comprehension of important facts, she might annotate one excerpt from the chapter as follows:

PRACTICE READING

Relationships with Maturing Children

Diane E. Papalia, Sally Wendkos Olds, and Ruth Duskin Feldman

1   Parenthood is a process of letting go. This process usually reaches its climax during the parents' middle age. It is true that, with modern trends toward delaying marriage and parenthood, an increasing number of middle-aged people now face such issues as finding a good day-care or kindergarten program and screening the content of Saturday morning cartoons. Still, most parents in the early part of mid-

dle age must cope with a different set of issues, which arise from living with children who will soon be leaving the nest. Once children become adults, parent-child ties usually recede in importance; but these ties normally last as long as parent and child live.

ADOLESCENT CHILDREN: ISSUES FOR PARENTS

It is ironic that people at the two times of life popularly linked with emotional   2
crises—adolescence and midlife—often live in the same household. It is usually middle-aged adults who are the parents of adolescent children. While dealing with their own special concerns, parents have to cope daily with young people who are undergoing great physical, emotional, and social changes.

Although research contradicts the stereotype of adolescence as a time of in-   3
evitable turmoil and rebellion . . . , some rejection of parental authority is necessary for the maturing youngster. An important task for parents is to accept children as they are, not as what the parents had hoped they would be.

Theorists from a variety of perspectives have described this period as one of   4
questioning, reappraisal, or diminished well-being for parents. However, this too is not inevitable, according to a questionnaire survey of 129 two-parent, intact, mostly white, socioeconomically diverse families with a firstborn son or daughter between ages 10 and 15. Most vulnerable were mothers who were not heavily invested in paid work; apparently work can bolster a parent's self-worth despite the challenges of having a teenage child. For some other parents, especially white-collar and professional men with sons, their children's adolescence brought increased satisfaction, well-being, and even pride. For most parents, the normative changes of adolescence elicited a mixture of positive and negative emotions. This was particularly true of mothers with early adolescent daughters, whose relationships generally tended to be both close and conflict-filled (Silverberg, 1996).

There is a great deal of variation among families, but parents who work usually adjust to the empty nest more easily.

WHEN CHILDREN LEAVE: THE EMPTY NEST

Research is also challenging popular ideas about the empty nest, a supposedly difficult transition, especially for women. Although some women, heavily invested   5
in mothering, do have problems at this time, they are far outnumbered by those who, like Madeline Albright, find the departure liberating (Antonucci & Akiyama, 1997; Barnett, 1985; Chiriboga, 1997; Helson, 1997; Mitchell & Helson, 1990). Today, the refilling of the nest by grown children returning home (discussed in the next section) is far more stressful (Thomas, 1997).

The empty nest does not signal the end of parenthood. It is a transition to a   6
new stage: the relationship between parents and adult children. For many women, this transition brings relief from what Gutmann called "the chronic emergency of parenthood" (Cooper & Gutmann, 1987, p. 347). They can now pursue their own interests as they bask in their grown children's accomplishments. The empty nest does appear to be hard on women who have not prepared for it by reorganizing their lives (Targ, 1979). This phase also may be hard on fathers who regret that they did not spend more time with their children (L. B. Rubin, 1979).

In a longitudinal study of employed married women with multiple roles, the   7
empty nest had *no* effect on psychological health, but cutting back on employment *increased* distress, whereas going to work full-time *decreased* it (Wethington & Kessler, 1989). On the other hand, in a comparison of stress at various stages of life, men in the empty-nest stage were most likely to report health-related stress (Chiriboga, 1997).

WHEN CHILDREN RETURN: THE REVOLVING-DOOR SYNDROME

8   What happens if the nest does not empty when it normally should, or if it unexpectedly refills? In recent decades, more and more adult children have delayed leaving home. Furthermore, the revolving door syndrome (sometimes called the *boomerang phenomenon*) has become more common, as increasing numbers of young adults, especially men, return to their parents' home, sometimes more than once. The family home can be a convenient, supportive, and affordable haven while young adults are getting on their feet or regaining their balance in times of financial, marital, or other trouble.

9   According to the National Survey of Families and Households, at any given moment 45 percent of parents ages 45 to 54 with children over age 18 have an adult child living at home; and three out of four 19- to 34-year-olds have lived in the parental home after turning 19 (in four out of ten cases, more than once). Thus this "nonnormative" experience is becoming quite normative, especially for parents with more than one child. Rather than an abrupt leave-taking, the empty-nest transition may be seen as a more prolonged process of separation, often lasting several years.

10   The way this transition plays out for parents is "strongly related to children's progress through the transition to adulthood" (Aquilino, 1996, pp. 435–436). Most likely to come home are single, divorced, or separated children and those who end a cohabiting relationship. Leaving school and ending military service increase the chances of returning; having a child decreases them.

11   As common as it has become, the revolving-door syndrome contradicts most parents' expectations for young adults. As children move from adolescence to young adulthood, parents expect them to become independent. Their autonomy is a sign of parental success. As the timing-of-events model would predict, then, an unanticipated return to the nest may lead to tension. Serious conflicts or open hostility may arise when a young adult child is unemployed and financially dependent or has returned after the failure of a marriage. Relations are smoother when the parents see the adult child moving toward autonomy, for example by enrolling in college.

12   Disagreements may center on household responsibilities and the adult child's lifestyle. The young adult is likely to feel isolated from peers, while the parents may feel hampered in renewing their intimacy, exploring personal interests, and resolving marital issues (Aquilino & Supple, 1991). The return of an adult child works best when parents and child negotiate roles and responsibilities, acknowledging the child's adult status and the parents' right to privacy.

Revolving door is more likely to arouse stress because some people view adult children living at home as a sign that they have failed as parents.

GUIDELINES for Annotating and Underlining for Recall

- **Mark the most important ideas.** Use underlining to outline a passage, highlighting those parts that express important ideas—topic sentences instead of supporting details, unless they too are significant. Notice that the reader does not underline anything in paragraphs 6 and 7, which illustrate a point made in the first sentence of paragraph 5:

   Research is also challenging popular ideas about the empty nest, a supposedly difficult transition, especially for women. Although some women, heavily invested in mothering, do have problems at this time, they are far outnumbered by those who, like Madeline Albright, find the departure liberating (Antonucci & Akiyama, 1997; Barnett, 1985; Chiriboga, 1997; Helson, 1997; Mitchell & Helson, 1990).

- **Don't underline too much.** Underlining nearly every sentence blurs distinctions between important concepts and minor details. Be selective, highlighting only the most important ideas and information. Of course, the amount you underline depends on what you read. A passage with heavily concentrated information may require lots of underlining. Passages that list examples or provide background may not be underlined at all. Judgment, derived through experience, offers the best guidance.

- **Mark with rereading in mind.** Underline words that clearly and briefly express important ideas. You needn't underline entire sentences if there are phrases that capture main ideas. Sometimes parts of different sentences can be connected to form a single statement, as in the following example:

   > In recent decades, more and more adult children have delayed leaving home. Furthermore, the revolving-door syndrome (sometimes called the *boomerang phenomenon*) has become more common, as increasing numbers of young adults, especially men, return to their parents' home, sometimes more than once. The family home can be a convenient, supportive, and affordable haven while young adults are getting on their feet or regaining their balance in times of financial, marital, or other trouble.
   >
   > According to the National Survey of Families and Households, at any given moment 45% of parents ages 45 to 54 with children over age 18 have an adult child living at home; and three out of four 19- to 34-year-olds have lived in the parental home after turning 19 (in four out of ten cases, more than once). Thus this "nonnormative" experience is becoming quite normative, especially for parents with more than one child.

- **When the author's words are not convenient or clear, use your own.** If a passage is not phrased in words suitable for underlining, rephrase the main idea in a marginal note. The reader of our sample passage wrote marginal notes to summarize ideas in paragraphs 4 and 11. Capsulizing important concepts in your own words helps you understand what you read. When people talk about "writing to learn," one of the things they mean is that when students recast difficult or unfamiliar ideas in their own words, their ability to understand and recall those ideas is enhanced. In some sense, they assume ownership of concepts that may initially have seemed obscure and alien.

- **Use special symbols to signal the most important passages.** Since some of the passages you mark are more important than others, highlight them by placing symbols beside them in the margins. Stars, asterisks, checks, and exclamation or question marks make important passages stand out.

- **Mark only your own books.** Because no two readers think exactly alike as they read, no one likes to read books that other people have marked. Writing in books borrowed from the library or friends is both a discourtesy and an act of vandalism. Use stick-on notes, or make photocopies of any borrowed materials that you want to mark. Of course, you are strongly urged to mark books that belong to you.

Annotating and Underlining for Recall

Like the *Newsweek* editorial on page 83, the following article concerns relationships between college students and their parents. As you read it, try to connect the views of the author, a college president, with those expressed in the *Newsweek* piece. Then reread with a pencil, annotating specific facts and concepts. Be careful to mark any passages that might help you better understand, modify, or contradict views held by the author of the *Newsweek* editorial.

PRACTICE READING

Keeping Parents off Campus

Judith R. Shapiro

Every September I join our deans and faculty to welcome first-year students and their families to the Barnard [College] campus. It is a bittersweet moment; while the parents are filled with pride, they also know they now must begin to let go of their children. Parents must learn to back off.

Confidently, with generosity and grace, most parents let their children grow up. They realize that the purpose of college is to help young people stand on their own and take the crucial steps toward adulthood while developing their talents and intellect with skill and purpose.

But this truth is often swept aside by the notion that college is just one more commodity to be purchased, like a car or a vacation home. This unfortunate view gives some parents the wrong idea. Their sense of entitlement as consumers, along with an inability to let go, leads some parents to want to manage all aspects of their children's college lives—from the quest for admission to their choice of major. Such parents, while the exception, are nonetheless an increasing fact of life for faculty, deans, and presidents.

Three examples, all recently experienced by my staff, illustrate my point. One mother accompanied her daughter to a meeting with her dean to discuss a supposedly independent research project. Another demanded that her daughter's academic transcript be sent to her directly, since she was the one paying the tuition bills. And one father called his daughter's career counselor so he could contact her prospective employers to extol her qualifications.

I have had my own awkward encounters on this front. I have met with parents accompanying their daughters on campus visits who speak in "third person invisible." The prospective student sits there—either silently or attempting to get a word in edgewise—while the parents speak about her as if she were elsewhere. I always make a point of addressing the student directly; although this initially feels as if I were talking to a ventriloquist's dummy, I find that, if I keep at it, I can shift the conversation to one between the young woman and me.

Stories abound of parents horrified by a child's choice of major and ready to do battle with faculty or deans. These parents fail to understand that passion and curiosity about a subject, coupled with the ability to learn, are the best career preparation.

We are living in times when educational pressures on families begin when children are toddlers and continue relentlessly through the teenage years. Four-year-olds may face a battery of tests to get into a desirable preschool. As they face the college admissions process, parents attuned to the barrage of media coverage believe that the best colleges accept only superhumans—a belief encouraged, admittedly, by some universities—and strive to prepare their sons and daughters accordingly. (One father even took a year off from his job to supervise the preparation of his daughter's admissions portfolio.)

By the time their children enter college, parents have become so invested emotionally in their success that they may not understand why it is crucial that they remain outside the college gates. The division of responsibility between parents and colleges during the undergraduate years is a complex matter, as is the question of how much responsibility young people should be expected to take for themselves. We have been hearing much of late about a return to the *in loco parentis* approach that fell out of favor in the late 1960s. The same baby boomers who fought to end these restrictions want to bring them back, perhaps out of dismay that their own children may have to make some of the same mistakes that they did.

Colleges should do as much as they can to provide a safe and secure environment. More important, they must help students learn to take care of themselves and to seek guidance on life's tough decisions. Neither colleges nor parents can make the world entirely safe for our young people and, hard as it may be to accept, there are limits to our ability to control what life has in store for our children.

Parents do best when they encourage their college-bound children to reach out enthusiastically for opportunities in the classroom and beyond. And if they can let go, they will see the results that they want and deserve: young people, so full of intelligence, spirit, and promise, transformed into wonderful women and men.

Annotating to Stimulate Response

Now let's look at a passage from an essay by historian and novelist Wallace Stegner. In this case, a student in a history course has been assigned a collection of readings about public-land policy in the West. Students will discuss these readings before taking an essay exam testing their ability to make connections—to recognize points of agreement and disagreement—among the readings. The reader's annotations show that he is reading for more than just information:

PRACTICE READING

Some Geography, Some History

Wallace Stegner

1 How many now?

Within the six Rocky Mountain states there lived in 1960 less than seven million people. They were densest in Colorado, at 16.9 to the square mile, and thinnest in Nevada at 2.6. Surprisingly, they were more urban than rural. Over half of Colorado's people were packed into the ten counties along the eastern face of the Rockies; the rest were scattered thinly across fifty-three counties. More than two-thirds of Utah's population made a narrow dense band of settlement in the six counties at the foot of the Wasatch. The cause for this concentration is the cause that dictates so many aspects of Western life: water. As Professor Webb said, the West is an oasis civilization.

2 Fewer than 3 per sq. mi.!

3 Scarcity of H₂O means population is concentrated in few areas

Room, then—great open spaces, as advertised. In reality as in fiction, an inescapable fact about the West is that people are scarce. For comparison, the population density of the District of Columbia in 1960 was 13,000 to the square mile, that of Rhode Island 812, that of New Jersey 806, that of Massachusetts 654. By the criterion of space, California at 100 to the square mile had already in 1960 ceased to be West, if it ever was, and Washington at 42.8 was close to disqualification; but Oregon, thanks to its woods and its desert eastern half, was still part of the family at 18.4, which is less than half the density of Vermont.

The natural resources of these open spaces are such as cause heartburn among corporations and individuals who wish the West were as open as it used to be, and were not watched over by so many federal bureaus. Now that the pineries of Wisconsin and Michigan are long gone, the Northwest holds our most valuable forests. Now that the Mesabi Range approaches exhaustion, Iron County, Utah, becomes a major source of iron ore; the steel industry based upon Utah ore and limestone, and Utah, Colorado, and Wyoming coal is a first step on the road that led to Pittsburgh and Gary. It has been estimated that the Upper Colorado River basin contains a sixth of the world's known coal reserves. The oil shales of Utah and Colorado, already in experimental reduction in Parachute Canyon, lie ready for the time when petroleum reserves decline. The Rocky Mountains contain most of our gold, silver, lead, zinc, copper, molybdenum, antimony, uranium; and these, depending on the market of the moment, may produce frenzies comparable with the gold rushes of the last century. A few years ago, on a road across the Navajo Reservation near the Four Corners, I was stalled behind an oil-exploration rig that had broken an axle fording Chinle Wash after a cloudburst. Behind me, in the hour I waited, stacked up fifteen or twenty cars and parts of three other exploration outfits. And who pulled the broken-down rig out and let us go on? A truck loaded with twenty tons of uranium ore. This on a road that only a little while earlier had been no more than ruts through the washes, ducks on the ledges, and periodic wallows where stuck travelers had dug and brushed themselves out of the sand.

Enormous potentials for energy—coal, oil, oil shale, uranium, sun. But one source, water, has about exhausted its possibilities. The Rockies form the nation's divide, and on them are generated the three great western river systems, the Missouri, Columbia, and Colorado, as well as the Southwest's great river, the Rio Grande. Along these rivers and their tributaries most of the possible power, reclamation, and flood-control damsites have been developed. Additional main-stem dams are not likely to recommend themselves to any close economic analysis, no matter how dam-building bureaus promote them, and conservationist organizations in coming years can probably relax a little their vigilance to protect the scenery from the engineers.

Margin notes:

5 Calif. isn't "West"; Fla isn't "South." Sounds like one of those writers who tells you what is and isn't Southern

8 With natural resources of East and Midwest depleted, corporations eye riches of the West

10 Unusual word: Erratic business cycles cause frenzies and panics

12 Paradoxes: sparsely populated but urban, great natural wealth but no water

4 Paradox: lots of land, not much of it livable

6 Developers suffer physically from their own greed

7 Where's this?

9 Now the steel industry is declining. Does development start a chain of events culminating in poverty?

11 Precious minerals but no water

This reader's annotations are more complex and varied than those of the first reader, who was more concerned with memorizing facts and understanding concepts. This reader's marginal notes fall into several categories:

- **Summary.** Notes 3, 4, 8, and 11 differ little from the marginal annotations in the excerpt from the psychology textbook. The reader is simply trying to recast Wallace Stegner's ideas in his own language.
- **Questions.** Questions help identify the "gaps" that exist in almost any text— places that cause confusion or arouse doubts and reservations, places where a reader would like more detail or explanation. In his first marginal note, for example, the reader ponders how much the population of the Rocky Mountain states has grown in the past thirty-five years. Is Stegner's assessment, published in 1969, still valid? Does Stegner foresee shifting trends in population growth? Have natural barriers to dense settlement kept the region relatively immune to radical changes brought on by development, as Stegner seems to forecast?
- **Personal reactions.** A reader may react either to the ideas presented in a passage or to the author's manner of expressing them (tone, vocabulary, bias). Note 2 illustrates the first type of reaction, which may voice agreement, disagreement, outrage, skepticism, or various other responses. (Note 2 says little more than "Imagine that!") Reactions become more complex when a reader calls on personal experience or draws connections to facts outside the text. In note 5, for example, the reader is saying something like this:

    Isn't it striking that Stegner should say that California, the westernmost of the lower forty-eight states, isn't "really" western? It reminds me of how many people say that Florida, the southernmost state, isn't "really" southern. Stegner sounds like an old-time native talking to an audience of outsiders or newcomers who don't know from western.

This note addresses the relationship between Stegner (as "speaker") and the reader (as "listener"). More specifically, the reader consciously resists the role of passive listener, one who might not question a subjective interpretation of where the West begins and ends.

Notes 6 and 10 comment on vocabulary. Specifically, they point to Stegner's tendency to describe the greed of corporations and developers in terms of illness (*heartburn*) and mental disturbance (*frenzy*). Alongside the natural abundance of the West, attempts to exploit and plunder its wealth are portrayed as symptoms of disease. Again, an alert reader recognizes a careful writer's efforts to influence interpretation and response.

- **Extrapolations.** To *extrapolate* is to take a given set of facts or ideas and to project, predict, or speculate about other facts or ideas that are not known or not provided in the text. For instance, a business executive, examining sales figures for the previous three years, might try to extrapolate how much future sales are likely to increase or decline in the coming months. Readers extrapolate when they take a writer's ideas and extend them, expand on them, or apply them in other contexts that the writer may have overlooked, suppressed, or failed to anticipate. In note 9, for instance, the reader points out that since Stegner wrote his essay, the steel industries of Pittsburgh and Gary, Indiana, have also suffered economic decline, just as the upper Midwest had earlier.

This leads the reader to extrapolate an idea about business cycles—an idea that is not stated (and perhaps not even implied) by Stegner.

• **Inventories.** Sometimes readers detect recurring ideas, images, or patterns of language in a passage. Or, perhaps during a second reading, they recognize connections among their own annotations. For example, when the reader connects Stegner's use of the words *heartburn* and *frenzy* to describe corporate behavior, he is starting to make an inventory in his mind. Note 12 is an attempt to put another type of inventory into writing: The reader sees that Stegner describes the West through a series of contradictions or paradoxes.

Not every annotation you make when reading with a pencil will fall neatly into one of these categories. However, the important thing is to record thoughts and responses that come to mind as you experience a text. As readers become more proficient at this process, they start to engage in conversations or dialogues with the texts they read. In the process, they become more independent, relying less on rules and rigid categories of response.

EXERCISE | Annotating to Stimulate Response

Imagine that you are a student in the same history course and that you have been asked to read the following review of the book *What You See in Clear Water: Life on the Wind River Reservation,* by western writer and television producer Geoffrey O'Gara. Specifically, you are expected to draw connections between information and ideas brought forth in the passage by Stegner and those presented in the review of O'Gara's book, published more than thirty years later. Read through the review; then read it again, annotating to stimulate response. Annotate the text in a way that would help you contribute to class discussion and, perhaps, prepare you to make connections between these two readings on the same general topic.

PRACTICE READING

Not a Drop to Drink

Timothy Egan

Nearly every story about American Indians—past or present, on the reservation or off—ends the same way. We know what's going to happen because it's what always happens: the Indians lose. And nearly every story about water rights in the American West also has a predictable ending: the rich and powerful get what they want, usually aided by a huge government subsidy. So suspense is not one of the sensations a reader feels while following Geoffrey O'Gara along in his exploration of water rights and tribal intrigue in that lovely, lonely, storm-scoured rectangle in the middle of Wyoming labeled the Wind River Indian Reservation.

   Water is power in the West, something Mark Twain noticed during his initial journalistic forays to the other side of the hundredth meridian: whiskey is for drinking, he wrote from Nevada, water is for fighting over. It continues to drive everything from the pathological sprawl of Phoenix to presidential-level debates over whether some dams should give way to fish. Wyoming is unique only in that the players are largely unknown outside the Mountain Time Zone, and the stakes, while enormously consequential within the small world drained by the Wind River, are unlikely to affect anyone's subdivision in a major city.

"What You See in Clear Water" is centered around a moderate-size river that draws its sustenance from snowmelt draining from an arc of ancient stone above 13,000 feet in the center of the state. The higher reaches of the valley are full of pine, fir, elk, and deer, and the lower elevations are flatter, more like the Great Plains, but cold—marginal cropland. It is hard to imagine many people wanting to live there year-round without, say, at least a good generator and maybe satellite television. The inhabitants, in fact, largely arrived by government incentive—coercion, in the Indians' case, and an exaggerated claim of irrigation-born farm riches in that of the whites.

The Indians are an odd pairing. From one side came the Eastern Shoshone, a people who roamed all over the Great Basin chasing bison and elk. Early on, they sided with whites, even helping the Army harass other tribes. They were ordered onto the reservation with their longtime enemy, the Northern Arapaho, a tribe that traces its roots to people of the Algonquian language group. Originally, the reservation was 44 million acres, probably big enough for the two tribes to sustain themselves and get along. But it has been shrunk, by Congressional mandates and real-estate schemes masquerading as Indian policy, to some 2 million acres. The whites came in the early 1900s and are the prime beneficiaries of an irrigation system drawing off the Wind River, which has cost American taxpayers more than $70 million. In one of many ironies, O'Gara, also the author of *A Long Road Home*, notes that the initial funds to build the homesteaders' water diversion came from money supposed to go to Indians.

The book chronicles a long fight—cultural, legal, and political—in which the Indians finally win from the United States Supreme Court the right to control water within the reservation, only to have that power taken away from them by a state court ruling. In some ways, the story has parallels to the South before the Civil Rights Act of 1964, when local powers essentially ignored federal law.

O'Gara is a lyrical writer when sketching pictures of the land. He is fair and evenhanded in trying to explain a complex issue freighted with emotion. He lets his characters have their say, revealing the racism of some white ranchers, and the desperation that hangs like low fog in so many reservations. . . . In the end, the Indians are left with nothing but a certain moral high ground, and, as they say in the West, you can't eat the scenery.

Keeping a Reading Journal

There are times when writing marginal notes may not be the most effective reading strategy. Perhaps you have borrowed a book from the library or from a friend, or you may want to expand the range of your responses to a particular reading (i.e., write at greater length than you would be able to do comfortably in the margins of a book). On such occasions, a reading journal is a good way to stimulate the same type of active engagement with a text that takes place when you write marginal notes.

Consider how one reader has commented on the following passage, which opens the book *Zen and the Art of Motorcycle Maintenance*. The reader is taking a course in contemporary literature and has selected Pirsig's book from a list of nonassigned readings. Asked to compose a paper that explains and develops her interpretation of the book's narrator, she decides to use a reading journal as stimulus for reflection. First read the passage and then observe how the reader reflects on it in a reading journal:

PRACTICE READING

From Zen and the Art of Motorcycle Maintenance

Robert Pirsig

What follows is based on actual occurrences. Although much of it has been changed for rhetorical purposes, it must be regarded in its essence as fact.

I can see by my watch, without taking my hand from the left grip of the cycle, that it is eight-thirty in the morning. The wind, even at sixty miles an hour, is warm and humid. When it's this hot and muggy at eight-thirty, I'm wondering what it's going to be like in the afternoon.

In the wind are pungent odors from the marshes by the road. We are in an area of the Central Plains filled with thousands of duck-hunting sloughs, heading northwest from Minneapolis toward the Dakotas. This highway is an old concrete two-laner that hasn't had much traffic since a four-laner went in parallel to it several years ago. When we pass a marsh, the air suddenly becomes cooler. Then, when we are past, it suddenly warms up again.

I'm happy to be riding back into this country. It is a kind of nowhere, famous for nothing at all and has an appeal because of just that. Tensions disappear along old roads like this. We bump along the beat-up concrete between the cattails and stretches of meadow and then more cattails and marsh grass. Here and there is a stretch of open water, and if you look closely, you can see wild ducks at the edge of the cattails. And turtles. . . . There's a red-winged blackbird.

I whack Chris's knee and point to it.

"What!" he hollers.

"Blackbird!"

He says something I don't hear. "What?" I holler back.

He grabs the back of my helmet and hollers up, "I've seen lots of those, Dad!"

"Oh!" I holler back. Then I nod. At age eleven you don't get very impressed with red-winged blackbirds.

You have to get older for that. For me this is all mixed with memories that he doesn't have. Cold mornings long ago when the marsh grass had turned brown and cattails were waving in the northwest wind. The pungent smell then was from muck stirred up by hip boots while we were getting in position for the sun to come up and the duck season to open. Or winters when the sloughs were frozen over and dead and I could walk across the ice and snow between the dead cattails and see nothing but grey skies and dead things and cold. The blackbirds were gone then. But now in July they're back, and everything is at its alivest and every foot of these sloughs is humming and cricking and buzzing and chirping, a whole community of millions of living things living out their lives in a kind of benign continuum.

You see things vacationing on a motorcycle in a way that is completely different from any other. In a car you're always in a compartment, and because you're used to it, you don't realize that through that car window everything you see is just more TV. You're a passive observer, and it is all moving by you boringly in a frame.

On a cycle the frame is gone. You're completely in contact with it all. You're in the scene, not just watching it anymore, and the sense of presence is overwhelming. That concrete whizzing by five inches below your foot is the real thing, the same stuff you walk on; it's right there, so blurred you can't focus on it, yet you can put your foot down and touch it anytime, and the whole thing, the whole experience, is never removed from immediate consciousness.

Here are the annotations that the reader wrote in her journal:

1. Well, the title is certainly interesting, and the author's note [in italics] is amusing. Most writers probably aren't so quick to tell you that something may not be factual.

2. Funny how this starts off seeming <u>not</u> to be the sort of thing I'd choose to read: I'm not an outdoorsy person, and I've been on a motorcycle exactly once—thought I'd never walk again after thirty-four miles of it! Maybe it's guilt feelings, sitting in the car openly admitting that the scenery is OK but sort of dull after a while, something for seeing through windows. Maybe I'm not, as Pirsig suggests, old enough to appreciate it. I don't like to sweat—have a compulsion about being clean, and I'm none too secure about the idea of being inches from pavement that could skin me clean if I made one wrong move.

3. I like what he says about smelling things, though. The smell of lawns being watered, wet pavement, honeysuckle, the ocean, even rotting logs. I used to find the smell of Greyhound buses exciting—the lure of adventure. I guess the motorcycle thing is like that, though maybe both Pirsig and I have been influenced by movies. I did sort of enjoy my one and only ride on a cycle, but I've never felt safe repeating the experience.

4. The narrator seems to be hinting at something about safety and risk. He's riding with his son—surely he's no hot-dogging type; you don't risk your children that way. So the risk is something else. My boyfriend once suggested how wonderful it would be to spend the rest of your life sailing around the world. I disagreed, since I'm afraid of drowning, sharks, sunburn (too many movies again?). He added, "However long it might be." There are various kinds of risk, not all of them physical. It's sobering to think how attached I am to safety. I've certainly taken some risks in my life, though seldom physical.

5. I wonder if the narrator is talking about this a bit when he says that you become part of the scene instead of just an observer.

This response to reading lies at the opposite extreme from the notes and underlines written in the psychology textbook. It is a highly personal response, as well as a greatly elaborated one. Of course, neither extreme (nor any one approach in between) is inherently better. Partly, it is a matter of individual preference, but mostly it is a case of tailoring your approach to your purposes for reading. The student responding to the excerpt from *Zen and the Art of Motorcycle Maintenance* is deliberately trying to explore her personal response to the character and voice of the narrator. She is doing this not because she is necessarily a more intuitive or imaginative person than the first reader; rather, she is trying to meet the demands of an academic task that calls for her subjective response to a text.

The responses in this student's reading journal fall into several categories:

• **Reactions to details outside the immediate text.** In her first annotation, the reader has attended to the author's prefatory note and reflected on the title of the book. In doing so, she draws on previous reading experiences.

- **Inferences.** In her fourth annotation, the reader begins to draw conclusions about how the narrator reveals himself as a person. This type of response will prove useful later, when she develops her thoughts into a more formal piece of writing aimed at a particular audience. Notice how the free play of seemingly irrelevant ideas in previous annotations appears to have primed the pump—to have led the reader spontaneously to focus her inquiry and form inferences.

- **Speculations.** Making an inference often arouses further reflection. In her fifth annotation, the reader extends and amplifies ideas from the previous annotation.

No list of categories will exhaust the range of responses that can appear in a reading journal. Independent of rules and formulas, experienced readers have learned to be inventive and even playful in their journal entries. However, if you have not used a reading journal before, you may want to try out some of the following suggested techniques, or *prompts:*

- Select a quotation from the reading:
  —Explain it.
  —Apply it to your life.
  —Explain precisely why it is not clear.
  —Supply a concrete illustration of one of its ideas.
  —Rewrite it so it communicates more clearly.
  —Examine its unstated assumptions.
  —Examine its logic or evidence.
  —Argue with it.
  —Examine its implications and significance.
- Make a list of words you did not know and their definitions.
- Take a long or complex passage and boil it down to key points.
- Try to pin down definitions of key terms.
- Pick out several impressive sentences or images.
- Point out internal contradictions or inconsistencies.
- Study relationships among facts, opinions, generalizations, and judgments.
- Examine the treatment of opposing views. Are they ignored? tolerated? refuted? ridiculed?
- Examine the structure or organization of the text.
- Characterize the audience that the text appears to target.

A variation on the reading journal is the **double-entry notebook,** in which the reader draws a vertical line down the middle of each page and writes the usual kinds of journal responses in the left-hand column. Later, she records further reflections on those responses in the column at the opposite side of the page. Many readers find the double-entry notebook an effective way to stimulate critical analysis by opening up a conversation or dialogue with themselves as well as with the text. Here is how some of the journal responses to the passage from *Zen and the Art of Motorcycle Maintenance* might look in a double-entry notebook:

Respond in this column to the text as you read it.	Reflect later on those responses here in the right-hand column.

I like what he says about smelling things, though. The smell of lawns being watered, wet pavement, honeysuckle, the ocean, even rotting logs. I used to find the smell of Greyhound buses exciting—the lure of adventure. I guess the motorcycle thing is like that, though maybe both Pirsig and I have been influenced by movies. I did sort of enjoy my one and only ride on a cycle, but I've never felt safe repeating the experience.

The "nature" thing is really a diversion. Not sure why, but I don't think he's going to be raving on about nature.

The narrator seems to be hinting at something about safety and risk. He's riding with his son—surely he's no hot-dogging type; you don't risk your children that way. So the risk is something else. My boyfriend once suggested how wonderful it would be to spend the rest of your life sailing around the world. I disagreed, since I'm afraid of drowning, sharks, sunburn (too many movies again?). He added, "However long it might be." There are various kinds of risk, not just physical. It's sobering to think how attached I am to safety. I've certainly taken some risks in my life, though seldom physical.

When he talks about being part of the scene, I also think of the idea that what's worth doing is worth doing well. The catch is, of course, that we can excuse any failure by saying, well, it wasn't worth doing.

I wonder if the narrator is talking about this a bit when he says that you become part of the scene instead of just an observer.

People say that all the time—"it's stupid"—just because it turned out bad. There are a lot of people just going through the motions because they decide too quickly that the results won't be worth real involvement; so the bad outcome is predetermined.

In her double-entry notebook, this reader has managed to sustain a dialogue between Pirsig's text and the personal associations that it arouses in her mind. Notice, for example, how the first annotation in the right-hand column carries the reader from the purely personal reflection found in its corresponding entry in the left-hand column back to an observation about Pirsig's text. The two following pairs of entries, on the other hand, move in the opposite direction.

Successful college students learn to adjust their reading processes to address various purposes. The different strategies presented in this chapter—annotating and underlining to recall specific facts and details, annotating to stimulate response, and keeping a reading journal—can help you regulate your reading processes, making them serve the needs at hand.

▉ READING SELECTIONS

The following two articles appeared in the "Education Life" supplement to the *New York Times*. The author, Glenn C. Altschuler, is Dean of the School of Continuing Education and Summer Sessions and professor of American studies at Cornell University.

Learning How to Learn

GLENN C. ALTSCHULER

1   As they begin their first year of college, many students do not know how to study—in no small part because they have not been challenged in secondary school, where their transcripts are embellished by grade-point inflation.

2   A nationwide survey by the University of California at Los Angeles of over 364,000 students in 1999 found that only 31.5% reported spending six or more hours a week studying or doing homework in their last year of high school. That was down from 43.7% in 1987, when the question was first asked. And 40.2% said they studied fewer than three hours a week, while 17.1% owned up to studying less than one hour a week.

3   No surprise then that so many college freshmen who insist they know all the material wonder why their first battery of exams do not go so well. No surprise either that offering courses that teach "learning strategies" has become a cottage industry. (Professionals think the term "study skills" too narrow, and they have banished the stigmatizing word "remedial" from the lexicon of higher education.)

4   For the bookish, *How to Study in College*, by Walter Pauk, the standard text in the field, is available in its seventh edition, at more than four hundred pages. For those inclined to the Internet, hundreds of institutions have established Web sites with mcnuggets of advice on how to study and to advertise the services of learning strategies centers. The University of St. Thomas, in St. Paul, Minn., for example, insists that successful students commit daily MURDER (Mood, Understand, Recall, Digest, Expand, Review).

5   Over 1.6 million students are enrolled in learning strategies courses in two- and four-year colleges and universities, according to the National Association for Developmental Education; an additional 900,000 take advantage of tutoring and supplemental instruction, individually or in groups.

At the Learning Resource Centers at the New Brunswick, Newark, and Camden, **6** N.J., campuses of Rutgers, about 13,000 students in 34,000 visits a year are supported in a variety of settings. They include workshops with descriptions like "Cramming for exams—and the consequences—in the social sciences" and "Identifying and understanding one's individual learning style for success in ecology courses."

Nonetheless, it is not easy to get the students who most need assistance to use the **7** resources available to them. Doing so, suggests Janet Snoyer, a learning-strategies specialist at Cornell University, means "breaking down the relentless high-school mindset that 'help' is designed for laggards and ill-equipped minds." Professionals know that although they will require those with manifestly inadequate preparation to see them and will exhort all first-year students to come in early in the semester, many students will not make an appointment until they receive a disappointing grade, and others not even then.

Sometimes, a lack of motivation, procrastination, and difficulty managing time **8** on the part of students are symptoms of emotional or personal distress. For such students, Ms. Snoyer says, "Study skills tips barely reach the tip of the iceberg," and a referral to peer counseling or psychological services is appropriate.

But for many students learning how to learn is the iceberg. Fortunately, it can be **9** chipped away at, or even melted. Professionals begin by getting students to acknowledge that being an undergraduate is a full-time job, requiring forty hours every week including attendance in class and course-related work. Accounting for how they have spent every hour for a week or two (including snoozing and schmoozing) helps students assess their ability to set priorities, manage time and, if necessary, to create a new schedule and monitor their adherence to it.

When they hit the books, students should also consider where, how long, and **10** with whom they will study. Will proximity to a telephone, television, refrigerator, friend, or potential date lead into temptation? Can extended exposure to an isolated library carrel cause narcolepsy?

A Cornell student, Paul Kangas, discovered that trying to study "while lying in **11** bed was a good antidote for insomnia but not the best way to memorize a list of German vocabulary words." But no matter how conducive to studying their accommodations may be, few undergraduates work more effectively at night than during the day.

And even fewer can concentrate for more than ninety minutes without a break. **12** That is why, as Michael Chen, an instructor in the Center for Learning and Teaching at Cornell, puts it, "Time between classes is prime time, not face time."

In his book, Mr. Pauk advises undergraduates to carry pocket work so that they **13** can read an article or memorize vocabulary for Spanish class while waiting at the doctor's office or the airport. Even if this approach seems a bit compulsive, a specific goal—one chapter, three problem sets—and a reward when it is reached, makes study less daunting. That reward, whether it is a coffee break or an update on the Jets game, works only if it lasts no more than half an hour.

Although students often spend their study time alone, study in groups can be ex- **14** tremely helpful. Carolyn Janiak, a Cornell student, said she found that she always learned more when working with others because discussions "force me to focus on the bigger picture and argument." As she clarified her opinions, she said, she was able to memorize details as well.

Group sessions work best if each student has already reviewed (and if necessary **15** memorized) all the material required for an assignment or exam; parceling out the work for vicarious learning is risky. Leslie Schettino, who teaches learning strategies courses in New York State at Tompkins Cortland Community College and Ithaca College, asks members of study groups to compare lecture notes, read problems aloud, pretend they are tutors in, say, the math lab and end a meeting only when everyone understands the most important concepts. Often students discover that the best way to master material is to be forced to explain it to someone else.

16   But groups are not for everyone. Andrew Janis of Cornell tries to study when his roommate is out because "complaints about organic chemistry distract me." He plays "quiet jazz" or turns his radio to "an AM station that is all fuzz." As he examines notes, handouts and review sheets, he uses an online encyclopedia to help with dates and other pertinent information.

17   Effective note-taking is essential. It takes time for students, who are used to high-school teachers who signal them with the phrase, "Now this is really important," to recognize the "architecture" of a lecture—the introduction and summary, inflection, emphasis and pause, the use of *therefore,* the digression—and to figure out what is worth taking down. Successful students read over their notes nightly, identifying the theme and two or three crucial points. If anything is not clear, they ask the instructor for clarification as soon as possible. To review notes for the first time the night before an exam is to court disaster.

18   Notes on a text should be taken on a separate sheet of paper or a computer. Students might begin by skimming to identify the "geography" of the book—its subheadings, graphs, maps, and tables, and its main lines of argument. I advise students to throw out their highlighters: those who use them are passive learners who do little more than paint their books yellow. Students who summarize a chapter in their own words, in a few paragraphs, tend to understand the material better and remember it longer. Questions might be recorded in the margin of the book, to be raised in discussions or in office hours.

19   Learning how to learn is not easy. It requires will and discipline, what the nineteenth-century English biologist Thomas Henry Huxley called "the ability to make yourself do the thing you have to do, when it ought to be done, whether you like it or not."

20   But just about everyone can do it. And the rewards—emotional, intellectual, and financial—reach well beyond a grade in a college course.

Adapting to College Life in an Era of Heightened Stress

GLENN C. ALTSCHULER

1   The first week of her freshman year at Cornell University, Kate Wilkinson of Plymouth, Mass., made a big mistake. She agreed to play Trivial Pursuit with several other students in her dormitory. Kate was embarrassed that she did not know what element was converted to plutonium in the first nuclear reactor, what one-time Yugoslav republic is shaped like a boomerang, or even the longest American war. Far worse, everyone else did (or seemed to).

2   Kate called her mother and, between sobs, gave voice to her fear that she was not smart enough to succeed at the university.

3   While some first-year students experience little or no anxiety, most freshmen have a stress story like Kate's, be it academic or personal—about family or financial responsibilities, inadequate high-school preparation, or pressure to do well in today's increasingly competitive environment.

4   In a 1999 survey of 683 colleges and universities conducted in the first days of school by the University of California at Los Angeles, 30.2% of freshmen acknowledged that they frequently felt overwhelmed, almost double the rate in 1985.

The number of appointments at Cornell's counseling and psychological services   5
has risen by 29% in the last four years. More than 40% of first-year students at Johns
Hopkins University visit its counseling center.

According to Dr. Samuel Parrish, medical director of the Student Health and Well-   6
ness Center at Johns Hopkins, better record keeping, greater awareness of on-campus
services, and additional staff and office hours account for some of the increase. And,
he said, now "there is no stigma in asking for help."

Mental health professionals say that young adults today appear to be under much   7
more stress than past generations were. Many of them have fewer "stabilizing forces in
their lives," said Dr. David Fassler, chair of the American Psychiatric Association's
Council on Children, Adolescents, and Their Families and author of *Help Me, I'm Sad*.

"Many live far away from their extended family, or they've moved a lot of times,   8
so they're less connected to their neighborhoods," he said.

At the extreme end of the continuum, more students may be arriving on campus   9
with diagnosed psychological problems. After documenting a rising incidence of depression among students, Harvard University issued a report last year recommending,
among other steps, that more psychologists be hired, that residence assistants and tutors receive instruction on mental problems and that two rooms be set aside in every
living unit for students experiencing emotional crises.

While academic pressure may not cause mental illness, it can act as a trigger.   10
"Some kids have a genetic predisposition for depression and are more likely than others to get depressed," said Dr. Fassler, ticking off the warning signs—"sadness, decreased energy and appetite, loss of interest in usual activities, decreased interest in
sex, any thoughts of suicide."

The vast majority of students, of course, are not clinically depressed but are expe-   11
riencing the self-doubt and anxiety typically associated with the critical transition
from high school and home to college, and will adjust. Ms. Wilkinson, for example,
has made that transition and is now doing well.

In an attempt to minimize the trauma of freshman year, most colleges and   12
universities supply peer counselors, residence hall advisers, faculty advisers, an academic advising center, a mental health clinic, and suicide-prevention services. At Cornell, students can call the Empathy, Assistance, and Referral Service (EARS); at the
State University of New York at Albany, the Middle Earth Peer Assistance Program
sponsors a telephone line, a campus radio talk show, a weekly advice column, and
peer theater performances about student problems.

Even the traditional organized activities of freshman year—ice cream socials,   13
wilderness-reflection weekends, wrestling parties in kiddie swimming pools filled with
yogurt—have therapeutic undercurrents to help students let off steam and face the
seemingly monumental task ahead.

Noting that students who accept stress as normal and even beneficial tend to re-   14
spond more creatively to its demands, therapists, counselors, and faculty members offer a variety of advice for coping with the freshman year.

In *Beating the College Blues*, Paul A. Grayson and Philip Meilman advise students   15
who are frequently irritable, anxious, or angry or who have difficulty sleeping to try
relaxation techniques: warm baths; slow, deep breathing; meditation; guitar playing; a
long walk.

Dr. Grayson and Dr. Meilman, who direct counseling services at New York Univer-   16
sity and Cornell, also recommend making an inventory of commitments (say, a five-
course load, twenty-hour-a-week job, crew team practice at 6:00 a.m., a steady girlfriend) and personal habits (procrastinating or partying too much?) as well as

impressions of college life. That exercise helps students determine whether to drop a course or change study habits. A reality check by peers and parents can also identify flawed thinking ("I'm the only person here who has not chosen a major").

17   Students tend to waste time between classes, then try to read and to write papers at night, when they are tired and are tempted to socialize. It is better to complete three to four hours of course-related work, six days a week, before dinner.

18   Students who get eight hours of sleep, get up early, and study during the day, starting with the first week of classes, do not have to scramble as the assignments pile up. (This schedule has another advantage: the first person up in the morning gets immediate access to the bathroom and a hot shower.)

19   Freshmen should get to know at least one adult on campus fairly well, starting with a faculty adviser. Alas, many students stand at the adviser's door with a hand on the knob, seeking a signature and speedy get-away, afraid to interrupt a Nobel Prize-winning experiment.

20   More often than not, those who plant themselves in a chair ready to discuss their backgrounds, their academic and professional aspirations, and uncertainties and their personal interests will get a warm response. Students who take the initiative to meet with advisers and visit professors' offices—not only after doing poorly on an exam but also to discuss a required text or ask how a professor became interested in a subject—learn that many teach better in private than in a large lecture hall. And the college, whatever its size, begins to seem far less impersonal.

21   In the midst of the forced social interaction that characterizes college life, it takes time and many false starts to make a real friend. Roommates do not have to be best friends, but they can be a freshman's first friend. Eating dinner with a roommate, even if she is only "just OK," and meeting others in the dormitory and in class will help students get through those sometimes lonely first weeks.

22   Participating in an extracurricular activity during the first semester provides contact with students who share interests. With their regular practice schedules, the marching band or rugby team may inspire discipline and efficiency.

23   Noting that Henry David Thoreau went to the woods because he wanted to live deliberately, Professor Allan Emery, who teaches English at Bowling Green State University in Bowling Green, Ohio, reminds his freshmen students to pause at least once a day to examine their lives.

24   Too often, as students drive through day after busy day, waiting to vegetate, lubricate, or unleash a primal scream on the weekend, college resembles anything but Walden Pond.

25   "Seize opportunities to reflect on life—your life and the lives of others," Professor Emery suggests, "and you will be far less likely to lose your equilibrium."

26   "That's what those well-stocked libraries, tree-lined avenues, and peaceful quadrangles are for."

Freewriting

Write for ten to fifteen minutes about your thoughts as you read Altschuler's articles. What do you learn from them? Which parts confirm personal experiences and observations? Are there parts that don't? Do your experiences or observations contradict any points made by the author or the experts he quotes? Can you think of other ways to develop study skills or to manage stress that Altschuler might have added to either article? Would you have approached the first weeks of college differently if you had read one or both of these articles?

Group Work

As freewrites are read aloud by each group member in turn, jot down notes whenever you hear ideas you wish to comment on or question. Discuss what you have written, taking note of similarities and differences in your responses. (For example, do you respond similarly to the assertion that entering college students usually don't spend enough time studying?) Do group members find the survival strategies discussed in these articles realistic and helpful?

Review Questions

1. How does Altschuler account for the poor academic performance of many first-year students whose academic records indicate that they are well prepared for college?

2. Why do so few students take advantage of the help offered through courses and workshops that teach study skills?

3. What factors contribute to the increasing stress that college students feel?

Discussion Questions

1. Each of these articles ends with a philosophical quotation. What do you suppose Altschuler is trying to accomplish through this technique? That is, how do you think he is trying to influence readers? Does he succeed? Are the quotations well chosen?

2. Do you see any evidence that high schools are attempting to better prepare their graduates for college life? What factors may impede their ability to do so?

3. Altschuler does not attempt to correlate size, location, or type of institution (e.g., liberal arts college, technical institute, two-year community college, research university) with the challenges that face first-year students or with the availability of services that help them meet those challenges. Is this a serious oversight? Try to speculate on what he might have found had he pursued this line of inquiry.

Writing

1. Examine your college catalog, Web site, and any brochures or other sources of information distributed among entering students or readily available to them. Take note of every type of service or facility designed to address the issues of adjustment discussed in Altschuler's articles. Write a report that assesses the adequacy of the support system at your school and how it

compares with those that Altschuler refers to. You may wish to conclude with recommended changes or additions.

2. In paragraph 4 of "Learning How to Learn," Altschuler asserts that "hundreds of institutions have established Web sites with mcnuggets of advice on how to study and advertise the services of learning strategies centers." Try to locate a dozen or so of such Web sites and report what you find. Specifically, you might list frequently offered advice, unusual or innovative suggestions, and strategies most and least conducive to your individual learning style.

WRITE, READ, and RESEARCH the NET

1. *Write:* Suppose you have been asked to speak to graduating seniors at your former high school. Use one of the prewriting strategies detailed on pages 19–24 to generate ideas about what you might say.

2. *Read:* Review the two following Web sites:
   http://www.washington.edu/doit/Brochures/Academics/survival.html
   http://www.clemson.edu/collegeskills/

3. *Research:* Using the Internet, find Web sites from various colleges and universities that list and describe survival skills for entering students. Draft a report that reviews and evaluates several of these Web sites.

ADDITIONAL READINGS

The following readings explore topics introduced previously in this chapter. Roland Merullo examines the needs and frustrations of college students whose cultural backgrounds and personal histories differ significantly from those of classmates whose families are college-educated. In "Class Struggle," Ron Suskind profiles one such student, Cedric Jennings, whose ambitions and strong academic record took him from an inner-city high school to a summer program at MIT. The final selections consider parent-child relationships from two very different perspectives. Roger H. Martin, president of Randolph-Macon College, relates his anxieties over his daughter's first weeks away from home. Finally, Jeffrey Zaslow writes about a controversial proposal to invite parents to visit their adult children's workplaces.

The Challenge of First-Generation College Students

ROLAND MERULLO

1   A friend of mine, a dean of long standing at a prestigious Midwestern university, talks to me sometimes about her most interesting or most troubled students. She is careful to protect their anonymity, changing names and details—as I will do here—but the force of these stories is preserved. After listening to them, I am reminded again of both

the psychological resilience and fragility of young adults: their apparent maturity, on the one hand, and, on the other, the fact that people in their late teens and early to mid twenties are still assembling a grown-up persona, still solidifying the belief system by which they will live, still struggling to find the place that feels like home.

Of all the stories that my friend, whom I will call Catherine, has told me, the one   2
that touched me most deeply concerned a young man from just north of the United States-Mexico border. His parents were of Mexican and Indian ancestry and had immigrated to the United States before he was born. Both of them lacked advanced English skills and worked at menial jobs. They had not graduated from high school; no one in their families and no one in either their Mexican or American neighborhoods had ever attended college. Not long after settling in the United States, they gave birth to a son—Miguel, I will call him—who showed a spark of brilliance from the time he could speak, and who excelled in school from his first day.

Not surprisingly, by the time he reached his last years of high school, Miguel was   3
interested in several top-rank colleges, and they were interested in him. He chose the one where my friend Catherine works, arriving there on a cool September day with thousands of other excited first-year students, all of them going about the same rounds: locating dormitory buildings, buying textbooks, taking their places in classrooms.

But Miguel's excitement had a shadow over it. No one he had ever been close to   4
had lived in a college dormitory room, paid for textbooks, been left on his own with a schedule of classes and a campus map, been thrown together so intimately with thousands of strangers.

He made friends quickly, as many freshmen do, but none of those friends came   5
from a world quite like his. In many ways, purely by virtue of his age and intellectual interests, he had much in common with them. But there were other, subtler ways in which he felt completely alone in his new environment, a smart refugee washed up on the shore of a luxurious island. Short and stocky, with a protuberant Mayan brow and dark skin, he did not look like any of his classmates. Their ironic humor and casual references to travel and inherited wealth, their taste in food, the upper-middle-class values by which they'd been raised, their choice of words, their speech patterns, and posture—Miguel had some acquaintance with those things, naturally. It wasn't, after all, as if he'd been brought up on Mars. And yet there was a way in which the behavior of his new acquaintances seemed alien, and gave rise, within him, to a painful friction.

He did not understand that friction clearly, and did not have words—in either of   6
his languages—to describe it. Not until he failed his first course and was sent to see my friend did his real feelings peek out from beneath the shadows.

Catherine met with Miguel several times during his second term. Without prob-   7
ing, without pretending to be a therapist or a friend, she tried to help him clear away the internal obstacles that kept him from performing in his classes the way both of them knew he could. But by then he had begun to soothe his discomfort with alcohol and drugs. Soon he fell in love, desperately, and the affair drew him farther away from his scholastic responsibilities. His talks with Catherine became islands of clarity in what was now a blurred and perilous seascape, and he sailed from one meeting to the next through winds and currents she could only imagine. Despite her generous efforts, and the intervention of school counselors, Miguel failed four courses in his second term and went back home towing his enormous potential behind him, like a smashed-up new boat.

The reason that Miguel's story struck me so profoundly was that it is a more   8
extreme version of my own. I grew up in a working-class, mostly Italian-American neighborhood near Boston, on a street where some of the forty-eight adults had not finished high school and only one had been to college. That lone graduate was my

mother, and even she had gone to school for something practical—physical therapy—rather than any kind of purely intellectual broadening. We weren't as poor as Miguel, nor as isolated, and not as likely to be the victims of racial or ethnic prejudice, but in 1969, when I left home for Phillips Exeter Academy as a junior in high school, I believe that I experienced some of what he must have felt during his year at college, and something like what thousands of American students experience every fall.

9   On the surface, like Miguel, I fit in well enough. I played sports, made friends, suffered no obvious psychological trauma (unlike him, I managed to pass my courses). But, despite high scores on the entrance exams and a history of A's in junior high and two years at a Catholic high school, I didn't do well for the first three terms at Exeter. The material wasn't beyond me; the teachers weren't inattentive. But the part of me that might have focused on my studies was focused instead on something invisible to me, and mysterious: in some buried psychological workshop, I was trying to find a way to weld two very different worlds.

10   In the Exeter world, there were no crucifixes or pictures of saints on the walls; the food was bland and unappetizing; the adults seemed almost comically reserved and proper compared with my aunts and uncles at home; my friends knew how to play bridge, how to order in expensive restaurants; some of them had been raised by nannies and had lived abroad, or at least gone with their families on exotic European vacations. My nextdoor neighbor in the dormitory used the word *guinea* once, in my presence, a fighting word back home; and, in front of the common-room television on a winter afternoon, some classmates—innocently, perhaps—chanted "Beat the wop!" when Emile Griffith fought the middleweight Italian champion Nino Benvenuti. (When Benvenuti knocked out Griffith in the later rounds, I found myself on top of a common-room table, dancing and gloating.) There were plates of brie in faculty apartments—I had never tasted it—and copies of the *New Yorker*, a magazine I'd never seen in my parents' or relatives' houses. The cartoons were puzzling to me, and the advertisements carried a whiff of snobbery that I took as a personal affront. As a scholarship boy, I was required to wait on faculty tables at dinner one out of every three terms, a practice that has since been discontinued at that school.

11   It would be inaccurate to give the impression that I went through my years at Exeter embittered and alone. I did not. Almost all of my memories of that place, and, later, of Boston University and Brown University, are happy ones. It would also be false to claim that class and cultural dislocation are the only, or even the primary, reasons that bright students fail to work to their potential. Indeed, at Exeter, some of the most troubled students I knew came from wealthy clans that had been sending sons to the school since before the Civil War. Those students arrived on campus with a heavy weight of expectation in their luggage, too, but it was a different kind, a different challenge. When Catherine tells me stories about students pressured by their ambitious, upper-middle-class families or students who suffer from poor health, depression, indolence, addiction, or some general post-adolescent confusion, I feel a certain basic human empathy for them, but none of the twist in my chest that Miguel's story elicited.

12   In the United States over the past thirty years, colleges have come to a better understanding both of the delicacy of young-adult psychology and of the unique predicament faced by first-generation students. Most institutions have begun to work harder to help people like Miguel make the adjustment to campus life. In the course of writing this article, I talked with administrators at a number of places, ranging from Smith College—small, private, single-sex—to the University of Texas at Austin. Both of those colleges, like so many others, offer carefully thought-out orientations designed to help students like Miguel, to soften the discordance between the ghetto, barrio, or hollow and the neatly tended lawns and careful speech patterns of academe.

Smith has a month-long program in July for those entering freshmen it calls "ed-   **13**
ucationally disadvantaged." It pays their travel and other expenses and, in September,
allows them to take a lighter course load for a term and assigns them a faculty adviser
who got to know them in the July program.

The University of Texas at Austin has programs for transfers, first-generation col-   **14**
lege students, and others who face unusual transitions. At Austin, about 30% of these
students are Hispanic, 30% African-American, 30% from poor white families, and 10%
from Asian or "other" backgrounds. There and elsewhere, what they have in common
is an extra weight in their backpacks, a burden composed of cultural dislocation (in
some cases, just the act of leaving their families at a young age to pursue an education
is culturally inappropriate); economic hardship (many of them, even those with full
scholarships, feel obliged to work while in college, in order to contribute to the family
income); and the inability to look to their relatives for guidance about campus life.

But even now there are institutions that have no such programs, or that offer only   **15**
special orientations aimed exclusively at minority students. And even the colleges
that go to extra lengths to identify and rescue their troubled freshmen still see people
like Miguel, students with tremendous potential who seem bent on self-destruction.

As someone who comes from a sort of demilitarized zone between the poorest of   **16**
the poor and the most comfortable of the rich, between street fights and Sophocles, I
believe that I have a clear view of part of that self-destructive picture—the part that
has to do with the psychological obstacles raised by movement between cultures and
between economic classes. Miguel's story says a great deal to me, not only about him,
or Hispanic Americans, or college life, but about the hidden damage caused by the inequities in American society. Hearing about Miguel, I thought immediately of the
kinds of interior trauma experienced by someone like O. J. Simpson—raised in the
projects, living in Beverly Hills. And the late comedian Freddie Prinze—who grew up
in a part of Manhattan that he called "a slum with trees," became a millionaire, and
then, at the height of his success, committed suicide. And Frank Sinatra, another millionaire product of a poor upbringing, rubbing shoulders with presidents one day and
punching reporters the next. I thought of Dorothy Allison, Maya Angelou, and Claude
Brown, who struggled to heal the wounds in themselves and bridge the gap between
American worlds with language, with art.

The number of poor, and poorly prepared, students who succeed in college and   **17**
beyond undercuts the simplistic notion that economic or educational disadvantage is
an excuse for failure, violent behavior, or indulgence in drugs. For every Miguel, there
are thousands of first-generation college students who take to their studies like salmon
to the open sea. For every O. J. Simpson, there are hundreds of kids who grow up in
housing projects, make a success of themselves in the wealthier world, and subdue
whatever demons that radical transition may have spawned.

But I am fascinated by the ones who fail, and by the reasons for their failure, and by   **18**
the ways we might move beyond knee-jerk conservative and liberal theorizing and probe
more deeply into how external success resonates, internally, for the children of the poor.

I believe it is almost impossible for those well-off educators and administrators   **19**
who are themselves products of educated parents to imagine what someone like
Miguel actually feels when he walks across their campus; what chord is struck in him
when his fellow students casually—almost innocently—make jokes, say, about the
people serving and cleaning up in the cafeteria line ("wombats," we used to call them
at Exeter). I believe it is difficult for those educators to comprehend, on something
other than an intellectual level, that the child of the ghetto, the barrio, or the white
working-class neighborhood was raised to believe that there is an oppressor just on
the other side of some invisible border.

20   In my case, it was "the high mucky-mucks" my father worked with in his state job and the people in the wealthier suburbs west of Boston. Hundreds of times in my childhood I heard comments about these faceless snobs, people who believed they were superior to us, who had things we would never have—stock portfolios, summer homes, new cars, skiing vacations, servants, the *New Yorker* on the coffee table; who were determined to keep us in the neat cage of our semi-success even as they mouthed the platitudes of American opportunity. Our litany of complaint came out of a confusion of wounded pride and frustrated ambition, but there was never any question about the existence of an enemy out there, people who were not like us and did not wish us well. How much more pervasive and powerful that litany must be for poor black, Hispanic, or American Indian boys and girls, for the daughters of white coal miners in Appalachia or the sons of Kmart clerks in western Kansas—eighteen-year-olds dropped into college life from what must sometimes seem like another universe.

21   And how terrible it must be when these young adults (and sometimes they are not so young, having returned to school after years in the working world) suddenly find themselves on the other side of that invisible border, consorting with the enemy. Have they not become the very people their parents and peers despised? Or at least become friends with them, sharing their jokes and tastes? In the film *Good Will Hunting*, when the character played by Matt Damon leaves behind his lower-middle-class South Boston roots and ventures into the wider world—drawn by a Harvard girlfriend and propelled by his own brilliance—his friends cheer him on. The film ends, predictably, on an upbeat note. But, watching the last scenes through a surprising spurt of tears, I wondered what demons Will Hunting was carrying with him into that world. What bitter internal conflicts would he face in his twenties and thirties and middle age? What kinds of guilt, doubt, and anger? And I wonder now if any college administrator has yet devised an orientation program that will come close to healing someone like him, at that deep level.

22   In my own teaching life, I have encountered dozens, perhaps hundreds, of students from uneducated families, three of whom stand out in memory. The first, a young man, was raised in the poorest section of northern Vermont; the second, a young woman, in a series of factory towns from central Massachusetts to western Pennsylvania; the third, an older student, had been abandoned at birth and raised by uneducated parents, among undereducated friends, in eastern New Hampshire. I spent a good deal of time with all three of them, working, as my friend Catherine did with Miguel, to clear up their confusion and redirect their energies. I listened and talked to them for hours on end, shared a few of my own experiences, helped them with papers and applications, wrote recommendations for jobs and grants, read their novels-in-progress. They responded variously, the first clinging to his bitterness, drinking, criticizing everything he saw, very nearly failing to graduate. The second set her past difficulties aside (like the ornaments on an elaborate Tibetan deity, which are said to be its lusts and angers, hammered, thanks to a lifetime of meditation and good works, into mere decoration) and created, in herself and in her writing, a beautiful blend of the toughness of her upbringing and the refinement of the learned world. The third earned his degree not long before his first grandchild was born and then set about building a successful career as a teacher.

23   In the end, as it was with those students, success or failure is mostly an individual matter, a mysterious blend of fate and will. As Dostoyevsky argued in his novels, people from all walks of life fail and succeed, act well and act badly, for reasons that no amount of scientific study can ever fully comprehend. But, for those of us, teachers and administrators, who deal with first-generation college students, perhaps it is useful simply to try to imagine the complexity of their predicament, the uniqueness of it.

Perhaps it might be helpful to think about another friend of mine, someone who grew up in a large, lower-middle-class, Irish-American family and was the only one of seven children to go to college. Recently she told me that her older brothers and sisters not only had failed to read to her as a child, but had pointedly chosen not to read to her, urging her, instead, in the direction of television and toys. The clear message was that reading would bring her nothing but trouble, would link her to the oppressor in a way that the rest of the family found distasteful.

To those of us who value education and the richness it has brought to our lives, an attitude like that seems counterintuitive, even absurd. But for thousands of students it is part and parcel of what they carry to campus on that thrilling first day. We can counsel them, support them, talk with them without condescension or syrupy, self-conscious "generosity"; we can try to design programs that help them fulfill their potential, personally and intellectually. Many of them will make good use of our kindness and vault into the high scaffolding of the educated classes. But some—too many—will fall back into the shadows of a free and democratic society that, more and more with each passing year, builds stone walls between the well-off and the poor, decorates them with ivy, and tacks up a sign: Please Apply. **24**

Class Struggle

RON SUSKIND

In a dormitory lobby, under harsh fluorescent lights, there is a glimpse of the future: a throng of promising minority high schoolers, chatting and laughing, happy and confident. **1**

It is a late June day, and the fifty-one teenagers have just converged here at Massachusetts Institute of Technology for its prestigious minority summer program—a program that bootstraps most of its participants into MIT's freshman class. Already, an easy familiarity prevails. A doctor's son from Puerto Rico invites a chemical engineer's son from south Texas to explore nearby Harvard Square. Over near the soda machines, the Hispanic son of two schoolteachers meets a black girl who has the same T-shirt, from an annual minority-leadership convention. **2**

"This is great," he says. "Kind of like we're all on our way up, together." **3**

Maybe. Off to one side, a gangly boy is singing a rap song, mostly to himself. His expression is one of pure joy. Cedric Jennings, the son of a drug dealer and the product of one of Washington's most treacherous neighborhoods, has worked toward this moment for his entire life. **4**

Cedric, whose struggle to excel was chronicled in a May 26 page-one article in [the *Wall Street Journal*], hails from a square mile of chaos. His apartment building is surrounded by crack dealers, and his high school, Frank W. Ballou Senior High, is at the heart of the highest-crime area in the city. Already this year, four teenagers from his district—teens who should have been his schoolmates—were charged in homicides. Another six are dead, murder victims themselves. **5**

For Cedric, MIT has taken on almost mythic proportions. It represents the culmination of everything he has worked for, his ticket to escape poverty. He has staked everything on getting accepted to college here, and at the summer program's end he will find out whether he stands a chance. He doesn't dare think about what will happen if the answer is no. **6**

7   "This will be the first steps of my path out, out of here, to a whole other world," he had said not long before leaving Washington for the summer program. "I'll be going so far from here, there'll be no looking back."

8   As Cedric looks around the bustling dormitory lobby on that first day, he finally feels at home, like he belongs. "They arrive here and say, 'Wow, I didn't know there were so many like me,'" says William Ramsey, administrative director of MIT's program. "It gives them a sense . . . that being a smart minority kid is the most normal thing to be."

9   But they aren't all alike, really, a lesson Cedric is learning all too fast. He is one of only a tiny handful of students from poor backgrounds; most of the rest range from lower-middle-class to affluent. As he settles into chemistry class on the first day, a row of girls, all savvy and composed, amuse themselves by poking fun at "my Washington street-slang," as Cedric tells it later. "You know, the way I talk, slur my words and whatever."

10   Cedric is often taunted at his nearly all-black high school for "talking white." But now, he is hearing the flawless diction of a different world, of black students from suburbs with neat lawns and high schools that send most graduates off to college.

11   Other differences soon set him apart. One afternoon, as students talk about missing their families, it becomes clear that almost everyone else has a father at home. Cedric's own father denied paternity for years and has been in jail for almost a decade. And while many of the students have been teased back home for being brainy, Cedric's studiousness has earned him threats from gang members with guns.

12   Most worrisome, though, is that despite years of asking for extra work after school—of creating his own independent-study course just to get the basic education that students elsewhere take for granted—he is woefully far behind. He is overwhelmed by the blistering workload: six hours each day of intensive classes, study sessions with tutors each night, endless hours more of homework.

13   Only in calculus, his favorite subject, does he feel sure of himself. He is slipping steadily behind in physics, chemistry, robotics, and English.

14   In the second week of the program, Cedric asks one of the smartest students, who hails from a top-notch public school, for help on some homework. "He said it was 'beneath him,'" Cedric murmurs later, barely able to utter the words. "Like, he's so much better than me. Like I'm some kind of inferior human being."

15   A crowd of students jostles into a dormitory lounge a few evenings later for Chinese food, soda, and a rare moment of release from studying. Cliques already have formed. There are whispers of romances, and lunch groups have crystallized, almost always along black or Hispanic lines. But as egg rolls disappear, divides are crossed.

16   A Hispanic teenager from a middle-class New Mexico neighborhood tries to teach the opening bars of Beethoven's *Moonlight Sonata* to a black youngster, a toll taker's son from Miami. An impeccably-clad black girl from an affluent neighborhood teaches some dance steps to a less privileged one.

17   Tutors, mostly minority undergraduates at MIT who once went through this program, look on with tight smiles, always watchful. The academic pressure, they know, is rising fast. Midterm exams start this week—along with all-nighters and panic. Some students will grow depressed; others will get sick from exhaustion. The tutors count heads, to see if anyone looks glum, confused, or strays from the group.

18   "They're going through so much, that a day here is like a week, so we can't let them be down in the dumps for very long," says Valencia Thomas, a graduate of this program and now a twenty-year-old sophomore at nearby Harvard University. "Their identities are being challenged, broken up, and reformed. Being a minority and a high achiever means you have to carry extra baggage about who you are, and where you belong. That puts them at risk."

Tonight, all the students seem to be happy and accounted for. Almost.   **19**

Upstairs, Cedric is lying on his bed with the door closed and lights off, waiting for   **20**
a miracle, that somehow, he will "be able to keep up with the others."

It is slow in coming.   **21**

"It's all about proving yourself, really," he says quietly, sitting up. "I'm trying, you   **22**
know. It's all I can do is try. But where I start from is so far behind where some other
kids are, I have to run twice the distance to catch up."

He is cutting back on calls to his mother, not wanting to tell her that things aren't   **23**
going so well. Barbara Jennings has raised her boy to believe that he can succeed, that
he must. When Cedric was a toddler, she quit her clerical job temporarily and went on
welfare so that she could take him to museums, read him books, instill in him the importance of getting an education—and getting out.

"I know what she'll say: 'Don't get down; you can do anything you set your mind   **24**
to,'" Cedric says. "I'm finding out it's not that simple."

Cedric isn't the only student who is falling behind. Moments later, Neda   **25**
Ramirez's staccato voice echoes across the dormitory courtyard.

"I am so angry," says the Mexican-American teen, who goes to a rough, mostly   **26**
Hispanic high school in the Texas border town of Edinburg. "I work so hard at my
school—I have a 102% average—but I'm realizing the school is so awful it doesn't
amount to anything. I don't belong here. My father says, 'Learn as much as you can at
MIT, do your best and accept the consequences.I said, 'Yeah, Dad, but I'm the one who
has to deal with the failure.'" By the middle of the third week, the detonations of self-
doubt become audible. One morning in physics class, Cedric stands at his desk, walks
out into the hallway, and screams.

The physics teacher, Thomas Washington, a black twenty-four-year-old PhD can-   **27**
didate at MIT, rushes after him. "I told him, 'Cedric, don't be so hard on yourself,'"
Mr. Washington recounts later. "I told him that a lot of the material is new to lots of
the kids—just keep at it."

But, days after the incident, Mr. Washington vents his frustration at how the deck   **28**
is stacked against underprivileged students like Cedric and Neda.

"You have to understand that there's a controversy over who these types of pro-   **29**
grams should serve," he says, sitting in a sunny foyer one morning after class. "If you
only took the kids who need this the most, the ones who somehow excel at terrible
schools, who swim upstream but are still far behind academically, you wouldn't get
enough eventually accepted to MIT to justify the program."

And so the program ends up serving many students who really don't need it. Cer-   **30**
tainly, MIT's program—like others at many top colleges—looks very good. More than
half its students eventually are offered admission to the freshman class. Those victors,
however, are generally students from better schools in better neighborhoods, acknowledges Mr. Ramsey, a black MIT graduate who is the program's administrative director.
For some of them, this program is little more than résumé padding.

Mr. Ramsey had hoped it would be different. Seven years ago, when he took over the   **31**
program, he had "grand plans, to find late bloomers, and deserving kids in tough spots.
But it didn't take me three months to realize I'd be putting kids on a suicide dash."

A six-week program like MIT's, which doesn't offer additional, continuing sup-   **32**
port, simply can't function if it is filled with only inner-city youths whose educations
lag so far behind, he says: "They'd get washed out and everything they believe in
would come crashing down on their heads. Listen, we know a lot about suicide rates
up here. I'd be raising them."

Perhaps it isn't surprising, then, that while 47% of all black children live in   **33**
poverty in America, only about a dozen students in this year's MIT program would

even be considered lower-middle class, according to Mr. Ramsey. Though one or two of the neediest students like Cedric find their way to the program each year, he adds, they tend to be long shots to make it to the next step, into MIT for college. Those few, though, Mr. Ramsey says, are "cases where you could save lives."

34   Which is why Cedric, more than perhaps any other student in this year's program, hits a nerve.

35   "I want to take Cedric by the hand and lead him through the material," says physics instructor Mr. Washington, pensively. "But I resist. The real world's not like that. If he makes it to MIT, he won't have someone like me to help him."

36   "You know, part of it I suppose is our fault," he adds. "We haven't figured out a way to give credit for distance traveled."

37   So, within the program—like society beyond it—a class system is becoming obvious, even to the students. At the top are students like the beautifully dressed Jenica Dover, one of the girls who had found Cedric's diction so amusing. A confident black girl, she attends a mostly white high school in wealthy Newton, Mass. "Some of this stuff is review for me," she says one day, strolling from physics class, where she spent some of the hour giggling with deskmates. "I come from a very good school, and that makes all this pretty manageable."

38   Cedric, Neda, and the few others from poor backgrounds, meanwhile, are left to rely on what has gotten them this far: adrenaline and faith.

39   On a particularly sour day in mid-July, Cedric's rising doubts seem to overwhelm him. He can't work any harder in calculus, his best subject, yet he still lags behind other students in the class. Physics is becoming a daily nightmare.

40   Tossing and turning that night, too troubled to sleep, he looks out at the lights of MIT, thinking about the sacrifices he has made—the hours of extra work that he begged for from his teachers, the years focusing so single-mindedly on school that he didn't even have friends. "I thought that night that it wasn't ever going to be enough. That I wouldn't make it to MIT," he says later. "That, all this time, I was just fooling myself."

41   As the hours passed, he fell in and out of sleep. Then he awoke with a jolt, suddenly thinking about Cornelia Cunningham, an elder at the Washington Pentecostal church he attends as often as four times a week with his mother. A surrogate grandmother who had challenged and prodded Cedric since he was a small boy, "Mother Cunningham," as he always called her, had died two weeks before he left for MIT.

42   "I was lying there, and her spirit seemed to come to me. I could hear her voice, right there in my room, saying—just like always—'Cedric, you haven't yet begun to fight,'" he recounts. "And the next morning, I woke up and dove into my calculus homework like never before."

43   The auditorium near MIT's majestic domed library rings with raucous cheering, as teams prepare their robots for battle. Technically, this is an exercise in ingenuity and teamwork: Each three-student team had been given a box of motors, levers, and wheels to design a machine—mostly little cars with hooks on the front—to fight against another team's robot over a small soccer ball.

44   But something has gone awry. The trios, carefully chosen and mixed in past years by the instructors, were self-selected this year by the students. Clearly, the lines were drawn by race. As the elimination rounds begin, Hispanic teams battle against black teams. "PUERTO RICO, PUERTO RICO," comes the chant from the Hispanic side.

45   Black students whoop as Cedric's team fights into the quarterfinals, only to lose. He stumbles in mock anguish toward the black section, into the arms of several girls who have become his friends. The winner, oddly enough, is a team led by a Caucasian boy from Oklahoma who is here because he is 1/128 Potawatomi Indian. Both camps are muted.

In the final weeks, the explosive issues of race and class that have been simmering   46
since the students arrive break out into the open. It isn't just black vs. Hispanic or
poor vs. rich. It is minority vs. white. At a lunch table, over cold cuts on whole wheat,
talk turns to the ultimate insult: "wanting to be white." Jocelyn Truitt, a black girl
from a good Maryland high school, says her mother, a college professor, "started early
on telling me to ignore the whole 'white' thing. . . . I've got white friends. People say
things, that I'm trading up, selling out, but I don't listen. Let them talk."

Leslie Chavez says she hears it, too, in her largely Hispanic school. "If you get   47
good grades, you're 'white.' What, so you shouldn't do that? Thinking that way is a
formula for failure."

In an English class discussion later on the same issue, some students say assimila-   48
tion is the only answer. "The success of whites means they've mapped out the territory for success," says Alfred Fraijo, a cocky Hispanic from Los Angeles. "If you want
to move up and fit in, it will have to be on those terms. There's nothing wrong with
aspiring to that—it's worth the price of success."

Cedric listens carefully, but the arguments for assimilation are foreign to him. He   49
knows few whites; in his world, whites have always been the unseen oppressors. "The
charge of 'wanting to be white,' where I'm from," Cedric says, "is like treason."

A charge for which he is being called to task, and not just by tough kids in Bal-   50
lou's hallways. He has had phone conversations over the past few weeks with an old
friend from junior high, a boy his age named Torrance Parks, who is trying to convert
Cedric to Islam.

"He just says I should stick with my own," says Cedric, "that I'm already betray-   51
ing my people, leaving them all behind, by coming up to a big white university and
all, that even if I'm successful, I'll never be accepted by whites."

Back in Washington, Cedric's mother, a data-input clerk at the Department of   52
Agriculture, is worried. She hopes Cedric will now continue to push forward, to take
advantage of scholarships to private prep schools, getting him out of Ballou High for
his senior year, "keeping on his path out."

"He needs to get more of what he's getting at MIT, more challenging work with   53
nice, hard-working kids—maybe even white kids," she says. The words of Islam,
which she fears might lead toward more radical black separatism, would "mean a re-
treat from all that." She adds that she asks Torrance: "What can you offer my son
other than hate?"

She is increasingly frustrated, yet unable to get her son to discuss the issue. When   54
recruiters from Phillips Exeter Academy come to MIT to talk to the students, Cedric
snubs them. "They have to wear jacket and tie there; it's elitist," he says. "It's not for
me."

Still, in the past few weeks, Cedric has been inching forward. Perseverance finally   55
seems to be paying off. He has risen to near the top of the group in calculus. He is improving in chemistry, adequate in robotics, and showing some potential in English.
Physics remains a sore spot.

He also has found his place here. The clutch of middle- and upper-middle-class   56
black girls who once made fun of him has grown fond of him, fiercely protective of
him. One Friday night, when Cedric demurs about joining a Saturday group trip to
Cape Cod, the girls press him until he finally admits his reason: He doesn't have a
bathing suit.

"So we took him to the mall to pick out some trunks," says Isa Williams, the   57
daughter of two Atlanta college professors. "Because he doesn't have maybe as many
friends at home, Cedric has a tendency of closing up when he gets sad, and not turning to other people," she adds. "We want him to know we're there for him."

58   The next day, on the bus, Cedric, at his buoyant best, leads the group in songs.

59   Though he doesn't want to say it—to jinx anything—by early in the fifth week Cedric is actually feeling a shard of hope. Blackboard scribbles are beginning to make sense, even on the day in late-July when he is thinking only about what will follow classes: a late afternoon meeting with Professor Trilling, the academic director. This is the meeting Cedric has been waiting for since the moment he arrived, when the professor will assess his progress and—most important—his prospects for someday getting accepted into MIT.

60   Cedric, wound tight, gets lost on the way to Professor Trilling's office, arriving a few minutes late.

61   Professor Trilling, who is white, ushers the youngster into an office filled with certificates, wide windows, and a dark wood desk. Always conscious of clothes, Cedric tries to break the ice by complimenting Mr. Trilling on his shoes, but the professor doesn't respond, moving right to business.

62   After a moment, he asks Cedric if he is "thinking about applying and coming to MIT."

63   "Yeah," Cedric says. "I've been wanting to come for years."

64   "Well, I don't think you're MIT material," the professor says flatly. "Your academic record isn't strong enough."

65   Cedric, whose average for his junior year was better than perfect, 4.19, thanks to several A+ grades, asks what he means.

66   The professor explains that Cedric's Scholastic Aptitude Test scores—he has scored only a 910 out of a possible 1600—are about 200 points below what they need to be.

67   Agitated, Cedric begins insisting that he is willing to work hard, "exceedingly hard," to make it at MIT. "He seemed to have this notion that if you work hard enough, you can achieve anything," Professor Trilling recalls haltingly. "That is admirable, but it also can set up for disappointment. And, at the present time, I told him, that just doesn't seem to be enough."

68   Ending the meeting, the professor jots down names of professors at Howard University, a black college in Washington, and at the University of Maryland. He suggests that Cedric call them, that if Cedric does well at one of those colleges, he might someday be able to transfer to MIT.

69   Cedric's eyes are wide, his temples bulging, his teeth clenched. He doesn't hear Mr. Trilling's words of encouragement; he hears only MIT's rejection. He takes the piece of paper from the professor, leaves without a word, and walks across campus and to his dorm room. Crumpling up the note, he throws it in the garbage. He skips dinner that night, ignoring the knocks on his locked door from Isa, Jenica, and other worried friends. "I thought about everything," he says, "about what a fool I've been."

70   The next morning, wandering out into the foyer as calculus class ends, he finally blows. "He made me feel so small, this big," he says, almost screaming, as he presses his fingers close. "'Not MIT material'. . . . Who is he to tell me that? He doesn't know what I've been through. This is it, right, this is racism. A white guy telling me I can't do it."

71   Physics class is starting. Cedric slips in, moving, now almost by rote, to the front row—the place he sits in almost every class he has ever taken.

72   Isa passes him a note: "What happened?"

73   He writes a note back describing the meeting and saying he is thinking of leaving, of just going home. The return missive, now also signed by Jenica and a third friend, tells Cedric he has worked too hard to give up. "You can't just run away," the note says,

as Isa recalls later. "You have to stay and prove to them you have what it takes. . . . We all care about you and love you." Cedric folds the note gently and puts it in his pocket.

The hour ends, with a work sheet Cedric is supposed to hand in barely touched. **74** Taking a thick pencil from his bookbag, he scrawls "I AM LOST" across the blank sheet, drops it on the teacher's desk, and disappears into the crowd.

Jenica runs to catch up with him, to commiserate. But it will be difficult for her to **75** fully understand: In her meeting with Professor Trilling the next day, he encourages her to enroll at MIT. She shrugs off the invitation. "Actually," she tells the professor, "I was planning to go to Stanford."

On a sweltering late-summer day, all three air conditioners are blasting in Cedric's **76** cramped apartment in Washington. Cedric is sitting on his bed, piled high with clothes, one of his bags not yet unpacked even though he returned home from Cambridge several weeks ago.

The last days of the MIT program were fitful. Cedric didn't go to the final ban- **77** quet, where awards are presented, because he didn't want to see Professor Trilling again. But he made friends in Cambridge, and on the last morning, as vans were loaded for trips to the airport, he hugged and cried like the rest of them.

"I don't think much about it now, about MIT," he says, as a police car speeds by, **78** its siren barely audible over the air conditioners' whir. "Other things are happening. I have plenty to do."

Not really. Most days since returning from New England, he has spent knocking **79** around the tiny, spare apartment, or going to church, or plodding through applications for colleges and scholarships.

The calls from Torrance, who has been joined in his passion for Islam by Cedric's **80** first cousin, have increased. Cedric says he "just listens," and that "it's hard to argue with" Torrance.

But inside the awkward youngster, a storm rages. Not at home on the hustling **81** streets, and ostracized by high-school peers who see his ambition as a sign of "disrespect," Cedric has discovered that the future he so carefully charted may not welcome him either.

Certainly, he will apply to colleges. And his final evaluations from each MIT class **82** turned out better than he—and perhaps even Professor Trilling—thought they would. He showed improvement right through the very last day.

But the experience in Cambridge left Cedric bewildered. Private-school scholar- **83** ship offers, crucial to help underprivileged students make up for lost years before landing in the swift currents of college, have been passed by, despite his mother's urgings. Instead, Cedric Jennings has decided to return to Ballou High, the place from which he has spent the last three years trying to escape.

"I know this may sound crazy," he says, shaking his head. "But I guess I'm sort of **84** comfortable there, at my school. Comfortable in this place that I hate."

When a Dad Says Goodbye to His Daughter

Roger H. Martin

It is 5:00 a.m. as we drive toward the airport, and I am struggling to come up with **1** something meaningful to say to my younger daughter as she leaves for a preorienta- tion wilderness hike sponsored by Tufts University, the Boston-area college she will soon enter as a freshman.

2   Emily is a bright, self-confident, and extremely capable young woman whose only shortcoming is that she sometimes puts things off until the last minute. But I am her father, and fathers always worry about their daughters. So I'm wondering, will Emily survive college without her mother and father around to give advice? Can she balance the social demands of college with the academic? More immediately, will she lose herself in the wilds of New Hampshire? In my imagination at least, the permutations of what can go wrong seem mind-boggling.

3   We arrive at the Richmond International Airport and unload an extremely heavy knapsack, packed very hurriedly the night before. As designated pack mule—always the father's role in these matters—I am lugging through the airport eighty pounds of the assorted stuff Emily says she needs for her wilderness trip, including designer hiking boots, snacks, rain gear, shampoo, more snacks, and her teddy bear.

4   Emily is now very emotional. Where two days ago my wife and I were pesky nags, imploring her to clean up her room and pack her bags, we are now long-lost parents. She is crying as though she will never see us again.

5   With more than a tear in my own eyes, I utter the brilliant send-off I have been laboring to compose: "Emily, I have two words of advice: 'Plan ahead.'"

6   My daughter—a slight five feet four inches—disappears down the jetway and into the plane. I should have told her how much I love her.

7   Fathers usually miss out on the mixed emotions of watching their children depart for the first day of school. That is what mothers do. But fathers who say goodbye to their college-bound daughters get a pretty close sense of it. Few record the experience. I did.

8   August 31: We are now making the five hundred-mile trip from Richmond to Boston in a rented van packed with more stuff, most of which will be hauled back home on parents' day two months hence. I know this from experience, not only as a college president but also because my older daughter, Kate, a senior at Tufts, made the same mistake.

9   September 1 (a.m.): Move-in day is a father's nightmare. This is the point where middle-aged men get hernias. Emily's room is on the fifth floor of a residence hall with no elevators. What was the architect thinking?

10   Like most parents who got up at dawn to make the trip to campus and then moved mountains of junk up five floors, I am in a daze. So is everyone else. Parents are running red lights. Distracted freshmen are walking in front of moving cars. But where is my daughter? As I begin to unpack the van, Emily is spotted limping across the parking lot, with an uneasy smile on her face. She had a blast in the wilds of northern New England, but the ill-fitting hiking boots have apparently ruined her feet.

11   September 1 (p.m.): Nothing goes according to plan. We miss lunch because Emily wants a shower. As a consequence, we also miss the matriculation ceremony. And then we are in the parking lot again saying goodbye. All three of us are choked up. This time, I remember to say, "I love you, Emily."

12   September 2: Emily's first call home. "I'm overwhelmed and stressed out," she sniffles. "Overwhelmed" is a universal condition of new college students. Emily is obviously homesick. We later learn from her sister Kate that Emily left her meal ticket in someone else's room and therefore cannot get into the dining hall.

13   September 3: Emily calls to confess that she has lost her meal ticket and is starving. But not to worry. She will buy food in the student union convenience store.

14   September 4: Emily's blistered feet are infected, requiring a visit to the infirmary. She tells us she is on antibiotics. Emily has also hit the jackpot on the registration lottery, getting first choice for all her courses, including one entitled "Love and Sexuality." I ask her what this course is about.

"It's English composition, Dad," Emily says somewhat indignantly.   15

September 5: It's late Sunday night, and Emily calls her mother in a panic. She   16
and five friends decided to explore downtown Boston, but she got separated from the
pack and is now in a phone booth in an underground "T" station. She cannot take a
cab back to school because she asked one of her pals to carry her wallet for her since
her jeans have no pockets. She cannot walk very far because of the condition of her
feet.

Emily: "Mom, how do I get back to campus?"   17

Mom: "I really don't know, sweetheart. I live in Virginia. What is the name of the   18
'T' station?"

Emily: "I don't know."   19

Mom: "OK. Calm down. Go to the token booth and ask them how to get back to   20
Davis Square." Emily gets back to campus in short order and even calls us to say that
she is there safely.

September 8: It has been three days without a phone call. We figure Emily must   21
be settling in. She is now calling to say that she made the sailing team, which surprises
us, since Emily never sailed before. The story is that at a fraternity party she was met
with the eager stares of at least a dozen men. Tufts's Division I sailing team hangs out
at the fraternity, and they were looking for ultralight women crazy enough to act as
crew—aka ballast—in their racing dinghies.

I quiz her, "What do you do as crew?"   22

Emily says, "Oh, it's kind of boring, Dad. My job is just to throw my body from   23
one side of the boat to the other."

She also reports that she found her meal ticket and, after surviving on pizza, has   24
finally eaten a real meal.

September 9: Emily calls with important news. "Love and Sexuality" is oversub-   25
scribed, and she has switched to a writing course on ecology, which she hates. So she's
planning to drop it and finish her composition requirement next semester. She is going to join the Outdoors Club, in addition to sailing. Before I can express concern
about her priorities, she says, "Got to go now, Dad. Lots to read for class. No time to
speak." I hear a young man's voice in the background and worry.

September 11: Emily is stressed out again. The infection in her feet is spreading.   26
With the demands of sailing, the Outdoors Club and other social life, she can't keep
up with homework. I suggest she go light on nonacademic activities. She tells me to
mind my own business.

And then, silence. No phone calls for almost a month!   27

October 8: Emily finally calls again. She seems to be a transformed person. No   28
more crises. No more complaints. The tenor of her conversation is entirely different.
"I just attended a class that was awesome," she says. She loves college! She is getting
her assignments in on time! She got a B on her first exam!

Clearly, Emily has learned from all the problems she has experienced. She has   29
conquered, or at least lived through, adversity, and she has done it on her own.

This is partly what college is about, after all: figuring out how to survive without   30
the presence of parents. Now, somehow, Emily has done it, becoming a self-sufficient
college freshman.

Take Your Parents to Work?

No Way, Says Adam Markey

JEFFREY ZASLOW

1   As Chicago gears up for its third annual "Take Your Parents to Work Day," Adam Markey is devising ways to keep his mother out of his office.

2   The twenty-seven-year-old marketing analyst offered to set a video camera on his desk so his mom can watch a tape of his day. He'll let her call from home and listen to his voice mail. He even says she can show up some Saturday "when no one is here." But on a workday? When coworkers are around? "It would be like wearing a sign on my forehead that said, 'Ridicule me at the water cooler,'" he says.

3   A self-described "aggressive mother," Judy Markey understands her son's reluctance. But as Parents Day, June 27, approaches, she has been begging to fly from Chicago to Atlanta, where her son works for Bondo Corporation, which makes automotive and home-repair products.

4   The rebuff of Ms. Markey is problematic because she happens to be a founding mother of the big day. She cohosts a show on WGN radio, where a listener first suggested the idea of bringing parents to work. That led to a proclamation from Chicago Mayor Richard Daley ("Whereas parents are often unaware of what their adult children do in the workplace . . . ") and a grassroots campaign built on the notion that, in "the city that works," residents would enjoy proving it to mom and dad.

5   The response, however, has been mixed. Some people embrace the chance to share their work lives with their parents. Others react like teenagers, still mortified by the idea of being seen with their parents.

6   It's unclear just how many hundreds or thousands of parents will participate in the event, since there's no registration. But about 85% of Parents Day visits are arranged at the behest of parents, and most visitors are mothers, organizers say.

7   In recent years, a handful of companies nationwide have held "Take Your Parents" days, with little fanfare. At career-guidance Web firm Vault.com (now Vault Inc.) in New York, parents were clueless about the Internet, says company founder Mark Oldman. But by the time milk and cookies were served to end Parents Day 2000, progress was made. "My mom learned to call the company Vault-dot-com," he says. "She'd been calling it Vaultcom."

8   Eric Ober, a former CBS News president, was Vault's chief executive at the time, and brought his eighty-seven-year-old, four-foot-ten mother, Sara. She happily answered employees' questions about Mr. Ober. They wondered: Why does he never wear socks? She told them, "He's a little *meshuga*"—Yiddish for crazy—and explained how she soft-pedals advice to her son. "I don't say, 'You should wear socks!' I say, 'You're not wearing socks?'" Mr. Ober loved watching his staff interact with his mother. "It was a highlight of my life," he says.

9   On the first two Parents Days in Chicago, many adult children felt like kids again, splashing at the swim club, screaming, "Hey Mom, look at me!" Still, they warn, there are risks in letting parents wade into the office pool.

10   Jennifer Bratt, a pharmaceutical sales representative, took her mother on sales calls to physicians' offices. Mom seized the opportunity for free medical advice. "She asked about her cholesterol, her decision not to go on estrogen, two fractures she had," says Ms. Bratt.

Lindsey Dunn, an Internet merchandising manager for J. C. Whitney and Company, had no picture of her mother at her office. Mom wasn't pleased. "She even had a picture of her dog on her desk," says Ms. Dunn's mother, Jeri Bus.   **11**

Some parents quickly made themselves at home in their kids' workplaces. At TGI Friday's, in Bolingbrook, Ill., Cheryl Clairardin followed her waitress daughter around and couldn't resist sitting at customers' tables to schmooze. "I'd plop myself down, and my daughter would roll her eyes and walk away."   **12**

Enthusiasm for Parents Day varies depending on company culture. Printer Joe Rizzo's mother insisted on visiting him at Saltzman Printing, in Maywood, Ill. "I couldn't keep her out," he says. In sympathy, Mr. Rizzo's bosses posted a sign-up sheet for other employees. There were no takers. "Everybody thought it was corny," says Mr. Rizzo.   **13**

But at family-owned ABT Electronics, in Glenview, Ill., forty employees brought parents to last year's Parents Day, and eighty are expected to do it this year. Martha Harpling, an ABT administrative employee, had her mother type a letter for her. Her mother had never used a computer before. "I kept hitting the keys too hard, like you do on a typewriter," says her mom, Dona Baker.   **14**

ABT sales manager Steve Shapiro says that his father, a retired salesman, was "raring to get out on the floor and help sell. Some customers wanted to hear what my dad had to say, but I told him to stay out of it. This was my gig." The day is now a sweet memory. Though Mr. Shapiro's dad had hoped to return for Parents Day this year, he died in April.   **15**

Previous Parents Days gave parents great insights into their kids' responsibilities. Arlene Weil's daughter is a Southwest Airlines customer-service agent. When flights were delayed, "I watched her take an incredible amount of abuse. I don't know how she kept that smile slapped on her face," says Ms. Weil, adding that she resisted the urge to throttle passengers who abused her kid. She was proud of her twenty-eight-year-old daughter. "To me, she just learned to tie her shoes last week."   **16**

Sharon Silver visited the Hinsdale, Ill., office where her son-in-law is an allergist and her daughter is office manager. She sat in the waiting room, chatting with patients—an incognito mother-in-law getting the skinny on her son-in-law. "They all said what a wonderful doctor he is," she recalls. "Then I'd say, 'Well, I'm his mother-in-law,' and they'd say, 'You must be so happy!'"   **17**

Ms. Silver's daughter, Deanna Jacobson, is encouraging the office staff to bring their parents back this year. "At work, people become disembodied from their families," she says. "It helps put coworkers into context when you meet their parents."   **18**

Chicagoans can track Parents Day vicariously by listening to WGN, as parents call in with updates.   **19**

Last year, the mother of a tile-setter called to say she was watching her son tile a customer's bathroom floor. When he closed in on a corner, she admitted, her heart began palpitating, as she wondered whether he'd measured correctly.   **20**

The mother of an air-traffic controller at Midway Airport called to say, "It was crazy! Six of them were talking at once." After two hours, feeling overwhelmed by the tension, she joined her son in the break room. That's when he explained that bad weather had closed East Coast airports, so it was an "easy" day. "They're all young," the concerned mother said, "and they all have gray hair."   **21**

Janet Hass, a Lutheran minister in Northlake, Ill., gave a sermon last year promoting Parents Day. This year, she plans to join her nineteen-year-old son, Andrew, at his job at a Fuddruckers restaurant. "She'll look about ten years younger in a Fuddruckers uniform," Andrew predicts.   **22**

23   "I don't see how a red shirt and apron will take ten years off my face," says Pastor Hass. "But it sounds good to me."

24   The Signature Room, the restaurant on the ninety-fifth floor of Chicago's John Hancock Center, is again offering Parents Day lunch specials. On Parents Day 2001, sixty-five downtown workers took parents to lunch there. "The parents try to pay, and the children argue with them," says coowner Rick Roman. "It's so darn cute."

25   In 2000, Diane Pienta spent Parents Day with two sons at the Chicago Board of Trade. When she arrived, one son said, "You don't want to stay all day, do you?" But as the morning wore on, her sons became gracious hosts, introducing her to coworkers, buying breakfast, and explaining their jobs.

26   "They were long. They were short. I didn't understand," she says, "but I was impressed."

27   At the end of the day, her older son told her, "I'm glad you came."

28   "He sent me off with a kiss," says Ms. Pienta. "For a mother, that says it all."

3 *Paraphrasing*

When you *paraphrase* a statement, a brief passage, or a longer excerpt from a text, you recast information and ideas in different words. College students engage in paraphrasing almost daily. When you take notes during class, for example, you try to capture the main points of your instructor's lecture in your own words. Likewise, essay examinations often ask you to distill important concepts from lectures, reading, and class discussion. In fact, the ability to present unfamiliar information and explain complex ideas in your own language is a crucial academic skill because it helps you demonstrate knowledge and understanding.

PARAPHRASE AS A READING STRATEGY

Let's begin with the most informal, and probably most frequent, use of paraphrase. Whenever skillful readers encounter a challenging passage, they try to construct an interpretation—to reach some understanding of it. One way they do this is to paraphrase. Consider the following sentence from *Talking Power,* a book by Robin Lakoff, a scholar of language study:

> When it is important that language be forceful, we attempt to buttress it in some tangible ways.

A fluent reader might pause for less than a second to process this sentence by mentally recasting it in different terms: "When we want people to pay attention to our words, we try to back them up with something concrete." Sometimes, readers write these interpretive paraphrases in the margins; other times, they simply read further to see whether their mental paraphrase turns out to be correct. In the case of Robin Lakoff's sentence, the accuracy of our paraphrase is confirmed by an illustration that appears later in the same paragraph:

> Nowadays we often think of . . . oaths as mere words themselves, *pro forma* declarations. But they originated as dire threats. . . . The very words *testify, testimony* recall one ancient link between words and reality. They are derived from the Latin *testes,* its meaning the same as in current English. In swearing, the Roman male . . . placed his right hand upon his genitals; the implication was that, if he swore falsely, they would be rendered sterile—a potent threat.

Sometimes, a marginal paraphrase proves useful later on. If, for example, you plan to review material for an exam, paraphrasing an important idea could be helpful. There are, however, limits to how much you can fit into the margins, just as there are limits to how much time you can devote to paraphrasing, either in your head or on paper. And since a paraphrase, unlike a summary, restates every idea from its source, writers seldom paraphrase more than two or three contiguous sentences. Proficient readers, likewise, rarely recast multiple sentences in their heads, even when they encounter a challenging passage such as the following, also from Lakoff's book:

> We are not mere passive recipients of manipulative communicative strategies. Orwell and other worriers ignore the truth, whether unpleasant or happy: we all manipulate language, and we do it all the time. Our every interaction is political, whether we intend it to be or not; everything we do in the course of a day communicates our relative power, our desire for a particular sort of connection, our identification of the other as one who needs something from us, or vice versa.

Adhering to one common, though naive, bit of advice, a baffled reader might look up every unfamiliar or confusing word and try to recast the passage in simpler language. After five minutes with a dictionary, this reader might render the first sentence as follows: "We are not inactive receivers of influencing talkative plans." The same industrious reader would learn also that *Orwell* refers to George Orwell, a British novelist and essayist who lived from 1903 to 1950. But all this effort produces little clarification. To make matters worse, the strategy is even less effective in dealing with the next sentence, in which the words are familiar to almost any English-speaking adult. Here, a dictionary offers no help at all.

Efficient readers, therefore, paraphrase sparingly. Often, they delay understanding for a few sentences to see whether subsequent text provides clarification. Later in the paragraph from which we have quoted, for example, Lakoff says, ". . . We are always involved in persuasion, in trying to get another person to see the world or some piece of it our way, and therefore to act as we would like them to act." Now, the foregoing sentences become clear, and most readers will not need to return to them for paraphrasing.

This first type of paraphrase lies at one end of a spectrum on which every act of reading and interpretation might be placed; more personal types of response lie at the opposite end. When we want to explore our individual responses and connections to a text, we read and write subjectively, less concerned with literal understanding of what the writer is trying to say. But when we want to get down exactly what a sentence or passage says, we paraphrase it. The figure below illustrates the spectrum of which we speak:

Responses to Reading

Objective   Subjective

←—————————————————————————————————→

Paraphrase   Personal Response
(author's ideas)   (reader's interpretation)

USING PARAPHRASE IN WRITING

Up to this point, we have treated paraphrase as a reading strategy—a way to understand or come to terms with concepts in academic texts. Whether performed mentally or recorded on paper, this private type of paraphrase differs from others in one important way: It is usually not accompanied by an ***acknowledgment phrase*** (e.g., "according to Robin Lakoff") or ***formal documentation*** (e.g., a parenthetical note keyed to a bibliographical entry). In other words, since this kind of paraphrase will not be read by anyone else, you are not obligated to identify its source explicitly. For example, if you wrote a marginal paraphrase of the main idea of this paragraph, you probably would not begin with "Veit and Gould say that . . ." or end with a note citing the authors' names and a page number.

Notice how we qualify this advice: A *private* paraphrase—one that *no one else is going to read*—is *usually* not accompanied by an acknowledgment phrase and documentation. However, if you were to place such a paraphrase in a notebook or index card or on a photocopied page that does not clearly identify the author, title, and location of the source, failure to acknowledge and document could prevent future use of the paraphrased ideas. If you ever wanted to cite or even refer to those ideas in any kind of writing intended for other readers (including your instructor), you would have to relocate the source and cite it appropriately. This is necessary because every public use of paraphrase—every use involving a reader other than yourself—demands acknowledgment and proper documentation.*

One public use of paraphrase involves rewording a difficult passage for an audience unfamiliar with its concepts or terminology. Legal experts often paraphrase complex, ambiguous texts such as contracts, court decisions, and legislation; and when they do so, they usually interpret as well as translate. Others may paraphrase an argument with which they disagree in an effort to demonstrate good faith and a willingness to listen and understand. Finally, in research projects particularly, writers paraphrase sources to cite important information, to place a topic or issue in context, or to support an interpretation or opinion. Subsequent sections of this chapter will consider each of these occasions for paraphrasing.

Before continuing, we must emphasize one crucial point about paraphrasing for *any* purpose. Whenever you paraphrase, you must *completely* rephrase your source, using your own words and your own style. Neither substitution of words nor rearrangement of word order produces a legitimate paraphrase of another writer's ideas. Suppose, for example, that you wanted to paraphrase the following sentence from an article about Walt Disney World written by columnist Manuela Hoelterhoff for the *Wall Street Journal:*

---

*The conventions of acknowledgment and documentation are presented in subsequent chapters. In particular, the parenthetical note, a short annotation usually citing the source of paraphrased ideas or quoted words and the page(s) on which they can be found, is explained in Chapter 5. Although the scope of the present chapter is confined to techniques of paraphrasing, the significance of proper documentation should not be overlooked or minimized.

The original
passage

> I did not have a great time. I ate food no self-respecting mouse would eat, stayed in a hotel that could have been designed by the Moscow corps of engineers and suffered through entertainment by smiling, uniformed young people who looked like they had their hair arranged at a lobotomy clinic.

The following sentence illustrates one of several acceptable paraphrases:

An acceptable
paraphrase

> Visitors to Disney World can expect unappetizing food, uncomfortable lodging, and sappy young singers and dancers who all look alike.

On the other hand, the following sentence would not be an acceptable paraphrase because it merely tinkers with Hoelterhoff's sentence:

An
unacceptable
paraphrase

> Don't expect to enjoy yourself. You will eat food unfit for rodents, let alone humans; sleep in a hotel that looks like a relic of the Soviet Union; and endure performances by grinning teenagers who look like they've had brain surgery.

Whenever you write a paraphrase that others will read, as in a research paper, you are bound by certain rules of fair play. Specifically, you must completely recast material borrowed from your source, using your own words and your own style. Failure to do so is *plagiarism,* an act of dishonesty. Unless you quote your sources exactly (either set off with quotation marks or indented as a blocked quotation), readers will assume that the language and style you use are entirely your own. You must also give full credit for a source's contribution to your writing.

Upcoming chapters will provide more detail about the use of sources in research writing, including paraphrase and quotation, citation of sources, and avoidance of plagiarism.

Paraphrasing for a Different Audience

Writers sometimes paraphrase a source in order to express its ideas more clearly for a particular audience. For example, a reference to Shakespeare might, in certain contexts, benefit from a clarifying paraphrase:

> "That which we call a rose," wrote the Bard, "by any other name would smell as sweet." His point is that we should not judge people by their names or things by the words that refer to them, since names do not alter essence.

The second sentence paraphrases the first. However, it does more than just restate an idea in different words (e.g., "A rose would be just as fragrant no matter what we called it"). It goes further, stating the implicit meaning of the source—a meaning that Shakespeare left unstated.

Likewise, a newspaper reporter might want to review recent discoveries in genetic engineering. Rather than quote extensively from articles in professional journals, where such discoveries are introduced and explained to scientists, the reporter would paraphrase crucial information in familiar, everyday language. The technical vocabulary and style appropriate to an audience of professional research scientists would confuse most newspaper readers.

Specialized and General Audiences

When you write for an audience that shares knowledge about a particular field, you customarily adopt the language, or **jargon,** appropriate to that field, even though it confuses most outsiders. (You can find a host of magazines and journals aimed at specialized audiences in the periodical section of your college library.) Writers for *Field and Stream* expect readers to understand specialized words and abbreviations relating to game animals and rifle scopes; an article in *PC Computing* would not explain the difference between RAM and ROM; and authors who publish in the scholarly journal *Linguistic Inquiry* assume that readers are familiar with terms like *anaphoric dependencies* and *surface filters*. We all have special interests that allow us to interpret texts that baffle others.

Often in research writing you must translate the specialized jargon of a source into a clearer, more accessible language that suits the needs of a general audience. Paraphrasing technical information for laypersons is therefore a useful skill for college students.

Consider two passages relating to periodicity, the rhythmic behavior exhibited in many plant and animal species. The first passage, from *Physiological Zoology,* a scientific journal, presents difficulties for most readers:

> Recent studies have provided reasons to postulate that the primary timer for long-cycle biological rhythms that are closely similar in period to the natural geophysical ones that persist in so-called constant conditions is, in fact, one of organismic response to subtle geophysical fluctuations which pervade ordinary constant conditions in the laboratory (Brown, 1959, 1960). In such constant laboratory conditions a wide variety of organisms have been demonstrated to display, nearly equally conspicuously, metabolic periodicities of both solar-day and lunar-day frequencies, with their interference derivative, the 29.5-day synodic month, and in some instances even the year. These metabolic cycles exhibit day-by-day irregularities and distortions which have been established to be highly significantly correlated with aperiodic meteorological and other geophysical changes. These correlations provide strong evidence for the exogenous origins of these biological periodisms themselves, since cycles exist in these meteorological and geophysical factors.
>
> —Emma D. Terracini and Frank A. Brown, Jr., "Periodisms in Mouse 'Spontaneous' Activity Synchronized with Major Geophysical Events"

Passage for a specialized audience

If you were researching periodicity, you might get the gist of this specialized writing. But if you wanted to report information to readers who do not share your background and interests, you would paraphrase parts of the passage in more familiar language.

In the second passage, Frank Brown recasts some of the same information for an article published in the less specialized *Science* magazine:

> Familiar to all are the rhythmic changes in innumerable processes of animals and plants in nature. . . .
>
> These periodisms of animals and plants, which adapt them so nicely to their geophysical environment with its rhythmic fluctuations in light, temperature, and ocean tides, appear at first glance to be exclusively simple responses of the organisms to these physical factors. However, it is now known that rhythms of

Passage for a less specialized but professional audience

all these natural frequencies may persist in living things even after the organisms have been sealed in under conditions constant with respect to every factor biologists have conceded to be of influence. The presence of such persistent rhythms clearly indicates that organisms possess some means of timing these periods which does not depend directly upon the obvious environmental physical rhythms. That means has come to be termed "living clocks."

—Frank A. Brown, Jr., "Living Clocks"

Though accessible to many educated adults, this passage assumes the reader's interest in scientific research (a valid assumption about people who subscribe to *Science* magazine).

Notice how Brown once again paraphrases the same basic information, this time adapting it to a still broader audience for an article published in the *Saturday Evening Post:*

Passage for a general audience

One of the greatest riddles of the universe is the uncanny ability of living things to carry out their normal activities with clocklike precision at a particular time of the day, month, and year. . . .

Though it might appear that such rhythms are merely the responses of organisms to rhythmic changes in light, temperature, or the ocean tides, this is far from being the whole answer. For when living things . . . are removed from their natural habitat and placed under conditions where no variations occur in any of the forces to which they are generally conceded to be sensitive, they commonly continue to display the same rhythms they displayed in their natural environment.

—Frank A. Brown, Jr., "Life's Mysterious Clocks"

In each of these cases, writing is adapted to the needs of a particular group of readers. The first passage targets research scientists. Consequently, the authors avoid assigning "agency"—telling who performs critical actions. They say, for example, that "*recent studies* have provided reasons" and that "organisms *have been demonstrated* to display"; they do not say "*scientists* have provided reasons" or "*we and our colleagues* have demonstrated." Although writing that does not assign agency is often harder to understand, scientists prefer this style because they consider it more objective. In the third passage, written for the *Saturday Evening Post*, the author uses simpler vocabulary (like *living things*) and explains concepts (like *controlled conditions,* described as "conditions where no variations occur in any of the forces to which [living things] are generally conceded to be sensitive").

You may wonder whether writers ever paraphrase in language more formal than that of an original source. Because the results may sound peculiar or pretentious, writers who do this often seek a comic effect. For example, in a well-known essay about misuses of language, George Orwell translates a passage from the Old Testament into modern political jargon. The original passage, from *Ecclesiastes,* reads:

I returned, and saw under the sun, that the race *is* not to the swift, nor the battle to the strong, neither yet bread to the wise, nor yet riches to men of understanding, nor yet favour to men of skills, but time and chance happeneth to them all.

Ridiculing what he calls "modern English," Orwell paraphrases the source as follows:

> Objective consideration of contemporary phenomena compels the conclusion that success or failure in competitive activities exhibits no tendency to be commensurate with innate capacity, but that a considerable element of the unpredictable must invariably be taken into account.

Orwell's aim is not to communicate the ideas or sentiments expressed in a source, but to show how a particular type of language renders them obscure and inelegant. The paraphrase draws attention to its own vocabulary and style and away from the content of its source.

The following sentence from a magazine that targets an audience of gay men presents a different situation in which a writer might paraphrase a source in more formal language:

> Chubby, fat, and obese queers suffer outcast status.

The word *queer*, used in reference to homosexuals, is a stereotypical and abusive term that offends many readers. (However, since the author of the source is himself a gay man, clearly he does not mean to be offensive.) Words like *chubby, fat,* and *obese* also carry negative connotations—implicit meaning, as opposed to objective "dictionary" definition. Therefore, if our aim is to report ideas objectively, an appropriate paraphrase might be the following:

> According to one observer, gay men are repelled by obesity.

Some may object to this paraphrase because it substitutes intentionally strong language with euphemisms (polite equivalents for unpleasant or controversial words), blunting the impact of the original source. Therefore, a better strategy might be a carefully introduced quotation:

> Writing for *Outweek* magazine, Jay Blotcher asserts, "Chubby, fat, and obese queers suffer outcast status."

Notice that in each case, the writer stands at a distance from the paraphrased or quoted source. This is often appropriate when citing controversial or highly subjective opinions. Some textbooks, in fact, distinguish between *informative paraphrases*—those that adopt the tone of a source, reporting facts and opinions as though the writer accepted their validity—and *descriptive paraphrases*—those that take a more detached stance, *describing* a source rather than *reporting* its information or opinions without qualification. Thus, an informative paraphrase of the forgoing sentence might begin this way:

> Textbooks sometimes differentiate between informative and descriptive paraphrases. . . .

An informative paraphrase

A descriptive paraphrase, on the other hand, might open like this:

> Veit and Gould report that textbooks sometimes differentiate between informative and descriptive paraphrases. . . .

A descriptive paraphrase

Though valid, the distinction between informative and descriptive paraphrases is not emphasized in this chapter; instead, we demonstrate how and when writers may detach themselves from certain sources. (The principle will be discussed also in Chapter 12.)

| EXERCISES | **Paraphrasing for a Different Audience** |

1. The following sentences appear in another article about periodism, or "biological clocks," the topic addressed in preceding excerpts. This article, also by Frank Brown, was published in *Biological Bulletin.* Try to paraphrase the sentences for a general audience, similar to the one targeted in Brown's article in the *Saturday Evening Post:*

   Much has been learned, particularly in recent years, as to the properties, including modifiability, of this endogenous rhythmicity. The fundamental problem, however, that of the timing mechanism of the rhythmic periods, has largely eluded any eminently reasonable hypotheses. . . .

2. Recast the passage from the article in the *Saturday Evening Post* (page 132), adapting it to *National Geographic World,* a magazine for children of elementary-school age.

3. Copy a passage from a textbook for one of your advanced courses that some people might find difficult. Write a paraphrase accessible to most readers.

4. The following referendum initiative appeared on ballots in New Jersey. Write a paraphrase to assist voters who are nonnative speakers of English:

   Should the "Jobs, Science, and Technology Bond Act of 1984" which authorizes the State to issue bonds in the amount of $90,000,000.00 for the purpose of creating jobs by the establishment of a network of advanced technology centers at the State's public and private institutions of higher education and for the construction and improvement of technical and engineering-related facilities and equipment as well as job training and retraining programs in high-technology fields at these institutions; and in a principal amount sufficient to refinance all or any such bonds if the same will result in a present value savings; providing the ways and means to pay that interest of such debt and also to pay and discharge the principle thereof, be approved?

Formal and Informal Writing

When you paraphrase a passage from the *Saturday Evening Post* for the readers of *National Geographic World,* as you did in the preceding exercise, you write something that sounds different from the original. After all, the two versions satisfy different purposes and target different audiences. Good writers, able to negotiate a range of styles and levels of formality, have learned to adapt what they say to specific occasions. Official documents often demand formal usage, while notes to friends call for a more casual tone. Between these extremes lies a range of stylistic levels. Examples that follow illustrate various points along this spectrum.

First is a passage from the Gospel of Saint Luke in the King James Bible, a translation undertaken by English scholars of the early seventeenth century, the age of Shakespeare:

And it came to pass in those days, that there went out a decree from Caesar Augustus that all the world should be taxed. (And this taxing was first made when Cyrenius was governor of Syria.) And all went to be taxed, every one to his own city. And Joseph also went from Galilee, out of the city of Nazareth, into Judaea, unto the city of David, which is called Bethlehem (because he was of the house and lineage of David) to be taxed with Mary his espoused wife, being great with child. And so it was that, while they were there, the days were accomplished that she should be delivered. And she brought forth her firstborn son, and wrapped him in swaddling clothes and laid him in a manger, because there was no room for them in the inn.

   And there were in the same country shepherds abiding in the field, keeping watch over their flock by night. And, lo, the angel of the Lord came upon them, and the glory of the Lord shown round about them, and they were sore afraid. And the angel said unto them, "Fear not: for, behold, I bring you good tidings of great joy, which shall be to all people." For unto you is born this day in the city of David a Saviour, which is Christ the Lord. And this shall be a sign unto you: Ye shall find the babe wrapped in swaddling clothes, lying in a manger. And suddenly there was with the angel a multitude of the heavenly host praising God and saying, "Glory to God in the highest, and on earth peace, good will toward men." And it came to pass, as the angels were gone away from them into heaven, the shepherds said one to another, "Let us now go even unto Bethlehem and see this thing which is come to pass, which the Lord hath made known unto us." And they came with haste and found Mary and Joseph and the babe lying in a manger. And when they had seen it, they made known abroad the saying which was told them concerning this child.

The language of this passage is lofty and formal. Its vocabulary is elevated, even obscure in places; there are no contractions or colloquialisms (words or expressions more appropriate to conversation than public speech or writing). Still, a great many, probably most, English-speaking adults are so familiar with this narrative that it presents no real difficulties for them.

   However, the following passage from *The Best Christmas Pageant Ever,* a play by Barbara Robinson, shows how this biblical passage might confuse some native speakers of English. In this scene, the mother is directing a rehearsal for a nativity play. The Herdmans—Ralph, Leroy, Claude, and Imogene—have never attended a Christian worship service:

Mother: All right now *(finds the place and starts to read).* There went out a decree from Caesar Augustus that all the world should be taxed . . . *(All the kids are visibly bored and itchy, except the HERDMANS, who listen with the puzzled but determined concentration of people trying to make sense of a foreign language.)* . . . and Joseph went up from Galilee with Mary his wife, being great with child. . . .

Ralph: *(Not so much trying to shock, as he is pleased to understand something.)* Pregnant! She was pregnant! *(There is much giggling and tittering.)*

Mother: All right now, that's enough. We all know that Mary was pregnant. *(MOTHER continues reading, under the BETH-ALICE dialogue.)* . . . And it came to pass, while they were there, that the days were accomplished that she should be delivered, and she brought forth her firstborn son. . . .

Alice: *(to BETH)* I don't think it's very nice to say Mary was pregnant.

Beth: Well, she was.

Alice: I don't think *your mother* should say Mary was pregnant. It's better to say she was "great with child." I'm not supposed to talk about people being pregnant, especially in church.

Mother: *(reading)* . . . and wrapped him in swaddling clothes and laid him in a manger, because there was no room for them in the inn. . . .

Leroy: What's a manger? Some kind of bed?

Mother: Well, they didn't have a bed in the barn, so Mary had to use whatever there was. What would you do if you had a new baby and no bed to put the baby in? . . .

Claude: What were the wadded-up clothes.

Mother: The what?

Claude: *(pointing to the Bible)* It said there . . . she wrapped him in wadded up clothes?

Mother: *Swaddling* clothes. People used to wrap babies up very tightly in big pieces of material, to make them feel cozy. . . .

Imogene: You mean they tied him up and put him in a feedbox? Where was the Child Welfare?

To Alice (described in the cast of characters as a "prim, proper pain in the neck"), informal words like *pregnant* seem irreverent in this context. However, stage directions—the parenthetical comments in italic type—show that the Herdmans intend no irreverence. Thus, the excerpt highlights an important fact about language: As our nation grows more culturally diverse, we are less justified in assuming that any one way of phrasing information and ideas is inherently better, clearer, or more appropriate than all others.

Consider how the same Gospel passage appears in a more recent version of the Bible:

At that time Emperor Augustus ordered a census to be taken throughout the Roman Empire. When this first census took place, Quirinius was the governor of Syria. Everyone, then, went to register himself, each to his own home town.

Joseph went from the town of Nazareth in Galilee to the town of Bethlehem in Judea, the birthplace of King David. Joseph went there because he was a descendant of David. He went to register with Mary, who was promised in marriage to him. She was pregnant, and while they were in Bethlehem, the time came for her to have her baby. She gave birth to her first son, wrapped him in cloths and laid him in a manger—there was no room for them to stay in the inn.

There were some shepherds in that part of the country who were spending the night in the fields, taking care of their flocks. An angel of the Lord appeared to them, and the glory of the Lord shone over them. They were terribly afraid, but the angel said to them, "Don't be afraid! I am here with good news for you, which will bring great joy to all the people. This very day in David's town your Savior was born—Christ the Lord! And this is what will prove it to you: you will find a baby wrapped in cloths and lying in a manger."

Suddenly a great army of heaven's angels appeared with the angel, singing praises to God: "Glory to God in the highest heaven, and peace on earth to those with whom he is pleased!"

When the angels went away from them back into heaven, the shepherds said to one another, "Let's go to Bethlehem and see this thing that has happened, which the Lord has told us."

This version of the narrative uses familiar words, like *pregnant,* yet few people would consider it fundamentally less reverent than the King James version.

Paraphrasing in a Different Style	**EXERCISES**

1. The following texts are *parodies,* works that adopt—and often exaggerate—the language and style of a specialized field or variety of text. After reading each, try to determine what type of language or document it parodies.

a. Postal System Input Buffer Device

Robertson Osborne

Although no public announcement of the fact has been made, it is known that the United States Post Office Department for some time has been installing Postal System Input Buffer Devices as temporary information storage units on pseudo-randomly selected street corners. Several models are in use: some older ones are still to be found painted in a color which may be described as yellow-greenish in hue, low saturation, and low in brilliance, but a significantly large proportion are now appearing in a red, white, and blue combination which seems to provide greater user satisfaction although the associational-algebra value-functions remain obscure. Access to the majority of these devices is from the sidewalk, although a recent modification (including a 180-degree rotation about a vertical centerline) makes some of them accessible from an automobile, provided that the vehicle is equipped with either (a) a passenger in normal working condition, mounted upright on the front seat or (b) a driver having at least one arm on the right-hand side which is six feet long and double-jointed at the wrist and elbow. Figure 1 shows a typical sidewalk-access model Postal Input Buffer Device.

Most normal adults without previous experience can be readily trained to operate the machine. Children and extremely short adults may find it necessary to obtain assistance from a passerby[1] in order to complete steps 4 (Feed Cycle) and 6 (Verification), or both. The machine is normally operated as described below.

1. Position of Operator. Locate the Control Console (see Figure 1). Stand in front of the machine so that the control console is facing you.[2]

2. Initial Setup. Grasp the Multi-Function Control Lever (Figure 1). This lever performs several functions, each being uniquely determined by that portion of the Operation Cycle during which it is activated. The lever may be grasped with either hand. With the other hand, position the input in preparation for step 4 (Feed Cycle).

3. Start Operation. Pull the Multi-Function Control Lever toward you until it is fully extended. It will travel in a downward arc, as it is attached to a mechanical But Gate hinged at the bottom. (The But Gate, so named because it allows but one operation at a time, is specially designed to make feedback extremely difficult.) Pulling the Multi-Function Control Lever at this time accomplishes an Input Buffer Reset and Drop-Chute Clear. These actions are of interest only to the technician, but are mentioned here in preparation for the following note.

---

[1]In this context, *passerby* may be defined as a member of the set of human beings having a maximized probability of occupying the event space.

[2]The Novice Operator Trainee may prefer to face the console.

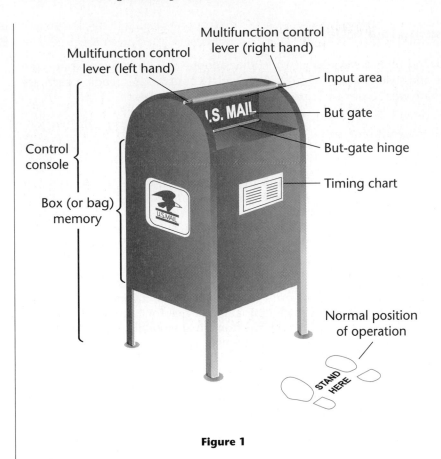

Multifunction control lever (left hand)

Multifunction control lever (right hand)

Input area

But gate

But-gate hinge

Control console

Timing chart

Box (or bag) memory

Normal position of operation

STAND HERE

Figure 1

NOTE: The lever should move freely. If it does not, the memory is full and cannot accept further information until it has been unloaded. The operator may elect to (a) wait for a Postal System Field Engineer (a "mail carrier") or (b) find another Postal System Input Buffer Device. If choice (b) is elected, refer to Description, above; also see Figure 1.

WARNING: Under no circumstances should the operator attempt to clear the unit; loss of a ring or wristwatch may result. In extreme cases, some individuals have lost thirty years.

4. Feed Cycle. Visually check to see that the input area is clear. The input area may be recognized because it is totally dark and makes a 90-degree downward turn; obstructions are hence not visible under normal circumstances. While holding the Multi-Function Control Lever in the extended position, start the input feed by manually inserting the information package.[3]

[3]Perhaps better known to some readers as a "letter" or "postcard."

NOTE: One particularly advantageous feature of the Postal Service Input Buffer Device is that, at this stage, the address field may be mixed alphanumerics (including special characters) and may be presented to the unit in normal format (reading left-to-right and top-to-bottom), backward, or even upside down.

5. Transfer Cycle. Release the Multi-Function Control Lever. The machine will now automatically transfer the input to the delay-box memory (delay-bag in some models). The operator will soon become familiar with the typical "squeak" and "clank" signals, provided on all models to indicate satisfactory operation of the But Gate. Actual transfer of the information, however, is not signalled unless the information is very densely packed, in which case a "thump" signal may occasionally be heard.

NOTE: A "boing" signal indicates that the information is unsuited to the Input Buffer Device and that a programming error has therefore occurred.

6. Verification. Pull the Multi-Function Control Lever again (see step 3), check to see that the Input Zone (Figure 1) is clear (see step 4), and release the lever. This completes one full Operation Cycle. Additional cycles, when necessitated by large input quantities, may be initiated by returning to step 1 (above).

NOTE: Step 6 is not actually necessary for machine operation. The Postal Service Input Buffer Device has been designed to permit this step, however, to satisfy the requirements of the overwhelming "Post-Mailing Peek Compulsion," which affects most users of the unit and which has been linked by some writers[4] to the "Unsatisfied Sex-Curiosity" Syndrome.

[4]*Op. cit.*

b. The Etiology and Treatment of Childhood[1,2]

Jordan W. Smoller, University of Pennsylvania

Childhood is a syndrome that has only recently begun to receive serious attention from clinicians. The syndrome itself, however, is not at all recent. As early as the eighth century, the Persian historian Kidnom made reference to "short, noisy creatures," who may well have been what we now call "children." The treatment of children, however, was unknown until this century, when so-called "child psychologists" and "child psychiatrists" became common. Despite this history of clinical neglect, it has been estimated that well over half of all Americans alive today have experienced childhood directly (Suess, 1983). In fact, the actual numbers are probably much higher, since these data are based on self-reports, which may be subject to social desirability biases and retrospective distortion.

The growing acceptance of childhood as a distinct phenomenon is reflected in the proposed inclusion of the syndrome in the upcoming *Diagnostic and Statistical Manual of Mental Disorders, 4th Edition,* or *DSM-IV,* of the American Psychiatric Association (1985).

[1]The author would like to thank all the little people.
[2]This research was funded in part by a grant from Bazooka Gum.

Clinicians are still in disagreement about the significant clinical features of childhood, but the proposed *DSM-IV* will almost certainly include the following core features:

1. Congenital onset
2. Dwarfism
3. Emotional lability and immaturity
4. Knowledge deficits
5. Legume anorexia

CLINICAL FEATURES OF CHILDHOOD

Although the focus of this paper is on the efficacy of conventional treatment of childhood, the five clinical markers mentioned above merit further discussion for those unfamiliar with this patient population.

Congenital Onset

In one of the few existing literature reviews on childhood, Temple-Black (1982) has noted that childhood is almost always present at birth, although it may go undetected for years or even remain subclinical indefinitely. This observation has led some investigators to speculate on a biological contribution to childhood. As one psychologist has put it, "we may soon be in a position to distinguish organic childhood from functional childhood" (Rogers, 1979).

Dwarfism

This is certainly the most familiar marker of childhood. It is widely known that children are physically short relative to the population at large. Indeed, common clinical wisdom suggests that the treatment of the so-called "small child" (or "tot") is particularly difficult. These children are known to exhibit infantile behavior and display a startling lack of insight (Tom & Jerry, 1967).

Emotional Lability and Immaturity

This aspect of childhood is often the only basis for a clinician's diagnosis. As a result, many otherwise normal adults are misdiagnosed as children and must suffer the unnecessary stigma of being labelled a "child" by professionals and friends alike.

Knowledge Deficits

While many children have IQ's within or even above the norm, almost all will manifest knowledge deficits. Anyone who has known a real child has experienced the frustration of trying to discuss any topic that requires some general knowledge. Children seem to have little knowledge about the world they live in. Politics, art, and science—children are largely ignorant of these. Perhaps it is because of this ignorance, but the sad fact is that most children have few friends who are not, themselves, children.

Legume Anorexia

This last identifying feature is perhaps the most unexpected. Folk wisdom is supported by empirical observation—children will rarely eat their vegetables (see Popeye, 1957, for review).

CAUSES OF CHILDHOOD

Now that we know what it is, what can we say about the causes of childhood? Recent years have seen a flurry of theory and speculation from a number of perspectives. Some of the most prominent are reviewed below.

Sociological Model

Emile Durkind was perhaps the first to speculate about sociological causes of childhood. He points out two key observations about children: 1) the vast majority of children are unemployed, and 2) children represent one of the least educated segments of our society. In fact, it has been estimated that less than twenty percent of children have had more than a fourth-grade education.

Clearly, children are an "out-group." Because of their intellectual handicap, children are even denied the right to vote. From the sociologist's perspective, treatment should be aimed at helping assimilate children into mainstream society. Unfortunately, some victims are so incapacitated by their childhood that they are simply not competent to work. One promising rehabilitation program (Spanky & Alfalfa, 1978) has trained victims of severe childhood to sell lemonade.

Biological Model

The observation that childhood is usually present from birth has led some to speculate on a biological contribution. An early investigation by Flintstone and Jetson (1939) indicated that childhood runs in families. Their survey of over eight thousand American families revealed that over half contained more than one child. Further investigation revealed that even most non-child family members had experienced childhood at some point. Cross-cultural studies (e.g., Mowgli & Din, 1950) indicate that familial childhood is even more prevalent in the Far East. For example, in Indian and Chinese families, as many as three out of four family members may have childhood.

Impressive evidence of a genetic component of childhood comes from a large-scale twin study by Brady and Partridge (1972). These authors studied over 106 pairs of twins, looking at concordance rates for childhood. Among identical or monozygotic twins, concordance was unusually high (.92), i.e., when one twin was diagnosed with childhood, the other twin was almost always a child as well.

Psychological Models

A considerable number of psychologically-based theories of the development of childhood exist. They are too numerous to review here. Among the more familiar models are Seligman's "learned childishness" model. According to this model, individuals who are treated like children eventually give up and become children. As a counterpoint to such theories, some experts have claimed that childhood does not really exist. Szasz (1980) has called "childhood" an expedient label. In seeking conformity, we handicap those whom we find unruly or too short to deal with by labeling them "children."

TREATMENT OF CHILDHOOD

Efforts to treat childhood are as old as the syndrome itself. Only in modern times, however, have humane and systematic treatment protocols been applied. In part, this increased attention to the problem may be due to the sheer number of individuals suffering from childhood. Government statistics (DHHS) reveal that there are more children alive today than at any time in our history. To paraphrase P. T. Barnum: "There's a child born every minute."

The overwhelming number of children has made government intervention inevitable. The nineteenth century saw the institution of what remains the largest single program for the treatment of childhood—so-called "public schools." Under this colossal program, individuals are placed into treatment groups based on the severity of their condition. For example, those most severely afflicted may be placed in a "kindergarten" program. Patients at this level are typically short, unruly, emotionally immature, and intellectually deficient. Given this type of individual, therapy is of necessity very basic. The strategy is essentially one of patient management and of helping the child master basic skills (e.g., finger-painting).

Unfortunately, the "school" system has been largely ineffective. Not only is the program a massive tax burden, but it has failed even to slow down the rising incidence of childhood.

Faced with this failure and the growing epidemic of childhood, mental health professionals are devoting increasing attention to the treatment of childhood. Given a theoretical framework by Freud's landmark treatises on childhood, child psychiatrists and psychologists claimed great successes in their clinical interventions.

By the 1950s, however, the clinicians' optimism had waned. Even after years of costly analysis, many victims remained children. The following case (taken from Gumbie & Poke, 1957) is typical.

> Billy J., age eight, was brought to treatment by his parents. Billy's affliction was painfully obvious. He stood only four feet, three inches, high and weighed a scant seventy pounds, despite the fact that he ate voraciously. Billy presented a variety of troubling symptoms. His voice was noticeably high for a man. He displayed legume anorexia, and, according to his parents, often refused to bathe. His intellectual functioning was also below normal—he had little general knowledge and could barely write a structured sentence. Social skills were also deficient. He often spoke inappropriately and exhibited "whining behavior." His sexual experience was nonexistent. Indeed, Billy considered women "icky."
>
> His parents reported that his condition had been present from birth, improving gradually after he was placed in a school at age five. The diagnosis was "primary childhood." After years of painstaking treatment, Billy improved gradually. At age eleven, his height and weight have increased, his social skills are broader, and he is now functional enough to hold down a "paper route."

After years this kind of frustration, startling new evidence has come to light which suggests that the prognosis in cases of childhood may not be all gloom. A critical review by Fudd (1972) noted that studies of the childhood syndrome tend to lack careful follow-up. Acting on this observation, Moe, Larrie, and Kirly (1974) began a large-scale longitudinal study. These investigators studied two groups. The first group comprised thirty-four children currently engaged in a long-term conventional treatment program. The second was a group of forty-two children receiving no treatment. All subjects had been diagnosed as children at least four years previously, with a mean duration of childhood of 6.4 years.

At the end of one year, the results confirmed the clinical wisdom that childhood is a refractory disorder—virtually all symptoms persisted and the treatment group was only slightly better off than the controls.

The results, however, of a careful ten-year follow-up were startling. The investigators (Moe, Larrie, Kirly, & Shemp, 1984) assessed the original cohort on a variety of measures. General knowledge and emotional maturity were assessed with standard measures. Height was assessed by the "metric system" (see Ruler, 1923), and legume appetite by the Vegetable Appetite Test (VAT) designed by Popeye (1968). Moe et al. found that subjects improved uniformly on all measures. Indeed, in most cases, the subjects appeared to be symptom-free. Moe et al. report a spontaneous remission rate of ninety-five percent, a finding which is certain to revolutionize the clinical approach to childhood.

These recent results suggest that the prognosis for victims of childhood may not be so bad as we have feared. We must not, however, become too complacent.

Despite its apparently high spontaneous remission rate, childhood remains one of the most serious and rapidly growing disorders facing mental health professionals today. And, beyond the psychological pain it brings, childhood has recently been linked to a number of physical disorders. Twenty years ago, Howdi, Doodi, and Beauzeau (1965) demonstrated a six-fold increased risk of chicken pox, measles, and mumps among children as compared with normal controls. Later, Barby and Kenn (1971) linked childhood to an elevated risk of accidents—compared with normal adults, victims of childhood were much more likely to scrape their knees, lose their teeth, and fall off their bikes.

Clearly, much more research is needed before we can give any real hope to the millions of victims wracked by this insidious disorder.

2. Translate two or three paragraphs from either of the above texts into a fundamentally different type of language: informal (adapted to the readers of newspapers and popular magazines), colloquial (conversational), or slang.

3. Write a short parody similar to either of the above, imitating or exaggerating a particular type of specialized language or document.

Paraphrasing an Argument

Objectivity is difficult when you must paraphrase an argument with which you disagree. Nevertheless, fairness and accuracy allow you to present yourself as a person of integrity and good will whose views deserve careful consideration.

The need to paraphrase an argument with which you disagree may arise under various circumstances, but let's consider one of the most familiar. Suppose you want to refute a commonly held opinion. You may wish to begin by demonstrating that you understand, have considered, and respect that opinion. One obstacle may be your *personal commitments.* Consider the following sentence from an essay by English professor Paul McBrearty, who argues for the elimination of anonymous student evaluations of college instructors:

> Anonymity in student evaluations virtually assures lowered academic standards and inflated grades. The pressures on teachers to *give* good grades so as to *get* good grades are severe, pervasive, unremitting, and inescapable.

A source that makes an argument

Though we happen to disagree with this argument, we do not consider the following a fair, objective paraphrase of the first sentence:

> Some college professors fear that students will use anonymous evaluations as a way of getting even for unfair grades.

An unacceptable paraphrase

This paraphrase states a claim that the author of the original passage is not really making. Specifically, it implies that *because* some college professors grade unfairly, they are afraid of student reprisals. What McBrearty is actually saying is that instructors should be able to grade both fairly and rigorously without fear of reprisal.

Another obstacle to paraphrase is overdependence on familiar patterns or *schemas.* Schemas are recurrent structures that help us make predictions about what a writer or speaker is going to say next. Most of the time, schemas allow us to read and listen efficiently. For example, the fourth sentence in the previous paragraph—"One obstacle can be your personal commitments"—leads most readers to expect that another obstacle will be discussed in a subsequent sentence or paragraph. A problem with schemas is, of course, that readers may take too much for granted and draw hasty assumptions about what a writer is about to say. Consider, for instance, the second sentence in the excerpt from McBrearty's article:

The original phrasing

> The pressures on teachers to *give* good grades so as to *get* good grades are severe, pervasive, unremitting, and inescapable.

At first glance, the following sentence may seem an appropriate paraphrase:

A hasty para-phrase

> Professors are tempted to bribe students with high grades.

Having encountered this claim before, a reader might be tempted to conclude that the author is preparing to make the same argument. Later in his essay, however, McBrearty asserts:

A statement made later in the same source

> Whenever student evaluations are used in any way by administrators as a basis for the denial of promotion, retention, or salary increase, or for assigning a less-than-satisfactory rating to a faculty member, the faculty member is denied the constitutional right of due process if not permitted to confront what are in effect his or her accusers.

Although we still do not find this argument valid, we must recognize that McBrearty is not suggesting that popular instructors are offering bribes, but rather that they may be responding to pressure in order to protect their jobs. Therefore, the following is a fairer paraphrase of the second sentence from the original passage:

A fairer para-phrase

> Professors fear that they will face the consequences of poor student evaluations if they grade rigorously.

Sometimes, writers must paraphrase arguments that not only diverge from their own opinions but also challenge their personal values. On these occasions, the best approach is to be explicit in attributing such an argument to its source. Suppose, for example, a writer who opposes censorship had to paraphrase the following passage from an essay by Barbara Lawrence titled "Four-Letter Words Can Hurt You":

A source that makes an argu-ment

> Obscene words . . . seem to serve a similar purpose: to reduce the human organism (especially the female organism) and human functions (especially sexual and procreative) to their least organic, most mechanical dimension; to substitute a trivializing or deforming resemblance for the complex human reality of what is being described.

A writer might emphasize that Lawrence's argument is incompatible with her own views by engaging in what we have referred to as descriptive paraphrase. In other words, she might use an **attribution phrase** to distance herself from the source—perhaps "According to Barbara Lawrence" or one of these alternatives:

Acceptable attribution phrases

> In an essay often cited by proponents of censorship, Barbara Lawrence argues . . .
>
> Lawrence presents an argument often raised by those who wish to suppress pornography. . . .

On the other hand, it would not be fair to use a slanted or loaded attribution phrase like "According to radical feminist Barbara Lawrence."

Earlier in this chapter, we spoke of the rare occasion for paraphrasing a source that uses language offensive to many readers. Equally unusual is the need to cite arguments that violate the generally permissive boundaries of academic inquiry and conversation. Though scholars must respect those with whom they disagree, we sometimes encounter ideas so hateful that we feel compelled to express disapproval. A number of years ago, one of our students found a periodical in the university library that he considered abusive and insulting to gay men and women as well as to religious minorities. To voice his indignation, the student wrote to the head librarian and, hoping to get his point across, paraphrased some of the views expressed in the periodical. Considering the circumstances, he felt justified in using these judgmental attribution phrases:

> Here we find the familiar homophobic claim that . . .
> Overt anti-Semitism emerges later, when . . .

Judgmental attribution phrases

Determining when to express judgment about paraphrased sources—or deciding that a particular opinion is out of bounds and therefore unworthy of paraphrase—is a sensitive issue in academic communities. However, it is generally best to avoid judgmental citations of sources unless there are clear and compelling reasons for doing so.

Paraphrasing an Argument

EXERCISE

Try to paraphrase each of the following arguments. Paraphrase only the argument, which appears in italic type; preceding sentences merely provide context.

a. The SAT has become a symbol—or, in the language of literary criticism, the objective correlative (that is, the object that correlates to the emotion)—of all the anxieties, concerns, fears, and frustrations in the college-admissions system. *The underlying issue,* I am forced to conclude, *is not, in fact, the test, but rather the nature, character, and degree of competition now endemic in college admissions—and in higher education generally.*
   —Lee Bollinger, "Debate over the SAT Masks Perilous Trends in College Admissions"

b. Standardized testing in public education was introduced to set a minimum standard of performance after thirty years of "education reform" was shown to be a failure—resulting in expensive schools run by educational bureaucrats who have miserably failed minority communities and inner-city students.
   Mastering standardized tests is a skill that is necessary to obtain credentials in just about any field—like it or not. Real education can easily accompany standardized tests.
   —Jeffrey Geibel, letter to the editor, *New York Times Magazine*

c. Sociologists have never demonstrated a firm connection between which college Americans attend and their success later in life.
   Ivy League graduates tend to do well financially, but it is unclear whether that reflects the added value of their elite education or merely that they were already primed for success when they applied to college.
   —Walter Shapiro, "Rejected by College of Choice? Relax"

Paraphrasing in Research Papers

As we have said earlier in this chapter, research writing often uses paraphrases sources in order to cite important information, to place a topic or issue in context, or to support an interpretation or opinion. In these cases, a writer must be careful to identify sources by name (usually in the form of parenthetical notes, which will be introduced in Chapter 6.)

Uses of paraphrase in research writing—particularly conventions of style and documentation—will be explained in greater detail in Chapter 12. The following examples simply illustrate various contexts in research writing that might call for paraphrase.

Paraphrasing to Cite Information

Suppose you are writing a research paper arguing for curtailed consumption of red meat. Using a direct quotation, you might open your paper this way:

Quoting to cite information

In his recent book, *Beyond Beef: The Rise and Fall of the Cattle Culture,* Jeremy Rifkin cites the following facts:

> Some 100,000 cows are slaughtered every twenty-four hours in the United States. In a given week, ninety-one percent of all United States households purchase beef. . . . Americans currently consume twenty-three percent of all the beef produced in the world. Today, the average American consumes sixty-five pounds of beef per year (154).

On the other hand, you might paraphrase the source to better effect. Consider this alternative:

Better: paraphrasing to cite information

> Americans are so addicted to beef that every week ninety-one percent of all families in the U.S. buy it. Because of this dietary preference, our country lays claim to nearly a fourth of the world's supply. Individually, each of us devours, on average, sixty-five pounds of beef each year, requiring a daily slaughter of 100,000 cows (Rifkin 154).

Although it may be easier simply to quote Jeremy Rifkin, there is no compelling reason to do so. Since there is nothing particularly unusual about his vocabulary or style, the basic information that he reports can be presented just as effectively in your own words.

Paraphrasing to Place a Topic or Issue in Context

Suppose that the college you attend has imposed restrictions on the use of air conditioning during summer sessions. Responding to outcries of opposition, you write an objective, researched study of the possible consequences of this unpopular measure—both its advantages as a conservation measure and its inevitable drawbacks. Recognizing the need for open-minded inquiry, you begin your report by addressing the widely held belief that air conditioning has become an indispensable comfort for nearly everyone in the United States. You might do this by paraphrasing the following passage from an essay by Frank Trippett:

A source that provides context for an issue

> [Air conditioning has] seduced families into retreating into houses with closed doors and shut windows, reducing the commonality of neighborhood life and all but obsoleting the front-porch society whose open casual folkways were an appealing feature of a sweatier America. Is it really surprising that the public's often

noted withdrawal into self-pursuit and privatism has coincided with the epic spread of air conditioning? Though science has little studied how habitual air conditioning affects mind or body, some medical experts suggest that, like other technical avoidance of natural swings in climate, air conditioning may take a toll on the human capacity to adapt to stress (Trippett 75).

Your opening paragraph might begin like this:

> Although most of us regard air conditioning as an unqualified blessing if not an absolute necessity, our dependence on it carries seldom examined consequences. Author Frank Trippett enumerates some of these consequences. For one thing, air conditioning has altered notions of neighborliness, luring people away from the front porch and into air-tight rooms where they have little contact with anyone outside the family. This seclusion may contribute to certain antisocial tendencies, such as self-absorption and extreme competitiveness. Also, Trippett suggests that while it remains an unproven theory, some scientists have suggested that air conditioning impairs our ability to cope with stress (75).

A paraphrase of the source

Notice that the author of the source, Trippett, is cited at the beginning of this paraphrase rather than in the parenthetical note at the end. (The parenthetical note must be retained, however, to identify the precise location of the borrowed ideas—page 75 of the magazine in which Trippett's article was published.)

Paraphrasing to Support an Interpretation or Opinion

Suppose that you are writing a paper arguing that the recording industry has grown too powerful. In the course of your research, you find the book *Music for Pleasure: Essays in the Sociology of Pop,* in which Simon Frith, a scholar of popular culture, argues that one consequence of the recording industry's power is suppression of certain kinds of musical talent:

> The industrialization of music means a shift from active musical production to passive pop consumption, the decline of folk or community or subcultural traditions, and a general loss of musical skill. The only instruments people like me can play today are their [CD] players and tape-decks (Frith 11).

A source that expresses an opinion

A paragraph in your research paper might open as follows:

> One consequence of the recording industry's power is the gradual decline of amateur musical talent. Simon Frith, a scholar of popular culture, has argued that the mass marketing of CDs has discouraged music-making by amateurs and undermined regional and ethnic traditions, thus limiting the acquisition and exercise of individual talent. Says Frith, "The only instruments people like me can play today are their [CD] players and tape-decks" (11).

A paraphrase of the source

There are two things to note about this paraphrase. First, when you use a source to support an opinion or interpretation, you normally choose a recognized authority. You are therefore more likely to identify the source in an acknowledgment phrase rather than a parenthetical note. (Notice that the paraphrase also cites the basis of Frith's authority—his being a scholar of popular culture—though it would not do so if he were a universally recognized person like Albert Einstein or Hillary Clinton.) The other thing you may notice about this paraphrase is that it incorporates a direct quotation. Since there really isn't any way to rephrase the last sentence without losing something, it is best to quote it directly.

Paraphrasing in Research Papers

For each of the following quotations, write a paraphrase appropriate to the situation at hand. Remember that you may choose to name the source before you paraphrase, or you may put the last name(s) of the source in a parenthetical note at the end, along with the page number.

a. You are enrolled in two thematically linked courses: History 203, American History from 1865 to the Present and English 224, Survey of American Literature. Students in these courses read and respond to common texts that relate to wealth in the United States. A paraphrase of the following source, which includes facts and information about the lives of wealthy people in the 1920s, allows you to place the setting of *The Great Gatsby* in historical context:

Source:
An article by James B. Twitchell, Professor of English at the University of Florida and author of the book *Living It Up: Our Love Affair with Luxury.* The quotation appears on page B7 of an article in the *Chronicle of Higher Education.* (*Note:* Dom Perignon is a type of champagne.)

Quotation:
Generations ago the market for luxury goods consisted of a few people who lived in majestic houses with a full complement of servants, in some time-honored enclave of the privileged. . . . They ordered their trunks from Louis Vitton, their trousseaux from Christian Dior, their Dom Perignon by the case, and spent lots of time looking out over the water. Their taste, like their politics, was determined largely by considerations of safeguarding wealth and perpetuating the social conventions that affirmed their sense of superiority.

b. You are enrolled in an anthropology course that introduces the aims and methods of archeology. A paraphrase of the following quotation illustrates the difficulty and urgency of identifying architectural landmarks that are not particularly old or historical and thus places zealous preservationism in some perspective.

Source:
An article by interior designer Brad Dunning in the *New York Times Magazine.* Dunning decries the demolition of a California house designed in 1963 by architect Richard Neutra, whose work is sometimes compared with that of Frank Lloyd Wright. The quotation appears on page 72.

Quotation:
Now that important modern architecture has finally achieved iconic stature, this is especially painful. Perhaps twenty years ago this wanton act might have been less shocking; the style had yet to achieve its lofty status. But at this point, when contemporary architecture has moved so far from the idealism and social engineering [it] intended—and realized—by these surviving gems, the thought that a house of this caliber would be in jeopardy escaped even the most paranoid preservationists.

c. As a student in an introductory education course, Teacher, School, and Society, you are asked to write a paper assessing the effectiveness of the abstinence movement as an alternative to sex education in public schools. You wish to support your opinion that the movement communicates a mixed message.

Source:
An article by Susan Dominus, editor of *Nerve,* a magazine about sex and culture. The quotation appears on page 10.

Quotation:
No wonder teenagers are drawn to Britney Spears, a proudly self-identifying virgin who practically pole-dances on prime-time TV and then says she's waiting for true love. In one navel-baring, camera-ready package, she personifies teenagers' semiotically schismatic world. . . . Spears saturates kids with sexuality; then . . . she tells them to guard their chastity.

GUIDELINES for Effective Paraphrasing

The general principles set forth in this chapter can be summed up in the following guidelines for effective paraphrasing:

- Paraphrasing involves a special kind of reading and response, appropriate when the occasion calls for close literal reading and accurate reporting.

- When you paraphrase a passage to make it suitable for a different audience, you should make appropriate adjustments in style, vocabulary, and degree of formality.

- When you paraphrase an argument, particularly one with which you disagree, you must be fair and objective.

- When you paraphrase a source in your research writing, you must completely recast information and ideas in your own language and style. Simple word substitution does not constitute a legitimate paraphrase; neither does rearrangement of word order.

READING SELECTION

With a PhD in biology, Barbara Ehrenreich began her career as a political essayist and social critic. In researching her most recent book, *Nickel and Dimed: Surviving in Low-Wage America,* Ehrenreich worked in a variety of jobs at the minimum wage. The following essay, which describes one of her jobs, appeared in the *New York Times.*

Another Day, Another Indignity

BARBARA EHRENREICH

Only a person of unblemished virtue can get a job at Wal-Mart—a low-level job, that   1
is, sorting stock, unloading trucks, or operating a cash register. A drug test eliminates the chemical miscreants; a detailed "personality test" probes the job applicant's horror of theft and willingness to turn in an erring co-worker.

2   Extreme submissiveness to authority is another desirable trait. When I applied for a job at Wal-Mart in the spring of 2000, I was reprimanded for getting something "wrong" on this test: I had agreed only "strongly" to the proposition, "All rules have to be followed to the letter at all times." The correct answer was "totally agree."

3   Apparently the one rule that need not be slavishly adhered to at Wal-Mart is the federal Fair Labor Standards Act, which requires that employees be paid time and a half if they work more than forty hours in a week. Present and former Wal-Mart employees in twenty-eight states are suing the company for failure to pay overtime.

4   A Wal-Mart spokesman says it is company policy "to pay its employees properly for the hours they work." Maybe so, but it wasn't a policy I remember being emphasized in the eight-hour orientation session all new "associates" are required to attend. The session included a video on "associate honesty" that showed a cashier being caught on videotape as he pocketed some bills from the cash register. Drums beat ominously as he was led away in handcuffs and sentenced to four years in prison.

5   The personnel director warned us, in addition, against "time theft," or the use of company time for anything other than work—"anything at all," she said, which was interpreted in my store as including trips to the bathroom. We were to punch out even for our two breaks, to make sure we did not exceed the allotted fifteen minutes.

6   It turns out, however, that Wal-Mart management doesn't hold itself to the same standard of rectitude it expects from its low-paid employees. My first inkling of this came in the form of a warning from a coworker not to let myself be persuaded to work overtime because, she explained, Wal-Mart doesn't pay overtime. Naively, I told her this was impossible; such a large company would surely not be flouting federal law.

7   I should have known better. We had been apprised, during orientation, that even after punching out, associates were required to wait on any customers who might approach them. Thanks to the further requirement that associates wear their blue and yellow vests until the moment they went out the door, there was no avoiding pesky last-minute customers.

8   Now some present and former employees have filed lawsuits against Wal-Mart. They say they were ordered to punch out after an eight-hour shift and then continue working for no pay. In a practice, reported in the [New York] *Times,* that you might expect to find only in a third-world sweatshop, Wal-Mart store managers in six states have locked the doors at closing time, some employees say, forcing all present to remain for an hour or more of unpaid labor.

9   This is "time theft" on a grand scale—practically a mass mugging. Of course, in my brief experience while doing research for a book on low-wage work, I found such practices or milder versions of them by no means confined to Wal-Mart.

10   At a Midwestern chain store selling hardware and lumber, I was offered an eleven-hour shift five days a week—with no overtime pay for the extra fifteen hours. A corporate-run housecleaning service paid a startling wage of only $6.65 an hour but required us to show up in the morning forty minutes before the clock started running—for meetings and to prepare for work by filling our buckets with cleaning supplies.

What has been revealed in corporate America . . . is a two-tiered system of morality: Low-paid employees are required to be hard-working, law-abiding, rule-respecting straight arrows. More than that, they are often expected to exhibit a selfless generosity toward the company, readily "donating" chunks of their time free of charge. Meanwhile, as we have learned from the cases of Enron, Adelphia, ImClone, WorldCom, and others, many top executives have apparently felt free to do whatever they want—conceal debts, lie about profits, engage in insider trading—to the dismay and sometimes ruin of their stockholders.

But investors are not the only victims of the corporate crime wave. Workers also   **11**
suffer from management greed and dishonesty. In Wal-Mart's case, the moral gravity
of its infractions is compounded by the poverty of its "associates," many of whom are
paid less than $10 an hour. As workers discover that their problem is not just a rogue
store manager or "bad apple" but management as a whole, we can expect at the very
least widespread cynicism, and perhaps an epidemic of rule-breaking from below.

Freewriting

Freewrite for ten to fifteen minutes about Ehrenreich's account of working conditions at Wal-Mart. You may write about anything you've learned, perhaps comparing or contrasting your own experiences as an employee with those of the author. On the other hand, you might consider whether and how this essay changes
your perspectives as a customer or consumer.

Group Work

Share freewrites in your group, each member reading aloud while others are taking notes. As you listen, try to develop a list of rules (often unwritten) and expectations (often unstated) that influence employee behavior, relationships between
workers and employers, and notions about ethical conduct in the workplace.

Review Questions

1. What screening techniques do Wal-Mart managers use to avoid hiring persons they consider undesirable?

2. How does Wal-Mart define "time theft"? In what sense, according to Ehrenreich, does the company itself engage in a different variety of time theft?

3. What "two-tiered system of morality" does Ehrenreich perceive in corporate culture?

Discussion Questions

1. Do you think Ehrenreich's audience, readers of the *New York Times*, is any
   more or less likely to shop or work at Wal-Mart than Americans in general?
   Does it matter? How do you think Ehrenreich hopes to influence her audience? That is, what would she like them to feel, understand, or do?

2. Is Ehrenreich challenging or appealing to the traditional American work
   ethic? If both, which aspects of the work ethic does her article challenge,
   and which does it validate?

3. While coworkers struggled to make a living, Ehrenreich was conducting sur-
   reptitious research. Does this affect her reliability as an observer or reporter?
   If so, how? How do you suppose her coworkers would respond to her article?

Writing

1. Citing the same kinds of information that Ehrenreich presents in her article, freewrite for at least fifteen minutes about your worst (or best) job. Using details from your freewriting along with information from Ehrenreich's article, write an essay that explains and illustrates the defining features of a bad (or good) job.

2. Each December, *Multinational Monitor* names its "Ten Worst Corporations"; in January, *Fortune* magazine releases its annual list of "The 100 Best Companies to Work for in America." Locate the appropriate issues of both periodicals for the past three years, looking either in your college library or the two following Web sites:
   <http:// www.essential.org/monitor>
   <http://www.fortune.com/fortune/lists/bestcompanies/index.html>
   Use your findings to develop criteria for evaluating a future workplace.

WRITE, READ, and RESEARCH the NET

1. *Write:* Freewrite for fifteen minutes about anything you have read, observed, or experienced regarding work in the retail sector. If this proves difficult, you may focus your freewriting on low-wage work in general or on your experiences and observations as a shopper in one or more of the larger discount chains (Kmart, Target, Wal-Mart).

2. *Read:* Consult the following two Web sites:
   <http://www.walmartstores.com/wmstore/wmstores/HomePage.jsp>
   <http://www.walmartwatch.org/>

3. *Research:* Using the index to the *Wall Street Journal,* which should be available online or in hardbound volumes in your library, scan the brief descriptions of articles listed under the heading "Wal-Mart." You may also consult the Wal-Mart homepage:
   <http://www.walmartstores.com/wmstore/wmstores/HomePage.jsp>
   Using any information you can gather about Wal-Mart's record as an employer and its response to criticism, write an essay assessing the reliability of Ehrenreich's article.

■ ADDITIONAL READINGS

The following readings deal with various types of low-paying work. First is a review of Iain Levison's *A Working Stiff's Manifesto,* a memoir similar to Barbara Ehrenreich's *Nickel and Dimed.* Following are articles by Lisa Black, a reporter for the *Chicago Tribune,* and Peter King, writer for the *Los Angeles Times,* who both argue for the long-term benefits of such jobs.

Get a Job

JONATHAN MILES

"In the last ten years, I've had forty-two jobs in six states," Iain Levison tells us. He can now add "writer" to a résumé that includes film-set gofer, fish cutter, oil truck driver, cook, mover, crab fisherman, and thirty-six other job titles. Anyone who finds these numbers startling probably hasn't put in any time behind a restaurant prep line or a retail counter lately, or has missed reading Barbara Ehrenreich's *Nickel and Dimed* and Ben Cheever's *Selling Ben Cheever,* two similar recent first-person chronicles about zigzagging through the lower levels of the American workplace. As Levison notes, "a million others" could have written the same book he has, a claim worth disputing on a literary level only.

"I have become, without realizing it, an itinerant worker, a modern-day Tom Joad," Levison writes, between pungent recountings of his on-the-clock misadventures. This revelation comes as something of a surprise to Levison, who—fresh out of college and the Army, and ripe with all the correct intentions—expected something different. "There was an unspoken agreement between me and the Fates that, as I lived in the richest country in the history of the world, and was a fairly hard worker, all these things"—a house, a wife, a serviceable car, a fenced-in yard—"would just come together eventually." In February, touting his economic proposals, George W. Bush proclaimed that jobs lead to "more independence, more self-esteem and more joy and hope." But while Bush's own job may have provided him those blessings, Levison and millions of other Americans have discovered that hourly jobs lead not to joy or to hope but only to different hourly jobs. "It's surviving," Levison says, "but surviving sounds dramatic, and this life lacks drama. It's scraping by."

To be fair, Levison is often a lousy hire. His overeducation makes him impatient lugging other people's stuff around, even though it qualifies him for little else. From a chi-chi Manhattan grocery he steals as much Chilean sea bass as he can fit into his pants. He cooks the log books on trucking runs, blows up the head of a lawn statue he mistakes for a heating-oil tank by pumping fuel into it, and on job applications he writes "the moon" for where he went to grade school and "compulsive masturbation" for his hobbies. But this last tack, like many of his others, is reactive rather than proactive, to crib from the current corporate parlance. "They'll hire me on nothing but a drug test," he writes, so what's the use? And this, more than anything else, is what chafes him.

Despite scattered grumblings, Levison's beef with his myriad employers isn't about money. "The real problem is with the expendability of us all. One human is as good as the next. Loyalty and effort are not rewarded."

The last ten years have supposedly seen the demise of the "Organization Man," the archetype of employee-employer fidelity that William H. Whyte posited in his 1956 classic of that name. The breakdown of that conformist ideology has proved a boon to white-collar workers, enabling them to manage their career arcs far more independently. For the unskilled labor pool, however, it has yielded few rewards. Working the same job all your life may strike many as a nightmare out of the 1950s, but for those like Levison it sometimes sounds like a merciful dream. "I have a job," he writes glumly. "Here we go again."

Unlike Ehrenreich and Cheever, who ventured into workplaces as undercover reporters, Levison is the real deal, less a correspondent than a combatant. Levison's account lacks the Michael Harrington-like[1] ambitions of Ehrenreich's book and the

---

[1]Michael Harrington (1928–89), author of *The Other America*, brought public attention to economic inequities in America (editor's note).

writerly *savoir faire* of Cheever's, but it bears an immediacy that neither of those authors can quite match. That said, "A Working Stiff's Manifesto" is at times lopsided, knee-jerk, and braying; but it is also bracing, hilarious, and dead on. "It wasn't supposed to be like this," Levison writes, but if there's naïveté involved (and there is), it's a communal naïveté. It's called the American Dream.

Before College, Start with a Side Order

Lisa Black

1 For all you high-school graduates preparing for college this fall, here are two words of advice:

2   Wait tables.

3   You will hone organization skills and learn humility, find out how to best approach a group of strangers, and recognize when to stay away.

4   You will be tested on math, learning to count back change from the deep crevices of bill-stuffed aprons.

5   And you will perfect a fake smile, for those times when old ladies bring in their own tea bags or a family begins arguing over their nachos or when small children blow their straw wrappers at you.

6   You will figure out why it's never a good idea to chew gum while taking orders. And you will be reminded what's important about getting your college education, anyway. (No offense to career waiters, but anxiety dreams featuring endless tables awaiting service is not normal.)

7   Best of all, working in the restaurant business provides a daily melodrama rivaling any soap. The waiters date the bartenders, the bartenders date the patrons, and the patrons date one another.

8   The gossip can get you promoted, or fired, as was the case when one financially challenged waitress bragged that she routinely added a quarter to her soft drink sales and pocketed the profit.

9   On the floor, you realize just how funny some people are about food. ("I'll have a plain hamburger, cut in half, mayonnaise on the side, without the bun.")

10   Groups of women always want to divide the checks. And often are more stingy about tipping.

11   At the bar, you will rarely know the regular customers by name, but think of them by drink order. For instance, Mr. Miller Lite/Wild Turkey-shot-on-the-side, or Ms. Brandy Alexander. In every college town, there's always the cheap-tipping-coffee-drinking-guy-who-hogs-booth-all-night-to-study.

12   The hours are flexible. At least, if you are. Working split shifts and double-shifts gives you the opportunity to budget your time wisely.

13   And talk about sharpening those problem-solving skills.

14   Consider these real-life situations from one English pub, where waiters would occasionally receive after-hour shots of ouzo in lieu of tips:

A man walks in, looks at the wine list, and orders a "Red Rose Chablis" (pronounced cha-bliss). Do you:

a. Laugh hysterically at his pronunciation of chablis?

b. Mix the three types of wine together in one glass?

c. Explain politely that you're out of cha-bliss and you'll bring him the red rose? This isn't one of those high-falutin' white tablecloth places, anyway.

Or four college students have begun pyramids with their empty beer cans, those super-size twenty-four-ounce kind, and are singing German folk songs. Loudly. Do you:

a. Pretend one of them asked for the check and hope they're too drunk to argue?

b. Join them when they ask for your company?

c. Knock down their pyramid and run away, giggling?

Or say you spy someone stealing a ten-dollar tip from a neighboring table minutes after the occupants have left. Do you:

a. Add ten dollars to the thief's bill?

b. Chew them out, lie, and tell them you're a single mother whose children haven't eaten solid food in a month and, by God, they should be ashamed of themselves?

c. Sneak something special under their hamburger bun, a choice bug, for instance?

The answer to all these questions is C, of course.

15 With all seriousness, if you take an extended break from college and lose your way for a while, you'll find few better ways to motivate your return than being forced to sweep french fries and cracker crumbs out from under tables at 2:00 a.m.

16 You'll learn to treat people better when you're sitting on the other side of the serving table, maybe even forgive them if they drop a drink in your lap.

17 Mostly, you'll find that paying for rent with crumpled bills and quarters makes for one very hard way to earn a living.

Revisiting the Lessons of Youth

Peter H. King

1 It is twilight. I am standing outside a locked wire fence that surrounds the feedlot where I worked three summers as a teenager. A new owner, I'm told, is attempting to revive the operation yet again, but for now the place seems a ghostly wreck.

2 Pens that once held as many as fifty thousand head of cattle are all but empty. The grain elevators and storage tanks sleep under blankets of rust. Squirrels dart about everywhere on frantic sundown missions.

3 Of course, twilight always was a strange, melancholy time at Noble's Land and Cattle Company feedlot. At dusk the hiss and thrum of the mill would cease, and the cattle would rise up by the thousands and shuffle about inside their pens. This stirring would send up thick clouds of dust that, backlighted by the fading sun, turned golden red. And the dominant sound was that of tens of thousands of hooves thudding against the dirt—a herd on the march to nowhere.

4 I have come back here to make a list. It is a list of all the things I learned nearly thirty years ago in three summers at this feedlot. My list-making was triggered by a newspaper headline. "Summer Work Is Out of Favor with the Young," the headline declared. When I spotted this headline my first reaction was: Good for the young.

5 I was remembering, sourly, how difficult it had been to haul my then skinny frame out of bed at 4:30 a.m. every day, six days a week, for the thirty-five-mile drive to the feedlot and twelve hours of low-wage work. I was forgetting all that I learned in those summers. For instance, how to cool beer with a fire extinguisher. . . .

6 On slow Saturday afternoons the mill hands would gather in the cinder-block control room with a six-pack of beer. They'd set the cans against a wall and blast them with the gas of a fire extinguisher, chilling the beer in a flash. This, though, was not the only lesson I took away from my summer work experience. In fact, I am a bit startled by the length of the list I've built in the half-hour I've been here, peering through the fence at the ghost mill, remembering.

7   Here was where I learned how to talk to truck drivers. They'd pull in by the score each morning, hauling grain, and as they waited to dump their loads, they'd share with me, the sixteen-year-old grain-tester, stories from the road. These tended to fall into two main categories: stories about outwitting the California Highway Patrol and stories about carnal adventures at truck stops.

8   Here I learned about work, hard, physical work in the oven that is the [San Fernando] Valley in August. This probably explains why the jobs I've held since all have been of the kind that require soft chairs and indoor "work" stations.

9   My views on immigration were formed here. I worked alongside men from Mexico. They were not "aliens," though I assume some were a bit short in the paperwork department. They were not "invaders." They were just men who worked hard and talked dreamily about saving enough money to return home and start cattle ranches of their own.

10   I learned about maintaining perspective. A good day was one spent driving air-conditioned trucks through the pens, delivering feed to the cattle. On a bad day they'd hand us a shovel and send us out to scoop manure from the troughs.

11   "It all pays the same," one of the veteran hands would say with a shrug.

12   I learned about mistakes. I once managed with one wrong pull of a skip loader lever to unleash a river of molasses across the feedlot. It took the entire crew all day to clean up the mess, a massive operation, and the total damage was calculated to be in the tens of thousands of dollars. The foreman who informed me how much I had cost the company said he wasn't going to fire me or even chew me out. It was clear, he said softly, I already felt rotten enough.

13   I learned not everybody is born lucky. There was a worker named Alvin, a stumpy little man who once had a job flagging for a crop duster. He was standing in the road one day, waving a flag to show the pilot where to spray, when a woman in a Cadillac struck Alvin and dragged him some amazing distance. He lived, only to be sued by the motorist for the damage his face caused to her bumper. This story was told on Alvin again and again in the little cafeteria where we ate lunch. He didn't seem to mind. He'd listen, blush, and smile his broken smile, ruefully shaking his head at his own misfortune.

14   I could keep going, but the point should be clear by now. When I was young and ignorant of the world, I landed by luck on the other side of this fence and found out some things no college or summer camp could have taught me—a common enough experience. And please don't get me wrong. I am not saying that I learned the answers to all of life's riddles at this feedlot; I suspect I didn't even learn a fraction of the right questions.

15   For instance, none of my rustic tutors ever told me how tedious, seemingly endless, twelve-hour workdays with distance will become mere tics in a life that seems to race along all too fast. Nobody in that lunchroom ever suggested that in thirty years I might come back and find all of them scattered and gone and the place overrun by squirrels.

4 *Reading for the Main Idea*

The reading strategies presented in Chapter 2 serve a number of purposes. One of the most important is to help you see, quickly and clearly, what a writer is getting at. Normally, when readers approach a text, the first question that confronts them is "What is this about?" or "What is the ***main idea***?" Being able to recognize, understand, and restate the main idea of a text is useful in carrying out a variety of academic tasks, including library research.

Defining main idea as a concept, however, is not so easy. Chapters 1 and 2 have demonstrated how individual readers *create meaning* when they bring their unique personal histories to a text. Consequently, no two readers are likely to experience a long, complex piece of writing (the novel *Moby Dick*, e.g.) in precisely the same way. In an effort to account for this diversity, one modern philosopher has declared that "every reading is a misreading." In the face of such views, you may ask how it is possible to arrive at anything like the main idea of a reading.

There is no easy answer to that question because the meaning of a written text does not belong entirely to the writer, nor entirely to the reader. Instead, readers and writers negotiate meaning collaboratively. Under ideal circumstances, this is how reading operates. But in order for the negotiation to proceed smoothly and predictably, both writer and reader must agree on and abide by certain established conventions. When you tried reading a passage in Chapter 2 that defied one of those conventions—an informative title—the collaboration between you and the writer suffered.

Basically, writers plant clues and signals, while readers respond to them in relatively consistent and predictable ways. This chapter focuses on the unwritten rules of this reciprocal process. Familiarity with these rules should help you hold up your end of the transaction between writer and reader.

GENERAL AND SPECIFIC CATEGORIES

When the main idea of a written text can be captured in a sentence, that sentence is a *general* statement, broader than other statements in the same text, which are more *specific.* Distinguishing between general and specific is an important aspect of reading for the main idea. Following is a list of words that illustrates the distinction:

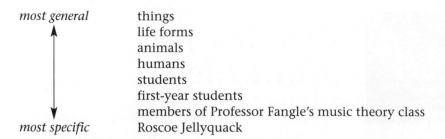

most general → things
life forms
animals
humans
students
first-year students
members of Professor Fangle's music theory class
most specific → Roscoe Jellyquack

Each item in the list is more specific, and therefore less general, than the one above it. As a category, each encompasses fewer members. The first item includes everything in the universe, while the last includes only a single individual. Roscoe belongs to each category; his dog Elmo belongs to just the first four; and Elmo's flea collar is a member of only the most general category, things.

Statements can also be arranged in general-to-specific order:

- Some people have qualities not shared by everyone.
- Jo Ann has many exceptional traits.
- Most notable is her superhuman will power.
- She can stick to her diet no matter how great the temptation.
- Monday, when I offered her a pastry, Jo Ann turned it down for an apple.

Again, each statement is a more specific instance of the statement before it. Each bears a *for example* relationship to the one it follows, and the examples cover less and less territory. The last one is a very specific, **concrete** statement, one that presents a picture you can visualize in your imagination—a particular event at a particular time involving particular people. In contrast, the first one is a very general, **abstract** statement, one that calls up an idea but not a specific event that you can see with your mind's eye. Recognizing the relationship between general, abstract statements and specific, concrete statements is essential to efficient reading.

EXERCISES | **General and Specific Categories**

1. Arrange the following lists in order from the most general to the most specific:

a. loafer
footwear
casual shoe
Colonel Eggslump's right loafer
garment
product
shoe

b. The College of Arts and Sciences
higher education
Natural History of Intertidal Organisms 553
The Marine Biology Option

Zenith State University
Department of Biology
Division of Physical Sciences

c. Madame DeShamble lacked concern for her fellow creatures.
Madame DeShamble cut off the tails of blind mice with a carving knife.
Madame DeShamble was a heartless person.
Madame DeShamble was cruel to animals.

d. Words can affect their hearers.
The cry "Give me liberty or give me death" aroused support for independence.
Political oratory can be particularly stirring.
Some statements provoke people's emotions.

2. For each of the following categories, provide one that is more general and another that is more specific:

a. chair
b. circus performer
c. Walter loves Connie.
d. Parents often urge their teenaged children to do well in school.

DEDUCTIVE AND INDUCTIVE ORGANIZATION

Within almost any passage, some statements are more general than others. Often, the way a writer arranges general and specific statements is important. Notice, for example, that the passage on page 86, which you examined in Chapter 2, contains four levels of generality. If we number those levels from 1 (most general) to 4 (most specific) and indent each level of specificity farther to the right, relationships among sentences become visible.

1 Scarfe was always a tyrant in his household.
　2 The servants lived in constant terror of his diatribes, which he would deliver whenever he was displeased.
　　3 One of the most frequent causes of his displeasure was the food they served him.
　　　4 His tea, for example, was either too hot or too cold.
　　　4 His soup had either too much or too little seasoning.
　　3 Another pet peeve was the servants' manner of address.
　　　4 God help the butler who forgot to add *sir* to every sentence he spoke to Scarfe, or the chauffeur whose tone was deemed not properly deferential.
　　　4 On the other hand, when one of the more timid parlor maids would hesitate in speaking so as to be certain her words did not give offense, he would thunder at her, "Out with it, you stupid girl."
　2 Scarfe's wife and children were equally the victims of his tyranny.

The most general sentence, at level 1, presents the main idea of the entire passage—that Scarfe was a tyrant in his household. Each level-2 sentence identifies victims of his tyranny. Likewise, level-3 sentences specify the supposed provocations of these victims, and level-4 statements provide concrete examples of those provocations. For the most part, then, sentences in the passage are arranged in a general-to-specific sequence.

Unlike the Scarfe passage, the explanatory paragraph you have just read ("The most general sentence . . .") is arranged in a specific-to-general order. Its first three sentences make specific statements before the last sentence sums them up in a general conclusion.

In general-to-specific, or *deductive,* passages, the writer begins by stating the main idea in a general way, then demonstrates it with specific examples or explanations. In specific-to-general, or *inductive,* passages, the writer takes you through a sequence of discovery, with the main idea coming as a conclusion reached after specific evidence has been presented.

Deductive arrangements are far more common than inductive, although few passages are as neatly organized or as multileveled as the one about Scarfe.

EXERCISES | **Deductive and Inductive Passages**

1. Decide whether each of the following passages is arranged in a deductive (general-to-specific) or inductive (specific-to-general) order:

a. Gold permeates our culture—and our language. There's the Golden Gate Bridge in San Francisco, and the golden rule. The golden age and the gold card. The Golden Gloves and Gold's Gym. High-quality goods are "good as gold." In the Olympics—as in so many other realms—gold is a symbol of excellence, wealth, and enduring value.

—Daniel Gross, "All That Glitters"

b. "Grilled slice of fresh foie gras served with a stew of corn, red beans, chickpeas, green peas, and duck jus."

"Beef short ribs braised in a rich Khmer broth with fresh ginger, garlic, young coconut juice, mushroom soy, tamarind, and chiles."

"Roasted lamb loin with a light curry sauce, garnished with plantain, mango, raisins, and couscous tabouleh."

"Tuna tartare with fresh wasabi, Sevruga caviar, cucumber, radish, and a Meyer lemon coulis."

These descriptions, drawn from different menus, exemplify the modern restaurant practice of listing as many exotic components as possible.

—Cullen Murphy, "From Soup to Nuts: The Categorical Imperative"

c. . . . While good things often happen to people at the movies, from first kisses to healing laughter, bad things happen too. John Dillinger got nailed by the F.B.I. while leaving a gangster movie in Chicago. Frank Sinatra had his clothes ripped off by young fans at the Paramount Theater in Brooklyn. When the song *Rock around the Clock* started playing during *Blackboard Jungle,* teenagers all over got so riled up that the police were called in. Lee Harvey Oswald went to the movies to hide after

John F. Kennedy's assassination in Dallas. Patty Hearst first met terrorist Kathy Soliah at a Oakland drive-in theater. Gang violence broke out in 1979 at Walter Hill's *Warriors,* and twelve years later, there was a shooting incident at a screening of *New Jack City* in Brooklyn. And who can forget Paul Rubens, aka Pee-Wee Herman, and his big adventure in a porn theater in Florida?

—Bob Morris, "Baltimore Babylon"

2. This paragraph, which describes a scholarly book by Gershon Legman, *The Rationale of the Dirty Joke,* contains several levels of generality. Try to number each sentence in the same fashion as the Scarfe passage on page 159.

A passionately felt personal manifesto—like all of Legman's work—the *Rationale* boils over with learned allusions, psychoanalytic evaluations, value judgments, and irrational attacks. In the space of a single page, he might dabble in philosophy, attack medicine, engage in literary critique, and offer a personal anecdote about his intimate relationships with women. His prose is always full of liberating verve, color, and exhaustively documented diatribes, relieved from time to time by wonderfully slanderous attacks on famous people and attention to scarcely relevant minutiae. At one point, for example, apropos of nothing, he launches into a rant against the regression to the anal stage that he claims is behind the interest in deodorants: "The natural odors of the woman are to be washed away as 'dirt,' and are to be replaced by the anal and genital secretions of deer (musk), skunks (civet), beavers (castors), and diseased whales (ambergris) at $30 an ounce. . . ."

—Mikita Brottman, "The Scholar Who Found a Life's Work in Dirty Jokes"

3. How would you characterize the organization of the following poem?

Lying in a Hammock at William Duffy's Farm in Pine Island, Minnesota

James Wright

> Over my head, I see the bronze butterfly,
> Asleep on the black trunk,
> Blowing like a leaf in green shadow.
> Down the ravine behind the empty house,
> The cowbells follow one another
> Into the distances of the afternoon.
> To my right,
> In a field of sunlight between two pines,
> The droppings of last year's horses
> Blaze up into golden stones.
> I lean back, as the evening darkens and comes on.
> A chicken hawk floats over, looking for home.
> I have wasted my life.

4. Write another version of the second paragraph of the Scarfe passage, beginning with the sentence "Scarfe's wife and children . . . ," inventing details for your sentences as needed. Make the sentences in your paragraph follow this pattern: 2, 3, 4, 4, 3, 4, 4.

THESIS STATEMENTS AND TOPIC SENTENCES

Sometimes, as the preceding examples have demonstrated, writers condense the main idea of a passage into a single sentence. When one sentence states the main idea of an entire essay (or a longer text, such as a research paper or a book chapter), it is called a *thesis statement.* When a statement within a single paragraph states its main idea, it is called a *topic sentence.*

Identifying Topic Sentences

Not every paragraph has a topic sentence (in fact, fewer than half do), just as not every longer text has an explicit thesis statement. When topic and thesis sentences appear, however, they are valuable reading clues, helping readers recognize a writer's intentions and anticipate what may follow. It pays to notice them. Since a deductive arrangement is much more common than an inductive one, topic sentences appear most frequently at the beginning of paragraphs, introducing and preparing for the supporting sentences that follow. Less often, they come at the end of a paragraph, summing up or drawing conclusions from preceding statements. As you read the following paragraphs, see if you can identify topic sentences.

> The effect of an ice age is dramatic. It does not just ice up the poles but drops temperatures everywhere around the world by about ten degrees centigrade. The world's wildlife gets squeezed into a band near the equator and even here life is hardly comfortable. The vast polar ice packs lock up a lot of the earth's water, disrupting rainfall and turning previously lush tropical areas into drought-stricken deserts.
>
> —John McCrone, *The Ape That Spoke*

> In the Medieval Glass of Canterbury Cathedral, an angel appears to the sleeping wise men and warns them to go straight home and not return to Herod. Below, the corresponding event from the Old Testament teaches the faithful that each moment of Jesus's life replays a piece of the past and that God has put meaning into time—Lot turns round and his wife becomes a pillar of salt (the white glass forming a striking contrast with the glittering colors that surround her). The common themes of both incidents: don't look back.
>
> —Stephen Jay Gould, *The Flamingo's Smile*

The first paragraph opens with a topic sentence that is perfectly straight-forward: *The effect of an ice age is dramatic.* This sentence facilitates reading by indicating what will follow: examples that illustrate the idea expressed in the topic sentence—in this case, with three dramatic consequences of an ice age. The second paragraph, arranged inductively, offers no such clue at the beginning. Instead, the author begins with specific evidence: He describes stained-glass representations of two biblical episodes. A topic sentence comes at the end, drawing a general conclusion from the evidence: Both episodes illustrate a common theme.

Identifying Topic Sentences

1. Identify the topic sentences in each of the sample paragraphs in Exercise 1 on pages 160–61.

2. Identify the topic sentence in each of the following passages:

a. People have always been disposed toward giving unsolicited advice. Now, with end-less television channels, the Internet, and a self-help publishing industry as active as the herpes virus, some of us are so thoroughly inebriated with knowledge that the only way to get it out of our systems, apparently, is by expelling it at others. There are wilderness survival guides by enterprising eggheads; party-giving tips from publi-cists who entertain on corporate budgets; change-your-spirituality books by personal trainers; a marriage primer by a divorced woman; an advice column by Pamela An-derson slated for *Jane* magazine and a new manners book, *Choosing Civility: The Twenty-Five Rules to Considerate Conduct,* by a professor at Johns Hopkins University.

—Bob Morris, "Advice from the Clueless"

b. If you meet a person who lives near you in a big city and you don't like her, that's fine: you can conduct your life so that you never have to speak with that person again. But in a village of 250, you don't have that luxury. You will see each other, day following day. You will sit side by side at town meetings or at other people's din-ner tables. You will work together on school committees or at the annual fair. You're stuck with each other.

—Geraldine Brooks, "Timeless Tact Helps Sustain a Literary Time Traveler"

c. To explain the tantalizing notion of broken symmetry, one of the key ideas in particle physics, . . . invoke the image of diners at a circular table. Between the settings are salad plates—a perfectly symmetrical situation that presents each guest with a prob-lem. Which plate to use, left or right? There is no compelling reason to prefer one over the other. But once one diner has arbitrarily made a choice, the effect ripples around the table, with each guest forced to abide by the decision. The symmetry is broken.

—George Johnson, "Out of Kilter: A Physicist Examines the Nature of Assymetry"

RESTATING THE MAIN IDEA

Because you want to understand what you read, recognizing topic sentences is more than just an exercise. To read efficiently, you must see what a writer is get-ting at; you must understand the main idea. A topic sentence that states the main idea neatly provides valuable help. Sometimes, however, topic sentences are not so explicit as they are in the preceding examples. As you read the following para-graphs, try to identify the writer's main idea:

Our files show us that most men are unhappy with the state of their bodies. They would prefer to have the kind of torso that provokes oohs and ahs from admiring women. They would like to have bulging biceps that will win the respect and envy of other men. They seek the pride and confidence that comes from possess-

ing a truly well-developed physique. They want the kind of body that any man
can build by subscribing to the Jack Harrigan Dyna-Fit Program.

—An imaginary advertisement

Almost everyone has hitherto taken it for granted that Australopitheca [our female hominid ancestor who lived more than a million years ago], since she was
primitive and chinless and low-browed, was necessarily hairy, and the artists always depict her as a shaggy creature. I don't think there is any reason for thinking this. Just as for a long time they "assumed" the big brain came first, before
the use of tools, so they still "assume" that hairlessness came last. If I had to visualize the Villafranchian hominids, I'd say their skin was in all probability quite as
smooth as our own.

—Elaine Morgan, *The Descent of Woman*

In the case of the body-building ad, you may wonder whether the first or last sentence should be called the topic sentence. An argument can be made for either.
The first sentence is a general statement, contending that most men are dissatisfied with their physiques. The remaining four sentences restate that contention
more specifically. On the other hand, the writer's main idea is not just to describe
this dissatisfaction but to provoke a response, namely to convince male readers
that they should spend their money on the Dyna-Fit Program. Perhaps, then, the
last sentence is more appropriately viewed as the topic sentence. Actually,
though, since the main idea of the whole paragraph combines information from
both the first and last sentences, supplemented by what you infer about the author's intentions, you can best capture the main idea in a general statement of
your own: *Men who wish to improve their physiques should invest in the Harrigan
Dyna-Fit Program.*

   A similar question arises in regard to the paragraph about Australopitheca.
Here, the author's main idea is stated twice—first in the short second sentence
and again, more concretely, in the final sentence. But since neither sentence expresses the entire idea of the paragraph, you could once again formulate your
own statement of the main idea: *Despite most people's assumption to the contrary,
Australopitheca was probably no hairier than modern woman.*

Paragraphs with Implied Main Ideas

Many paragraphs have no explicit topic sentence. Often, these paragraphs deal
with several different ideas joined together for convenience, as in the following
example:

[Joseph] Smith set up the first Mormon community in Kirtland, Ohio, in 1830,
but persecutions drove the Mormons to Missouri and then to a spot on the east
bank of the Mississippi which the Prophet named Nauvoo. At first the Mormons
were welcomed in Illinois, courted by both political parties and given a charter
that made Nauvoo practically an autonomous theocracy. The settlement grew
rapidly—even faster than Chicago; by 1844, with fifteen thousand citizens,
Nauvoo was the largest and most prosperous city in Illinois. It was at Nauvoo
that Joseph Smith received the "revelation" sanctioning polygamy, which he
and the inner circle of "elders" were already practicing. Although supported by

Isaiah iv. 1, "And in that day seven women shall take hold of one man," this revelation split the church. The monogamous "schismatics" started a paper at Nauvoo; Smith caused the press to be broken up after the first issue; he and his brother were then arrested by the authorities for destruction of property and lodged in the county jail, whence, on June 27, 1844, they were pulled out by a mob and lynched. Brigham Young, who succeeded to the mantle of the Prophet, and to five of his twenty-seven widows, directed retaliation; and for two years terror reigned in western Illinois. The Mormons were a virile, fighting people, but the time had come for them to make another move, before they were hopelessly outnumbered.

—Samuel Eliot Morrison, Henry Steele Commager, and
William E. Leuchtenburg, *The Growth of the American Republic*

This paragraph narrates a series of events in the early history of the Mormon church, but no one sentence summarizes everything.

Sometimes, a single-topic paragraph does not need a topic sentence because the main idea can be easily inferred from the context. Here is an example of such a paragraph:

Thin soup served in a soup plate is eaten from the side of the spoon, dipped into the liquid away from you. Thick soup may be eaten from the tip and dipped toward you. Soup served in bouillon cups is usually sipped (silently) from the spoon until cool and then drunk—using one handle or both. Eat boneless and skinless fish with a fork, but to remove the skin or bones it is necessary to use a knife. According to the best modern practice, you may cut a piece of meat and lift it at once on the fork in the left hand to the mouth while holding the knife in the right.

—*Britannica Junior* (1956), "Etiquette"

If the authors had wanted to introduce this paragraph with a topic sentence, they might have written something like this: *Polite people follow certain rules of table etiquette when they eat.* But since preceding paragraphs undoubtedly address other aspects of etiquette, including table manners, no topic sentence is needed in this context. In many situations, however, topic sentences are useful. One common mistake of inexperienced writers is to omit such sentences when they might aid the reader.

Restating the Main Idea   EXERCISES

1. Identifying topic sentences can be useful, but the important thing is to recognize the main idea of a passage. Remember that the two do not always coincide.

For each of the following paragraphs, try first to identify a topic sentence. If no one sentence adequately states the author's main idea, write your own one-sentence statement of that idea. Then consider whether the paragraph would have been more readable if the author had included your topic sentence. If so, should it go at the beginning, middle, or end of the paragraph?

a. Obsessed? You say I'm obsessed? With what, obsessed? Oh, you mean these Studebakers. Well, in fact, they happen to be the largest collection of Studebakers in North America, if you don't count Phillips in Bismarck, N.D., with his to-say-the-least questionable "rebuilt" engines. I don't think so. How do you like these Zippo lighters—1,110, if you're counting. I certainly am. What about my Marilyn Monroe movie furniture, my Trekkie memorabilia, my Daisy Buchanan, my Holy Grail, my double helix? Call me obsessed? What do you think of this church ceiling? Took me ten years hanging in the air to get the God's-hand-to-Adam right. Do you think I did get it right? Should I start over?

—Roger Rosenblatt, "Still Obsessive after All These Years"

b. In [the year] 2100 there are still Joseph Turner landscapes of inanimate beauty in many parts of the world. People still enjoy snow-covered mountain peaks, wave-dashed headlands, and white-water rapids tumbling into deep, still pools. But what of living nature? The huge human population, having at last leveled off at nine to ten billion, occupies the entire habitable part of the planet, which has been turned into a tight mosaic of cropland, tree farms, roads, and habitations. Thanks to massive desalinization, put in place by 2100, new methods of freshwater transport and irrigation, drier regions have turned from brown and yellow to green. Global per-hectare food production is well above 2000 levels. More of the fifty thousand species of potentially palatable kinds of plants are in agricultural use, while genetic engineering has been applied to tweak older crop species toward their productive limits.

—Edward O. Wilson, *The Future of Life*

2. In the following passages, topic sentences have been replaced by ellipses (. . .). Using context to infer the main idea of each, try to guess what the topic sentence might be.

a. . . . A nice shirt—no Henleys, turtlenecks or mocks. Nice trousers—no jeans or cut-offs, no big-and-baggy cargo pants or any other element of hoodlum manqué. The front can be flat or have pleats. Why? Because flat is nice, and pleats are nice. Is it chilly? Here, take this nice sweater and very nice windbreaker, just in case. Winter? Wear this nice down parka. Now stand back and look in the mirror. Don't you look nice!

—Ellis Weiner, "Within the Style of No-Style"

b. At a gas station the other day, I saw an advertisement attached at eye level near the fuel hose. I have also seen ads on shopping carts and heard commercials on the phone when a business puts me on hold. And I begin each day at my computer beneath an avalanche of e-mail sales pitches for laser printer cartridges, low-interest mortgages, and cut-rate Viagra.

As I'm deleting all this junk, I sometimes think of William Forster Lloyd, the English economist who, in the 1830s, described the problem of the commons. "Why are the cattle on a common so puny and stunted?" Lloyd asked. "Why is the common itself so bare-worn and cropped so differently from the adjoining enclosures?"

His answer was that it was in the interest of everyone using the common pasture to exploit it maximally. Each herdsman could benefit by adding another cow, but when all the herdsmen acted this way, as they inevitably would, the benefit of the commons was lost to everyone. . . .

—Daniel Akst, "Ubiquitous Ads Devalue All Messages"

3. Like an inductive paragraph, which ends by stating a conclusion, many scientific experiments can be called inductive, in that they lead to discovery. So too the

following might be called an inductive exercise because it asks you to draw conclusions from your discoveries.

a. From books, magazines, or other kinds of texts, find one paragraph that begins with a topic sentence and another that ends with a topic sentence. Transcribe (or photocopy) them both and bring them to class.

b. Examine an example of each of the following:
   - college-level textbook
   - novel
   - biography
   - newspaper article
   - magazine article

From each, select ten paragraphs at random and see how many (1) begin with a topic sentence, (2) end with a topic sentence, (3) have a topic sentence imbedded within, (4) have an implied topic sentence, or (5) have no unifying concept at all.

c. Now draw some conclusions from this experiment: How easy is it to find topic sentences? When they occur, where are topic sentences most likely to be placed? Are certain types of writing more likely than others to make use of topic sentences? If so, why? Can you draw any general conclusions about how writers construct paragraphs?

Detecting Implications

The preceding section of this chapter demonstrates how paragraphs can have topic sentences that are implied rather than explicitly stated. In such cases, discerning the main idea is left to the reader. But that is only one of many tasks involved in comprehension. Writers also leave gaps in the meaning they wish to communicate, and they expect alert readers to fill them in.

Even in everyday conversation, we do not always state everything we mean. Consider, for example, the *implication,* the unstated but intended meaning, in the following conversation between two students:

COLIN: I signed up for Professor Sneederbunk's course.

DANEEN: I hope you've got a large supply of caffeine tablets.

Without saying so explicitly, Daneen is implying that Professor Sneederbunk's course is difficult and requires long, late study hours. For Colin to understand her, he must draw connections, relying on past experience with college life and with how people use language. A less sophisticated listener, say, an eight-year-old, might not be able to bridge the gap between what Daneen says and what she actually means.

Being a sophisticated listener or reader demands skill at drawing inferences. Not everyone derives the same meaning under the same circumstances. Gaps can often leave messages open to more than one interpretation. In the preceding example, Colin was probably already aware of the reputation of Professor Sneederbunk's course and therefore understood exactly what Daneen meant. But someone else overhearing her remark might draw a different conclusion, inferring perhaps that Professor Sneederbunk's classes are so boring that students have difficulty staying awake. Successful communication depends on knowing your audience and adapting your message so that they can infer what you mean.

Writers also rely on implications. Consider the following paragraph, taken from an essay about the bizarre treatment the author receives because he is blind:

> For example, when I go to the airport and ask the ticket agent for assistance to the plane, he or she will invariably pick up the phone, call a ground hostess and whisper: "Hi, Jane, we've got a seventy-six here." I have concluded that the word *blind* is not used for one of two reasons: either they fear that if the dread word is spoken, the ticket agent's retina will immediately detach, or they are reluctant to inform me of my condition of which I may not have been previously aware.
>
> —Harold Krents, "Darkness at Noon"

The writer expects us to infer that a "seventy-six" is an airline code for a blind passenger. He also assumes our understanding that ticket agents whisper into phones because they do not want people in the vicinity, including Krents himself, to hear what they say. Earlier in his essay, Krents writes, "There are those who assume that since I can't see, I obviously also cannot hear." Having read this, a reader can infer that the whispering agents foolishly imagine that Krents will neither hear nor understand their words. The final sentence of the paragraph demands even more sophistication in drawing implications. Krents probably expects readers to infer a meaning that can be spelled out like this:

> The agents don't really believe they will go blind if they say the word, and Krents isn't sincere when he suggests that they may. The agents also can't really think that Krents doesn't know that he is blind. But as silly as either conclusion would be, the real reasons behind the agents' behavior are almost as absurd: they apparently think of blindness as a condition too embarrassing to be spoken of to a blind person. They aren't giving Krents credit for being able to notice that they are evading the topic. Worse, they aren't even able to realize that a blind person is a human being with the same capacities for hearing and thinking as anyone else.

You can easily see that the passage, with its unspoken implications, is far more effective than it would have been if Krents had spelled out everything he meant. By causing us to think for ourselves and to draw conclusions, Krents enlists us as partners in creating meaning. That sense of partnership makes us more receptive to his purpose in writing. After reading the paragraph, you might draw the following, more general conclusion:

> Perhaps I, the reader (now that I see the airline agents' behavior as ridiculous), should give some thought to how I treat blind people or others with disabilities.

Drawing inferences is an important part of reading, and good readers are as alert to implied meaning as they are to that which is explicitly stated.

Detecting Implications

1. What might you infer from the following bits of overheard conversation?

   a. A well-dressed couple in their thirties are dining in an elegant restaurant.

      Man: But darling, you've never given brandy a *chance.*

      Woman: Well excuse the hell out of me, Mister Connoisseur.

   b. **Investor:** Are you suggesting that I sell my shares of Pushmore Pharmaceuticals?

      Broker (quoting Shakespeare): There is a tide in the affairs of men, which, taken at the flood, leads on to fortune; omitted, all the voyage of their life is bound in shallows and in miseries.

2. Though the words in each of the following passages express a relatively clear and explicit meaning, they don't explain everything that was on the author's mind. What inferences can you draw as you read each passage?

   a. On the third floor [of Minnesota's Mall of America] was the only obvious sign of September 11 I could find: a small store called USA America Pride, which sold various clothes and knickknacks on a patriotic theme. . . .

      Not a single item in the USA America Pride store was made in America. I knew that already, just from common sense, but I began looking at the labels anyway. Blue baseball cap with the letters "FDNY" in white outlined in black on the front: Honduras. Black T-shirt with "Born in the U.S.A." in red-white-and-blue letters: Honduras. Black baseball cap with "American Pride" in red-white-and-blue spangles: Bangladesh. T-shirt with comical image involving bin Laden and a camel: Dominican Republic. Coffee mug with picture of Twin Towers: China. And so on. I asked the young man behind the counter if the store had ever sold any products made in America, and he said he thought there might have been one or two, but he couldn't remember. "If we did sell stuff made in America, you couldn't afford it," he said. "It's just not cost-effective to make such small items."

      —Ian Frazier, "The Mall of America"

   b. Man, it is so hard to live down that sugar-and-spice rep. We women try, Lord do we try, and still people are shocked—shocked!—when we are mean to each other, humiliate our partners, scream at our children, spread nasty rumors, lie on our résumés, embezzle from our employers, demean our employees, give slower drivers the finger, have extramarital affairs, commit murder, enter the military, join the Aryan Nation or the Islamic Jihad, and fail to send Christmas cards to the family. How dare women behave like . . . like . . . people?

      —Carol Tavris, "Are Girls Really as Mean as Books Say They Are?"

■ A FURTHER COMMENT ON PARAGRAPHS

We reemphasize the point that relatively few paragraphs contain explicitly stated topic sentences. The paragraph is actually a less structured unit of text than is often supposed. Most writers usually do not plan paragraphs as they compose. Instead, they often use the paragraph break as a form of punctuation—sometimes to signal a new idea or a change in direction, sometimes to provide emphasis. At other times, long topics may be divided rather arbitrarily into paragraphs, to provide pauses and to make a text appear less formidable.

Eye appeal is frequently a factor in paragraphing. Essays written in a sprawling handwriting are likely to have (and need) more paragraph breaks than typed essays. Newspapers, because of their narrow columns, contain shorter paragraphs than those found in most books. Psychologists have discovered that readers find material easiest to process when it is divided into short to medium-length paragraphs.

For all these reasons, no two writers create their paragraphs in exactly the same way. Given passages such as those featured in the following exercise, from which all paragraph breaks have been removed, any two professional authors or writing instructors chosen at random will probably disagree about where the breaks belong.

EXERCISES   **Supplying Paragraph Breaks**

1. Paragraph breaks have been removed from the following passages. Decide where you would put them and indicate your choices, using the paragraph symbol (¶). Remember that there are different yet appropriate responses to this exercise.

a. Where is the "official" birthplace of Route 66? This question has been asked many times over the years, and now we finally have the answer. On October 20, 1925, the Joint Board on Interstate Highways issued its "final" report that selected the system of roads to be known as United States Highways. The report designated 75,884 miles of road as the interstate system, with each road given a specific routing and number. The report was approved by the Secretary of Agriculture on November 18, 1925, forwarded to the American Association of State Highway (and Transportation) Officials (AASHTO) and accepted at their annual meeting. The Joint Board was then dissolved, and the Executive Committee of AASHTO was empowered to make "minor" changes in the recommended system "as appeared necessary or desirable." Between November 1925 and final approval of the system on November 11, 1926, the committee acted on 132 requests, many of which were not minor, resulting in changes to the route numbers and expansion of the system to 96,626 miles. This is the story of one of those changes.

—James R. Powell, "The Birthplace of Route 66"

b. Inevitably there were some lapses of judgment, but in general the sheer scale of the American landscape made it relatively easy to tuck a superhighway away unobtrusively among its folds. Problems arose where scale changes required a more delicate touch. This was often the case along coastlines, for example, where highway planners understandably wished to provide scenic drives with views of the ocean. Sometimes this was achieved brilliantly, as in Monterey and San Luis Obispo counties, California, where California's Route 1 (not part of the Interstate System) snakes gracefully above the Pacific, affording spectacular vistas of Big Sur and Carmel without in any way interfering with the grandeur of the landscape. Farther north along the Pacific coast, however, there are too many instances of highways encroaching clumsily on beach areas, some of these roads being built on landfills that have altered for the worse the relationship between land and sea. The California Highway Commission permitted the razing of centuries-old redwoods to facilitate the construction of the Redwood Freeway, while in a number of instances national and state parks have been disfigured by thoughtless routing. In general, though, the rural sections of the Interstate System can be considered a success. The real problems occurred when the superhighways approached cities and penetrated the urban fabric itself.

—Christopher Finch, *Highways to Heaven: The AUTO Biography of America*

2. Compare your responses to the first exercise with those of classmates. Was there general agreement about the number of paragraph breaks you supplied? Did you agree with the authors of the two passages (who, as it happens, presented them in five paragraphs and one paragraph, respectively)? What conclusions might you draw from this exercise?

▪ READING SELECTION

The following article was published in February 2002, just as a series of books about aggressive behavior among girls and women began to gain public attention. Margaret Talbot is a frequent contributor to the *New York Times Magazine,* where the article originally appeared.

Girls Want to Be Mean

MARGARET TALBOT

1 This focus on the cruelty of girls is, of course, something new. For years, psychologists who studied aggression among school children looked only at its physical and overt manifestations and concluded that girls were less aggressive than boys. That consensus began to change in the early 1990s, after a team of researchers led by a Finnish professor named Kaj Bjorkqvist started interviewing eleven- and twelve-year-old girls about their behavior toward one another. The team's conclusion was that girls were, in fact, just as aggressive as boys, though in a different way. They were not as likely to engage in physical fights, for example, but their superior social intelligence enabled them to wage complicated battles with other girls aimed at damaging relationships or reputations—leaving nasty messages by cell phone or spreading scurrilous rumors by e-mail, making friends with one girl as revenge against another, gossiping about someone just loudly enough to be overheard. Turning the notion of women's greater empathy on its head, Bjorkqvist focused on the destructive uses to which such emotional attunement could be put. "Girls can better understand how other girls feel," as he puts it, "so they know better how to harm them."

2 Researchers following in Bjorkqvist's footsteps noted that up to the age of four girls tend to be aggressive at the same rates and in the same ways as boys—grabbing toys, pushing, hitting. Later on, however, social expectations force their hostilities underground, where their assaults on one another are more indirect, less physical, and less visible to adults. Secrets they share in one context, for example, can sometimes be used against them in another. As Marion Underwood, a professor of psychology at the

University of Texas at Dallas, puts it: "Girls very much value intimacy, which makes them excellent friends and terrible enemies. They share so much information when they are friends that they never run out of ammunition if they turn on one another."

3   In the last few years, a group of young psychologists, including Underwood and Nicki Crick at the University of Minnesota, has pushed this work much further, observing girls in "naturalistic" settings, exploring the psychological foundations for nastiness and asking adults to take relational aggression—especially in the sixth and seventh grades, when it tends to be worst—as seriously as they do more familiar forms of bullying. While some of these researchers have emphasized bonding as a motivation, others have seen something closer to a hunger for power, even a Darwinian drive. One Australian researcher, Laurence Owens, found that the fifteen-year-old girls he interviewed about their girl-pack predation were bestirred primarily by its entertainment value. The girls treated their own lives like the soaps, hoarding drama, constantly rehashing trivia. Owens's studies contain some of the more vivid anecdotes in the earnest academic literature on relational aggression. His subjects tell him about ingenious tactics like leaving the following message on a girl's answering machine—"Hello, it's me. Have you gotten your pregnancy test back yet?"—knowing that her parents will be the first to hear it. They talk about standing in "huddles" and giving other girls "deaths"—stares of withering condescension—and of calling one another "dyke," "slut," and "fat" and of enlisting boys to do their dirty work.

4   Relational aggression is finding its chroniclers among more popular writers, too. In addition to Wiseman's book, this spring will bring Rachel Simmons's *Odd Girl Out: The Hidden Culture of Aggression in Girls,* Emily White's *Fast Girls: Teenage Tribes and the Myth of the Slut,* and Phyllis Chester's *Woman's Inhumanity to Woman.*

5   In her book, the twenty-seven-year-old Simmons offers a plaintive definition of relational aggression:

> Unlike boys, who tend to bully acquaintances or strangers, girls frequently attack within tightly knit friendship networks, making aggression harder to identify and intensifying the damage to the victims. Within the hidden culture of aggression, girls fight with body language and relationships instead of fists and knives. In this world, friendship is a weapon, and the sting of a shout pales in comparison to a day of someone's silence. There is no gesture more devastating than the back turning away.

Now, Simmons insists, is the time to pull up the rock and really look at this seething underside of American girlhood. "Beneath a façade of female intimacy," she writes, "lies a terrain traveled in secret, marked with anguish and nourished by silence."

6   Not so much silence, anymore, actually. For many school principals and counselors across the country, relational aggression is becoming a certified social problem and the need to curb it an accepted mandate. A small industry of interveners has grown up to meet the demand. In Austin, Tex., an organization called GENaustin now sends counselors into schools to teach a course on relational aggression called Girls as Friends, Girls as Foes. In Erie, Pa., the Ophelia Project offers a similar curriculum, taught by high-school-aged mentors, that explores "how girls hurt each other" and how they can stop. A private Catholic school in Akron, Ohio, and a public-school district near Portland, Ore., have introduced programs aimed at rooting out girl meanness. And Wiseman and her Empower Program colleagues have taught their Owning Up class at sixty schools. "We are currently looking at relational aggression like domestic violence twenty years ago," says Holly Nishimura, the assistant director of the Ophelia Project. "Though it's not on the same scale, we believe that with relational aggression, the trajectory of awareness, knowledge and demand for change will follow the same track."

Whether this new hyper-vigilance about a phenomenon that has existed for as   **7**
long as most of us can remember will actually do anything to squelch it is, of course,
another question. Should adults be paying as much attention to this stuff as kids do, or
will we just get hopelessly tangled up in it ourselves? Are we approaching frothy adolescent bitchery with undue gravity or just giving it its due in girls' lives? On the one
hand, it is kind of satisfying to think that girls might be, after their own fashion, as aggressive as boys. It's an idea that offers some relief from the specter of the meek and
mopey, "silenced" and self-loathing girl the popular psychology of girlhood has given
us in recent years. But it is also true that the new attention to girls as relational aggres-
sors may well take us into a different intellectual cul-de-sac, where it becomes too easy
to assume that girls do not use their fists (some do), that all girls are covert in their cru-
elties, that all girls care deeply about the ways of the clique—and that what they do in
their "relational" lives takes precedence over all other aspects of their emerging selves.

Nowadays, adults, particularly in the upper middle classes, are less laissez-faire   **8**
about children's social lives. They are more vigilant, more likely to have read books
about surviving the popularity wars of middle school or dealing with cliques, more
likely to have heard a talk or gone to a workshop on those topics. Not long ago, I
found myself at a lecture by the best-selling author Michael Thompson on "Understanding the Social Lives of Our Children." It was held inside the National Cathedral
on a chilly Tuesday evening in January, and there were hundreds of people in attendance—attractive late-forties mothers in cashmere turtlenecks and interesting scarves
and expensive haircuts and graying but fit fathers—all taking notes and lining up to
ask eager, anxious questions about how best to ensure their children's social happiness. "As long as education is mandatory," Thompson said from the pulpit, "we have a
huge obligation to make it socially safe," and heads nodded all around me. He made a
list of "the top three reasons for a fourth-grade girl to be popular," and parents in my
pew wrote it down in handsome little leather notebooks or on the inside cover of
Thompson's latest book, *Best Friends, Worst Enemies*. A red-haired woman with a fer-
vent, tremulous voice and an elegant navy blue suit said that she worried our children
were socially handicapped by "a lack of opportunities for unstructured cooperative
play" and mentioned that she had her two-year-old in a science class. A serious-
looking woman took the microphone to say that she was troubled by the fact that her
daughter liked a girl "who is mean and controlling and once wrote the word *murder*
on the bathroom mirror—and this is in a private school!"

I would never counsel blithe ignorance on such matters—some children are truly   **9**
miserable at school for social reasons, truly persecuted and friendless and in need of
adult help. But sometimes we do seem in danger of micromanaging children's social
lives, peering a little too closely. Priding ourselves on honesty in our relationships, as
baby-boomer parents often do, we expect to know everything about our children's
friendships, to be hip to their social travails in a way our own parents, we thought,
were not. But maybe this attention to the details can backfire, giving children the impression that the transient social anxieties and allegiances of middle school are
weightier and more immutable than they really are. And if that is the result, it seems
particularly unfortunate for girls, who are already more mired in the minutiae of relationships than boys are, who may already lack, as Christopher Lasch once put it, "any
sense of an impersonal order that exists independently of their wishes and anxieties"
and of the "vicissitudes of relationships."

I think I would have found it dismaying if my middle school had offered a class   **10**
that taught us about the wiles of Marcie and Tracie: if adults studied their folkways,
maybe they were more important than I thought, or hoped. For me, the best antidote
to the caste system of middle school was the premonition that adults did not usually

play by the same rigid and peculiar rules—and that someday, somewhere, I would find a whole different mattering map, a whole crowd of people who read the same books I did and wouldn't shun me if I didn't have a particular brand of shoes. When I went to college, I found it, and I have never really looked back.

11   And the Queen Bees? Well, some grow out of their girly sense of entitlement on their own, surely; some channel it in more productive directions. Martha Stewart must have been a Q.B. Same with Madonna. At least one of the Q.B.'s from my youth—albeit the nicest and smartest one—has become a pediatrician on the faculty of a prominent medical school, I noticed when I looked her up the other day. And some Queen Bees have people who love them—dare I say it?—just as they are, a truth that would have astounded me in my own school days but that seems perfectly natural now.

12   On a Sunday afternoon, I have lunch with Jessica Travis and her mother, Robin, who turns out to be an outgoing, transplanted New Yorker—"born in Brighton Beach, raised in Sheepshead Bay." Over white pizza, pasta, cannoli, and Diet Cokes, I ask Robin what Jessica was like as a child. "I was fabulous," Jessica says.

13   "She was," her mother agrees. "She was blond, extremely happy, endlessly curious, and always the leader of the pack. She didn't sleep because she didn't want to miss anything. She was just a bright, shiny kid. She's still a bright, shiny kid."

14   After Jessica takes a call on her pumpkin-colored cell phone, we talk for a while about Jessica's room, which they both describe as magnificent. "I have lived in apartments smaller than her majesty's two-bedroom suite," Robin snorts. "Not many single parents can do for their children what I have done for this one. This is a child who asked for a pony and got two. I tell her this is the top of the food chain. The only place you can go from here is the royal family."

15   I ask if anything about Jessica's clique bothers her. She says no—because what she calls "Jess's band of merry men" doesn't "define itself by its opponents. They're not a threat to anyone. Besides, it's not like they're an A-list clique."

16   "Uh, Mom," Jessica corrects. "We are definitely an A-list clique. We are totally A-list. You are giving out incorrect information."

17   "Soooorry," Robin says. "I'd fire myself, but there's no one else lining up for the job of being your mom."

18   Jessica spends a little time bringing her mother and me up to date on the elaborate social structure at her high school. The cheerleaders' clique, it seems, is not the same as the pom-pom girls' clique, though both are A-list. All sports cliques are A-list, in fact, except—"of course"—the swimmers. There is a separate A-list clique for cute preppy girls who "could play sports but don't." There is "the white people who pretend to be black clique" and the drama clique, which would be "C list," except that, as Jessica puts it, "they're not even on the list."

19   "So what you are saying is that your high school is littered with all these groups that have their own separate physical and mental space?" Robin says, shaking her head in wonderment.

20   When they think about it, Jessica and her mom agree that the business with the rules—what you can wear on a given day of the week and all that—comes from Jessica's fondness for structure. As a child, her mom says she made up games with "such elaborate rules I'd be lost halfway through her explanation of them." Besides, there was a good deal of upheaval in her early life. Robin left her "goofy artist husband" when Jessica was three, and after that they moved a lot. And when Robin went to work for Oracle, she "was traveling all the time, getting home late. When I was on the road, I'd call her every night at eight and say: 'Sweet Dreams. I love you. Good Night.' "

21   "Always in that order," Jessica says. "Always at eight. I don't like a lot of change."

Toward the end of our lunch, Jessica's mother—who says she herself was more a   22
nerd than a Queen Bee in school—returns to the subject of cliques. She wants, it
seems, to put something to rest. "You know I realize there are people who stay with
the same friends, the same kind of people, all their life, who never look beyond that,"
she says. "I wouldn't want that for my daughter. I want my daughter to be one of
those people who live in the world. I know she's got these kinds of narrow rules in her
personal life right now. But I still think, I really believe, that she will be a bigger person, a person who spends her life in the world." Jessica's mother smiles. Then she
gives her daughter's hair an urgent little tug, as if it were the rip cord of a parachute
and Jessica were about to float away from her.

Freewriting

Freewrite for ten to fifteen minutes about Talbot's account of relationships among
girls in early adolescence. You may write about anything that reaffirms or challenges your own perceptions, whether they are based on personal experience, observation, or other reading. Or, you may wish to consider how serious a problem
relational aggression is.

Group Work

Share freewrites in your reading group, each member reading aloud while others
are taking notes. After everyone has read, try to reach some consensus about the
reliability of Rosalind Wiseman as an observer and Margaret Talbot as a reporter
and about the implications of relational aggression as a social problem. If your
group cannot reach a consensus, try to agree on a clear presentation of conflicting views.

Review Questions

1. When and how did scholarly interest in cruelty among girls get started?
   What directions has it taken more recently?

2. How might adults take recent discoveries about relationships among girls
   too seriously? How could this affect their parenting?

3. What was Talbot like as a teenager? How have the "Queen Bees" of her
   adolescence developed as adults?

Discussion Questions

1. Which television programs and films depict meanness and aggression
   among adolescent girls? Do they usually treat it dramatically, comically, or
   both? Which, in your opinion, are most and least realistic?

2. What do you suppose Talbot means by the "superior social intelligence" of
   girls as compared to boys? Might one make a similar comparison between

women and men? If so, what are some possible implications for family relationships, friendships, or the workplace?

3. Would you say that Jessica Travis is a well-adjusted teenager? Would you expect her to become a successful adult? How do you think Talbot would respond to these questions?

Writing

1. The paragraph by Carol Tavris on page 169 introduces an article that takes issue with Talbot and others who have studied and written about aggressive behavior among girls and women. Locate the complete text of Tavris's article (*Chronicle of Higher Education,* July 5, 2002) in your college library. Write an essay that either affirms Talbot's claims and refutes Tavris's (or vise versa) or that attempts to reconcile views expressed by the two authors.

2. Using paragraph 18 of Talbot's essay as a model, write a short description of high-school culture and relationships as you recall them from your own experience.

3. Write an essay responding to one or more of the questions that Talbot poses in paragraph 7.

WRITE, READ, and RESEARCH the NET

1. *Write:* Freewrite for fifteen minutes about bullying and peer pressure among adolescents of both sexes.

2. *Read:* Review the two following Web sites:
   <http://www.williampollack.com/voices_intro.html>
   <http://www.msnbc.com/news/735673.asp#BODY>

3. *Research:* Using the Internet, locate Web sites that address the topics of bullying and peer pressure in junior and senior high schools. Use the information you collect to write a paper assessing whether recent books and discussions have accurately portrayed (or exaggerated) issues of safety in public schools.

■ ADDITIONAL READINGS

The following selections further explore connections among gender and violence. First is an excerpt from the book *Real Boys' Voices* by clinical psychologist William Pollack. Pollack's book reports the results of his extensive interviews with adolescent boys regarding "the things that hurt them" and their reluctance to acknowledge them openly. Following this are two newspaper articles reporting horrific hate crimes provoked by the victims' transgressions against the sexual mores enforced by other persons of their gender.

Listening to Boys' Voices

WILLIAM POLLACK

In my travels throughout this country—from the inner-city neighborhoods of Boston, New York, and San Francisco to suburbs in Florida, Connecticut, and Rhode Island; from small, rural villages in New Hampshire, Kentucky, and Pennsylvania to the pain-filled classrooms of Littleton, Colorado—I have discovered a glaring truth: America's boys are absolutely desperate to talk about their lives. They long to talk about the things that are hurting them—their harassment from other boys, their troubled relationships with their fathers, their embarrassment around girls and confusion about sex, their disconnection from parents, the violence that haunts them at school and on the street, their constant fear that they might not be as masculine as other boys. **1**

But this desperate coast-to-coast longing is silenced by the Boy Code—old rules that favor male stoicism and make boys feel ashamed about expressing weakness or vulnerability. Although our boys urgently want to talk about who they really are, they fear that they will be teased, bullied, humiliated, beaten up, and even murdered if they give voice to their truest feelings. Thus, our nation is home to millions of boys who feel they are navigating life alone—who on an emotional level are alone—and who are cast out to sea in separate lifeboats, and feel they are drowning in isolation, depression, loneliness, and despair. **2**

Our sons, brothers, nephews, students are struggling. Our boyfriends are crying out to be understood. But many of them are afraid to talk. Scotty, a thirteen-year-old boy from a small town in northern New England, recently said to me, "Boys are supposed to shut up and take it, to keep it all in. It's harder for them to release or vent without feeling girly. And that can drive them to shoot themselves." **3**

I am particularly concerned about the intense angst I see in so many of America's young men and teenaged boys. I saw this angst as I did research for *Real Boys,* and then again in talking with boys for this book. Boys from all walks of life, including boys who seem to have made it—the suburban high-school football captain, the seventh-grade prep-school class president, the small-town police chief's son, the inner-city student who is an outstanding cartoonist and son of a welfare mother—all were feeling so alone that I worried that they often seemed to channel their despair into rage not only toward others but toward themselves. An ordinary boy's sadness, his everyday feelings of disappointment and shame, push him not only to dislike himself and to feel private moments of anguish or self-doubt, but also, impulsively, to assault, wound, and kill. Forced to handle life's emotional ups and downs on their own, many boys and young men—many good, honest, caring boys—are silently allowing their lives to wither away, or explode. **4**

We still live in a society in which our boys and young men are simply not receiving the consistent attention, empathy, and support they truly need and desire. We are listening only to parts of what our sons and brothers and boyfriends are telling us. Though our intentions are good, we've only developed a culture in which too often boys feel comfortable communicating a small portion of their feelings and experiences. And through no fault of our own, frequently we don't understand what they are saying to us when they do finally talk. **5**

Boys are acutely aware of how society constrains them. They also notice how it holds back other boys and young men, including their peers, their male teachers, and their fathers. "When bad things happen in our family," Jesse, an astute twelve-year-old boy from a large middle-class suburb of Los Angeles, recently told me, "my father gets blocked. Like if he's upset about something that happened at work, he can't say **6** anything, and we have no idea what he's thinking. He just sits in front of the television, spends time on the Internet, or just goes off on his own. You can't get through to him at all. He just gets totally blocked." Of course, Jesse is teeming to do the same. And if we don't allow, even teach, boys like Jesse to express their emotion and cry tears, some will cry bullets instead.

A NATIONWIDE JOURNEY

7   I began a new nationwide journey to listen to boys' voices last summer in my native Massachusetts. In one of the very first interviews, I sat down with Clayton, a sixteen-year-old boy living in a modest apartment in Arlington, a medium-sized suburb of Boston. Clay introduced me to his mother and older sister and then brought me to his attic hideaway, a small room with only two small wooden windows that allowed light into the room through a series of tiny slits. Clay decided to share some of his writing with me—poetry and prose he had written on leaves of white and yellow paper. His writings were deeply moving, but even more extraordinary were the charcoal sketches that, once he grew comfortable with my presence, he decided he would also share. His eyes downcast, his shoulders slumped inward, he opened his black sketchbook and flipped gently through the pages.

8   On each consecutive sheet of parchment, Clay had created a series of beautiful images in rich, multicolored charcoal and pastels. "You're a talented artist," I said, expressing my real enthusiasm.

9   "I haven't shown these to too many people," he said, blushing. "I don't think anyone would really be too interested." Clay's pictures revealed his angst and in graphic, brutal detail. There was a special series of drawings of "angels." They were half human, half creature, with beautiful wings, but their boyish faces were deeply pained. Soaring somewhere between earth and heaven, the angels seemed to be trying to free themselves from earthly repression, striving for expression, longing to reach the freedom of the skies. They evoked the mundane world where Clayton's psychological pain felt real and inescapable, yet they also evoked an imaginary place where he could feel safe, relaxed, and free.

10   In our conversation, Clayton revealed that his inner sense of loss and sadness had at times been so great that on at least one occasion he had seriously contemplated suicide.

11   "I never actually did anything to commit suicide. I was too afraid I'd end up in a permanent hell . . . but that's how bad I felt. I wanted to end it all."

12   I thought to myself that maybe that's what these tortured angels were about—a combination of heavenly hope mixed up with a boy's suppressed "voice" of pain.

13   Clayton then revealed "The Bound Angel," a breathtaking sketch of one of his winged, half-man creatures bent over in pain, eyes looking skyward, but trunk and legs bound like an animal awaiting slaughter.

14   Clayton explained, "His hands are tied, and his mouth is sealed so he cannot speak. He's in pain, but he has no way to run from it, to express it, or to get to heaven."

15   "Your angel wants to shout out his troubles to the high heavens, but he is bound and gagged. He wants to move toward someone, but he is frozen in space. He needs to release his voice, but he cannot and fears he will not be heard. That's why he's so tortured."

16   "Yes, exactly," he said.

17   "I guess if he's tied up long enough," I responded, "and can't release that voice, he'll want to die, like you did."

18   "I think so," Clay said.

19   There is no reason we should wait until a boy like Clay feels hopeless, suicidal, or homicidal to address his inner experience. The time to listen to boys is now.

Vengeance Destroys Faces, and Souls, in Cambodia

SETH MYDANS

It is a form of revenge that is intended to be worse than murder. Every time the victim looks into the mirror she will know: I am ugly now.   **1**

The fleeting smile of Som Rasmey is still disconcertingly beautiful. But her face is ribbed and ruined by acid, her left eye red and staring, her burned scalp barren.   **2**

After the screaming, thrashing attack twenty months ago the scorned wife who drenched her with acid, Minh Rinath, returned to make the message explicit. "He is mine now," she said. "He will never want you again."   **3**

Miss Som Rasmey, who is now twenty-four, had a particular kind of beauty—lustrous, proud, the kind that could be as intimidating as it was alluring.   **4**

The attack, in which three other women held her down by her arms and legs and hair, has not only robbed her of her looks; it has crushed her soul.   **5**

"I have the soul of a dead woman now," she said as tears streamed down her face. "My body is alive but my soul is dead."   **6**

In the past two years, there has been a horrific surge in acid attacks in Cambodia, most of them carried out—in contrast to places like Bangladesh—by wives against the lovers of their husbands. One local human rights group, Licadho, recorded twenty such attacks last year in a sort of imitative mass hysteria.   **7**

"The wife does not want you to die," said Maniline Ek, an American volunteer at a women's shelter here. "They want you to live and suffer. It's torture. People look at your face and they say, 'Oh, she took someone else's husband.' "   **8**

These are battles among the oppressed, the harsh intersection of mutual tragedies—woman against woman. In Cambodia, power belongs almost exclusively to men. The philandering husbands are almost never the targets of attack.   **9**

A local women's aid group, the Cambodian Women's Crisis Center, recorded only one instance last year in which a husband was the target. And it was the only instance in which the attacker was tried and punished.   **10**

It is common in Cambodia for men—particularly men of power—to take an unofficial second wife. The betrayal of the official wife is so familiar that popular songs have been written about it.   **11**

"Our society does not condemn the men," said the director of the crisis center, Chanthol Oung. "It feels their behavior is acceptable."   **12**

The most highly publicized attack was carried out in late 1999 by a woman named Khourn Sophal, the wife of Svay Sittha, undersecretary of state at the Council of Ministers.   **13**

The victim, an eighteen-year-old actress and singer named Tat Marina, was horribly disfigured when the woman and several bodyguards poured about five quarts of acid over her.   **14**

A government spokesman, Khieu Thavika, described the attack as a personal matter "for the first and second wife to resolve." Although charges have been brought against Mrs. Khourn Sophal, no move has been made to arrest her. Relatives of her victim say Mrs. Khourn Sophal telephones periodically to insult the young woman.   **15**

Three years ago, the wife of an even higher official was implicated in the shooting death of Cambodia's most popular singer, Piseth Pilika. That official is the prime minister himself, Hun Sen. No one has been arrested or charged in that attack.   **16**

Typically, the girlfriends or second wives of powerful men are poor young women who have little but beauty to offer them hope or prospects for the future. And when that leads to conflict, they are powerless.   **17**

18   At the age of fifteen, Miss Som Rasmey dropped out of school to earn money for her family by selling coconuts, cigarettes, and gasoline at the roadside. Three years ago she graduated to serving drinks at a restaurant.

19   Like many other young women who serve drinks, she soon attracted a patron, a powerful military colonel named Lim Sok Heng. Her life was transformed: beautiful clothes, holidays at the beach, even a trip to Hong Kong. And then a baby.

20   With time, Miss Som Rasmey said, she grew frightened by the colonel's brutality and by increasing threats from his wife. She tried to leave him but he imprisoned her in a small house under constant guard.

21   His obsession with her must have driven his wife mad. When at last she attacked, she was raging.

22   "I'll throw the acid now!" she shouted as her friends pinned her victim to the floor. Miss Som Rasmey had been nursing her seven-month-old daughter and had just time enough to toss her out of the way.

23   Her lips tighten as she describes what followed and her speech is clipped and angry.

24   "She emptied a bottle over my head," she said. "Then another half bottle. I was burning all over. I struggled and I tried to break free. I ran into the yard, and she ran after me. She had one more bottle, and she wanted to throw it. She was shouting, and I was shouting, 'I'm burning; please help me.' "

25   The attack ended when a group of neighbors surrounded Mrs. Minh Rinath with hatchets in their hands.

26   As they heaved Miss Som Rasmey onto a pallet to rush her to a hospital, she could hear her little girl screaming, the last time she would hear the baby's voice. After the attack, Colonel Lim Sok Heng and his wife took the baby home and Miss Som Rasmey cannot be sure whether she is now alive or dead.

27   Following the attack, the colonel seized Miss Som Rasmey from the hospital and imprisoned her again, this time in Vietnam, for fear she would make trouble. Six months later, she escaped and returned to her home, so disfigured that at first her family did not recognize her.

28   Her anger has not subsided. Miss Som Rasmey is the first victim to pursue her attacker in court, demanding compensation and the return of her child.

29   And it is here that the fundamental law of Cambodia asserted itself: impunity. Cambodian courts consistently bow to the power of position and the persuasion of cash.

30   As Miss Som Rasmey put it: "The rich and the poor are completely different. Prison is only for poor people. But people like Lim Sok Heng and his wife can do whatever they want and get away with it."

31   At the trial last fall, the judge, Tith Sothy, displayed impatience with Miss Som Rasmey, cutting her off and ordering her not to waste his time "talking about romance."

32   But he was not an unsympathetic man. He could see who had been wronged here. The scorned wife, he said, had acted out of understandable feelings of jealousy.

33   The judge dismissed Miss Som Rasmey's demand for the return of her child. He sentenced her attacker, Mrs. Minh Rinath, to two years in prison for misdemeanor assault, suspended.

Murder of Teen Resembles Case
That Became Movie *Boys Don't Cry*

YOMI S. WRONGE AND PUTSATA REANG

Three Newark, Calif., men who became enraged after learning that the stunningly   1
beautiful girl at their late-night party was actually a seventeen-year-old cross-dressing
boy punched the youth, dragged him into the garage, and strangled him with a piece
of rope, according to court documents released Friday.

   Eddie Araujo's body was then wrapped in a sheet and buried in a shallow grave   2
near Placerville, about 150 miles from his family's home in Newark, police said.

   On Friday, the three main suspects—Jose Merel, Jaron Chase Nabors, and Michael   3
Magidson—made their first appearance in court, where they each face one count of
murder, with a hate-crime enhancement. The enhancement could add up to four
years of a prison term. All are being held without bail.

   Paul Merel, Jr., of Newark was also arrested but later released when the district at- 4
torney's office determined there was not enough evidence to prosecute him. Police
have not ruled out other suspects.

   Judge Dennis McLaughlin agreed to delay the arraignment of all three. Merel is   5
expected to enter a plea on October 21. Nabors, who has hired attorney Robert Beles,
and Magidson are scheduled to be arraigned October 24.

   "I feel when all the facts are known, my client will be found not guilty," said Be-   6
les. "He's a college student with no crime in his background."

   Nabors's parents, who quickly left the courtroom, declined to comment about   7
their son but said simply, "It's a hard time for us right now."

   Nabors, who was arrested October 15 after being questioned by police, led investi- 8
gators to the shallow grave where detectives found the remains of the boy wrapped in
a sheet with his hands and feet bound. The victim was wearing several pieces of
jewelry.

   Araujo, who went by the name "Gwen," normally favored jeans and blouses, ac-   9
cording to his mother. But on October 3, for the first time, he left home wearing a
denim miniskirt and peasant top to attend a party at the home of Jose Merel, who she
said was a friend.

   At the party, a witness told Newark Police, she saw Araujo flirting with all the   10
men. At some point during the late-night gathering, a partygoer went into the bathroom with Araujo and learned his true gender.

   She told one of the three alleged killers, a scuffle broke out, and Araujo was   11
punched, dragged into the garage, and strangled, according to witness statements.

   The official cause of death is strangulation and blunt trauma to the head, accord- 12
ing to Frank Gentle, with the Alameda County Coroner's bureau.

   Araujo's mother, Sylvia Guerrero, said Friday that she had asked her son to change 13
before going to the party. She last saw him that night as he reached for a pair of pants
but then decided to wear what he had on. Something about the ensemble of a skirt,
shirt, and flip-flops screamed, "man," to her, Guerrero said.

   "It was the shoes," Guerrero said. "He didn't have a pedicure, and his feet looked   14
manly. It was a dead give-away."

   The case eerily resembles the high-profile murder of Teena Brandon, a girl who   15
dressed as a boy and was murdered in a small town in Nebraska after her attackers discovered Brandon was a she—a case that was later turned into the 1999 movie, *Boys*

Don't Cry. It falls on the heels of the four-year anniversary of the murder of Matthew Shepard, a gay youth in Laramie, Wyo.

16   Two years ago in Santa Clara County, in the murder case involving the death of a nineteen-year-old man who dressed as a woman, a jury rejected prosecutors' request for a first-degree murder conviction and found the defendant guilty of second-degree murder. Jurors also determined that the crime was not a gender-based hate crime.

17   Friends and family describe Araujo's tragic story as that of a boy who lived his life as a girl and faced harassment because of the lifestyle.

18   Although witnesses told police that Eddie may have been romantically involved with at least one of the suspects, Guerrero said he told her he would never engage in sexual intercourse with anyone until he had a sex change.

19   Students at Newark Memorial High School and Bridgepoint were stunned by the arrests and say they can't imagine any of the men committing such a crime.

20   For as far back as anyone can remember, Eddie fought to be accepted. Old school chums remember him as effeminate, even as a little boy, and how he suffered for it.

21   "He was harassed all the time, especially by boys," said Tara Rodriguez, who met Eddie in the fifth grade. She had a crush on him, but kept it to herself for fear of rejection.

22   "He never said he was gay, but he wasn't interested in girls in that way," she said.

23   The teasing continued through middle school and seemed to intensify as Eddie became more accepting of his transgendered identity. His sister, Pearl, said that he began experimenting with make-up at a young age, and by the time he hit high school, Eddie wore full face and wigs and was arguably one of prettiest "girls" in town.

24   At one point, he dyed his hair pink to match that of his idol and namesake, singer Gwen Stefani from the band No Doubt. But when his hair grew long he colored it jet black, instantly turning into the spitting image of his mother.

25   He was so attractive, "other girls were jealous of him," said Lisa Santana, a longtime family friend and nextdoor neighbor.

26   He dropped out of school because of the relentless harassment and had a tough time finding a job because he dressed like a woman.

27   On Friday, friends at Bridgepoint High, a continuation school in Newark where he did independent study, gathered for a memorial.

5 *Summarizing*

A *summary* of a text or passage is a brief distillation of its salient points—its main ideas and essential information—that excludes any supporting details, such as examples or illustrations. Summaries save time, but they serve other purposes as well, such as focusing attention and stimulating recall. A textbook chapter, for example, may end with a summary that reinforces new concepts and reemphasizes important information. A scientific or technical article may open with an *abstract,* a summary of findings that allows a reader to recognize the main point quickly and, perhaps, decide whether to proceed through the entire text.

As a student, you have probably written a fair number of summaries already. A book review or "report on the literature" requires you to summarize the contents of one or more texts. A lab report contains a brief account of your experimental procedures and results. An argumentative paper (like a trial lawyer's *brief*) may conclude with a forceful summation of the evidence you have presented. Less familiar, perhaps, are the uses of summary in research writing. As you consult sources filled with detailed information and expert analysis, you must determine which is most important and relevant, recording only that on your note cards. In fact, your completed research paper is by nature a summary, a carefully condensed and focused presentation of what you have discovered during the course of an investigation.

Whenever you read, your mind engages in something like summarizing: seeking out main ideas, making connections among them (as well as drawing associations with your other experiences), and creating a framework for efficient storage in your memory. You can assist that process when you annotate your reading. For example, a student reading a textbook to learn how the human eye works might write this summary note in the margin:

> In the human visual system the initial coding of the image occurs in the *retina,* a layer of neural cells at the rear of the eyeball. The retina contains a two-dimensional layer of sensory cells, called *rods* and *cones,* which are sensitive to light. Each of these cells is a *transducer* that is capable of generating a neural signal when struck by light.
>
> —Neil A. Stillings, *Cognitive Science: An Introduction*

Rods and cones in the retina encode images

Writing the note helps the student see the main point of the passage and remember it.

◼ SUMMARY AND PARAPHRASE

Although marginal annotations often *paraphrase*, the preceding note *summarizes:* it omits details, including definitions of terms. As you will see, summary and paraphrase share similarities in both form and function. Before introducing those similarities, however, we need to consider two ways that summary and paraphrase differ. First, unlike a paraphrase, a summary may quote a phrase or two, or even a short sentence, from the original source, provided that it is set off with quotation marks. Second, summarizing involves decisions about what is most important and what can be left out. In the following passage, a British author writes about the processing and marketing of groceries:

The original source

All these techniques, originating in the United States and vigorously marketed by American businessmen, have spread across the industrialized communities of Europe.

One of these has been a significant change in shopping habits. When food retailers still purchased their supplies in bulk—flour and sugar by the sack, tea in a chest, butter in a keg, and cheeses whole—the local store was a place of resort. It was a social center as well as a distribution point. Standard articles, prepackaged and preserved by canning or freezing in a large-scale modern factory, are distributed with more efficiency, even if with the loss of social intercourse, in an equally efficient large-scale supermarket. Hence it is reasonable to suggest that one of the effects American food technology has had on the character of European society has been to accelerate the extinction of the general store on the street corner, of the specialized butcher, baker, greengrocer, and dairy and to substitute the supermarket. Great Britain, moving forward a decade behind the United States, possessed 175 supermarkets in 1958, 367 in 1960, and 4,800 in 1970.

—Magnus Pyke, "The Influence of American Food Technology in Europe"

Notice the difference between a paraphrase and a summary of this passage. A student wishing to use the information in a research paper might paraphrase as follows:

A paraphrase of the source

New methods of processing and distributing food, developed in America and sent overseas, have brought social change to Europe. For one thing, many Europeans no longer shop for groceries as they once did when stores bought large containers of flour, sugar, tea, and butter and whole cheeses. In those days, the food store was a place to meet friends as well as to buy groceries. Though impersonal by comparison, today's supermarkets are more efficient, selling products that come individually packaged from the factory, where they have been canned or frozen to keep them fresh. Consequently, American methods have led to the gradual disappearance of butcher shops, bakeries, produce markets, and dairy stores, all of which have been supplanted by supermarkets. The number of supermarkets in Britain, which is about ten years behind trends established in the U.S., grew from 175 in 1958 and 367 in 1960 to 4,800 in 1971 (Pyke 89–90).

This paraphrase alters the writer's language, while retaining all his ideas, including examples and minor details. The following summary, on the other hand, presents only the most important ideas:

American innovations in the production and distribution of food have brought supermarkets to Europe. Once a neighborly "place of resort," the corner store has been supplanted by the more efficient, though less sociable, supermarket (Pyke 89–90).

A summary of
the source

Notice that the summary omits details and examples found in the paraphrase. Nevertheless, it provides a faithful representation of the author's ideas and attitudes. You may also notice that this particular summary retains a phrase from the original source, placed in quotation marks.

A summary, like a paraphrase, makes an author's ideas clear, perhaps even clearer than they are in the original. Unlike a paraphrase, a summary may incorporate a quotation—a phrase or short sentence from the source—if it is set off with quotation marks. Both summary and paraphrase, however, must acknowledge their common source in a parenthetical note.

Summary and Paraphrase

EXERCISE

A process for writing summaries appears in the next section of this chapter, but you already can summarize a passage with a main idea. The following excerpt from a book by Mark Boren explores the early history of student revolt. First paraphrase the passage; then write a brief summary. Both the paraphrase and summary should be written in your own words, although you may wish to quote a short phrase or two in the summary. Avoid making reference to the author's name, ending both the paraphrase and summary with a parenthetical note (Boren 9).

> Universities were originally not founded as safe havens for pursuit of knowledge but begun by the sons of the well-to-do and rising middle class for the express purpose of wielding economic power and for generating financial leverage against host towns and cities. Thus the powers of and behind modern universities have deep roots. As a collective of students, the University of Paris, for instance, threatened to withdraw from the city in 1200 and successfully extorted significant legal and economic concessions from it; the events leading up to the threat centered around an already classic type of "town-and-gown" altercation: shortly after the cathedral school became a university, a student's servant was apparently thrown out of a Paris tavern after insulting the innkeeper and his wife. In protest, the servant's master and a contingent of other students rushed into the establishment and attacked the innkeeper and a few inebriated locals; responding to the innkeeper's call for aid, town officials and a number of enraged townies retaliated by hunting down and viciously attacking the students, beating a number of them to death.

WRITING SUMMARIES

One method of summarizing short passages parallels the process you performed in Chapter 4 when you created topic sentences for paragraphs with main ideas that were implied but not stated: *Read the passage once or twice until its meaning is clear, put it aside, and then write a brief summary from memory.* As the length of a passage increases, however, summarizing becomes more of a challenge. Since college students are expected to summarize a variety of texts and passages, some of which are long and complex, you can benefit from a reliable, efficient method of composing summaries. The following process can save time and minimize frustration. As in all other types of writing, time spent in the preliminary stages pays off later on.

GUIDELINES for Summarizing Longer Passages

- *Read carefully.* To summarize a text or a passage, you must understand it thoroughly. Read it, look up unfamiliar words, and discuss its meaning with others.

- *Read with a pencil.* Underlining and marginal notes can increase comprehension. Be selective; underline main ideas only. Use your own symbols and marginal comments to highlight important ideas. Good notes and underlining will make later review quick and easy, so it pays to concentrate the first time through.

- *Write a one-sentence paraphrase of the main idea.* If the text or passage has a thesis statement, paraphrase it. If not, state what you take to be the main idea in your own words. This statement should provide a focus for everything else in the summary.

- *Write a first draft.* Compose a miniature version of the text or passage based on portions you have underlined and marginal notes you have written. Keep this draft simple, following the order of ideas found in the original. Paraphrase where possible, although parts of the first draft may still be close to the phrasing of the original.

- *Paraphrase your draft.* Treat your draft as a passage to be paraphrased. Restate its ideas and information in your own language and style, quoting no more than an isolated phrase or two or a single short sentence if there is an idea you cannot express as effectively in your own words. Remember that a summary expresses the ideas of the text or passage smoothly and clearly as well as concisely. Provide transitions, eliminate unnecessary words, combine ideas, and clarify any confusing sentences.

To illustrate this process, let's suppose you need to summarize the following passage from pages 76–78 of *Telling It Like It Isn't,* a book by J. Dan Rothwell, a scholar of semantics, the study of how language affects the way we think. First, read it with care until you are sure that you understand it (step 1).

Once you are satisfied that you understand the passage, go back and reread it with a pencil (step 2). Following is the passage as it was marked by one reader. (Since readers differ, it is unlikely that you would have marked it in exactly the same way.)

PRACTICE READING

Stereotyping: Homogenizing People

J. Dan Rothwell

We all carry around images of what members of particular groups are like. For instance, what image is conjured in your mind for a dope smoker, New York cab driver, black athlete, college professor, construction worker? These images are often shared by others. Typically, they stress similarities and ignore differences among members of a group. These images, then, become stereotypes—the attribution of certain characteristics to a group, often without the benefit of firsthand knowledge.

Stereotypes are judgments . . . of individuals not on the basis of direct interaction with those individuals specifically . . . but based instead on preconceived images for the category they belong to. Stereotypes, however, are not inherently evil. Some stereotypes, when predicated upon personal experience and empirical data, can be valid generalizations about a group.

Some stereo-
types are
valid?!

There are several potential problems with stereotypes, however. First, these preconceived images of groups may produce a frame of reference, a perpetual set in our minds concerning the group as a whole. Then, when faced with an individual from the group, the preconceived image is applied indiscriminately, screening out individual differences. Individuals become mere abstractions devoid of unique qualities, pigeonholed and submerged in the crowd, a crowd that is thought to be homogeneous.

①
The group
becomes more
important.

Indiscriminate application of stereotypes is particularly troublesome because stereotypes are not necessarily grounded on evidence or even direct experience. The classic study of stereotyping by Katz and Braly (1933) clearly revealed that stereotypes are often formulated in ignorance. They reflect attitudes toward labels, racial, ethnic, and others, frequently without benefit of actual contact with members of the group stereotyped. Student subjects held Turks in low esteem, yet most had never interacted with any member of this group.

A second problem with stereotypes is what general semanticists term *allness*. This is the tendency to characterize an individual or an entire group in terms of only one attribute or quality. This one characteristic becomes all that is necessary to know about a person. Once you realize that the person is a woman, or a Jew, or a Southerner, no more information is sought. This unidimensional view of a person is nothing more than a simplistic conception of an individual. You may be a Jew but also a brother, son, brilliant lawyer, charming compassionate individual, devoted father, loving husband, and so forth. Allness sacrifices complexity and substitutes superficiality. Racial and ethnic characteristics do not lend themselves to change, yet racial or ethnic labels may be the prepotent characteristic that supersedes all others. In fact, allness orientation may produce exaggerated perception of group characteristics. Secord et al. (1956) showed "prejudiced" and "unprejudiced" subjects several pictures of blacks and whites. The prejudiced observers exaggerated the physical characteristics of blacks such as thickness of lips and width of nose. Racial labels accentuated the stereotyped differences between "races" for prejudiced (allness-oriented) subjects.

②

A final problem associated with stereotyping is that it can produce frozen evaluations. Juvenile delinquents or adult felons may never shed their stigmatizing label despite "going straight." Zimbardo and Ruch (1977) summarize studies conducted at Princeton University over several decades regarding stereotypes by

③
When we see
stereotypes,
we can't see
people!!

Princeton students of various ethnic groups. While the stereotypes did change, they tended to do so relatively slowly. In 1933, blacks were deemed superstitious by 84% of Princeton students, 41% in 1951, and 13% in 1967. Thirty-four years is a very long time for people to acquire an accurate image of blacks on this one item.

Summary of above

Stereotypes are thus troublesome because they are often indiscriminate, exhibit an allness orientation, and can produce frozen evaluations. Considering the pervasiveness of stereotyping in our society, one should not take it lightly. When we stereotype, we define a person, and this definition, superficial at best, can be quite powerful.

To stereotype is to define, and to define is to control, especially if the definition is widely accepted regardless of its accuracy. In a male-dominated society women may be stereotyped as empty-headed and illogical. The fact that the stereotype has persisted for years manifests the control men have over women, control that excludes women from executive positions and relegates them to mindless housekeeping duties. Women's liberation is fundamentally the struggle to define, to reject male stereotypes of females.

vicious circle

Stereotypes are sometimes seductive, however. When women are told repeatedly that they are stupid, they may begin believing it. A self-fulfilling prophecy may develop. Low self-esteem produced from male definitions of women as unintelligent can lead to poor performance and the consequent belief that the stereotype has merit. The stereotype is thus nurtured and perpetuated. Stereotyping can thus control, insidiously imprisoning its victims in constraining roles.

SUMMARY
★

So while stereotyping isn't intrinsically evil, most stereotypes lack empirical foundations and are assertions of power and dominance over less powerful groups. Reduced to an abstraction, victims of stereotyping must struggle to define themselves or be content to accept roles others have carved out for them. It is little wonder our society has been experiencing turmoil.

Now write the thesis, a sentence stating the main idea of the passage (step 3):

Thesis

Stereotypes are judgments of people based on preconceived images about a group they are supposed to belong to.

Next, a first draft might look like this (step 4):

A first draft

We all carry around images of what groups are like, and these images are often shared. They stress similarities and ignore differences. Stereotypes assign certain characteristics to a group without benefit of firsthand knowledge. They are judgments of individuals based on preconceived images, not on direct interaction. However, stereotypes are not inherently evil. Some are valid.

Nevertheless, there are problems with stereotypes. When you have a preconceived image of a group, it induces a perceptual set that screens out individual differences. Indiscriminate stereotypes are not grounded on evidence and are often formulated in ignorance without actual contact. A second problem is allness: characterizing an individual or group in terms of only one attribute or quality. When you realize someone is a woman, a Jew, or a Southerner, you may not look for other information. This is a very simplistic idea of a person. It is superficial and does not account for the complexities that real people exhibit. A final problem with stereotypes is frozen evaluations: judgments that have stayed the same for a long time and change relatively slowly.

So we can see that stereotypes are dangerous because they are indiscriminate, are inclined toward allness, and give a frozen evaluation. They also define and control people if the stereotypes are widely accepted. Women, for example, have to struggle to reject men's stereotypes of females. Sometimes stereotypes are seductive. People believe these images, so they become self-fulfilling. An image can control its victims, imprisoning them in roles. Even though most stereotypes aren't valid, victims of stereotyping must either struggle to define themselves or accept the bad image others have made up for them.

The final step is to revise and proofread (step 5). Here you can concentrate on condensing, on avoiding repetition, and on focusing the sentences around the thesis. Because you are seeking economy, see if your first draft can be shortened. The result is a final draft that is, in effect, a summary of a summary, as in this final version:

Stereotypes are perceptions of individuals based on unexamined assumptions about a group they belong to. Although some stereotypes may be valid, they often create problems. First, stereotypes prevent us from regarding people as individuals. Second, they cause us to characterize people or groups on the basis of only one superficial attribute, a problem known as *allness*. Third, stereotypes become frozen and take years to change. When these false images are widely accepted, they define and therefore control people so thoroughly that unless victims struggle to disprove a stereotype, they often subscribe to it themselves (Rothwell 76–78).

The final draft

Writing Summaries   EXERCISES

1. Use the process outlined on page 186 to summarize the following passage from "Understanding Road Rage," an article by Read Mercer Schuchardt in *Counterblast: e-Journal of Culture and Communication*. Close your summary with a parenthetical citing only the name of the author, because electronic journals do not carry page numbers.

   Road rage is the incredibly unbearable frustration of being unable to successfully make the switch from the electronic to the mechanical universe while driving. It happens outside the car all the time, under different names. ADD, Going Postal, and a host of other modern phenomena will undoubtedly one day be linked to this inability of the human species to click from "reality" to "simulated reality" seamlessly without any psychic scars. Road rage is the intense anger you feel at not being able to click out of the traffic jam you're stuck in. Without knowing why you're so angry, you feel trapped in your car, claustrophobic, and anything—including violence—is better than suffocating under those conditions. . . . Now notice what a gun actually is: it's a live-action remote control—you use it to switch people to other channels, or rather, to get them off the one you're on. Seen another way, the gun is a live-action mouse—you just point and click, and boom, a new reality appears through the monitor screen of your windshield. To me, the truly amazing news about road rage is that so little violence has actually happened. . . . I have friends and students who have told me that when they come to a traffic jam, they will deliberately take the nearest exit and drive in the opposite direction just so they can keep driving, even though it takes them further from their destination.

2. Summarize the following article, which appeared on page 16 of the *Times* of London on the hundredth anniversary of air conditioning.

The King of Cool Celebrates a Century

James Bone

Even when temperatures soar into the nineties and beyond, it is easy to forget the little electrical box droning incessantly in the corner of the room. Yet that humble device is what made possible the summer blockbuster film, the all-glass skyscraper, retirement in Florida, the computerized office, the political rise of the "sunbelt states" and even mankind's mission to the moon.

The ubiquitous air conditioner, which transformed America as much as the railroads or the telegraph, turns one hundred this week, and its fans are seeking recognition for its unsung inventor, Willis Haviland Carrier.

"We could last a few days without air conditioning, but I think in the long run it would be difficult the way we have configured our buildings, our machines, our productivity," Marsha Ackermann, the author of *Cool Comfort: America's Romance with Air Conditioning,* said.

"Many people in other countries, particularly countries that happen to be cooler than ours, see it as an example of American excess," she notes. "But I have spent a lot of time in Britain, and there are very few days you need A/C. In our climate, it has really improved the living standard of a great many Americans."

Humans have tried to cool air at least since the Roman Emperors ordered snow to be brought down from the mountains to make their gardens more bearable. In the nineteenth century, a doctor in Florida invented a method of blowing air over buckets of ice hanging from the ceiling to keep malaria patients comfortable.

But the first mechanical system—marrying the twin innovations of electricity and refrigeration—was invented in 1902 by Carrier, a dreamer just a year out of Cornell University who was being paid just $10 a week by the Buffalo Forge Company in upstate New York.

The Sackett-Wilhelms Lithographic and Publishing Company in Brooklyn, one of Buffalo Forge's clients, complained that the paper it used for its printing jobs—including the popular humor magazine *Judge*—was expanding and contracting so much that the printers could not align the ink. Carrier's system was installed at the printing house on July 17, 1902.

Though few realized it at the time, the "Age of Air Conditioning" had begun. America had long prided itself on being "Nature's Nation," and its inhabitants prided themselves on their connection with the land. At first, few workplaces and even fewer homes adopted the new technology. The first dwelling to get air conditioning was a Minneapolis mansion in 1914.

But the prospect of a "weatherless" world fuelled Utopian dreams. Soon the new "picture palaces" embraced air conditioning in order to keep their audiences through the summer.

The early systems had vents in the floor and moviegoers sometimes had to wrap their legs in newspaper to fend off the cold. In 1925, Carrier installed a new system with ceiling outlets in the Rivoli Theater. "The Rivoli Cooled by Refrigeration Always Sixty-Nine Degrees," the marquee proclaimed.

Railway "club cars" and department stores' stuffy "bargain basements" followed, and the politicians in sweaty Washington decided that they should not be left out. The windowless House and Senate chambers in Congress were air-conditioned in 1928 and Herbert Hoover's White House outfitted the next year.

> "I date the end of the old republic and the birth of the empire to the invention of air conditioning," Gore Vidal, who grew up in the U.S. capital, wrote in 1982. "Before air conditioning, Washington was deserted from mid-June to September. The President—always Franklin Roosevelt—headed up the Hudson and all of Congress went home.
>
> "But since air conditioning and the Second World War arrived, more or less at the same time, Congress sits and sits while the Presidents and their staff never stop making mischief."
>
> It was only after the War that air conditioning entered ordinary American homes. By 1960, 12% of the nation's homes and 10% of its cars were air-conditioned, compared to 83% and 98% today.
>
> Raymond Arsenault, a professor at the University of South Florida, noted in a 1984 scholarly article that in the 1960s, for the first time since the Civil War, more people moved into the South than out. He attributed that "startling" statistic to the twin successes of the civil rights movement and air conditioning.
>
> Even the outcome of the disputed 2000 presidential election, decided in Florida, would have been different without air-conditioning. From being a relatively unimportant state of just 2.7 million people in 1950, Florida has grown into the fourth-largest state in the union, with 16 million people. Mr. Arsenault estimates that only 8 million would live there if it were not almost entirely air conditioned.

USES OF SUMMARY

Thus far we have said little about why a writer might summarize a text or a passage, beyond the obvious reason of saving the reader's time. Basically, however, summary serves most of the same purposes as paraphrase. The marginal note beside the textbook passage on page 183 shows how summary, like paraphrase, can help you understand and internalize complex and important ideas. Likewise, you can use summary to make a challenging passage accessible to others who may be unfamiliar with its terminology and concepts. (Our summary on page 185 of Magnus Pyke's account of European grocery shopping provides an example.)

Summarizing an Argument

Another frequent use of summary is to demonstrate understanding of a controversial point of view or argumentative text. Suppose you need to summarize the following excerpt from an essay about nonsexist language written by conservative columnist William Safire:

> It makes sense to substitute *worker* for *workingman* . . . , *firefighter* for *fireman,* and *police officer* for *policeman.* Plenty of women are in those occupations, and it misleads the reader to retain the old form. . . .
>
> But do we need *woman actor* for *actress,* or *female tempter* for *temptress?* And what's demeaning about *waitress* that we should have to substitute *woman waiter* or the artificial, asexual *waitron?* We dropped *stewardess* largely because the occupation was being maligned—a popular book title suggesting promiscuity was *Coffee, Tea, or Me?*—a loss that also took the male *steward* out the emergency exit,

A source that makes an argument

and now we have the long and unnecessarily concealing *flight attendant*. We were better off with *steward* and *stewardess*.

The abolition of the *-ess* suffix tells the reader or listener, "I intend to conceal from you the sex of the person in that job." Thus, when you learn that the *chairperson* or *chair* is going to be Pat Jones or Leslie Smith, or anyone not with a sexually recognizable first name like Jane or Tarzan, you will be denied the information about whether that person is a man or a woman.

Ah, that's the point, say the language police, sex-eraser squad: it should not matter. But information does matter—and does it really hurt to know? What's wrong with *chairwoman* or *Congresswoman?* Let's go further: now that the anti-sexist point has been made in this generation, wouldn't it be better for the next generation to have more information rather than less?

Regardless of whether you agree with these views, you probably would employ an attribution phrase, rather than just a parenthetical note, to call attention to their source. Notice how the underlined phrases in the following summary do that:

A summary
with attribution
phrases

<u>Some purists argue</u> that certain forms of nonsexist language are awkward and unnecessary, contributing little if anything to gender equity. <u>These writers contend</u> that occupational titles like *flight attendant* and *waitron* are awkward or silly and that they conceal relevant information about people's identities. <u>One such critic, William Safire, believes</u> that the injustices of sexist language have been sufficiently addressed already and that some traditional job designations should be retained (10).

EXERCISE | ## Summarizing an Argument

Write a summary of the following argument excerpted from another editorial by Safire. Since your summary will refer to the author by name, the closing parenthetical note should indicate only that the passage appears on page A17.

As every bigamist should know, *polygamy* is the condition of having more than one spouse at the same time, while *polyandry* is sex-specific—the marriage of a woman with more than one man.

I estimate that 98% of the 30,000 bigamists are males with plural wives, which means that there are probably fewer than 600 polyandrists in active practice today, presumably in a conservative ratio of one woman to two men. These 200 women and their 400 husbands (whose identities are unknown to snooping neighbors) deserve a discreet salute for quietly pioneering America's future lifestyle.

One woman, in the security of being doubly beloved and beneficiaried, can surely provide life-extending companionship to two men. And when one husband passes on, either to his Maker or to some gold-digging bimbo, the long-lived polyandrist would still have the remaining man for mutual comfort and support.

The Polyandry Movement, first espoused in this space five years ago, met an underwhelming response. Aberrant fogies like me, married nearly forty years to one woman, are selfishly disinclined to share, but two generations from now—given the woeful diminution of exclusive marriage commitment and the lengthening of life—the two-husband home may be the bedrock of the newest morality and the salvation of what's left of the American family.

Summarizing in Research Papers

Summary serves the same purposes as paraphrase in research writing: to cite important information, to place a topic or issue in context, and to support an interpretation or opinion. (It is, of course, equally important to use parenthetical notes to identify summarized sources.) The following examples illustrate these occasions for using summary in research writing.

Summarizing to Cite Information

Suppose you are writing a research paper about homelessness. One of your sources, an article by David Levi Strauss, cites the following facts:

> "Home" has increasingly become a site of violent conflict and abuse. Half of all homes are "broken" by divorce; many more are broken by spousal abuse. Child abuse in the home is a national epidemic. Poverty kills twenty-seven children every day in America. Ozzie and Harriet are dead, and the Cosbys don't live around here.
>
> Every year in the United States a million and a half kids run away from home. Many of them end up on city streets. Right now, today, there are some thirty thousand kids living on the streets of New York City. Contrary to popular belief, most of them run away not because they want to but because they have to; because even the streets are safer than where they're running from, where many of them have been physically and sexually abused by their families. Even so, they are not running *to* anything but death. Nationwide, more than five thousand children a year are buried in unmarked graves.

A source that cites information

A summary of these facts might be useful in a paragraph that dispels misconceptions about homeless people, including the belief that they are primarily adults who have made poor choices. Your summary might look like this:

> One of the most brutal facts about homelessness is the number of victims who are minors. Driven from their families by domestic violence, huge numbers of children (30,000 in New York alone) have taken to the streets, vainly hoping to find safety. Thousands of them die (Strauss 753).

A brief summary

Basically, this summary presents facts, including one statistic. Though obliged to identify your source in a parenthetical note, you probably would not cite the author's name in an acknowledgment phrase, since there is nothing about the manner in which you present these facts that is uniquely his. If, on the other hand, you wanted to quote a bit, you probably would employ such a phrase. A slightly longer summary, then, might look like this:

> One of the most brutal facts about homelessness is the number of victims who are minors. One reason is a dramatic increase in domestic violence, especially in poor neighborhoods. As journalist David Levi Strauss puts it, "Ozzie and Harriet are dead, and the Cosbys don't live around here." Strauss points to some alarming facts: on any given day, thirty thousand children are homeless in New York City; thousands of homeless children die every year in the United States (753).

A longer summary quoting the source

Summarizing to Place a Topic or Issue in Context

Suppose that a member of the student government on your campus has voiced opposition to Black Culture Week, arguing that such an event is unwarranted without a comparable celebration of white European culture. If you wished to examine and refute this familiar argument in a research paper, you might wish to demonstrate that most white Americans know far less about African cultures than they suppose—certainly a great deal less than most African Americans know about western European culture. In the course of your research, you locate a book review by Neal Ascherson, which includes the following paragraph:

A source that provides context for an issue

> This is a book perfectly designed for an intelligent reader who comes to the subject of Africa reasonably fresh and unprejudiced. Unfortunately, those are still fairly uncommon qualifications in Europe. The first category of baffled consumers will be those who until yesterday spent much energy denying Africans their history. They did not quite say, like [one] Cambridge professor, that Africa had no history at all. They said that anything ancient, beautiful, or sophisticated found on the continent could have had nothing to do with the talentless loungers incapable of making a decent cup of tea or plowing in a straight line. The ruins of Great Zimbabwe had been built by the Phoenicians; the Benin bronzes were probably Portuguese; and all ironwork was Arab. A more sophisticated version of this line was that although Africa had made a promising start, some unknown disaster or lurking collective brain damage had immobilized Africans halfway down the track. This meant, among other things, that the history and archaeology of Africa belonged to the Europeans, who had dug it up and were alone able to understand it. Back to Europe it went and there, to a great extent, it remains.

A summary of this passage would allow you to place Black Culture Week in a different context from the one in which your fellow student views it. Consequently, your paper might include a paragraph like this somewhere in its introduction:

A paragraph summarizing the source

> Black Culture Week is more than just an occasion for celebrating African heritage. It is an opportunity to dispel some of the demeaning misperceptions and stereotypes that diminish respect or even curiosity among white Americans. Among these is the belief, held by many educated people of European descent, that Africa has no native history or culture at all—that whatever artifacts are found there were brought by non-Africans, who are also the only people capable of understanding or appreciating their beauty or significance (Ascherson 26). Black Culture Week, therefore, is not so much a matter of promoting African heritage as it is a matter of correcting pervasive misinformation so that educated people can decide whether to study a field that many assume to be nonexistent or unworthy of serious attention.

Summarizing to Support an Interpretation or Opinion

When we discussed the paraphrasing of arguments in Chapter 3, we examined various ways of citing the source of a debatable point of view. Specifically, we looked at these options:

- Stating an argument without an attribution phrase, but putting both the author's name and appropriate page number(s) in a parenthetical note.

- Identifying the source with an attribution phrase and leaving only the page number(s) in the parenthetical note. (Attribution phrases that might be used to introduce a paraphrase of Barbara Lawrence's argument appear on page 144.)

- Expressing judgment about the credibility of the source in an attribution phrase. (Judgmental attribution phrases used in a letter to a library director appear on page 145.)

The effects of attributing an opinion to its source are equally important in the case of summary. Consider the following passage from an essay by Charles R. Lawrence, III, a professor of law at Georgetown University. Lawrence argues that racial insults are not protected by the constitutional guarantee of free speech when they occur on college campuses.

> If the purpose of the First Amendment is to foster the greatest amount of speech, racial insults disserve that purpose. Assaultive racist speech functions as a pre-emptive strike. The invective is experienced as a blow, not as a proffered idea, and once the blow is struck, it is unlikely that a dialogue will follow. Racial insults are particularly undeserving of First Amendment protection because the perpetrator's intention is not to discover truth or initiate dialogue but to injure the victim. In most situations, members of minority groups realize that they are likely to lose if they respond to epithets by fighting and are forced to remain silent and submissive.
>
> Courts have held that offensive speech may not be regulated in public forums such as streets where the listener may avoid the speech by moving on, but the regulation of otherwise protected speech has been permitted when the speech invades the privacy of the unwilling listener's home or when the unwilling listener cannot avoid the speech. Racist posters, fliers, and graffiti in dormitories, bathrooms, and other common living spaces would seem to clearly fall within the reasoning of these cases. Minority students should not be required to remain in their rooms in order to avoid racial assault. Minimally, they should find a safe haven in their dorm rooms and in all other common rooms that are part of their daily routine.
>
> I would also argue that the university's responsibility for insuring that these students receive an equal educational opportunity provides a compelling justification for regulations that insure them safe passage in all common areas. A minority student should not have to risk becoming the target of racially assaulting speech every time he or she chooses to walk across campus.

A source that expresses an opinion

If you were arguing in favor of a speech code that prohibits racial insults, you could cite Lawrence's claims by summarizing the passage as follows:

> The First Amendment was designed to protect the free exchange of ideas, but racial insults are designed to injure or intimidate others, to discourage rather than promote discussion. It would be different if minority students were able to walk away from such insults, but when they occur in dorms and other university buildings, offended students are compelled to endure them (Lawrence B1).

A paragraph summarizing the source

If you wanted to add the weight of authority to this opinion, you might introduce your summary with an attribution phrase—for example, "Georgetown University law professor Charles Lawrence concludes that . . ." or "Some legal experts argue that. . . ."

If, on the other hand, you disagreed with Lawrence, you certainly would introduce your summary with an attribution phrase—perhaps, "Professor Charles Lawrence expresses views typical of those who argue that protecting the interests of minorities takes priority over preserving unrestricted free speech." You might even consider a more judgmental attribution phrase—for example, "Professor Charles Lawrence rationalizes the abridgment of free speech, presenting it as a means of promoting equality and justice."

EXERCISE | **Summarizing in Research Papers**

Write a summary of each of the following passages—one that is appropriate to the given situation. Remember that you may either identify the source at the beginning of your summary or put the last name(s) of the author(s), along with page number(s), in a parenthetical note at the end.

a. *Source*

The following passage appears on page A1 of an article by Denise Grady, staff writer for the *New York Times.* The article reports findings of recent research regarding the children of first cousins.

Situation

Enrolled in a biology course titled Genetics in Human Affairs, you are writing a research paper about cultural beliefs regarding incest and how they correlate with scientific fact.

Passage

Contrary to widely held beliefs and longstanding taboos in America, first cousins can have children together without a great risk of birth defects or genetic disease, scientists are reporting. . . .

In the general population, the risk that a child will be born with a serious problem like spina bifida or cystic fibrosis is three to four percent; to that background risk, first cousins must add another 1.7 to 2.8 percentage points. . . .

Although the increase represents a near doubling of the risk, the result is still not considered large enough to discourage cousins from having children.

b. *Source*

The following passage appears on pages 27–28 of *Fast Girls: Teenage Tribes and the Myth of the Slut,* a recent book by freelance writer Emily White.

Situation

You are writing a research paper about high-school drug-education programs for your psychology course, Drugs and Behavior. You want to demonstrate the difficulty, as well as the importance, of integrating these programs into the overall curriculum and of tailoring them to an audience of high-school freshmen and sophomores.

Passage

In 1999 a warning pamphlet was circulated through public high schools. Called *The Marijuana Addict, at a Glance,* it's a remarkable piece of administrative prose that reveals a lot about the debased and contradictory way America addresses its teenagers.

The Marijuana Addict at a Glance

WHAT THEY THINK THEY ARE	vs.	WHAT THEY ARE
Believe they have good personal insight and awareness.		Are out of touch and deluded; live in a dream world.
Believe that success, fame, and fortune are just a matter of time.		Have grandiose illusions which have little chance of becoming reality.

After puzzling over this pamphlet repeatedly, I finally realized the irony. The marijuana addict being described and dissected (after being "glanced" at) was not much different from a dyed-in-the-wool American dreamer, the kind of man we learned about in social-studies class who walked two miles through the snow to school and believed "that success, fame, and fortune are just a matter of time." And while the pamphlet recognizes "living in a dream world" as a sign of deviance, the same kids who are being warned against the dream's dangers are reading *The Great Gatsby* in freshman lit. In Fitzgerald's irresistible perception, no matter how pathetic the dreamer becomes, he still possesses a glamorous beauty, a beauty ripe for idolatry and imitation.

c. *Source*

The following passage appears on page B14 of an article by Richard Kamber, professor of philosophy, and Mary Biggs, professor of English, both at the College of New Jersey. Kamber and Biggs argue that grade inflation has compromised the integrity of higher education and, as a result, diminished the value of a diploma.

Situation

You are writing a research-based article on college grade inflation for a journalism workshop. Your article will be considered for publication in the campus newspaper.

Passage

By passing students for going through the motions of learning, faculty members and their institutions are adopting the practice of social promotion that has stripped high-school diplomas of credibility. Thousands of college graduates are staffing businesses, teaching children, providing critical social services, and even winning admittance to graduate and professional schools without having mastered college-level skills or knowledge.

With four out of five students graduating with GPAs of B-minus or better, with a college degree ensuring neither knowledge of subject matter nor basic skills, employers and graduate schools have had to rely on other measures to sift through applicants. Standardized test scores and institutional "reputation" have become more important than the judgments of teachers and scholars. The discouragement of excellence, the concealment of failure, the torpedoing of our own credibility: harsh accusations, hard to believe, and yet these are the consequences of grade [inflation].

GUIDELINES for Effective Summarizing

The general principles set forth in this chapter can be summed up in the following guidelines for effective summarizing:

- Like paraphrasing, summarizing calls for close literal reading, but it also involves recognizing main ideas—distinguishing them from minor points and illustrative details.

- Like a paraphrase, a summary is written in your own language, although it may contain a short quotation or two—never more than a single sentence.

- Although there is no single correct way to compose a summary, one useful method is detailed on page 186.

- Summaries serve the same basic functions in research writing as paraphrases do.

■ READING SELECTION

The following article is one of the many attempts to put the terrorist attacks of September 11, 2001, into perspective. Roland Merullo, who also wrote "The Challenge of First-Generation College Students" (pages 110–15), teaches fiction writing at Amherst College.

America's Secret Culture

ROLAND MERULLO

1   In Robert Stone's third novel, *A Flag for Sunrise,* published twenty years ago, one of the major characters is an American professor of anthropology named Frank Holliwell. Partly because he wants to reconnect with an old friend, and partly because he's curious about political developments in Central America (the story is set just before the Nicaraguan revolution of 1979), Professor Holliwell finagles a speaking invitation at the Autonomous University of Compostela. Compostela is a fictional neighbor of Stone's fictional Tecan—a nation that very much resembles Nicaragua—and the small audience that assembles for Holliwell's speech is composed of American expatriates, Compostelan intellectuals, and a group of easily offended right-wing zealots worried about the spread of communism.

2   Holliwell prepares for his speech by drinking Scotch on an empty stomach. He writes it in Spanish but, at the last minute, is asked to give it in English. Then, standing at the lectern, confronted by his audience's prickly anticipation, he makes a decision that nearly gets him killed: He will ad-lib.

3   In the course of his drunken, rambling, brilliant diatribe on America and its relationship to the rest of the world, Holliwell says this: "Our popular culture is machine-made, and it's for sale to anyone who can raise the cash and the requisite number of semiliterate consumers. . . . Yet I would like to take you into my confidence in one regard, ladies and gentlemen and esteemed colleagues—and here I address particularly those of my listeners who are not North Americans—we have quite another culture concealed behind the wooden nutmeg and the flash we're selling. It is a secret culture. Perhaps you think of us as a nation without secrets—you're wrong. Our secret culture is the one we live by."

4   Like most of Stone's work, *A Flag for Sunrise* is strewn with substance abusers and driven by large ideas. It touches on communism, capitalism, materialism, the source of cruelty and insanity, the friction between faith and doubt, and the variability of loyalty and

love. And it circles around the notion that forms the heart of Holliwell's drunken tirade: America's secret culture. Does such a thing exist? If it exists, of what is it composed?

Those questions are more urgent and interesting now than they were before the 5 recent late-summer morning on which four commercial airliners were hijacked and three thousand innocent people killed. We know a little bit about the hijackers' movements before September 11, something about their financial backing and ideological motivation. But we have not probed very deeply into the real source of their anger. What do they see in American culture that infuriates them so? How much of what they see is truly there? What is it they don't see? What is it we don't see?

In the days after the attacks, some commentators on the left, while decrying the 6 violence and expressing sympathy for the loss of life, seemed to be suggesting that we'd gotten our just deserts. Cheeseburgers in Riyadh, warships in the Gulf—what did we expect, really?

And some commentators on the right, equally sympathetic to the victims and at 7 least as outraged at the perpetrators, were quick to close off that avenue of national introspection, eager to turn a blind eye to the bitter poverty from which so much Middle Eastern hatred has sprouted.

But what we heard then, and what we've been hearing since, are, in fact, only dif- 8 ferent voices coming from the same choir. Liberals and conservatives are linked, in some essential way that transcends their differences, by the culture of their native land—its language, its spiritual foundations (without always being aware of it, we are steeped in the stories and lessons of the Old and New Testaments), its political and military history, and some intangible other force as well—our secret culture.

My left-leaning friends have a note of mockery in their voice when they talk 9 about their fellow townspeople driving around with Old Glory flapping on the back of their pickups. And my right-leaning friends respond with a note of derision; they're quick to question the mockers' patriotism. Secret tribunals for suspected terrorists? Your reaction to that idea sets you on either side of a line that cuts through American society: the National Rifle Association, Rush Limbaugh, and Idaho versus the American Civil Liberties Union, Mario Cuomo, and Massachusetts.

The terrorists, though, and the radical sects that finance them and foment their 10 hatred, make no such distinction. Conservative or liberal, pious or agnostic, you're still American, and you therefore bear the stain of America's wicked history. Osama bin Laden said as much when he asserted that the people in the World Trade Center were legitimate military targets, as complicit as soldiers in America's rape and pillage of the rest of the world. He and his sympathizers look at us through a lens clouded by their own subjectivity—what Robert Stone called, in a *New York Times Magazine* essay about the attacks, their "stories." They don't see us as we are. (Just as, quite likely, we don't see the Yemenis or Tajiks as they are.) If they saw us as we are, they might have more accurately anticipated our response to the September attacks: a tidal wave of charitable donations on the one hand and, on the other, a raging, largely unquestioned military campaign that quickly succeeded in flushing the Taliban from power. Blinded by their compelling but inaccurate narratives, they could not imagine that America might transcend their caricature of it, and they have paid a terrible price for that mistake.

What I have not seen in recent commentary, on either the left or the right, is the 11 eerie resemblance between the way radical Islamic sects depict America and the way it was depicted by Soviet propaganda through much of the twentieth century. The caricatures could pass as twins. For twenty-eight months between March 1977 and March 1990, I worked in the Soviet Union on a series of cultural-exchange exhibitions organized by the United States Information Agency, an arm of the State Department. My first job there, a job that lasted for most of 1977, was to stand with twenty-four other

Russian-speaking Americans on the floor of the "Photography USA" exhibit and answer questions. The questioners were Soviet people from every corner and layer of that enormous nation: collective farmers, gulag veterans, propaganda-shouting KGB provocateurs, scientists, journalists, actresses, plumbers, and tough old kerchiefed women who had survived the siege of Leningrad.

12   Admission to the ten thousand-square-foot exhibit was free, and visitors squeezed into the building at the rate of fifteen thousand per day. They'd stand before the displays of cameras and the pictures in the portrait gallery, then surround the exhibit guides three or four deep and drown us in streams of questions: Why did you drop the atomic bomb in Hiroshima and Nagasaki? Why can't black people and white people sit together in your restaurants? Why are the police always beating students? Why did Elvis Presley kill himself with drugs? Isn't it true that you got this job only because you're the son of a wealthy industrialist?

13   Our assignment was to stand there, little islands of Americana in a sea of propaganda-saturated Soviets, and answer questions like that six hours a day, six days a week—in Moscow, in Siberia, in Stalinist backwaters like the Ural Mountains city of Ufa. We were free to say anything we wanted about America, to criticize, boast, even to deride. And, to the confusion of some visitors, we did all of those things.

14   It was the perfect way to get a sense of what might be called the Soviet Union's secret culture—its bizarre combination of public meanness and private hospitality, naïveté and harsh experience, sadism and sympathy. And it wasn't a bad way, either, of being made to look over our shoulders at the country we'd left behind.

15   Starved of objective information as they were, even some highly educated Soviets saw us then the way the fundamentalists in the Middle East see us now: as nothing more than a nation made rotten by phenomenal wealth, a people turned soft by lucky history, a culture doomed to fail—and soon—because it had embraced the demon of capitalism. It goes without saying that, in both cases, the caricature is based partly in fact. Though the story we tell ourselves rarely acknowledges this, we have thrived thanks to a fortunate combination of geographical location, climate, and soil. We did build our nation on the tombs of another culture, on the backs of slaves and unsuspecting immigrants. We do tolerate an inexcusable degree of distance between our rich and our poor. And we continue to manipulate economic markets, incite or ignore coups d'état, and throw our military weight around simply to further our own interests.

16   But to stop there is to see only the wooden nutmeg and the flash. It is a kind of seductive simplification and underestimation that has proved fatal to a series of anti-American ideologies over the centuries, and may prove, eventually, to be fatal again where the violent wing of fundamentalist Islam is concerned.

17   To get to the essence of America's secret culture, one must pass beyond that caricature, then vault over a razor-wire-topped fence of homegrown cliché. We are too big and complicated to be encapsulated in a sketch of Uncle Sam. We are something more than a capitalist demon and something less than the Statue of Liberty. We are the people who welcome immigrants from Guatemala . . . and train the Guatemalan secret police in the science of torture. We are the people who soak our rich topsoil in pesticides manufactured by profit-blinded corporations . . . and give away millions of tons of food. We support dictators—Duvalier, Somoza, the Shah of Iran—and risk our lives to depose dictators—Hitler, Milosevic, Mohammad Omar. We are Disney, and we are National Public Radio, Las Vegas and the Metropolitan Museum of Art, Harvard Square and Birmingham, tenth-generation WASP investment bankers and first-generation Somalian nursing-home aides.

18   We are a sort of anti-tribal juggernaut in a world that has been evolving, for millennia, from tribalism toward something larger, more inclusive, less closed. That evo-

lution has been marked by the worst kinds of violence and arrogance—from the Crusades to the conquistadors to the Chinese invasion of Tibet—and we certainly bear on our collective soul some of the sins of colonialism and imperialism.

But, ultimately, we are the riddle wrapped in a mystery inside an enigma. Only, instead of closing ourselves off to the outside world—as the Soviet Union did for seventy-five years—in true American fashion we offer the world an image of welcome and openness. We are a big, smiling Mickey Mouse, knocking people over in his rush to make everyone as happy as he is. There is a person hidden inside—sweating, overfed, bumptious—and he'll help you if he can. That sometimes disingenuous charitability is the color you get when you mix the colors of all the people who have come here. They came to escape poverty or repression or pogroms; to be free to make a fortune, burn a flag, buy a pair of blue jeans and the latest jazz CD. But, within a generation or so, those motivations fade and something new and mysterious evolves, something both self-absorbed and generous and particularly American. . . .   **19**

Clumsy, corny, well-meaning, adolescent, brainy, aggressive and tough, sentimental and gracious, overly proud, guilty of sin and preaching redemption, we are the people who drop five thousand-pound bombs and food packages on Afghanistan at the same time. Show me another culture in the history of humankind that can match that mixture of yin and yang. Show me another people who would send the Uzbek tribesmen of northern Afghanistan peanut butter instead of *plov*, and then brag about it. Show me another country that could produce Colin Powell—a Harlem-born Republican with African, Irish, Scottish, Jewish, and Arawak Indian blood—and send him on behalf of the descendants of slaveholders to negotiate with sheiks, tribal elders, and dictators.   **20**

Boiled down to its last hard ounce, our secret culture is nothing more than a kind of tolerance—grudging, bigotry-speckled, soaked in self-interest—for the contradictions within ourselves. Embracing and expanding that tolerance is the larger purpose of American academicians and artists. Because the acceptance, even the pursuit, of contradiction is the essence of our work.   **21**

Novelists, playwrights, theoretical physicists, art critics, anthropologists—the best of them, at least—make their careers in the muddy waters of human complexity. It is often a thankless and frustrating life, a pursuit of the certainty of uncertainty, the unifying force of individuality, or a formula that posits where an electron is likely to be at any given point in time. How much more existentially comforting to be a carpenter who, at the end of the day, can be sure that he has accomplished something, or a fireman who has saved a life, or a businesswoman who has turned a profit.   **22**

But America's secret culture is a slippery creature, composed of the ghosts of Iroquois and Pilgrims, anarchists and tycoons, ruffians and household saints. Try taking hold of something like that.   **23**

It is fitting that Robert Stone chose as his American hero a professor who holds all our contradictions within himself. At the close of *A Flag for Sunrise*, Frank Holliwell has risked his life to befriend an outcast colleague, fallen in love with and then betrayed a nun, and murdered a Latino drug addict. But he is still alive, still hopeful, and, as he insists, still "capable of honor." Mixed and mixed up, but capable of honor. American to the core.   **24**

The culture that produces millions of Holliwells has often been described as adolescent, and that is surely true. And yet, is it not also true that one measure of maturity is the ability to accept ambiguity, to grow beyond the simple answers favored by religious fanatics and ideologues? In the end of ends, as the Russians say, this is what saves us. Homosexual or heterosexual, celibate or promiscuous, luxury-loving or ascetic, pious or irreverent, scholarly or stupid, hypnotized by our pop culture or marching against it—we rant and mock and threaten . . . and in the end let each other be.   **25**

And so, naturally, like Professor Holliwell, we are exactly the kind of people who drive the religious zealot and the political iconoclast absolutely mad.

Freewriting

In your notebook, write for ten to fifteen minutes about Merullo's characterization of America's hidden culture. Try to capture in your own language, as clearly and precisely as you can, the contradictions that Merullo regards as the defining features of this culture. You may wish to identify other contradictions that you perceive in the actions, beliefs, or values of some Americans or to cite other examples of the contradictions that Merullo highlights. Or, you may wish to describe individuals (including celebrities, fictional characters, or historical figures, as well as personal acquaintances) who, in their public or private lives, exemplify these contradictions.

Group Work

Share freewrites in your reading group, each member reading aloud while others are taking notes. As you listen to each person read, try to develop a list of contradictions within our national culture that, if recognized and explored, might help Americans and non-Americans to better understand themselves or each other. Try to phrase each contradiction in a way that indicates inconsistency (e.g., "We say . . . , but we still do . . ." or "We believe . . . , yet we also believe . . .").

Review Questions

1. How, according to Merullo, have commentators on the left reacted ineffectively or inappropriately to the terrorist attacks of September 11, 2001? How, in his view, have commentators on the right also misconstrued those events?

2. How do the perceptions of Islamic radicals resemble those of many Soviet citizens during the Cold War?

3. What does Merullo see as the appropriate role of academicians and artists in America?

Discussion Questions

1. Merullo is critical of both liberals and conservatives. Is he more harshly critical of one than the other? Does he say anything to suggest what his own political affiliations might be?

2. Why do you suppose the fictional Frank Holliwell nearly gets killed for his ad-libbed comments about America's hidden culture?

3. What public figures, other than Colin Powell, represent the complex contradictions of America? (Consider celebrities as well as historical and political figures.)

Writing

1. Write an essay that identifies, defines, and illustrates the contradictions found within a group, organization, or subculture to which you belong or about which you have some knowledge.

2. In paragraph 8 of "America's Hidden Culture," Merullo states that "without always being aware of it, we are steeped in the stories and lessons of the Old and New Testaments." Later, he refers to an essay by Robert Stone, in which the author states: "The power of narrative is shattering, overwhelming. We are the stories we believe; we are who we believe we are. All the reasoning of the world cannot set us free from our mythic systems. We live and die by them."

   In a similar vein, essayist Joan Didion has stated:

   > [N]ot only have I always had trouble distinguishing between what happened and what merely might have happened, but I remain unconvinced that the distinction, for my purposes, matters. The cracked crab that I recall having for lunch the day my father came home from Detroit in 1945 must certainly be embroidery, worked into the day's pattern to lend verisimilitude; I was ten years old and would not now remember the cracked crab. . . . And yet it is precisely that fictitious crab that makes me see the afternoon all over again, a home movie run all too often, the father bearing gifts, the child weeping, an exercise in family love and guilt.

   Regardless of whether one agrees with Merullo, Stone, or Didion, their experience as writers and storytellers complicates notions of truth vs. lie, fact vs. fiction, that most people accept as axiomatic. Write an essay that contrasts these two points of view, relating them to some specific event, public or private (e.g., a familiar legend or story), that you have witnessed or are at least familiar with.

WRITE, READ, and RESEARCH the NET

1. *Write:* Freewrite for fifteen minutes in response to some or all of the questions and assertions raised in paragraph 5 of Merullo's essay.

2. *Read:* Review the following Web site:
   <http://www.msnbc.com/news/649424.asp?cp1=1>

3. *Research:* Using the Internet, locate Web sites that address the controversy surrounding the adoption of Deryl Davis's book *Approaching the Qu'ran* (keep in mind the alternate spelling, *Koran*) as a required reading for first-year students at the University of North Carolina at Chapel Hill. Write an essay that fairly represents the strongest argument in support of and the strongest argument in opposition to the university's decision.

■ ADDITIONAL READINGS

"Elements of Tragedy" is a collection of memoirs relating to the terrorist attacks of September 11, 2001, contributed to the *New York Times Magazine* by eight prominent authors, five of whom are novelists. Among them is the response of Robert Stone to which Roland Merullo refers in paragraph 10 of "America's Secret Culture." Following is a condensation of the final chapter of a recently published book, *Sweet Freedom's Song: "My Country, 'Tis of Thee" and Democracy in America,* coauthored by the late Robert James Branham and Stephen J. Hartnett. Branham was a professor of rhetoric at Bates College. Hartnett, a musician and poet, teaches speech communication at the University of Illinois. The authors trace the history of the British national anthem and its American counterpart, often referred to by its opening line: "My country, 'tis of thee."

Elements of Tragedy

The Image

COLSON WHITEHEAD

1   Fort Greene Park in Brooklyn has hills that look out on Lower Manhattan. On the morning of September 11, people were staked out in small groups, strangers trading misinformation and speculation. What was sure and known was that the towers were burning; we could see that from the northern slope of the park. The trees at the edge below us obscured all but the highest landmarks: the tips of the Manhattan Bridge, the roofs of the more ambitious corporate headquarters. The top halves of the twin towers had always overpowered the scene like bullies.

2   We picked out a spot, and I told my wife, "You should take a picture." Because it was a very nice shot, well composed. The three men in the foreground were obviously strangers, standing together, but not so close as to violate any rules about personal space. They were of different races; one had a dog that looked away from the scene at a bird or something; one had abandoned a bicycle on the ground. The bicycle was a nice touch—couldn't have placed it better myself. In the sky before the men, the towers burned. The right part of the frame was unblemished blue sky, the left a great wash of brown and black smoke. The dynamic event, the small human figures. It was a nice shot. Call it "The Watchers" or "The Spectators." Frame it. Keep it away.

3   Then the wind shifted for a second, and where the second tower should have been, it wasn't. All that time, I had assumed that the smoke had merely hidden it, but it hadn't been there at all. And then Tower 2 sighed. The top floors buckled out, spraying tiny white shards, and the building sank down into itself, crouching beneath the trees and out of frame. I shouted, "Oh, my God!" It had been a nice shot. And certainly it had been easier to shape the horror into an aesthetic experience and deny the human reality. There was safety in that distance. A man picked up his bike and walked away. My wife and I went home. There had never been any safety at all.

The Simile

RICHARD POWERS

I was preparing to meet my undergraduate writing class at the University of Illinois when   **4**
I heard the news. The day's topic was to have been figurative speech: metaphor and simile in fiction. On my way out the door, I saw the first headlines. Then the images and the
repeating, unreal film. And every possible class lesson disappeared in that plume.

With the rest of the world, I found myself losing ground against the real. The an-   **5**
chors, the reporters, the eyewitnesses, the experts: all fighting against the onset of
shock, all helpless to say what had happened, all working to survive the inconceivable. And when the first, stunted descriptions came, they came in a flood of simile.
The shock of the attack was like Pearl Harbor. The gutted financial district was like Nagasaki. Lower Manhattan was like a city after an earthquake. The gray people stream-
ing northward up the island covered in an inch of ash were like the buried at Pompeii.

And in this outpouring of anemic simile, again and again with startlingly little   **6**
variation, people resorted to the most chilling refrain: like a movie. Like *Independence
Day*. Like *The Towering Inferno*. Like *The Siege*. Like bad science fiction. Like a Tom
Clancy novel. (Clancy, talking to CNN, seemed to find the plot more unbelievable
than any plot of his own.) The magnitude of this day could not be made real except
through comparison to fiction. Nothing but the outsize scale of the imaginary was big
enough to measure by.

Failed similes proliferated throughout the afternoon. Blocks like the apocalypse.   **7**
Wall Street executives wandering like the homeless. Streets like Kinshasa. Rubble like
Beirut or the West Bank.

No simile will ever serve. In its size and devastation and suddenness, the destruc-   **8**
tion of September 11 is, in fact, like nothing, unless it is like the terrors experienced in
those parts of the world that seemed so distant on September 10.

I met my class, although I could pretend to no teaching. It was not like a wake; it   **9**
was one. We shared the shortfall of our thoughts. "It's like a dream," my students said.
And more frightening still, "Like waking from a dream." The America they woke to on
Tuesday morning was, like the skyline of New York, changed forever. The always-
thereness of here was gone.

The final lesson of my writing class came too soon. There are no words. But there   **10**
are only words. To say what the inconceivable resembles is all that we have by way of
learning how it might be outlived. No comparison can say what happened to us. But
we can start with the ruins of our similes, and let "like" move us toward something
larger, some understanding of what "is."

The Villains

ROBERT STONE

In 1993, I wrote a *New York Times* Op-Ed article about the bombing of the World Trade   **11**
Center that occurred that year. Writing then, I offered the readers the mind's eye of an
anonymous conspirator watching from a safe house in Queens or New Jersey, praying for
the explosion, knowing it was God's will. Those towers thrusting so immodestly more
than a thousand feet in the air, I wrote, must have mocked his passionate intensity.

I was thinking of "The Second Coming," by Yeats, the chilling prophetic dream of   **12**
"mere anarchy" loosed on the world. "The best lack all conviction," Yeats wrote,
"while the worst are filled with passionate intensity."

13   A dozen or so individuals as human as we fly planes full of doomed, terrified people into the Pentagon and the World Trade Center, a teeming city in the air. Are they moral monsters? Are they really the worst, driven by sheer evil?

14   Though we are being judged, despite our grief and loss, we cannot really judge. We are steeped in relativism, as confined by our narrative as the murderers are confined by theirs. History is a story we have accepted; our lives are the stories we tell ourselves about the experience of life.

15   In the Middle East, where the gods were born, the ancient narratives are glorified again. After the 1967 war, for example, Jewish settlers awaiting the Messiah founded settlements among their ancestral stones, risking their lives, ready to kill and to die in the name of a sacred narrative, soon to be vindicated.

16   So in the Muslim world the sacred historical destiny of Islam is reasserted. The will of God is to be done on earth. One narrative contained in the Koran speaks of the people of Ad. "Their sin is arrogance," the book says. The people of Ad rely on their power and their material wealth to prevail in the world. "They will be brought low."

17   The unreality we experienced on September 11 was of something fictive. We witnessed, in the elemental horror that our conscious minds denied, the violent assault of one narrative system upon another. People deeply enclosed in their sanctified worldviews were carrying out what they experienced as a sacred command to annihilate the Other.

18   The expressions from Washington are nothing surprising—assurances of "resolve" and retribution. But in various ways, our internal narrative, our social and political foundations, circumscribe our capacity for revenge. The internal narrative of our enemies, their absolute ruthless devotion to an invisible world, makes them strong. Our system, too, is a state of mind. We need to find in it the elements that will serve our actual survival.

19   The power of narrative is shattering, overwhelming. We are the stories we believe; we are who we believe we are. All the reasoning of the world cannot set us free from our mythic systems. We live and die by them.

The Hero

JAMES TRAUB

20   One of the running gags of the Giuliani years was "the bunker"—press shorthand for the $15 million Emergency Command Center the mayor built on the twenty-third floor of 7 World Trade Center in 1998. The bunker symbolized the mayor's bunker mentality—his love of crisis, his almost delighted sense that a besieged city needed an untiring and unsmiling defender.

21   Now that bunker lies in a great heap of rubble. On the morning of the disaster, which infinitely exceeded even his own direst imaginings, the mayor and his chief aides abandoned the Emergency Command Center for another installation and fled that one in turn only ten minutes before it was destroyed, killing the men who stayed behind. In the news conferences he gave that afternoon, the mayor spoke of his own escape from death and of the many friends who had died. There was a delicacy in his manner, an anxious concern for the sufferings of others that few had ever associated with him. Giuliani's stoicism in the past had seemed to come of unfeeling; this was the stoicism of deep feeling held rigorously in check.

22   At one point during the day, Ed Koch, the former mayor, suggested that America obliterate the capital of any nation that continued to harbor terrorists. You couldn't

help feeling grateful that Koch was no longer mayor. Mayor Giuliani issued no such threats. Quite the contrary: he assured New Yorkers that the Bush administration would find the appropriate response, whatever that was, and urged them to refrain from all forms of hatred, especially "group hatred" directed at Muslims. And then he apologized for having even to suggest something that was beneath the dignity of New Yorkers. The mayor is normally the least graceful of men, but on that day he brought to mind Hemingway's phrase "grace under pressure."

The time will come when our sense of crisis will settle into a kind of permanent   23
substrate, and New Yorkers will return to their perennial concerns—the schools, the streets, the parks. By November, when voters choose a new mayor, they may not regard grace under pressure as the cardinal mayoral virtue. You could, in fact, argue that by defusing New York's fixed atmosphere of crisis, Mayor Giuliani has made the city safe for a very different kind of successor. The candidates might embrace this logic themselves if doing so wouldn't implicitly diminish them.

Indeed, the World Trade Center disaster magnifies the widespread sense that the   24
men hoping to succeed the mayor are smaller than he. But we should remind ourselves that Giuliani himself wasn't always so magisterial a figure; the hothead candidate of 1993 probably could have started a nuclear war on his own. The crisis shapes the man as much as the other way around; he is, if he has any substance at all, fired in the crucible of office. Giuliani's bearing at this moment of anguish ensures that he will be remembered fondly, at least by many; New Yorkers can hope that the man they elect may someday surprise them with the same gifts.

The Weapon

Stephen King

People keep saying "like a movie," "like a book," "like a war zone," and I keep thinking: No, not at all like a movie or a book—that's no computer-generated image, because you can't see any wash or blur in the background. This is what it really looks like when an actual plane filled with actual human beings and loaded with jet fuel hits a skyscraper. This is the truth.

Certainly, it seems to me that the idea of an enormous intelligence breakdown is   26
ludicrous; again, this was not like a book, not like a movie; this was men armed with nothing but knives and box cutters relying on simple speed to keep people off balance long enough to accomplish their goals. In the case of the plane that crashed in Pennsylvania, they failed. With the other three, however, they succeeded quite nicely. Cost of weaponry? Based on what we know now, less than a hundred dollars. This qualifies them as cut-rate, low-tech, stealth guerrillas flying well under the radar of American intelligence. We must realize this and grasp an even more difficult truth: although it is comforting to have a bogeyman, and every child's party needs a paper donkey to pin the tail on, this Osama bin Laden fellow may not have been the guy responsible. It wouldn't hurt to remember that the boys who shot up Columbine High School planned to finish their day by hijacking a jetliner and flying it into—yes, that's right—the World Trade Center. Dylan Klebold and Eric Harris weren't exactly rocket scientists, and the guys who did this didn't have to be either. All you had to be was willing to die, and these guys were. It could happen again. And now that crazos the world over see that it's possible to get seventy-two hours of uninterrupted air time on a budget, it will almost certainly happen again.

The Technology

JENNIFER EGAN

27   I first learned of trouble at the World Trade Center from my husband, who watched the second plane's explosion from inside a Q train on the Manhattan Bridge. He reached me at home on his cell phone. It was only after we had hung up that the thought of him suspended there, above the East River in a subway car, began to unsettle me. Still, I felt curiously calm. He's fine, I thought. After all, I just talked to him.

28   Of course, that was no guarantee of anything. Throughout the disasters of September 11, people harnessed communications technology from the most extreme circumstances imaginable. Barbara Olson, a passenger on American Airlines Flight 757, used her cell phone to report early details of the hijacking. Friends and families of workers in the World Trade Center used e-mail to exhort their loved ones to flee the building. Some of those trapped in the rubble used their pagers or cell phones to call for rescue. The sheer density of such exchanges makes the boundary between those inside and outside Tuesday's disasters seem difficult to establish.

29   Still, there is an eerie poignancy about those high-tech goodbyes from people trapped inside burning buildings and runaway planes. A similar quality clung to the story of Rob Hall, the leader of a doomed 1996 expedition up Mount Everest. Marooned in a snowstorm, Hall reached his pregnant wife in New Zealand by radio-phone, and together they chose a name for their unborn child. The imbalance is almost crushing: if they could hear each other's voices, name a child, say goodbye, how could he not have been rescued?

30   We in the developed world have come a long way toward eliminating time and space as determining factors in our lives. We can whisper into the ear of someone across the globe. We can trade intimacies with people whose whereabouts are unknown to us—beside the point, even. Without a doubt, Tuesday's tragedies showcase the extraordinary rewards of the communications revolution. Yet never have the limits of communication been more stark. One person is inside a burning building and one is outside. Their voices may meet in the digital void, but they can't pull each other to safety across it.

The Bond

ROGER LOWENSTEIN

31   I was in Chicago, preparing a speech about uncertainty as an inherent part of business, when the need arose, obviously, to get back to the East Coast, to get home.

32   Mass transport had stopped, and the car-rental companies were booked. In another time, I might have put out a thumb, but all I could think of was to connect with other travelers, so I jogged to the Hilton nearby. A quartet of young to middle-aged businessmen were camped in the lobby. My luck that they had rented a van and were bound for New York, and doubly so that they were of a mind to share it.

33   Because I wanted to feel a part, I bought water and Snickers bars for the gang, but I needn't have; on Tuesday, you could connect with anyone. My companions were part of what is called the global economy; they worked for a company with a German parent that sold, I gathered, digitally enhanced machines all over America. Until a few hours before, each of them had been wining and dining clients at pricey restaurants.

34   Now we were eating up highway in states I had seen before only from the air. We talked about the attack, of course, and we murmured into our cell phones. In Toledo, we stopped for gas; I looked at the other drivers in line, and they nodded as if to say, "I'm here for the same reason you are."

As we rolled by the unrelenting scenery, we heard the same news, transmitted   **35**
through distinct geographic filters: school closings in Chicago, people giving blood in
Dayton. Commentators spoke of Pearl Harbor, but the country seemed too vast to believe it would all shut down or be shunted, ultimately, off its course. The farms in Indiana looked like giant combines; on the pastures in Ohio, the cattle grazed as ever.

The sky darkened, and somebody joked about finding a strip joint. But we were   **36**
beyond that. The men were calling their wives, and nobody ingested anything
stronger than Maalox and Camels. The oldest of the salesmen was frantically trying to
learn about a colleague in the World Trade Center. The youngest was telling his wife to
keep his kids away from the television. One by one, we lost our batteries, our technological connection.

Inevitably, the men talked about themselves a little. I gathered that they liked   **37**
their lives, their work. The oldest had been involved in bailing people out in Vietnam.
They didn't want, any of them, to go back to that America of turmoil.

We stopped for the night at a Holiday Inn in eastern Ohio. We went into a bar for   **38**
dinner, and even with the televisions showing the awful footage, some locals were
carousing with what struck us as too much gaiety. My companions had the grace to remember that perhaps we in the East hadn't paid enough mind to the tragedy in Oklahoma City; perhaps, I thought, that was one reason the president seemed slow to connect to this one.

We hit the road early Wednesday and didn't stop until lunch at a Denny's, in the   **39**
eastern part of Pennsylvania now. We ran into a caravan of businesswomen driving
westward to Michigan—our opposites, so to speak, and it seemed that the entire country had reverted to a pretechnological form of travel. I sensed that they would be
ready, if need be, to forsake even automobiles, but not the unceasing motion and energy of our wonderfully restless country.

The Thrill

Judith Shulevitz

So this is what it's like to go to war, real war, in which real Americans die and toler-   **40**
ance for people with dangerous ideas seems frivolous compared with the need to stop
them. Just a couple of weeks ago, I would have dismissed the exchange of civil liberties for safety as a false trade-off. But then I didn't know what it felt like to see even
network news anchors grow nervous inside their New York skyscrapers. Every other
American-fought war taking place during my adulthood has felt, by comparison, like a
media event. Grenada? The Gulf War? Army exercises and fireworks displays, with the
same relationship to national defense as a burlesque extravaganza has to romantic intimacy. Now I understand the urgent patriotism Steven Spielberg was trying to get
across in *Band of Brothers,* in retrospect the most prescient television program of the
days before the attack.

This sense of seriousness, of having a role to play in history, is why war engenders   **41**
so much nostalgia despite its atrocities. Somewhere deep in my heart, I have always
longed for a catastrophe like the present one. Such wishes may seem appalling once
they have come true, but we harbor them nonetheless. The novelist Don DeLillo has
called this our "tone of enthusiasm for runaway calamity." I have sometimes imag-
ined, while panting up a mountain, that I'm sneaking away from a ghetto to join
some partisans in the forest. Others dress up in Civil War uniforms and reproduce his-
toric battles, or just watch the History Channel.

The desire for a collective purpose seems almost as great as the desire for a per-   **42**
sonal one. Indeed, if you ask people who have lived through periods of intense

national challenge—veterans of World War II, of course, or of the Czechoslovakian Velvet Revolution—about the high points of their lives, you might conclude that they value their memories of struggle more than those of peace. There's nothing like being under attack to clarify what's important and to sweep away the nonsense on which we tend to squander our public attention: petty political squabbling, the enervating celebrity gossip. Never again to have to think about Gary Condit or Britney Spears! To focus as a nation on our future and that of our children! These are instinctively attractive and ennobling ideas. Only once those other topics disappear, if they disappear, do we begin to appreciate how lucky we had been to be obsessed by them.

"America," "God Save the Queen," and Postmodernity

ROBERT JAMES BRANHAM AND STEPHEN J. HARTNETT

1   The 1831 premiere of Samuel Smith's "America" in Boston's Park Street Church featured a well-drilled children's choir and the moral pretensions of temperance[1] activists gathered to celebrate a properly righteous July Fourth unsullied by the drunken revelry of their social inferiors. For much of the rest of the nineteenth century the song was employed in a variety of similarly ceremonial but also frequently oppositional occasions. Whether using Smith's original lyrics in dignified celebrations of the nation or any number of the hundreds of parodied variations used to protest the nation's failures, most of the grassroots activists using "America" held the song to be an iconic symbol of American identity. One might argue about whether the promises and ideals of "sweet freedom's song" had been filled and were cause of celebration or whether in fact they had been buried beneath generations' worth of hypocrisy and fear and were cause for protest, but it was generally agreed that democracy was an evolving experiment and that using one's politics, both individually and collectively, was a healthy and productive way of making sure that the nation continued to learn (albeit it slowly, painfully slowly) how to be more true to its foundational principles. Thus, while "America" was a universally popular *and* contested song, one senses that the myriad groups appropriating it shared the assumptions that democracy was serious business and that participating in political struggle—particularly via song—was part of what it meant to be an American.

2   The gradual development of mass media led, however, to the production of a culture awash in an almost infinite number of images, sounds, and commodities, hence to the creation of a world in which very little is agreed on, let alone shared as an icon worth fighting for. Not surprisingly, "My Country, 'Tis of Thee," played a central role in the evolution of this situation, for it was among the first songs recorded and sold on a mass scale, contributing to the production of what scholars now refer to as "the culture industry." The first commercial recordings were developed in 1889 for use in phonograph parlors, where patrons paid a nickel, spoke the name of a song into a tube, and listened to their selection through a separate tube connected to a phonograph in the room below. In 1890, North American Records developed the first cylinder duplication machinery. Jules Levy, who billed himself "the world's greatest cornet player" and was the first major musician to be exclusively recorded, scored a number-one hit with his 1893 version of "America," as did the Columbia Mixed Double Quartet in 1916. Two different

---

[1]The temperance movement was an effort to discourage the consumption of alcoholic beverages and to outlaw their sale (editor's note).

versions, one by "March King" John Philip Sousa's band, charted in 1905. Sousa then included the song in his collection *National, Patriotic, and Typical Airs of All Countries,* which became the standard text for American service bands for the next fifty years. . . .

But the culture industry is not monolithic, as both its products and its means of   **3**
mass marketing have always been open to appropriation by groups of all political and religious persuasions. For example, in 1910, the Mormon Tabernacle Choir achieved national celebrity through the release of their recording of twelve hymns and patriotic songs, including "America." Just twenty-three years earlier, the Mormons had been considered un-American by Congress, which had forced legal and social reforms through the Edmunds-Tucker Act. In response to such persecution, the Choir's recordings blended church songs and patriotic anthems to assert their patriotism. Perhaps as a nod to the complicated costs and benefits of this quintessential example of assimilation, "America" has been regularly featured in the Choir's concerts ever since. The sense that "America" was the nation's unofficial hymn—a claim that . . . was pushed forcefully by the song's author, Samuel Smith—thus merged nicely with the new means of production and distribution enabled by the recording industry. It is wonderfully appropriate, then, that the 25,000-voice choir of the evangelist Billy Sunday recorded "America" in 1918. The song was then included in *Songs for Service,* the popular evangelistic hymn collection compiled by Sunday's musical director, Homer Rodeheaver. Thus, by the early twentieth century, "America" had crossed many contexts—secular and scared, home and stage—to become a staple element of American public life and a touchstone for the discussion of what it means to be an American. One is forced to wonder, however, if the ever-accelerating capability for mass-producing recorded songs and corresponding songbooks—all fetching fancy profits as commodities—has come to the point where there are simply too many objects of consideration for any one of them to fire the collective imagination the way "God Save the King" and then "America" did from roughly 1750 through 1932.

The fact that one can discuss national songs and immediately think of "America"   **4**
is evidence of the foreshortening of our national sense of history and tradition, which in turn closes off options for cultural productions and protest. Indeed, . . . "America" has been sung for the past 260 years *mostly* as a vehicle of protest. One wonderful example of how our forebears used "America" to lampoon a nation rocketing along on what many thought was a fast track to destruction was George S. Kaufman and Morrie Ryskind's 1931 Broadway musical *Of Thee I Sing.* With its title drawn from Smith's "America," *Of Thee I Sing* lampooned campaign politics in the midst of the Depression. Candidate John P. Wintergreen is elected to the presidency by ignoring the social catastrophes all around him, instead playing up his romance with Mary Turner, who has promised to marry him if he wins. His campaign song (written by George and Ira Gershwin) turns Smith's "America" into a wickedly ironic pop hit:

> Of thee I sing, baby,
> You have got that certain thing, baby.
> Shining star and inspiration
> Worthy of a mighty nation,
> Of thee I sing! . . .

At a time when political leaders seemed incapable of dealing with the country's   **5**
social problems, *Of Thee I Sing* used "America" to parody vacuous political sloganeering and to caricature the decline of democratic politics into a deadening distraction of romantic and patriotic spectacle.

Four years after *Of Thee I Sing* opened on Broadway, sixteen-year-old Ella Fitzgerald recorded a similar parody of Smith's "America" with the Chick Webb Orchestra.   **6**

Her "Vote for Mr. Rhythm," released at the height of the Depression, describes an imaginary feel-good candidate:

> Everyone's a friend of his.
> His campaign slogan is:
> "Change your woes
> Into a-wo-de-ho."
> Vote for Mr. Rhythm,
> Let freedom ring,
> And soon we'll be singing,
> Of thee I swing.

With its platform of promised good times, Fitzgerald's "Vote for Mr. Rhythm" is played over the closing credits of D. A. Pennebaker's revealing documentary of the 1992 Clinton presidential campaign, *The War Room*. A song performed as an ironic critique of feel-good politics during the depression is thus revised as an equally ironic critique of feel-good politics in the age of the Teflon presidency.

7   Whereas Smith's 1831 "America" sings of proud citizens whom we know first gathered to sing the song in a choral form in a temperance gathering in a church, this 1935 parody (and its 1992 appropriation) speaks of cynical citizens who come to recognize democracy as a lark, a romp, "a-wo-de-ho" that leaves the masses swinging. Following Fitzgerald's 1935 "Vote for Mr. Rhythm" and the Gershwins' 1931 title song from *Of Thee I Sing*, "America" was used in the second half of the twentieth century mostly as a humorous prop symbolizing political naïveté and the surreal politics of conventioneers' straw hats and slogan-adorned banners. Indeed, it would appear that the song has become either a token of lost innocence, immediately identified as nostalgic musical quotation, or an object of merciless pastiche in which a song's promises are not only no longer taken seriously but lampooned as the deluded rhetoric of hopelessly idealistic dreamers. . . .

8   For example, Charles Gross's musical soundtrack to Everett Aison's 1968 film *Post No Bills* uses eleven comical variations on "America" (including bluegrass, Dixieland, and cocktail-lounge versions). The ten-minute film opens with a shot of a beautiful lake surrounded by trees; the camera pans to a billboard with the exhortation "Drink Beer!" In the next image, a lone man (Bob Brady) tears down the billboard and burns it, then moves on to destroy another. A police officer catches him in the act and arrests him. As he exits the courthouse after sentencing, he is met by a crowd of cheering supporters who are holding signs protesting billboards. They lift him on their shoulders and carry him to a bar to celebrate by drinking beer, the very activity urged by the billboard he had destroyed. He becomes a celebrity and appears on a television talk show; as he is applauded by the mindless studio audience, he smiles and lights a cigarette. The film ends with this bitter image dissolving to a shot of the protagonist's image displayed on a billboard with the slogan "Smoke the Rebel's Cigarette." Gross's multiple variations on "America" are dispersed throughout the film. Thus, in the year of the assassinations of Kennedy and King, the Tet Offensive, and the riotous Democratic National Convention in Chicago, Smith's song is used to illustrate the voracious banality of a nation in which protest and patriotism have been absorbed as little more than the raw material for corny sloganeering and commercial kitsch. Gross's point would appear to be clear: democracy has become little more than a joke, a façade for consumerism—believing in the promises and possibilities of democracy amounts then to a kind of naïve sentimentalism as outdated as "America."

9   A similar critical use of the song may be found in Chip Lord's 1981 video short *Get Ready to March!* Newly inaugurated president Ronald Reagan is shown waving to

the crowd at a parade while the text rolls by explaining that the president's proposed budget for the National Endowment for the Arts will be less than the allocation for military bands. The brilliant soundtrack accompaniment is a trumpeter stumbling through "America," thus symbolizing the perilous predicament of the arts in an age of unprecedented military expenditures. Addressed to an implied audience whose opposition to Reagan has been outvoted, Lord's video concludes with the admonition: "Get Ready to March!" America the nation and "America" the song are here mutually botched by Reagan's headlong rush into barbarism. While Aison's *Post No Bills* and Lord's *Get Ready to March!* offer wickedly biting commentaries, they also illustrate the paradoxical role of "My Country, 'Tis of Thee" in postmodernity. Indeed, whereas prior generations of activists used the song both to criticize the nation and to celebrate its utopian promises, in these two films the song stands as little more than an outdated symbol, a throwback, a decayed reminder of just how completely democracy has slid into meaninglessness. In this sense, then, Aison's and Lord's appropriations of "My Country, 'Tis of Thee" recall "Bitter" Ambrose Bierce's[2] despair. But whereas Bierce and his Gilded-Age contemporaries bemoaned a nation sinking beneath the weight of gross political corruption and deadly capitalist exploitation, our postmodern predicament is generally understood, for better or worse, as more properly cultural, as a result of the incredible multiplicity of images and sounds and tastes and other commodities. . . .

One final observation is in order regarding the incomprehensible, almost comi- **10** cally obscene use of "America" for commercial purposes. The list here could be extended at will, but one example will suffice; in this case, the guilty party is AT&T. In a full-page ad in the *New York Times,* complete with a full-size picture of a cordless phone painted in the Stars and Stripes, large letters announce "Two Hundred More Reasons to Let Freedom Ring." Smith's original version of the song . . . was complicated by a variety of tricky intentions and subtle exclusions, yet there is no doubt that he envisioned his song speaking of *political* freedoms. In 1831 "let freedom ring" was a call for the realization of the nation's then-and-still radical promises of justice and equality for all. But in 2000 the phrase "let freedom ring" is a call for a "fifty-dollar-cash-back" deal that, when you sign on to the AT&T juggernaut, includes "NO ROAMING, NO LONG-DISTANCE CHARGES." One cannot imagine a more representative example of the conflation of politics with commerce, of the confusion of the individual's consumption with the community's political obligations.

In contrast to the . . . vulgar advertising version of AT&T, our sense is that one of **11** the most significant factors in the long popularity of "My Country, 'Tis of Thee" is the simple beauty and inescapable presence of the human voice. At the April 1997 Central States Communication Association Conference in St. Louis, for example, Bob [Branham] presented some of the materials in this book to a packed room of fellow historians, rhetorical critics, and music lovers. While Bob told the story of the song, complete with slides and video, friends read some versions of the song while I and others sang some of the variations of the song. The presentation was greeted with something I have never seen before at an academic conference: a standing ovation, complete with some members of the audience crying. It would seem that even the most ironic of postmoderns still want to love their country, still thrill at the sheer depth and wonder of a historical story when well told, and still cherish the simple pleasure of hearing their friends and colleagues and neighbors burst out in a good song—"My country, 'tis of thee, / Sweet land of Liberty, / Of thee I sing," indeed.

[2]Ambrose Bierce (1842–1914) was a writer of fiction, satirist, and social critic (editor's note).

6 *Synthesizing*

In previous chapters, you have paraphrased and summarized isolated texts and passages. More typically, research writing involves combining, or *synthesizing,* ideas and information from several sources. If, for example, you wanted to learn more about dirigibles or the early history of your hometown, you probably would consult books and articles. If you reported your findings, you would synthesize information from those sources.

There are several strategies for synthesizing multiple sources, and we begin with the simplest. It consists of two steps: writing separate summaries or paraphrases of each source and then linking them with transitional passages. Following is a demonstration.

A BRIEF SUMMARY REPORT

Suppose you are writing a report on advertising and sports. You have chosen the following articles from a list of sources provided by your instructor. As a first step toward writing your report, you would read each article with care, searching for important ideas and underlining noteworthy information.

PRACTICE READING

The Anglophile Angle*

Terry Lefton

It's an age of logo ubiquity, wherein every establishment, from the hotel where you happen to be staying to your local marina, sells apparel based on logo appeal. Add some sports equity to that logo, and those with a vested interest in the organization are easily convinced that their logo is the equivalent of the New York Yankees' familiar trademark, a perennial top seller.

It is helpful sometimes to recall that wasn't always the case, and Wimbledon is a good place to start. The licensing history of the tennis icon shows how long-

*This article appears on pages 28–29 of the June 6, 1999, issue of *Brandweek.*

term brand management was able to transform a ramshackle licensing program erected upon a shaky legal foundation into a blue-chip equity, one that has deftly played off the non-commercial purity and prestige of the underlying property to support an extraordinary range of products, from men's suits to Japanese bento boxes, that collectively generate some $100 million in annual revenues.

Mark McCormack, founder and chairman of Cleveland-based agency IMG, recalls that at his first meeting with principals from the All England Lawn Tennis and Croquet Club in 1967, he surprised them by saying that a Wimbledon highlights film might have commercial value. A little later, he suggested that foreign broadcast rights could be worth far more than the $75,000 the club was then receiving. A slightly skeptical board authorized him to sell foreign broadcast rights, but hedged its bet by making the first $75,000 of any new deals sans commission. . . .

Another revenue stream McCormack and IMG created for Wimbledon may be its most creative, since it was a licensing program for a property without a logo and whose name, taken from the municipality in which the tournament is held, was largely in the public domain.

Up until the late 1970s, the club, which stages Wimbledon as the governing body for tennis in England, had generally eschewed licensing as too commercial. As a result, some companies were paying to use the name, while others used it haphazardly and on products of varying quality, without much fear of retribution. Tournament officials had almost no quality control, even though legal and illegal licensees were borrowing on their equity.

McCormack and IMG suggested cleaning up the program with some licensing expertise and a dose of brand management. Once again, those in charge of tennis' top tourney weren't exactly thrilled about what McCormack was proposing, but assigned IMG the rights anyway in the late 1970s, with the caveat that IMG "shouldn't spend more buying or protecting trademarks than you are going to make licensing them." IMG bought up some licensing agreements from the likes of Bancroft and Nike and shut down some others that weren't paying for use of the name. To get off the shaky legal ground of using a municipal name as a trademark, IMG later launched what today has become the well-known "flying W" logo. Using another device that is now standard, McCormack and IMG negotiated a minute or so of TV time of their own in each broadcast agreement, then used that time to push both the Wimbledon brand and its licensees, adding valuable TV exposure for the new logo. Whether it was foresight or just good fortune, the tennis boom of the 1970s and early 1980s came just after the Wimbledon trademark began to be managed as a brand. "I don't think tennis will ever see that kind of growth spurt again," said IMG licensing chief Rick Isaacson. "All of a sudden, not only playing the sport but looking like you played—the tennis lifestyle— became a big fashion statement."

With an early assist from the forces of fashion, IMG built up the Wimbledon licensing program to a point where it now brings in more than $100 million in annual worldwide retail sales. That's easily bigger than any other tennis tourney's licensing revenues: by comparison, the U.S. Open generates $7 million annually. The Wimbledon universe has around forty licensees, with sales fairly evenly split between Europe, the U.S., and Japan. As you'd expect, there are a number of tennis equipment licensees, with LBH Group and Little Miss Tennis two of the larger tennis apparel licensees in the U.S. But it's the non-endemic areas that make the Wimbledon licensing program so compelling.

Hartmarx has a longstanding deal for tailored clothing, leveraging not the logo but rather the cachet of the name for a brand of fine clothing, like wool blazers and pants. In the U.S., you can also buy bracelets earrings, rings, and necklaces ranging from $30 to $3,000 from the Continental Buying Group along with $30 to $300 Wimbledon blankets from Chatham. Overseas, there's an even wider assortment of Wimbledon-licensed products, like chocolate, eyewear, shortbread, preserves, and teas. One could sip that tea between matches from Wedgwood's Wimbledon tea service and accompany that with some Wimbledon frozen yogurt served in some licensed Wimbledon crystal from Waterford. Most of those products could be bought at a year-round Wimbledon-branded shop at the Royal Arcade in London.

Japan's many Anglophiles can purchase towels and soaps, along with Wimbledon-branded bento boxes, chopsticks, coffee, and tea sets. While they are no longer on the market, Japanese fans once could even buy Wimbledon-branded wicker furniture and fishing rods. Japan is also the only place in the world where you can purchase Wimbledon tennis balls.

Why does Wimbledon work so well as a licensing brand? Over several weeks, officials of the tightly staffed club were not available to discuss the program, but IMG execs suggested Wimbledon's very noncommercial nature allows it to translate well to so many product categories.

"You've got the purity and prestige of a 120-plus-year-old event, combined with the pomp and circumstance of the royal box and the Anglophile appeal," said IMG vice president and director of fashion and apparel licensing Jeffrey Ceppos. "That means a lot to a lot of markets." McCormack still has enough affinity for Wimbledon for it to be one of the few IMG clients he continues to personally direct.

"I just like what it stands for," he said. "If you ask golfers what championship they dream about winning, you'd have a split between the U.S. Open, the British Open, and the Masters. If you asked a hundred tennis players, they would all say Wimbledon. It denotes tradition, heritage, prestige, quality, and that British lifestyle. So if there's a company out there trying to get across any of those qualities, it fits."

PRACTICE READING

Brand Builders
Open for Business*

Gerry Khermouch

Back in 1995, Heineken decided to pull its considerable international clout out of golf sponsorships and instead beef up its exposure to tennis. Gone from its promotional calendar were such major golf events as the Heineken Dutch Open, the Australian Open, and the World Cup of Golf. Filling the vacuum the next years was an ambitious five-year sponsorship with the U.S. Tennis Association that elevated the Dutch beer brand to the top-tier status of a USTA "Corporate Champion," joining such other megabrands as IBM, Citizen, Nissan Infiniti, and Prudential Securities. Suddenly the red star and green bottle had marshalled a presence at events that include one of the highest-visibility tournaments in the country, the U.S. Open in Flushing, N.Y. Outsiders pegged the value of the sponsorship at about $30 million over its five-year lifetime. . . .

As for the pragmatics, while golf may be hot lately, it is a much more difficult sport for a sponsor to "own" on account of the greater diversity of activities that would have to be acquired and orchestrated to have a meaningful impact.

*This article appears on pages 18–21 of the October 5, 1998, issue of *Brandweek*.

At the same time, the major U.S. brewers generally have eschewed tennis for team sports and more downscale non-team activities such as car racing, activities that are appropriate for premium beers but not necessarily for an above-premium European import like Heineken.

And there is a timing issue: the U.S. Open occurs during the crucial Labor Day beer-consumption period. For domestic brewers, that signals the end of the core summer selling season, but for less seasonal specialty beers like Heineken, it inaugurates a fall season.

Tennis "is in a transition period, and we're in on the ground floor," said Heineken brand manager Scott Hunter Smith, a former Coca-Cola executive and avid tennis player, who came to the brand after the tennis commitment was established. "Yes, golf is hot, and a Tiger Woods can help you do those things. But the Williams sisters are creating a lot of energy around tennis. And this is something Heineken can own, and do with a flair."

Take the most visible manifestation of Heineken's marketing against the recently concluded U.S. Open: a television spot via agency Lowe and Partners/SMS, New York, exploited a clever conceit by translating the activity of the familiar ball retrievers to Heineken's main habitat, a bar environment, where the blurred images of the young men are seen whisking away green Heineken bottles the moment they are emptied. The "Ball Boys" spot, which leverages the on-premise ubiquity that has been a key to Heineken's success through the decades, aired heavily on VH 1 and CBS coverage of the Open, as well as in six local markets, including such high-end-import meccas as Atlanta, Boston, and Chicago. As with the core campaigns of the past couple of years, the company has placed a premium on repeated images of the green bottles and red-star icon against the backdrop of urban sophisticates' watering holes.

Radio ads took a parallel, but not identical, tack, drawing an analogy between the one-upmanship games played between friends or ex-lovers and the blistering volleys that characterize a good U.S. Open competition. In doing so, the ads similarly act in harmony with Heineken's core campaigns, which have featured the on-premise exchanges of affluent, sometimes overly verbal members of the youthful end of Heineken's urban demo.

Thus, one of the radio spots employs the audio backdrop of two grunting tennis players engaged in an intense volley as two supposed buddies engage in a game of one-upmanship that grows to encompass jobs, money, material possessions, and women.

"I just bought a boat," one of the men casually informs his drinking buddy. "Yeah?" says the other, with a mixture of defensiveness and skepticism.

"Yeah. And I'm taking Rachel Novak on it this weekend."

"Rachel Novak? Geez, I broke up with her ages ago. You might like her, though," the other says as the sound of the winning volley is heard along with the announcement: "Game. Set. Match." Tagline: "Heineken. Proud sponsor of the U.S. Open, and grudge matches everywhere."

The spots, with the emphasis on more urbane wit, contrast sharply with the often broader humor of ads for domestic premium brands like Bud, Bud Light, or Miller Lite, with their talking frogs, work-shirking husbands, and grunting wrestlers. "There are two kinds of fun," Smith said. "This is a classier kind of fun."

Not coincidentally, the USTA has been employing younger people in its own ads in a similar effort "to create change and excitement.

"They know they need to open the door and have more fun with themselves," Smith said. "Our campaign certainly helps to show that we're having fun with it."

Certainly, for the USTA, it's a refreshing and much needed change to have sponsors serving up active marketing communications around its events. The game's most mainstream exposure in the past decade has been through a handful of superstars in Nike or Reebok ads, and yet now the sneaker giants are reevaluating their broad endorsement rosters and media expenditures. As for corporate sponsorships, tennis has long been a destination for high-end marketers who didn't necessarily advertise to a mainstream audience, and who bought their rights more for the élan of hospitality, schmoozing in the sport's rarified air, than for active promotional use. . . .

"They're a terrific sponsor and partner for us," said J. Pierce O'Neil, USTA marketing director. "They truly understand the marketing power of the U.S. Open in particular, and tennis in general, and are helping us to position it as a relevant, fun, and important part of the U.S. sports landscape."

PRACTICE READING

Endangered Species*

Leigh Gallagher

Which is a tougher marketing challenge—creating a brand from scratch or bringing one back from the grave? Ask Daniel Barth, the elegant-looking president of Devanlay, the U.S. subsidiary of the French manufacturer of Lacoste apparel. Barth has the very daunting task of resurrecting Lacoste's name and its little green crocodile logo.

"There isn't anyone who doesn't remember the crocodile," insists Barth in a thick French accent. Unfortunately what many shoppers remember is the cheap polyester version that sold for as little as $20 at Marshalls and other discounters in the 1980s. That's when General Mills owned the brand.

What most consumers don't recall is the shirt's proud origins. French tennis great René Lacoste, nicknamed "Le Crocodile" because of his exceptionally long nose and speed on the court, first wore the crocodile on a white, short-sleeved tennis shirt in 1926. In 1951 he brought it to the U.S., where it became an instant hit.

Therein lies Barth's challenge. Devanlay, part of the French apparel maker ten-percent controlled by the Lacoste family, spent $32 million to reclaim the U.S. rights to the Lacoste name and the crocodile logo six years ago.

Rescue might be a better word. In a brand-buying spree that included outdoor-clothing maker Eddie Bauer and golf brand FootJoy, General Mills had bought the U.S. licensee for Lacoste in 1969 for $30 million. Over the next decade the cereal maker built Izod into a full line of crocodile-adorned wear, including jackets, sweaters, socks, and ties. By 1982 sales reached $400 million. But fashion is not General Mills' strength.

Figuring knit shirts weren't much different from toasted oats, the company stopped importing the shirts from France in 1975 and began making them in Hong Kong, and U.S. consumers started noticing changes. No more "capped" sleeves with reinforced bands around the ends. Instead of one hundred percent cotton, the shirts now came in a cotton-polyester blend.

When sales began to slow in 1983, General Mills cut prices and relaxed its distribution policy, dumping hundreds of thousands of shirts on discounters.

*This article appears on page 105 of the May 31, 1999, issue of *Forbes*.

By 1985 the badly overexposed croc had little cachet left. Sales had fallen to $50 million. Conceding defeat, General Mills spun the Lacoste licensee off that year to shareholders as Crystal Brands, which continued to struggle. In 1993 Devanlay bought the U.S. distribution rights to the name *Lacoste* and the crocodile logo. (Two years later Phillips-Van Heusen bought Crystal Brands, which then included the Izod name as well as Gant shirts.) But the damage to the croc had been done.

Today all Lacoste knit shirts are made in France from Swiss yarn and mother-of-pearl buttons. In fifty-four colors, they sell for $69, compared with $52 for a Ralph Lauren polo shirt or $44 for a Tommy Hilfiger.

Will shoppers go for it? Barth is banking on a classic strategy: Make something inaccessible, and it becomes more desirable. Thus Barth is doing very little advertising—only $4 million a year—minuscule for the rag trade. But he makes sure the croc shows up on the right people, like golfer Jose Maria Olazabal and *NBC Today* show host Matt Lauer.

Barth consciously limits the distribution. Croc shirts are available in country-club pro shops and a few catalogs like Bullock and Jones and Ben Silver. Only a few hundred upmarket retailers like Mettlers in Florida or Bergdorf Goodman in New York carry them. Nine Lacoste shops—in places like Bal Harbour and Beverly Hills—offer the shirts, along with $500 sweater sets and $400 jackets.

Barth and his team are also banking on a new crop of consumers: shoppers in their teens and twenties who missed the crocodile's first go-round. For these buyers—the same people who flock to Banana Republic for its minimalist preppy look—Barth is hoping the crocodile has just the right retro feel.

So far, so good. Devanlay turned its first profit on a forty percent sales gain last year, to $26.5 million. Barth wants to extend the crocodile franchise into footwear, eyewear, and fragrances. But he's got a lot of image-repair work to do before that can happen. "This is the real product," he says. "What you remember—but much better than you remember."

A simple strategy for composing your report is to summarize the sources individually and then link the summaries with connecting comments. Writing the summaries should be easy enough, but you also need to unify your report with a theme that relates to all three sources. Certainly, they all concern commercial aspects of professional tennis. But is there a single statement that can connect all three? To find out, you can start by paraphrasing the main idea of each source as we have done below:

- Overcoming some initial reluctance, Wimbledon sponsors have realized huge profits by allowing manufacturers to attach the name and logo of the world's most prestigious tennis tournament to a wide variety of high-quality products.

- Heineken's radio and television spots during the U.S. Tennis Open target a more elite clientele than most other beer advertisements.

- Efforts to reintroduce the once-fashionable Izod crocodile logo popularized by tennis legend René Lacoste have been complicated by memories of cheap sportswear sold by General Mills when it owned the trademark.

In search of a unifying theme, we can begin with these three observations:

- It seems wise to restrict the licensing of tennis logos to expensive, high-quality merchandise produced in relatively small volume.
- Commercials for less expensive products like beer also target an elite clientele when they are broadcast during tennis tournaments.
- A tennis logo can quickly lose prestige and marketing appeal if it is not reserved for upscale merchandise.

From these observations, you can discern a central idea that provides a unifying theme for your report: *Hoping to profit from the current enthusiasm for tennis, advertisers and promoters of the sport have learned to target an affluent clientele.*

Writing the report now becomes easier. You can begin with two or three sentences introducing the topic, state your central idea, then follow it with summaries of the three sources, as in the essay that follows. Notice that the sources are acknowledged both by notes within parentheses and in a list of works cited at the end of the report.

Pitching Tennis: Go Slow on Logos

Though less influenced by the directors of exclusive clubs, professional tennis is still surrounded by an aura of genteel sophistication. The growing popularity of the sport has not diminished the elitist appeal of Wimbledon, the U.S. Open, and other major tournaments. In fact, that appeal has become a marketable commodity. Hoping to profit from the current enthusiasm for tennis, advertisers and promoters of the sport have learned to target an affluent clientele.

Marketing of the Wimbledon name and logo is an excellent example. In 1967, members of the club that sponsors the tournament hesitantly agreed to sell foreign broadcast rights. A decade later, they approved a plan to regulate commercial use of the tournament's name and "flying W" logo. Today, as a result of those timely decisions, yearly revenues have reached $100 million. Much of this income derives from sales of tennis equipment and clothing, but growing sources of profit include jewelry, gourmet food, and premium household goods including fine linens and china. Marketers agree that a crucial ingredient of this success is the aura of prestige and integrity that surrounds Wimbledon. Despite these large profits, the public continues to perceive the tournament as uncorrupted by commercialism (Lefton 28-29).

Advertisements for less expensive goods have also been adapted to the elitist image of tennis. Heineken, for example, a mass-marketed beer, recently became a corporate sponsor of the U.S. Open. During the tournament, however, the company's broadcast commercials differ from those of most other brewers, targeting an urbane, affluent clientele. Tournament officials regard the sponsorship as beneficial to the sport, widening its appeal to a younger audience more in tune with popular trends (Khermouch 18-21).

The fate of one trademark associated with professional tennis offers an example of what to avoid. The crocodile icon inspired by French tennis legend René Lacoste appeared on an exclusive line of sportswear long before the trademark was purchased by manufacturing conglomerate General Mills. Hoping for quick profits, the American company attached the crocodile to a cheaper line of apparel which was eventually spurned by disaffected consumers. Today, a French company, owned in part by the Lacoste family, is trying to restore the prestige of the logo with a line of expensive clothing marketed to an exclusive clientele. Success may depend upon whether wealthy customers can forget that a once-prestigious trademark was compromised by its association with inferior products (Gallagher 105).

Tennis is still in transition. Renewed enthusiasm for the sport, first aroused during the 1970s and 1980s, has now started to wane. If this trend continues, promoters might attempt to dispel the aura of elitism that surrounds tennis. But while that strategy could broaden the popular appeal of tennis and attract new players, it could dilute also advertising profits. From a commercial standpoint, it is a dubious ploy.

[New Page]   Works Cited

Gallagher, Leigh. "Endangered Species." Forbes 31 May 1999: 105.

Khermouch, Gerry. "Brand Builders: Open for Business." Brandweek
       5 Oct. 1998: 18-21.

Lefton, Terry. "The Anglophile Angle." Brandweek 6 June 1999:
       28-29.

There are several things to note about this report. First, it concludes with a paragraph that extends the main idea stated in the introduction. Second, it is divided into paragraphs: one to introduce the main idea, one to conclude the paper, and one for each summary. Although this report could have been a single long paragraph, indentations assist the reader by signaling changes in topic. On the other hand, if the writer had used more or longer sources or had taken more information from each source, more paragraphs might have been needed.

There are, of course, other ways to synthesize the same three sources. For example, a writer might devote one paragraph to the marketing of sportswear, drawing information from Lefton and Gallagher, and another paragraph to sales of other items, drawing information from Khermouch and Lefton.

Regardless of how such a report is structured, it is called *objective* because it presents information from sources without any overt expression of the report writer's opinions. (In Chapter 7, we consider subjective, critical reporting, in which a writer analyzes or evaluates sources.) Nevertheless, objectivity is relative. For example, this particular report places less emphasis on the creative aspects of advertising and demographic research than the original sources. This may reflect the report writer's personal interests and observations, as well as her experience with tennis and her attitudes toward the sport. Suppose, however, that the same three sources had been read and synthesized by someone very different from this writer—say, a recreation or marketing major, an ardent fan of hockey or professional wrestling, an investor in General Mills or one of the other companies mentioned in the articles. An objective report by the recreation major might emphasize the history of tennis and the influence of advertising on the sport. Struck by the incongruity of genteel sportsmanship and mercenary greed, the hockey fan might focus his objective report on the double standard of tennis promoters. The investor's objective report might consider which of the companies profiled in the articles are most likely to profit from their associations with tennis. The point is that each of these readers and, indeed, all readers unavoidably—and often unconsciously—connect what they read with other texts as well as with personal experiences and interests.

In short, no synthesis is ever entirely objective. Nor is any synthesis a completely definitive report on a topic. Consider, for example, how the writer of the foregoing synthesis might change her approach after reading the following article as a fourth source.

PRACTICE READING

Corporate Ties Squeeze the Life out of Sports*

Joe Cappo

The older I get, the more challenging it becomes to remain a loyal fan of baseball.

Actually, this has less to do with my age than it does with the ultimate commercialization of what used to be the national pastime. The business—I hesitate to call it a sport anymore—is being run by a bunch of rich guys who have little or no regard for the tradition and dignity of baseball. This includes most of the owners and a lot of the players.

I was reminded of this when it was disclosed that Major League Baseball wants to entice corporate sponsors to put their logos on the uniforms of baseball players. This practice has not been allowed among the major sports until now.

For decades, of course, Nascar race cars and drivers' uniforms have been festooned with dozens of corporate logos, representing the investment and alliances these companies have with the racing teams. A few years back, professional tennis players started wearing discreet, but still visible, logos on their playing outfits.

In the beginning, a lot of these deals were barter arrangements: "You display my logo, and I will provide you with my whole line of tennis apparel, or racing tires, or a new car, free of charge." We have since progressed to a more mercenary level, where anybody with the ability to attract a sizable number of public eyeballs is charging money to give exposure to a product, service, or company.

It wasn't that long ago that college football bowl games did not have name sponsors. Now, they all do.

The movie business is loaded with this kind of guerrilla marketing, called product placement. Years ago, if a movie character was eating cereal, the producer would create an imaginary brand and package to use in the filming. "Not anymore," said an acquaintance in the movie industry. "Whenever you see a recognizable brand being used in a movie, I will guarantee you that money changed hands to get that product into the picture."

The practice has reached the point where some legislators want to require producers to list these product placements in the credits of the movies. Maybe

*This article appears on page 8 of the April 12, 1999, issue of *Crain's Chicago Business*.

they should run a subtitle every time there is a product placement in a movie, or sound a chime to get attention. Of course, some movies hawk so many products, it would make them sound like *The Bells of St. Mary's*.

Anyone being subjected to advertising should be able to tell the difference between the advertising and the programming. Most publishers go to great lengths to differentiate between the editorial product and "advertorials."

Don't get me wrong. Baseball has every right to put logos on team uniforms; I guess they can even force players to have logos tattooed on their foreheads. But why push things to the limit? There is nothing wrong with a little restraint, even if you pass up the chance to make a few extra bucks.

If the writer who synthesized the first three sources had considered this article, she might have reached a different conclusion. For example, she might connect the four sources with a thesis like this: "Attempting to profit from the elitism of tennis, advertisers and promoters of the sport risk alienating the individual fan."

| EXERCISE | **Writing a Brief Summary Report** |

Here are three appraisals of Thomas Kinkade's paintings, included in a feature column in the *Chronicle of Higher Education*. The column opens with this headnote:

> Thomas Kinkade's landscapes and gift merchandise have made him the most popular artist in America, and his franchise earned more than $2 billion in 2000. Known as "the painter of light," Kinkade has brought art to the masses through shopping malls and QVC, and next month he will publish the first of several novels inspired by his paintings. But can he get any critical respect? We asked several experts to explain his appeal.

Write a report synthesizing information from the three following sources:

a. Read each with a pencil, underlining important information.

b. Write a one-sentence summary of each writer's main idea.

c. Consider whether a theme links the three sources. If so, state that theme in a sentence that can serve as the thesis statement for your report.

d. Write the report. Begin with your thesis statement, follow it with three summaries (in whatever order you consider appropriate) linked with transitional phrases if necessary, and end with a general concluding statement. For now, you can omit parenthetical notes and a list of works cited, both of which are discussed later in this chapter.

Karal Ann Marling*
Most of his works are landscapes with little houses in them. They are suffused with nostalgia, but the people I've interviewed about them think his paintings create a sense of safety and light in a darkened world. So in a way, they're a perfect metaphor

*Professor of art history and American studies, University of Minnesota-Twin Cities.

for the re-nesting of America. There's nothing controversial about his painting; there's often something religious at least in their implication. He also puts a number of Scripture verses in his pictures, and he shows his devotion to family by putting his wife's initials in the pictures. They repay close attention to detail.

I'm sitting here in my office surrounded by Thomas Kinkade picture puzzles, Thomas Kinkade calendars, Kinkade throws to put on the end of your couch. Clearly this is a major cultural phenomenon, and I thought it was interesting that no one seemed to pay any attention to it. The *New Yorker,* the snottiest of American magazines, wrote a kind of exposé—as though the rest of us didn't already know this. This is popular art, this is how it's made, and all of a sudden, all of these people who've never heard of Thomas Kinkade—presumably they never go to the mall—are insulted by this art movement they know nothing about.

I'm not so sure the critical reception is what counts in any event. People who flock to the Guggenheim don't want to see another damn thing except the Norman Rockwells. It's about time we started paying some respect to artists who manage to engage the popular imagination.

Kinkade knows what he's doing—he writes about it quite compellingly, in fact. He's seen artists such as Albert Bierstadt in the nineteenth century who used landscape painting to say great things about American westward expansion and patriotism. Bierstadt was able to bridge the gap between fine and popular art. We've lost that sensibility, and Kinkade knows about that stuff. He's not some ignorant pissant out there making velvet paintings to hang in the gas station. He's really tapped a deep wellspring of need.

Brooke Cameron[†]

Kinkade is reinventing the wheel: His work is like Currier and Ives. It presents no particular challenge; it's just a nice, nostalgic look at the little stone cottage. His only gimmick is [that] he's the painter of light. So the lights are on in the houses. But this is not exactly breaking new ground. Plenty of painters did this in the nineteenth century. He's offering a warm, fuzzy buzz for people. And if that's what they want, fine. I'm not against that, but he's gotten way more than his due.

I can't imagine why somebody would want one of these things when they could have a real Currier and Ives print. I own some, and I'm very fond of them. They're real. But no way in my darkest day would I ever consider buying a Thomas Kinkade; if I'm going to pay money for art, I want it to offer me something either that I have not seen before or that's an authentic piece of art history. When all is said and done, no one's going to remember Thomas Kinkade as an artistic innovator. They may remember him as a businessman. He's selling something that's very comfortable. There's no poetry in there—it's kitsch. He's sort of a male Martha Stewart.

Mark Pohlad[‡]

He fulfills a need for people to surround themselves with what we used to call craft, which provides for escape and is lovely, and is something that doesn't really ask questions but provides solace and something predictable. It would be so easy to trash Thomas Kinkade, but he meets some kind of need for a great many people who are bright, reasonable, and articulate.

What you can really do with Thomas Kinkade's art that you can't do with real art or great art is own it. If you like something of his work, you can buy a great Thomas Kinkade for $1,500, and he makes it really easy. In the same way, if you go to the Van

---

[†]Professor of art, University of Missouri at Columbia.

[‡]Associate professor of art and art history, DePaul University.

Gogh exhibition, the final room is a gift shop. They seem to know that people want to have something to prove their artistic experience. There's this appetite to own things that he's good at supplying. They are clearly [in] hideous taste, but there's a sense in which a million people can't be wrong. It's really easy to shrug it off and say it's crap, the equivalent of a Schwarzenegger movie, but something has to be going on there.

■ AN OBJECTIVE REPORT ON SOURCES

Some reports focus not so much on a topic—on the information *within* sources—as on the sources themselves. This kind of report can be approached in much the same way as a brief summary report. The main difference is that a report on sources refers specifically to its sources, saying, in effect, "Source A says this; Source B says this; Source C says this. . . ." A report on sources can be subjective (presenting your own analysis and opinions), but for now we will consider objective reports. Following is an example.

Suppose you are reporting on two editorials that debate the legality of excluding gays and atheists from the Boy Scouts. Since your report presents the opinions of other writers, it must refer specifically to both sources. Before reading the editorials, look at their titles and subtitles, which indicate that one writer supports the Scouts' policy of exclusion and the other opposes it. Next, try to locate each writer's thesis statement. Finally, read both editorials with a pencil, marking important information and ideas.

PRACTICE READING

Scout's Honor
The Boy Scouts Are under Relentless Legal Assault
Because They Are an Affront to the Age

E. V. Kontorovich*

For more than eighty years, the Boy Scouts of America have sent young boys on arduous, fortnight-long hikes; taught them to survive alone in the wilderness; and guided them through countless other physical and mental challenges that have helped transform them into mature, responsible men. But now the organization faces a challenge greater than all of these: Can it survive . . .?

Recently, a New Jersey appellate court forced the Boy Scouts to give a scoutmaster post to James Dale, a gay activist and editor at *Poz*, a magazine for HIV-positive people. The divided bench overturned an old Scout policy of not allowing "avowed homosexuals" to serve as scoutmasters. What is particularly shocking about the opinion is its unabashed political expression. The court found that the Boy Scouts cannot discriminate against anyone, on any basis, because the organization is a "public accommodation," like restaurants and parks. Actually,

*This article appears on pages 40–42 of the Aril 6, 1998, issue of *National Review*.

the judges admitted that it wasn't much like a public accommodation as defined by the law, but they held that such limited definitions "would frustrate our goal of eradicating the 'cancer of discrimination' in New Jersey."

New Jersey is but one front in the nationwide attack on the Boy Scouts of America. Illinois was the venue of two recent defeats for the Scouts. Last year, a Chicago court ordered the reinstatement of a gay scoutmaster on the grounds of employment discrimination, despite the fact that the position is voluntary and unpaid. In February, the City of Chicago severed all its ties with twenty-eight Scout troops, to settle a suit brought by the American Civil Liberties Union.

The ACLU claimed that the arrangements with the Scouts violated the separation of church and state. This is an odd contention given that BSA is not a church, or a religious organization of any kind. The Boy Scouts are under relentless legal assault because they are an affront to the age. It is a nonsectarian group that simply insists that its members honor some sort of divinity in accordance with the dictates of their conscience. But instead of preparing to fight, several other municipalities have preemptively thrown the Scouts overboard.

The ACLU, captivated by vague emanations from the penumbra of the establishment clause, has completely forgotten the more concrete First Amendment right of free association—the right to fraternize with whomever one wants, a crucial underpinning of civil society.

This is a principle the California Supreme Court would do well to remember when it rules in two suits currently before it. In one, a pair of twins from Anaheim insist on retaining their membership in the Scouts despite their refusal to recite the Scout's oath, which acknowledges the existence of God. In effect, the twins' parents and supporters are using the courts to change the core credo of a voluntary organization. The California judges will also decide another suit brought by a gay scoutmaster. Arguments in similar cases will soon be heard by D.C.'s Human Rights Commission.

At this rate, it's no wonder that girls are starting to sue, because the Boy Scouts, by definition, discriminate against them. The California Supreme Court is considering discrimination charges brought by a teenage girl who thinks the Boy Scouts' exclusion of females is unfair because Girl Scout activities aren't as much fun. A similar suit has been filed in Florida.

The wave of litigation against the Scouts is not ultimately about the rights of gays, or atheists, or females. It is a challenge to the BSA's right to exist in its present form. Such an attack should not be surprising; if anything, it's odd that the Boy Scouts have hung on for so long.

The organization is a holdover from a vanished era. The *Boy Scout Handbook* still bears Norman Rockwell paintings of scouting activities, offered without a trace of irony. Even the BSA's bylaws talk about "character building." The Scouts' charter still calls on leaders "to teach [the boys] patriotism," and members still take an oath "to do my duty to God and my country."

The BSA has always been an apolitical, nonpartisan organization. But today its leaders and lawyers must defend its membership policies by saying it stands for "conservative moral views." The BSA's policies have not changed significantly since it was chartered by Congress in 1916. What has changed is the underlying society.

Endorsing specific, non-negotiable values has become a conservative position. The existence of the Scouts irritates the ideologues of modernity—and so hordes of litigators, the antibodies of a dissolute culture, have responded by attacking the foreign body. If the courts find in favor of the plaintiffs in the undecided cases, the meaning of the Boy Scouts will be greatly eroded. The organization will become the Gay Godless Girl/Boy Scouts of America. It is only the right to restrict membership and insist that members follow rules that can give a civic group definition.

In that light, consider the plaintiffs' order of battle: the ACLU; the Lambda Legal Defense Fund; the Parents, Families, and Friends of Lesbians and Gays; and the American Atheists. Yes, the American Atheists: united by common disbeliefs.

Fundamentally, it is meaninglessness that lies at the core of the attack on the Boy Scouts. This is a competition not between rival sets of values but between the idea of values and an antinomian moral vacuousness. The comments of plaintiffs and judges show that the intent is not just to destroy the Scouts; it is to deconstruct them.

For example, the Scout's oath has a clause about "keeping myself . . . morally straight," a provision the BSA says is on its face incompatible with homosexual activity. "There is nothing in [the Scout's oath] about homosexuality," says Timothy Curran, the California gay seeking reinstatement as a scoutmaster. "It says you must be 'morally straight,' but you can define that any way you want." Which is precisely what New Jersey's jurisprudes chose to do.

There are tough days ahead for the Scouts, but they vow that they are in it for the long haul; all parties agree that the U.S. Supreme Court will finally have to rule on these issues. Until then, how can one support the Scouts? Perhaps one can give their enemies a taste of their own medicine. Religious believers should join the American Atheists in droves and introduce Sunday Mass, daily prayers to Mecca, and the donning of tefillin at every meeting.

But no, that's not right—it wouldn't be in keeping with the Scouts' spirit of fair play. Instead, the Scouts need donations to fund their ongoing appeals and fill the gap left by cowardly towns and cities.

PRACTICE READING

The Bigoted Scouts of America*

Barbara Dority

Imagine a national organization with wide-ranging government support that continues to discriminate against persons on the basis of sexual orientation and religion. There is only one such group in the United States: the Boy Scouts of America. This huge organization (in contrast to the more liberal Girl Scouts) is making it abundantly clear that it knows exactly what it's doing—and that it has no intention of changing. While the Boy Scouts did finally prohibit racially segregated units, the group doggedly clings to its loathing of atheists and homosexuals.

The BSA has the general support and encouragement of all sorts of influential institutions, most notably the United States government. In Scout Explorer programs, government employees conduct valuable and unique training classes for high-school-age youth. Agencies such as police and fire departments run Explorer Posts according to the discriminatory rules prescribed by the BSA. This results in the clearly unconstitutional activity of government employees asking children to sign an oath regarding their religious beliefs. If the child refuses to sign a statement that "America's strength lies in her trust in God," the police officer, fire-

*This article appears on pages 35–37 of the July-August 1998 issue of the *Humanist*.

fighter, or member of the National Guard is required to deny that youth entrance into this tax-supported program. In effect, the Boy Scouts has enlisted the government to monitor our attitudes on religion and even to punish individuals of whom they disapprove.

Atheists and gays are by no means the only people excluded from the BSA. A few years ago, the Muslim father of a Cub Scout was expelled from his position as a Cub Scout leader by the sponsoring organization, a Protestant church. The church felt that leadership of its Scouts should be restricted to Christians. The BSA stood behind this move, declaring that any sponsoring group could enforce whatever additional religious requirements it liked.

The Boy Scouts has spent hundreds of thousands of dollars during the past few years defending its bigotry in courtrooms around the country. In 1996, the Pennsylvania Human Rights Commission ordered the BSA to admit an atheist as an adult leader and her child as a Scout. The organization has refused to comply, thereby committing itself to another long and unavoidably expensive court battle. Clearly, it is prepared to fight any attempt to be enlightened, with all the considerable resources at its command. Ironically, when the Scouts and its most important source of funds—the United Way—solicit donations to fund such tremendous legal expenses, they don't question the religion or sexual orientation of prospective benefactors.

Among the recent legal defeats against the BSA is one regarding the Randall twins, two young atheists from California whose family was recently named 1998 Humanist Pioneers by the American Humanist Association in recognition of their efforts to combat BSA bigotry. The Randalls filed suit when the BSA challenged the twins' membership because they refused to recite the portion of the Scout oath relating to "duty to God." The suit was based on California's Unruh Act, which forbids any California business from participating in religious and other discrimination.

A lower court ruled in favor of the Randalls, but the Boy Scouts appealed. The court ruled that the Randalls could work toward their Eagle badges while the litigation continued. In the meantime, the Randalls' case was combined with a similar challenge to the banning of gays. The BSA prevailed, however, when the state supreme court declared that the Boy Scouts is a "private group" and, as such, can restrict membership as it sees fit. As humanist Patrick Inniss, a Boy Scout discrimination activist, states: "This California Supreme Court decision upholding the rights of a 'private' organization to exclude anyone for apparently any reason demonstrates that, even in states with anti-discrimination laws more rigorous than federal law, the BSA is impervious to direct attack."

This ruling is similar to the one in Chicago's 1993 Welsh case, which established that, for the purposes of federal civil rights legislation, the BSA cannot be considered a "public accommodation." While these suits have served an important role in bringing the problem to the attention of the public, and the possibility of more legal challenges remains, we may be unable to use the law directly to force the Scouts to change.

However, there has been a major legal victory. In March 1998, a New Jersey appeals court ruled against the BSA in a discrimination suit involving a gay Scout. James Dale was a nineteen-year-old Eagle Scout when he was expelled in 1990 after it was discovered through a newspaper article that he was gay. He sued and lost, then appealed and won in the state's appellate court. The court ruled that the BSA is "a place of accommodation" within the meaning of the law and is, therefore, bound by the state's anti-discrimination law. BSA spokesperson Gregg Shields insists that the Scouts "has a right, as a voluntary association . . . , to establish membership and leadership standards" and says the group plans to appeal this ruling to the New Jersey State Supreme Court.

There have also been several small victories. In April, for instance, the Boy Scouts was booted from a San Francisco charity drive that raises hundreds of thousands of dollars from city employees because of the group's stance against admitting gays. "We have a longstanding policy not to do business with groups that discriminate," said the city council in a statement, "and we feel very strongly about this." (Last year, city employees allowed $563,098 to be deducted from their paychecks and donated to charities, including the Boy Scouts.)

"The Boy Scouts are hated because they represent traditional morality in a Judeo-Christian context," claims Catholic League President William Donohue. What a turn-around! The Boy Scouts requires its members and leaders to be, among other things, "morally straight." It says that means it must exclude gays and atheists. Who is engaging in hatred here? "Oh, certainly not us," the BSA declares. "We're just a private, voluntary organization that insists on maintaining traditional values and freedom of association."

The BSA does have a huge vulnerability which we can and should exploit. No such organization can survive without the support of the community, and community standards are increasingly inclusive of all elements of society. The Boy Scouts can't survive without the government agencies, community organizations, and corporate entities that provide indispensable support.

A few breakthroughs occurred in this area in 1991 and 1992, when the Bank of America and Levi Strauss both withdrew financial support for the Scouts. Unfortunately, these actions did not prompt other financial backers to do likewise. On April 15, 1998, at a national conference of Boy Scout sponsors and leaders, Joe Velasquez, director of the AFL-CIO's Department of Community Services and a BSA executive board member, eloquently summed up the situation in a statement of the union's position—a position that humanists can certainly endorse:

> The AFL-CIO's relationship with the Boy Scouts of America has deep historical roots. In 1912, when the first leader of our organization, Samuel Gompers, met with the first leader of the Boy Scouts of America, James E. West, to talk about working together, the Boy Scouts of America had been in existence less than two years.
>
> The AFL-CIO has worked with the Scouts for these eighty years because we share many values. . . . The BSA has always offered the labor movement an opportunity to help America's youth. . . . We believe it is our duty to pass those values along to our children, to teach them the things that are important: an understanding of service and personal responsibility, a love of their country, and a deep respect for the personal dignity and individual rights of every American.

And he goes on to clearly denounce the BSA's policy of exclusion:

> Because you're different from me, because you're lower than me, because you aren't really an individual with individual rights and personal dignity, because you're a member of a group I don't like or I don't understand, it follows that not only can I discriminate against you, I can beat you up, I can even kill you, and it doesn't really matter because you're different from me. Is this a lesson we want to teach our young people? That it's okay to hate people who are different from us? to discriminate against them? to deny them opportunities because they're different?

Indeed, this is the crux of the matter. It's clear that this egregious situation has got to change—now.

As in the case of the previous report, a logical step now is to formulate briefly the main idea of each article:

- Writing in *National Review*, E. V. Kontorovich argues that lawsuits aimed at forcing the Boy Scouts to extend membership to gays and atheists are part of an effort to harass the organization because of its unfashionably traditional ideals.

- In an editorial published in the *Humanist*, Barbara Dority contends that the Boy Scouts of America enjoys many forms of governmental subsidy while engaging in practices that are incompatible with public policies regarding discrimination.

Following the steps used in the exercise on pages 224–26, we can now write the report:

Can the Boy Scouts Legally Discriminate?

E. V. Kontorovich and Barbara Dority hold sharply differing views about recent court decisions involving the Boy Scouts of America. Kontorovich believes that law suits in behalf of homosexuals and atheists who have been denied membership in the organization are part of an effort to redefine the values of scouting, undermining its commitment to religion and patriotism. He dismisses appeals to the separation of church and state as well as arguments that the Boy Scouts operates as a "public accommodation" legally barred from discrimination. He insists that every private organization has the right to define itself by deciding who it wishes to accept as members (40-42).

Dority, on the other hand, claims that the Boy Scouts of America is not a truly private organization. She points to the tax-funded contributions of police and fire departments and National Guard units, all of which support programs sponsored by the Boy Scouts. She also notes that the Scouts receives direct funding from charitable agencies, such as the United Way, which solicit contributions from homosexuals, atheists, and some of the religious minorities who have been excluded from participation in scouting activities. Given the inconsistent record of the courts, however, Dority concludes that the most effective way to challenge discrimination is to influence the government agencies, civic organizations, and companies on whose support the Boy Scouts depends (35-37).

[New Page]   Works Cited

Dority, Barbara. "The Bigoted Scouts of America." Humanist
    July-Aug. 1998: 35-37.

Kontorovich, E. V. "Scout's Honor: The Boy Scouts Are under
    Relentless Legal Assault Because They Are an Affront to
    the Age." National Review 6 Apr. 1998: 40-42.

Three things should be noted about the way this report is written. First, it lacks a concluding paragraph or statement. Although one could have been added, a short report like this does not usually require a separate conclusion, since the reader does not need to be reminded of its purpose. Conclusions are unnecessary also when you have nothing new to add to what you already have written. Second, the report is presented in two paragraphs. Since the introduction is a single sentence, the first editorial need not be introduced with a paragraph break. There is a break for the second paragraph, however, because here the reader needs to be alerted to the change in subject. Finally, the report aims to be objective, presenting the views of both editorialists without commentary. (The phrase "Kontorovich believes . . ." in the first paragraph shows that the opinion expressed in that sentence is not necessarily that of the person writing the report.) One question to ask, however, is whether the order in which the summaries are presented makes a difference. Would the report have a different effect if the editorials had been summarized in reverse order?

ACKNOWLEDGING SOURCES: AN OBLIGATION

Whenever you compose a summary report or any other type of writing that relies on sources, you create something new for others to read. Although what you produce may seem less than earth-shaking in significance, you are nevertheless adding, in however small a way, to the sum of the world's knowledge. You are making a contribution to the domain of scholarship. That may sound lofty, yet it is still true that your writing makes you a member of the fellowship of scholars, past and present, subject to all the benefits and obligations of that august body.

One of the principal benefits of being a scholar is that you are entitled to read—and to use—the scholarship of others. You have a right, for example, to write a summary report based on any sources you can find. Presenting your research and ideas for others to use is, in fact, one of the obligations of scholarship. We must work together, sharing our findings, if humanity's search for knowledge and understanding is to progress.

Another of your obligations as a scholar is to acknowledge your sources. For example, in the summary report found on pages 220–22, the writer uses parenthetical notes and a list of works cited to identify sources of information. Likewise, in the report on sources found on pages 231–32, the writer makes it clear that the ideas and opinions presented have been expressed by others.

Whenever your writing is based on research, you should make sure that readers know which ideas and discoveries are your own and which you have taken from sources. You must give your readers accurate and complete information about what those sources are and where they can be found. Acknowledging your sources is important for two reasons:

- Credit must be given where it is due. Creators of ideas deserve to be recognized. Whenever you present material without acknowledging an outside source, readers assume that you are the author of that material. When students err in this regard, they usually do so unintentionally, because of inexperience. However, when writers deliberately present another's work as their own, they are guilty of *plagiarism.* (See pages 397–400 for a further discussion.)

- Readers need to know where they can locate your sources so they can consult the original versions. This allows them not only to check the accuracy of your citations, but also to find additional material beyond what you have presented.

A List of Works Cited

A writer adds a list of works cited to a research paper to indicate sources. The list provides enough information for readers to identify each source and to locate it if they wish. Although this information might be presented in various ways, writers generally follow a standard *format,* a prescribed method of citing information.

Different fields adhere to separate formats. If you are writing a paper for a psychology course, for example, you may be expected to follow a format different from the one you would use for a history paper. The lists of works cited for the two preceding summary reports follow a format known as **MLA style,** which is prescribed by the Modern Language Association, an organization of scholars in English and other literatures and languages. Research papers written for composition courses use this format more often than any other, and it is the one that we feature throughout this book. (Other widely used formats are explained in Chapters E and F of Part II.)

Each different type of source—a book, say, or a government document or a motion picture—is presented in a particular way in an MLA-style list of works cited. For now, we will examine only four of the most common types of sources: books, articles in magazines, newspaper items, and essays in edited anthologies or collections. Formats for other sources, along with more detailed information about MLA-style documentation, can be found in Chapter A of Part II.

Suppose that you have used a passage from a book titled *Intimate Readings: The Contemporary Women's Memoir* by Janet Mason Ellerby. Here is how you would cite that source in an MLA-style list of works cited:

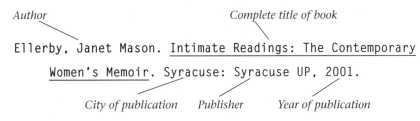

The entry consists of three general categories of information, each of which is followed by a period. They are presented in this order:

1. *The author's name.* Give the author's last name, followed by a comma, then the author's first name, followed by middle name or initial (if either is cited in the book's title page).

2. *The complete title of the book, including any subtitle.* Capitalize the first word of the title (and of the subtitle, if there is one) and of all subsequent words except for articles (*a, an, the*), conjunctions (*and, or, but, nor*), and prepositions (*in, from, to, between,* etc.). Underline (or italicize) both the title and the subtitle (*Note:* The subtitle should be preceded by a colon, which follows the title.)

3. *Information about publication.*

   —The city (and state, if the city is not a major one) in which the book was published. Follow this with a colon.

   —A shortened form of the publisher's name. The shortened form always omits articles, business abbreviations (*Inc., Corp., Co.*), and words such as *Press, Books,* and *Publishers.* If the name of the publisher is that of an individual (e.g., William Morrow), cite the last name only; if it consists of more than one last name (e.g., Prentice Hall), cite only the first of them. If the

name contains the words *university press*, they must be signified by the abbreviation *UP*. Follow the publisher's name with a comma.

—*The year of publication.* End the entry with a period.

Now suppose you have also used an article in *Newsweek*. Here is how you would cite it:

Author   *Title of article*

Christenson, Elise. "Firefighters Looking for Ways to Stop the

    Exodus." <u>Newsweek</u> 7 Oct. 2002: 8.

    Name of magazine   *Publication date*   *Page on which article appears*

This entry consists of the same three categories of information, with only slight variations in the last two. Instead of being underlined, the title of the article is punctuated with a period and placed in quotation marks. Information about publication is presented as follows:

1. ***The name of the magazine.*** Underline (or italicize) it. Do not follow it with any mark of punctuation.

2. ***The publication date.*** List the complete date—day, month, and year (in that order)—for a weekly or biweekly magazine; month(s) and year only for a monthly or bimonthly magazine; or season and year for a quarterly magazine. Abbreviate all months except May, June, and July. Put a colon after the date.

3. ***Page number(s).*** After the colon list the page number(s) on which the article appears. Do not include the word *page(s)* or any abbreviation such as *pg., p.,* or *pp.* If the pages are not continuous (e.g., if an article is printed on pages 34, 35, and 40), cite the number of the first page *only,* followed by the symbol +.

Entries for newspaper items are much the same. Following are two typical examples:

Author   *Title of article*   *Name of Newspaper*

Shimron, Yonat. "Anger and Spirituality." <u>News and Observer</u>

    [Raleigh] 14 June 2002: 3E.

        Publication date   *Page on which article appears*

Brown, Patricia Leigh. "A Push to Save Reno's Landmarks as

    Divorce Capital." <u>New York Times</u>, natl. ed.: sec. 3: 7.

                         Edition   *Section*   *Page*

One difference between these entries and the example for magazine articles is that a section of the newspaper is cited. When the section is designated by a letter, as in the first instance, it is incorporated into the page number; when designated by a number, as in the second instance, it is cited separately with the abbreviation *sec.* You will also notice that the second entry cites *natl. ed.,* since the *New York Times* appears in separate late and national editions. The name of the edition is abbreviated in lowercase letters, as shown. Finally, when the title of a city newspaper (as opposed to a national paper such as the *Wall Street Journal* or *USA Today*) does not include the city in which it is published, the name of that city should be enclosed in brackets—not parentheses—after the title.

An entry for an essay in an edited anthology cites the author and title of the essay, followed by the title of the anthology and the name of its editor(s). Information about publication is followed by page numbers for the essay:

Author   *Title of essay*   *Title of anthology*

Montwieler, Katherine. "Marketing Sensation: Lady Audley's

    Secret and Consumer Culture." <u>Mary Elizabeth Braddon in</u>

    <u>Context</u>. Ed. Marlene Tromp, Pamela Gilbert, and Aeron

    Haynie. Albany, NY: SUNY P, 2000. 43-61.

            Editors   *Pages on which essay appears*

List entries alphabetically. If the author of a source is not named, introduce the entry for that work by title and alphabetize accordingly (ignoring the words *a, an,* and *the*). Do not number the items. Entries that occupy more than a single line are **outdented** (the reverse of indented); that is, the first line begins at the left margin and each subsequent line is indented half an inch. Notice how this format is applied in the following excerpt from the list of works cited in a report on the cultural implications of interstate highway construction.

Crouch, Andy. "Interstate Nation." <u>Christianity Today</u> 10 June

    2002: 55.

Finch, Christopher. <u>Highways to Heaven: The Auto Biography of</u>

    <u>America</u>. New York: Harper, 1992.

Gillespie, Angus Kress, and Michael Aaron Rockland. <u>Looking for</u>

    <u>America on the New Jersey Turnpike</u>. New Brunswick, NJ:

    Rutgers UP, 1992.

"Interstate Highway System." <u>Civil Engineering</u> Nov.-Dec. 2002:

    140.

```
Kilborn, Peter T. "In Rural Areas Interstates Build Their
        Own Economy." New York Times 14 June 2001, late ed.:
        A1.
St. Clair, David James. The Motorization of American Cities.
        New York: Praeger, 1986.
Weingroff, Richard F. "The Genie in the Bottle: The Interstate
        System and Urban Problems, 1939-1957." Public Roads
        Sept.-Oct. 2000: 2-25.
```

Consult Chapter A of Part II for more information relating to lists of works cited.

A Brief List of Works Cited

Suppose you have been asked to report on grade inflation using the following sources. Write an MLA-style list of works cited. Be careful to follow the guidelines governing format precisely.

a. A book by Alfie Kohn titled *What to Look for in a Classroom and Other Essays*, published in San Francisco, California, by Jossey-Bass in 2000.

b. An article by Gregory Stanley and Lawrence Baines titled "No More Shopping for Grades at B-Mart: Re-Establishing Grades as Indicators of Academic Performance," published in the March–April 2001 issue of *Clearing House*, on pages 227–30.

c. An article titled "Who's Been Cheating?" published in the October 5, 2002, issue of *The Economist*, on page 15. No author is cited.

d. An article by Richard Rothstein titled "Doubling of A's at Harvard: Grade Inflation or Brains?" published in the December 5, 2001, late edition of the *New York Times*, on page 8 of section D.

Parenthetical Notes

A list of works cited identifies your paper's sources *in their entirety*. A **parenthetical note**—a note placed in parentheses within your paper—identifies the *specific* location within a source from which you have taken a quotation or a bit of paraphrased information. Unlike the more complicated and cumbersome footnotes and endnotes, parenthetical notes employ a clear and efficient type of shorthand:

They supply the least amount of information needed to identify a source about which more detailed information can be found in the list of works cited.

The beauty of parenthetical notes is their simplicity. MLA-style notes usually contain only two items: the author's last name and the page(s) from which the quotation or paraphrased information has been taken. For example, assume that one of your sources is Terry Lefton's article on tennis and advertising, which appears on pages 214–16. You would cite it in your list of works cited as follows:

```
Lefton, Terry. "The Anglophile Angle." Brandweek 6 June 1999:

     28-29.
```

Any notes within your paper need only refer the reader to this citation. To indicate that the following sentence is a paraphrase of information found on page 28 of that article, you would provide a parenthetical note:

```
In 1967, the governing board of Wimbledon hesitantly

allowed an American promoter to sell broadcasting rights for the

tournament in overseas markets (Lefton 28).
```

The note is placed at the end of the sentence but preceding the period. Observe also that the note tells you only the *specific page* on which this information appears. (In contrast, the entry in the list of works cited shows the page numbers on which the *entire article* is printed.) However, when notes refer to an article as a whole—as do the notes on pages 221–22—then they too cite the pages on which the entire article appears.

When the author's name is unknown, cite instead the first word or two of the title. Suppose, for example, you wanted to paraphrase something from the fourth item in the list of sources concerning highway construction. That anonymous article is cited as follows:

```
"Interstate Highway System." Civil Engineering Nov.-Dec. 2002:

     140.
```

Your parenthetical note would look like this:

```
("Interstate" 140)
```

If you name the author (or, in the case of an anonymous article, if you cite its title) within the text of your paper, thus identifying the source, a parenthetical note provides only the page number(s). See, for example, the two notes for "Can the Boy Scouts Legally Discriminate?" on pages 231–32. As you can see, the theory behind parenthetical notes is to provide the least information needed to identify sources.

Consult Chapter B of Part II for more information relating to parenthetical notes.

| **Providing Parenthetical Notes** | **EXERCISE** |

Suppose you have written a report on interstate highway construction using the sources listed on pages 236–37. Show what the following parenthetical notes would look like:

a. A note referring to information on page 18 of Finch's book.

b. A note referring to the article in *Civil Engineering* as a whole.

c. A note referring to information taken from the last two pages of Weingroff's article.

▮ READING SELECTION

The following chapter from the recently published book *Mosquito: A Natural History of Our Most Persistent and Deadly Foe* provides an account of the ambitious— yet unsuccessful—effort to rid the world of malaria by killing mosquitoes with dichlorodiphenyl trichloroethane (DDT), a toxic compound currently outlawed in the United States and most other developed countries. Experiences related in the first person are those of Andrew Spielman, a professor at the Harvard Medical School. Coauthor Michael D'Antonio is a journalist.

The Great Mosquito Crusade

ANDREW SPIELMAN AND MICHAEL D'ANTONIO

[Shortly after World War II,] the Greek government had begun an all-out war on malaria using the . . . super weapon, DDT. **1**

Greece had a history of malaria outbreak that predated Hippocrates. Most recently, in 1942, half the country's population had been infected. In 1947, a war of eradication was declared with the goal of freeing Greece once and for all from malaria. The mosquito in question was *Anopheles sacharovi,* a notorious malaria carrier that breeds in brackish water around the Mediterranean. With DDT supplied by the United Nations and with military veterans doing the spraying, the Greeks went after the mosquito with warlike intensity. . . . **2**

As far as most Greeks were concerned, the campaign was a glorious success. Spray crews were housed and fed by local villagers who welcomed them as a liberating army. Pilots in biplanes skimmed twenty feet above the ground to attack swamps with DDT fog. And where olive farmers were lucky enough to have their groves catch some of the spray, the collateral deaths of destructive caterpillars meant a much bigger haul at harvest-time. In every town, residents were thrilled to discover that flies, fleas, lice, roaches, and other pests disappeared along with their mosquitoes. DDT became so popular that a few pilots took unauthorized turns over neighborhoods where friends and family lived just to kill sand flies. **3**

4   Except for the accidental deaths of some silkworms and honeybees, the Greek DDT offensive seemed an unblemished success. In 1948, malaria appeared to be essentially gone. Whereas sixteen percent of Greek children had previously tested positive for malaria parasites, none could then be found. Then something strange happened. The flies came back. Soon afterward a malariologist eating lunch at a country inn noticed something even more troubling: several of the dreaded *Anopheles sacharovi* mosquitoes flitting about a room that had been treated with DDT. Finally, in 1951, the men who had just sprayed a village noticed that these mosquitoes had returned in a matter of days and had recommenced biting.

5   Laboratory investigators demonstrated that *Anopheles sacharovi* could adapt, due to natural selection, to the presence of DDT. Some officials hoped that the Greek mosquitoes were somehow special, and other species might not pull off the same trick, but they were wrong. Resistance was being noted in Lebanon and Saudi Arabia. And then came the worst news of all: massive DDT resistance in *Anopheles albimanus* created by the agricultural use of DDT in cotton fields in El Salvador. In that case, the mosquitoes were adapting even before an impending antimalaria campaign could begin.

6   The lowly mosquito's ability to resist DDT had political as well as scientific implications. As every student of history knows, the West's cold-war hostilities with the Soviet Union began immediately after the end of World War II. As the Communists worked to bring one nation after another into their sphere, the United States and Western Europe responded accordingly.

7   In the geographical competition, new technologies yielded the best propaganda material. Whether it was *Sputnik,* atomic energy, or even new vaccines, the competing systems presented every advance as evidence of a superior political and economic system. Whenever possible, breakthroughs were delivered to allies and potential allies in order to extend political influence. At the head of this effort, the United States, through its Agency for International Development (AID), created countless programs designed to use American money and know-how in this way.

8   DDT was going to be a major weapon against communism as well as mosquitoes, bringing health to a world that would have to notice that it came from America. The resistance problem threw an unexpected and disturbing variable into the picture—time. Although many mosquitoes ultimately adapted to DDT, liberal and broadscale use of this extraordinary insecticide would disrupt transmission of malaria long enough for the disease to begin to disappear. Other forces might then break the cycle of transmission. This is what happened in Greece, where, in the end, the mosquitoes survived but malaria did not. . . .

9   Seven years was how long it seemed to take for resistance to arise in mosquitoes under attack from DDT and to become an insuperable obstacle to its continued use. If we were to employ this chemical wonder in an all-out attempt to rid the world of malaria, our goal would have to be accomplished within that span of time. This was the conclusion reached in 1956 in a seminal report issued by the International Development Advisory Board (IDAB) to the U.S. State Department.

10   Guided mainly by Dr. Paul Russell, Soper's* colleague and a true believer in eradication, the IDAB laid out a bold plan requiring $520 million in 1955 dollars (the equivalent today would be many billions of dollars) to defeat malaria worldwide.

---

*Fred Soper was Regional Director of the International Health Division of the Rockefeller Foundation from 1927 to 1942 and Director of the Pan American Sanitary Bureau from 1947 to 1959. He coordinated an aggressive campaign to eradicate mosquito populations through massive applications of DDT. (Editor's note.)

"Eradication is economically practicable today only because of the remarkable effectiveness of DDT and related poisons," the board declared. But because of resistance, it added, in capital letters, "TIME IS OF THE ESSENCE."

The humanitarian reasons for a world war on malaria were obvious, but the report suggested other justifications for America paying the bill for the assault. The first was economic. Malaria was debilitating workers and consumers in countries that trade with the United States. Their lost labor made goods that the United States imported more expensive. Their malaise also retarded development, meaning fewer markets for high-priced American goods. Ultimately, America paid a hidden, $300 million "malaria tax"—in higher prices and lost sales—every year.   **11**

But beyond dollars, the board saw potential political benefit from a huge malaria eradication initiative; it would win America friends. Unlike other development programs, which rarely lead to "visible evidence of progress," a malaria eradication project made life better, immediately, for every family it touched. The point was obvious. DDT spray teams that appear twice a year with mosquito-killing agents labeled "Made in USA" would reinforce America's positive image. . . .   **12**

The IDAB message—that America should immediately fund a program literally to douse the world with DDT and end malaria—could not have surprised anyone who knew the board's scientific adviser, Paul Russell. Just one year before, Russell had published a book with the audacious title *Man's Mastery of Malaria*. In it, he expressed an evangelical zeal for eradication. "The verb *to master* does not imply an end to the matter," he writes, "rather it suggests that, having prevailed over an opposing force, one has moral responsibility for keeping it under control."   **13**

Here was the sum of Russell's medical, scientific, and even family background coming to the fore. The son of a New England preacher, Russell had wanted to serve both God and man as a medical missionary. In his work with malaria, he found a true moral purpose. He was excited by DDT, which he called a "wonder," and his faith in eradication was all but unshakable.   **14**

The DDT evangelists were persuasive enough to convince the State Department and then two prominent senators—John F. Kennedy and Hubert H. Humphrey—that victory over malaria was attainable. The timing couldn't have been better. In 1957, the Soviets' launch of the *Sputnik* satellite revved America's competitive spirit to an almost paranoid pitch. The government was ready to do anything to prove the might of American science. A project to use an American-manufactured technology (DDT) to rid the world of malaria fit perfectly.   **15**

Congress approved the program and the Agency for International Development quickly organized itself to run it. USAID virtually took over the existing World Health Organization program, greatly accelerating and expanding the work underway. President Eisenhower, and later President Kennedy, delivered speeches that declared all-out war on this mosquito-borne disease.   **16**

In 1958, DDT was shipped by the ton to dozens of countries that stood on the front lines in the great war against malaria. The commitment to this strategy was total, so much an article of faith in American science that grants for malaria research disappeared almost overnight. If the great solution—DDT—had been found, then what was the point of research? This became dogma, even at universities. At Harvard, for example, the faculty simply avoided teaching and doing research in malariology. To continue would have been seen as subversive.   **17**

The demand for total loyalty that swept the field of tropical medicine may have been a product of the urgency felt by so many at the top. They understood best the time pressure in our gamble. Wherever DDT was applied, it would have to work its   **18** magic fast. But there was another factor to fear: recolonization. No country that rid itself of malaria would be safe if its neighbor did not join in the effort. Mosquitoes and travelers could inevitably reintroduce the infection. Here lay one final, terrible problem. A population that has been rendered malaria-free for a few years loses its immunity. And if the pathogen returns, everyone will be more vulnerable to severe disease than they were before they received the benefit of this intervention. Immunity works to modulate the symptoms of malaria but does not prevent reinfection.

19   With the terrible possibilities of DDT resistance and recolonization hanging over their heads, the U.S. Agency for International Development and the World Health Organization worked at a fevered pitch. Training institutes were opened, malaria surveys were conducted, manuals were assembled. By 1960, sixty-six countries were embarked on the prescribed spray campaign. Another seventeen were either planning or negotiating to get involved. . . .

20   By 1961, just three years into the offensive, the proponents of eradication were adding up their victories. More than twenty percent of the people once plagued by malaria lived in cleared areas. Wherever near total coverage was achieved, malaria was beaten. And the only resistance the program officers had met was not in the mosquitoes but in the offices of the bureaucrats who managed their funds.

21   Well before the end of the five-year timetable, Americans were bragging about their role in this effort. At a mosquito-control conference in California, one federal official made the claim to glory: "Where else could sixty million pounds of insecticide be mobilized in one single year for this fight overseas?" asked Roy F. Fritz. "Where else could we obtain the number of vehicles and spray equipment which can withstand eight to ten hours a day's use, day in and day out, year in and year out? Where else could that be produced? It isn't produced anywhere else." . . .

22   Exactly one year after Roy F. Fritz crowed about American technology and the coming defeat of malaria, the Royal Society of Tropical Medicine and Hygiene met at Manson House, a brick row building in London named for Sir Patrick Manson. These scientists gathered to review the progress, or lack of it, in antimalaria battlefield reports from around the world.

23   "It appears," noted scientist M. J. Colbourne, "that resistance is seriously interfering with progress in several countries." Though he suggested that a change of insecticides might save the day, there were still other difficulties, including those dangerous "exophilic" species that flitted indoors to bite but refused to rest long enough to be killed by DDT residue. In the end, said Colbourne, "the achievement of worldwide, or even continent-wide eradication does not appear practicable in the near future." . . .

24   Failure was going to be noted, soon, all over the globe after the seven-year time span and large-scale American funding expired. Taiwan held to its eradication record, but Sri Lanka began to see the beginning of a malaria comeback that would produce half a million cases in 1969. (In the same year, the World Health Organization officially recognized the failure of eradication.)

25   In other countries the story was to be the same—the gradual appearance of resistant mosquitoes and the subsequent emergence of malaria. In Indonesia, malaria increased fourfold between 1965 and 1968. India held on longer than most, but a massive epidemic announced malaria's return in 1976, when an estimated twenty-five million people were stricken. Due to the malaria eradication effort, many people had lost all immunity to the parasite: their new infections were particularly dangerous.

26   In the early 1960s, those who pushed the military-style assault on mosquitoes with DDT clung to their strategy. If only a little more time and DDT were applied, they argued, the desired result would occur. But the money, the energy, and, most important,

faith in the solution had been running out. The final blow, at least as far as public opinion in the developed world was concerned, came in the form of a book by a middle-aged biologist who once showed her students the strange mating behavior of polychete sea worms near the dock at the famous Woods Hole Marine Biological Laboratory.

Published in 1962, Rachel Carson's *Silent Spring* took on a host of nascent ecological issues, including problems associated with radiation, but its major effect was to challenge the widespread assertion that DDT was safe. Beginning with convincing evidence linking the pesticide to the decline of certain bird populations, Carson went on to describe health problems in workers who handled the chemical and liver cancers in exposed fish. She argued for restraint. **27**

It was from Carson that the general public learned that DDT was found in mother's milk and could accumulate in the bodies of their babies. And it was Carson who told the public that as early as 1950, the federal Food and Drug Administration warned, "It's extremely likely that the potential hazard of DDT has been underestimated." **28**

Silent Spring was one of the first popular works to bring environmental concerns to a broad audience. It also revealed that science was not a monolith. Indeed, in one passage after another, Carson presented the work of respected researchers who challenged the DDT establishment. They described how in some cases DDT spraying killed other animals and allowed for an explosion in the abundance of certain pests. She also explained in clear terms how insecticide resistance developed. **29**

"Spraying kills off the weaklings," she wrote. "The only survivors are insects that have some inherent quality that allows them to escape harm." These are the parents of the new generation, which, by simple inheritance, possess all the qualities of "toughness inherent in its forebears." Under Carson's guidance, it's pretty easy for any reader to understand how insect populations that give rise to new generations in a matter of days can quickly defy a pesticide. **30**

As convincing as her science may have been, it was Carson's gift with prose that was more persuasive. "The 'control of nature' is a phrase conceived in arrogance, born of the Neanderthal age of biology and philosophy, when it was supposed that nature exists for the convenience of man," she concluded. "The concepts and practices in applied entomology for the most part date from the Stone Age of science. It is our alarming misfortune that so primitive a science has armed itself with the most modern and terrible weapons, and that in turning them against the insects, it has also turned them against the earth." **31**

Silent Spring was published eight years before the creation of the U.S. Environmental Protection Agency. But almost immediately, several states began reviewing the use of pesticides, and by 1968, half a dozen had banned particular chemicals. Four different national research commissions conducted studies on DDT and recommended that its use be phased out. A year later, the United States Department of Agriculture began banning its use on certain crops. In 1971, the EPA held hearings on DDT that resulted in nine thousand pages of testimony. On December 31, 1972, the agency issued a press release announcing that "the general use of DDT will no longer be legal in the United States after today." **32**

DDT's supporters continue to argue that, despite the application of more than 1.3 billion pounds of the chemical in the United States, not one human death can clearly be attributed to its use. But this argument could not stand against the perceived long-term danger. And with the chemical banned in America, the prospect for its use overseas dimmed as well. How many leaders abroad would be able to assure citizens that a pesticide that Americans no longer produced, and feared using themselves, was actually safe? **33**

34   Nevertheless, a worldwide ban on DDT would be a severe loss for public health workers because the pesticide has properties that render it an invaluable tool against malaria. When used for this purpose, it is applied close to where people sleep, on the inside walls of houses. After biting, the mosquitoes generally fly to the nearest vertical surface and remain standing there for about an hour, anus down, while they drain the water from their gut contents and excrete it in a copious, pink-tinged stream. If the surfaces the mosquitoes repair to are coated by a poison that is soluble in the wax that covers all insects' bodies, the mosquitoes will acquire a lethal dose.

35   No chemical compares to DDT as a weapon against the resting mosquito. First, it is potent. Just two grams of DDT per square meter of wall surface is more than enough to kill a mosquito within its usual one-hour resting period. Second, it is inexpensive. It is also easily stored and transported, and relatively safe for the person doing the spraying. Best of all, it remains effective for many, many months.

36   The total ban on DDT's use in the United States deprived American public health officials of a weapon that could have been safely used. Even today, when there are many chemicals available to kill mosquitoes, DDT retains many advantages. It is the ideal insecticide of first use. This is because the resistance that mosquitoes develop after being exposed to DDT does little to protect them against the other, more expensive insecticides that wait on the sidelines. However, mosquitoes hit first with one of those other compounds—such as malathion, sevin, or permethrin—develop a broader resistance that partially protects them from DDT as well. A spray program based on the use of chemicals in any of these alternatives also tends to be about three times as expensive as one based on DDT. When used correctly and with restraint, DDT appears to be irreplaceable in antimalaria programs.

37   In the year 2000, DDT was nearly outlawed worldwide under the terms of a United Nations Environmental Program treaty. It was to be classified as one of the unsafe "dirty dozen" of the Persistent Organic Pesticides, known as POPs. In December 2000, however, a treaty conference held in South Africa agreed to a "dirty eleven." DDT was excluded from proscription. The chemical is now manufactured only in China and India, and it is to remain available solely for use in antimalaria programs. This most recent battle over DDT's status was intense and the outcome crucial for helping to protect human health around the world.

38   By the time that the postwar effort to eradicate malaria waned, many of the important vector species had developed some degree of resistance. Where malaria workers turned to substitute insecticides, some mosquitoes learned to resist those too. At the same time, the malaria parasite itself began to demonstrate its ability to evolve resistance to our best medicines, and drug resistance accelerated as these medicines became more readily available. In too many poor households people obtain the medicine, use just enough to ease their symptoms, and then hoard the remainder for the next wave of illness. Malaria parasites frequently are exposed to sublethal doses of drug. In this manner, malaria sufferers turn their bodies into ideal breeding sites for drug-resistant parasites. . . .

39   No history of the monumental malaria eradication campaign would be completed without acknowledging several key points. Although malaria continues to destroy human lives and impede happiness, the recent eradication campaign preserved human health and lives, at least temporarily, around the globe. It's reasonable to suppose that many millions of people escaped death because they got through their vulnerable childhood years without infection. Sadly, many of their children and grandchildren will not now be spared a malarious fate, as this infection continues to stage its raging comeback.

It is also necessary to acknowledge America's own major failure to destroy a cer-   **40**
tain dangerous mosquito species. Under pressure from Latin American countries that
had run the yellow fever vector out of their territories, the United States promised to
eradicate *Aedes aegypti* from the Americas in the mid-1960s. There was more than a little irony in this situation. After all, America had gone to war with Spain, in part, because of the danger of yellow fever spreading from Cuba into nearby lands. Now the
same Latin American countries that had been blamed for sending pests north were
quite understandably demanding protection from the same mosquito harbored in the
United States.

Mainly a container-breeding insect, *Aedes aegypti* would be attacked by DDT appli-   **41**
cations and by crews that located and removed disused tires, jars, and other man-
made containers that collected water and supported breeding. Thousands of workers
were trained for the task. Fleets of trucks were equipped with sprayers. Nine states,
from Texas to South Carolina, were notified that they harbored the mosquito and
would be battlegrounds in the war against it. A determined government notified laboratories that used the mosquito for research that these colonies would be destroyed.
This "guinea pig" of the medical entomology laboratory was to be lost, even in northern cities where these insects could not survive the winter.

Once the effort began in earnest, so did the opposition. Laboratories successfully   **42**
fought the order to destroy the mosquito colonies that they used for experimental
studies. And in one community after another, the U.S. Public Health Service encountered residents who didn't want anyone traipsing through their backyards looking for
old tires or blanketing their neighborhoods with DDT. They had read (or heard of)
Silent Spring and would have none of it.

As legal costs mounted, the eradication effort slowed. Then the EPA banned DDT.   **43**
The war was over. Latin America would continue to live under the threat that the yellow fever vector could return via the United States. It was another victory for the mosquitoes. (This fact became clear to me on the day I visited the *Aedes aegypti* eradication
program's headquarters near Atlanta and found the little devils breeding in a can that
had been discarded near the agency's parking lot.)

When the great war on mosquitoes was begun, Fred Soper and Paul Russell de-   **44**
clared victory for their theories of eradication as a solution to malaria. Generations of
experts had argued over whether eradication was really feasible, and for many years
those who favored more cautious "control" or "suppression" programs had prevailed.
But with the U.S. government's embrace of the eradication concept, the matter
seemed completely settled. It became such an article of faith that students who hoped
to enter the field were warned that they had joined a dying profession. The vector
mosquito was soon to be wiped off the face of the earth.

As failures mounted, however, and it became clear that worldwide eradication   **45**
would never be achieved, Soper and Russell quite literally ceased discussing the matter
in scientific forums. Russell, who had accepted a position at Harvard in 1959, demonstrated his disappointment by avoiding the subject altogether and steadily withdrawing from contact with students and faculty. By 1968, he had retired to an isolated village in Maine. Soper remained a heroic figure because of his work in Brazil, but he
distanced himself from the global malaria initiative. Remarkably, his 1977 memoir,
Ventures in World Health, makes no significant mention of this grand attempt to apply
his theory. . . .

In reality, mosquitoes are a pest and a threat that require people to mount a con-   **46**
sistent, sophisticated, and even strategic defense. The impulse to smash the enemy

must be measured against the knowledge that, in the case of a weapon like DDT, it is possible to go too far. . . .

47   Today a map shaded to illustrate the worldwide distribution of malaria does not look much different from one drawn in 1955, before the great mosquito crusade. A few island nations, most notably Taiwan and Jamaica, have joined the nations of the Northern Hemisphere where malaria has disappeared. But across much of the tropical part of the globe, the parasite predominates. Today's map looks even more ominous when it is marked to indicate where drug-resistant parasites—entirely absent from the world scene in 1955—now roam. Chloroquine can't destroy these parasites, and even our modern multidrug cocktails are sometimes ineffective. Almost every country in sub-Saharan Africa suffers from this more deadly kind of malaria, along with half of South America and much of Asia from Afghanistan to New Guinea. Billions of people are at risk. Every year, ten percent of the world's population suffers from malaria. Every twelve seconds a malaria-infected child dies.

Freewriting

In your notebook, write for fifteen minutes about the "Great Mosquito Crusade" conducted after World War II. You may wish to consider whether, on the whole, it was a worthwhile venture, or you may want to draw connections to other human attempts to control or defy nature—cloning, genetic engineering, atomic energy, strip mining, supersonic transport, "unsinkable" ships. On the other hand, you might assess the motives and methods of Fred Soper, Paul Russell, and other advocates of mosquito eradication.

Group Work

Share both freewritings with members of your peer group by having each member read aloud as others take notes. Try to arrive at some consensus about whether any historical lesson emerges from the "Great Mosquito Crusade" and, if so, what that lesson is and the extent to which it has been understood and accepted.

Review Questions

1. What were the political implications surrounding the use of DDT to eradicate mosquito populations?
2. Why was it important to pursue the eradication campaign quickly as well as aggresively?
3. What factors contributed to the ban on DDT production and use in the United States?
4. What have been the ultimate effects of the eradication campaign on the worldwide distribution of malaria?

Discussion Questions

1. Would you say that Spielman and D'Antonio are fair and objective in their presentation of Fred Soper, Paul Russell, and their associates? If not, do you feel that they are too harsh or too lenient?

2. In one section of their book, Spielman and D'Antonio refer to the eradication campaign as "the kind of deception that people practice when they are trying their very hardest to do something good, even heroic, in the face of a terrible problem." Try to think of other possible examples of this type of deception—either public historical events or private experiences and observations. After doing so, can you say that this type of deception is ever justified? If not, do you feel that there is any moral difference between this and other types of deception?

3. Spielman and D'Antonio argue that total rejection of the production and use of DDT in the United States and most other countries was an overreaction to the publication of Rachel Carson's *Silent Spring*. Can you account for the fact that other, more dramatic events (e.g., the nuclear accident at Chernobyl, the oil spill from the *Exxon Valdez*) have not resulted in similar consequences?

Writing

1. Write a brief summary report on any of the following sets of readings:

   a. "Pay Your Own Way! (Then Thank Mom)" (p. 83), "Relationships with Maturing Children (pp. 90–92), and "Keeping Parents off Campus" (pp. 94–95).

   b. "Learning How to Learn" (pp. 104–06), "Adapting to College Life in an Era of Heightened Stress" (pp. 106–08), and "The Challenge of First-Generation College Students" (pp. 110–15).

   c. "Another Day, Another Indignity" (pp. 149–51), "Get a Job" (pp. 153–54), and "Before College, Start with a Side Order" (pp. 154–55).

2. Using the Internet, or with the help of your instructor or a reference librarian, find two articles about one of the following technological advances: disposable diapers, enriched bread, laundry detergent, frozen or fast food, styrofoam. One article should address the benefits of this technology; the other should examine some of its unanticipated consequences. Write an objective report on sources that synthesizes the two articles.

WRITE, READ, and RESEARCH the NET

1. *Write:* Brainstorm a list of historically important inventions, beginning perhaps with those listed in the preceding writing suggestion 2.

2. *Read:* Review the two following Web sites:
<http://www.lib.lsu.edu/sci/chem/patent/srs136.html>
<http://www.totallyabsurd.com/>

3. *Research:* Using the Internet, locate biographies of several of the inventors cited in the first of the two Web sites listed above. Look for similarities and differences in their backgrounds, personality traits, and personal histories. On the basis of what you find, write a short essay about what seems to foster innovative and experimental impulses.

■ ADDITIONAL READING

The following readings deal with discoveries and inventions that have profoundly affected American culture as well as influenced the course of world history. In each case, technology brought both immediate benefits along with unanticipated long-term consequences.

George B. Kauffman, professor emeritus of chemistry at California State University, Fresno, relates the circumstances under which Thomas Midgley, Jr., developed tetraethyl lead (TEL), a crucially important gasoline additive, and chlorofluorocarbons (CFCs), substances used in air conditioning and refrigeration. Though highly effective and quickly adopted, TEL and CFCs eventually proved harmful to the environment, with the production and use of both eventually curtailed. Kauffman depicts Midgley as a compulsive inventor (he held 117 patents) whose premature death was caused by one of his less famous innovations.

Midgley: Saint or Serpent?

GEORGE B. KAUFFMAN

1   This year marks the centenary of the birth of Thomas Midgley, Jr., discoverer of the antiknock gasoline additive tetraethyl lead (TEL) and of chlorofluorocarbons (CFCs), a class of stable, nontoxic, nonflammable refrigerants, propellants, and blowing agents. These two everyday materials, though useful, have brought environmental effects that took years to manifest themselves. They thus typify the delicacy of the risk-benefit balance of modern technology.

2   Midgley, born on May 18, 1889, in Beaver Falls, Pa., inherited his inventiveness from both parents; his father, Thomas Midgley, Sr., was a prolific inventor in various fields, especially automobile tires. His mother was the daughter of James Emerson, inventor of the inserted-tooth saw. Midgley attended public school in Columbus, Ohio, where his talent for invention surfaced. In high school, where he played on the baseball and football teams, he used an extract of the inner bark of the slippery elm to impart to a baseball the slipperiness needed for maximum curving effect. The technique was later practiced extensively by many pitchers. In 1905 he entered the Betts Academy, a small, private college preparatory school in Greenwich, Conn. His chemistry teacher, Henry M. Robert, Jr., son of the writer of *Robert's Rules of Order* and later professor of economics at the U.S. Naval Academy, first introduced Midgley to the periodic table, which later led him to his two greatest discoveries. . . .

Midgley decided on a career in research [and] in 1916 joined the Dayton Engi-   3
neering Laboratories Company (Delco), which Charles F. Kettering had established to
develop his own inventions and to manufacture starting, lighting, and ignition equipment for automobiles. Midgley's first two assignments were to develop an indicator
for the degree of charge of storage batteries and to improve mercury-cooled exhaust
valves. His third assignment from "Boss Ket" led to what was called in 1944 "the most
important automotive discovery of the last two decades."

One of Kettering's inventions was a home-lighting system for farms. He had modified an internal-combustion engine to use kerosene because fire laws prevented the
storage of gasoline on residential property. However, this kerosene-fueled engine de-   4
veloped a violent knock that sometimes was strong enough to crack the cylinder head
and pistons, and Kettering assigned Midgley the task of discovering the cause of
knocking and how to eliminate it. Kettering and Midgley thought that the less volatile
kerosene knocked worse than gasoline because kerosene vapors were full of droplets
that vaporized upon combustion, resulting in an explosive knock. Midgley developed
what became known as the Midgley Indicator—a high-speed camera with a series of
optical lenses attached to the engine to magnify and record the shape of the explosive
pressure wave within the engine. This device, which he later patented and which won
him the Franklin Institute's Longstreth Medal in 1925, showed that the knock was
caused by the rapid rise in pressure after ignition rather than during preignition, as
Kettering and he had supposed.

SERENDIPITY STRIKES

An incorrect theory and a fortunate accident led to the first antiknock agent. Remembering from his boyhood that the reddish flowers of the trailing arbutus (*Epigaea
repens*) bloom early in the spring, Kettering theorized that perhaps the red color ab-   5
sorbed more heat than did the other flowers, thus causing the early blooming. Either
he or Midgley speculated that dyeing kerosene red might cause it to absorb heat faster
so that the droplets might vaporize enough to prevent knocking.

Calculations would have shown that this theory was untenable. However, Midgley decided that it was easier to try it out than it was to do the calculations. One Saturday afternoon, December 16, 1916, Midgley went to the Delco lab storeroom look-   6
ing for an oil-soluble red dye, but none was available. Fortunately, the chemical
supply houses in Dayton were closed, so his colleague Fred L. Chase suggested that
Midgley try a small amount of iodine, which turns kerosene reddish. The dyed fuel
performed beautifully without producing a single knock.

On Monday morning, when the supply houses opened, Midgley bought a dozen
different red dyes, but none prevented knocking. Apparently, color had nothing to do
with antiknock properties, for Midgley showed that colorless iodine compounds, such   7
as ethyl iodide, had a modified antiknock effect. Although the arbutus theory had led
to the discovery of an antiknock agent, it now had to be abandoned. Unfortunately,
iodine not only added more than a dollar to the cost of a gallon of fuel but also was
very reactive and corroded the engine parts. In Midgley's words, "Carburetor and
gasoline piping gradually changed into copper and zinc iodides, the cylinders were
transformed into iron iodide and so on. It was clear that no car could be an iodide factory and a good automobile at the same time."

Nevertheless, the discovery of iodine's effects had shown that antiknock agents   8
existed, and the search for a suitable substance continued, largely by use of the
Edisonian trial-and-error method of research, of which Kettering said, "Why don't
they call it the 'trial-and-success' method? That is what it really is."

9   When the United States entered World War I, a better aviation gasoline was badly needed, and what had begun as a minor problem became an urgent matter. Collaborating with the U.S. Bureau of Mines, the Delco laboratory staff now attacked the antiknock problem under Midgley's leadership. . . . Midgley and his co-workers tested every substance that they could find for antiknock activity, "from melted butter and camphor to ethyl acetate and aluminum chloride, and most of them had no more effect than spitting in the Great Lakes."

ULTIMATUM

10   Weeks became months, and months became years, and the search continued without success. Finally, Midgley and his coworkers were given a week to find a better antiknock agent than iodine. According to Midgley, "We thought we had worked hard up to this day, but our work was mere idleness compared to the feverish activity that we crowded into the next seven days."

11   On Jan. 30, 1919, Midgley and his team found that 2 mL of aniline was a more effective antiknock agent than a gram of iodine. Encouraged by this success, Midgley continued the search. Derivatives of aniline and other nitrogen-containing organic compounds were found to be effective, but their effectiveness varied widely, depending on the hydrocarbon groups attached to nitrogen. Hydrogen peroxide, bromine, carbon tetrachloride, nitric acid, hydrochloric acid, and nitro compounds were found to increase the knocking when added to the fuel and air mixture. . . .

12   Midgley, disgusted with the slow, wasteful Edisonian hit-or-miss procedure, now abandoned it in favor of what he called a "fox hunt"—narrowing the field by a systematic investigation of compounds based upon a periodic table arranged by MIT's Robert E. Wilson and based on Irving Langmuir's theory of atomic structure. In view of the antiknock activity of selenium oxychloride, the corresponding compound of sulfur, sulfur oxychloride, was prepared and also turned out to be an excellent antiknock agent. Now, as Midgley expressed it, "predictions began fulfilling themselves instead of fizzling." The new approach zeroed in on metallorganics, and within four months Midgley had demonstrated that antiknock activity is a periodic function of the elements that increases with increasing atomic weight within a group.

13   Diethyl selenide was effective. Diethyl telluride, the corresponding compound of tellurium—the element that lies directly below selenium in the table—was even better, but it had "a satanified garlic odor . . . and a single exposure to the stuff would cling to you for weeks." Midgley plotted antiknock activity vs. atomic number for fluorine, oxygen, nitrogen, and carbon groups. He found that antiknock activity increased not only within a group with increasing atomic weight but also increased from right to left in the table. Tetraethylin was more effective than expected. Midgley therefore predicted that the corresponding compound of lead, the element immediately below tin in the table, should be even more effective.

TETRAETHYL LEAD

14   On December 9, 1921, after about 33,000 compounds had been tested, in the Fuel Division of the General Motors Research Corporation, "Tab" Boyd—in the presence of Midgley and [Carroll A.] Hochwalt, who had prepared TEL ($Pb[C_2H_5]_4$)—tested 0.025% of it in kerosene in a Delco-Light engine and found that it gave better results than 1.3% of aniline, their adopted standard. A spoonful of the new compound was enough to convert a gallon of gasoline from a rattling, knocking nuisance into a smooth-running motor fuel. The long search for a satisfactory antiknock agent had

ended, and the work of manufacture, development, and marketing was to begin. When Midgley presented his paper on TEL at the National ACS Meeting in Pittsburgh in September 1922, he filled the stage of the Carnegie Music Hall with an elaborate apparatus and gave impressive demonstrations of engine knocking, both in a glass tube and in an actual engine, and showed how TEL could stop it.

After the discovery Midgley stated: 15

> The popular idea might be that when we found tetraethyl lead we shouted hosannas for it and all marched in to ask the boss for a raise. Actually, there wasn't a pause in the program. We started spending more money, doing more research, and looking for other ingredients to go with tetraethyl lead, to make up a commercially practical compound that could transfer the antiknock qualities of tetraethyl lead to a gallon of gasoline. Thousands of miles were run in various types of automobile tests, hundreds of hours of operation were put in by engines on dynamometer blocks, running day and night. We thought we knew what we had, but we knew very little about it. We had to find the answers, the right answers, to many questions.

For example, Midgley . . . found that TEL left a slight deposit of grayish yellow lead 16
oxide (PbO) in the engine cylinders, which eventually eroded spark plugs and burned valves. Boyd was assigned the problem, and by the summer of 1922 he found that adding ethylene dibromide to gasoline converted the lead oxide to volatile lead bromide and thus minimized the buildup of nonvolatile lead deposits. . . .

Other problems remained, and Midgley was involved in most of them. For exam- 17
ple, Charles A. Kraus of Clarke University developed a cheaper, more practical process for synthesizing TEL. Robert A. Kehoe of the University of Cincinnati College of Medicine determined the toxic hazards of antiknock additives and worked on their control. Earl W. Webb established business policies and marketing details. Before "ethyl gas," a term coined by Kettering, showed a profit and became a commercial success, its sponsors had spent more than $3 million.

Kettering believed that the new product's deficiencies could be remedied more 18
quickly if customer reactions were observed. He thus pushed for marketing it even before the problem of lead deposits in the engine had been solved. The first public sale of ethyl gas occurred on the morning of February 1, 1923, at the Refiners Oil Company station at Sixth and Main Streets in Dayton. Two months later the General Motors Chemical Company, with Kettering as president and Midgley as vice president, was formed as a Delaware corporation to market the product. In May, Boyd suggested that ethyl gas be dyed red with Sudan IV to distinguish it from regular gasoline. Kettering and Midgley persuaded some of the drivers in the 500-mile race at Indianapolis on Memorial Day to use it, and the first three places were won by cars that used ethyl gas. In August 1924, General Motors and Standard Oil of New Jersey founded the Ethyl Gasoline Corporation (renamed the Ethyl Corporation on April 9, 1942), with Kettering as president and Midgley as second vice president and general manager.

The question of TEL toxicity has been addressed for more than sixty years. The 19
manufacturing process is hazardous and led to new and stringent safety regulations. On December 20, 1922, U.S. Surgeon General Hugh S. Cumming issued a warning about the substance, and in February–March 1923, Midgley spent a month in Florida to rest and recuperate from the effects of excess exposure to it. Several months later, on Midgley's request, the Bureau of Mines began "to make an exhaustive and impartial experimental investigation on the possibility of poisoning from the lead in automobile exhaust gases from gasoline containing lead tetraethyl and to make the results public, regardless of what they might be."

20   During 1924 and 1925, fifteen workers died at three plants manufacturing TEL. Midgley became so depressed that he considered abandoning the entire TEL program. As early as July 8, 1924, Kehoe had announced to the Bureau of Mines that the actual problem was the manufacturing process rather than the public's exposure to the product, a judgment confirmed by subsequent investigations. On October 25, 1924, an accident at the Bayway, N.J., "semiworks" operated by Standard Oil of New Jersey resulted in the illness of about forty workers, five of whom died. Some of the fatally ill became insane and had to be confined in strait jackets before their deaths. Journalists covering the tragedy coined the term "loony gas" for ethyl gasoline, and the term persisted for some time.

21   The Ethyl Corporation publicized the first reports of the Bureau of Mines, which concluded that exhaust gases from engines using ethyl gasoline were apparently harmless to humans, and in an interview on October 30, 1924, Midgley, a consummate showman once again now that he had recovered from his depression, rubbed some TEL on his hands to prove that its was not toxic in small amounts. In May 1925, Ethyl Corporation suspended sales until the health hazard question was settled. In 1926 the surgeon general issued Public Health Bulletin 163, titled *The Use of Tetraethyl Lead and Its Relation to Public Health*. The report found no health hazard to the public and concluded that "there are at present no good grounds for prohibiting the use of ethyl gasoline with a composition specified as a motor fuel, provided that its distribution and use are controlled by proper regulation." On May 1, 1926, Ethyl put TEL back on the market and issued new safety regulations for its manufacture and distribution.

22   For the next quarter-century, Kehoe continued his research for Ethyl Corporation on the health aspects of lead and became the world's foremost authority on its toxicity. In the 1950s, as concern for the environment surfaced, new questions arose about automobile exhaust emission and air pollution. Ethyl improved TEL and created a related compound—tetramethyl lead ($[CH_3]_4Pb$, TML). Ethyl also developed an entirely new additive—methylcyclopentadienyl manganesepentacarbonyl $CH_3C_5H_5Mn(CO)_5$. In 1956 the Midwest Research Institute, an independent research group in Kansas City, concluded that lead did not contribute to the smog problem. By the mid-1950s Ethyl had developed an exhaust device to minimize emission problems, and the device was approved by Los Angeles authorities. However, in 1964 the major automobile manufacturers announced that their 1966 models would comply with California's air standards, the most stringent in the nation, in an entirely different way, that is, by concentrating on the intake system, thus eliminating the market for an exhaust device.

23   On January 14, 1970, Edward N. Cole, president of General Motors, announced that GM planned to install a catalytic converter to achieve the air quality of engine exhaust specified by federal regulations. Because leaded gasoline would inactivate the platinum catalyst, TEL would have to be phased down or out. The Clean Air Act of 1970 authorized the Environmental Protection Agency to determine whether any fuel additives would endanger public health. For the next five years Ethyl Corporation testified before EPA, claiming that automobile exhaust from ethyl gas made only an inconsequential addition to atmospheric contaminants; that leaded gasoline had been made a "lead herring," drawing attention and resources away from lead-based paint, the real environmental problem; and that tremendous amounts of crude oil would be wasted in obtaining high-octane gasoline if TEL were not used. However, the reports *Lead in the Human Environment* (National Academy of Sciences, Washington, 1980) and D. Bryce-Smith and R. Stephens's *Lead or Health* (Conservation Society, London, 1981) both identified automobile exhaust as the greatest source of atmospheric lead pollution.

During these years of hearings and litigation, Ethyl Corporation developed lean　**24** reactor engines operating on very low fuel-to-air ratios that reduced emissions to levels below the standards set in all states except California. Ethyl contested the EPA regulations but ultimately lost in the courts. On August 30, 1984, Lawrence E. Blanchard, Jr., vice chairman of Ethyl Corporation, in testimony at the EPA's public hearing on lead phasedown, stated that the EPA had failed to consider the 55% increase in the prime replacement for TEL—aromatics such as benzene, which are known to be carcinogenic—and that the EPA was trying to make lead in gasoline "the scapegoat for other environmental problems." . . .

On the positive side, TEL banished the obstacle of knock and ushered in a great　**25** era of progress in transportation and petroleum technology. Billions of gallons of automobile and aviation gasoline have been improved by TEL since its discovery in 1921. For more than six decades it . . . enabled automotive engineers to increase the power, performance, and efficiency of their engines by raising compression ratios, and it has also promoted the conservation of petroleum by increasing the efficiency of its use. TEL has saved the public an estimated one-third of the total gasoline costs that would have been paid had TEL not been discovered.

CHLOROFLUOROCARBONS

In contrast to the discovery of TEL, which required more than five years, the discovery　**26** of dichlorodifluoro methane (CCl_2F_2), a member of a group of compounds known as CFCs (and known by the DuPont trademark Freons), required only three days. By 1930 the field of artificial refrigeration was growing by leaps and bounds. However, the most widely used refrigerants—ammonia, methyl chloride, and sulfur dioxide— are toxic, and the first two are also fire hazards.

One day Lester S. Keilholtz, chief engineer of the Frigidaire Division of General　**27** Motors, came to Dayton with a message from Kettering to Midgley to develop a nontoxic, nonflammable, cheap refrigerant. At lunch with co-workers Albert N. Henne and Robert MacNary, Midgley expressed doubt that he could find such a single substance, but he hoped that mixing nonflammable, toxic substances with flammable, nontoxic substances might lead to nonflammable, considerably less toxic refrigerants than were currently on the market. Midgley's skepticism aroused Henne's interest, and after lunch the three searched the *International Critical Tables* for stable, nontoxic, nonflammable, volatile organic compounds with boiling points between 0° and −40°C. The discovery that the tables erroneously listed the boiling point of carbon tetrafluoride (CF_4) as −15°C rather than the correct −128°C focused their attention on fluorine compounds.

Realizing that the ICT tables were incomplete—and possibly recalling his earlier　**28** success in discovering TEL—Midgley again turned to the periodic table. He quickly found that only the elements on the right-hand side of the table form sufficiently volatile compounds. Eliminating volatile compounds of boron, silicon, phosphorous, arsenic, antimony, bismuth, tellurium, and iodine as too unstable and toxic, and the noble gases as too low in boiling point, he concentrated on the remaining elements: carbon, nitrogen, oxygen, sulfur, hydrogen, fluorine, chlorine, and bromine; every commercial refrigerant had been made from combinations of these elements. Flammability decreased from left to right, and toxicity decreased within each group from the heavier elements at the bottom of the table to the lighter elements at the top. Thus fluorine appeared as the most likely possibility. Although elemental fluorine is toxic, corrosive, and the most reactive of all the nonmetals, apparently no one had considered that it might be nontoxic and nonreactive in some of its compounds.

29   According to Midgley, "plottings of boiling points, hunting for data, corrections, slide rules, log paper, eraser dirt, pencil shavings, and all the rest of the paraphernalia that take the place of tea leaves and crystal spheres in the life of the scientific clairvoyant were brought into play." Deciding that dichlorofluoro methane ($CHCl_2F$) would be the best starting point for experimentation, Midgley ordered five one-ounce bottles of the then-rare reagent antimony trifluoride (SbF_3) . . . to react with carbon tetrachloride to form the desired compound.

30   Midgley and Henne prepared a few grams of dichlorofluoro methane from one of the five bottles of antimony trifluoride chosen at random. They were delighted to find that a guinea pig placed under a bell jar with the substance was unharmed. However, when the experiment was repeated with dichlorofluoro methane made from the second bottle, the guinea pig promptly died. When they repeated the experiment, they detected the odor of phosgene ($COCl_2$), a poisonous, volatile substance used as a war gas. They removed the phosgene with a simple caustic wash to render the product perfectly safe. Four of the five bottles had been contaminated with a double salt containing water of crystallization, which produced lethal amounts of phosgene.

31   Midgley concluded his address on receiving the Society of Chemical Industry's Perkin Medal as follows:

> Of the five bottles marked "antimony trifluoride" one had really contained good material. We had chosen that one by accident for our first trial. Had we chosen any one of the other four, the animal would have died as expected by everyone else in the world except for ourselves. I believe we would have given up what would then have seemed a "bum hunch." And the moral of this last little story is simply this: You must be lucky as well as have good associates and assistants to succeed in this world of applied chemistry sufficiently well to receive the Perkin Medal.

With his flair for the dramatic and his love of showmanship, Midgley [then] filled his lungs full of Freon vapor, exhaled, and extinguished a lighted candle, thus vividly demonstrating to his audience its nontoxicity and nonflammability.

32   Dichlorofluoro methane (CFC-21) was the first chlorofluorocarbon to be used as a refrigerant. Other members of this family included trichlorofluoro methane (CCl_3F, CFC-11), dichlorodifluoro methane (CCl_2F_2, CFC-12, the most common member of the group), 1,2-dichloro-1,1,2,2-tetrafluoro ethane (CFC-114), 1-chloro-1,1-difluoro ethane (CFC-142), and 1,1,1-trichloro-2,2,2-trifluoro ethane (CFC-113). The CFC numbers, which indicate the formulas, are used commercially to avoid the possibility of confusion and error that might arise if the chemical names were used.

33   Like TEL, CFCs may prove to be a mixed blessing. CFCs have been used not only for refrigeration and air conditioning but also for aerosol spray propellants; foam for insulation, bedding, and packing; and solvents and cleaners for the electronics industry. Furthermore, halons (CFCs containing bromine) currently provide the only safe method for extinguishing fires in computer installations and aircraft cockpits without harming people or equipment.

34   In a 1974 article, Mario J. Molina and F. Sherwood Rowland first suggested that CFCs were destroying the ozone layer in the earth's stratosphere. Ironically, the chemical inertness that made them commercially useful allows them to remain in the atmosphere for forty to fifty years. Some scientists believe that photodissociation of CFCs in the stratosphere produces chlorine atoms, which have decreased the ozone layer by about 0.5% per year.

35   This decrease in the Earth's ozone layer, which shields the planet's surface from damaging ultraviolet radiation, is said to have far-reaching environmental consequences, the most publicized of which is an increase in the number of skin cancers.

Even more ominous, as Carl Sagan and others have warned, is the extreme vulnerability to increased ultraviolet radiation of phytoplankton—the tiny marine plants at the bottom of the ocean's food chain. Also, CFCs are said to be implicated in the greenhouse effect and may have deleterious effects on global climate.

Other scientists stress that no confirmed data substantiate these claims. They **36** strongly doubt that CFCs play any role in the fluctuations of the "ozone hole" over Antarctica. A strong biennial variation in the hole's size and strength recorded in 1988 has forced many scientists to admit that chlorine chemistry alone could not account for the fluctuations. Having admitted the existence of such dynamic processes, it is relatively easy to explain the occurrence of the hole without requiring any unusual chemical destruction of ozone.

However, even without conclusive evidence, in 1978 the EPA banned the use of **37** CFCs in aerosols in the United States, and a number of chemical companies have developed non-chlorine-containing replacements such as 1,1,1-trifluoro-2-fluoro ethane (CF_3CH_2F or HFC-134a). Although regulating the use of CFCs in spray cans was the beginning of a solution to this complex problem, other countries did not follow the United States' example. American manufacturers, who produce 40% of the world's CFCs, have argued that unilateral action will only place them at a disadvantage without protecting the atmospheric ozone layer, and that any action to phase out CFCs must be an international one.

The Montréal Protocol, adopted in the fall of 1987 by twenty-four governments, **38** and now ratified by thirty-nine nations, requires those countries to halve their production and use of CFCs . . . and to freeze the use of halons at 1986 levels. Many less-developed countries, such as China and India, have not signed this agreement because of concerns about the costs of replacing CFCs and equipment using CFCs. F. Sherwood Rowland, a leading authority on the problem, claims that even if the Montréal Protocol were fully effective, reductions would have only a minor effect. . . . On May 5, 1989, delegates from eighty-one countries closed a four-day United Nations conference at Helsinki by calling for a complete phase-out of the production and use of CFCs . . . and for a ban on the use of halons as soon as feasible.

OTHER ACHIEVEMENTS

Midgley's TEL and CFCs were only the two best known of his numerous contributions **39** to science and technology. Midgley was a prolific contributor to the technical and scientific literature and held 117 patents. He obtained his knowledge of chemistry mostly by studying it himself and working at it. Midgley said that for years he "ate and slept chemistry." He also took an active role in the commercialization of ideas that he had conceived.

During World War I he made the first synthetic high-octane aviation fuel; he de- **40** veloped a practical method for purifying benzene of sulfur and for hydrogenating it to cyclohexane by using a nickel catalyst. He produced fuel consisting of 70% cyclohexane and 30% benzene, which allowed the compression of airplane engines to be boosted by 2-3 ratios, but the Armistice brought the project to an end. Also during the war and more than a quarter-century before Nazi Germany's V-1 and V-2 rockets, as Kettering's assistant, Midgley was one of a group of engineers who pioneered the first flying bomb—a pilotless airplane steered gyroscopically that carried 300 pounds of explosives. . . .

Midgley's death was tragically premature. In the fall of 1940 he contracted po- **41** liomyelitis, which deprived him of the use of his legs and rendered him a semi-invalid. He calculated the probability of a man his age contracting polio as "substantially equal to the chances of drawing a certain individual card from a stack of playing cards as high as the Empire State Building." But, with his characteristic wit, he said, "It was my tough luck to draw it." With typical courage and energy, he continued many of his professional activities. Still the prolific inventor, he devised a harness with pulleys to aid himself in rising from bed. He somehow became entangled in it and was accidentally strangled in his home in Worthington, Ohio, on November 2, 1944. He was only fifty-five.

7 *Analyzing Texts*

During a break between classes, a friend asks your opinion of the latest music video by a currently popular group. "I didn't like it," you say. "It seemed repetitive. It's like I've heard and seen it all before. They've lost their edge." After some half-hearted agreement or disagreement with this appropriately imprecise comment, the topic drifts to a recent party, an upcoming exam, the weather, or lunch. This is typical of informal conversation; it wanders from here to there, rarely pursuing any particular topic in depth.

But in a different context, your offhand comment could be disastrous. If, for example, you submitted the same response in an exam for a course in popular culture, you would fail. In that situation, your analysis would be inadequate. It has a thesis ("I didn't like it") and some support ("repetitive," "lost their edge"), but both are too superficial for formal writing.

Although the transition from the looseness of conversation to the demands of formal writing can be difficult, the distinction is critical. You rarely need to provide much support for the ideas and opinions expressed in conversation, but that is not true of writing. It is not so much a matter of right and wrong; it is, rather, that each type of communication adheres to its own conventions. As a member of an academic community, you should know and observe these conventions. When a friend casually asks your opinion of a music video, a lengthy analysis of cinematography is uncalled for; a "correct" response must be brief. In any situation, the needs and interests of your audience determine the ideas you explore, the specificity of detail you provide, and the language you choose.

As we noted in Chapter 4, the structure of most academic writing is influenced by the movement between general and specific, the process by which we make abstract ideas explicit and concrete. Writers support general statements with details, reasons, examples, and illustrations. They belong to a community of people who not only express what they think, but also explain their reasons for thinking it. In a sense, the general ideas and opinions they express are implied promises to readers, promises they fulfill by developing and linking claims and observations to specific facts and examples. When writers don't keep their promises, readers are disappointed. That's why good writers deliver.

Good readers also deliver. No educated adult wants to be a passive consumer of information. To be a contributing member of a literate community, you must be an active, analytical reader and writer. When you write about reading, you learn to read more carefully and to develop more perceptive observations. This chapter is designed to help you analyze what you read and to become a more effective interpreter of ideas and reporter of information.

ANALYZING THE PARTS

Whenever you analyze something—a chess move, an automobile engine, a political theory, or a poem—you break down its complexity by examining its components. As you look at these components individually, you observe their features and consider how they operate together.

To understand anything complex, scholars begin by analyzing its parts. Political scientists, for example, continually analyze the differences between free-market and managed economies—how they manufacture and deliver consumer goods, the profits they produce, the restrictions they impose on imports. Experts can then compare the two systems by analyzing money, people, goods, laws, attitudes, and other elements. They disassemble the whole to see how each component works; then they study the ways those components operate together.

Whenever you analyze a text, you do the same thing—you examine components separately, then see how they function together as a whole. Since writing is a flexible medium—there is no recipe for composing an essay, and success is often a function of originality—there is no formula for analyzing a text. It depends on what you read and why you read it. You look for different qualities in epic poems, satires, and scientific reports. You approach recreational reading differently than you approach sources for a research paper.

Nevertheless, some features are common to most written texts. Every piece of writing attempts to do something with concepts or information, addressing and developing a main idea in an organized sequence that helps readers comprehend and respond appropriately. The following five elements can be examined in a textual analysis:

- The *purpose* for which the text was written
- The way the author has adapted the text to an intended *audience*
- The *main idea* of the text
- The *development* or *support* for the main idea
- The *organization* and *coherence* of the text.

We will first look at each of these elements individually, then consider how they can be coordinated in a comprehensive analysis.

Purpose

Every text must be approached in terms of what it is supposed to accomplish. It is pointless to disparage a zany movie because it adopts a superficial view of human nature, an article about comparative linguistics because it lacks humor, or a fantasy adventure because it is unrealistic.

Some writers try to change our minds; others simply want to tell us something we haven't known. Some hope to provoke action; others seek to entertain, cajole, shock, or educate. As a critical reader, you must be alert to these possibilities. Misinterpreting a writer's intentions can be catastrophic—or hilarious.

Although we cannot always know exactly what an author is thinking, the basic purpose of a text is usually evident. But things are not always what they initially seem. You must be alert to satire as well as to other types of manipulation. You must detect a writer's biases and be wary of slanted evidence or outright deception. Sometimes writers are candid about where they stand; other times they expect you to read between the lines, inferring their intentions on the basis of past reading experiences and knowledge of human nature.

In the following passage, David Sacks and Peter Thiel do not conceal their bias—a disdain for the efforts of universities to raise students' consciousness of cultural diversity:

> "Orientation is designed to disorient you," announced Stanford professor James Adams to an auditorium of 1,600 puzzled freshmen at the beginning of the new school year. Assembled for one of the many orientation-week programs on "diversity," the freshmen soon learned what he meant. A lesbian activist spoke first about "challenging your sexuality" and encouraged the seventeen- and eighteen-year-old students to "overcome" their "fears of being queer." Next, a black musician performed an electric-guitar solo as police sirens wailed in the background. He concluded his demonstration by dropping suddenly to the floor and convulsing his body in a reenactment of the Rodney King beating.

After quoting Professor Adams's statement about the objectives of orientation, the authors ridicule those objectives by describing the more controversial—some might say outrageous—activities included. Various clues signal the authors' attitudes. For example, they place the word *diversity* in quotation marks and describe the audience of first-year students as puzzled. A more subtle tactic is reminding readers that some first-year college students are, legally, minors. Because they are forthright in revealing their bias (and since their article was published in the conservative *National Review*), the writers cannot be accused of deception. We may disagree with them—we may even dislike their methods of argument—but they give us every reason to expect a discussion that reflects a particular bias. An intelligent reader will examine Sacks and Thiel's article skeptically, aware that theirs is not the only perception of freshman orientation at Stanford University.

EXERCISES | **Analyzing Purpose**

1. Try to determine the author's purpose in writing the following column from the *New Yorker*.

Dept. of Commitment
Unmarital Bliss

Rebecca Mead

Dorian Solot and Marshall Miller are the founders of the Alternatives to Marriage Project and the authors of the newly published book *Unmarried to Each Other: The Essential Guide to Living Together as an Unmarried Couple,* which advocates for the rights of couples who live together without being legally wed. Solot and Miller have been unmarried for nearly a decade, since they were undergraduates at Brown, and they decided to write the book because they were frustrated by the presumption of matrimony by which they were often met—the prospective landlord who wanted to know when they were getting hitched; the car-rental company that charged extra to allow Solot to be listed as a second driver. *Unmarried to Each Other* addresses couples in all kinds of unmarriages: those who can't marry because they are gay; those who won't marry because of political objections to the institution; and those who just haven't yet made up their minds. It includes practical information about how to obtain domestic-partnership rights, as well as tips to help couples figure out whether they are ready for unmarriage, such as "It would be a rude surprise to find out a year from now that your partner saw cohabitation as an unspoken engagement when you thought it would be a good way to save on rent and see how things unfolded."

The book's publication was celebrated at a party the other day, in the Upper West Side home of Ashton Applewhite and Bob Stein, who have been unmarried to each other for going on ten years. At the party, Solot, who is twenty-nine, said that when she met Miller, who is twenty-eight, she did not immediately think, Here's the man I want to be unmarried to for the rest of my life. "It was not one of those head-over-heels things," she said. Neither Miller nor Solot had actually ever popped the question of whether to become unmarried; their relationship had just evolved in that direction. Though both agree that everything is working really well as it is now, Miller said he did not rule out the possibility that things could end in un-unmarriage. "We joke that we can't get married because we've written this book," he said. "But we never say never."

Among the guests were other happily unmarried couples in their late twenties, like Joe Lowndes and Priscilla Yamin, who are both finishing their PhDs in political science at the New School. Lowndes said that he had always wanted to be unmarried—"I was an activist and anarchist for years, and I am not comfortable with my private relationships being wrapped up with state politics," he explained—but that it was not until he met Yamin that he knew he had found the woman he wanted to be unmarried to. After seven years together, they held what they called a "Commitzvah," at which they exchanged vows, drank from a kiddush cup, and handed out little bells that friends and family were asked to ring at the moment the unmarriage was sealed. The Commitzvah is described in a chapter of the book about commitment ceremonies. ("There's no reason why you can't wear the white dress, walk down the aisle, exchange I do's and rings, and dance the Electric Slide all night long.") Yamin said that being formally unmarried did add an unexpected emotional dimension to the relationship, and that both families enjoyed the Commitzvah. "My mother was very happy—she was like, 'I'll take whatever you're giving me,' " Yamin said.

Other guests at the party were uncertain about whether unmarriage was right for them. Michael Oates Palmer, a writer for *The West Wing,* said that his recent experience of unmarriage had been unnerving. "I was just unmarried to someone for the last five months," he said. "It was a relationship where I was hoping it would make the transition to not-being-unmarried status, but she decided it should make the transition to not-being-in-a relationship status." Palmer's friend Lockhart Steele was at the party with Salma Abdelnour, whom he said he had been seeing for nine months. Their unmarital status, though, was still somewhat undefined. "I'm unmarried to her, but we're not unmarried in Dorian and Marshall's sense of it," Steele said. "You might even say we're just dating."

2. A short column by the chairman and chief executive officer of a major airline introduces each issue of the company's in-flight magazine. The following column appeared in July 2002.

Control and Choice
You're in Charge When You Research and Book Your Travel Online

Leo Mullen

If you like plenty of control and choice when you're making travel plans, then online travel purchase sites may be the right place for you to shop.

At Delta's own *delta.com,* as well as through other e-travel options such as Orbitz (*orbitz.com*), Travelocity (*travelocity.com*), Expedia (*expedia.com*), and Priceline (*priceline.com*), you set the pace and decide what you want to know and when you want to know it. Because of the easy availability of Internet purchase channels, online shopping is increasingly popular. The number of U.S. online travel buyers is expected to double, growing from 18.6 million in 2001 to 38.6 million in 2007. But with so many sites to choose from, how do you decide which site is right for you?

Naturally, we think *delta.com* is a great first choice—and outside observers agree. In the latest NPD Airline Tracking Study, our site was ranked number-one in every major category, including ease of use, offers and deals, and breadth of choice. The site is easy to access and navigate, even for first-time users. *Delta.com* also allows us to expand the range of personalized services we offer our customers. Not only can you check for schedules and fares—including sales and special promotions—and make reservations, you can also review your itinerary and select your seat. But the opportunities don't stop there—you can also check current airport wait times and find links to other travel-related information. The services on *delta.com* are all part of Delta's commitment to minimizing potential hassles related to the travel experience—making your travel as easy as possible.

If you're a member of SkyMiles, our easy-to-join club for frequent flyers, you can also take advantage of even more time-saving services. For instance, you can:

- Check in and print your boarding card.
- Redeem award tickets.
- Check your SkyMiles balance online.
- Sign up for fast notification of flight delays or cancellations.

Delta customers are increasingly attracted to the ease of the Internet and the personalized service we can bring to customers through its speed and power. We know, though, that when it comes to Web shopping, one size does not fit all. As a result, we've partnered with online agencies such as Orbitz, Travelocity, and Expedia as well as with Priceline to give you even more options.

Orbitz, the most recently launched online travel agency site, combines the power of a revolutionary search engine with an industry-leading customer interface that is easy to use and customize. Because of its comprehensive pricing engine—currently the best available—as well as its extensive connections throughout the travel industry, Orbitz brings customers one-stop Web shopping and more unbiased choices than any other online travel agency.

Travelocity and Expedia are two additional e-travel options providing a broad array of innovative services. And for passengers with complete flexibility in terms of both airline flown and time of travel, Priceline lets you name the maximum you're willing to pay for travel. As long as the price you name is higher than the price the site has set for the ticket, the purchase is made for you automatically.

Already, travel is the largest category of purchases made online. As more and more customers embrace the Internet as an effective means to research and purchase travel, they quickly realize the added convenience and control it provides. At Delta, we are constantly evaluating opportunities to provide customers with greater choice along with high levels of service—and continuing to offer you the best in online travel options is an important part of reaching those goals.

a. Several purposes emerge from this text. How many can you recognize?

b. Does any one purpose take priority over others? Are any in conflict with each other? Which ones are more challenging to present or justify to an audience of passengers?

c. What strategies (e.g., phrasing, order of presentation) does the writer use to communicate information or influence the behavior of customers?

Audience

Sometimes authors write to express themselves, but more often their purpose is to influence readers. They usually have a particular audience in mind and adapt their writing to the needs and interests of those readers. Consequently, when they analyze a text, readers should consider the audience to which it was addressed and examine it accordingly.

In the following brief article from an edition of the *Weekly Reader* that targets fourth-graders, the writer considers the needs of young readers:

Maron-1: Robo Helper

When you are at school or hanging with friends, do you wonder what your dog is doing in your house? If so, a new robot might be just what you need.

The robot, called Maron-1, is made by a company in Japan. Maron-1 looks like a cartoon copy of R2-D2. It weighs about 11 pounds and stands about 2 feet high. When it goes on sale in Japan next year, the robot will cost about $1,600.

The makers of Maron-1 say their robot is better than the other kinds of robots that you can buy at toy stores. "Our robot is different from pet robots. It's useful," said a representative of the company that makes Maron-1. . . .

Maron-1 can detect whether someone or something is moving in front of it. If it "sees" something moving, it says, "An intruder found." It can also call you on a cell phone to tell you about the intruder.

The amazing computer can do many other things as well. It can turn on electronic equipment, such as a TV or VCR. Maron-1 can move around, but it cannot go up or down stairs.

Notice the clear, connected way in which information is presented. The short sentences, basic vocabulary, and lack of technical detail indicate the writer's consideration of audience.

It would be unfair to disparage this article because of its superficiality. If you were investigating robotics for a research project, you would not use it as a source. On the other hand, the following passage from *Aviation Week and Space Technology,* an engineering journal, might be equally unsuitable:

STS-111 astronauts Franklin Chang-Diaz and Philippe Perrin from France performed three extravehicular activities (EVAs) to install the new 1.5-ton $254 million MD Robotics Mobile Base System (MBS) on the [International Space] station's truss-mounted mobile transporter and to change out the wrist roll joint on the station's arm.

The starboard truss section is to be launched in late August on *Atlantis,* but engineers are checking whether the addition of the starboard, and then a port section planned in October, will stress the station's degraded attitude control gyro system. One of the station's four 800-pound control-moment gyros (CMGs) failed on June 8, the day after *Endeavour* docked. The 6,600-rpm gyros exert torque to change attitude without the use of Russian propellant. The CMGs were being used to maneuver the 700,000-pound station/orbiter stack, when CMG-1 began to fly apart in its housing in the Z-1 truss above the Node 1.

In this case, the writer's vocabulary and assumptions about what readers know, as well as the information reported, indicate an audience of experts. To characterize this passage as dense and unreadable would also be unfair.

Audience, however, is reflected in more than just vocabulary and assumptions about prior knowledge. It also involves attitudes and values that readers are expected to share. Consider, for example, the opening paragraphs of a chapter from *The Inner-Bitch Guide to Men, Relationships, Dating, Etc.*, a self-help manual by Elizabeth Hilts:

The Inner-Bitch Way of Dealing with Men

The inner-bitch deals with men who are romantic possibilities the same way she deals with anyone—which is to say honestly. It's just easier that way. It is vital, however, to recognize some simple truths about how men approach life.

Men, apparently, love a challenge. Theory has it that this is a basic biological fact, though I wouldn't know because I flunked basic biology. According to some people who seem to live in a parallel universe (you know who you are), this information entitles women who seek relationships with men to behave poorly.

Here's how it works in that parallel universe: If you want a man, you have to play hard to get.

The variations in this theme are endless—don't make it "easy" for them; men are supposed to rearrange their schedules around you, but you never do the same for them; don't ever go Dutch on a date; don't call him; and the ultimate, rarely return his calls.

There's a word for this kind of behavior—*RUDE!*

Not to mention archaic, antithetical, manipulative, and . . . RUDE! I mean, really, what are they thinking? This isn't behavior you'd put up with from other people, is it? If a man treated you this way, you'd have nothing to do with him, right? (The only correct answer to this question is "Right!") Do you honestly want to indulge in rudeness yourself?

I don't think so.

The vocabulary of this passage is unpretentious; its style is informal. The writer uses contractions, asks questions, and directs conversational asides to readers. Although the word *bitch* offends many people, the author probably assumes that women who read a book with this word in its title understand that it is used ironically. (Actually, Hilts connects the word with behavior that contradicts what overt sexists typically characterize as "bitchy.") More important than vocabulary, however, are other clues that reveal the author's assumptions about her audience. For example, when she appeals to the reader's preference for honesty and comfort in relationships, Hilts envisions an audience of women who are not naïve or blindly romantic. Without becoming jaded or cynical, these readers may be exasperated with self-defeating behaviors that frequently undermine dating relationships. Proclaiming her ignorance of biology, the author appeals to an audience that resists—or even mistrusts—academic experts while valuing the practical insights of a clear-thinking, experienced peer. Finally, Hilts skillfully allows readers to distance themselves from the foolish behavior she ridicules. Attributing this behavior to "*some people* who seem to live in a parallel universe," she adds in a sly parenthetical aside, "you know who you are." Likewise, five paragraphs later, Hilts shifts from judgmental third-person references (e.g., "I mean, really, what are *they* thinking?") to personal appeals: "If a man treated *you* this way, *you'd* have nothing to do with him, right? . . . Do *you* honestly want to indulge in rudeness *yourself?*"

These techniques contribute to a comfortable relationship, allowing Hilts to identify with an audience of forthright women who defy conventions that put them at a disadvantage. Together, they can laugh at past mistakes and brush off the stigma of "bitchiness" assigned to them by people who accept self-defeating behaviors as a normal part of dating.

Analyzing audience may entail little more than gauging how much information and terminology readers are supposed to be familiar with; more often, it involves detecting subtle clues about the attitudes, values, interests, and experiences shared by a community of readers.

Analyzing Audience	**EXERCISES**

1. The following texts concern irritable bowel syndrome (IBS) or irritable bowel disorder (IBD), a condition that afflicts one in five Americans. Using clues such as style, vocabulary, content, and assumptions about what readers know, characterize the audience to which each text is addressed and explain how the author addresses the needs of that audience. It should be helpful to know that the first source appeared in the science section of the *New York Times,* the second in the *Tufts University Health and Nutrition Letter,* and the third in the *IBD Humor Web site.*

a. A Common Syndrome Seldom Discussed

Jane E. Brody

Jean's problem started in high school, with repeated bouts of abdominal cramps, a perpetual bloated feeling, and the need to visit the bathroom dozens of times a day for long periods at a time but without much relief. Now through college, married and working, Jean has to get up hours ahead to get in enough bathroom time for her chronically constipated bowel before she goes to work.

Neither doctors nor dietary changes have provided more than a brief respite from the symptoms, which cause her considerable anxiety and embarrassment and make her unwilling to stay anywhere, including at her in-laws' home, where there is only one bathroom.

Jean, who lives in Phoenix, suffers from a condition called irritable bowel syndrome, a chronic disorder of a seemingly normal gut that national surveys have indicated afflicts as many as one person in five, seventy percent of them women.

Lillian, has a different version of the same problem. Instead of the chronic constipation that plagues Jean, Lillian is beset by unpredictable bouts of diarrhea that can occur many times a day. She says: "IBS affects every aspect of my daily life. I can't ride on a city bus or go to the park because there is no bathroom. With the things that I can do, I constantly have to make allowances like leaving extra time in case I experience an episode."

Despite the high incidence of the syndrome, it is common for a sufferer to see many doctors over a period of years before getting a proper diagnosis. Many patients endure costly, difficult tests that reveal nothing, although some tests may be needed to rule out more serious conditions. Experts estimate that up to seventy percent of sufferers do not seek medical help. . . .

The syndrome has long been misunderstood. Through the years it has been called many things, some of which are inaccurate, including colitis and mucous colitis (unlike real colitis, there is no inflammation in IBS), spastic colon, and functional bowel disease. Contrary to widespread belief among the public and in medicine, irritable bowel syndrome is a real condition. It is not a psychosomatic disorder, although its symptoms can be aggravated by stress, anxiety, depression, or emotional trauma.

Rather, the syndrome is believed to stem from abnormal nerve connections between the brain and gut, resulting in extreme sensitivity to bowel contractions and the passage of gas and fluids. Nerves that control muscles in the gut seem to overreact to gas or to food after a meal, resulting in painful spasms that may either speed or slow the passage of stool and cause diarrhea or constipation. In some sufferers, symptoms alternate between diarrhea and constipation.

b. Irritable Bowel Syndrome Linked to Emotional Abuse

It has been known for some time that Irritable Bowel Syndrome, or IBS, is largely psychological in nature. That is, while the severe abdominal pain, cramping, flatulence, and diarrhea (and/or constipation) are all too real, researchers have traced the symptoms not to a physical cause but to an emotional one—stress. Now investigators are beginning to try to pin down exactly what types of stress might be most likely to lead to the disorder, which afflicts nearly 35 million Americans, mostly women. What they are finding is that stress resulting from emotional abuse in adolescence or adulthood may play a role.

When University of Toronto scientists compared twenty-five young and middle-aged women with IBS to twenty-five women who had similar symptoms but from bowel disorders with a clear medical cause, they found that the IBS sufferers were more likely to have been verbally threatened, put down, or denied personal or economic independence. They were also more likely to blame themselves for negative life events and to hold in their feelings while keeping others' needs in front of their own.

Previous studies have linked physical and sexual abuse to IBS, so the scientists are not surprised by the findings. But lead investigator Alisha Ali . . . cautions that it's much too early to say abuse of any kind causes the problem. At this point, she says, all we have is an association between abuse and IBS. Additional studies are necessary.

In the meantime, anyone suffering from IBS might want to consider seeing a psychotherapist to reduce stress, whether from abuse or some other cause. IBS sufferers should also seek the help of a physician, who can at least prescribe a medication like Donnatal or Levsin to reduce spasms in the intestine that cause pain. Dietary strategies, such as reducing fatty foods, may also help mitigate flareups; fatty foods could stimulate intestinal contractions.

c. From IBD Humor Web Site

IBD is *not* funny. It is a chronic condition that causes pain, cramps, fever, bloating, diarrhea, and many other unpleasant symptoms. However, if you look for the humorous things that happen to us, as the following IBD afflicted have done, maybe, just maybe, these stories will brighten your day. So, sit back, move your mouse (or your bowels if need be) and read what us IBDers have to say about this "fun" disease. Some are better than others. Keep reading; you'll find at least a couple that may sound just like you wrote them. . . .

Most of you know Crohn's disease flareups are not *limited to our lower ends. They can attack the stomach and esophagus, too. (Sorry if this is news to any of you.) When the disease does "go to town" in the upper area, vomiting is sometimes frequent and, like the diarrhea, you get little or no warning. I was being "processed" very late one night by an unhappy hospital clerk who also seemed to enjoy throwing around the little authority she had. This was especially irritating to those of us (me) who needed to be admitted to use the more private commode in a room as opposed to the one in the admissions area rest room and because she seemed especially obnoxious to the elderly folks waiting. (This is Florida, so the elderly outnumbered me.) I listened to her treat one older gentleman like he was retarded, making him repeat information and practically shouting questions at him, then refusing to proceed until his wife went home and came back with some form or another. And the whole time I was wondering just when my personal explosion would come. After another half hour of pointless waiting, she decided she would start my paperwork. Slowly, so slowly, she asked questions, filled in forms, and generally dragged the whole thing on and on and on. I finally told her I really needed her to move a little faster, and just as she reared back to denounce me as impertinent (and God knows what else), I threw up all over her desk, the forms, the computer, and her. You've never seen such shock! Of course, I was terribly embarrassed at the time, but my husband put it into perspective when he dropped back as I was being carted away in the requisite wheelchair to say, "And that was just for being rude to the old man ahead of us. Be glad my wife wasn't upset at you for prolonging her misery!"*

2. The following passage appeared in a syndicated newspaper column for investors. The author, Malcolm Berko, is responding to a reader who, though deeply in debt, considers using an inheritance of $105,000 to finance his son's college education. Try to infer the attitudes, values, interests, and experiences shared by Berko's audience. As much as possible, connect your inferences to specific details in the text.

> Don't be stupid. You guys are in hock up to your earballs, and soon as you get a gift from God, you're hot to trot to spend it. Suckers like you who pledge their incomes ten years hence are seldom given a second chance . . . in life. And most that do fail because they can't discipline themselves for the future. It must be genetic! . . .
>
> Forget Junior's college education. Frankly, many colleges today are nursery schools for teenage high-school mutants. Most colleges have lowered their testing standards so that almost anyone with sixth-grade qualifications can get a degree. And the College Board in March 1994 made its SAT questions so simple that applicants with room-temperature IQs earn acceptable scores.
>
> In my opinion college degrees are fraudulent diplomas certifying an education that never happened. Today's students believe that paying four years of tuition entitles them to a degree, and so many colleges have acquiesced, that we have created a new national social disease called the "dumbing down of America." Tell Junior to join the armed services. . . .

Main Idea

As you saw in Chapter 4, the first question a reader asks when engaging with a text is what, specifically, it is about. Writers often announce their main point in a single sentence—a thesis statement. But since many good writers develop ideas in other ways, you cannot always expect a one-sentence presentation of the main idea in an opening paragraph. Sometimes the main idea appears in the middle of a text, sometimes at or near the end, and sometimes throughout the text without being summarized in a single sentence. And since not all writers are careful, some texts wander from point to point without ever arriving at a focus.

There are, then, two questions to consider when you analyze a text: (1) What is the main idea? (2) Does the writer stay on topic, providing a coherent exploration of that main idea? The best way to determine the main idea of a text is to read it attentively and actively. Reread as necessary, using a pencil to underline key passages and to insert marginal comments. Then try to summarize the main idea in your own words.

| EXERCISES | **Analyzing the Main Idea** |

1. Applying skills introduced in Chapter 4, underline important statements as you read the following article; then state the main idea in your own words.

Who Cares, as Long as It's Natural?

Daniel Akst

If there's a sure-fire way to sell something these days, it's to claim the thing is natural—even if it's a cigarette. "Natural American Spirit Products," the Santa Fe Natural Tobacco Company Web site, says solemnly, "were created based on our belief in the traditional Native American usage of tobacco—in moderation, in its natural state. Our brand name was chosen as a symbol of respect for this tradition."

Above those words is a row of mannered photographs showing hipsters smoking what are presumably Natural American Spirit cigarettes. It's a seductive lineup; you can just see yourself puffing away, joining this gallery of quirky individualists.

The Natural used to be Roy Hobbs, Bernard Malamud's mythic baseball player, but now it's an obsession that many of us seem to share about a life we have somehow lost. In the grip of something like lapsarian fever, people buy natural cigarettes presumably to be sure that when the cancer comes, it wasn't caused by any horrible chemical additives. They shop at health-food stores and pay outrageous prices for herbal remedies to be consumed in blissful indifference to the absence of scientific support or approval by the Food and Drug Administration. A new book, *The Soul of the New Consumer* by David Lewis and Darren Bridger, says the key to success in business is to give people authenticity, and, of course, suggests a few sophisticated techniques for accomplishing this.

Natural? Authentic? Some fairyland of trees and grass that we can traverse in our sport utility vehicles? For women, a truly natural life probably means having a dozen babies and spending all the time in between breast-feeding. For men, I imagine, it's spearing mammoths and dying at thirty of gangrene in a broken leg.

The truth is that people have never before lived so far from anything like "the natural"—or worked harder to widen the distance. And a good thing, too. The sooner we stop pretending, the sooner businesses will stop fooling us with natural folderol. I myself lead as unnatural life as possible, and I'm proud of it. If you are reading these words, you shouldn't need reminding that primitive hunter-gatherer societies had a terrible time getting home delivery of the *New York Times*.

At some level, of course, people know that they are pretending. They drive cars to natural childbirth classes. They buy natural European spring water bottled in plastic and shipped thousands of miles. They object in Internet discussion groups to genetically engineered products. Is it any wonder that businesses respond by marketing pretend "natural" products?

Oh, to wake up one day in a world that knows the state of nature is no more hospitable than the state of North Korea. Then we'll all demand hard proof that herbal remedies are safe and effective, instead of simply assuming that being herbal makes them OK. We'll recognize that some of the nastiest toxins we ingest are made by Mother Nature without capitalism's help. And we'll be open to more "unnatural" technologies that actually increase safety, like food irradiation.

For now, though, if you're selling something, natural goes with traditional, as long as the second term is used the right way. Clever marketers like Restoration Hardware, for instance, know that people hanker for "simpler times" and stock the shelves accordingly.

Among the group that David Brooks has christened Bobos (for bourgeois bohemians, from his book *Bobos in Paradise*), the natural fetish extends even to children's toys. One mother I know believed for a while that children shouldn't play with stuff made of plastic, only wood. What difference does it make? Who knows?

Personally, I'm hoping for more products like Gatorade. My favorite flavors are Riptide Rush, Alpine Snow, and, in a truly marvelous aqua hue, Glacier Freeze. Not only do they taste great, but there is no pretense whatsoever of any naturalness about them.

Mine remains an unfashionable opinion. I bought a tasty electric-blue sports drink once from a California sales clerk who scorned its artificiality.

"But what's natural?" I asked.

"From the earth," she replied disdainfully.

Apparently she has never visited the Natural American Spirit Web site, which (at the government's behest) offers the perfect rejoinder: "No additives in our tobacco does NOT mean a safer cigarette."

2. Following is an excerpt from the opening handout for an upper-level college course. A list of class policies is not usually thought to have a purpose apart from announcing the policies themselves. Nevertheless, see if you can detect a theme, a main idea, that runs throughout the excerpt. If you can, summarize it in a sentence.

Attendance policy: Since regular attendance is an essential requirement of this course, roll is taken at each meeting. While there is no penalty for as many as three absences, each absence beyond that limit, unless excused for a legitimate reason, lowers the final course grade one letter. Students who are absent more than six times (for any reason) have missed too much to receive credit for the course and should withdraw to avoid a failing grade. Attendance is taken at the beginning of each class. (Please do *not* submit excuses for the first three absences—no matter how noble— since none is needed.)

Late arrival: You must be here on time. Since late arrival disrupts the class, it is penalized. Three arrivals after attendance has been taken are counted as one absence. Should you arrive late, it is *your* responsibility to check with me after class in order to be marked present; otherwise, you will be counted absent.

Reading assignments: You are expected and required to be well prepared for each class meeting. To contribute constructively to discussions and to benefit from lectures, you must have read assignments with care. Unannounced quizzes are frequent; and scores are a significant factor in final grading decisions, since they reflect your participation in the course. Continuous study is essential; this is not a course in which students can wait until exam-time to begin studying.

Exams: Four exams are given, after each quarter of the semester. Failure to take any of these exams at the assigned time results in a failing grade for the course. Make-up exams are given only in the event of a documented medical or other emergency. All make-ups are given during the final exam period (following the final exam) and are more difficult than the regularly scheduled exam. It is your responsibility to know the date and time of the final exam and to plan accordingly. Make-up exams are *not* given to accommodate conflicting engagements, jobs, or early vacations.

Course grade: Your final grade is based principally on the four exams and a paper. Passing grades on the exams and paper range from A+ (4.33) to D- (0.67). Failing grades are F (0), F- (-1.0), and F-- (-2.0). The average of the five grades determines the course grade. Quiz scores are the deciding factor when a student's average is within 0.1 of another grade. More than six absences, cheating, not taking an exam, or not submitting the paper automatically results in a failing grade for the course. Please take note: The course grade is determined strictly by a calculation based on your performance. I do not "give" grades; your grade in this course is the grade you have earned.

A final observation: You are expected to be a serious, self-disciplined, conscientious student in this class, and responsibility for your actions and performance is entirely yours, not the instructor's. In the past, students who have worked conscientiously and have consistently come to class prepared have done well. Persons with poor work habits have found themselves having to repeat it.

Development

If merely stating an idea were enough, there would be no books or essays. Every expository text could be reduced to a topic sentence. Of course, more is needed. Writers must explain, expand, and support ideas. Sometimes facts or logic is called for, sometimes narration of events, sometimes reasons and examples. A math text relies on clear, sequential explanation, with examples and exercises that reinforce each lesson. Interpretations of history demand background, evidence, and support from authoritative sources. The best way to develop a main idea depends on the purpose of a text and the audience to whom it is addressed.

Good writers develop their ideas by supporting them with specific, concrete evidence. In the following excerpt, the writer answers her opening question with a series of examples.

> Who were the influential male models of appearance and behavior in turn-of-the-century America? Sports figures like boxer John L. Sullivan were important, as were businessmen and industrialists. In addition, western cowboys were also admired. They had inherited the mantle of the frontiersman and Indian fighters after Owen Wister apotheosized their lives as cattle raisers into a saga of gun-slinging drama in his 1901 novel *The Virginian*. But there were others whose image was softer and whose aggressive masculinity was countered by sophistication and humor.
>
> Cosmopolitan men of the theater, for example, were popular. This was the age, after all, when the Barrymores first rose to prominence. In the 1890s many stationery and jewelry stores displayed in their windows photos of Maurice Barrymore holding an elegant demitasse cup and saucer in his hand and garbed in full dress as in one of his famed portrayals. . . .
>
> —Lois W. Banner, *American Beauty*

For much of the writing you do in college, you must support your ideas with research. Outside sources provide the information you need, and expert testimony lends prestige and authority to what you write. The authors of the following excerpt rely on outside sources to support their views about science education:

The design of this science classroom . . . is also based on the notion that schools are not just buildings, and that all people are life-long learners. The need for relevance in the experiences of school children and for applicability and currency in teacher-training programs is not a new one; however, these needs are not often met.

   In *Educating Americans for the 21st Century,* a National Science Board Report, technology and an understanding of technological advances and applications were recognized as basic. While initial effects of the infusion of computers into instruction might not have produced desired results (Greenburg 107), the relevance of technology education is still apparent. Kids learn differently today, differently from the learning modes familiar to us. In the twentieth century people were "paper" trained. Youngsters of the twenty-first century are "light" trained, i.e., comfortable with video- and computer-based material. Matching learning styles with delivery systems is crucial for success.

—Richard J. Reif and Gail M. Morse, "Restructuring the Science Classroom"

To support their thesis about classroom technology, the authors cite a report of the National Science Board. Even when they cite another source (Greenburg) that disputes some of their claims, Reif and Morse show readers that they are well informed and have considered other points of view.

Analyzing Development   EXERCISE

Read each of the following excerpts and respond to these questions: What is the main idea? What specific facts, ideas, or examples does the author present to support and develop that idea? What, if anything, demonstrates the author's authority to address the topic? Would a different approach (e.g., citing more sources or personal experiences) be more effective?

a. In Good Company

Kostya Kennedy

> *The most lonely, frustrated people I have worked with have not been the loners but the people who are addicted to social interaction. Afraid to encounter themselves in solitude, they fill their lives with shallow social interactions that keep them from ever coming face to face with their own solitary spirit.*
> —John Selby, *Solitude*

I arrive at dusk, after a long and traffic-marred drive. By the time I unpack, make the bed, and put a few things into the fridge, darkness has fallen. I find myself alone in a quiet and unfamiliar place, a month looming ahead of me and facing what Doris Grumbach describes in her 1994 book, *Fifty Days of Solitude,* as "that frighteningly reflexive pronoun, *myself.*"

   The cabin in which I will live out the next twenty-eight days measures eight paces long by five wide. There are a table and two chairs, a small bathroom, a half-sized refrigerator, two burners for cooking, an oval sink, and a comfortable, full-sized bed. The screened-in porch where I will spend my days working looks out onto a glade of rough, uncut grass.

A summer storm is rolling in and I go to bed early. Before I left New York, a friend wished me luck and said, "Call if you get lonely up there." As I sit up in bed, reading lamp on and not ten hours removed from home, I very nearly dial her number. *What am I doing here?* I wonder. Thunder rumbles in the distance.

Instead of phoning, I reach for my bedside table stack and pull out *Walden*. The book, Henry David Thoreau's meditation on the two years he spent living by himself at Walden Pond in Massachusetts, came out in 1854 and to this day remains the most influential work on solitude in American literature. Thoreau's portrayal of a hardy, quiet life in nature, a life of simplicity and self-sufficiency, still touches deeply on the American nerve. Each year thousands of visitors travel great distances to see the land on which Thoreau lived.

I begin the book this first night, and soon I come to a passage that stokes me for the time ahead. "I find it wholesome to be alone," Thoreau writes. "I never found the companion who was so companionable as solitude."

At this, I stop reading and turn out the light. . . .

A daily routine may seem a drag in ordinary life, but when you are alone and secluded, a routine proves essential. The routine itself becomes company, and this was mine: I woke when sunlight filled the cabin. I took breakfast outside and watched robins bob for worms. I wrote for a few hours, then stopped and went for a short walk. Sometimes I gathered blackberries. I returned to work until about midday, when I broke for lunch. After eating, I strolled to the post office for mail or to the village for a newspaper. In the afternoon I read over my morning's work and, if the weather was good, went for a good, long swim in the bay. I prepared simple dinners and usually listened to a ball game on the radio. I read myself to sleep, and in the morning I began again.

Once a week I drove a half hour to the nearest supermarket and did a large shop. Otherwise I relied on a small grocery store nearby. Each Friday I took myself to the movies, and on a few other nights during that month, I met a friend for dinner.

I was not entirely without human interaction. (Neither, incidentally, had Thoreau been; he regularly walked into Concord center to chat with the locals and to visit his mother, who baked cookies for him.) But days would pass without my having a conversation with anyone beyond greetings. For the vast majority of the time I was alone, involved in my work.

Here's another rule for an extended period of solitude: Have something to immerse yourself in. It could be gardening, sewing, reading, hiking, cooking, painting, or whatever. But having a project to fill the hours is essential.

Solitude has been a common refuge for writers. This is true not only of those who wrote about the solitude itself but also for many who wrote about other things altogether. Franz Kafka lived a life of extreme isolation and believed that "one can never be alone enough when one writes." Emily Dickinson was so extravagantly reclusive that she did not leave her house for the final ten years of her life and even refused to receive visitors.

Great writers, sure, but Dickinson was a depressed, forlorn soul, and Kafka lived on the verge of psychosis. My bet is that their seclusion didn't help. I rapidly learned that when you're alone, with no one to check your irrational thoughts, no one to laugh at a joke with, no one to reassure you in moments of insecurity, no one to get your mind off *yourself*, it's easy to slip into paranoia. Sensing—falsely, it turned out—that someone was lurking around the cabin at night, I took to sleeping with a light on. It was no longer the prospect of loneliness that worried me, but a larger concern: Would I go mad? When left to itself, the mind can do funny things. . . .

"Some people need a little solitude, and some need a lot of it," says Dr. William Galbreath, a psychotherapist in Florida. "But everyone needs some. When I spend a few days alone, it strengthens me when I come back to society."

That rings true. My time alone helped me reenter my life of work and friends, dates and dinners, conversations and obligations, with new vigor. There is an inescapable human truth that we are each of us alone. Only you know how the words resonate in your head, how the type appears on the page.

Yet I also found an opposite truth during my time alone. Thoreau wrote that there existed a part of himself that was not himself, but rather a spectator. My realization proved similar: I am in fact not alone and never will be. Because I, and all of us, have more than one self: another self who is a singer, a poet, a woodcutter. I am at once an adult and a child, a happy man and an angry one.

That, then, is the result of my experiment—the discovery of a detached but deeply interested other self. A protector of a sort, and a companion who will be with me to the end.

b. In the Dough

Rebecca Gray

Sugar is part of the very definition of a cookie: "a hand-held, flour-based *sweet* cake—either soft or crisp" as stated in *Food Lover's Companion: Comprehensive Definitions of Over 4000 Food, Wine, and Culinary Terms.* Thus the people of Persia, one of the first countries to produce sugar, are credited with creating a cookie-like sweet cake. The word "cookie," however, comes from the Dutch *koekje,* meaning "little cake." And given that the Dutch in New Amsterdam were the first to successfully industrialize sugar refinement in the 1600s, it presumably was they who also introduced the cookie into the colonial American cuisine.

One interesting cookie fact says that each one of us will consume in our lifetime some 35,000 cookies. Although cookies can be made in six basic styles—drop, hand-formed, bar, pressed, rolled, and refrigerator—probably the most popular ones in the United States are those based on a simple dough made of eggs, butter, flour, and, of course, sugar. . . .

Originally available only as an import from England, animal crackers . . . became popular, and by the late 1800s American bakers began producing them. In 1902, the newly formed National Biscuit Company trademarked the Barnum's Animals as a cracker for children, even designing the now-famous red box with a string handle for hanging on a Christmas tree. Nabisco, as the company is now known, hasn't changed its animal-cracker recipe in a century of production, making only modifications in the variety—there are twenty two of them. . . .

My practiced dissection of the animal cracker as a child was perhaps a foreshadowing of my behavioral approach to another kind of cookie as an adult. I carefully pull my Oreos apart, trying to leave the white cream on one side of the chocolate wafer. And I'm sure that many of you readers have done the same.

The Oreo might be unique, but it's not the true original. The Hydrox chocolate sandwich cookie came first. In 1908, Hydrox, the signature product of the Sunshine Bakery, dominated the chocolate sandwich cookie world until Nabisco introduced its amazingly similar Oreo cookie in 1912. With better distribution, marketing, and, let's face it, a much better name, the Oreo quickly eclipsed the Hydrox. In 1998, Oreo sales reached $374 million, while Hydrox sales tallied only $16 million. The Sunshine founders, hoping to create an image of goodness and purity, truncated two simple elements, hydrogen and oxygen to form the word *Hydrox*. This ill-conceived word, unfortunately, didn't work: When Sunshine sold it to Keebler in 1996, surveys indicated that even the most loyal Hydrox patron reacted negatively to the name. Keebler has now adopted a new name: Droxies. Meanwhile Oreos have become the number-one-selling cookie in the United States. . . .

Now, it's hard for a commercially produced cookie to earn comfort-food status, especially when compared to the homemade variety. What homemade cookies lack in shape (often irregular) they make up for with freshness and uniqueness. And as Ruth Wakefield learned after inventing the original Toll House cookie, a great production can sometimes be the result of chance. In 1930, Wakefield and her husband purchased an eighteenth-century toll house near Boston, which they converted into the Toll House Inn. One day, while making a batch of Butter Drop Do cookies from a favorite old colonial recipe, Ruth added pieces of a Nestlé chocolate bar to the dough, expecting them to melt. Instead, they held their shape, and the rest is history.

Ruth Wakefield never kept her recipe a secret: initially publishing it in a Boston newspaper, she later made an agreement with Nestlé to print it—first on the chocolate-bar wrapper and then on the chocolate-morsel package—partly in exchange for a lifetime supply of chocolate.

Like Wakefield's Toll House treats, [other] great cookies have key ingredients: tradition and technique. There's no better example than the cookies crafted at Termini Brothers Bakery on Eighth Street in South Philadelphia. This family business was founded in the 1920s by brothers Giuseppi and Gaetano. And Giuseppi's son, Vincent, and his grandsons, Joseph and Vincent, run the still-thriving business today. Giuseppi, at the age of eight, apprenticed to a master baker in Sicily. When he came to the United States, he brought with him those cookie recipes—never written down, but locked in his head. The pastry shop has changed little over time, and its baked goods have become part of a Christmas tradition in South Philadelphia. Termini Brothers now offers over a dozen different cookies, as well as torrone and cannoli. It has four stores: two in South Philly, one in Reading, and one in suburban Ardmore. There is also a mail-order business for those not fortunate enough to live nearby. More than 7,000 tins of cookies are hand-packed annually. . . .

Even this non-Italian can taste the love and authenticity that go into a Termini Brothers cookie. Actually, I'm seriously considering making half of those 35,000 cookies that I'll eat in my lifetime the Termini Brothers' pignoli.

Organization and Coherence

Good writing demonstrates courtesy. Like good hosts, writers are considerate of their readers. Of course, great poets, novelists, and playwrights often challenge their audiences through experimental techniques. But nonfiction writers, whose usual aim is to inform or persuade, tend to be more straightforward. Typically, they make their point early and stick to it. Their readers expect clarity, order, and logic. As one writing theorist, the late Kenneth Burke, expressed it, writers have a duty to take readers by the hand, walking them through a text and helping them see connections among ideas, sentences, and paragraphs.

Readers should ask the following questions about organization and coherence: Does the writer indicate where the text is heading? Can you follow the progression of ideas, or are you sometimes puzzled, lost, or taken by surprise? Is the text logically organized? Is there a clear link between the main idea and supporting details (reasons, examples, testimony)? Is the supporting material arranged sensibly? Does the writer make the passage accessible by providing transitions when new ideas are introduced?

Not every writer gives readers the help they need. The following passage leaves us to shift for ourselves; it is so poorly organized that we cannot accurately predict where it will go next. The writer arouses expectations about one topic but then veers off in other directions.

> You wouldn't believe my son Jason. He was so unbelievably wild and inconsiderate yesterday, I got one of my headaches. They come on with a vengeance, with no warning. I was so crazy with pain last week, it will be a miracle if my sister-in-law ever speaks to me again. I've been to specialist after specialist, and none of them can find the problem. A lot of money they get paid, for what? Fancy offices and fancy diplomas so they can charge fancy fees. When I think about doctors, I get another headache. My head throbs, and my eyes don't focus. I don't want anything to do with people, and I'm as miserable to Jason as he is to me. Maybe Jason will be lucky enough to become a doctor someday and then the money can stay in the family.

This writer disregards organization, writing whatever comes to mind. He leads us to think the paragraph will be about Jason's behavior, but it turns into a discussion of his headaches, with frequent detours to other topics. Later, we expect to find out what he said to his sister-in-law, but that topic is abandoned with no concern for the reader's unsatisfied curiosity. The topic of doctors is introduced, then forgotten, then finally reintroduced near the end, without logical explanation.

In contrast, the essays in the following exercise are coherent, readable, and logical because the writers have considered how to present their ideas to readers. They have organized the movement of their thoughts by providing signposts. Coherence, however, is relative. Some readers may find one of the essays more carefully organized than the other.

Analyzing Organization

EXERCISE

After reading each of the following essays carefully, explain as specifically as you can how the writer has organized the text. Why is it arranged as it is? How does the writer move from one idea to the next? from general to specific? How are sentences and paragraphs linked to each other? How does the writer guide you through the text? Are there digressions or gaps in either essay? Does one essay seem more cohesive than the other?

a. The Financial Page
The Talking Cure

James Surowiecki

When you think of Wall Street, candor is probably not the first word that leaps to mind, but in the past few months the Street has been gripped by it. Merrill Lynch now warns, on the first page of each of its research reports, that it may be seeking "investment banking or other business relationships from the companies covered in this report." (That is to say, the analysis may be tainted.) The New York Stock Exchange, meanwhile, has proposed a rule that would bar a stock-market analyst from talking to newspapers that fail to disclose the analyst's conflicts of interests. Even the CEO of Goldman Sachs, one of Wall Street's most discreet firms, has chimed in with a public *nostra culpa* on behalf of the industry and has exhorted his peers to restore "trust in our system."

This outbreak of straight talk is Wall Street's way of addressing the collapse of its credibility. Everyone agrees that conflicts of interest riddle the securities and accounting industries—research analysts touting dubious companies to win their business, auditors signing off on dubious numbers to keep it—and that something must be done, so Wall Street has decided to adopt the talking cure. The problem with the conflicts of interest, the argument goes, is that no one knows about them. Fess up, and the problem goes away.

It's a nice thought, but the diagnosis is facile, and the remedy won't work. Start with the central tenet: that during the boom the conflicts of interest were kept secret. The truth is, people knew more than they like to admit. Back in 1998, a *Business Week* cover story called "Wall Street's Spin Game" put the matter succinctly: "The analyst today is an investment banker in sheep's clothing." When Merrill Lynch hired Henry Blodget as an Internet analyst in 1999, the media explained the decision by saying that Blodget, with his rosy predictions, would help the firm bring in more investment-banking business. Jack Grubman, the former Salomon Smith Barney analyst, bragged of his intimate relationship with the companies he was supposed to be evaluating objectively. And the problems in the accounting industry were even more obvious. Though the firms maintained their game face, it was no secret, by the late 1990s, that the game itself was rigged. Most investors accepted this state of affairs with the genial tolerance of pro-wrestling fans.

Why? One reason, clearly, was the boom itself—people didn't care why an analyst recommended a stock, as long as it went up. But there was something else: it turns out that people think conflicts of interest don't much matter. "If you disclose a conflict of interest, people in general don't know how to use that information," George Lowenstein, an economics professor at Carnegie Mellon, says. "And, to the extent that they do anything at all, they actually tend to underestimate the severity of these conflicts."

Usually, conflicts of interest lead not to corruption but, rather, to unconscious biases. Most analysts try to do good work, but the quid-pro-quo arrangements that govern their business seep into their analyses and warp their judgments. (Warped judgments subvert the market; although even honest analysts have a hard time picking stocks, everyone benefits from the flow of sound information.) "People have a pretty good handle on overt corruption, but they don't have a handle on just how powerful these unconscious biases are," Lowenstein says.

To test the idea, Lowenstein and his colleagues Don Moore and Daylian Cain devised an experiment. One group of people (estimators) were asked to look at several jars of coins at a distance and estimate the value of the coins in each jar. The more accurate their estimates, the more they were paid. Another group of people (advisers) were allowed to get closer to the jars and give the estimators advice. The advisers, however, were paid according to how high the estimators' guesses were. So the advisers had an incentive to give misleading advice. Not surprisingly, when the estimators listened to the advisers their guesses were higher. The remarkable thing is that even when the estimators were told that the advisers had a conflict of interest, they didn't care. They continued to guess higher, as though the advice were honest and unbiased. Full disclosure didn't make them any more skeptical.

In the course of the experiment, Lowenstein discovered something even more startling: that disclosure may actually do harm. Once the conflict of interest was disclosed, the adviser's advice got worse. "It's as if people said, 'You know the score, so now anything goes,' " Lowenstein says. Full disclosure, by itself, may have the perverse effect of making analysts and auditors more biased, not less.

Obviously, we shouldn't keep conflicts of interest secret. But revealing them doesn't fix a thing. To restore honesty to analyses and audits, you need to get rid of the conflicts themselves. That means completely separating research from investment banking, as Citicorp did in October, and barring auditors from serving as consultants—and making companies bring in new auditors every few years, as regulators have proposed.

It has become a truism on Wall Street that conflicts of interest are unavoidable. In fact, most of them only seem so, because avoiding them makes it harder to get rich. That's why full disclosure is suddenly so popular: it requires no substantive change. "People are grasping at the straw of disclosure because it allows them to have their cake and eat it too," Lowenstein says. Transparency is well and good, but accuracy and objectivity are even better. Wall Street doesn't have to keep confessing its sins. It just has to stop committing them.

b. Retailers' Siren Song

Elizabeth Razzi

Have you ever gone shopping for pants and come home with a Mr. Coffee? Or run into the store for a quart of milk and walked out with a shopping cart filled with groceries? Odds are you have, and probably haven't thought much about it. But *someone* has thought about it. The retail industry has literally turned studying the habits of shoppers into a science. Before you venture into the retail jungle again, you should realize that your buying habits are being mapped almost as closely as the human genome, manipulated like Pavlov's dog, and seduced like the American electorate every fourth November.

THE HAPPINESS FACTOR

The homey tabletop display of cherries, Cuisinarts, and pie plates just inside the doors of Williams-Sonoma isn't about selling pie plates or food processors. The bountiful tableau welcomes you, slows you down, and (the retailer hopes) puts you in a friendly frame of mind. . . .

Something as subtle as a pleasant aroma or a free sample of nectarine can trigger that happy feeling, which actually *changes the way we think,* says Alice Isen, a professor of marketing in the Johnson Graduate School of Management at Cornell University. When you're happy, "you can think in more creative ways about alternative uses of things," she says. This state of "positive affect" is strongest with regard to emotionally neutral things, such as a display of dish towels at Williams-Sonoma. (Come to think of it, the whole store has a wonderful, vaguely herbal scent.) Instead of thinking of the drudgery of drying dishes, a happy shopper is likely to think of ways to use a towel to dress up a basket. . . .

Touching an item also increases the odds that you will buy it. And if a salesperson talks to you, the odds of your buying a piece of clothing increase by half, says [Paco] Underhill [author of *Why We Buy*]. Store clerks talking to us and recommending items make us feel wanted, he explains. And we may even pay more to shop where we feel wanted.

The chances you'll buy a garment double if the salesperson talks to you and you try it on. So what's the script in a quality clothing store? As soon as you pull an item off the rack, a friendly clerk offers to "start a dressing room" for you, freeing your hands to touch more items. The hook is set. . . .

MORE IS BETTER

Here's a scary conditioned response: Humans obey when retailers tell us to buy more. Brian Wansink, professor of marketing and director of the Food and Brand Laboratory at the University of Illinois at Urbana-Champaign, performed a study with full-price Snickers bars in a convenience store. The researchers put up a sign that said "buy some for the freezer." They also tried a sign that said "buy 18 for the freezer." Few people actually bought 18 candy bars, but they did buy 1.5 times more than when the sign simply read "buy some." Wansink says: "Even in the face of zero discount, it still ends up influencing people. It's a really powerful effect." . . .

Another way our shopping habits can be used against us is by manipulating our concept of space. Why have grocery stores grown so huge? One reason is that people tend to shop the perimeter of the store, where they find the "boutique" departments: the dairy, the butcher, the greengrocer, and the baker. "The average visit to a supermarket lasts only seventeen minutes," says [Martin] Roberts [president of a Grid2 International, a store-designing firm]. We cruise the perimeter for, say, a dinner of mesclun greens and roast chicken, grab fresh juice and rolls for breakfast, and head for the express lane. Grocers are desperate to entice us to walk up and down the aisles. Their chief tool is the "end-cap" display, where the merchandise is usually (but not always) discounted. "Hopefully, the end cap will lure you down the chip aisle and convince you to buy something at full price," says Roberts.

Cavernous stores, Humvee-size carts, and pillowcase-size produce bags—combined, they give us the perception that we're buying fewer things. . . .

PRICED TO SELL

Retailers know you probably won't buy the most expensive item or the cheapest item, but, like Goldilocks, you'll go for the middle. So guess how they set the price range? "They can manipulate what people buy by how high that high end is," says [marketing professor Julie] Irwin. "Kmart will have three levels of irons, or whatever. And people will buy the middle one. It's irrational because you're being manipulated into buying something because of what else is on the shelf."

The effect can carry over from the store shelf to the whole store. "So often in stores they have exorbitantly expensive things that make you think, who would buy this? In fact, nobody buys it," says Irwin. "It's there to make you feel as if you're getting a bargain on what you are buying." So maybe that $50 cotton sweater at the Austin Saks wasn't a great buy; it only seemed that way compared with the gloriously impractical $230 shoes we soberly left on the rack earlier in the day.

Not only do people usually prefer to shop where they find reasonable prices, but they also like to shop where they'll find lots of variety. But how do we judge variety? We size up the selection in "signal categories," says Wansink. We may judge a whole store by how broad the variety is in the cereal department, the produce section, or even the beer cooler, depending on our tastes. And the more jumbled it appears, the better people seem to like it. "The more random and unpredictable it is, the more people perceive that there is a variety of products," he says. That's why you find socks next to picture frames at T.J. Maxx, and why Campbell's never puts its soups in any logical order.

Irwin says that jumble adds to the thrill of the hunt that draws people to discount stores and outlets. "It's totally true that you do not always get the best price at such places. That's how they stay in business. Often, near the door, there are items with a really high markup. You're not paying attention; you're just grabbing. And that's where they end up getting the money from you."

Whether it's a mountain of portobello mushrooms blocking the produce aisle at Central Market or a table of $25 lotions and bath salts blocking the cosmetics aisle in Saks, retailers are trying to slow you down and make you look around. "It's not easy to figure your way out of Central Market," says Irwin. "They want you to find yourself in front of the mustards and say, 'Wow, I never knew there were so many types of mustard.' " And if they stock so many varieties, the implicit message is that an urbane shopper like you must need at least one.

KEEPING YOUR HEAD

If these methods aren't exactly diabolical, they are seductive, especially if you're just browsing to see what catches your fancy. But don't think that planning alone can insulate you from bad buys. Guess who makes the largest number of impulse buys at the grocery store. The shopper who carries a list. About 34% of the items in the cart of a list-toting shopper are unplanned purchases, compared with 20% of the items in the cart of a list-free shopper, says Wansink. "People who've actually written things down see the shopping trip as a scheduled event," he explains. "They spend a little longer in the store. It's more of a pleasurable activity for them." And the longer you stay, the more you buy.

So what's a shopper to do? Remember that no matter how well the scientist figures out the behavior of the cheetah, now and then the cheetah has a scientist for lunch. Here's how to keep your claws sharp:

- Have a price in mind before you go, so the store doesn't bump up your idea of "reasonable."
- Save your splurging until you're on your way out of the store. You'll minimize the what-the-hell effect, and you might skip the purchase altogether.
- Shop online, if only to research your selections before you head to the mall. It's the right-brainer's way to go. You won't be beholden to one merchant's manipulation of low, middle, and high prices. And they haven't figured out how to make a scent of cinnamon buns waft out of your computer—yet.

■ WRITING A BRIEF READING ANALYSIS

Purpose, audience, main idea, development, organization, and coherence—these are the most important, but by no means the only, things to consider when you analyze a text. In addition to considering these general elements, you should approach a text on its own terms. Because texts are not all alike, and because engaged readers often respond to the same text in different ways, there is no formula for analysis. Though it is always important to read carefully and perceptively, it is also wise not to strive for a "correct" interpretation or analysis.

Having studied each of the five elements of analysis separately, you should now understand how they work together. When you analyze a complete text, you should consider all five elements. Read the following editorial carefully and analytically, contemplating each of the elements we have presented.

PRACTICE READING

"Ernie's Nuns" Are Pointing the Way

Molly Ivins

Way to go, college students!

Reebok, the sports shoe manufacturer, admitted this week that conditions at two of its factories in Indonesia were distinctly sub-par and says its subcontractors have spent $500,000 to improve them. Reebok's actions came after a boycott of its shoes on campuses around the country coordinated by United Students against Sweatshops, a nationwide student coalition. Nice going, good win.

Reebok also deserves credit: in response to the boycott and criticism from human-rights groups, the company commissioned a study of working conditions in its foreign factories fourteen months ago and has apparently followed up on the findings. "We hope that this will also break through and encourage more companies to do something like this," said a Reebok vice president.

USAS also urged students to join a new group—the Worker Rights Consortium—that will set a strict code of conduct for overseas factories that make clothes with university names.

USAS then pressed universities to withdraw from the Fair Labor Association . . . on grounds that the group's practices are insufficient. The specific criticisms of Fair Labor include letting manufacturers choose which plants will be monitored and giving advance notice of inspections. Another very smart move by the college students. In my day, we referred to this as "not getting co-opted by the Establishment."

Several human-rights groups have helped with the anti-sweatshop movement, but the bulk of the energy seems to have come from the campuses.

USAS has become quite sophisticated about how to guarantee independent monitoring and is also working for living wages for foreign workers, based on economic conditions in each country. These laptop activists have already had a major impact on the collegiate licensing industry and should in time be able to affect the entire apparel industry.

The apparel industry is—to use a word I loathe—paradigmatic, in that it is completely globalized and notoriously exploitative. Apparel manufacturers are actually design and marketing firms that "outsource" production to independent contractors all over the world. This model is increasingly copied by other industries as they seek to lower labor costs and avoid worker organizing.

Any Texan can get a look at the results by visiting the maquiladoras just on the other side of the Tex-Mex border. The toxic dump in Matamoras is worth a visit all on its own.

Tom Friedman, the *New York Times*'s foreign affairs columnist, has observed: "For many workers around the world the oppression of unchecked commissars has been replaced by the oppression of the unregulated capitalists, who move their manufacturing from country to country, constantly in search of those who will work for the lowest wages and lowest standards. To some, the Nike swoosh is now as scary as the hammer and sickle."

Middle-aged activists who waste time bemoaning apathy on campus could help by getting off their duffs and helping spread word about the USAS boycotts.

Lest you think hideous working conditions are found only in the Third World, consider the case of Big Chicken, the poultry industry in America.

Workers in chicken factories endure conditions that would shame Guatemala or Honduras. Many stand for hours on end in sheds that reek of manure, or chop chickens all day in cold, dark plants, or are constantly scratched by live chickens that have to be crammed into cages by the thousands.

The *New York Times* reported that the Reverend Jim Lewis, an Episcopal priest whose assignment is to improve the lives of poultry workers, once led a wildcat strike against a plant where a worker was fired after he had a finger cut off. The wages are so low, workers often qualify for welfare. And as Texans know from our experience with Big Chicken in East Texas, these plants are often notorious polluters as well, fouling both air and water.

The point of the *Times* article on Lewis was to demonstrate that hundreds of priests, ministers, and rabbis are involved in struggles to improve conditions for American workers on the bottom rungs of society.

This seems to me at least as newsworthy as the latest bulletin from the Christian right that Tinkie-Winkie, the purple Teletubbie, is gay or that Harry Potter books are Satanic.

If you were asked to analyze Molly Ivins's editorial, you might begin by freewriting about each of the five elements, producing preliminary notes such as these:

Purpose: Ivins hopes to do more than provoke a response from her audience; she intends to rouse them to action. She talks about people "getting off their duffs," as if she wants to shame them into supporting boycotts. Newspaper opinion pieces like this often elicit a disengaged--even contemplative--response, asking readers to reconsider conventional attitudes or opinions, appealing to fairness and detached skepticism. But rather than urging her readers to consider new or controversial ideas, Ivins appeals to their <u>consciences</u>, almost shouting at them to take action. She opens her essay with an exclamation and ends with dark sarcasm. In the few places where she adopts the more polite, sophisticated language of "think pieces"--using words like paradigmatic and outsource--she seems at pains to distance herself from it.

Audience: Ivins opens as though she were speaking directly to college students, and she continues in that vein throughout her first two paragraphs. But in paragraph 5 it becomes clear that she really is talking about the actions of a specific group of students--"Another very smart move by the college students." The word you doesn't appear until paragraph 12: "Lest you think hideous working conditions are found only in the Third World. . . ." Here, it sounds like she's talking down to her readers, the "middle-aged activists" she has scolded in the previous paragraph. But in spite of her exasperation with their inertia, Ivins exhorts these readers who share her values; she doesn't try to win over corporate executives or conservatives. She identifies herself as a Texan when she says "as Texans know from our experience," but I think that's because she writes a column in the Fort Worth newspaper; the issues she deals with are international in scope, and there are people throughout the world who share Ivins's concerns.

Main Idea: Ivins wants readers to know that savvy, committed activists are bringing abusive labor practices to light and are fighting to eliminate them. Ivins says that middle-aged, middle-class Americans who share her views ought to participate in those efforts.

Development: In her first seven paragraphs, Ivins presents evidence that may have come from a news story written for the Associated Press or one of the other wire services. In the next several paragraphs, she reveals knowledge of the broader economic implications of franchising and outsourcing. In paragraphs 9, 12, and 13, she leads us to understand that she has observed the inhumane working conditions in Mexico and Texas. She also quotes an article from the New York Times and refers to another.

Organization and Coherence: In her first five paragraphs, Ivins sounds triumphant, like she's gloating over the fact that someone is at last taking action. She sounds like a cheerleader: "Way to go . . .! Nice going, good win." The next five paragraphs place a specific event (one manufacturer's response to student activism) within a global economic context. In the following three paragraphs, Ivins alerts her audience of "middle-aged activists" to the urgency of the issue. It's not just news from some Third World country that receives brief coverage in newspaper; it's something that well-meaning Americans permit to happen within or close to their own communities. Finally, Ivins refers to one particular activist, Jim Lewis, and to the conditions he opposes and what he's doing to change them.

These notes are a beginning. You would next compose a draft to be revised and edited. Finally, a polished analysis might look like this:

Analysis: " 'Ernie's Nuns' Are Pointing the Way"

Molly Ivins, a syndicated columnist for the <u>Fort Worth</u> <u>Star-Telegram</u>, addresses an audience of aging Baby Boomers, many of whom were Civil Rights activists and war protestors during their college years in the 1960s. By applauding the commitment and savvy of present-day students who have organized boycotts to improve working conditions in garment factories overseas, Ivins tries to shame readers into action. Specifically, she upbraids them for "bemoaning apathy on campus" and enjoins them to get "off their duffs" to "spread word about the . . . boycotts."

Unlike some Op-Ed authors, Ivins does not try to appear objective or disengaged from the issue. She assumes that readers share her values and political views, and she makes no effort to persuade anyone who doesn't. She appeals to our consciences rather than pursuing the kind of detached inquiry often found in journalistic think pieces. In fact, Ivins mocks the vocabulary of politically disengaged writing. She tries to distance herself from the word <u>outsource</u> by placing it in quotation marks and, when forced to use the word <u>paradigmatic</u>, she inserts a sarcastic aside: "to use a word I loathe."

To earn the moral authority to which she lays claim, Ivins must demonstrate knowledge of the issue--a challenging task in so short an essay. Her familiarity with the focusing event that introduces this essay--the successful boycott of Reebok by the United Students against Sweatshops--is a good start. However, many readers are aware that information like this is readily available through newspaper wire services, which editorial writers routinely consult. More impressive is Ivins's grasp of the economic implications of franchising and outsourcing, a preemptive response to people who might otherwise dismiss her views as naively idealistic. Ivins further enhances her credentials with specific references to working conditions in Texas and Mexico.

Ivins's essay consists of three parts. In the first five paragraphs, Ivins gloats over a successful boycott. Her tone is gleeful and exultant: "Way to go . . . Nice going, good win." The next five paragraphs demonstrate knowledge and credibility: Ivins places the boycott in a global context with heroes (labor activists) and villains (greedy corporations). Then, in her final paragraphs, Ivins appeals for action. She describes the horrible working conditions in chicken factories, tells how one person is combatting the abuse, and urges readers to join the struggle.

Writing a Brief Reading Analysis   ASSIGNMENT

Analyze the following essay, using this procedure:

- Read the essay twice, underlining important ideas and writing in the margins.
- Freewrite about each of the five elements of analysis.
- Compose and carefully revise a draft. Begin with a description of the essay (its purpose, audience, and main idea); then analyze development, organization, and coherence. Edit your draft thoroughly.

■ READING SELECTION

The following editorial by the vice president for academic affairs at Southern Oregon University appeared in the *Chronicle of Higher Education*.

Opening Ourselves to Unconditional Love in Our Relationships with Students

SARA HOPKINS-POWELL

1 The concept of unconditional love may seem an unlikely topic for college faculty members to consider in this time of sexual-harassment charges and consensual-relationship policies. And yet, one of the greatest gifts we have as teachers, mentors, and co-creators of learning is the ability to care so deeply for individual students that we hold them in our hearts regardless of whether we agree with their life choices.

2 This definition of unconditional love is not an abstract concept for me, but one that I have experienced as both the receiver and the giver. My passion is the power of education to transform people's lives, and it follows that an intimacy can sometimes occur in the process that transcends the typical student-teacher relationship. I am not suggesting that faculty members establish such a relationship with every student; in fact, you are privileged if it happens more than once or twice in your lifetime.

3 Disturbingly, when I began research for this essay on the Internet, the most frequent hits for the term "unconditional love" were sites related to pedophiles, who use the phrase to cloak their real intent. The second most-common use of the term was in the context of religion and theology, with emphasis on the relationship between God and humanity. It is difficult to find references to unconditional love between parents and children, and few sites use the term even remotely as an emotion between adults.

4 How do we experience unconditional love in our teaching? While this happens with students who share our interests, one of the surprises is that frequently the student in question does not mirror our own interests or personality, although the affinity of a shared experience sparks the initial contact. The student may differ in temperament, background, or interests.

5 Sometimes, it's someone you initially overlooked in the classroom. These are often the students who are quiet in class but who ask the insightful questions. Unconditional love does not develop immediately but results from repeated interaction either in class or in other settings. Faculty members teaching large lectures may never have the time to share an intimate relationship with three hundred students, but it could be the one student who routinely comes to office hours. More likely, the possibility for this kind of friendship arises during a seminar or the supervision of thesis or dissertation work, or with a student who works in a laboratory or studio.

6 Let me describe my own personal experience with such a relationship. When I was in graduate school, I was assigned an adviser. My first meeting with him was difficult. He found normal conversations trying, and he took an eternity to get to the point. I quickly learned that if I waited, not only would I receive an answer, but an eloquent one at that.

7 I took a class from him my first semester, although it was not a subject that I thought would interest me. His classroom demeanor was similar to his office persona. During class, he would stare out the window, chalk dust spattered all over his clothes,

and then he would turn to us and talk about the importance of social justice. I began to see him during his office hours in part because I did not quite grasp the assignments, but as the term progressed, we discovered that we enjoyed many of the same interests.

8   Over the next five years, our relationship grew, and he eventually became my dissertation adviser. He bought me champagne when I passed my orals and cheered when my overseas research was arranged. He deftly guided me through the dissertation process, and then he served as an adviser as I got my first job and shared the joy of a marriage. He was always there with a ready ear to listen to whatever was plaguing me at the moment.

9   Through all of this, I learned about his family, his children and grandchildren, his love of opera and twentieth-century prints. He was one of the few people I could go to who would hear me out—without judgment. If he offered advice and I didn't take it, there was never any hint of recrimination or guilt.

10   I have also experienced the other side of the coin—as a faculty member interacting with a student. That student came to the first class I ever taught at my current institution. She was nervous and shy and would begin shaking when you asked her a question in class. Even presenting her research was enough to make her almost sick, but her writing showed great promise.

11   She began to visit me during office hours and then asked if I would be her adviser. She took every class I taught, and, as time went on, she became more confident and self-assured. She was noticed by other faculty members, who were equally impressed with her intellect.

12   As she began to contemplate her future, my behavior may have appeared less accepting—I was somewhat relentless in urging her to make plans beyond graduation. Eventually, I backed off (remembering one of the precepts of unconditional love), and she discovered her own way. She joined the Peace Corps and went to Central Asia. In an early letter to me, she wrote that she had finally found what she needed to do with her life. She is still working abroad today and routinely checks in to let me know where she is. During a rare visit home, we talked about a new relationship in her life. When I convinced her of my total acceptance, she cried. She is an exceptional young woman with a deep sense of justice and caring, and I am proud to know her.

13   Without extrapolating too much from these personal stories, I want to say that both relationships went beyond mentoring and friendship. My interactions both as receiver and giver with these two people were qualitatively different from those with other students and mentors.

14   In both cases, the relationship started out with an uneven power relationship—that of teacher-student. Over time, the nature of the connection grew first into friendship, then into unconditional love. These were not relationships in which we socialized with each other frequently. There might be an occasional lunch or something more formal, but most of the interactions took place in an office setting or a classroom. I am aware enough to realize that the needs of both the individuals and my own played into the relationships, but I have found that by careful tending, platonic love grows.

15   While discussing the joys of this sort of relationship, it is equally important to identify the potential problems. A faculty member is clearly personally vulnerable in this relationship, as is the student, but the nature of love is that you must be open to both joy and sorrow. If you are giving unconditionally, there could be a time when the other wounds you in some way.

Other issues to be aware of are the inherent power differential and the potential   16
for oppression within the relationship. Faculty members must constantly remain
sensitive to relationships that change from platonic to sexual—whether real or imag-
ined—particularly with younger students or those who are mentally fragile. Boundaries need to be maintained and spoken about in an open and thoughtful way. We
faculty members must also guard against pushing these students to be clones of ourselves, pursuing questions of interest only to us. That is the true test of unconditional
love: the ability to let the other make different decisions.

Ultimately, I am grateful that I experienced unconditional love as a student—   17
partly so I could then share this gift as a faculty member. If we begin to model this
type of relationship on our campuses, perhaps it will help us get beyond the issues of
harassment and consensual relationships that plague us. If we as faculty members are
strong enough to maintain clear boundaries, then perhaps the all-too-common yet
inappropriate sexual relationships between students and faculty members can be
avoided.

Why is unconditional love so important to recognize, when it is fraught with dif-   18
ficulty and occurs so rarely? It is because we are human beings, and practicing this
love can carry us past the indifferent students and the endless meetings. It is because,
as a colleague of mine from Mexico says, "teaching is the most important work in the
world, and we do it one student at a time." When you are enriched by another's love
and friendship, it is a deep breath of life.

And there is another reason I think it is important to practice this type of rela-   19
tionship: some faculty members, out of fear of sexual-harassment charges, have
completely shut students out of their lives. They have no personal interactions with
students, even with the door open. I view that as a tremendous loss, both for the faculty members and the students. With care and maturity—and a degree of courage—we
professors can open ourselves up to deep intimacy and love with a person whom we
bring into our hearts, and hold there for a lifetime.

Freewriting

In your notebook, freewrite for at least ten minutes, making the strongest argument to support the benefits of the kind of student-teacher relationship that
Hopkins-Powell describes. Regardless of whether you agree with her views, develop a list of reasons, facts, examples, personal observations, or experiences that
lend support to her beliefs. Then freewrite for at least another ten minutes, making the strongest argument you can to support the opposite point of view (i.e.,
that this type of relationship is inappropriate).

Group Work

Share freewritings with members of your peer group by having each member read
aloud as others take notes. Try to reach some consensus about the validity of
Hopkins-Powell's claims. If you are unable to do so, try to reach a fair rendering of
two (or more) conflicting viewpoints.

Review Questions

1. How does Hopkins-Powell define unconditional love?

2. What two specific illustrations does Hopkins-Powell provide to help readers understand a faculty member's unconditional love for a particular student?

3. What are the potential problems with the type of student-teacher relationship that Hopkins-Powell describes?

Discussion Questions

1. How do paragraphs 15 and 16 help to support Hopkins-Powell's claims?

2. How do you suppose Hopkins-Powell would respond to the argument that what she is talking about is really nothing more than being a "teacher's pet"? Should she have anticipated and attempted to refute that argument?

3. A college instructor teaches thousands of students during her career. A typical student in a four-year degree program will take classes from thirty to forty instructors. Given these facts, how likely is it that any one student will enjoy the type of relationship that Hopkins-Powell describes? That any one instructor will do so? Is this an important consideration? That is, does it strengthen or weaken the author's case?

Writing

1. Hopkins-Powell addresses an audience of college professors and administrators. Write a summary of her ideas directed to an audience of college students, their parents, or persons who have never attended college.

2. Write a brief reading analysis of either of the additional readings in this chapter.

3. Write a brief summary report that synthesizes Hopkins-Powell's editorial with the two additional readings in this chapter.

WRITE, READ, and RESEARCH the NET

1. *Write:* Freewrite for fifteen minutes about a particularly rewarding or particularly difficult relationship you have had with a teacher.

2. *Read:* Review the following Web site:
   <http://www.ala.org/BookLinks/v09/students.html>

3. *Research:* Using the Internet, locate Web sites that deal with student-teacher relationships. Using the five elements of analysis presented in this chapter, write a brief analysis of any one of the Web sites you locate.

■ ADDITIONAL READINGS

The following readings address issues involving relationships between teachers and students. The first, written by an English professor at Monroe Community College, was, like Hopkins-Powell's essay, an editorial in the *Chronicle of Higher Education*. The second reading, by Adam Farhi, originally appeared in the educational journal *Clearing House*.

Crossing the Fine Line Between Teacher and Therapist

M. GARRETT BAUMAN

1 The first day, his wheelchair was backed against the side wall, empty seats separating him from his fellow students in the rest of the room. Knowing how difficult it is to maneuver a wheelchair in cluttered classrooms, I slid some desks aside and invited him to move nearer the others.

2 He wore wraparound, mirrored sunglasses and slowly panned the class, forcing down curious eyes. Then he turned to me and said, "I'm OK." He looked about fifty and wore a T-shirt whose rolled sleeves exposed tattoos of snakes and the American flag on his thin arms. When I reached his name on the roster and called "James," he corrected me: "The name's Jimmy."

3 During the first weeks of our college writing class, Jimmy slumped in his wheelchair, taking no notes, grunting minimal replies to questions directed to him. He became animated only during a discussion of Vietnam.

4 Few of his classmates were even born then, so Jimmy described how his unit had evacuated a flooded village. "A hundred people piled carts with stuff. Sarge says they can bring only one thing each, 'cause the boat's overloaded. This woman has a baby under one arm and a pig under the other. 'One thing!' Sarge says, so the woman throws the baby into the river."

5 A young woman in class gasped, "What did the soldiers do?"

6 Jimmy's face was impassive, his eyes hidden behind his mirrored glasses. "Nothing. That's the way it was in Nam. A pig was worth something." The class shrank back as if a cobra had spit at them.

7 After class, Jimmy rolled to my desk. "My counselor says I got to find out why I been gettin' low grades." I pointed out that his papers were much too short and suggested that he visualize more details, as he had done with his oral story. He said, "I got nothing to say on these topics. I tell it like it is. After that it's just bullshit." I reminded him that he chose the topics. He sighed.

8 "Yeah, yeah. But nothing ever happened to me my whole life but one thing."

9 I sat down to be on his level. My own distorted reflection shone in his sunglasses—bulging, insect-like. Is that how he sees me? I wondered. Or is it how I feel—the soft professor who never saw a child thrown in a river. Vietnam was so long ago. Yet I felt those years now, like an old shard of shrapnel under the skin. As Jimmy's classmates were being born and I was raising a family and maturing professionally, he was stuck in the jungle. All those years he remained a teenager serving time in a broken, old man's body. I said, "So write about that one thing."

10 He barked a laugh. "No way! Too much'd come out I don't want out again." He clenched the wheelchair. I suggested that a good paper would make something posi-

tive of his experience, that writing might even help exorcise it. He snorted. "Nah! You don't want that out."

11   Maybe not, but if education was to help him discover his strengths, it had to go where the energy was. In his curved lenses I watched my lips say, "I do," and I wondered what my advice would cost him.

12   His next paper described his wounding, near the war's end. Jimmy was shuffling to the latrine at night when the first rounds hit.

13   "They couldn't even see me," he wrote. A machine-gun bullet tore through his kneecap. Two more shattered two vertebrae in his lower back. He collapsed like a deflating balloon, his kneecap gone, both legs paralyzed. Jimmy said he was "stupid" to be crippled because he couldn't "hold a leak." He concluded, "I got a medal, but I was no hero. None of us were heroes. We were just lucky or stupid. I was stupid."

14   I puzzled over *stupid*. Wasn't *unlucky* the right word?

15   When it was time for the students to discuss their papers, I worried about how Jimmy would react to their comments about his work. A silly comment could light his fuse.

16   Yet after a few awkward moments, they began to hotly debate heroism and luck. They wanted more details to fill in their fathers' shadowy tales of Vietnam. At first, Jimmy bristled at what he took for patronizing. Yet by the end of class he seemed to sense that the students respected his authority. Nodding at their suggestions for his paper, Jimmy acted as if he owned something valuable.

17   Having a real topic led him to sharper details, bumping his grades from D-'s to C's and B's, and Jimmy tentatively edged into more of his mined landscape. His next paper described rehab and sagging through tedious years with other broken men in veterans' hospitals.

18   "All for nothing," he snarled in my office.

19   "It got you to college."

20   He shook his head. "It was college or welfare, they told me. Politicians are tired of us hardbodies. I been draining the system twenty-four years."

21   "If you can take three bullets, you can take a few D's."

22   He laughed. "You don't know what all I took, Teach. You lay flat on your back for a year. Being crippled ain't just a thing that happens to you once. I got a son. Yeah. He was born while I was in Nam. I saw him twice since I been back. The last time he was nine."

23   "Why don't you visit him?"

24   "Like this?" He slapped the chrome wheelchair. "He's better off without a daddy to shame him. I ain't dragging him down with me. The kid thinks I'm a hero. What a word. I sucked weed and got nailed going to the can. I mailed him my medals. They're better than the real me."

25   "He might see past the wheelchair," I said.

26   I was a teacher, not a therapist. Yet to treat Jimmy as a purely educational issue would be not only heartless but truly stupid.

27   While it may seem best to keep academic and personal issues separate, it's hypocritical. Personal heartaches, neuroses, and rage account for part of the vitality of great books and their best teachers. Surely it is the same for our students and their studies. Jimmy's crippled body and psyche were an unhealed wound in our collective spirit, and part of his intellectual contribution to our class.

28   Jimmy went on. "Yesterday, I was rolling to the river to fish, when I had this creepy feeling my daddy was behind me. I could hear him thinking, 'So that's my Jimmy. He looks so stupid with his fishing gear and beer strapped to that chair. He'd a been better off kilt, poor sumbitch.' I don't want my kid thinking that about me."

"Your son's in his twenties. How can you be bad for him? You love him." I had intruded where professors are not supposed to go, but I didn't care. **29**

"I'm trash. Pin a degree on me, an' I'll still be trash." **30**

"You don't have to be a rotten father because yours was." **31**

He pounded his armrest. "I already am, dammit! If that's not stupid, what is? Yeah, I love the kid. I know he's a man, but he's gonna stay a kid to me! So what?" He pushed violently on his wheels and rammed the door, escaping. **32**

I collapsed into my chair. How little I knew of what it was to be him. Could I really teach him unless I did? I lifted my feet and shoved my hands against the desk so I rolled in my desk chair across the office. I stranded myself in the center where I could reach nothing. I told myself to remember that feeling. **33**

Jimmy's writing sometimes transformed his pain into insight; sometimes it enraged him. I didn't have a plan, didn't know if I pushed him to deliverance or disaster. But we slogged together through the tangled places he'd inhabited for twenty-four years. He was eager just to move somewhere. No matter what else he did, he wrote, and I hoped we both might stagger into one of education's ordinary miracles, when learning ought to be impossible but happens anyway. **34**

I told myself that shortly after the middle of the term, when Jimmy punched a police officer who had arrested him for selling pot. **35**

He railed in my office. "Who cares if I smoke dope? Am I going to be a doctor? Fly an airplane? Play shortstop?" **36**

He was hunkering down in his miserable foxhole, and I prodded him. "You didn't hit the cop because he arrested you." **37**

He took off his purple mirrored sunglasses, and I saw his old, exhausted eyes for the first time. The skin around them was sickly white from lack of sunlight. "That's right." **38**

I rolled my chair closer and said what had been brewing in me. "Daddy's gone. The cops are not the army. You can't get even with anonymous bullets. Let go of what you were—that boy's dead. Live what's left!" **39**

He laughed and rolled back a few inches. "This is life? See, my big problem is, what's a hardbody do with a diploma? Jerk off a computer all day? Wear a suit?" **40**

"See your son. Write your papers. It's not what it could have been, but it's better than rotting in Vietnam for the rest of your life." **41**

He sighed and nodded. **42**

Jimmy's GPA turned ugly despite the C+ he was earning in my class. By December he looked exhausted. During finals week, I heard the familiar whizzing, and Jimmy rolled into my office. "I got to tell you something." **43**

"You're dropping out?" I hate students' choosing failure, but I knew Jimmy was not surrendering. He was pricking the bubble of hypocrisy that said we could help, could atone for the loss he had suffered on behalf of all of us. And I knew he had fought harder in college and learned more than most A students. **44**

He shrugged. "Sure. But I finished your last paper. Here." He swallowed. "I also . . . uh . . . wanted to tell you . . . I ain't been honest with you. I got some leg movement. I can crab around with crutches; I just don't practice. Watch." **45**

He slowly straightened one leg parallel to the floor, then the other. I had noticed them twitching before, but had said nothing. "I don't have to be in this chair." **46**

"Show me," I said. Jimmy shook his head. My hand hung in the air between us. **47**

"I walk like an epileptic duck," Jimmy said. I extended my hand closer, and he took it. I felt the full weight of him as I pulled. **48**

Hollywood Goes to School
Recognizing the Superteacher Myth in Film

ADAM FARHI

1   "The power of cinema," says filmmaker Steven Spielberg, "is a lot stronger than the power of literature" (Taylor, 1992, p. 23). Although Spielberg may be a bit biased in his assessment, there is no denying that movies have become so embedded in our culture that it is often difficult to determine when they are reflecting society and when they are affecting it. Since the early 1980s, the reach of film has vastly expanded: Through cable television and VCRs, Americans have the ability to watch a film of their choice again and again. They are bombarded with images and ideas.

2   In 1992, Elliot measured the power of the film *JFK* by having college seniors view it. He found that 68% of the audience accepted the facts presented in the film as true. A skillfully made film, he learned, can "integrate its message with existing messages and create a reality for its audience" (p. 31). That phenomenon brings up an important issue for the education community: How are teachers being portrayed to movie audiences that include impressionable students and taxpaying adults?

3   The answer is disturbing. With some exceptions, films that center around teachers tend to show them as almost superhuman, capable of permanently changing lives in a short period of time. By forcing them to compete with their cinematic counterparts, the superteacher myth places an impossible burden on real teachers.

4   The superteacher formula is fairly simple. Take one teacher, often male, ranging from someone who has "different" ideas to someone who is an outright rebel. Give him an uncaring or unwilling administration, incompetent or lackluster coworkers, and students whom everyone else has given up on. With little assistance from anyone and teaching methods that are barely existent, the teacher is able to overcome the odds and quickly transform the class. Frequently the teacher, who has no personal life of his own, becomes something of a cult figure and proceeds to solve the students' personal problems. Along the way, the teacher alienates someone in a position of power, thus putting his job on the line. The students, of course, join together to pledge their support, because the teacher has changed their lives forever. The end.

5   One of the most common elements in teacher films is the class full of unruly students. This portrayal of students has evolved over the years, from the cranky, working-class English kids in *To Sir, with Love* (1967) to the criminals who roam the halls at the start of *Lean on Me* (1989). The first line in *Teachers* (1984), which is directed at the student body, is, "All right, you little animals." Such an opening, common in the genre, is remarkably similar to the start of many western movies: The town is in chaos; the townspeople are scared; and no one is brave enough to do anything about it. Now the search is on for a gunslinger (or superteacher) who cares enough to make a difference.

6   Often, it is not only the kids who are out of control. Consider *Summer School,* a hit film from 1986. Freddy Shoop is a phys ed teacher pressed into summer duty as a remedial English teacher. Very quickly, we learn that the class is made up of kids who are "not real students." But then the film flits the odds against Mr. Shoop even further: It presents him as an untrained loser, someone who "only got into this teaching gig" to get his summers off. (As the film progresses, however, Mr. Shoop will magically be transformed into a superteacher.)

7   Then there is the film *The Principal* (1987), which revolves around James Belushi's character, whose arrest for a drunken assault leads to his being "promoted" to principal of a nightmarish urban school. The violent students are unexpellable, and the po-

lice have no jurisdiction over the school. The notion that a school like that could exist is ridiculous, but there is Belushi, about to become a hero. His secret identity as a superteacher is foreshadowed early in the film when someone tells him, "You should've worn your cape."

Belushi's heroic principal is rare, however; most of Hollywood's teachers are saddled with an administration that does not care about them or their students. In *Up the Down Staircase* (1968), a young teacher is warned on her first day not to "even try to communicate with these students." More often than not, the principals are presented in this stereotypical fashion, which has the effect of making the superteacher seem that much more noble. In one typically outlandish example, the principal in *Dangerous Minds* (1995) exists for no other reason than to provide resistance to teacher Louanne Johnson. He refuses to talk to a troubled student because the student didn't bother to knock before entering his office. After being kicked out of the office, the student, who was seeking refuge, is gunned down. As a result, Ms. Johnson looks even more heroic because she is obviously the only one in the school who cares about the students.   **8**

Class of 1984 (1982) puts a rookie teacher in a school that is the ultimate urban nightmare, and when he is threatened by students, the principal does nothing about it. That situation gives the teacher a chance to utter the quintessential superteacher line: "I can't leave my job. I'm worth something as a teacher." The principal in *Teachers,* while more sympathetic, serves the same function. His philosophy is, We're here to get as many kids through the system as we can with what we've got. When John Kimble, who is actually an undercover cop, takes over a kindergarten class to track a suspect in *Kindergarten Cop* (1990), he has no educational training. Yet the principal not only gives him no help; she hopes he will fail.   **9**

There can be only one superteacher in a movie. Many times, that means that the other teachers in the school are incompetent, bitter, or drab and boring. Frequently those coworkers have given up on the students. They are burned-out individuals who warn the hero not to bother trying. "I would row home if I could," Mr. Thackary is warned at the start of *To Sir, with Love.* One of the coworkers in *Teachers* is nicknamed "Ditto" because his daily class routine is made up of the students silently completing worksheets with their chairs facing away from the teacher.   **10**

Dead Poets Society (1989) stars Robin Williams as Mr. Keating, a character who is more of an actor than a teacher. Consider the way in which Keating is introduced: We see three successive scenes at a stuffy, 1950s New England prep school. Chemistry, Latin, and calculus are all presented as deadly boring—the teachers are monotonous; they have no personality. When the audience has been sufficiently dulled, Mr. Keating wanders in, whistling, and leaves. The curious students follow as if the Pied Piper had just walked through. "Weird," one of them remarks about Mr. Keating, "but different."   **11**

That sort of portrayal is one of the major problems with the superteacher myth. It implies that a teacher has to be unconventional to be qualified, making it difficult, if not impossible, for real teachers to measure up. Anyone opposed to Mr. Keating is the enemy, even if that means creating false situations. In his essay on *Dead Poets Society,* Heilman (1991) notes, "First you've got this guy on a white horse charging in to save the place. So you need some set-up black hats to make him look like a hero instead of a moral egoist" (p. 417).   **12**

Providing another unrealistic expectation for real teachers, Hollywood's teachers are able to cause nearly instantaneous transformations for the better among their students. *Renaissance Man* (1994) is a perfect example. We are told that the soldiers in Bill Rago's class have "sawdust for brains," yet they begin to comprehend *Hamlet* immediately. How is Rago able to work such magic on his students? We never find out. The   **13** film is too busy cutting to shots of Rago beaming with pride. Instant gratification, rare in the real world of education, is common in Hollywood's classrooms.

14   *Dangerous Minds* is just as misleading. Note the steps Louanne Johnson follows to control her unruly class. On day one, she has so little control over the students that she flees the school after just a few minutes. That night, she reads a book about discipline and proclaims her new attitude: "OK, you little bastards." On day two, she has changed her outfit from a beige skirt to a black leather jacket. She gets the class members' attention by giving them a karate lesson. On day three, the same students who forced their previous teacher to quit are literally sitting with their hands folded, waiting for the class to begin.

15   This type of rapid evolution is common. Of *Dead Poets Society,* Heilman (1991) notes that "we never do see Keating *teaching anything*" (p. 418). In fact, we rarely see Hollywood's teachers teaching at all. Filmmakers tend to show the end result of the teaching process without bothering to show the process itself.

16   In many movies, superteachers don't need to teach because their students have always been smart. Their misbehavior is the fault of the previous teachers, who didn't care enough to expose the pearl in the oyster. This is why Bill Rago's students, nicknamed the "Double Ds" ("dumb as dogshit"), manage to pick up Shakespeare so quickly. Sometimes, however, special measures need to be taken. When *Summer School*'s Mr. Shoop is asked how he finally got a class full of underachievers to start learning, he answers with pride, "Bribed 'em." Louanne Johnson is equally honest about her teaching methods in *Dangerous Minds*. She announces that she's "gotta find a gimmick." And she does: She tosses candy bars to the students who speak up in class.

17   So what, then, do most of these cinematic teachers actually do? Perhaps they have so little time to teach because they are too busy trying to solve all of their students' personal problems. "How you gonna save me?" a troubled student asks Louanne Johnson. The word *save* comes up two other times in the film, as Johnson makes it her mission in life to help her students.

18   Like the superteachers in *The Principal* and *Lean on Me,* she makes unannounced visits to a troubled student's home. *Summer School*'s Mr. Shoop takes the blame when two of his underage students are caught with alcohol. Shoop is arrested, but the judge lets him off without any penalty. Then he goes a step further and actually commends Shoop for his "dedication" to his students. The teacher, in other words, does not really care about his students unless he is willing to put his reputation on the line for them.

19   A great way to judge how the superteacher myth has evolved over the last thirty years is to compare *To Sir, with Love* with its made-for-TV sequel, *To Sir, with Love Part 2* (1996). The original film, on the whole, doesn't subscribe to the superteacher formula. Sidney Poitier's Mark Thackary works hard to teach his students respect. He is not a savior; he is a good teacher.

20   In the sequel, Mr. Thackary has changed. He begins making unannounced visits to his students' homes. He conceals a felony and lets himself be fired, all to protect a student with a gun. Then comes the ultimate act of heroism. He follows a troubled student into a junkyard at night, and, to protect this student, Mr. Thackary puts his own life in danger by walking into the path of a loaded gun. He manages to convince an armed thug to put down his weapon, leaving us with a disturbing question: How can real teachers be expected to match this kind of behavior?

21   With such superteachers, it should come as little surprise that the students in these films are intensely loyal. Should something happen to put their teacher's career in jeopardy, the students will be there. Inevitably, something does happen. Witness the conclusion of *Dead Poets Society,* in which Mr. Keating is blamed for a student's suicide

and fired by the stodgy headmaster. In the final scene, some of his students (who all signed a document implicating him in the suicide) defy the headmaster and stand up on their desks in support of Mr. Keating. One by one they get up and pledge their allegiance by reciting from the poem "O Captain! My Captain!" But what, if anything, has Mr. Keating actually taught them? Film critic Roger Ebert (1996) makes an excellent observation: "At the end of a great teacher's course in poetry, the students would love poetry; at the end of this teacher's semester, all they really love is the teacher" (p. 142).

It should be noted that it is possible to make a film about a teacher that rises above the superteacher myth. Along with *To Sir, with Love, Conrack* (1974), *Stand and Deliver* (1987), and *Mr. Holland's Opus* (1995) are all examples of films in which teachers are presented as actual human beings who work hard to teach their students. These are three excellent films that do not fall back on clichés.   **22**

It has become so easy for movies to follow the superteacher formula, however, that the formula threatens to overrun the entire teacher genre. Although unrealistic characters are not uncommon in movies, an alarmingly disproportionate number of teacher films present the protagonist as a superteacher. Never mind that schoolchildren in the audience—and their parents—are wondering why their teachers are not as funny/dedicated/charming/offbeat/devoted as the Mr. Keatings and Louanne Johnsons of the silver screen.   **23**

Furthermore, there is little protection against the influence of film. Any kid with cable TV or a VCR has probably seen *Summer School* at least once, which means that he or she has witnessed the film's "inspiring" ending. After being transformed into a superteacher, Mr. Shoop, using no visible teaching methods, brings about an amazing change in his students. Their test scores have soared. But the vice principal wants to see him fired, and as Mr. Shoop's students stand behind him while his job is in doubt, the principal discovers the results that Mr. Shoop has produced.   **24**

"Now, that's teaching!" exclaims the principal.   **25**

No. That's Hollywood.   **26**

References

Ebert, R. (1996). *Roger Ebert's movie home companion* (1996 ed.). Kansas City: Andrews McMeel.

Elliot, W. R. (1992, March). Synthetic history and subjective reality: The impact of Oliver Stone's *JFK*. Paper presented at the annual meeting of the Association for Education in Journalism and Mass Communication. Montreal (ERIC Document Reproduction Service No. ED 352 682).

Heilman, R. (1991). The great teacher myth. *American Scholar, 60* (3), 417–423.

Taylor, P. M. (1992). *Steven Spielberg: The man, his movies, and their meaning*. New York: Continuum.

8 *Beginning a Research Project*

Suppose you are a smoker who has finally decided to kick the habit. Knowing that your addiction will be hard to overcome, you wonder if you should try to cut down in successive stages, or if you should take the more drastic step of quitting cold turkey. Determined to succeed, you visit the library and find that people who quit all at once have the best results. You also learn that you can expect withdrawal symptoms, but that after seventy-two hours, the worst of these are over. You grit your teeth, toss your remaining cigarettes in the garbage, and resolve that you, not tobacco, will prevail.

In Chapter 1, you learned that research is another name for finding out what you need to know. In the case at hand, reading about nicotine addiction carries a clear personal benefit. However, research often helps others as well. A college *research project* is an undertaking that should not only satisfy your own curiosity but also inform anyone else who reads the paper in which you present your findings.

THE RESEARCH PAPER

A *research paper* is one way to report your findings. However, the paper itself is only the final step in a project that seeks out and discovers information about a particular topic. After making your discoveries, evaluating and selecting among them, and then organizing the material you wish to report, you finally present what you have learned in a documented paper. Of course, not all research papers are alike; in years to come you probably will make frequent use of research in your writing, though not always in what you may think of as "research papers."

Although papers that draw on research can take many different forms, most fall into one of two categories. The more common of the two is the *research-based paper.* Papers of this type consist largely of information found through research; the writers of such papers present relatively few of their own opinions or discoveries. For example, a student seeking to learn whether the fearsome reputation of great white sharks is justified could write a paper based almost entirely on what she found from reading and from interviewing experts. Her own observations on the subject might play only a small part in her paper. In contrast, the *research-supported paper* presents the writer's own ideas, with research findings used to support or supplement them. Argumentative essays are frequently research-supported. For example, a student arguing for increased funding for intramural athletics could use research in part of his paper; he could demonstrate feasibility by citing published budgetary figures, and he could support his own arguments with expert testimony on the need for greater fitness. Still, his original ideas would constitute the heart of his paper.

In practice, the distinction between research-based and research-supported writing is far from absolute. It is not possible to present information in a completely impersonal or neutral way. Assume, for example, that the student writing about great white sharks tried to make her paper objective and impersonal, presenting only the facts and ideas she had learned from her reading and offering no personal opinions or speculations. Even so, the paper she wrote would be very much hers, since it was she who interpreted her sources, selected which facts and ideas to include, and shaped the material so that it represented her understanding of what great white sharks are like. Whatever type of research writing you engage in, you are expected to *think;* even research-based papers are written by human beings, not by computers.

PRIMARY AND SECONDARY RESEARCH

We can also distinguish between types or methods of research. Most library research undertaken for college papers is *secondary research,* so called because it involves the second-hand discovery of information. Through secondary research we learn what others have previously discovered or thought about a topic. In contrast, when we make our own original discoveries, we engage in *primary research.* To give an example of primary research, an agricultural scientist might plant a standard variety of corn in one field and a new hybrid variety in another to test which provides higher yields and is more resistant to drought and disease. On the other hand, a farmer who reads a report written by that scientist to find out the best seed to plant is engaging in secondary research.

As a college student, you will have opportunities to undertake both primary and secondary research. When you conduct an experiment to test the behavior of laboratory rats or survey voter reactions to a presidential speech, you engage in primary research. When you read a history or a chemistry textbook, consult an encyclopedia, or get a printout from a computer database, you engage in secondary research.

However, not every use of a print source is secondary. Written sources can be either primary or secondary. A historian researching the slave trade in colonial America would seek sources from that era. Newspaper stories about slavery, diaries written by freed slaves and slave owners, slave auction notices and bills of sale, tracts written by abolitionists, and census figures and other records from that time are all examples of *primary sources.* In addition, the historian would consult such *secondary sources* as books and articles by other historians who have also researched and written about the slave trade.

In your upcoming research project, you may have occasion to make both secondary discoveries (in library works) and primary discoveries (by interviewing or corresponding with sources). The research you do is determined by the nature of your project and the resources at your disposal.

BENEFITS OF DOING RESEARCH

If research papers were not a requirement in college classes, it is doubtful that many students would have the opportunity or motivation to undertake such projects on their own. By the same token, few instructors are surprised when students, after their projects are completed, say that they were glad to have had the opportunity. Often students say they have gained more from the experience than they expected. They find that research writing can have unanticipated benefits.

Learning an Essential Skill

One aim of this book is to help you become a competent college researcher with all the tools you need to produce quality research papers. A more general—and important—aim is to give you the confidence and skills to discover and use available information about any topic that arouses your curiosity.

It is likely that you will need to write many research papers during your college career and afterward. In other classes, you may be asked to gather information on a topic and report what you discover. After college, in your professional career, you may be faced with questions that you will have to answer through research. In these cases, you will need to consult what others have written, to evaluate and select what is pertinent from this information, and to write reports on your findings.

One reason you are being asked to do one or more research projects in your current course is to give you the experience you will need to conduct future projects with confidence. Practice now will make things easier later. When you are assigned to write a research paper in an art history, marketing, or anthropology class, for example, your instructor will not have time to tutor you in the basics of research. And after you graduate, you will have no instructor at all. College students and college graduates are simply expected to have mastered these skills. Now is the time for you to become an experienced researcher.

While students in a college composition course have the opportunity to learn research skills, they are also at a disadvantage compared with other researchers. Others do research not to practice a skill but to learn about specific topics. What they are discovering is important to them, and the research process is merely a means to that end. In the composition class, however, learning about the research paper can be an end in itself, and the topic you are writing about may seem of only peripheral importance. In that regard, your research project may seem artificial to you, an exercise that is useful in teaching skills for later use but one that has no real importance of its own. This *can* happen, but it is up to you to make sure it does not. For that reason, it is essential for you to choose with care the topic that you will research and write about. Because you will be spending much time and effort on this project, you should become as involved as you can with your topic. If you pursue a topic you genuinely care about, you will gain many rewards: Not only will you spend your time profitably, but you will also write a far better paper and, in the process, learn what you need to know about research methods. If you take an interest in your topic and pursue it avidly, the skills you are seeking to acquire will take care of themselves.

Contributing to Scholarship

Although competence in research and research writing are practical skills, there is yet another reason to engage in research besides its personal usefulness to you. By doing research and then making your discoveries public in a paper, you are benefiting your readers as well.

Research is at the very heart of education—it represents the cooperation that is essential to learning. Most knowledge that you have gained is a result of such cooperation. None of us would have been able to figure out the principles of algebra, to mention just one example, if we had been left entirely on our own. Fortunately, throughout the centuries, mathematicians have shared the results of their discoveries with each other and (through our school algebra classes and textbooks) with us as well. A major function of higher education is to share with students the most important thoughts and discoveries of other scholars.

School classes are not the only means by which scholars share their work with us. They also publish their findings so that we and other scholars can have access to them. To make this sharing even easier, the books and articles they produce have been gathered in a central, accessible place: the college library. Engaging in research is simply taking advantage of what other scholars have learned. Like all scholars, you have the right to read about and learn from the discoveries of others. But scholarship is more than just passively receiving the gift of knowledge. As a scholar, you play an active role. Even when you write a research-based paper reporting on the findings of others, you are still creating something new, a fresh synthesis of information, shaped with your own wisdom and insights, a *new source* that was not available to scholars before. Every research paper makes at least a modest contribution to the domain of knowledge. As a student researcher, you are fully entitled to think of yourself as a scholar engaged in a scholarly enterprise. It is for this reason that you are expected to share your findings in a written, public form.

Gaining Personal Knowledge

In traditional college research writing, the author's aim is to report findings, to share information with readers. Authors of these papers keep their writing focused on their topic, while directing attention away from themselves as authors. (The word *I* rarely appears in conventional research writing.) But while you write such a paper to inform others, no one benefits more from your project than you yourself. Before you can inform your readers, you must first inform yourself about your topic through research. Research writing is a sharing of the knowledge you have gained.

Even the act of writing contributes to your learning. Creating a focused, unified paper forces you to see your topic in new ways. It causes you to bring together information from various sources, to make connections, to take vague ideas and make them concrete. Writing has been properly called a *learning tool;* research writers continue to gain personal knowledge while they are writing about what they have read.

On some occasions, however, personal benefit is not just a byproduct but your principal motive for conducting research. At times, you need to seek answers to questions important to you personally. Writing about such privately motivated research can be just as beneficial and worthy as carrying out conventional research projects. For that reason, one type of paper that has become increasingly popular in composition courses is the **personal research paper.*** Unlike the standard research paper, this paper does not call for impersonal writing; as its name implies, it aims to be intensely personal. If you write a personal research paper, you should pick a topic that has real importance to you—or as one author puts it, you should let a topic pick you (Macrorie 66).† Perhaps your research will help you make a decision, such as what major or career to choose, or even which motorcycle to buy or what vacation to take. Perhaps it will just satisfy some strong curiosity. In any case, a personal research paper is a record of your quest for answers. You write your paper not only about *what* you found but also about *how* you went about finding it. The word *I* appears often in personal research writing. Even when such projects are approached with purely personal goals in mind, they provide far wider benefits. Besides being informative, they can be especially instructive because a strong motivation to find answers is the best teacher of research skills. Although personal research papers center on the writer's interest and focus on the writer's experiences, readers often find them interesting. The writer's deep involvement in the subject usually translates into lively writing.

▮ THE RESEARCH PROCESS

Like all other forms of writing, a research paper does not happen all at once. Many steps are involved. Although a research paper may seem complicated and difficult, you can learn to produce one quite capably if you take one step at a time. This and the next five chapters examine each stage in the research process. To illustrate the tasks involved, we will trace the experiences of two first-year college students as they undertake research and write papers for their composition classes. By examining the steps they follow, the problems they encounter, and the solutions they discover to overcome them, you can observe the skills that go into

---

*It was also given the name "I-search paper" by Ken Macrorie in his book *The I-Search Paper,* rev. ed. (Portsmouth, NH: Boynton, 1988).

†As Chapter 6 explained, "Macrorie 66" is a form of shorthand telling the reader that the authors are citing an idea by Ken Macrorie on page 66 of his book (identified in the preceding footnote).

writing a research paper. The same procedure can be adapted for research writing in your other courses and in your future career.

A RESEARCH ASSIGNMENT

In any given semester, students in different composition classes receive a wide variety of assignments for research projects. Some are given open-ended assignments with many options, whereas others are assigned more focused tasks, such as projects related to a particular theme the class has explored in reading and discussion.

Emily Gould and Justin Stafford, first-year college students enrolled in composition courses, were given different assignments by their instructors. In Emily's class, each student was asked to write a standard college research paper. Students in Justin's class were offered the option of writing either a standard or a personal research paper. In both classes, students were asked to choose their own topics.

Following is an assignment similar to the one that students in Justin's class received. Your own research assignment may differ from it, and your instructor may provide additional criteria for the length, scope, and format of your paper. Make careful note of any ways in which your own instructor's assignment differs from the one given here.

Research Paper	ASSIGNMENT

Investigate a question or problem that intrigues you and write an informative essay, based on your findings from research. Observe the following guidelines, depending on the option you choose or are assigned.

Option A: The Standard College Research Paper

- *Subject.* Frame your research task in the form of a question that you want your investigation to answer. You may explore any subject that arouses your curiosity and interest. You might choose a topic related to your career goals or the field you plan to major in. Perhaps a certain topic in one of your other courses has aroused your curiosity. Perhaps an event or person from recent or earlier history would be worth learning more about. Perhaps in your reading, in conversation, or in viewing a film or television documentary, you have encountered a subject you would like to explore.

- *Audience.* Assume that the other members of your class are your audience. Write a paper that is appropriate for this audience—one that they will find informative and interesting.

- *Voice.* You are the author of this paper, and it should be an honest presentation of what you have learned. But remember that your readers' interests, not yours, should come first. Although sometimes research writers use the word *I* in their papers (e.g., when they present their personal experience as a source), the focus of the paper should be on the subject matter, not on you as a person.

- *Information and opinion.* Be certain that your paper is principally based on the findings of your research rather than on personal speculation. This does not mean, however, that your paper must avoid any ideas and opinions of your own. Your paper may adopt a point of view, but if it does, you should make it clear to your readers from the beginning.

- *Length.* A typical paper is six to twelve pages long, but the length of your paper should be determined by the nature of your subject.

- *Sources.* Your paper should be based on a variety of research, including (where appropriate) such secondary sources as books, periodicals, and newspapers. If you find that additional sources are appropriate for your topic, you should also interview or correspond with experts or participants. Most papers will cite between eight and sixteen sources. In upcoming classes, you will learn how to locate appropriate sources, how to make use of what you learn from them, and how to acknowledge them in notes and in a works-cited page—that is, how to give your sources credit for their contributions to your paper.

Option B: The Personal Research Paper

Most of the guidelines for the standard research paper apply here as well, but there are some differences.

- *Subject.* You should pick a topic that is already a personal concern in your life. That is, you should seek a question you have a good reason to answer, one that can benefit you directly. Any topic that can help you make a decision or that can provide you with information that will enhance your life in some way is likely to be a good choice.

- *Voice and audience.* You should write honestly and unpretentiously about your research experience. Since your topic is of personal interest to you, the word *I* may occur often in your paper. However, you should also write so as to inform readers who may share your interest.

- *Form.* Unlike the standard paper, which is limited to the subject of the writer's research, the personal paper tells about the writer's process of discovery as well. Although no pattern for what to include and how to arrange it is right for all papers, here is a typical pattern suggested by Ken Macrorie. If you choose, your paper can follow this general outline, found in Macrorie's book *The I-Search Paper:*

  1. What I Knew (and didn't know about my topic when I started out).
  2. Why I'm Writing This Paper. (Here's where a real need should show up: The writer demonstrates that the search may make a difference in his life.)
  3. The Search [an account of the hunt, usually in chronological order; what I did first, what I did next, and so on].
  4. What I Learned (or didn't learn. A search that failed can be as exciting and valuable as one that succeeded). (Macrorie 64)

Parts 3 and 4 can be merged if it makes sense to combine your accounts of what you found and how you found it.

- *Sources.* Interview experts, people who are likely to have the answers you want or who know where you can find answers. Consult these primary sources as well as library materials and other secondary sources.

You are also asked to keep a research notebook (explained on pages 337–38) throughout your research project. Save all your notes, outlines, and rough drafts (more about these later), and submit them in a folder with your completed paper. Your current priority is to choose one of these options and to begin focusing on a specific topic. Use the time between now and the next class to think more about potential topics for your paper.

When their instructors announced the assignment, Emily and Justin had a reaction typical of most first-year college students in this situation: a sinking feeling in the stomach, followed by varying degrees of anxiety. It seemed more intimidating than the papers they had written before. Although both are competent writers, they weren't sure they could do it. At least momentarily, they were afraid their deficiencies would be exposed, that they would be revealed as imposters impersonating college students.

As grim as this sounds, there is nothing unusual about what Emily and Justin felt. All writers are apprehensive at the beginning of an assignment, especially one as unfamiliar and as complex as this research paper seemed. But despite their early fears, Emily and Justin not only wrote their papers but also received high grades for them. Afterward they admitted that the project was not the ordeal they had expected. In fact, it was not only rewarding but also interesting, informative, and, despite much hard work, even enjoyable.

What Emily and Justin did you can do. The trick is to divide the long project into a sequence of smaller, manageable tasks. As we examine these tasks, we will consider these two students' experiences as examples—following the progress of research from chaos to clarity, from panic to finished product. Since you will be making a similar trek, the journeys of Emily and Justin are worth your attention.

◼ THE FINISHED PRODUCT

Before you examine all the steps Emily and Justin took to produce their papers, first look at where they ended up. Their polished, final drafts—the completed papers that were the results of all their work—appear on the following pages.

A Sample Standard Research Paper

First is Emily's response to option A, her research paper on teenage workers in fast-food restaurants. Note that despite her impersonal voice, Emily's paper expresses her point of view about a controversial topic.

Emily Gould

English 12

Professor Katherine Humel

4 October 2002

Fast Food Comes at a High Price for Workers

McDonald's, Burger King, KFC, Wendy's, and other popular chains have brought countless innovations to the restaurant industry, delivering food fast and at low cost year after year. Convenience and value have come at a price, however, and many believe that benefits to the public are outweighed by the costs that this giant industry imposes on its workers.

In his best-selling book Fast-Food Nation, Eric Schlosser shows just how much such popular chains revolutionized America's eating habits. In 1970, Americans spent $6 billion on fast food. By 2000, that figure had soared to $110 billion. Schlosser says Americans "spend more on fast food than on movies, books, magazines, newspapers, videos, and recorded music--combined" (3). Every day about a quarter of the U.S. adult population eats fast food in some form. Few, however, give much thought to the workers who prepare and deliver their meals.

Hiring teenagers to serve us food in a fast-food setting has become "so natural, so normal, and so

Gould 2

inevitable that people often think little about it," says
Stuart Tannock, a lecturer in social and cultural studies
at the University of California at Berkeley (qtd. in Ayoub
A20). Nevertheless, while fast-food workers have become an
essential component in the service industry, a fast-food
job is usually viewed as undesirable, dead-end work.

　　　One-third of all workers under the age of 35 have
gotten their first jobs working for restaurants (Yum!
Brands), and about one-eighth of all workers in the United
States have, at some point, worked for McDonald's
(Schlosser 4). Yvonne Zipp of the Christian Science
Monitor observes that such jobs have become "a teen rite
of passage as universal as driver's ed" (1). They are
ideal for teens because they require no special skills,
and many believe that such jobs provide the educational
benefit of teaching responsibility and good time and money
management. These benefits may be more than offset by
costs, however. Zipp cites a study by the National
Research Council and the Institute of Medicine in
Washington that teens who work more than 20 hours a week
are "less likely to get enough sleep and exercise, less
likely to go on to higher education, and more likely to
use alcohol or drugs." These findings are disturbing,
since four-fifths of American teens work at least part-

time during the school year, and of these, half work more than 20 hours weekly (Zipp 1).

Child labor laws offer some protection, governing the number of hours teens can work and the kinds of work they can do. Those who are 14 or 15 years of age may work up to three hours on a school day and up to eight hours on other days, for a maximum of 18 hours during a school week and 40 hours during a non-school week. They may work only between the hours of 7 a.m. and 7 p.m., except in the summer, when the hours extend to 9 p.m. Once they reach 16, however, teens may work an unlimited number of hours ("General").

These boundaries were set by the Fair Labor Standards Act of 1938, and many believe they are no longer suitable to current realities. At the beginning of the twentieth century, most teens left school at 16, and restrictive laws for children up to 15 years of age were designed to introduce them to the workforce before becoming full-time workers at 16. Today, however, 90% of teens graduate from high school at 18, and most work primarily for extra spending money or luxuries such as new cars. Relatively few now work to help support their families (Zipp 1).

Since 2000, Congress has been debating the Young American Workers' Bill of Rights, a bill that would update the 1938 labor law. If it is enacted as law, 14- and 15-

Gould 4

year-olds could work no more than 15 hours weekly, and teens 16 and 17 would be limited to a 20-hour work week (Kiger). While this bill would only affect work hours, some critics of teen employment, such as Janine Bempechat, assistant professor in Harvard's Graduate School of Education, want to keep teens away from fast-food counters altogether, claiming that they can get a similar sense of responsibility and self-esteem from jobs such as peer tutoring or volunteer work. Others, however, noting that some teens use their paychecks to save for college, worry that limiting hours could keep them from earning enough to pay for tuition (Zipp 1).

Teens are also restricted in the kinds of work they can do. Workers at 14 or 15 are not allowed to cook and are limited to jobs such as cashier, bagger, or member of the cleanup crew. More options are available to 16- and 17-year-olds, who can cook but cannot use hazardous machinery such as automatic slicers, grinders, choppers, or machines that form hamburger patties ("Prohibited"). Even though such regulations are intended to ensure safety in the workplace, many employers are either not obeying the laws or not doing enough to protect young workers. A teen gets injured on the job every 40 seconds, and one dies from a work-related injury every five days. Responding to these alarming statistics, the U.S. Department of Labor

has tried to crack down on violations of child labor laws
with heavy fines (Kiger). Funding for these efforts has
increased, with money going toward inspection of workplaces,
investigations, and occasional sweeps of industries
suspected of serious violations. The Department can impose
fines of up to $10,000 on employers who willfully break
labor laws and can sentence individuals to six-month jail
terms for each employee working in violation of the law.
One of the largest fines was incurred by a fast-food
company in Ohio, when a 15-year-old cut her finger while
using a meat slicer, a piece of equipment that should have
been off-limits to her according to federal law. The
company was ordered to pay $333,450 after it was found to
have 32 other unauthorized employees using similar
equipment, including one under the age of 14 (Pass and
Spector).

In recent years, reported cases of employer
misconduct have declined, but the injury rate among teens
at work has not seen a similar drop. Although fines for
violators are steep, critics worry that the Labor Department
is not doing enough to reduce violations. Only a thousand
inspectors are responsible for the safety of all 100
million workers in the nation. As a result, most employers
are not fined until someone is injured. Under the proposed
Young American Workers' Bill of Rights, an employer who

Gould 6

willfully ignores child labor laws could be sentenced to
as long as five years in prison for each teen who is
seriously injured on the job and up to ten if a teen dies
as a result of the employer's neglect. Regardless,
however, of whether stricter child labor legislation is
passed, companies and young workers alike have a strong
economic incentive to break whatever laws are on the
books. U.S. businesses save an estimated $155 million each
year by employing teens, and the economic gains that
result from hiring them to do jobs meant for older, more
experienced workers often outweigh the consequences of
getting caught (Kiger). Furthermore, teens are unlikely to
refuse an illegal assignment and risk losing the only job
they are qualified to hold.

Because most fast-food jobs require little skill,
they are among the worst paying in the United States. The
fast-food industry pays minimum wage to a higher proportion
of its workers than any other sector of employment. While
a minimum-wage job may be a good source of spending money
for a teenager living at home, it is nearly impossible
for an adult to live off such wages, much less support a
family. Between 1968 and 1990, the boom years for
fast-food restaurants, the purchasing power of the minimum
wage dropped 40 percent, and even now, despite increases
mandated by federal law, it still purchases about 27

percent less than it did in 1968. At the same time, the earnings of restaurant executives have risen dramatically. Nevertheless, the National Restaurant Association opposes any further increase in the minimum wage, and some large fast-food chains, such as Wendy's and Jack in the Box, have backed legislation that would allow states to exempt certain employers from federal minimum-wage regulations (Schlosser 73).

Critics of a higher minimum wage fear the effects of increased labor costs on the restaurant industry. Scott Vincent, director of government affairs for the National Council of Chain Restaurants, says, "A lot of chains are franchised, which means they're small businesses with thin profit margins that can't handle more labor costs" (qtd. in Van Houten). Higher wages, he maintains, would result in reduced hiring, layoffs, or even closings. The only way to compensate would be price increases, which would lessen the appeal of fast food to customers with limited means and therefore reduce business.

A spokesperson for the Coalition on Human Needs expresses a contrary view, asserting that the effects of previous increases in the minimum wage suggest that no serious consequences to the restaurant business would result, while low-income neighborhoods would derive the greatest benefits from a minimum-wage increase

Gould 8

(Van Houten). Author Eric Schlosser calculates that an
increase of one dollar in wages would cause the price of a
hamburger to increase only two cents (73). Furthermore,
Jill Cashen, a representative of the United Food and
Commercial Workers Union, argues that better wages and
working conditions for workers would actually benefit the
consumer:

> The service that customers get when going to
> shop is one of the main reasons why they'll come
> back and be repeat customers. . . . When workers
> are happier--when they have better wages and
> feel like they have a voice at work--their
> service is going to be better, and customers are
> going to come back, and that's what helps build
> a good company.

Without a minimum-wage increase, however, the pay
that fast-food workers receive is unlikely to rise because
they have so little bargaining power. The industry
recruits part-time, unskilled workers, especially young
people, because they are more willing to accept lower pay.
Today, fast-food restaurants also hire disabled persons,
elderly persons, and recent immigrants, for similar
reasons (Schlosser 68, 70). When such employees grow
dissatisfied, they are replaced quickly and easily, with
little disruption of the restaurant's operations.

Fast-food restaurants see an annual turnover rate in employees of over 75% (White). To accommodate easy replacement of workers, companies are steadily reaching a goal of "zero training" for employees by developing more efficient methods and adopting the most advanced kitchen technology. The fast-food kitchen is like an assembly line. Food arrives at the restaurant frozen, and preparation, which involves little actual cooking, is regimented by a manual, which includes such details as how hamburger patties are to be arranged on the grill and the thickness of the fries (Schlosser 68-72). One college student who worked at Wendy's said, "You don't even think when doing work, and you never make any decisions. You're always told what to do. When you make hamburgers there are even diagrams about where the ketchup goes" (Williams). All these factors have contributed to the "de-skilled" nature of fast-food jobs, which corporations believe to be in their best interest because it increases output and reduces the cost of training and wages.

Others, however, claim that the high turnover in fast-food jobs costs employers more than they save through low wages. Fast-food restaurants lose at least $500 for each employee who has to be replaced. Managers are forced to spend time in recruiting, hiring, and training new employees, and additional staff is often needed to help process applications. Current employees are also burdened with extra responsibilities when they pick up the tasks of replaced workers (White).

Other controversies involving wages have plagued the fast-food industry. In 1998, a Washington state jury found Taco Bell guilty of cheating as many as 13,000 workers out of overtime pay (Broydo 20), which, according to federal law, must be paid whenever an employee works more than 40 hours in a week and must be at least one and a half times the normal hourly wage ("General"). In the Taco Bell case, the jury found that managers had forced workers to wait until the restaurant got busy to punch in, had them work after punching out, and failed to record hours correctly. One worker claimed that she regularly worked 70 to 80 hours a week but was paid for only 40. While these are among the worst violations, there is evidence that many other companies deprive workers of earned overtime pay. The Employment Policy Foundation estimates that employees lose $19 billion in unpaid overtime wages every year (Broydo 20).

Fast-food restaurants adopt several other tactics as well to lower costs. Workers are employed "at will," meaning that they are employed only as needed, so if a restaurant is not busy, a manager can send them home early. Managers also avoid the cost of benefits for full-time

employees by hiring large crews and keeping all workers
employed for less than 30 hours per week. Fast-food chains
often reward managers who keep labor costs down, leading
to such abuses as compensating workers with food instead
of money and requiring them to clean the restaurant on
their own time. When such abuses do occur, corporations
try to distance themselves from responsibility. For
example, the McDonald's corporation has no formal wage
policies, so it accepts no blame for the abuses of its
franchisees (Schlosser 74-75).

    In various industries, dissatisfied workers have
turned to labor unions to gain a voice in the workplace
and to secure better wages and working conditions. At
fast-food restaurants, however, union representation is
rare. Organizers attribute their failed attempts to
unionize McDonald's restaurants during the 1960s and 70s
to the high turnover of workers and the corporation's
opposition to unions. John Cook, U.S. labor-relations
chief for McDonald's during the 1970s, said, "Unions are
inimical to what we stand for and how we operate" (qtd. in
Royle 40).

    While the company no longer publicizes its anti-union
stance, its efforts to forestall unions have continued. In
1998, two McDonald's employees in Ohio claimed that they
were fired for trying to organize a union (Hamstra). In

Gould 12

1973, during a union drive at a McDonald's in San Francisco,
a group of employees claimed that they had been threatened
with dismissal if they did not agree to take polygraph
tests and answer questions about their involvement in
union activities. The company was found in violation of
state law and was ordered to stop; nevertheless, the
attempt to unionize was unsuccessful (Schlosser 76).

Ads for fast-food companies always show smiling,
well-scrubbed, contented workers, and the corporations
boast of their employee-friendly policies. Restaurants
recruit workers with slogans such as "Everybody's Somebody
at Wendy's" (Wendy's) and "A Subway restaurant is a really
neat place to work" (Subway). On its website, McDonald's
proclaims, "We're not just a hamburger company serving
people; we're a people company serving hamburgers," and it
claims that its goal is "to be the best employer in each
community around the world" (McDonald's). While many
thousands of teenagers who annually accept work serving
fast food find the experience rewarding, many others
regard the job as anything but friendly. As author Eric
Schlosser concludes, "The real price [of fast food] never
appears on the menu" (9).

Gould 13

Works Cited

Ayoub, Nina C. "Nota Bene." Rev. of Youth at Work: The
    Unionized Fast-Food and Grocery Workplace, by Stuart
    Tannock. Chronicle of Higher Education 25 May 2001:
    A20.

Broydo, Leora. "Worked Over." Utne Reader Jan./Feb. 1999:
    20-21.

Cashen, Jill. Personal Interview. 10 Sept. 2002.

"General Information on the Fair Labor Standards Act
    (FLSA)." U.S. Dept. of Labor Employment Standards
    Administration Wage and Hour Division. 29 Sept. 2002
    <http://www.dol.gov/esa/regs/compliance/whd/
    mwposter.htm>.

Hamstra, Mark. "Unions Seek Momentum from Canadian McD's
    Certification." Nation's Restaurant News 7 Sept.
    1998: 3. MasterFILE Premier. EBSCOhost. 15 Sept. 2002
    <http://web3.epnet.com/>.

Kiger, Patrick. "Risky Business." Good Housekeeping Apr.
    2002: 114. MasterFILE Premier. EBSCOhost. 15 Sept.
    2002 <http://web3.epnet.com/>.

McDonald's USA. "Why McDonald's Has a People Promise and a
    People Vision." 22 Sept. 2002.
    <http://www.mcdonalds.com/corporate/promise/>.

Pass, Caryn G., and Jeffrey A. Spector. "Protecting
    Teens." HR Magazine Feb. 2000: 139. MasterFILE

Premier. EBSCOhost. 15 Sept. 2002 <http://
      web3.epnet.com/>.

"Prohibited Occupations for Non-Agricultural Employees."
      U.S. Dept. of Labor. Elaws--Fair Labor Standards Act
      Advisor. 29 Sept. 2002 <http://www.dol.gov/elaws/esa/
      flsa/docs/haznonag.asp>.

Royle, Tony. "Underneath the Arches." People Management 28
      Sept. 2000: 40.

Schlosser, Eric. Fast Food Nation: The Dark Side of the
      All-American Meal. Boston: Houghton, 2001.

Subway Restaurants. "Subway Job Opportunities." 22 Sept.
      2002 <http://www.subway.com/>.

Van Houten, Ben. "Moving on Up?" Restaurant Business 1
      July 2001: 15. MasterFILE Premier. EBSCOhost. 15
      Sept. 2002 <http://web3.epnet.com/>.

Wendy's International. "Welcome to Wendy's Career Center."
      22 Sept. 2002. <http://www.wendys.com/w-5-0.shtml>.

White, Gerald L. "Employee Turnover: The Hidden Drain on
      Profits." HR Focus Jan. 1995: 15. InfoTrac OneFile.
      21 Sept. 2002 <http://infotrac.galegroup.com/>.

Williams, Tamicah. Personal interview. 24 Sept. 2002.

Yum! Brands. "Great Jobs." 22 Sept. 2002. <http://
      www.yumjobs.com/>.

Zipp, Yvonne. "Virtues of Work vs. Finishing Homework."
      Christian Science Monitor 15 Dec. 1998: 1. MasterFILE

Gould 15

<u>Premier</u>. EBSCOhost. 15 Sept. 2002 <http://
web3.epnet.com/>.

A Sample Personal Research Paper

True to the nature of personal research papers, Justin's paper on whether he should pursue a career in pharmacy is more personal and informal than Emily's paper on fast-food restaurants. Justin's style, however, is fully appropriate for the kind of paper he is writing.

Justin Stafford

ENG 102

Prof. Richard Veit

8 Oct. 2002

Becoming a Pharmacist: Prescription for Success?

I. Why I Am Writing This Paper

Next to finding the person I will marry, selecting the profession that will occupy me for the rest of my life is the most important decision I am likely to make. At various times as a boy and a teenager, I dreamt about exciting jobs, such as being an astronaut, a soldier, a senator, and a rock star. Lately, however, my plans have become more practical, and for the last year I have given serious thought to a career with considerably less sex appeal. Rather than piloting the space shuttle or winning a Grammy, I have begun to think that I can be successful and happy by becoming a pharmacist.

Because the consequences are so great, I do not want to make a hasty decision, and this assignment has given me an opportunity to learn if pharmacy is the right choice and, if so, what I will need to do to pursue this career path.

Stafford 2

II. What I Knew

Science has always been one of my interests and
strengths, so I have focused on science-related fields,
including pharmacy as well as medicine, dentistry,
electrical engineering, and marine biology. All have their
attractions as well as drawbacks. Doctors, for example,
have high incomes and great prestige, but their hours can
be irregular, and their stress level is high. Marine
biology fascinates me, but the number of interested
students far exceeds the number of available jobs.

Although I was much less informed about pharmacy
before writing this paper than I am now, I did know that a
pharmacist spends fewer years in school than either a
doctor or a dentist. I had heard about a nationwide
shortage of pharmacists, so jobs are easy to get and the
pay is excellent. Unlike engineers, pharmacists work on a
daily basis with the general public, something I enjoy. My
guidance counselor in high school raised the possibility
of a career in pharmacy, and the idea appealed to me from
the first. In my hometown, our neighbor, Mr. Eric
Marshburn, was a pharmacist who drove a restored classic
Thunderbird and had a good life. He was an excellent role
model, one of the people I admired growing up, and he is
one reason I am leaning toward this profession.

Stafford 3

About the required education, I knew that I would need to transfer to a pharmacy school, but the details were hazy. Learning the practical aspects of getting from where I am now as a first-year college student to the end point as a professional pharmacist was a major goal of my search. But first, and even more important, I needed to find out for certain if this profession was the right one for me.

III. The Search

My first step was a visit to the university's Career Services Center, where the receptionist directed me to books and brochures about health professions. At his suggestion, I also went online to the Center's career-planning page and took several tests intended to match me with professions suited to my skills and interests. Based on my answers, the "Career Key" test told me I scored highest in "investigative" jobs, followed by "social" and "enterprising." I scored lowest in the "artistic" category. The 70 "investigative" jobs listed on the program include biological scientist, speech pathologist, historian, and--I was pleased to see--pharmacist (Jones). The "Career Interests Game" from the University of Missouri combined several traits and narrowed the list of professions to a dozen choices, one of which, again, was

Stafford 4

pharmacy. The "Career Key" program also linked me to the Department of Labor's Occupational Outlook Handbook, which contained a wealth of information about the pharmacy profession and which provided still more links to Web sites of professional organizations such as the American Association of Colleges of Pharmacy.

I then went online to the university's library databases. I did not find any useful books on my topic, but I had much better luck with periodicals. I searched the EBSCOhost, InfoTrac, and Lexis-Nexis databases using various keywords, including "pharmacy career," "pharmacy education," "pharmacy degree," and "pharmacist shortage," and I was led to many useful articles. I also did an Internet search with the Google search engine using similar phrases. The phrase "pharmacy degree" led me to several sites of universities that offer pharmacy degrees, and I learned about their requirements and the application process. I visited the public library and found one helpful reference book on pharmacy careers.

I next read about the pre-pharmacy major in our university catalog, and I talked with the pre-pharmacy advisor, Ms. Claudia Stack. She gave me information about what courses I would need to take in the next three semesters to be eligible to transfer to a pharmacy program after sophomore year. Finally, when I had read widely

Stafford 5

enough to ask intelligent questions, I undertook what
turned out to be the most valuable step in my search, an
interview with a working pharmacist. I called the Target
discount store and spoke to Mr. Blake Barefoot, the head
pharmacist, who readily agreed to speak with me. We made
an appointment to talk during the slowest part of his day,
and during the twenty-minute interview, he answered all my
questions and discussed the pros and cons of his
profession.

At this point I had an abundance of information. I
was not only informed but enthusiastic and ready to put it
all together. Later, as I made note cards and began
writing, I found some gaps and had further questions,
which caused me to conduct additional searches in the
library's databases.

IV. What I Found

As everyone knows, pharmacists dispense drugs
prescribed by doctors. In the past they mixed ingredients
to form powders, tablets, and ointments, but today most
drugs are packaged by pharmaceutical companies in pills
and capsules in a standard dosage ("Pharmacists," Bureau).
Nevertheless, pharmacists must still be experts in
medications so they can advise patients and doctors about
the effects and dosages of drugs. They must be able to

Stafford 6

protect patients by identifying errors in prescriptions, and they must keep careful records of all the drugs prescribed to each customer by different physicians to be able to identify duplicate drugs or combinations of drugs that can lead to harmful side effects or interactions ("Pharmacists," Encyclopedia 103).

Skills in dealing with people are just as important for pharmacists as scientific skills. Pharmacists advise patients about the proper use and effects of drugs, answer questions about symptoms, and advise about non-prescription medications such as vitamins and cough syrups. Being a drug counselor is an increasingly important role for pharmacists as many doctors have less time to spend with patients than in the past ("Pharmacists," Encyclopedia 103).

Winning the trust of patients and being able to give clear, careful advise are vital since one third of all Americans have "low health literacy" (Kaufman). Todd Dankmyer of the National Association of Retail Druggists says, "If patients don't feel comfortable talking with their pharmacist, they may discontinue prescribed medication on their own, make wrong treatment decisions, or avoid seeking medical help until the side-effects become life-threatening" (qtd. in "Your Local"). Blake Barefoot, the chief pharmacist at the Wilmington Target store, says, "Good people skills are essential, and

pharmacists who lack them usually hate their work."
Others, like Barefoot, consider working with the public
"the most valuable and rewarding part of my job."

In addition to skill in both science and communication,
pharmacists must be orderly and meticulous. Qualifications
listed in the Encyclopedia of Careers and Vocational
Guidance include the following:

> You must be diligent in maintaining a clean and
> ordered work area. You must be exceedingly
> accurate and precise in your calculations, and
> possess a high degree of concentration, in order
> to reduce the risk of error as you compound and
> assemble prescriptions. You must be proficient
> with a variety of technical devices and computer
> systems. ("Pharmacists," Encyclopedia 104)

Clearly, not every personality is suited to this
profession.

When most people think of pharmacists, they picture
the druggists they encounter when getting their
prescriptions filled, but a pharmacy degree can lead to
many different career options. In addition to drug stores
and retail chains, pharmacists can work in primary-care
clinics and nursing homes. They can be employed by
government agencies such as the U.S. Public Health Service
and the Indian Health Service, or they can assess the

Stafford 8

safety and effectiveness of drugs as agents of the Food
and Drug Administration (American, "Career"). They can
also work to discover new drugs as university research
pharmacists, or they can work for a drug manufacturer,
where they can test the chemicals that go into the
company's products, supervise their preparation, or make
sure the company's literature and advertising about drugs
are truthful ("Pharmacists," Encyclopedia 105).

Even being a pharmacist in the local community
presents several career choices, including working in a
hospital, owning an independent pharmacy, and being a
salaried employee in a retail store. Like the others,
hospital pharmacists dispense drugs, but an advantage of
a hospital setting is they can work more closely with
doctors and nurses on patient care as members of a
healthcare team--often right on a patient floor (Levenson).
They can also specialize in areas that may interest them
such as nuclear pharmacy, drug and poison information, and
intravenous therapy (American, "Hospital"). On the other
hand, hospitals are open around the clock, so working
hours are less regular and predictable. As an incentive,
some hospitals offer pharmacists the option of working
seven days on, seven days off, which gives them frequent
mini-vacations and can cut child-care costs in half.
Because hospitals pay pharmacists about six percent less

Stafford 9

than stores, some hospitals offer scholarships for pharmacy school as an incentive, paying for one year of schooling for each year the student agrees to work at the hospital after graduation (Costello 2).

Owning a retail drug store is potentially the most lucrative option, and it allows pharmacists to be their own boss and to set store policies. Retail pharmacists usually begin as salaried employees before gaining the funds and experience to be store owners or co-owners ("Pharmacists," Bureau). A drawback is that the initial capital investment is high and so are the risks. Competition is great, and independent pharmacies now account for only 17% of the prescription market, compared to chain stores at 30%. Mail-order companies (13%) and even supermarket pharmacies (9%) are also growing rapidly and capturing market share (Frederick 45). Profits are further threatened as health insurance companies and Medicare have cut the fees they pay for each prescription. Drug stores are now filling more prescriptions than ever but making less money doing so. One owner lamented, "All I can do is try to survive by controlling expenses and focusing on the part of my business that is profitable-- cards and gift items" (qtd. in Martinez).

Perhaps to avoid the problems of ownership, most pharmacists, by far, choose to work as salaried employees

Stafford 10

in retail stores, but they face problems there as well. In addition to filling prescriptions and advising patients, pharmacists spend on average almost 20% of their time on insurance claims and other paperwork related to payments (Mistretta 37). Hours can be long, but the biggest cause of stress comes from customers. Rafael Saenz, a pharmacy student who worked part-time for a chain drug store, gave an example:

> The clients could be incredibly rude. One Saturday, when we were filling out something like 500 prescriptions, a man demanded to know what was taking so long, and why we couldn't just count the pills and slap a label on the bottle. He didn't realize we were looking for drug interactions and fighting with his insurance company to pay for the medication. (Qtd. in Mangan A43)

To Blake Barefoot, the greatest cause of stress in his job is in "trying to be fast--everyone wants their prescription in five minutes." He says delays come when drugs cannot be refilled or people give the wrong insurance information.

On the positive side, pharmacists are in demand, and employers go to great lengths to make the job attractive. Dramatic growth in the number of pharmacies has led to

Stafford 11

over 5,600 unfilled openings for full-time pharmacists in
chain stores alone, and the shortage is expected to
continue for the foreseeable future ("Pharmacist
Shortage"). As a result, employers are offering high wages
and hiring assistants to take on more of the paperwork.
The average starting salary of full-time pharmacists in
2000 was $67,824 ("Pharmacists," Bureau). Entering
salaries of $80,000 are now common in mid-size cities and
can reach $120,000 in parts of New York and California
(Mangan). Chain stores also offer opportunity for
advancement, and a pharmacist who is willing to relocate
can become a chief pharmacist when a store is opened in a
new location (Barefoot).

    Until recently, a five-year college degree was the
standard for becoming a licensed pharmacist, but today
most states require a six-year Doctor of Pharmacy degree.
At colleges that do not offer this degree, students enter
a pre-pharmacy program in the first two years, where they
take a range of courses, with a focus on the sciences.
They then apply to transfer in their third year to a
pharmacy program to begin a demanding four-year course of
study leading to the D. Pharm. degree. Pre-pharmacy
students are advised that, since admission to a pharmacy
program isn't guaranteed, they should also be working
toward another major. In addition, they should get a job
in a pharmacy part-time or during the summer to gain

Stafford 12

experience and be certain they are choosing the right profession (Pre-Health 13-14).

Despite some negative aspects to the job, pharmacist Blake Barefoot enthusiastically recommends pharmacy, which he has found to be "a wonderful career" that provides "endless potential for personal growth and learning." It is also a job with good pay and security, since "people will always need medicine" (Barefoot).

V. Conclusion

My research has taught me much I did not previously know about pharmacy and has given me a solid basis for making the crucial career decision that faces me, although questions still remain in my mind. From aptitude tests I have learned that my personality and interests are suited to the demands of this career. Income and benefits for pharmacists are even better than I expected, and, at a time when the economy is questionable, it would be comforting to be in a high-paying profession where employment is all but guaranteed.

Still, I must be careful not to take too rosy a view of what may be in store. I must consider, for example, whether I am prepared to spend long hours filing Medicare claims or haggling with insurance companies over a patient's coverage. I must consider the stress and

Stafford 13

frustrations that pharmacists endure. Fortunately, I have
always thrived under pressure and enjoyed challenges. I
love talking and working with people, and I don't get
flustered or angry when confronted by rude or angry
people. I am also famous among friends and family for
being a "neat freak," so the detail and orderliness of the
job also appeal to me.

Writing this paper has solidified my intention to
become a pharmacist. I intend to take the pre-pharmacy
curriculum and apply to several pharmacy schools next
year. I will also be ready for a major in chemistry or
biology in case I am not accepted. During the school year
I am too busy to take a part-time job, but this summer I
will certainly work in a pharmacy to gain first-hand
experience before making a final commitment to the field.

The one question I am least close to answering is
which branch of pharmacy I will enter, because several
look attractive. I can picture myself, for example, as a
uniformed officer of the Public Health Service, traveling
to different assignments and assisting in disasters and
health emergencies. I can also imagine myself in a
laboratory doing drug research, although I would miss the
interaction with people that other options provide. Most
likely--and realistically--I will choose to become a
retail pharmacist, dispensing drugs and drug-related

Stafford 14

advice to neighbors in my community. Fortunately, I will not have to lock into any of these options until pharmacy school. During my study for the Doctor of Pharmacy degree, I will be able to take internships in several areas to learn which is right for me. Pharmacist Blake Barefoot told me, "I learned more doing my internship and in my first six months on the job than in my first four years of college."

My research into pharmacy has made me enthusiastic about my future. Although several momentous decisions lie before me, I am now increasingly hopeful and confident that this profession offers me the best prescription for my happiness and success.

Stafford 15

Works Cited

American Association of Colleges of Pharmacy. "Career
        Options." 16 Sept. 2002 <http://www.aacp.org/>.

---. "Hospital and Institutional Practice." 16 Sept. 2002
        <http://www.aacp.org/>.

Barefoot, Blake. Personal interview. 18 Sept. 2002.

"The Career Interests Game." U of Missouri Career Center.
        14 Sept. 2002 <http://success.missour.edu/career/>.

Costello, Mary Ann. "More than a Job." AHA News 5 Feb.
        2001: 2. Health Source. EBSCOhost. 15 Sept. 2002
        <http://web3.epnet.com/>.

Jones, Lawrence K. "The Career Key." 14 Sept. 2002.
        <http://www.careerkey.org/english/>.

Kaufman, Jeffrey. Report on health literacy. ABC World
        News Tonight. 16 Sept. 2002.

Levenson, Deborah. "Hospitals Struggle to Fill Pharmacy,
        Radiological Technology Staff Positions." AHA News 3
        Apr. 2000: 1-2. Health Source. EBSCOhost. 15 Sept.
        2002 <http://web3.epnet.com/>.

Mangan, Katherine S. "Pharmacy Schools Struggle to Fill
        Their Classes." The Chronicle of Higher Education 2
        Mar. 2001: A43.

Martinez, "Independent Druggists Feel the Pinch." Wenatchee
        Business Journal Mar. 1997: 1+. MasterFILE Premier.
        EBSCOhost. 15 Sept. 2002 <http://web3.epnet.com/>.

Stafford 16

Mistretta, A. J. "Pharmacists' Ranks Thinning as Demand
     for Recruits Grows." New Orleans CityBusiness 20 Aug.
     2001: 36-37.

"Pharmacist Shortage Is Long Term." Chain Drug Review. 5
     Aug. 2002. InfoTrac OneFile. 8 Sept. 2002.
     <http://infotrac.galegroup.com/>

"Pharmacists." Bureau of Labor Statistics. U.S. Dept. of
     Labor. Occupational Outlook Handbook, 2002-03
     Edition. Bulletin 2570. Washington: GPO, 2002.
     257-59. 14 Sept. 2002 <http://stats.bls.gov/oco/
     ocos079.htm>.

"Pharmacists." Encyclopedia of Careers and Vocational
     Guidance. Ed. Holli R. Cosgrove. Vol. 4. Chicago:
     Ferguson, 2000. 103-07.

"Pre-Health Professions Student Manual." UNCW. Handout.

"Your Local Pharmacist Could Be Your Lifesaver." Executive
     Health's Good Health Report Mar. 1995: 1-3. Health
     Source. EBSCOhost. 15 Sept. 2002 <http://
     web3.epnet.com/>.

Justin's paper is about a decision that may have important consequences for him. Personal research projects also work well with less momentous topics; any question that arouses your curiosity is a worthy candidate for such a paper. Emily's paper on fast-food jobs, for example, would also have worked well as a personal paper, particularly if she had her own experience with fast-food work. Likewise, Justin could have written his pharmacy paper as a standard research paper. In fact, he chose to keep himself out of one part of his paper, the "What I Found" section. You might try to imagine what each of these papers would have been like if its author had chosen a different format for it.

| EXERCISE | **Analysis and Discussion** |

Before reading on to learn how Emily and Justin went about researching and writing their papers, answer these questions about their final drafts:

a. What is your impression of the strengths and weaknesses of each paper? Does each have a clear focus; that is, can you give a brief summary of its topic or central idea? Do you find it interesting? informative? clearly written? well organized? Did the author seem to do an adequate job of researching his or her topic?

b. If you were the author's instructor, how would you respond to each paper? If you were the author, would you change it in any way to improve it?

Both Emily's paper about fast food and Justin's about his career decision impressed their instructors and classmates, but they did not get that way all at once. Many stages involving much labor, some frustrations, and many changes preceded the final versions. The history of their creation is as informative as the papers themselves.

■ YOUR RESEARCH SCHEDULE: PLANNING IN ADVANCE

Writing a research paper is a labor-intensive project. Between now and the time you submit your final draft, you will be busy. You will be choosing a topic, exploring it, refining it, chasing down leads, riffling through sources, taking notes, thinking, jotting down ideas, narrowing your project's focus, doing more research and more thinking, writing a tentative draft, revising and revising again.

Obviously, a research project cannot be completed in a day or two. You need to plan now so that you have enough time to undertake each step in the process and so that you can make efficient use of your time. Like Emily Gould, you may be assigned separate deadlines for the various steps in your project. Or you may be given only the final deadline for submitting the completed paper, in which case you

```
                           RESEARCH PROJECT
        Principal Deadlines:                              Due Dates:

        1.   Research prospectus due, including a
             statement of your research topic and a
             working bibliography (see page 381):         _____

        2.   Note cards and preliminary outline due
             (see page 438):                              _____

        3.   In-class editing of completed draft
             (see pages 455–56):                          _____

        4.   Typed good draft due (see page 488):         _____

        5.   Final draft due (see page 488):              _____
```

Figure 8.1 A schedule for a research project.

should establish your own intermediate deadlines for completing each stage. Emily's instructor gave the class a form much like the one shown in Figure 8.1, with a date for each deadline. You can use the form for recording your own schedule.

Some instructors may supply an even more detailed schedule, which may include dates for such additional activities as library orientation, additional editing sessions, and student–instructor conferences. Whatever your schedule, your instructor will certainly concur in this advice: Budget your time wisely, and get started on your project without delay.

A RESEARCH NOTEBOOK

At the beginning of your project you may already have a clear vision—or only the vaguest notion—of what your final draft will eventually look like. Nevertheless, it is probably safe to say that your final paper will be very different from anything you currently imagine. A research project involves many discoveries, and the act of writing usually inspires us to rethink our ideas. Rather than being *assembled,* research papers typically *evolve* through a process of development and change. Prepare for an adventure in which you discover what eventually emerges on paper.

Your finished paper is the end product of that adventure, the last of several stages in the research process. What you learn during that process is probably more important in the long run than the paper itself. It was for this reason that Emily's and Justin's instructors asked each student in their classes to keep a *research notebook.* At every stage of the project, researchers were expected to keep a personal record of their progress. The research notebook is like a diary. In it Emily and Justin recorded what they were doing and what they were expected to do. They wrote about what they had found, the problems they were facing, and their plans for their next steps. Justin used his notebook as the raw material for the "search" section of his personal research paper.

The writing you do in a research notebook should be informal, not polished. Unlike the research paper itself, the notebook is written to yourself, not to outside readers. When you are finished, you have a record of your research process. But there is also another benefit to keeping a notebook. Both Emily and Justin found that it helped them make decisions and focus their thoughts. In addition, many of the passages both writers used in their papers came from ideas they had scribbled in their notebooks.

You should use a spiral notepad that you can carry with you when you do research, though you may also want to use your word processor (if you have one) to record some entries. You will start using your notebook from the very beginning—now—as you select and focus your research topic.

YOUR RESEARCH TOPIC

Only on rare occasions do researchers have to *choose* a topic. Such an occasion might come about for a freelance writer of magazine articles who wants to select not only a fresh subject that will interest readers and an editor but also one about which she can find enough information through interviews, legwork, and library research.

In most cases, however, researchers already have their topics before them. A situation arises that demands exploration. For example, in order for a detective novelist to write convincingly about a counterfeiting ring, he must do research to learn how counterfeiters actually operate. A historian with a theory about the causes of the Russian Revolution would have to discover the available facts about the period as well as learn what theories other historians have proposed. A lawyer writing a brief for a criminal case must research legal precedents to know how similar cases have been decided in the past and to provide herself with convincing arguments. Most researchers begin with a strong curiosity about a topic and a need to know.

As you begin your own research project, you may already have decided on a topic. Perhaps your class has been reading and talking about an interesting issue such as nuclear policy, teenage suicide, the future of the family farm, or dating practices in foreign countries. Your discussion may have raised questions in your mind, questions that you can answer only through research. Besides satisfying your own curiosity, you can perform a service for your instructor and classmates by informing them about what you have learned. For you, a research paper is a natural.

On the other hand, you may not yet have chosen a specific topic. Perhaps your instructor, like Emily's and Justin's, has left the selection of a topic up to you. Perhaps you have been given a choice within a limited area, such as a current event, the life and views of a public figure, or your career goals. In any case, it is important for you to select a topic you can work with. Because many hundreds of topics may appeal to you, deciding on any one can be hard.

You begin with your curiosity. Your research is aimed at answering a question in your mind, at satisfying your urge to know. For that reason, it is usually helpful at the outset of a project to state your topic in the form of a ***research question.*** Rather than just naming a general area for your paper, such as "racial policy in the armed forces," it is often more useful to frame your project as a question to be answered, such as "How has the military dealt with discrimination?" or "How has the struggle against discrimination in the American armed forces compared with the struggle in the civilian world?" Perhaps you have formed a ***hypothesis,*** a theory that you would like to test. In this case your question would begin, "Is it true that . . . ?" For example, in reading about the plagues that devastated Europe during the thirteenth century, you might have speculated that in spite of modern scientific advances, the reactions of people to epidemics have not changed much in seven hundred years. If you decided to test this hypothesis through research, your question might be, "Are effects of the AIDS epidemic on our society similar to the effects of the Black Death on medieval Europe?"

Three factors are critical in framing a good research question. Your topic should have the following qualities. It should be

1. **Appealing.** This is the most crucial factor. Your research should be aimed at answering a question that genuinely arouses your curiosity or that helps you solve a problem. If you are not involved with your topic, it is unlikely that you will write an essay that will interest readers. The interest you have in your topic will also determine whether the many hours you spend on it will be rewarding or agonizing.

2. **Researchable.** You may be curious about the attitudes of college students in Japan toward religion, for example, but if you can locate only one or two sources on the subject in your local libraries, you will not be able to write a research paper about it.

3. **Narrowed.** If your question is "What is astronomy?" you will find no shortage of materials. On the contrary, you will certainly discover that your topic is too broad. You can find hundreds of books and entire journals devoted to astronomy. However, you cannot do justice to so vast a topic in a paper of a few thousand words. You will need to narrow your topic to one you can research and cover adequately. You may decide to concentrate on black holes, for example, as a more focused topic. Later on, as you continue your research and begin writing, you may narrow the topic still more, perhaps to a recent theory or discovery about black holes.

GENERATING IDEAS

Unless you already have a question in mind that you are eager to answer, or unless you are facing a pressing decision for which you need information, you will have to do some exploring and thinking about a general subject before you arrive at a properly appealing, researchable, and narrowed research question. Several techniques for stimulating ideas can help you in your selection, including brainstorming and clustering.

Brainstorming

If you were asked right now to declare some possible research topics, you might find it difficult to do so. After a few minutes of wrestling with the problem, you might finally come up with a few topics, but you might find them to be neither original nor exciting. Yet there are literally hundreds of topics that you not only would enjoy researching but also could write about well. The trick is to stimulate your mind to think of them. *Brainstorming* is one helpful technique. It is simply a way of forcing your mind to bring forth many possible topics, under the theory that one idea can lead to another and that, if enough ideas are brought forth, at least one will click.

On the day they announced the assignment, Emily's and Justin's instructors led their classes through several activities to stimulate their thinking. Following are some examples of brainstorming exercises.

EXERCISES   **Brainstorming: Random Listing**

1. We start with a light and unintimidating exercise. The following is a random list of concepts in no particular order and of no particular significance. Read the list rapidly and then, in your research notebook, begin your own list, adding as many items to it as you can. Give free play to your imagination. List whatever comes to mind without regard to whether it is serious or would make a reasonable research topic. Save those concerns for later. For now, write rapidly, and have some fun with your list.

surnames	water fountains	swimsuits
clowns	sea horses	salesmanship
cans	con artists	pro wrestling
lip sync	cremation	campaign buttons
lipstick	hiccups	prep schools
war paint	blueprints	sponges
juggling	Russian roulette	snuff
teddy bears	triplets	fads
cave dwellers	women's weightlifting	cavities
haircuts	chocolate	advertising jingles
ways to fasten shoes	frisbees	plastic surgery
high heels	coffins	bartending
hit men	chain letters	mirrors
cheerleaders	tanning	juke boxes
revenge	baldness	icebergs
bicycles	wigs	mermaids
televangelists	facial hair	tribal societies
silicon chips	earrings	fast food
college colors	longevity	cyclones
company logos	boomerangs	Beetle Bailey
roller skates	fuel injection	toilets

tractors	fertility	laughing
warts and birthmarks	nomads	cable cars
freckles	film editing	Mardi Gras
tattoos	spelunking	free gift with purchase

2. Because one idea leads to another in brainstorming, the ideas of other people can stimulate your own thinking. You can cross-fertilize your imagination by looking at other students' lists. After you have listed items for a few minutes, you can (a) exchange lists with one or more classmates or (b) join members of your class in calling out items (perhaps in orderly turns, perhaps randomly) as one or more people write them on the blackboard.

3. Stimulated by these new ideas, resume listing for another few minutes.

4. When you have finished, reread your list and circle the items that seem most interesting to you. What about these items stimulates your curiosity? See if you can now pose five or six questions about them for which you would like answers.

You may be concerned that some of the topics you listed or some of the questions you posed are not particularly serious or do not seem scholarly or deep. You need not worry, since any subject that provokes your genuine interest and curiosity is worth exploring and can be given serious treatment in a research paper. The item "lipstick" in the preceding list, for example, may seem frivolous at first, but it can lead to many serious questions: What is lipstick made of (now and in the past)? How long have people been using lipstick? How has society regarded its use in earlier times? Does it symbolize anything? Is its use widespread throughout the world? Is it ever prohibited by governments or by religions? Why do American women use it but not (for the most part) American men? Such questions point to an interesting and rewarding research project. A student who pursued them would find much information. In the course of research, the student could certainly narrow the topic—perhaps to "What has society thought about lipstick?"— and write an informative, worthwhile paper.

Brainstorming: Focused Listing

EXERCISE

This brainstorming exercise is more focused than the preceding one. In your notebook, list as many ideas as you can in response to the following questions. Write rapidly, listing whatever comes to mind. List phrases, rather than complete sentences. If one topic strikes you as having possibilities as a research topic, keep listing ideas about it until you have explored it to your satisfaction. You do not need to answer every question, but do not stop listing ideas until your instructor tells you that time is up.

- What have been your favorite courses in high school and college? What topics in those courses did you find interesting? For each topic, write as many phrases associated with it as you can.

- What major are you considering? List some particular subjects you hope to explore in your major.

- What career are you considering? What specific branches of that field interest you? What jobs can you imagine yourself holding in the future? List several possibilities.

- What recent or historical events or discoveries are associated with your career interests or major field? What notable persons are associated with these areas? List some things you know about them.

- List magazine articles, books, movies, and memorable television programs that you have encountered lately. List some specific ideas or topics that they bring to mind.

- List some events or controversies that concern you. What news stories have aroused your interest or concern? What historical events have you wanted to learn more about? What do you consider the major changes that have taken place during your lifetime in world affairs? In science and technology? In the way we lead our lives? What problems face us in the future?

- What topics have you read about because you needed or wanted to learn more about them? What problems do you now need to resolve?

- What decisions will you have to make soon? Decisions about school? career? lifestyles? morality? romance? friends? family? purchases? leisure time?

- What areas are you an expert in? What are your chief interests and hobbies?

- What are some of the major gaps in your background? What should you know more about than you do?

- What notable people do you most admire? What people have had achievements that mean something to you? Think of men, women, historical figures, living people, scientists, artists, athletes, politicians. What famous people do you pity or consider villains?

Emily's class spent about fifteen minutes listing ideas for the preceding exercise. Afterward, students shared lists with classmates and discussed their ideas. They also jotted down any new ideas that came to them. Emily's list filled two pages in her notebook. Here are excerpts:

Favorite subjects
   History
      —American history
      —20th century
   Government and politics—current events, law school?
Possible careers
   Journalism
      —TV news
      —print media—Time, Newsweek
      —politics based

. . .Controversies–healthy and unhealthy food
  –vegetarian vs. meat-eating
  –health risks
    obesity–heart disease, diabetes
    causes–fatty diets, fast food, large portions, overeating
  –risky diets, eating disorders
  –body image

Emily's list was not an orderly, logical outline, nor was it meant to be. However, this short excerpt shows her mind actively at work, listing and shaping ideas. Clearly she hadn't yet found her research topic at this point, but even at this early stage the germ of her topic was apparent in her list. Among the controversies she noted was unhealthy eating, and, almost as a tangential thought, she mentions fast food, which, several permutations later, would become the eventual topic of her paper. The complete list included many other ideas as well, most of which turned out to be dead ends. But several ideas captured Emily's interest and provided options as she journeyed toward her topic.

Here are some excepts from Justin's list:

. . .3. Careers
    a. Pharmacy—most promising
        benefits: income, job in demand
        skills: science, sales/personal
    b. Marine biologist
    c. Research chemist
    d. Physician's associate
    e. Other science-related
    f. Military—short-term
  4. Recent events
    a. Anthrax scare
    b. Ban on whale meat
    c. Medicare prescription benefits
    d. Required doctoral degree for pharmacists
. . .8. Major decisions
    a. Career
    b. Major
    c. Marriage
    d. Part-time job . . .

In contrast to Emily, Justin hit on his topic—his interest in pursuing a career as a pharmacist—almost immediately. The brainstorming question "What career are you considering?" coincided so exactly with a decision he was wrestling with that he knew instantly what he would research and write about. Justin's certainty about his topic at this point is a rarity. In many cases, brainstorming activities do not lead directly and immediately to a topic the writer recognizes as ideal. Instead, they open up many pathways for the writer to explore. When pursued, some of those paths will lead to still other paths for the writer to take, until eventually the right destination is reached.

Developing an Idea: Clustering

A more concentrated form of brainstorming can be called *clustering* or *mapping.* It is a technique designed to stimulate the development of many ideas related to one given idea. Emily's instructor gave her class the following exercise.

EXERCISE   **Clustering Ideas**

Review the lists you have made thus far and circle all the items that look promising as research topics. If you have time, ask one or two classmates to do the same thing, each using a different color ink. Finally, select one possible topic (this is not a final commitment) and write it in the center of a blank page in your notebook. Using it as a starting point, radiate from it whatever ideas come to mind. The clusterings of Emily and Justin are shown in Figures 8.2 and 8.3.

Figure 8.2 Emily's clustering.

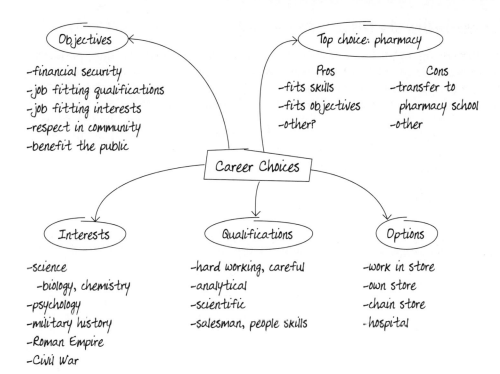

Figure 8.3 Justin's clustering.

Finally, Emily's instructor asked class members to call out question that arose from the idea they had listed (or new ones that occurred to them), while she wrote them on the board. Here are some typical questions offered by the students:

- Does having a baby increase a mother's IQ?
- What effects does El Niño have on weather?
- Are big-time college athletics corrupt?
- Do high CD prices represent price fixing?
- Was Susan B. Anthony an American hero?
- How is wireless technology changing American society?
- Are violent video games harmful to children?
- What strategies work in quitting smoking?
- What are causes of body dysmorphic disorder?
- Why do wealthy people shoplift?
- Is phonics a useful strategy for teaching reading?
- What are benefits and drawbacks of state lotteries?
- What role did music play in the Civil Rights movement?

Also on the list was a question from Emily, "What effects does fast food have on our health?"

Prewriting exercises are not magic formulas that instantly produce perfect research topics. Instead, if all goes well, they begin a chain reaction that leads you, however circuitously, to your eventual topic. The idea-generating exercises that Emily and Justin engaged in pointed them in helpful directions. Justin was that rare student who knew almost immediately exactly what would be the focus of his research. His mind was already occupied by a decision with an upcoming deadline: If he was going to enter a career in pharmacy, he would need to declare a pre-pharmacy major almost immediately. Emily, in contrast, arrived at her research topic by a far more indirect route. Most of her brainstorming centered around food-related health issues, a topic she had been reading about. As her clustering shows, she thought about vegetarianism, diets, and obesity. The latter led her to causes of obesity, including the eventual topic of her paper, fast food. At this early stage, she was focusing on the health effects of fast food, and it would still be some time before she settled on the ultimate topic of her paper, workers in fast-food restaurants.

A research project is like a puzzle. When you begin, you never know how it will turn out. After all, the purpose of research is to answer questions for which you do not currently have answers. When you start, you cannot know what answers you will find. You cannot even be sure your questions are good ones. These discoveries are made only as you undertake the actual research and as you begin to write about your findings. You are almost certain to find that the research paper you end up writing will be quite different from your current expectations. What you learn along the way will cause you to change plans and go in new and often unexpected directions. You are sure to meet surprises. A good researcher must be flexible, able to adapt to whatever new ideas and information present themselves. For this reason you need not be concerned if you now have only a tentative idea of the topic of your paper. Your topic will take firmer shape (and perhaps a very different shape) as you undertake your research. The following chapters show you how to conduct that research.

9 Tools for Finding Sources

■ BEGINNING YOUR RESEARCH

Having generated ideas about likely topics for papers, Emily and Justin needed to do preliminary research to learn more about these topics and to bring their research questions into sharper focus. A visit to the library and some exploration of the resources available to them via computer were the logical next steps. From their instructors they received assignments similar to the one that follows.

Do some preliminary research to explore the topic you are considering.

- Learn more about your topic by reading about it in encyclopedias and other general reference sources. If the topic seems appropriate, take notes and see if you can narrow your focus to a specific question.

- See if your topic is researchable by assembling a working bibliography of about a dozen sources that you intend to consult. (Working bibliographies are further explained in Chapter 11.) Use a variety of search tools (explained in this chapter), and include books, periodicals, newspapers, and electronic media, as appropriate for your topic. If, for example, you are writing about a recent event, newspaper articles will be a significant source of information. On the other hand, if you are writing about an event from ancient history, you may not discover any newspaper sources.

- If adequate sources are not available, see if you can broaden your topic or switch to another one. If you find too many sources, read more about the subject and narrow your paper's focus within more manageable limits.

- Make sure your sources are available. Find out if the library has the periodicals and newspapers you are seeking. Check books out. If necessary, order books from other libraries through InterLibrary Loan. Ask the circulation desk to recall desired books that have been checked out by others. If most of the books are gone, however, someone else is probably writing on your topic, and the sources you need may not become available in time. If so, avoid needless frustration by switching now to another topic.

- Do some quick reading in your sources to learn more about your topic. It might be wise to ask a professor or some other authority on your subject for suggestions about the topic and for further research sources.

- Decide what additional sources can provide valuable information for your project. Write letters to request information, if necessary. Arrange interviews in advance by setting up appointments. (Letters and interviews are discussed in Chapter 10.)

- Be sure to record your discoveries, questions, and other experiences with locating sources in your research notebook.

As they begin their first research project in college, few students are experts in using the library. Many are confused and intimidated by electronic resources such as online databases and the World Wide Web. By the time students have finished the project, however, they have learned how to find information in their library as well as to access other sources throughout the world via electronic communication.

YOUR CAMPUS LIBRARY

Your purpose in conducting a research project is not only to inform yourself about your topic by discovering information but to inform others as well by making your discoveries available in a paper. Learning is, after all, a cooperative venture, and scholars have an obligation to pass on to others what they have learned. For that reason, a wealth of important information and ideas produced by scholars has been collected and located in a convenient place for your use—your college library.

As any quick browse through the library will make abundantly clear, there are a great many potential sources out there—written about an almost unlimited number of topics. Finding information about any particular topic might seem an impossible task. Fortunately, however, the means are available for locating almost anything you are looking for. Your library offers not only *research sources* themselves, such as books and periodicals, but also *search tools,* which allow you to discover what research sources are available for your topic and to locate them. These tools include the library's book catalog, online and printed guides to periodical and newspaper sources, and reference librarians. Search tools can give you a great deal of power, allowing you to discover information on almost any topic. Of immediate interest to you, of course, is that they allow you to find sources for your research paper. This chapter, with its accompanying exercises, is intended to make you proficient in the use of various search tools.

ELECTRONIC RESOURCES

A generation ago, college students searched for books about their research topics by flipping through index cards alphabetized in drawers in a library's card catalog. To find periodical and newspaper sources, they paged laboriously through dozens of bound indexes. The computer revolution changed all that, and today most library searches are conducted at a keyboard in front of a computer screen. Not only have searches become simpler and more convenient, but today's students have easy access to vastly more sources than did scholars just a few years ago.

Electronic searches have themselves undergone rapid change. A few years ago, the student researcher had to visit many different library terminals, each dedicated to a particular index or database. Today it is typical for a college library to have a *central information system,* a single online site from which a student can locate all the library's holdings, find sources in any of dozens of electronic databases, and even read many sources directly on the viewing screen. Because most library information systems are accessible on the Internet, students may avail themselves of many library resources from their home computers or at computer workstations around campus.

Being able to link up with your college library from home is only a small part of the research power now available to you through computers. For example, if you wanted, you could also search the holdings of a university library in Australia, copy a file stored on a computer in Scotland, or ask a question of a scholar in Nigeria. Before we explore the various tools for locating sources, both within and outside the library, we need some general background about electronic resources. To understand electronic resources and acquire skill in using them, there is no substitute for hands-on practice, but the following can provide a useful introduction.

A collection of material that is available electronically (by computer) is generally referred to as a *database.* Databases can be classified as either portable or online. A *portable database* is one that can reside within a particular computer, such as a program on a diskette or a CD-ROM file. In contrast, an *online database* is located at a distant site, such as a host computer or another computer on a network. For you to access it, your computer must communicate with that site. A vast and ever-growing number of databases is available online. These include valuable search tools such as indexes that enable you to locate sources, electronic encyclopedias, and whole libraries of data.

Networks

To gain access to an online database, your computer terminal needs to be connected to another computer containing the database. Such an arrangement by which a number of computers can contact each other is called a *network.* Your college is likely to have its own *local network* in which most computers on campus are connected through a central computer, known as a *server.* This connectivity allows students and faculty to share files and use e-mail to communicate. Most *college library networks* are tied in with the larger campus network, providing patrons with access to library information from classroom, office, and dormitory computers. Since colleges put restrictions on who may use their network, you may need to apply for an **account** and receive an **address** and a **password.**

Smaller networks are often joined in a larger network. For example, your college library network may be joined with networks from other regional libraries, so that you can search for works in several different libraries simultaneously. The linking of libraries in such a consortium also enables students at one campus to find and borrow works owned by another campus.

Finally, networks throughout the world, most likely including your campus network, are joined together in the largest and grandest network of them all, the **Internet.** Originally begun by the U.S. government, this network has grown to allow computer users almost anywhere on the planet to communicate and share information. Any Internet user can send and receive messages with any other user via e-mail. For example, you could direct an inquiry about your research question to a scholar in Finland, provided you knew that person's e-mail address. You could also join one of countless **discussion lists** devoted to particular topics. A message sent to a list is automatically forwarded to all its subscribers. For instance, if you were researching voting patterns of women, you might post an inquiry on the PoSciM list, which is devoted to a discussion of political science issues (and maybe also to WmSt-L, a women's studies list). Other subscribers interested in your topic would be likely to reply. An index to thousands of discussion lists can be found online at http://paml.alastra.com.

Another way to follow an ongoing e-mail discussion about a particular topic is by consulting a **newsgroup** or a **bulletin board.** These are very much like actual bulletin boards, where anyone can read and post messages. Unlike discussion lists, where all items are e-mailed directly to subscribers, newsgroups and bulletin boards are "places" on the network that you can "visit" whenever you choose, but no messages are sent to your e-mail in-box.

By far the most popular component of the Internet is the **World Wide Web,** which allows users to read (and create) attractive presentations of text, graphics, and sound known as **Web pages.** Because virtually anyone can post material on the Web, there is no limit to the variety of available presentations. For example, you can explore your college's **home page,** which is linked to many other Web pages containing information about its programs, faculty, and resources. You can also read electronic "magazines" (often called *zines*) on the Web or consult the Web for instant news, weather, and sports updates. The variety is so great that "surfing the Net" has become a recreational obsession for many. However, because almost anyone can post whatever they choose on the Web without oversight or restriction, much information found on Web pages is of dubious merit. Students need to take special care in evaluating material from Web sources.

USING YOUR LIBRARY'S RESEARCH TOOLS

It is worth repeating that while search tools can give you access to a vast quantity of information, the *quality* of that information varies widely. More than ever, student researchers need to use careful judgment about the reliability of their sources and the usefulness of information they encounter. Since the number of channels by which you can access research sources is so great, the following sections of this chapter will focus on those most likely to be helpful. Still, many such tools—old and new—are described, and they can seem intimidating at first. Don't allow yourself to be overwhelmed. It is not necessary for you to absorb all the information in a single sitting. Nor do you need to memorize the names of all the available reference sources and the procedures for using them. Instead, regard this chapter as a guide that you can consult whenever you need it, now and in years to come. By examining the resources that are described here one at a time and by gaining experience with their use through the practice exercises, you will soon develop a solid and confident command of the tools needed for doing college research.

Most college libraries allow you access to a great variety of resources, and you can begin your search from one convenient online screen, the home page of the library's central information system. Once you log on to this page, you are presented with a menu of choices. Different libraries set up their home pages in different ways, but most have similar features, and we will explore some typical and important research tools likely to be available through your college library's online system.

The following two menu options are a staple of most college library systems:

- **Search the library catalog.** This option allows you to find books and other items in your library's holdings.
- **Search electronic indexes and databases.** This option allows you to find articles in journals, newspapers, and other periodicals.

In addition, the menu may allow you to learn library hours, view your own library record and renew items you have borrowed, see what materials your instructor has placed on reserve, and even search catalogs at other libraries.

Finding Books and Other Library Holdings

Let us begin by examining the first of the two options just mentioned, a search of your library's catalog. The library's holdings include books, periodicals, videocassettes, sound recordings, and many other materials—and all are indexed in its online catalog. The catalog menu will present you with a number of search options, including the following:

- Author search
- Title search
- Subject search
- Keyword search
- Call number search

If you know what author or book title you are seeking, you can do an *author search* or a *title search.* Merely enter the name of the author or title, and information is displayed.

When you are engaged in a research project, you will be looking to find what books are available on a particular topic, and you will want to conduct a ***subject search*** or a ***keyword search.*** In a subject search, you enter the subject you are searching. Only particular subjects are indexed, namely the subject headings designated by the Library of Congress. Since you may not know the exact subject heading, a keyword search may be the handiest way to begin your search for books on your topic.

Doing a Keyword Search

In a keyword search, you enter one or more words that are likely to appear in a work's title, in its subject, or in catalog notes about its contents. Imagine, for example, that you are interested in researching the widely believed myths known as "urban legends." These are popular but unfounded stories, such as the rumor that a certain brand of bubble gum contained spider eggs or the myth that alligators live in the sewers of New York City. If you entered "legend," you would find that hundreds of works in your library are referenced by this keyword, most of which would have nothing to do with urban legends. (In our library, the entries we found included a book about basketball legend Michael Jordan and a CD of Irish fairy tales.) To eliminate the clutter, you can narrow your search by typing in two or more words, such as "urban legend." Most library catalogues treat two words as a phrase and will search for instances of those words appearing side by side.

Library Catalog Searches

- Type in one or more words that may appear in the title, subject, author name, or notes.
- Multiple words are searched as a phrase: The entries "college English" and "English college" will produce different results.
- Use *AND* to search for entries containing *both* words (not necessarily together):

    alcohol AND law
- Use *OR* to search for entries containing *either* word:

    college OR university
- Use a wildcard symbol (asterisk) to represent missing letters: The entry "educat* polic*" will produce results for "educational policy" and "education policies," but also "educating police."

One limitation to keyword searches is that a computer is very literal-minded. If you include the word "legend," it will ignore instances of "legends." Most catalogs allow you to use a ***wildcard symbol***, usually an asterisk, to represent optional characters. For example, in a keyword search of our college catalog, we found

KEYWORD ⬥	urban legend*		UNC Coastal Library Consortium ⬥	Search	
	Sorted by Date				
Num	**Mark**	**KEYWORDS (1–6 of 13)**		**Medium**	**Year**
1	☐	Net crimes & misdemeanors : outmaneuvering the spammers, swi		Book	2002
2	☐	Encyclopedia of urban legends / Jan Harold Brunvand ; artwor		Book	2001
3	☐	The truth never stands in the way of a good story / Jan Haro		Book	2000
4	☐	Urban legends : the as–complete–as–one–could–be guide to mod		Book	2000
5	☐	Urban legends final cut [videorecording] / Columbia ; Phoeni		Videorecording	2000
6	☐	Spiders in the hairdo : modern urban legends / collected and		Book	1999

Save Marked Records   JUMP TO AN ENTRY 13

Figure 9.1 Results of a keyword search for "urban legend*" in a library catalog.

only one entry by entering just "urban legend." However, we found thirteen entries when we entered the term "urban legend*." Researchers must be judicious in
their use of wildcards, however, because they can sometimes make a search too
broad. For example, a search for "urban*" would return entries about urban legends, but also many unwanted entries containing the words "urbane," "urbaniza-
tion," "Pope Urban VIII," and "Urbana, Illinois." Partial results of our search using the keywords "urban legend*" are shown in Figure 9.1, in which the first six
of thirteen titles are shown on the screen.

You could make a list of all the works that interest you by checking the boxes
to the left of their titles. Later, when you have finished all your searches, you
could ask for a display of all the works you marked. Alternatively, you could examine entries immediately. For example, if you clicked on the sixth title in Figure
9.1, *Spiders in the Hairdo: Modern Urban Legends*, you would be shown a record,
part of which is reproduced in Figure 9.2. This screen gives much information
about the book, including its authors, title, publisher, and length (111 pages). The
fact that the book was published in 1999 tells you how current it is. The fact that
the book contains "bibliographic references" tells you that you might go to pages
110 and 111 to find a list of other works on the topic. The information in the
boxes tells you where to go to find the book (its location and call number) and

Author	Holt, David
Title	**Spiders in the hairdo : modern urban legends / collected and retold by David Holt & Bill Mooney**
Publisher	Little Rock, Ark. : August House, 1999

LOCATION	CALL #	STATUS
UNCW General Collection	GR105 .H63 1999	AVAILABLE

Description	111 p. : ill. ; 22 cm
Bibliography	Includes bibliographical references (p. 110-111)
Subject	Urban folklore -- United States
	Legends -- United States
	United States -- Social life and customs
Alt author	Mooney, William
Add title	Modern **urban legends**
ISBN	0874835259 (tpb. : alk. paper)

Figure 9.2 Excerpt from a book record.

that it is available (not checked out by another patron). When a book's status is "unavailable," you can ask the circulation desk to send a *recall notice* to the borrower, but you would receive no guarantee that it will be returned in time to meet your project's deadline.

Notice that in Figure 9.2, seven different items are underlined, which means that each is a computer *link* to further data, and each provides a useful way to find additional sources on your topic. If you were to use your mouse to click on the first author's name, "Holt, David," you would be shown a list of all the holdings in the library written by that author. If you clicked on the books's call number, you would be shown a list of works with similar call numbers. Since books are numbered according to their topic, this is a handy way to see what other related items (in this case, about folktales) are in your library. Finally, three different subject headings are listed. You could click on any one of them to do a subject search for this heading.

It should also be noted that your search need not be limited to the holdings in your own library. One useful tool for searching the holdings of over 40,000 libraries worldwide is the OCLC *WorldCom* database, which is available among the online tools on most college library Web sites. Our search on WorldCom for books using the keywords "urban legends" found forty-nine entries. For each entry, WorldCom noted if the work was available in our library. For a work not available locally, WorldCom provides a list of libraries in nearby states that hold the book. A work found in another library can be borrowed by your library through an *InterLibrary Loan*. You may find it useful to check the collections of libraries specializing in your subject. If you were researching automotive engineering, you would be wise to check libraries of major universities in Michigan, a state with a large automobile industry. Likewise, if you were researching manatees, you would expect to find more works on the subject at the University of Florida than, say, at the University of North Dakota. Ask your librarian for help in searching the collections of other libraries.

EXERCISES   ## Using Your Library's Central Information System

Use your college library's online catalog to answer the following questions. Although these exercises may remind you of a scavenger hunt, they are intended to familiarize you with the resources in your library and to practice important research skills that you will use many times in the future.

1. These questions can be answered by doing an author search on your college library's catalog:

    a. How many authors with the surname Churchill have works in your library?

    b. How many author listings are there for Sir Winston Churchill (1874–1965)?

    c. View the record for one book by Sir Winston Churchill (and print it, if your computer terminal is connected to a printer). What is the book's full title? its call number? Is the book currently available in your library, or has it been checked out? In what city was the book published? by what publisher? in what year? How many pages long is the book? What subject headings could you use in a subject search to find similar works on the same topic?

2. Do a subject search, using one of the subject headings found in 1c, above. How many works does your library have on that subject? What are the title, author, and call number of one of those works (other than the Churchill book)?

3. Find an author whose last name is the same as or close to your own. Record the title and call number of one book by this author.

4. How would you use your library catalog to locate works *about,* rather than by, Sir Winston Churchill? How many works does your library have about him? Record the author, title, and call number of one such book.

5. How many books does your library have with the title (or partial title) *Descent of Man?* Who are the authors of these books?

6. Do a call number search to answer these questions: How many works are there in your library whose call numbers begin with TL789? What subject(s) are books with this number about? Record the author, title, and call number of one such book.

7. To answer this question, you may need guidance from your instructor or librarian: How can you limit your call number search to only those works (with call number TL789) that were published after 1990? How many such works are there in your library's collection? Can you limit your search to TL789 works with the word "flying" in the title? How many such works are in your library?

8. Do a keyword search to find works on your research project topic (or another topic that interests you). What subject headings do you find for these works? Use the most appropriate of these headings to do a subject search. Now use the WorldCom database to see what additional works on your topic are available at other libraries in your state. Record information about works likely to help you in your research project.

Encyclopedias and Other General Reference Works

General reference works, books, periodicals, newspapers, and microforms are some of the resources in college libraries. Because so many sources are available, it is helpful to approach a search for information with a strategy in mind and to turn first to resources that are most likely to be of help. Before you search in particular directions, you need a broad overview of your topic. General reference works are often a good place to begin.

General reference works, such as encyclopedias and almanacs, offer information about many subjects. They are located in the reference section of your library, where they can be consulted but not checked out. Many encyclopedias, dictionaries, and almanacs are also available online or in CD-ROM format. In addition to text and pictures, some online works allow you to view film clips and hear audio as well. Another advantage of online encyclopedias is that they are frequently updated, and the latest edition is always available to you.

General encyclopedias have alphabetically arranged articles on a wide variety of subjects. *Encyclopedia Americana* and *Collier's Encyclopaedia* both contain accessible articles that can provide you with helpful introductions to unfamiliar subjects. The print version of the *New Encyclopaedia Britannica* is somewhat more complicated to use in that it is divided into various sections, including the "Micropaedia," which consists of short articles and cross-references to other articles in the set, and the "Macropaedia," which consists of longer, more detailed articles. Encyclopedias published on CD-ROM disks or available online include *Encarta* and *Britannica Online.* One-volume **desk encyclopedias,** such as the *New Columbia Encyclopedia,* can be quick and handy guides to basic information about a subject. **Almanacs,** such as *Information Please Almanac, Atlas and Yearbook,* and *The World Almanac & Book of Facts,* contain tables of information and are handy sources of much statistical information.

Specialized encyclopedias, restricted to specific areas of knowledge, can provide you with more in-depth information. Many such works are available—the online catalog at the university where we teach lists over a thousand works under the subject heading "Encyclopedia." By way of example, here are just a few from the beginning of the alphabet: *Encyclopedia of Adolescence, Encyclopedia of African-American Civil Rights, Encyclopedia of Aging and the Elderly, Encyclopedia of Alcoholism, Encyclopedia of Allergy and Environmental Illness, Encyclopedia of Amazons, Encyclopedia of American Social History, Encyclopedia of Animated Cartoons, Encyclopedia of Arms Control and Disarmament,* and *Encyclopedia of Assassinations.* You can use your college catalog to locate a specialized encyclopedia dealing with your research topic. You can also browse the reference section in the appropriate stacks for your topic; sections are marked by Library of Congress call numbers (e.g., BF for psychology, HV for crime, N for art, etc.).

EXERCISES | ## Using General Reference Works

1. Locate a specialized encyclopedia dealing with your research topic or another topic that appeals to you.
2. Look up that same topic in the print version of the *New Encyclopaedia Britannica* (look first in the index, which will direct you to either the "Micropaedia" or the "Macropaedia") and then in an online or CD-ROM encyclopedia. Compare the treatment and coverage of the topic in these different works.
3. Determine if information about the same topic can also be found in a desk encyclopedia or in an almanac.

4. Finally, write a one-page account of what you discovered. In particular, what kinds of information are found in the different reference works? How do the treatments of the topic differ?

FINDING ARTICLES: MAGAZINES, JOURNALS, AND NEWSPAPERS

Articles in magazines, journals, and newspapers are among the sources used most frequently by student researchers in composition classes, for several reasons: Articles are written on a variety of subjects; they make timely information available right up to the most recent issues; and, being relatively brief, they tend to focus on a single topic. Your college library is likely to have recent issues of hundreds of magazines and journals and of many local, national, and international newspapers. In addition, back issues of these publications are available either in bound volumes or on *microforms* (miniaturized photographic copies of the material). Many electronic indexes that you may use to find articles on your research topic allow you to view the articles directly on your screen, saving you the step of finding the article in print or on microform.

Locating Periodicals

If you are in doubt about whether your library has a magazine or journal you are looking for, you can consult a list of all the periodicals your library owns. Such a list is usually found in the library's online catalog. In most libraries, current issues of magazines and journals are shelved on open stacks; back issues are collected and bound by volume or copied onto microforms. Recent back issues, not yet bound, are sometimes available at a periodicals or service desk. If you have difficulty finding an article, ask at the periodicals or reference desk for assistance.

Microforms

As a space-saving device, many libraries store some printed materials on microforms, miniaturized photographic copies of the materials. The two principal types of microforms are *microfilm*, which comes in spools that resemble small movie reels, and *microfiche* (pronounced *MY-crow-feesh*), which comes in individual sheets of photographic film. The images they contain are so small that they can store large quantities of material. A projector is required to enlarge these images so they can be read. Most college libraries have projectors for both microfilm and microfiche. Some projectors also allow for photocopying of what appears on the projector's screen. Follow the directions on these machines or ask a librarian for assistance. Although sturdy, microforms are not indestructible, so it is important to handle them with care and to return them in the same condition as you received them.

Library Vandalism—A Crime Against Scholarship

Since scholarship is a cooperative enterprise, it is essential that all scholars have access to sources. Students who steal, deface, or mutilate library materials commit a crime against the ethics of scholarship. An unforgivable sin is to tear articles from magazines, permanently depriving others of their right to read them. Many a frustrated scholar, looking for a needed source only to find it stolen, has uttered a terrible curse on the heads of all library vandals—one that it might be wise not to incur. On the more tangible side, most states have made library vandalism a criminal offense, punishable by stiff fines and in some cases jail sentences.

Actually, there is no excuse for such vandalism. Short passages can be hand-copied. Longer excerpts, to be used for legitimate academic purposes, can be photocopied inexpensively. Most libraries have coin-operated or debit-card photocopy machines in convenient locations. (Some photoduplication violates copyright laws; consult your instructor or librarian if you are in doubt.)

■ USING ELECTRONIC DATABASES

Most college libraries provide links to electronic databases, which have replaced printed indexes as the most popular means for students to locate articles, electronic files, and other materials related to their research topics. These databases are either online (through an electronic connection to the database host site) or portable (stored on a CD-ROM disk). *Databases* are usually accessed through the library's central information system.

College libraries allow you access to dozens of databases, and the number is increasing at a rapid rate. In this chapter we will introduce a few of the more popular and useful databases, but you should explore your library to learn what databases are available. Most databases work in a similar way, and you need to master only a few simple principles to conduct a successful search. Once you have practiced searching one database, you should have little trouble negotiating most other databases as well. It is usually advisable to search several different databases when you are looking for articles and other information about your research topic.

A Sample Search for Periodical Sources

Your library may subscribe to several *online reference services*, such as EBSCO-host, FirstSearch, InfoTrac, Lexis-Nexis Academic Universe, ProQuest, and WilsonWeb. Each service allows you to search a number of databases either singly or simultaneously. As an example of how you could use an online reference service, we will demonstrate a search using the EBSCOhost service. Let us imagine you are doing a research project on college students who are binge drinkers.

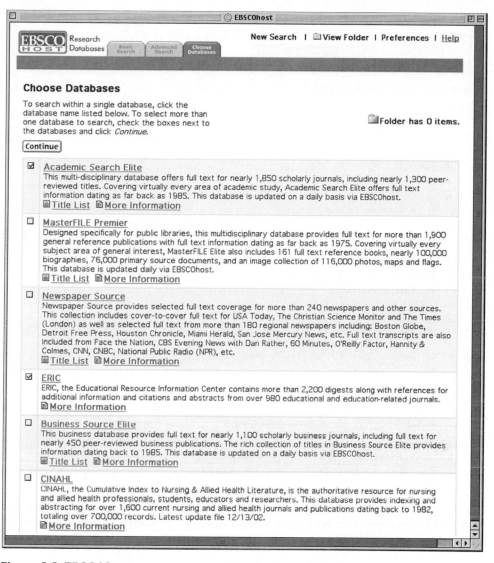

Figure 9.3 EBSCOhost menu screen with selection of databases.

Figure 9.3 shows part of the EBSCOhost menu of databases. Scrolling down the screen would reveal many other databases as well. To the left of each database is a box. As a first step in your search, you would click on the boxes of all the databases that might be pertinent. Let us assume you decided to search the Academic Search Elite database (a database of articles in scholarly journals) and ERIC (a database of education-related journals and documents). By clicking first in those two boxes and then on the *Enter* button, you bring up the search page shown in Figure 9.4.

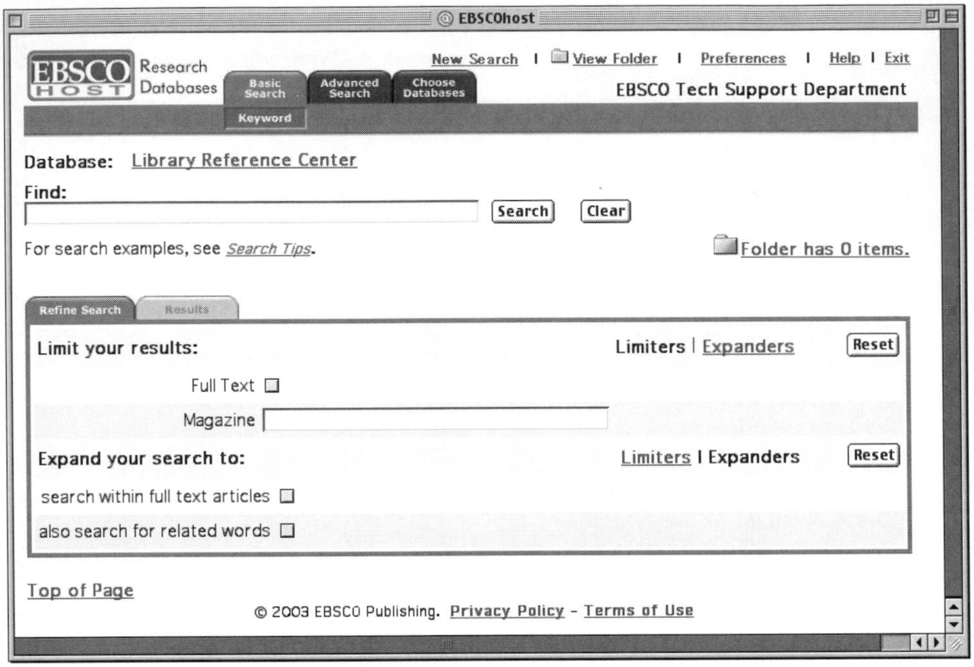

Figure 9.4 Search page in the EBSCOhost search engine.

Tips for Successful Keyword Searches

The next step in your search is to enter *keywords* on the screen in Figure 9.4 to tell the *search engine* (that's another term used to describe an online program that searches a database) what words or phrases to look for as it searches the titles and abstracts of articles. If you enter "binge drinker" in the *Find* box and then click on the *Search* button, a results list will soon appear with fifty-seven documents, the first several of which are shown in Figure 9.5. Although this may seem a respectable return, unfortunately it does not come close to capturing all the articles available on the subject.

But wait! Computers are very literal. You have asked the search engine to restrict its search just to that one phrase, greatly limiting the results. A useful tip is to use an asterisk as a ***wildcard character*** to find any of several related words. Entering "binge drink*" instead of "binge drinker" will broaden your search to any phrase that begins with those characters, including *binge drinker*, *binge drinkers*, and *binge drinking*. Click on the *Search* button, and instead of fifty-seven results, the search engine now reports it has found 393 items—a more satisfactory outcome.

But perhaps a search of these keywords is still too limiting. The EBSCOhost search engine assumes that two or more words side by side constitute a phrase, and it will look only for the words *binge* and *drink** when they occur next to each other, not when they are separated by other words. A solution is to conduct what is known as a ***Boolean search***, using the signals *AND*, *OR*, or *NOT*. For example, if

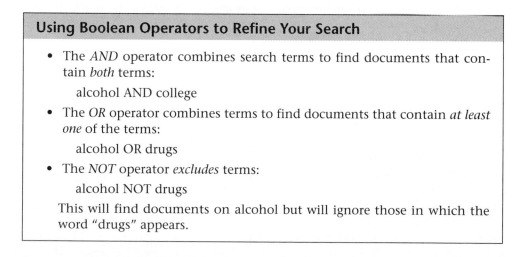

Figure 9.5 A "results list" in the EBSCOhost search engine.

Using Boolean Operators to Refine Your Search

- The *AND* operator combines search terms to find documents that contain *both* terms:

    alcohol AND college

- The *OR* operator combines terms to find documents that contain *at least one* of the terms:

    alcohol OR drugs

- The *NOT* operator *excludes* terms:

    alcohol NOT drugs

    This will find documents on alcohol but will ignore those in which the word "drugs" appears.

you asked EBSCOhost to search for "binge AND drink*," it will look for articles that contain both of those words, even if they are separated from each other. That is, it would find articles that contain "binge drinkers" as well as those that contain "drinkers who go on a binge" and so on.

More is not always better, however, and now your search may be too broad. You aren't interested in binge drinking among business executives, just among college students, so a useful strategy is to refine your search further to eliminate unwanted articles. Make the search topic "binge AND drink* AND college*" to eliminate any documents in which the words *college* or *colleges* do not appear. However, in some articles about binge drinking, the word *university* (or *universities*) may be used instead of *college*. You can use the OR operator to search for either *college** or *universit**. That is, you might have your best results if you search for the keywords "binge AND drink* AND (college* OR universit*)." The search results that EBSCOhost returned when different keywords were entered are shown in Figure 9.6.

The Next Step—Finding More Detail on Sources

In our sample search for articles about collegiate binge drinking, we used the keywords "binge AND drink* AND (college* OR universit*)," and EBSCOhost found 265 documents. The first screen of these results is shown in Figure 9.7. Each result gives the document's title and publication data. The next step is to examine the most promising articles to find useful sources. You can click your mouse on the title of an article to read an **abstract** (a brief summary) of its contents. Beneath the titles of the first article, the words "HTML Full Text" appear. If you click on these words, you can read the entire article on your screen. The second and third entries also give you the option to view photocopies of the original articles ("PDF Full Text"). For the fourth entry, an abstract is available online, but you would have to read the article in your library. To see if your library has back issues of the journal *International Journal of Eating Disorders*, you can click on the words "Check library catalog for title."

Keywords entered	Number of documents found
binge drinker	57
binge drinkers	66
binge drinking	356
binge drink*	393
binge AND drink*	427
binge AND drink* AND college*	250
binge AND drink* AND (college* OR universit*)	265

Figure 9.6 Number of documents found in an EBSCOhost search using different keywords.

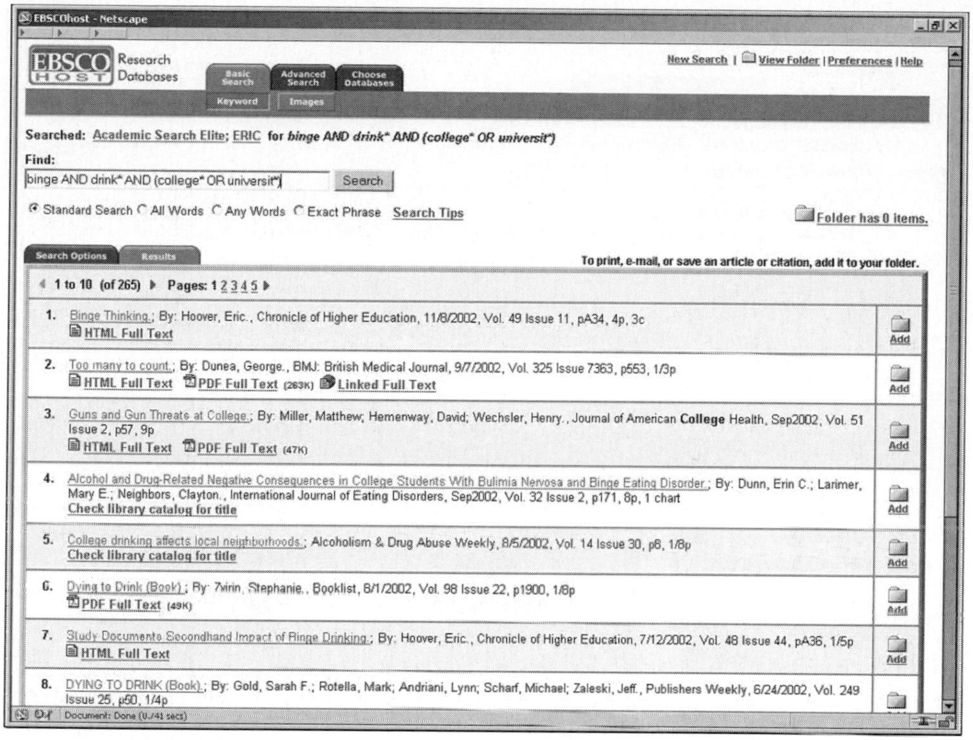

Figure 9.7 Search results for "binge AND drink AND (college* OR universit*)."

If you were to click on the title of the first item in Figure 9.7, "Binge Thinking," you would see the detailed information shown in Figure 9.8. In addition to the title, author, and source of the article, this screen contains several other useful items. The abstract summarizes the article and is your best guide to whether the article is likely to be a useful source for your research project. If so, you can read the full text by scrolling down the page or by clicking on "HTML Full Text" above the title. If you believe the article is a useful research source, you can take notes on the article immediately if you like. You also are given several other options at the top of the page. You can *Print* it for later use; *E-mail* the article to yourself (this is especially useful if you are working in a library); *Save* it on a diskette; or *Add to folder*. The last option allows you to select all the articles that you have found to be likely sources for your project.

Another useful feature of Figure 9.8 is the "Subject(s)" heading. This article is indexed under four different subjects. If you were to click on the third subject, "DRINKING of alcoholic beverages—United States," you would find additional articles related to that subject.

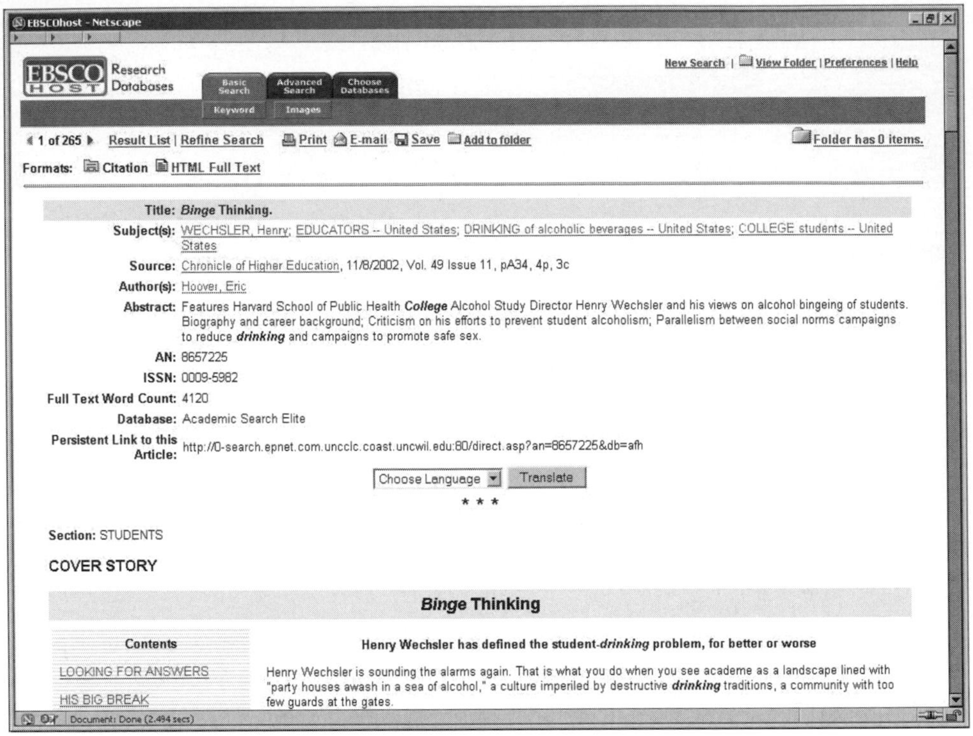

Figure 9.8 An EBSCOhost citation screen.

EXERCISES

Using an Online Reference Service

1. In Figure 9.3, which of the databases shown would be your best source to find articles in academic journals? Which database(s) would you search if you were writing a paper on the issue of social promotion in the schools? Which database(s) would be most useful to locate sources for a research project on student entrepreneurs who start Internet businesses? What is the difference between the MasterFILE Premier database and the Newspaper Source database?

2. Figure 9.4 shows an EBSCOhost search page. If you were looking to find articles about psychological warfare, what keywords would you enter in the "Find" box, and which of the four buttons immediately below the "Find" box would you click? What would you do if you were looking for articles about penguins in Chile? What if you were looking for articles about either anorexia or bulimia? If you were searching for articles about the town of Paris in Texas, how could you use Boolean operators to eliminate articles about the movie named *Paris, Texas*? What if you were looking for articles about the censorship of music or television in China or Vietnam?

3. In Figure 9.4, how could you limit your search to articles that can be read online? Which box would you check if you wanted to limit your search just to articles that

appeared in scholarly journals? What if you wanted to conduct the search for your keywords not just in the titles or abstracts of articles, but in the articles themselves?

4. In Figure 9.7, who were the authors of the article "Guns and Gun Threats at College"? In what publication did it appear? What is the length in pages of the article? Of the eight articles listed on screen, which ones can be read online? Which ones would you have to look for in your library? If you wanted to email articles numbered 1, 4, and 5 to your home, what would your first steps in the process be?

5. The page shown partially in Figure 9.7 gives the first ten of 265 documents. Where would you click with your mouse pointer to view the next ten results?

6. Figure 9.8 shows a citation page for an article. What is the title of the article? Where would you find a brief summary of the article? How many words long is the article? In what publication did it appear? Would clicking on any of the four listed subject headings be helpful in finding additional articles about binge drinking among college students? How could you read the full article?

7. Figure 9.9 shows a search screen using the InfoTrac search engine in which a student has filled in some of the boxes. What subject(s) is the student researching? In addition to entering keywords, what other limitations did the student put on the search?

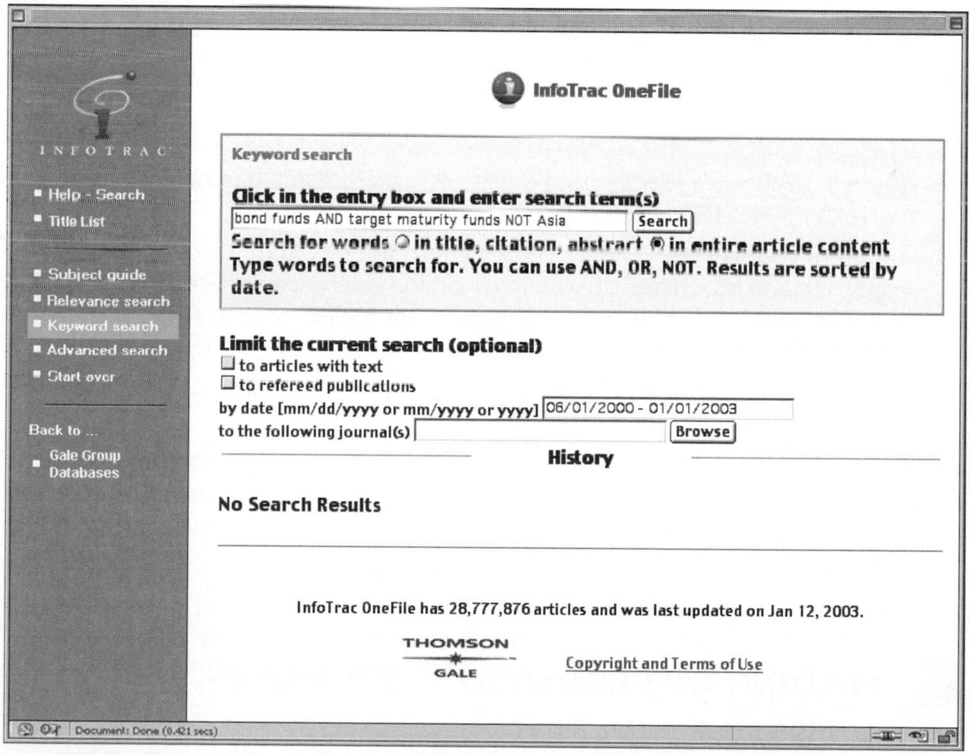

Figure 9.9 A keyword search using the InfoTrac OneFile search engine.

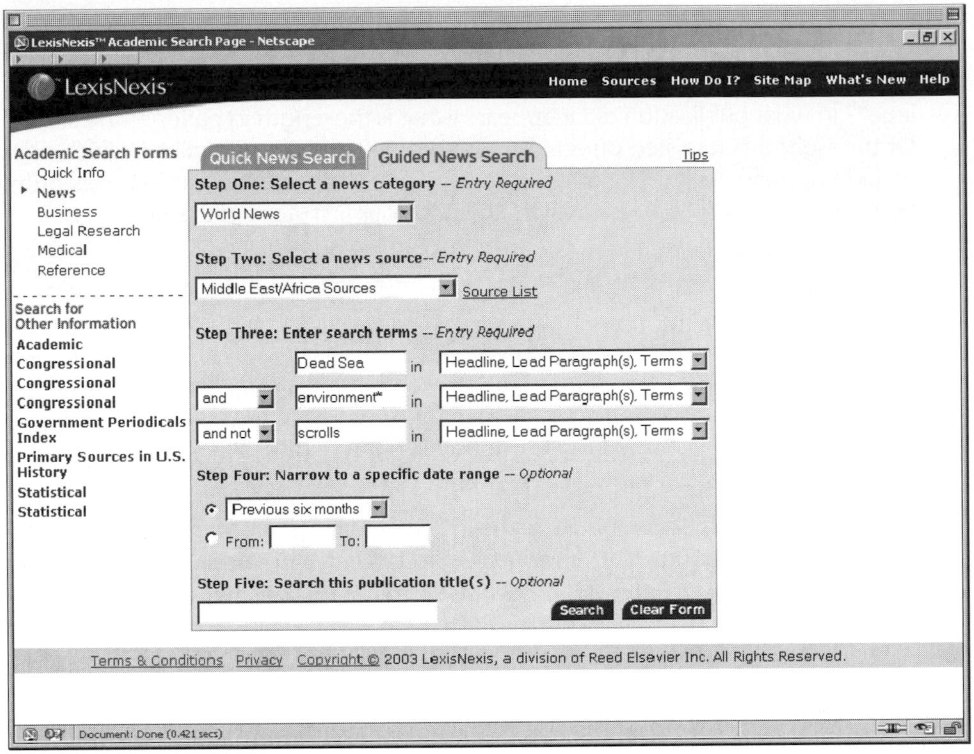

Figure 9.10 A LexisNexis™ search.

8. Figure 9.10 shows a search using the LexisNexis™ search engine. Describe what the student who filled in this page was seeking?

9. Log on to your college library's central information system. Does it allow you to search for articles online? If so, which online reference services (e.g., EBSCO-host, FirstSearch, LexisNexis, WilsonWeb) does it allow you to search? Are there other databases you can use to search for articles?

10. Use your college library's resources to find a newspaper article about Medicare fraud published within the past year.

11. Use a different database to find an article in an academic journal about the sleeping disorder known as sleep apnea. If you can, print out the citation screen for the article; if not, copy the name of the author, title, publication, date, and page numbers.

■ FINDING GOVERNMENT DOCUMENTS

The vast array of documents published by the U.S. government constitutes another useful resource for research in almost any field of study. Many government documents are available online. In addition, each state has at least one designated depository library that receives all documents distributed by the Government Printing Office (GPO), as well as several other partial depository libraries that receive selected government publications. Items not in your college library can usually be borrowed through the InterLibrary Loan service. Government documents are usually shelved in a special library section and identified by a call number (called a *GovDoc* or *SuDoc* number). Many library catalogs do not index all their government documents along with their book holdings. To find documents and their call numbers, you need to consult one of several indexes that can search GPO databases. The ***Catalog of U.S. Government Publications*** is a government-sponsored online search engine, located at http://www.access.gpo.gov/su_docs/locators/cgp/.

Another index is the ***GPO Monthly Catalog*** available in many university libraries through the FirstSearch online reference service. Imagine, for example, that you were writing a research paper on the prevalence and causes of teenage smoking. A search of the GPO Monthly Catalog using the keywords "teen*" and "smoking" would yield many documents, including one called "Changing Adolescent Smoking Prevalence: Where It Is and Why." Clicking on the title would call up on your screen the record of that publication shown in Figure 9.11.

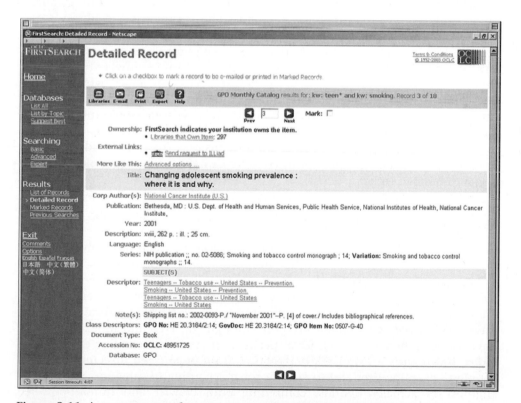

Figure 9.11 A government document record in the GPO Monthly Catalog.

Finding Government Documents

1. This exercise can be undertaken by one or two students who can report their findings to the class. Find out if your college library is your state's regional depository for U.S. government documents or a partial depository. If the latter, what percentage of available government items does it receive? Where are government documents shelved in the library? How can students gain access to government documents not in your library?

2. Figure 9.11 is the record of one of the government documents found from a search about teenage smoking. Which government agency authored the report? In what year was it published? On what subject heading(s) might you click to find more documents about teen smoking?

3. Use a GPO index to search for a government document related to your research topic. Report briefly on what you find.

INTERNET RESOURCES

Library sources can be accessed in systematic ways; by contrast, finding sources on the Internet is much more a hit-or-miss affair. Whereas the library's staff controls its collection and creates an index of all the library's holdings (its on-line catalog), no one runs the Internet, much less controls access to it or creates a comprehensive index. The Internet is really a vast interconnected network of smaller networks, which virtually anyone can access and where virtually anyone can publish anything. Navigating the Internet and finding resources that can aid your research project require much practice, some skill, and considerable luck.

The best Internet tutorial comes from hands-on exploration, aided by your curiosity and an adventurous spirit. Here we can give only some brief information and hints to get you started.

Web Search Engines

When you seek Web sources for a research project, you will probably not know the addresses for specific sites. Although no comprehensive index to the millions of Web pages exists, several commercial indexes (known as *search engines*) provide access to a large number of sites. Search engines are of two general types: Web crawlers and human-powered directories, which work in radically different ways. *Web crawlers* automatically pore through the Web and index what they have found. When you search for a specific term, the search engine examines its index and returns a list of relevant sites. A *human-powered directory* relies on people to examine sites and to classify them according to category. Most search engines are actually hybrids, combining both crawler and human-powered results.

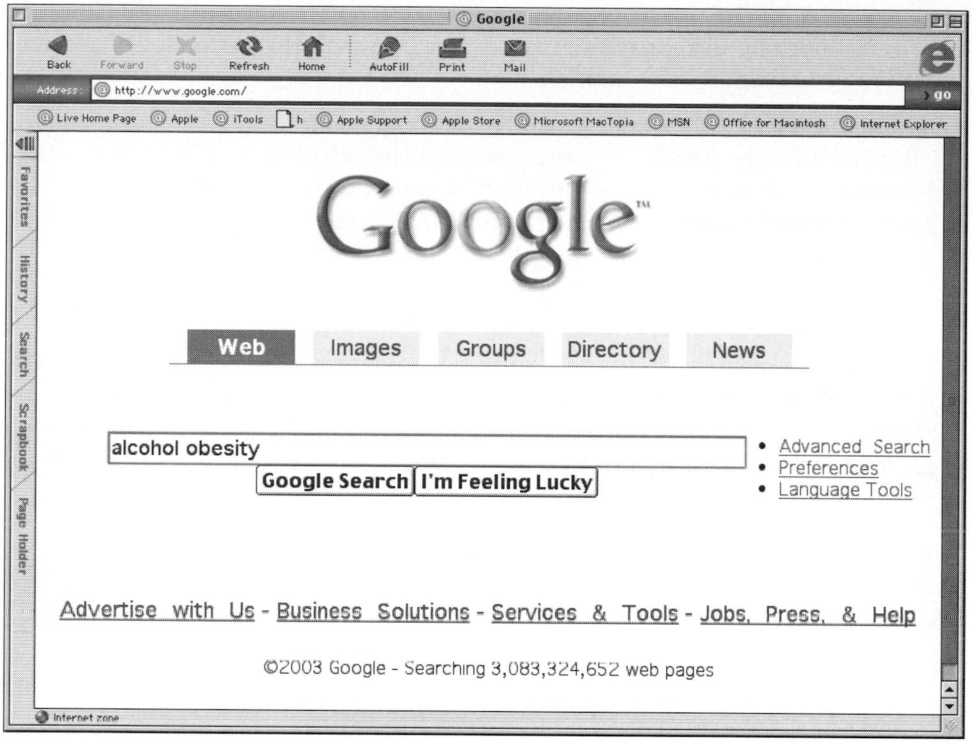

Figure 9.12 Screen for a basic Google search.

Tips for a Basic Google Search

- Google searches for entries with *all* the words listed:

    alcohol obesity

- Use quotation marks to search for phrases:

    censorship "high school"

- Google does not support wildcard characters such as *.

- Google ignores capitalization:

    pAris fraNCe

- Google ignores common words, such as *the, of, I, where,* and *how.* Entering *World War I* also provides results about World War II. Add a + sign before a common word to include it in the search, or place the word within quotation marks:

    World War +I

    "World War I"

- Use a minus sign to exclude a term. For a search on bass (the fish, not the musical term), enter

    bass −music

Because different search engines provide different results, it is often best to use more than one in researching your topic. Here are the addresses of some of the more prominent search engines:

Google	http://www.google.com
AllTheWeb.com (FAST)	http://www.alltheweb.com
Yahoo (crawler)	http://www.yahoo.com
Yahoo (directory)	http://dir.yahoo.com/
MSN Search	http://search.msn.com
Lycos	http://www.lycos.com
Ask Jeeves	http://www.askjeeves.com

One of the most popular and highly regarded search engines is Google. The Google address *www.google.com* produces the basic search screen shown in Figure 9.12 on page 369. Unlike most library catalogs and periodical search engines such as EBSCOhost, Google does not treat keywords as phrases; that is, it will search for

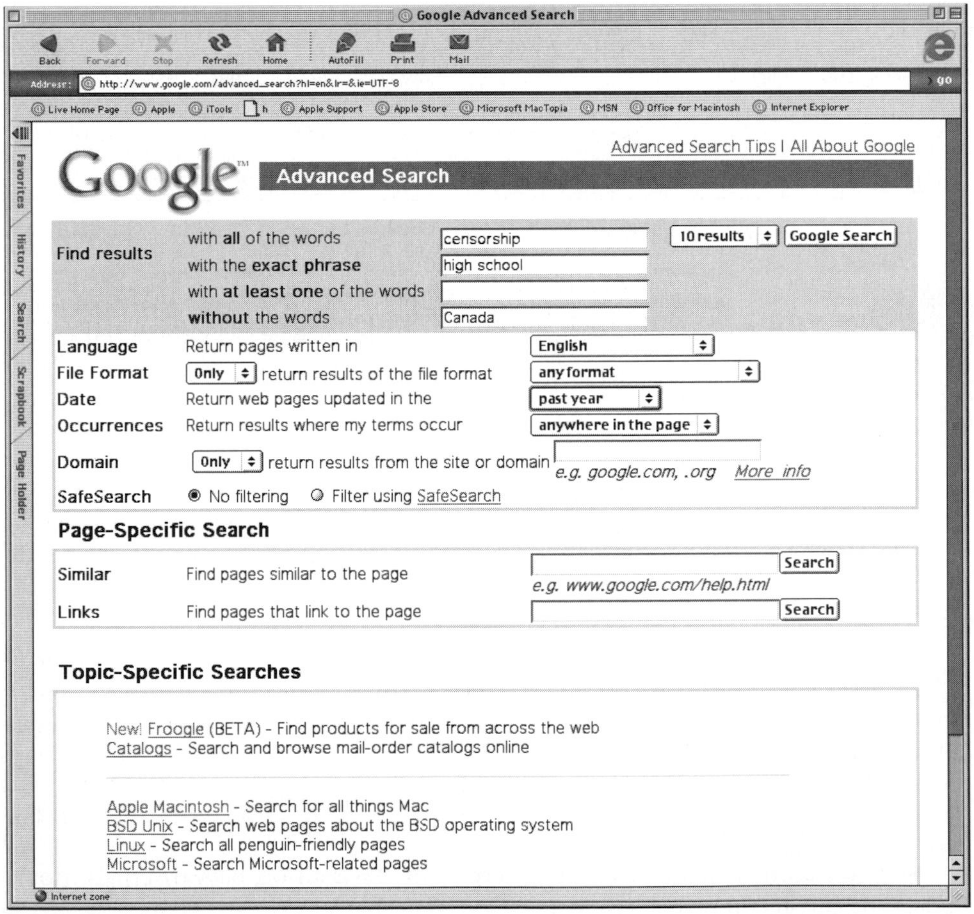

Figure 9.13 Screen for an advanced Google search.

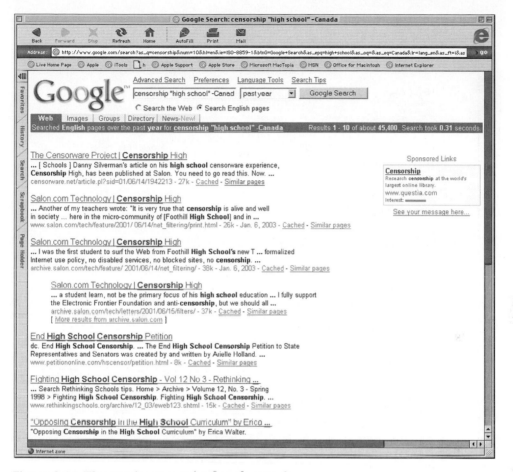

Figure 9.14 The results page of a Google search.

sites containing all the words listed, regardless of whether they occur side by side. If you were searching for sites about the relationship between alcohol and obesity, you could enter *alcohol obesity*. You don't need the *AND* operator between the words (in fact, Google ignores *AND* or *and*). See the box on page 369 for other tips about a basic Google search.

For greater control in an Internet search, click on the "Advanced Search" link. An advanced search can allow you to return the most pertinent results while excluding unwanted sites. For example, Figure 9.13 shows how you might search for pages in English produced within the last year about censorship in high schools, but not those in Canada. Figure 9.14 shows the results of this search. Because all search engines provide different results, it is often worthwhile to conduct searches on more than one search engine.

A second option for Web searching is to use the search engine's human-powered directory. Figure 9.15 shows the Yahoo directory at *dir.yahoo.com*. You can either browse the directory by following links through relevant categories

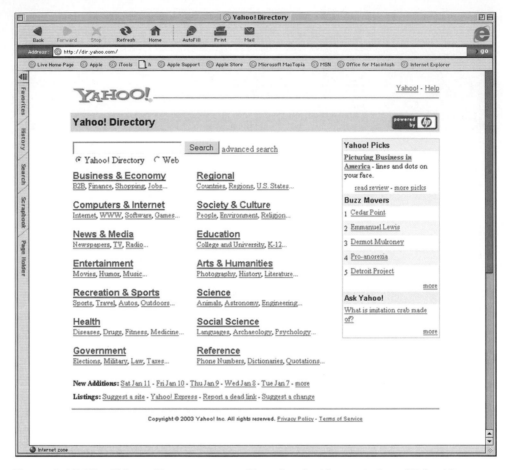

Figure 9.15 The Yahoo directory page. *(Reproduced with permission of Yahoo! Inc. Copyright © 2003 by Yahoo! Inc. Yahoo! and the Yahoo! logo are trademarks of Yahoo! Inc.)*

(e.g., *Science*, then *Biology*, then *Evolution*, etc.) or you can do a keyword search of the directory. Because items in the directory have been selected by humans, a search will provide fewer, but more selective results.

Some words of caution about Web searches are in order. Students should evaluate Web pages with a careful, critical eye. Remember than anyone can post Web pages, and so not everything on the Web is valuable or accurate. Find out who has created the document and how reliable or comprehensive it is. For example, if you are researching a scandal in the widget industry, you will likely find many widget pages. Knowing if the page is created by a widget trade organization (which would be expected to have a pro-widget bias) or by an anti-widget consumer group (with the opposite bias) is essential if you are to assess the sources and determine whether and how to use them.

Because Web searches often return hundreds, if not thousands, of results, visit only those that look promising. When you find worthwhile sites, you can take notes on them, print the pages, or bookmark them for later use.

| **Using the World Wide Web** | **EXERCISES** |

Do the following exercises using the World Wide Web:

1. See what you can find on the Web on the following three topics: identical twins, Peru, and archery. Use one or more of the above search engines to explore these topics. Follow links from page to page as your curiosity leads you. Write a narrative describing your search and discoveries.
2. The Yahoo directory at *dir.yahoo.com* is organized around a number of topics (business & economy, computers & Internet, etc.). Select one that interests you, and continue to choose from among options until you arrive at an interesting page. Print the page (if equipment allows) or summarize its contents.
3. Use other search engines to find Web sources on your research topic.

THE REFERENCE LIBRARIAN—THE MOST RESOURCEFUL RESOURCE

By far the most valuable resource in any library is the librarian, a professional who knows the library well and is an expert in locating information. Use the other resources in this chapter first, but if you become stuck or do not know where to look or cannot find the sources you need, do not hesitate to ask a librarian for help. College libraries have *reference librarians* on duty, usually at a station marked as the *reference desk.* Their job is to assist when you need help in finding sources. Reference librarians are almost always helpful, and they have aided many students with the same kinds of research problems and questions that you are likely to have.

There are some limits, however, to the services reference librarians can provide. One librarian requested that we mention some problems they are sometimes asked to solve but cannot. They cannot pick a topic for you, interpret your assignment, or answer questions about the format of your bibliographic citations. Those questions should be addressed to your instructor. The librarian's job is to assist when you need help locating library sources.

Although printed and electronic materials are of great value to researchers, they are not the only sources available. Chapter 10 discusses ways to use other sources in your research project.

10 *Finding Sources outside the Library: Conducting Interviews and Writing Letters*

■ INTERVIEWING SOURCES

In addition to print sources, interviews with experts can provide valuable material for your paper. Because the people you interview are primary rather than secondary sources, the firsthand information they provide is exclusively yours to present—information that readers will find nowhere else. Therefore, interviewed sources can make a favorable impression, giving readers the sense that they are getting expert testimony directly and reliably. Your own reliability and credibility may also be enhanced, since you demonstrate the initiative to have extended your search beyond the usual kinds of sources.

On a college campus, professors are an accessible source of expert information. Being familiar with research in their individual fields, they also can suggest published and unpublished resources you might not have found in your library research. You may also find experts living in your local community. In his research on a pharmacy career, Justin Stafford interviewed Blake Barefoot, a working pharmacist in a chain store in his city. Justin found it invaluable to talk with someone who had direct experience in the profession and could answer his many questions and give him expert advice. Similarly, Emily Gould gained valuable firsthand information about labor issues in fast-food restaurants when she interviewed Jill Cashen, an official for a union active in the food industry.

Participants and eyewitnesses are also valuable sources. Emily also interviewed Tamicah Williams, a fellow student with a part-time job in a fast-food restaurant. If you were researching, say, biological terrorism, you could interview persons responsible for emergency preparedness in your community, such as police and hospital staff. Be resourceful in considering interviewees who can contribute to your knowledge and understanding.

Conducting interviews may not be the first order of business in your research project, but because interviews require advance planning, it is important to set up appointments as early as possible—even before you are ready to conduct them. Soon after Justin had decided on his topic, he knew he would want to talk to a pharmacist. He wanted to do some reading first in order to be sufficiently informed to ask intelligent questions, but he also knew that pharmacists are busy during their work hours and that it would be wise to arrange an interview well in advance.

Arranging the Interview

Like every other stage in a research project, arranging interviews can lead to inevitable frustrations. For example, if you were researching a career in psychiatry, you might find it difficult to arrange an interview with a psychiatrist. After all, psychiatrists spend their days talking with patients; they may have little interest in giving up their precious free time to talk with someone else (without compensation).

When you telephone someone you don't know, be courteous and explain your purpose simply and clearly. For example, if you were calling an executive at a computer company to ask for an interview, you might say something like this:

> Hello, Ms. Smith, I'm [your name], a student at [your school]. I'm conducting a research project concerning the future of computers in the workplace. I'm particularly interested in talking to a person in the industry with your expertise, and I would like to learn your views on the topic. I wonder if I could meet with you briefly to ask you a few questions.

You can expect the person to ask you further questions about the nature of your project and about the amount of time the interview will take. If you are courteous and open and if your purposes seem serious, people are likely to cooperate with you to the extent that they are able. Be prepared to meet at a time and place convenient to the interviewee. Many interviews can be conducted in fifteen to thirty minutes. If you wish to tape-record the interview, ask for permission at the time you arrange the meeting.

Professors are usually available to students during office hours, but business people and other professionals are usually not so easy to reach. Before talking to the executive, you might have to explain your need to a receptionist or secretary, who might be reluctant to connect you. Often a letter written in advance of your telephone call can be effective in securing an interview. For example, a student who wishes to arrange an interview with a computer executive might send a letter like this one:

```
                                    202 Willow Street
                                    Wilmington, NC 28401
                                    2 March 2003

Ms. Denise Smith
Vice-President for Research and Development
CompuCosmos Corporation
Wilmington, NC 28401

Dear Ms. Smith:
     I am a student at the University of North Carolina at
Wilmington engaged in a research project concerning the future
of computer use in business offices. I have learned much about
```

the topic from written sources, but I still have some
unanswered questions. Your observations and expert opinions
would be invaluable for my report. I know your time is
valuable, and I would be grateful if I could meet with you for
a brief interview. I will telephone Wednesday morning to see if
I can arrange a meeting. If you wish, you can reach me by phone
at 555-1893.

                                        Sincerely,

                                        Blair Halliday

                                        Blair Halliday

Conducting the Interview

Some interviews may consist of a simple question or two, designed to fill specific gaps in your knowledge about your topic. Others may be extended question-and-answer sessions about a variety of topics. The success of your interviewing depends on your preparation, professionalism, and interpersonal skills. The following guidelines should be followed when you conduct an interview:

1. *Before the interview:*

    • **Be well prepared.** The most important part of the interview takes place before the questions are posed. Become as informed about your subject as you can so that you can ask the right questions. Use your reading notes to prepare questions in advance.

    • **Dress appropriately for the interview.** How you dress can influence how the interviewee behaves toward you; people are most comfortable talking with someone who dresses as they do. Business and professional people, for example, are more likely to take you seriously if you are wearing standard business attire. On the other hand, formal attire would be inappropriate when interviewing striking factory workers, who might be reluctant to speak freely with someone who looks like management.

    • **Arrive on time for your appointment.** Not only is arriving on time a matter of courtesy, but it is essential in assuring the interviewee's cooperation.

2. *During the interview:*

    • **Take careful and accurate notes.** If you intend to quote your source, you must be certain that you have copied the person's words exactly. A tape recorder can give you an accurate transcript of your interviews.

    • **Behave politely and ethically.** Be certain you have the interviewee's permission if you tape-record the conversation. If you take notes, offer to let the interviewee check the transcript later to ensure accuracy (doing so may elicit further elaborations and additional statements that you can use).

- **Be relaxed and friendly.** People who are not accustomed to being interviewed are often nervous at first about having their comments recorded. By being friendly and relaxed, you can win their confidence and put them at ease. The most fruitful parts of interviews occur when interviewees become absorbed in what they are saying and forget they are being recorded. Begin with general questions that can be answered with ease and confidence. Later introduce more specific and pointed questions. (For experienced interviewees, these precautions may not be necessary.)

- **Make your recording as unobtrusive as possible.** Many people will not speak freely and naturally when constantly reminded that their comments are being recorded. Place the tape recorder out of the interviewee's direct line of sight. Do not write constantly during the interview; write down key phrases and facts that will allow you to reconstruct the conversation immediately after the interview.

- **Be interested in what the interviewee says.** People will speak much more freely with you if they sense that you are responsive to their comments. It is a mistake for an interviewer to read one prepared question after another, while barely listening to the interviewee's responses. Such wooden interviewing produces an uncomfortable atmosphere and strained responses.

- **Stay flexible.** Do not be a slave to your prepared questions. Listen with real curiosity to what the person says and ask further questions based on what you learn. Request explanations of what is not clear to you. Ask probing questions when a topic is raised that you would like to learn more about.

- **Let the interviewee do the talking.** Remember that it is the interviewee's ideas that you are interested in, not your own. Avoid the temptation to state your own opinions and experiences or to argue points with the interviewee.

3. *After the interview:*

- **End the interview professionally.** Check your notes and questions to determine if any gaps still need to be filled. Thank the interviewee. Ask if the person would like to check your use of statements and information for accuracy, and whether you can call again if you have further questions. Offer to send the interviewee a copy of your paper when it is completed.

- **Be fair to the source.** When you write the paper, be certain that any ideas or statements you attribute to the source are true reflections of the sound and spirit of the person's answers and comments. Be accurate in quoting the person, but eliminate slips of the tongue and distracting phrases like *uh* and *you know.*

- **Send a thank-you note.** Whether or not you send a copy of your paper to the interviewee, you should send a note expressing your appreciation for the help that the person provided.

Justin prepared the following list of questions before he interviewed Blake Barefoot, a pharmacist at a chain store in his community:

Possible Interview Questions for Mr. Barefoot

- Why did you decide to be a pharmacist?
- Is your job what you expected?
- What do you do on a typical day?
- Are you "following doctor's orders" or do you make decisions affecting people?
- What are your working conditions?
- Is the job enjoyable and rewarding? What are the major satisfactions?
- Is it stressful? What are your major frustrations?
- Is there opportunity for advancement?
- What training did you have?
- What was pharmacy school like?
- Would you recommend this career to others?

Although he used his prepared questions as a point of reference, Justin found himself departing from them as he responded to Mr. Barefoot's comments. During his interview, Justin took notes in his research notebook. Here are some excerpts. (In some cases we have recast them to make them clearer to other readers.)

Notes from Interview with Mr. Barefoot

—Grew up in a small town. I wanted to be a lawyer, but my brother decided to go to pharmacy school and steered me in that direction.

—Most valuable work is interacting with people. Answer questions about side effects, alleviate their fears or steer them to other therapies. Check drug interactions.

—Long hours, not bad--no qualms. Target is a good company to work for.

—Stressful? High level of stress, trying to be fast. Everyone wants prescription in 5 minutes. Delays: no refills, people give us the wrong insurance company. Juggling 10 people's work schedules.

—Many argue they fill too many prescriptions in one day. What is safe? Stress factors involved.

—Advancement: extensive. Pharmacy business has done well, especially in last 5 years. Dramatic growth. If willing to relocate, if opening a new store, can be supervisor.

—5 years of school, now 6. 1 year of internship, "preceptor program." You can choose: retail, hospital, ER. I learned more doing my internships and in the first 6 months on job than in first 4 years of college.

—Retail: money is better. My personality lends itself to retail.

—Owning a store is very difficult nowadays. Insurance billing & low payments from insurance companies. Hard to be independent without specialization in something in addition to pharmacy. Hard to compete.

—Good people skills needed. Pharmacists who lack them usually hate pharmacy.

—Would definitely recommend. A wonderful career. Endless potential for personal growth and learning, plus good income. People will always need medicine.

WRITING FOR INFORMATION

It frequently happens that information helpful to your project is unavailable in the library. For example, if you were doing a project on nutrition in children's breakfast foods, you might visit a supermarket to record nutritional information and ingredients of various brands from the sides of cereal boxes. You could also write letters of inquiry to cereal manufacturers, such as the one that follows.

November 3, 2003

Public Relations Officer
Breakfast Foods Division
General Foods Corporation
250 North Street
White Plains, NY 10625

Dear Public Relations Officer:
    As a student at [your university], I am undertaking a research study of nutrition in breakfast cereals. I am particularly interested in learning if there is a market for low-sugar cereals targeted specifically for the children's market. Could you please tell me the sales figures for your low-sugar Post Crispy Critters cereal? I would also appreciate any additional information you could send me related to this subject.
    I would be grateful if you could respond before [date], the deadline for my research paper.

                        Sincerely,
                        [your signature]
                        [your name]

Business directories in the reference section of your library, such as the *Directory of Corporate Affiliations,* can help you find company addresses. Your library may also subscribe to online databases that provide corporate information, such as *Dow Jones Interactive.* You can also consult a "yellow pages" search engine, such as www.switchboard.com. If you need further assistance, consult with the reference librarian.

It is wise to tell correspondents how you plan to use the information you are requesting. They are more likely to respond if convinced that your project will not be harmful to their interests. (Some businesses, such as tobacco or liquor companies, are understandably leery about supplying information for studies that may attack them.) You can increase your chances of getting a response by including a self-addressed stamped envelope with your letter. If time is short, a telephone call, e-mail message, or a fax may get a speedier response than a letter.

STILL OTHER SOURCES

Researchers can avail themselves of many other sources besides library materials, interviews, and letters. *Lectures, films, television programs,* and *audio recordings* are among the sources often cited in student research projects. In your paper, for example, you might quote a person who appeared in a television documentary, or you might describe an event portrayed in a news program. A song lyric or a line from movie dialogue might effectively illustrate a particular theme.

On many campuses there is a *media center* in which videotapes (including television documentaries), films, and various audio recordings are available. It may be housed in the library or in a separate building. Some campuses belong to a regional network of media centers that share their materials, usually with little or no charge to the borrower. If your campus has a media center, ask how you can find what sources are available on your topic and whether it is possible for you to gain access to materials from other campuses.

11 *Putting Your Sources to Work*

■ A RESEARCH PROSPECTUS

A *prospectus* is a statement of your plans for a project. During the early stages of their projects, Emily Gould and Justin Stafford were asked by their instructors to submit a research prospectus. Emily's class received the following assignment.

Research Prospectus   ASSIGNMENT

Bring to our next class a prospectus of your research project. It should consist of the following elements:

1. **A statement of your research question.** Your topic may be tentative at this point, so you needn't feel locked into it. In upcoming days, you may decide to alter your question or shift its focus as you conduct further research and learn more about the subject.

2. **A paragraph or two about your progress so far.** You can summarize why you chose your topic, what you already know about it, and what you hope to discover. You can also discuss any problems or successes you have had with focusing your topic and finding sources.

3. **A working bibliography** (a list of the sources you have located so far). Use the MLA format (explained in Chapter A of Part II) for your bibliography. This is a list of raw sources—sources you have not yet had much chance to examine and evaluate—so it is likely to contain some items that you will not use in your paper and therefore will not appear in the works-cited page of the final draft.

Emily and Justin by now had a general idea of their topics. They had done some browsing in encyclopedias and other reference works, and each was beginning to assemble a list of potential sources. Following are some excerpts from Emily's research notebook, written as she was beginning her search. Emily's notes

are informal, in the style of journal entries. We have edited them somewhat to
make them clearer for other readers.

> [After searching for books,] I went to the library's
> database/article search [using my computer]. I clicked
> on EBSCOhost's "MasterFILE Premier" and searched several
> topics concerning fast food. I started by typing in
> "fast food and nutrition" and found quite a few articles.
> I knew that it would be easy to find articles that would
> accuse fast food of being a cause of obesity, so first I
> looked for articles that gave a balanced view, since
> I wanted to provide a variety of opinions in the paper.
> I found an article titled "Can Fast Food Be Part of a
> Healthy Diet?" which stressed the idea of moderation in
> diet above all. . . . The health issue involved spokespeople
> from fast-food restaurants and the restaurant business deny-
> ing responsibility for obesity and denying the fact that fast
> food was unhealthy. I found several interesting articles
> talking about meatpacking plants, but for the most part
> they were too graphic and many of the articles seemed too
> emotional.

Here is another entry from Emily's notebook a few days later:

> . . . I looked for articles about the labor issues in
> fast food. One of the first articles I found was called
> "Worked Over." I could not find the full text online,
> so I went to the library to make a copy from the actual
> [print] periodical. It discussed the abuses of workers by
> employers in fast food who required their employees to
> work overtime but shortchange them in their paychecks.
> I decided to check what the actual laws concerning work
> hours and pay were, so I used the "Search" tool on my
> browser to find the Web site for the U.S. Department of
> Labor and followed links to "Youth Employment" where
> I found a list of all of the labor regulations
> including pay and minimum wage, and age-labor
> regulations. . . .

After more searching with their college library's central information system and
online databases, Emily and Justin had settled on their topics and were ready to
write their prospectuses. Emily's prospectus and working bibliography are shown
in Figure 11.1. Her original interest in the health aspects of fast food had begun to
broaden, and she was also exploring the effects of fast food both on society and
on the employees in the restaurants.

Gould 1

Emily Gould

Research Prospectus

1. Research question: How has America's love affair with fast food changed our lives, and what have the consequences been?

2. After reading journalist Eric Schlosser's 2001 book Fast-Food Nation this summer, I became aware of many controversies surrounding fast food. I have decided to research the topic further, focusing on three aspects: The proliferation of fast-food restaurants has changed the eating patterns of Americans and other aspects of our culture. Second, these restaurants affect the lives of thousands of workers, whom they employ in low-wage, unskilled jobs. Finally, fast food itself has been blamed for causing obesity, diabetes, and heart attacks in thousands of Americans who had no knowledge that the food they were eating was unhealthy until recently.

My searches of the library catalog and of periodicals have turned up hundreds of books and articles on the topic. I have checked out a book and have printouts of the articles in my bibliography. If anything, I am finding too many sources and will probably narrow my topic as I do more research.

Figure 11.1 Emily's Research Prospectus.

Gould 2

3. Working bibliography

Broydo, Leora. "Worked Over." <u>Utne Reader</u>. Jan./Feb. 1999:
　　20-21.

Cardial, Denise. "Multicultural Breakdown." <u>Des Moines</u>
　　<u>Business Record</u>. 6 May 1996: 16. <u>MasterFILE Premier</u>.
　　EBSCOhost. 10 Sept. 2002 <http://web3.epnet.com/>.

Cooper, Marc. "The Heartland's Raw Deal." <u>The Nation</u> 3
　　Feb. 1997: 11-17.

"Fast-Food Explosion 'A Threat to Global Health.'" <u>Daily</u>
　　<u>Mail</u> 18 Feb. 2002. <u>Newspaper Source</u>. EBSCOhost. 10
　　Sept. 2002 <http://web3.epnet.com/>.

Greenburg, Jan C. "Fast-Food Lawsuits May Be Successful
　　Legacy of Big Tobacco Penalties." <u>Chicago Tribune</u> 30
　　Aug. 2002. <u>Newspaper Source</u>. EBSCOhost. 10 Sept. 2002
　　<http://web3.epnet.com/>.

Matorin, James. "Obesity Awareness Campaign Needed, but
　　Regulations Won't Curb Fast-Food Appetite." <u>Nation's</u>
　　<u>Restaurant News</u> 27 Aug. 2001. <u>MasterFILE Premier</u>.
　　EBSCOhost. 15 Sept. 2002 <http://web3.epnet.com/>.

Ritzer, George. <u>The McDonaldization Thesis: Explorations</u>
　　<u>and Extensions</u>. London: Sage, 1998.

Schlosser, Eric. <u>Fast-Food Nation</u>. Boston: Houghton, 2001.

Zipp, Yvonne. "Virtues of Work vs. Finishing Homework."
　　<u>Christian Science Monitor</u> 15 Dec. 1998: 1. <u>MasterFILE</u>
　　<u>Premier</u>. EBSCOhost. 15 Sept. 2002
　　<http://web3.epnet.com/>.

◼ THE WORKING BIBLIOGRAPHY

A *bibliography* is a list of research sources. One of the last tasks in your search project is to type a *list of works cited* at the end of your paper—a formal bibliography or listing of all the sources you have used in writing it. But this occurs much later in the research process. For now, your task is to continue gathering sources; that is, you need to use the library databases and other research tools described in Chapter 9 to locate books and articles for your paper. The list of possible sources you draw up as you begin your search is your *working bibliography.* You add to the working bibliography during the course of your project as you discover additional sources, and you subtract from it as some sources on the list turn out not to be helpful.

A working bibliography is tentative, informal, and practical. The only requirement for a good working bibliography is that you are able to use it conveniently. Since it is for your own use—not part of the paper itself—you can record the information you need any way you like. For example, when you find a likely book from a subject citation in the library catalog, you can jot down in your notebook the key information that will enable you to locate it—perhaps only its title and call number. On the other hand, there are advantages to including more complete information in your working bibliography, as Emily did, in that you will use this information later, at the end of the project, when you type your works-cited page. Therefore, you can save considerable time by including all the information you may need later. For that reason, it is important for you to be acquainted with the standard conventions for citing sources. Those conventions are detailed in Chapter A of Part II.

Once you have completed your prospectus and have had it approved by your instructor, you are ready to put your sources to work.

◼ USING YOUR WRITTEN SOURCES

The early stages of your project may have been easier than you expected. You selected a topic, did some preliminary browsing in the library, and assembled a list of sources to work with. So far so good. But now what? Is there some simple technique that experienced researchers use to get ideas and information *out* of their sources and *into* their writing?

In fact, there is a reasonably uncomplicated and orderly procedure for putting your sources to use, but it isn't exactly simple. You can't just sit down before a stack of sources, read the first one and write part of your paper, then read the second one and write some more, and so on until you are finished. Obviously, such a procedure would make for a very haphazard and disjointed paper.

You can't write your paper all at once. Because you have a substantial body of information to sort through, digest, select, and organize, you have to use good management skills in your project. Your course of action needs to consist of manageable subtasks: You need to (1) *read* your sources efficiently and selectively and (2) *evaluate* the information you find there. As you learn more about your topic, you should (3) *narrow your focus* and (4) *shape a plan* for the paper. And to make use of new ideas and information, you need to (5) *take notes* on what seems important and usable in the sources. Only then are you ready to begin the actual drafting of the paper.

This chapter examines each of these tasks in turn, but do not think of them as separate operations that you can perform one after the other. They must interact. After all, how can you know what to read and take notes on unless you have some plans for what your paper will include? On the other hand, how can you know what your paper will include until your reading reveals to you what information is available? In working on your paper, you can never put your brain on automatic pilot. As you read and learn from your sources, you must continually think about how you can use the information and how using it will fit in with (or alter) your plan for the paper.

Emily and Justin received an assignment like the following from their instructors.

ASSIGNMENT   **Note Cards and a Preliminary Outline**

Continue your research by reading your sources, evaluating them, taking notes on note cards, narrowing your focus, and shaping a plan (a preliminary outline) for your paper. This is the most time-consuming stage of your research project, so be sure to begin working on it right away. Continue to record your experiences and observations in your research notebook.

Reading Your Sources

At this stage, you need to undertake several tasks, the first of which is to **read your sources.** A research paper should be something new, a fresh synthesis of information and ideas from many sources. A paper that is largely a summary of only one or two sources fails to do this. Become well informed about your topic by reading widely, and use a breadth of information in your paper. Most likely you have found many sources related to your topic, and the sheer volume of available material may itself be a cause for concern. Because your time is limited, you need to use it efficiently. Following are some practical suggestions for efficient reading:

- **Read only those sources that relate to your topic.** Beginning researchers often try to read too much. Do not waste valuable time reading sources that do not relate specifically to your topic. Before reading any source in detail, examine it briefly to be sure of its relevance. Chapter titles in books and section headings or even illustrations in articles may give you a sense of the work's usefulness. If you find dozens of books devoted solely to your topic, that topic probably is too broad to treat in a brief paper, and your focus should be narrowed. (Narrowing your paper's focus is discussed later in this chapter.)

- **Read each source selectively.** Do not expect to read every source from cover to cover; rather, read only those passages that relate to your topic. With a book, for example, use the table of contents in the front and the index in the back to locate relevant passages. Skim through promising sections, looking for passages relating directly to your topic—only these should you read carefully and deliberately.

- **Think as you read.** Ask yourself if what you are reading relates to your topic. Is it important and usable in your paper? Does it raise questions you want to explore further? What additional research do you need to do to answer these questions? Find new sources as needed, discard unusable ones, and update your working bibliography.

- **Read with curiosity.** Do not let your reading become a plodding and mechanical task; don't think of it as plowing through a stack of sources. Make your reading an act of exploration. You want to learn about your topic, and each source holds the potential to answer your questions. Search out answers, and if you don't find them in one source, seek them in another. There are many profitable ways for researchers to think of themselves: as explorers discovering unknown territory, as detectives following a trail of clues, as players fitting together the pieces of an intriguing puzzle.

- **Use your hand as well as your eyes when you read.** If you have photocopied an article or book chapter, underline important passages while reading, and write yourself notes in the margins. (Of course, don't do either of these things unless you own the copy; marking up material belonging to the library or to other people is a grave discourtesy.) Getting your hand into action as you read is a good way of keeping your mind active as well; writing, underlining, and note-taking force you to think about what you are reading. An article from *Human Resources Focus* magazine that Emily photocopied and then annotated is shown in Figure 11.2.

- **Write notes about your reading.** Use your research notebook to "think on paper" as you read. That is, write general comments about what you have learned from your sources and the ideas you have gained for your paper. Use note cards to write down specific information that you might use in writing your paper. (Note cards are discussed in detail later in this chapter.)

Evaluating Your Sources

All sources are not equally reliable. Not all writers are equally competent; not all periodicals and publishers are equally respected; and not all statements from interviewees are equally well informed. Certainly not every claim that appears in print is true. Because you want to base your paper on the most accurate, up-to-date, and authoritative information available, you need to exercise discretion in *evaluating your sources.* Following are some questions you can ask about a source:

- **Is the publication respectable?** If you are researching flying-saucer sightings, for example, an article in an astronomy or psychology journal com-

Employee Turnover: The Hidden Drain on Profits

In today's economy, business owners and managers need to control expenses to increase profits. Employee turnover is one of the most frustrating areas. For many industries—such as fast food, retail, convenience stores, trucking and healthcare—turnover rates exceed 75 percent.

(!)

Although related costs are not always direct or budgeted, turnover drains profits and adversely affects the business' overall efficiency. For example, a company that operates on a 5 percent margin must add about $20,000 in sales for every $1,000 lost to turnover costs.

The U.S. Department of Labor estimates that it costs a company one-third of a new hire's annual salary to replace an employee. Using a wage rate of only $6 an hour, it would cost a company $3,600 for each departing employee. This estimate, however, may be too high. Many fast-food companies, in fact, calculate the cost at $500 to replace one crew person and about $1,500 to replace a manager. Thus, for a fast-food operation with 500 employees and 300 percent turnover, the annual cost would be $750,000 (500 x 1,500 new hires x $500). In the trucking industry, managers estimate the per-driver replacement expense between $3,000 and $5,000.

Cheap labor leads to turnover— but costs are not so cheap.

TANGIBLES AND INTANGIBLES

Tangible costs include time involved for recruitment, selection and training of new personnel. These are real costs in terms of advertising expenses and manpower. The time a manager spends in the hiring process could otherwise be devoted to managing his or her everyday functions. For large companies, high turnover also requires additional staff to process the huge volume of applicants who race through the proverbial revolving door. This further drains profits and indicates a weakness in the selection process.

Other employees pay the price

Intangible costs are reflected in increased workloads as coworkers take up the slack until new employees are hired; the turbulence inherent in companies with high turnover; and the adverse publicity that seems to follow high-turnover businesses.

managers and workers

Although these intangible costs are more difficult to quantify, they definitely have an adverse impact on overall efficiency and worker morale. And unless the cause of the turnover is identified, low morale may lead to more troubles, such as greater tension with management and disruptive behavior.

Hidden cost: morale

Unfortunately, turnover costs often reach critical levels before managers react. One well-known restaurant chain, for example, recently quantified its annual turnover cost at $67 million. Incredibly, these costs had never been tracked until this year.

Figure 11.2 Annotation of a photocopied source.

mands far more respect than an article like "My Baby's Daddy Came from a UFO" in a lurid supermarket tabloid. Between these two extremes are popular magazines, which cover a wide range of territory. Information that appears in a news magazine such as *Newsweek* or *U.S. News & World Report* is more likely to be accepted as balanced and well researched than information taken from a less serious publication such as *People* or *Teen*. You must use your judgment about the reliability of your sources. Because sources differ in respectability and prestige, scholars always identify their research sources so as to allow readers to make their own judgments about reliability. (Acknowledging sources is discussed in Chapter B of Part II.) As a general rule, works that identify their sources are more likely to be reliable than those that do not.

- **What are the author's credentials?** Is the author a recognized authority? An astrophysicist writing about the possibility of life in other galaxies will command more respect than, say, an amateur flying-saucer enthusiast who is a retired dentist. Expert sources lend authority to assertions you make in your paper—another reason for the standard practice of identifying your sources to your readers.

- **Is the source presenting firsthand information?** Are the writer's assertions based on primary or secondary research? For example, articles about cancer research in *Reader's Digest* or *Time* may be written with a concern for accuracy and clarity, but their authors may be reporters writing secondhand on the subject—they may not be experts in the field. You can use these sources, but be certain to consider all factors in weighing their reliability.

- **Does the source demonstrate evidence of careful research?** Does the author show by way of notes and other documentation that the statements presented are based on the best available information? Or does it appear that the author's statements derive from unsupported speculation or incomplete research? A source that seems unreliable should either not be used at all or else be cited as an example of one point of view (perhaps one that you refute using more reliable sources).

- **Is the source up-to-date?** Clearly, you do not want to base your paper on information that is no longer considered accurate and complete. For example, a paper on a dynamic field such as nuclear disarmament or advances in telecommunications would be hopelessly out-of-date if it is based on five-year-old sources. If you are writing a paper on a topic about which new findings or theories exist, your research should include recent sources. Check the publication dates of your sources.

- **Does the source seem biased?** Writers have opinions that they support in their writing, but some writers are more open-minded than others. Is the author's purpose in writing to explain or to persuade? Does the author provide a balanced presentation of evidence, or are there other perspectives and evidence that the author ignores? Be aware of the point of view of the author and of the publication you are examining. An article in a magazine of political opinion such as *National Review* can be expected to take a conservative stance on an issue, just as an article in *The Nation* will express a more liberal opinion. Your own paper, even when you are making an argument for a particular viewpoint, should present evidence for all sides. If you use opinionated sources, you can balance them with sources expressing opposing points of view.

- **Do your sources consider all viewpoints and theories?** Because many books and articles are written from a single viewpoint, it is important to read widely to discover if other points of view exist as well. For example, several works have been written claiming that ancient monuments such as the pyramids are evidence of past visits to our planet by extraterrestrials. Only by checking a variety of sources might a student discover that scientists have discredited most of the evidence on which these claims are based. Students writing about such topics as astrology, subliminal advertising, Noah's flood, holistic healing, Bigfoot, or the assassination of President Kennedy should be aware that these areas are controversial and that they should seek out diverse points of view in their research so they can be fully informed and present a complete picture of the topic to their readers.

Narrowing Your Paper's Focus

If you are like most students, the research paper assigned in your composition course may be the longest paper you have had to write, so you may feel worried about filling enough pages. Most students share that concern at this stage, but they soon find so much material that having *too much* to say (not too little) becomes their concern.

The ideal topic for your paper is one to which you can do justice—one you can write about with some thoroughness and completeness—in a paper of the length you are assigned. Most student researchers start out with a fairly broad conception of their topic and then make it more and more limited as their research and writing progress. As you learn how much information is available about your topic and as you discover through your reading what aspect most intrigues you, you should *narrow your paper's focus*—that is, bring your topic into a sharper and more limited scope.

From your first speculations about a topic until the completion of your final draft, your topic will probably undergo several transformations, usually with each new version more narrowly defined than the one before. For example, a student might begin with the general concept of her major, oceanography, and narrow it through successive stages as follows:

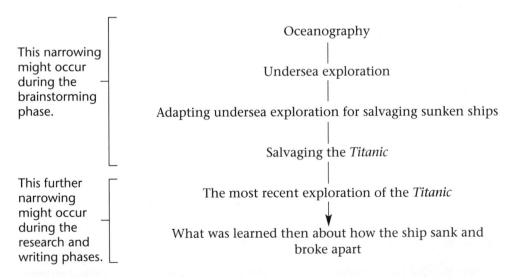

The path from the original germ of an idea to the eventual paper topic isn't always a matter of successive narrowing. As in Emily's case, it sometimes involves some turns and detours. In her clustering exercise on page 344, we can discern a narrowing process as she reached the topic of fast food.

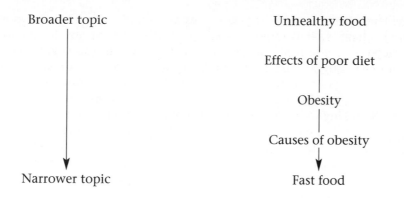

As she conducted her research, however, other aspects of fast food besides the health aspects also attracted her interest. By the time she wrote her prospectus, her topic had expanded to include the social issues and work issues associated with fast food. She would soon realize, however, that she was attempting too much, and once again her topic narrowed appropriately to just work issues in the fast-food industry. Do not be surprised, or discouraged, if your path to your topic takes similar twists and turns. Just keep in mind that *narrowing* your paper's focus is generally the best advice for making your project manageable and for producing the best result.

Narrowing a Topic

EXERCISES

1. Speculate on how each of the following general topics might be successively narrowed during the course of a research project. Write each topic in your notebook, and beneath it give three or four additional topics, each more specific and more narrowly focused than the one above it. (For example, if you were given the topic *oceanography,* you might create a list something like the one given on the facing page.)

    warfare   music   famous people   luxury goods

2. Now take your own research topic and make a general-to-specific list of its successive stages. First list the most general idea you started with and show how it narrowed to your present topic. Then speculate on how your topic might be narrowed even further as you complete work on your project.

Formulating and Refining a Plan

Writing is never an exact science or a tidy procedure, and the business of planning and organizing is the untidiest part of all. It would be nice if you could start by creating a full-blown outline of your paper, then take notes on the areas you have outlined, and finally write your paper from your notes, exactly as first planned. However, any writer can tell you it rarely if ever works that way.

Research papers evolve as you do research, and they continue to evolve as you write them, so it is important to remain flexible. As you learn more about your subject—as you read and take notes, and even as you begin writing—new directions will suggest themselves to you. Be prepared to adjust the focus and organization of your paper at every stage, right up to your final revision. Many a student has expected to write one paper, only to discover something quite different actually taking shape on the page. There is nothing wrong with making these changes—they are a natural part of the writing process. Writing is as much a process of discovery for the writer as it is a medium for communicating with readers.

As you start examining your sources, you may have only a hazy notion of the eventual contents of your paper, but the beginnings of a plan should emerge as you learn more and more. Shortly into your research you should be ready to pause and sketch a very general *informal preliminary outline* of where your paper seems to be going. Emily's first rough outline, shown in Figure 11.3, makes no

Figure 11.3 Emily's rough outline.

pretense of being complete or final or even particularly pretty—nor should it at this stage. Emily was "thinking on paper," making sense of her own thoughts and trying to bring some vague ideas into focus. She was doing it for her own benefit, not trying to impress any outside readers. Having established some sense of her paper's parts, Emily was then able to resume reading and taking notes with greater efficiency. She now had a clearer idea of what she was looking for. She was also aware that the organization of her paper would probably change as she continued writing.

Begin with a very general outline, perhaps listing just a few of the main topics you expect your paper to include. As you continue reading, taking notes, and thinking, your outline may become more fleshed out, as you continue to refine your preliminary plans. Remember that an informal outline is an aid to you in organizing and writing your paper. It is not a part of the paper and does not need to be in any kind of polished, orderly form. A formal outline, if you do one, can be written as one of the last steps of your project. (Formal outlines are discussed in Chapter C of Part II.)

Taking Notes on Note Cards

Clearly, you cannot put into your paper everything you read during the course of your research. Some sources will be more useful than others, but still you will use only a small portion of any one source. Note-taking is a way of selecting what you can use. It is also a way of aiding your memory and storing the information and ideas you find in a convenient form for use when you write the paper.

Good notes, then, have the virtue of being both selective and accessible. You could take notes in your notebook, but a notebook is far less easy to work with than *note cards,* which have the advantage of flexibility. Unlike entries in notebooks or on long sheets of paper, notes on index cards can be easily sorted, rearranged, and weeded out. When you are ready to write, you can group note cards according to topics and arrange them in the order in which you expect to use them in the paper. This greatly simplifies the task of writing.

Besides being selective and convenient, good notes have another quality—accuracy. You are obliged as a scholar to be scrupulously accurate in reporting and acknowledging your sources. In research writing, you must quote your sources accurately and paraphrase them fairly. (Quoting and paraphrasing sources are discussed more fully in Chapter 12.) Moreover, you should give credit to sources for their contributions and make it clear to your readers which words in the paper are your own and which are taken directly from sources. You can use your sources fairly and accurately only if you write from notes that you have taken with great care.

For an example of how a writer takes notes, look first at this passage that Emily read in one of her sources, "Virtues of Work vs. Finishing Homework," an article by Yvonne Zipp that appeared in the *Christian Science Monitor*:

> More than in other developed countries, in the US donning a McDonald's cap or Blockbuster khakis is a teen rite of passage as universal as driver's ed. Surveys show 4 in 5 American teens hold some kind of job during the school year, and half those who work are manning cash registers and flipping burgers more than 20 hours a week.

Everyone can rattle off the benefits of a job: It can instill a solid work ethic, build self-confidence, and teach teens responsibility, time management, and the value of the dollar—not to mention socking funds away for college.

But even though teen work is a proud American tradition—one that has held steady since the 1970s—many are now arguing that the cost to kids is too high.

Students who work more than 20 hours a week are less likely to get enough sleep and exercise, less likely to go on to higher education, and more likely to use alcohol or drugs, according to a recent report by the National Research Council and the Institute of Medicine in Washington.

Figure 11.4 is the note card that Emily made for this passage. Later, when Emily wrote her paper, she used this card to write the following:

> . . . Yvonne Zipp of the Christian Science Monitor observes that such jobs have become "a teen rite of passage as universal as driver's ed." They are ideal for teens because they require no special skills, and many believe that such jobs provide the educational benefit of teaching responsibility and good time and money management. These benefits may be more than offset by costs, however. Zipp cites a study by the National Research Council and the Institute of Medicine in Washington that teens who work more than twenty hours a week are "less likely to get enough sleep and exercise, less likely to go on to higher education,

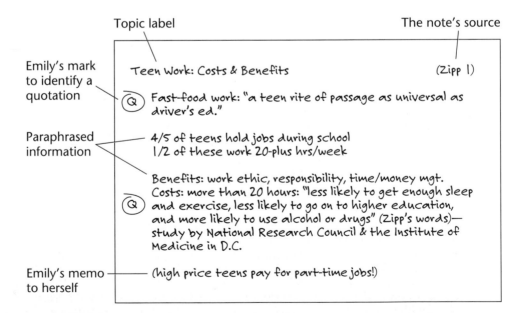

Figure 11.4 A Note Card

and more likely to use alcohol or drugs." These findings are disturbing, since four-fifths of American teens work at least part-time during the school year, and of these, half work more than twenty hours weekly (Zipp 1).

There are various systems for taking notes on cards, and you should use consistently a system that meets your needs. All good note-card systems have several features in common. In making note cards, you should follow these guidelines:

• **Put only related information on a note card.** That is, use one card for each important fact or idea. If you try to economize by crowding many unrelated notes from a source onto a single card, you will sacrifice flexibility later when you try to sort the cards by subjects. Some cards may contain long notes, whereas others may contain only a word or two. One source may provide you with notes on a dozen different cards, whereas another may give you only a single note (or no notes at all).

• **Label each card by topic.** A topic label helps you remember what a note card is about so that after you have finished taking notes from all your sources, you can easily arrange your cards according to topic. Emily selected the label *Teen Work: Costs & Benefits,* writing it in the upper left corner of the card. Similar labels appeared on two other cards that Emily prepared while reading different sources. When she was ready to organize her notes, Emily gathered these three cards together, discarded one of them that she knew she would not use, and arranged the remaining two in the order she was likely to use them in a first draft of her paper.

You should consider following a procedure similar to Emily's. Whenever you take a note, consider where within your subject the information might fit and give the note a label. The label may correspond to one of the divisions in your preliminary outline. If it does not, this may suggest that the organization of your paper is developing and changing and that you need to expand or revise your outline to reflect those changes.

• **Identify the source of each note precisely.** In the upper right corner of her note card, Emily identified her note's source: *(Zipp 1).* This is an example of a parenthetical note (explained in Chapter B of Part II), and its purpose is to tell Emily that the information on the card comes from page 1 of the article written by Zipp. Emily had recorded the full information about that source in her working bibliography, so she needed only the author's last name to identify it.

It is important for each note card to contain all the information you will need in order to cite its source when you write your paper—so you can give the source credit in a parenthetical note. You will find nothing more frustrating as a researcher than having to search through sources at the last minute to find a page reference for a passage that you forgot to identify on a note card. It is smart to identify each source, as Emily did, just as you will identify it in the paper itself—with a parenthetical note. For that reason, you should consult Chapter B before you begin taking notes.

- **Clearly identify the kind of information your note contains.** Three principal kinds of information can appear on note cards; you must make it clear which is which, so you do not get confused later if you use the card in writing the paper:

  Direct quotations. The passage "teen rite of passage . . ." on Emily's card is quoted directly from the author, Yvonne Zipp. *Any time you put a source's own words on a note card, place them within quotation marks.* Do so even if everything on the card is a quotation. It is essential that when you read a note card later, you can tell whether the words are a direct quotation or your own paraphrase of the source. For this reason, you might even use a backup procedure for identifying quotes, as Emily did. She put a circled Q next to each quotation on her cards to be doubly sure she knew these were her source's exact words.

  Your own comments. When you write a note from a source, it may inspire some additional thoughts of your own that you will want to jot down. You may also want to remind yourself later of how you intend to use the note in your paper. *Put your own comments in parentheses.* For example, at the bottom of Emily's note card, she wrote a note to herself about where she might use the material in her paper: "(high price teens pay. . .)." She placed these comments in parentheses to alert herself that these were her own ideas, not those of her source.

  Paraphrase. Like Emily's, your cards should consist largely of paraphrases of what you have found in your sources. *Anything on a card that is not in quotation marks or in parentheses is assumed to be your paraphrasing of the source.* To paraphrase, recast the source's words into your own language, using your own phrasing and style.

- **Be selective in your note-taking.** Because many beginning researchers fear they will not have enough material to use in writing their papers, they often take too many notes. When it comes time to write the paper, they soon discover that if they were to make use of every note, their paper would be dozens of pages long. In fact, for each student who cannot find enough source material for a paper, many others discover to their surprise that they have more than enough.

With experience, researchers learn to be selective, restricting their note-taking to material they stand a good chance of using. Of course, no one makes use of every note card. Especially in the early stages of reading, a researcher does not have a clear notion of what the paper will include or of what information is available. As reading continues, however, hazy notions become more substantial, and the researcher can take notes more selectively.

Figure 11.5 shows two cards that Emily wrote when she read the article in *Human Resources Focus* magazine shown in Figure 11.2 on page 388.

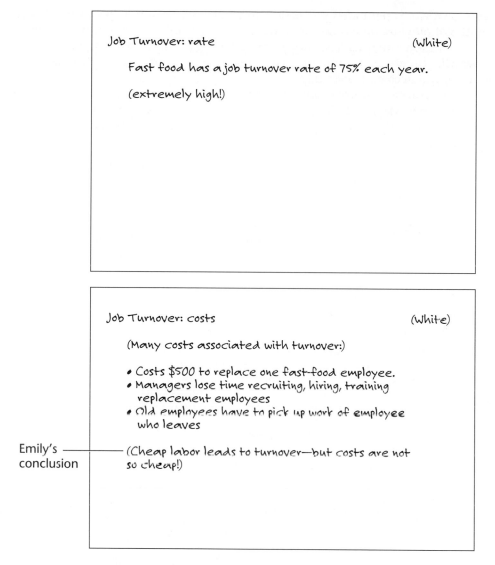

Emily's conclusion

Figure 11.5 Two additional note cards.

▉ AVOIDING PLAGIARISM

To ensure that you use your sources fairly and accurately, you should observe one additional guideline when you take notes: *Do your paraphrasing on the note card, not later.* If you do not intend to use a source's exact words, do not write those words on your card. (When you should and should not quote a source directly is discussed on pages 423–28.) It is wise to translate important information into your own words right after you read. This will save time and help you avoid unintentional *plagiarism*—using the source's words without quotation marks—when you begin to write from your notes. Paraphrasing and summarizing your sources now will also give you more focused notes, as well as force you to read and analyze your sources more carefully.

Since you cannot use everything in your sources, no matter how interesting, it is often necessary to boil down what you find into brief summaries of what is important. In general, the procedure for paraphrasing and summarizing a source is as follows:

1. When you have discovered a passage that you may want to use in your paper, reread it with care.

2. After you have reread it, put it aside and think about the essential idea you have learned. Then write that idea on your card in a brief version, using your own words and style. It is often best not to look at the passage while you write the note, so as to be less likely to plagiarize the original language.

Do not forget to indicate on your note card the specific source of the paraphrase.

Consider how Emily used material from one of her sources. First she read this passage from Eric Schlosser's book *Fast-Food Nation*:

The original source

> Although the McDonald brothers had never encountered the term "throughput" or studied "scientific management," they instinctively grasped the underlying principles and applied them in the Speedee Service System. The restaurant operating scheme they developed has been widely adopted and refined over the past half century. The ethos of the assembly line remains at its core. The fast-food industry's obsession with throughput has altered the way millions of Americans work, turned commercial kitchens into small factories, and changed familiar foods into commodities that are manufactured.

If Emily had written a note like the following, she might have plagiarized the passage when she used the note card to write her paper:

Note too close to the original

```
The McDonald brothers grasped the "throughput" concept
instinctively and applied it in their cooking system.
The scheme they developed has been copied and improved upon
over the past fifty years. It relies on an assembly-line
mentality. An obsessive concern for "throughput" has changed
the way countless Americans work, made restaurants into
factories, and turned restaurant food into a manufactured
commodity.
```

Notice how this passage—while it selects from the original, changes some words, and rearranges phrases—relies too closely on Schlosser's original wording. Now look at the note Emily wrote from this passage:

A legitimate note

```
McDonalds' founders revolutionized fast-food kitchens by
introducing assembly-line techniques and "changed familiar
foods into commodities that are manufactured."
```

In this note, Emily succinctly summarized her understanding of Schlosser's ideas in her own words. Where Schlosser's words were memorable and could not easily be paraphrased, she quoted them exactly.

Putting source information into your own words does *not* mean substituting a few synonyms now and again as you copy your source's sentence onto your note card. For example, consider how it would be possible to misuse the following sentences from an article in *Good Housekeeping* by Patrick Kiger:

> Twenty-five percent of teenage deaths in the workplace are caused by violence, mostly in the commission of a robbery. Yet, though more than half of all teen employees work in retail jobs, only about a third of young workers are given any training on what to do if they're confronted by an armed robber.

The source's words

> One quarter of all teen deaths at work are the result of violence, mostly when robberies are committed. Even though more than fifty percent of teenage workers have retail jobs, only a third of them are trained in any way about how to act if they encounter an armed robber.

A plagiarized note

Observe that this is really the Kiger passage with a few word substitutions (*one quarter* for *twenty-five percent*, *at work* for *in the workplace*, etc.). Putting sources aside when you write note cards is one way to avoid this plagiarism by substitution. It also ensures that your paraphrase will be a genuine expression of your own understanding of a source's idea. Of course, if the exact words are particularly memorable or effective, you may wish to copy them down exactly, within quotation marks, for possible use in your paper.

The foregoing can be summed up as follows:

GUIDELINES for Avoiding Plagiarism

1. Whenever you use ideas or information from a source but do not intend to quote the source directly, paraphrase the source. You must restate the material in your own words, using your own phrasing and style. Merely substituting synonyms for the source's words or phrases is not acceptable. Do your paraphrasing at the time you take notes.

2. Whenever you intend to use the source's words, copy those words exactly onto a note card and place them within quotation marks. To be doubly sure that you will not later mistake the author's words for your own, place a circled letter Q (or some other prominent device) on the card next to the quotation.

3. For any borrowed material—whether a direct quotation or your paraphrase of it—carefully note the source and page number(s) on your note card so that you can cite them in your paper.

4. In your paper, you will give full credit to the sources of all borrowed material, both those you quote directly and those you paraphrase. The only exception is for commonly available factual information. (For further guidelines, see the section "When Are Notes Needed?" in Chapter B of Part II.)

5. Observe the rules for acknowledging sources in your paper by providing acknowledgment phrases, parenthetical notes, and a list of works cited. (Further information about giving credit to sources can be found in Chapter 6 and Chapter B.)

EXERCISES | **Note-Taking**

Imagine that, in doing a research project on the subject of urban legends, you discovered the following sources. Using the guidelines provided in this chapter, write notes from these sources. On your note cards, you may want to paraphrase some passages, quote others, and offer your own comments or responses. You may take more than one note from a passage.

1. The following appeared on page 175 in an essay by Richard A. Reuss titled "Suburban Folklore." Write one note card that captures an explanation of what is meant by the term "urban legend." Then write a second card whose heading is "Urban legend: example." Include at least one passage that you might want to quote in your paper.

    Another major component of the verbal lore of contemporary suburbia is the so-called urban legend, which perhaps deserves equal billing in the folklorist's lexicon as the "suburban legend," since so large a percentage of these narratives are set, either explicitly or implicitly, in a suburban locale. These narratives typically are brief accounts of anonymous people caught up in bizarre and traumatic, occasionally supernatural or humorous, circumstances because of the violation of some unspoken community or social norm. They are most intensively communicated among teenagers but are widely disseminated throughout the rest of the suburban population as well. One cycle of these stories revolves around babysitters left alone with their young charges. In one narrative the parents call to notify the sitter of a later returning time only to be informed by the teenager spaced out on LSD that all is well and "the turkey is in the oven." Knowing no such food is in the house, the parents speed home to find their baby roasting in the oven.

2. Darcy Lockman wrote an article titled "What Fuels Urban Legends?" for *Psychology Today.* The following paragraph appeared on page 21. Write a note card that summarizes the researchers' discovery about what causes urban legends to succeed.

    Psychologists at Stanford and Duke universities had another theory. "We proposed that ideas are selected and retained in part based on their ability to tap emotions that are common across individuals," explains Chip Heath, Ph.D., an associate professor of organizational behavior at Stanford. Heath and his colleagues decided to examine anecdotes that inspire disgust (some 25 percent of urban legends fit the bill). They took 12 urban legends and presented undergraduates at Duke University with three increasingly revolting versions of each story. . . . Amused undergrads consistently repeated the version that elicited the most disgust. "Emotion matters," says Heath. "It's not informational value alone that causes these things to succeed."

 **12** *Reporting on Sources: Paraphrase and Quotation*

Mostly when you *do* research on sources, you find out what other people have thought, discovered, said, or written. When you *report* on your research, you tell your readers what you have learned. The following very different passages could all be called examples of reporting on research sources:

1. My old man says he can lick your old man.

2. "If man does find the solution for world peace," wrote General George C. Marshall in 1945, "it will be the most revolutionary reversal of his record we have ever known."

3. Senator Woodling made it clear today that she would shortly declare herself a candidate for the presidency.

4. The first words ever transmitted by telephone were spoken by Bell to his assistant: "Mr. Watson, come here, I want you."

5. The Stoics argued that it was the highest wisdom to accept triumph without elation, tribulation without regret.

6. V. O. Key, Jr., a leading political scientist, offered this positive assessment of the role played by interest groups in American politics:

   > At bottom, group interests are the animating forces in the political process. . . . The chief vehicles for the expression of group interest are political parties and pressure groups. Through these formal mechanisms groups of people with like interests make themselves felt in the balancing of political forces. (Qtd. in Lowery 63–64)

These six passages all report on sources, since each of them communicates what has been learned from someone else. They certainly do so in different ways and with different effects. The first statement, you might guess, is spoken by one child to another, reporting on what he learned from his father. As for its authority, a listener might be wise to doubt that his father said any such thing. The last statement, in contrast, is surely an example of writing, not speech, since it has all the earmarks of a passage from a scholarly paper or article. Its very form, its direct quotation, its acknowledgment of its source and claim for his expertise (*V. O. Key, Jr., a leading political scientist*), and its careful source citation (*Qtd. in Lowery 63–64;* i.e., the quotation was found on those pages in a work by Lowery) all lend it an impressive authority. The four middle passages could be either spoken or written.

There are other differences among them as well. Passages 2, 4, and 6 all present their sources' words through ***direct quotation,*** with the original language repeated in a word-for-word copy. Passages 1, 3, and 5, on the other hand, ***paraphrase*** their sources, with the source's ideas and information recast in different words. The identity of the sources in each statement is generally clear, although we are not told where the author of passage 5 learned about the Stoic philosophy; still, it is evident that the ideas presented are those of the Stoics and not the author. Of all these passages, however, only number 6 with its ***parenthetical note*** gives a careful ***citation*** of its source, the exact location from which the quotation was taken.

THE CONVENTIONS OF REPORTING

Like the reporting of journalists, the reporting of scholars aims to get at and present the truth. To ensure accuracy and clarity, both types of writing follow careful rules and procedures.

Often these practices are identical in both fields. Both journalism and scholarship, for example, require that sources be acknowledged and identified. Both pay scant attention to unsupported opinions. On the other hand, both pay great respect to expert testimony. In reporting on sources, both fields observe the same time-honored conventions, including rules for paraphrasing, quoting, and even punctuating quotations. If there is one outstanding difference between scholarship and journalism, however, it is that scholarly writing, with its careful conventions of documentation, follows even more stringent procedures for identifying the precise sources from which ideas and information are taken.

This chapter is in large part devoted to these conventions. While some of it involves technicalities (e.g., does a comma go to the left or right of a quotation mark?), even they are important extensions of the care that researchers take to be accurate and truthful. While you are expected to become familiar with most of the conventions here, you should also regard this chapter as a resource that you can turn to often throughout your college career for guidance in presenting the results of your research.

OPTIONS FOR PRESENTING SOURCES

Whenever you report on your research, you need to find a way of presenting to your readers what you have learned from your sources. Sometimes the appropriate method will be paraphrase; at other times, quotation. In fact, you have several options.

Imagine, for example, that in an introductory anthropology course, your instructor has assigned a research paper in which you are to analyze some aspect of American culture. You have chosen to write about the way Americans express their emotions, and in your research you come upon the following passage from page 248 of Ashley Montagu's book, *The American Way of Life*:

> To be human is to weep. The human species is the only one in the whole of animated nature that sheds tears. The trained inability of any human being to weep

is a lessening of his capacity to be human—a defect which usually goes deeper than the mere inability to cry. And this, among other things, is what American parents—with the best intentions in the world—have achieved for the American male. It is very sad. If we feel like it, let us all have a good cry—and clear our minds of those cobwebs of confusion which have for so long prevented us from understanding the ineluctable necessity of crying.

The passage expresses an interesting opinion—that American men have been trained, unnaturally, not to cry—and you want to use it in your paper. You can do so in many ways; the following are examples of your options.

Paraphrase

You can restate an author's ideas in your own words:

> Montagu claims that American men have a diminished capacity
> to be human because they have been trained by their culture
> not to cry (248).

Direct Quotation of a Sentence

You can quote an author's exact words, as in these three examples:

> In his book, The American Way of Life, Ashley Montagu writes,
> "The trained inability of any human being to weep is a
> lessening of his capacity to be human a defect which usually
> goes deeper than the mere inability to cry" (248).

> According to Montagu, "To be human is to weep" (248).

> "If we feel like it," writes Ashley Montagu, "let us all have
> a good cry--and clear our minds of those cobwebs of confusion
> which have for so long prevented us from understanding the
> ineluctable necessity of crying" (248).

Quoting Part of a Sentence

You can incorporate part of an author's sentence into a sentence of your own:

> One distinguished anthropologist calls the American male's
> reluctance to cry "a lessening of his capacity to be human"
> (Montagu 248).

```
Montagu finds it "very sad" that American men have a "trained
inability" to shed tears (248).
```

Quoting Longer Passages

You can quote more than one sentence:

```
Anthropologist Ashley Montagu argues that it is both
unnatural and harmful for American males not to cry:
            To be human is to weep. . . . The trained
            inability of any human being to weep is a
            lessening of his capacity to be human--a defect
            which usually goes deeper than the mere inability
            to cry. . . . It is very sad. (248)
```

In this chapter, we will study these options in some detail. We will first examine the precise methods of presenting sources through paraphrase and quotation. Afterward, we will look at strategies for using sources: when and where to use the options at our disposal. Chapter B of Part II considers the techniques for citing these sources in parenthetical notes.

ACKNOWLEDGING SOURCES

Whether you paraphrase or quote an author, it is important that you make it clear that it is the author's ideas, not your own, you are presenting. This is necessary for the sake of clarity and fairness—so that the reader knows which words, ideas, and discoveries are yours and which are your source's. Parenthetical notes, which cite a page reference and, if needed, the author's name, do that. Notice, too, that each of the preceding examples makes its indebtedness to its source clear through an *acknowledgment phrase,* such as "Montagu claims that. . . ." Other acknowledgment phrases that we might have used include the following:

Acknowledg-
ment phrases
```
Ashley Montagu maintains that . . .
Ashley Montagu, author of The American Way of Life,
        says that . . .
Montagu also believes that . . .
Professor Montagu argues that . . .
According to Ashley Montagu, the eminent
        anthropologist, American men . . .
```

A quotation should never be placed in a paper without acknowledgment. Even a parenthetical note is not enough to identify a quotation. You must always introduce a quotation, telling your readers something about it. Avoid writing passages like this with a "naked" quotation in the middle:

> When my grandfather died, all the members of my family--men and
> women alike--wept openly. We have never been ashamed to cry.
> "To be human is to weep" (Montagu 248). I am sure we are more
> human, and in better mental and physical health, because we are
> able to express our feelings without artificial restraints.

Bad: un-acknowledged quotation

Even though the parenthetical note identifies the source, readers find it awkward to read a quotation without knowing its origin in advance. Forcing them to skip ahead to find the note creates an undesirable interruption of the flow of the paper. These problems would not arise if the writer had used a simple phrase (e.g., *As anthropologist Ashley Montagu observed,*) to introduce the quotation:

> When my grandfather died, all the members of my family--men
> and women alike--wept openly. We have never been ashamed to
> cry. As anthropologist Ashley Montagu observed, "To be human
> is to weep" (248). I am sure we are more human, and in better
> mental and physical health, because we are able to express
> our feelings without artificial restraints.

Better: acknowledged quotation

Not only does the reader better understand the quotation's function with the introductory phrase, but the quotation has more impact as well because it has been attributed to a recognized authority.

Always give your readers enough information to identify your sources. The first time you refer to a source, give both the person's first and last names. Unless the source is a well-known figure, identify him or her so that the reader can understand why this particular person is being quoted.

> Winston Churchill said, . . .
>
> Cynthia Bathurst, author of <u>The Computer Crisis</u>,
>   believes that . . .
>
> According to Valerie Granville, British ambassador to
>   Bhutan during the Sherpa Riots, . . .
>
> Rock star Mick Jagger gave a flip answer: . . .

First references

After the first reference, the source's last name is sufficient:

Subsequent
references

```
Churchill said that . . .
Later Jagger remarked, . . .
```

Although acknowledgment phrases almost always introduce quotations, they are sometimes unnecessary with paraphrased material. As a general rule, use an acknowledgment phrase when the paraphrased material represents an original idea or opinion of the source, when the source's credentials lend the material authority, or when you wish to distance yourself from opinions with which you disagree.

Acknowledg-
ment phrase
for para-
phrased
material

```
Anthropologist Ashley Montagu argues that crying is a
distinctively human activity--as appropriate and necessary
for males as for females (248).
```

However, an acknowledgment phrase is not needed for largely factual information, as in these passages:

No acknowl-
edgment
phrase is
needed for
factual infor-
mation

```
At one point in his life, even Alex Haley, the author of
Roots, possessed only eighteen cents and two cans of sardines
(Powell 179).

One study has found that firstborns score better in
achievement tests that measure language and mathematics
skills (Weiss 51).
```

In such cases, the parenthetical notes provide adequate recognition of sources. (Parenthetical notes are discussed in Chapter B of Part II.) Use your best judgment about whether an acknowledgment phrase is called for with paraphrased material. When in doubt, however, provide the acknowledgment phrase. It is better to err on the side of *over-* rather than *under-*recognition of your sources.

■ RELYING ON EXPERTS

Besides being fair, acknowledging the contribution of a source can also add force to your own writing. In most cases, the sources you present will have greater expertise than you on the subject; a statement from one of them can command greater respect than an unsupported statement from you, a nonexpert. To illustrate this, assume that, in writing a research paper, you quote Montagu on the subject of crying and identify him to your readers as an eminent anthropologist. Could you have made the point equally effectively if instead you had written the following?

```
I think it is wrong that men in America have been brought up

to think it is not manly to cry. Crying is natural. Our

macho-man mentality takes a terrible toll on our emotions.
```

While you are entitled to your opinions, a reader who doubts your expertise on the subject is likely to question whether you have considered all aspects and implications of your position. After all, what reason does the reader have to trust you? However, when an expert such as Montagu is quoted, many of the doubts are removed and the statement carries greater weight.

This is not to say that experts are automatically right. Experts do not always agree with each other, and progress in humanity's quest for truth often comes as new ideas are introduced to challenge old ones. What it does mean is that experts are people who have studied their subjects thoroughly and have earned the right to be listened to with respect. Since you will not often begin with a thorough knowledge of the subjects you write about in research papers, your writing will rely heavily on what you have learned from expert sources.

■ PARAPHRASING SOURCES

Most of the time when you present ideas or information from sources, you will paraphrase them. To *paraphrase* a statement or a piece of writing is to recast it into different words. Paraphrase is the least cumbersome way of communicating what a source has said, as well as the easiest to read. Often the source is too technical for your readers or too wordy; you can present the source's point more clearly and succinctly using your own words. When you paraphrase a source, be accurate and faithful to what your source wrote, but use your own style and phrasing. Imagine, for example, that you wished to make use of this passage as a research source:

> Nearly forty years ago Damon Runyon nearly collapsed in laughter when he covered the trial of George McManus, a gambler, who was accused of shooting Arnold Rothstein, another gambler, who thereupon died. The cause of Damon Runyon's mirth was the sight of the witnesses and jurors in the case running out into the halls during court recesses to place bets with their bookies—even as they considered the evils of gambling in the city.
>
> —Edwin P. Hoyt, *The Golden Rot*

You can paraphrase this information in a briefer version, using your words:

```
According to Edwin P. Hoyt, Damon Runyon was highly amused          Good

that both witnesses and jurors in a gambling trial would

place bets with their bookies during court recesses.
```

What you must *not* do is simply change a word or two while keeping the structure of the original intact:

Bad

> Edwin P. Hoyt writes that about forty years ago Damon Runyon almost fell down from laughing when he was a reporter for the trial of gambler George McManus, accused of murdering another gambler, Arnold Rothstein.

You can avoid word-substitution paraphrase, as well as unintentional plagiarism, if you paraphrase from memory rather than directly from the original copy. Chapters 3 and 11 describe the best method as follows: *Read the passage so that you understand it; then put it aside, and write your recollection of its meaning on a note card, in your own words.* Be certain to observe the guidelines for avoiding plagiarism (see pages 399–400).

EXERCISE   ## Paraphrasing a Source

Imagine that each of the following is a source for a research project. Write a paraphrase of important information from each quotation as you would on a note card. Then write it as you would in the paper itself, giving credit to your source with a suitable acknowledgment phrase. *(Note:* You do not need to present all of the information from each passage in either your paraphrases or your acknowledgments.)

a. *Source:* Linus Pauling. He won Nobel Prizes for both Chemistry (1954) and Peace (1962).

   Quotation
   Science is the search for truth—it is not a game in which one tries to beat his opponent, to do harm to others. We need to have the spirit of science in international affairs, to make the conduct of international affairs the effort to find the right solution, the just solution of international problems, not the effort by each nation to get the better of other nations, to do harm to them when it is possible.

b. *Source:* Edwin P. Hoyt. This quotation is from his book, *The Golden Rot: A Somewhat Opinionated View of America,* published in 1964.

   Quotation
   Let there be no mistake, the pressures on government for destruction of wilderness areas will grow every time the nation adds another million in population. The forest service has been fighting such pressures in the West for fifty years. Any national forest visitor can gauge the degree of success of the "multiple use program" of the forest service very nicely by taking a fishing rod and setting out to catch some trout. He will find mile after mile of the public waters posted by private landowners who do not allow fishing or hunting on their property—or on the government property they lease. Inevitably this includes the best beaver dams and open stretches of water along the streams.

c. *Source:* Marvin Harris. He is an anthropology professor and author of several books on human behavior throughout the world.

Quotation
The trouble with the "confessions" is that they were usually obtained while the accused witch was being tortured. Torture was routinely applied until the witch confessed to having made a pact with the Devil and having flown to a sabbat [a witches' meeting]. It was continued until the witch named the other people who were present at the sabbat. If a witch attempted to retract a confession, torture was applied even more intensely until the original confession was reconfirmed. This left a person accused of witchcraft with the choice of dying once and for all at the stake or being returned repeatedly to the torture chambers. Most people opted for the stake. As a reward for their cooperative attitude, penitent witches could look forward to being strangled before the fire was lit.

d. *Source:* Jessica Mitford. She was a well-known muckraker, an investigative journalist who specialized in exposing scandals and abuses.

Quotation
True, a small minority of undertakers are beginning to face the facts and to exhibit more flexibility in their approach to customers, even to develop some understanding and respect for people who as a matter of principle do not want the full funerary treatment ordinarily prescribed by the industry. But the industry as a whole, and particularly the association leaders, are unable to come to grips with the situation that confronts them today because their whole operation rests on a myth: the assumption that they have the full and unqualified backing of the vast majority of the American people, that the costly and lavish funeral of today, with all its fabulous trimmings, is but a reflection of American insistence on "the best" in all things. It is particularly hard for them to grasp the idea that a person who has lived well or even luxuriously might *prefer* the plainest disposition after death.

QUOTING SOURCES

In research writing, sources are quoted less often than they are paraphrased, but quotation is more complicated and requires more explanation.

Punctuating Quotations

The conventions of punctuation have driven many a student nearly to distraction. They seem arbitrary and often illogical. If you were to set about tinkering with the rules of punctuating, you could very likely make some worthwhile improvements in the current system. Nonetheless, the system as it stands is well established and unlikely to change. Your consolation is that, even if it is complicated, it can be mastered, and it does serve its purpose of giving readers helpful signals that make reading easier. In the case of quotations, punctuation makes it clear just which passages are your own and which belong to your sources.

The following are the most important punctuation conventions for presenting sources. You should learn these guidelines and follow them carefully.

1. *Use double quotation marks (" ") before and after a source's words when you copy them directly.*

Double quotation marks

> At the Battle of Trafalgar, Admiral Nelson exhorted his
>
> fleet: "England expects every man to do his duty."
>
> The phrase "bats in the belfry" was coined by the writer Eden
>
> Phillpotts.

2. *Use single quotation marks (' ') before and after quoted material when it occurs within other quoted material—that is, when it occurs inside double quotation marks.*

Single quotation marks

> Charles and Mary Beard contend that the American government
>
> was not established as a <u>democracy</u>: "The Constitution did not
>
> contain the word or any word lending countenance to it,
>
> except possibly the mention of 'We, the people,' in the
>
> preamble."
>
> We used this example earlier in the chapter: "According to
>
> Ashley Montagu, 'To be human is to weep.'"

3. *Indent a quotation that takes up more than four lines in your paper.* In typing, indent one inch (ten spaces) from the left margin. Do not indent any additional spaces from the right margin. If you are quoting a single paragraph or less, do not indent the first line of the quotation any additional spaces:

Indent the left margin one inch (ten spaces). Do not indent the right margin.

> The millionaire Andrew Carnegie believed that free enterprise
>
> and private charity, not government social programs, offered
>
> the best solution to the problem of poverty:
>
> > Thus is the problem of Rich and Poor to be
> >
> > solved. The law of accumulation will be left
> >
> > free; the laws of distribution free.
> >
> > Individualism will continue, but the millionaire

> will be but a trustee of the poor; entrusted
> for a season with a great part of the increased
> wealth of the community, but administering it
> for the community far better than it could or
> would have done for itself.

However, if the indented quotation consists of two or more paragraphs, indent the first line of each paragraph an additional quarter inch or three spaces:

> Florence Nightingale questioned the unequal treatment
> of men and women in Victorian England:
>> Now, why is it more ridiculous for a man
>> than for a woman to do worsted work and drive
>> out everyday in the carriage? Why should we
>> laugh if we see a parcel of men sitting around
>> a drawing room table in the morning, and think
>> it all right if they were women?
>> Is man's time more valuable than woman's?
>> Or is the difference between man and woman
>> this, that women have confessedly nothing to do?

Indent paragraphs an additional quarter inch (three spaces)

These passages demonstrate other guidelines as well:

- **An indented quotation is never placed within quotation marks.** Quotation marks are unnecessary since the indenting already makes it clear that the passage is a quotation.
- **When typing, do not skip extra lines before or after an indented quotation.** The entire paper, including such quotations, is double-spaced.

4. *Accuracy is essential in quoting a source.*

- **Copy a quoted passage exactly as it is printed.** The only exception is for obvious typographical errors, which you should correct. Otherwise, make no changes in a quoted passage, even if you disagree with its wording or punctuation. For example, if you, rather than Andrew Carnegie, had been the author of the quotation that concludes on the top of this page, you might have used a colon or dash after the word *poor* instead of a semicolon. But since Carnegie used a semicolon, that is the way it must appear when you copy it.

- Insert *[sic],* **the Latin word meaning "thus," in brackets, immediately after an apparent error.** Do so only if you feel it necessary to identify it as your source's error, not your error in copying the passage.

```
The régime posted a proclamation on every streetcorner:

"Amnesty will be granted all mutineers who lay down their arms.

Die-heart [sic] traitors who persist in rebellion will be shot."
```

This device should be used only rarely. Avoid using *sic* to belittle a source with whom you disagree.

5. *Use punctuation to separate a quotation from an acknowledgment phrase or sentence.*

- **Use a comma or colon when the phrase comes before the quotation. A comma is preferred when the introduction is not a complete sentence:**

The introduction is not a complete sentence

```
Jacques Delille wrote, "Fate chooses our relatives, we

choose our friends."

As Al Jolson remarked, "You ain't heard nothin' yet, folks."
```

- **A colon is preferred when the introduction is a complete sentence:**

The introduction is a complete sentence

```
Edmund Burke believed that sadism is a component of human

nature: "I am convinced that we have a degree of delight and

that no small one, in the real misfortunes and pains of others."
```

Colon

```
The last words in Act II are spoken by Hamlet: "The play's

the thing / Wherein I'll catch the conscience of the King."
```

- **Use a colon to introduce an indented quotation:**

```
From his jail cell Martin Luther King wrote about the law:
        An unjust law is a code that a numerical or power

        majority group compels a minority group to obey

        but does not make binding on itself. This is

        difference made legal. By the same token, a just
```

```
law is a code that a majority compels a minority
to follow and that it is willing to follow
itself. This is sameness made legal.
```

- However, no punctuation is needed when a quotation is a continuation of the introductory sentence:

```
According to the Library Bill of Rights, libraries are
forums for information and ideas, and they have                    No colon
. . . the responsibility to provide . . .
all points of view on all questions and issues
of our times, and to make these ideas and
opinions available to anyone who needs or wants
them, regardless of age, race, religion,
national origin, or social and political views.
```

- Use a comma when the acknowledgment phrase comes after the quotation, unless the quotation ends in a question mark or exclamation point:

```
"When you have nothing to say, say nothing," wrote Charles        Comma
Caleb Colton.
```

But:

```
"Who can refute a sneer?" asked William Paley.                     No comma
```

- When the acknowledgment phrase is inserted within a quoted sentence, begin and end it with commas:

```
"Politics," said Bismarck, "is not an exact science."             Commas
```

- Use no punctuation at all (other than quotation marks) when you make quoted words part of your own sentence:

```
Robert E. Rogers's advice to the Class of 1929 at MIT was to      No comma
"marry the boss's daughter."
```

The word *that* incorporates a quotation that follows it into your sentence. Note carefully the difference in punctuation among the following three sentences:

–Quotation treated as an independent sentence:

Comma

Henry Ford said, "History is more or less bunk."

–Quotation incorporated into the sentence:

No comma

Henry Ford said that "history is more or less bunk."

–Quotation paraphrased:

No comma

Henry Ford said that history is nonsense.

6. *Capitalize the first word of a quotation when it is treated as an independent sentence. Do not capitalize it when it is incorporated into your own sentence.*

Uppercase
letter

Margaret Hungerford gave us the famous saying, "Beauty is in the eye of the beholder."

Lowercase
letter

Like Margaret Hungerford, many psychologists believe that "beauty is in the eye of the beholder."

7. *The trickiest rules apply to punctuation at the close of a quotation. Refer to the following examples whenever necessary.*
   • **Commas and periods are always placed inside a closing quotation mark:**

Comma inside
the quotation
mark

"From the sublime to the ridiculous is but a step," wrote Napoleon.

Period inside
the quotation
mark

Martin Joseph Routh offered timeless advice over a century ago: "You will find it a very good practice always to verify your references, sir."

Judge Learned Hand wrote, "I should like to have every court begin, 'I beseech ye in the bowels of Christ, think that we may be mistaken.'"

Period inside single and double quotation marks

- **Colons, semicolons, and dashes are placed outside a closing quotation mark:**

"Blood, toil, tears and sweat": these were the sacrifices Churchill promised to his country.

Colon outside the quotation mark

On his deathbed, O. Henry said, "Turn up the lights--I don't want to go home in the dark"; then he expired.

Semicolon outside the quotation mark

- **Questions marks and exclamation points go inside the closing quotation mark when they belong to the quotation, but outside when they do not:**

Macbeth asked, "What is the night?"

Question mark belongs to quotation

Who said, "Cowards die many times before their deaths"?

Question mark does not belong to quotation

Colonel Sidney Sherman first shouted, "Remember the Alamo!"

Exclamation point belongs to quotation

How dare you respond, "No comment"!

Exclamation point does not belong to quotation

- **For punctuation following a parenthetical note, see pages 562–63 or the quick reference guide on the inside back cover.**

8. *Follow these conventions for quoting poetry:*
   - **Use a slash with a space before and after it to divide quoted lines of poetry:**

Ogden Nash wrote, "Candy / Is dandy / But liquor / Is quicker."

Space, slash, space

- Longer passages of poetry are indented:

Emily Dickinson wrote

    "Faith" is a fine invention

      When Gentlemen can <u>see</u>--

      But <u>Microscopes</u> are prudent

      In an Emergency.

Indent the left
margin ten
spaces

Like other indented passages, poetry is not placed within quotation marks. The word *"Faith"* is in quotation marks because Dickinson punctuated it that way in her poem.

EXERCISES | **Punctuating Quotations**

1. The following passages that appear in brackets are quotations, printed with their original capitalization and punctuation. Remove the brackets and add whatever punctuation is necessary. Make whatever additions and changes are necessary to put each sentence into proper form.

   a. Anne Morrow Lindbergh wrote [The wave of the future is coming and there is no fighting it.].

   b. Rachel Carson was among the first to warn against the pollution of the environment [As crude a weapon as the cave man's club, the chemist's barrage has been hurled against the fabric of life.].

   c. [Gentlemen of the old régime in the South would say, "A woman's name should appear in print but twice—when she marries and when she dies."] wrote Arthur Wallace Calhoun in 1918.

   d. [Gentlemen] wrote Anita Loos [always seem to remember blondes.].

   e. How many students today believe with James B. Conant that [He who enters a university walks on hallowed ground.]?

   f. William Morris called this a [golden rule] [Have nothing in your houses that you do not know to be useful, or believe to be beautiful.]; a rather different conception of what a house should be is presented in a statement of architect Le Corbusier [A house is a machine for living in.].

   g. Freud never underestimated the role of religion in human culture [If one wishes to form a true estimate of the full grandeur of religion, one must keep in mind what it undertakes to do for men. It gives them information about the source and origin of the universe, it assures them of protection and final happiness amid the changing vicissitudes of life, and it guides their thoughts and motions by means of precepts which are backed by the whole force of its authority.].

h. Poverty is not portrayed as romantic in Keats's poem "Lamia"
[Love in a hut, with water and a crust,
Is—Love, forgive us!—cinders, ashes, dust.]

i. Gloating on his pact with the devil, Doctor Faustus asked [Have not I made blind Homer sing to me?].

j. [We was robbed!] shouted manager Joe Jacobs into the microphone in 1932, when the decision went against his fighter, Max Schmeling.

2. Create sentences that incorporate quotations according to the following guidelines:

a. Use this quotation by Mark Twain in a sentence that begins with an acknowledgment phrase:

Man is the only animal that blushes. Or needs to.

b. Use the following quotation by Havelock Ellis in a sentence that ends with an acknowledgment phrase:

The place where optimism most flourishes is the lunatic asylum.

c. Use the following quotation by George Santayana in a sentence with an acknowledgment phrase inserted within it:

Fanaticism consists in redoubling your efforts when you have forgotten your aim.

d. Incorporate a paraphrase of this quotation into a sentence that acknowledges its author, Congressman Grimsley Buttersloop:

My opponents have accused me of embezzlement, drinking, fooling around, and falling asleep during committee meetings. The only thing they haven't accused me of is not loving my country, and that they can never do.

e. When you quote the following, let the reader know that its author, Frank Winslow, deliberately misspelled the word *souperior* in a letter to his aunt, Martha Fleming:

All I can say of your clam chowder is that it was positively souperior.

Altering Quotations

Sometimes when you write about your research, you will want to use a quotation that does not precisely fit. Either it lacks a word or a phrase that would make its meaning clear to your readers, or else it contains too much material—unnecessary words that are not relevant to your point. For example, imagine that you found this quotation from a person named Vanessa O'Keefe:

I absolutely long to prove to the world, as I said in an interview yesterday, that a perpetual motion machine is not an impossibility.

Assume you wanted to introduce it with the phrase *Vanessa O'Keefe announced that she. . . .* Fortunately, there are methods that allow you to alter such a quotation to fit your needs. By using them, you can write

```
Vanessa O'Keefe announced that she "absolutely long[ed] to

prove to the world . . . that a perpetual motion machine is

not an impossibility."
```

As you can see, you can make certain alterations in quotations to suit your needs. When you do so, however, you must obey these two guidelines:

1. You must make it completely clear to your readers precisely what changes you have made.

2. Your alterations must not distort the meaning or essential phrasing of a quotation or make it appear to say something other than what the author intended.

The following methods may be followed to alter quotations.

Adding to Quotations: Brackets [ ]

Whenever a word, phrase, or suffix needs to be added to a quotation to make its meaning clear, you may insert it within **brackets.** Brackets are most commonly used to explain a reference. For example, it would not be evident to a reader of this quotation that it was the United States that José Martí was referring to as "the monster":

```
I have lived in the monster and I know its insides; and my

sling is the sling of David.
```

By using brackets when you quote this sentence, you can make the reference clear:

Insertion in brackets

```
In a letter to Manuel Mercado, Martí wrote, "I have lived in

the monster [the United States] and I know its insides; and

my sling is the sling of David."
```

Similarly, you can insert modifiers in brackets. The following insertion makes it clear which frontier is being referred to:

```
Churchill said, "That long [Canadian-American] frontier

from the Atlantic to the Pacific Oceans, guarded only by
```

neighborly respect and honorable obligations, is an example

to every country and a pattern for the future of the world."

Another use for brackets is to provide brief translations of foreign or archaic words:

Chaucer wrote, "A fol [fool] can not be stille."

Unusual terms may also require explanation. For example, if you used the following quotation in writing about doctors performing unnecessary operations, you might need to explain the term *arthroscopic surgery* to your readers.

According to Dr. Robert Metcalf, who teaches orthopedic

surgery at the University of Utah, the problem exists in

his field as well: "There's considerable concern that

arthroscopic surgery [a technique for repairing damaged

knees] is being overutilized and is sometimes being done in a

manner damaging to healthy cartilage."

When the unclear term is a simple pronoun, you can replace it altogether with the noun it refers to. For example, in the following quotation, instead of "They [the Americans] are the hope of the world," you can write

Baron de l'Aulne expressed a more favorable opinion in 1778:

"[The Americans] are the hope of the world."

Instead of brackets, however, sometimes the simplest solution is to incorporate the unclear portion into your own sentence:

Writing about Americans in 1778, Baron de l'Aulne expressed the

more favorable opinion that "they are the hope of the world."

Or better still:

In 1778, Baron de l'Aulne expressed the more favorable

opinion that Americans are "the hope of the world."

The best rule is to use brackets when they provide the simplest way of making the source's meaning clear to your readers. As you can see, bracketing is a useful tool that can solve several writing problems. At the same time, it should not be overused. As with other devices, when brackets appear again and again in a paper, readers will find them distracting.

Subtracting from Quotations: Ellipsis Dots (. . .)

You can omit irrelevant parts of a quotation and replace them with *ellipsis dots,* three typed periods separated by spaces. The part you omit can be a word, a phrase, one or more sentences, or even a much longer passage. As with everything you alter, there is one important condition: You must not distort the author's meaning or intentions.

Good writers edit their writing, paring away what is unnecessary, off the point, or distracting. Quotations are used most effectively when you select them carefully and when you keep only the pertinent parts and omit what is not needed. As an example, consider again the passage by Ashley Montagu quoted earlier:

> To be human is to weep. The human species is the only one in the whole of animated nature that sheds tears. The trained inability of any human being to weep is a lessening of his capacity to be human—a defect which usually goes deeper than the mere inability to cry. And this, among other things, is what American parents—with the best intentions in the world—have achieved for American males. It is very sad. If we feel like it, let us all have a good cry—and clear our minds of those cobwebs of confusion which have for so long prevented us from understanding the ineluctable necessity of crying.

As interesting as this passage is, you might be best able to make your point if you quote only parts of it. For example:

Anthropologist Ashley Montagu argues that it is both

unnatural and harmful for American males not to weep:

> To be human is to weep. ▓.▓.▓ The trained
>
> inability of any human being to weep is a lessening
>
> of his capacity to be human--a defect which usually
>
> goes deeper than the mere inability to cry. . . .
>
> It is very sad.

Ellipsis dots indicate a deletion

Whole sentences have been removed from the passage and replaced with ellipses. Parts of a sentence can also be omitted, as follows:

```
Montagu feels that "the trained inability . . . to weep is
a defect which usually goes deeper than the mere inability
to cry."
```

As with brackets, there is a danger in overusing ellipses. Not only can they become distracting to the reader, but they can also defeat your purpose in quoting, as with this monstrosity:

```
Montagu feels that "the . . . inability . . . to weep is
a defect which . . . goes deeper than the . . . inability
to cry."
```

The preceding sentence makes so many changes in the original quotation that it can no longer be said to communicate Montagu's phrasing, and the point of using direct quotation is lost. Paraphrase would make much more sense; for example:

```
Montagu feels that the inability to cry is a more significant
defect than many realize.
```

Ellipsis dots are not needed when it is already obvious that the passage you have quoted is only a part of the original:

```
A man's inability to cry, according to Montagu, is a
"lessening of his capacity to be human."
```

Ellipsis dots are
not needed

You should use ellipses, however, when it is not obvious that you are quoting only a portion of the source's complete sentence:

```
Montagu wrote, "The trained inability of any human being to
weep is a lessening of his capacity to be human. . . ."
```

When the omission comes at the front of a quoted sentence, you may capitalize the first word if you put the first letter in brackets:

```
Montagu offered this advice: "[L]et us all have a good
cry. . . ."
```

EXERCISES | **Using Brackets and Ellipsis Dots**

1. The following is part of the transcript of a reporter's interview with a political candidate, Paul Shawn. Read it and comment on the quotations that follow.

   Q: Your opponent, Darla Stowe, says you hunger for money. Is that true?

   A: If you mean, do I want to earn enough for my family to live decently, then yes, I hunger for money. I think that's true of almost everyone. But I hunger for other things as well: peace, justice, brotherhood, and national prosperity.

   Q: Your opponent also says you are using this race as a stepping-stone to higher office. Is this true?

   A: Actually, I'm quite certain I have no more desire for higher office than she has.

   Which of the following quotations can be justified on the basis of this interview? Explain why each of them is fair or unfair, and discuss its use of brackets, ellipses, and paraphrase.

   a. Paul Shawn says he "hunger[s] for . . . peace, justice, brotherhood, and national prosperity."

   b. Shawn admitted, "[Y]es, I hunger for money."

   c. Shawn's opponent accuses him of using this race to seek further political advancement, but he responds, "I have no more desire for higher office. . . ."

   d. Shawn believes that a "hunger for money" is "true of almost everyone."

   e. Quick in responding to an opponent's accusation, Shawn retorted that he has "no more desire for higher office than [Darla Stowe] has."

   f. While admitting he has the same interest as most people in earning a comfortable living for his family, Shawn says he has other goals as well: "peace, justice, brotherhood, and national prosperity."

2. Use quotations from the following passages according to the instructions given for each. Introduce each quotation with an acknowledgment phrase.

   a. Quotation

   I always dreamed of it as being a kind of earthly paradise where no troubles ever intruded.

   Speaker: Linnea Aycock

   Instructions:
   (1) Introduce the quotation with the acknowledgment phrase *Linnea Aycock said,* and use brackets to show that Aycock is talking about Tahiti. (2) Write another version, this time quoting only part of her sentence. Without using brackets, show that she is talking about Tahiti.

   b. Quotation

   Our inspiration was a cartoon that appeared in a children's magazine.

Speaker: A NASA scientist

Instruction:
Use brackets to indicate that the cartoon inspired the design of a new space helmet.

c. Quotation

My generation never thought of college in terms of making ourselves employable. It was OK to be interested in Plato or T. S. Eliot or Freud, but never in IBM or General Mills. It was easy then to regard jobs with contempt since there were so many of them. It is very different with today's job-conscious generation. The response to Shakespeare now is likely to be, "How will he help me in my job?"

Writer: Ronni Jacobsen

Instruction:
Quote two or three sentences that communicate the main idea of this passage. Use ellipsis dots to represent what you omit.

d. Quotation

My message to all you students is that hard work and self-discipline are the keys— and you should never forget this—to success in your college and business careers.

Speaker: Cyrus T. Pierpont

Instruction:
Begin with *Cyrus T. Pierpont told students that.* Omit unnecessary parts of the quotation, including the first eight words and the part that is surrounded by dashes. Although it is not necessary, you can change *your* to *their.*

e. Quotation

If idiots drive motor vehicles when they are drunk, this should happen: they should lose their licenses and be sent to jail—for 90 days or longer.

Speaker: Sergeant Robert Symmes

Instruction:
Introduce the quotation with the words *Sergeant Robert Symmes said that.* Alter the quotation by deleting the word *if,* inserting *who* after *idiots,* omitting *this should happen:,* and making whatever other changes are necessary.

WHEN TO QUOTE AND WHEN TO PARAPHRASE

One of the questions beginning research writers often ask their instructors is: "How many quotations should I put in my paper?" Their uncertainty is not usually allayed by the appropriate answer: "It depends." What it depends on are the circumstances of the individual case—and your own good judgment. While there is no easy answer to the question, some useful guidelines can help you decide how to use your sources.

1. *Do not overquote.* In fact, do not quote very much at all. Most beginning researchers quote far too much in their papers. Quotations should be saved for special occasions, and with good reason: Readers find papers that are filled with quotation after quotation unpleasant and hard to read. (By now you are probably tired of reading quotations in this chapter!) When they encounter a great many quotations, readers will often skim them or skip them entirely. No one likes to read a passage like this:

Bad (too many quotations)

"Early [Roman] amphitheaters," according to Fredericks, "were temporary wooden structures that often collapsed under the weight of spectators, with the result of great loss of life" (40). Bennett reports:

> The most famous of all buildings of this kind was the Flavian Amphitheater in Rome. Also called the Colosseum because of its size, it was begun by the emperor Vespasian and dedicated by his son Titus in A.D. 80. . . . After the 6th century it was used as a fortress and a quarry. (101)

Fredericks says, "Although accounts of the time report it held more than 80,000 spectators, modern estimates place its capacity at 50,000" (42). The architectural historian Anne Ramsey wrote:

> Structurally and functionally, the Roman Colosseum has been rivaled by no comparably sized arenas until the most recent age. Even today it remains a model of planning for rapid crowd access and exit and for unobstructed spectator sight lines. (17-18)

Of these four quotations, piled one on the other, all but the last, which expresses the opinion of an authority, should be rephrased in the writer's own words. The passage then becomes much more readable:

The first Roman amphitheaters were temporary structures   Better
built of wood. Because they could not long support the great
crowds who attended the spectacles, they often collapsed in
terrible disasters (Fredericks 40). Later they were replaced
by permanent facilities, the most famous of which was the
Flavian Amphitheater, better known as the Colosseum. Begun by
the emperor Vespasian, it was dedicated in A.D. 80 by his
son, Titus. It served as a sports and gladiatorial arena with
a capacity of 50,000 spectators until the sixth century. It
was then allowed to deteriorate, being used occasionally as a
fortress and frequently stripped of its stone for use in
other buildings (Bennett 101). Nevertheless, it survived and
remains today one of the most widely admired Roman buildings.
Architectural historian Anne Ramsey writes:

> Structurally and functionally, the Roman
> Colosseum has been rivaled by no comparably sized
> arenas until the most recent age. Even today it
> remains a model of planning for rapid crowd
> access and exit and for unobstructed spectator
> sight lines. (17-18)

The rule can be restated as follows: *If you have a choice between quoting and paraphrasing a source, paraphrase it.*

2. ***Always paraphrase a source, except when a direct quotation is needed.*** You should paraphrase most of your sources most of the time, especially under the following conditions.

- **Paraphrase if the source provides factual information.** Avoid quotations like the following:

The collapsing of bridges was a considerable problem in the   Unnecessary quotation
past: "In the latter half of the 19th century, American
bridges were failing at the rate of 25 or more per year!"
(Worth 29).

Instead, state this factual information in your own words:

Better

A century ago American bridges were far more dangerous than today, collapsing at an annual rate of 25 or more (Worth 29).

- **Paraphrase if you can say it more briefly or clearly in your own words.**

Wordy

Sun worshiper Andrea Bergeron claims that "Solists face grave and persistent discrimination, not the least of which is that which prohibits a fair hearing for our beliefs. Because our beliefs are not traditional we are dismissed as cultists" (202).

Very likely, you would need nothing more elaborate than this brief paraphrase to make your point:

Better

Andrea Bergeron feels that she and her fellow Solists (sun worshipers) are discriminated against and their religious views are not taken seriously (202).

3. *Quote a source directly when the source's words work better than your own.* If you use them sparingly, quotations can be effective in your research writing. Use them in the following cases:

- **Quote when the source's words are phrased in a particularly eloquent or memorable way.** Paraphrase could not do justice to the following quotations:

General Patton wrote, "A pint of sweat will save a gallon of blood" (987).

In 1947, physicist J. Robert Oppenheimer expressed the unease felt by many scientists about their role in developing the atom bomb: "In some sort of crude sense which no vulgarity, no humor, no overstatement can quite

extinguish, the physicists have known sin; and this is a
knowledge which they cannot lose" (1055).

You may not always find it easy to decide whether a statement from a
source is so well phrased that it should be presented to readers directly. Use
your best judgment. In cases where you are in doubt, the wisest course is to
paraphrase.

- **Quote when you are writing about the source or the source's words:**

  Ginter was never modest in his self-descriptions:
  "When I was born 42 years ago to a family of humble
  asparagus farmers, none suspected I would one day be
  the world's leading transcriber of baroque music for
  the banjo" (37).

  The advertisement promised "luxury villas with a
  spectacular ocean view," but only by leaning far out
  the windows of our ancient bungalow could we gain even a
  distant glimpse of the sea.

  Victor Hugo called Jean Henri Fabre "the Homer of the
  Insects" with good reason. Few naturalists wrote such
  vivid metaphors as Fabre does in this description of the
  praying mantis:

  > To judge by the term <u>Prègo-Diéu</u>, we should look
  > to see a placid insect, deep in pious
  > contemplation; and we find ourselves in the
  > presence of a cannibal, of a ferocious spectre
  > munching the brain of a panic-stricken victim.
  > (Qtd. in Lynch and Swanzey 51)

- **Quote when the source is an expert whose exact words will lend authority to a claim that you make:**

> Paratrupus schusterensis, the common swamp frogwort, is a
> delicacy among scavenger gourmets. Florence Demingo, author
> of A Field Guide to Edible Weeds, exclaims: "Ah, the frog-
> wort! No other plant offers such a thrill to the palate
> while fortifying the liver with such potent dosages of
> Vitamin B-8" (188).

> The public is often outraged when technicalities decide the
> outcome of important court cases, but as Justice Felix
> Frankfurter observed in 1943, "The history of liberty has
> largely been the history of the observance of procedural
> safeguards" (37).

> As anthropologist Ashley Montagu observed, "To be human is
> to weep" (248).

Usually, however, you can paraphrase an authority with the same good results:

> Florence Demingo, author of A Field Guide to Edible Weeds,
> finds the frogwort both tasty and rich in Vitamin B-8
> (188).

And one final consideration for quotation in research papers:

- **Do not restrict your quoting to already quoted material.** Many students
  quote only passages that appear within quotation marks in their sources;
  that is, they quote writers they have found quoted by other writers. It
  never occurs to them to quote their sources directly. Of course, you should
  not overquote, but on the other hand, do not be afraid to quote your
  sources themselves. If, for example, you were using this very paragraph as
  a research source, you could quote from it:

> Veit and Gould advise, "Do not restrict your quoting to
> already quoted material" (428).

| **Judging When to Paraphrase and Quote** | **EXERCISE** |

Decide if any of the quotations in the following passages should instead have been paraphrased by the writers. For those quotations, write a paraphrase that could be substituted for the inappropriate quotation. Omit any notes that you decide are unnecessary.

a. Pott's disease is "tuberculosis caries of the vertebrae, resulting in curvature of the spine. It was named after the physician who described it, Percival Pott (1714–88)" (Gleitman 110).

b. Geologists and seismologists are uncertain how to interpret the cryptic note found in McPhilibar's hand after the cave-in: "Major discover [sic]—8th strata, fault line demarcation—earthquake predictor. Eureka!" (Donnelly 192).

c. Harris argues that the animal-powered agriculture of India is not necessarily a problem to be corrected:

To convert from animals and manure to tractors and petrochemicals would require the investment of incredible amounts of capital. Moreover, the inevitable effect of substituting costly machines for cheap animals is to reduce the number of people who can earn their living from agriculture. . . . Less than 5 percent of U.S. families now live on farms, as compared with 60 percent about a hundred years ago. If agribusiness were to develop along similar lines in India, jobs and housing would soon have to be found for a quarter of a billion displaced peasants. (12)

d. Humans are not entirely logical creatures. Often we take our guidance from emotional and spiritual voices within us. As the philosopher Pascal observed, "The heart has its reasons which reason knows nothing of" (40).

e. "The word *ain't*," says Phillips, "has generated its share of controversy" (64). Frelling writes, "*Ain't* is widely accepted in casual conversation. It is rarely used in formal discourse and in writing" (6). A controversy arises especially over its use as a contraction for *am not.* Dwight Macdonald speaks in its behalf, noting that "there is no other workable contraction, for *amn't* is unpronounceable and *aren't* is ungrammatical" (144). Theodore Bernstein, on the other hand, says, "There can be no doubt that *ain't I* is easier to say than *aren't I* and *amn't I,* and sounds less stilted than *am I not. Nevertheless, what should be not always is" (13–14).

■ A FURTHER NOTE ON PLAGIARISM

Undoubtedly, the most often repeated exhortation in this book is your obligation as a scholar to acknowledge your sources. The message is so important that we don't want to risk its being missed. Feel free to make use of sources (after, all, that is what research is all about), but give them full credit when you do so. Failure to acknowledge a source, thereby making someone else's work appear to be your own, is plagiarism.

The most glaring cases of plagiarism are deliberate acts of cheating: students handing in papers that they did not write or copying articles from magazines and passing them off as their own work. These are dishonest acts that rank with library vandalism as among the most serious breaches of the code of scholarship. They are dangerous as well, since penalties for them are understandably severe, and instructors are much better than most plagiarists realize at spotting work that is not a student's own.

A less serious offense, but also one to be avoided, is an unintentional act of plagiarism. Most of the time when students plagiarize, they do so innocently, unaware that they are violating the rules of scholarship. They copy a sentence or two from an article, not knowing that they should either quote or paraphrase it. They change a few words in copying a sentence, sincerely believing that they are paraphrasing it. They do not provide a parenthetical note because they do not know that one is needed. They are not trying to cheat; they are not even aware that they are cheating. It is just that no one ever told them to do otherwise. Perhaps when they were in the fifth grade, they wrote papers that consisted of copying out passages from encyclopedia articles. That may have gone unreprimanded in grade school. It is never tolerated in college.

There is certainly no need to plagiarize, because you are allowed to use sources provided that you acknowledge them. In fact, there is no advantage in it either: Papers based on expert sources, fairly acknowledged, are what is wanted of scholars. They are exactly what instructors are looking for.

■ PRACTICE WITH USING SOURCES

The first part of this chapter—in which you learned to paraphrase and quote individual sources—can be compared to the on-the-ground instruction given to would-be parachutists. It is essential background, but the real learning doesn't take place until the first jump. In the rest of this chapter, we intend to push you out of the plane. Your jump will involve taking a selection of sources and using them to write a brief research-based essay.

Writing a Brief Objective Research Essay

When you do research, you have a purpose in mind: You are seeking to learn more about a certain topic and, often, to inform others about what you have discovered. As an example to illustrate the process involved in a brief research project, imagine that you have been assigned to report briefly to your political science class on a controversy surrounding the Constitution's Bill of Rights. Let's suppose that, having narrowed your topic, you decide to review the "Schillinger case." Here are excerpts from five (fictitious) sources that you have discovered in your research.

The following is a news article from the *Essex Herald-Journal,* 5 August 2003, on page 6:

State Seeks to Force Cancer Treatment

State authorities have asked the courts to grant them custody over the 13-year-old daughter of a clergyman so that she can receive the anti-cancer treatment doctors say she needs to stay alive.

The Rev. and Mrs. Paul Schillinger and their daughter, Cathy, are members of the Children of Prophecy church, which rejects all medical treatment and relies on faith to cure ailments. The Schillingers are contesting the state's attempt to force Cathy to undergo chemotherapy. Doctors say that she suffers from leukemia and will die within six months without treatment.

Claiming in his brief to the court that "the first duty of the state is to protect its citizens," State's Attorney J. Walker Dodson says he is "reluctantly" undertaking the action to save the girl's life.

At a press conference outside the courthouse, Cathy Schillinger affirmed her own opposition to the state's action. "I know there is a better place waiting for me in heaven. If God calls me, I am ready to die," she said.

If the court rules in favor of the state, the girl will be placed in Memorial Hospital until the course of treatments can be completed.

A ruling is expected later this month.

This excerpt is from an article by Cathy's father, the Rev. Paul Schillinger, "Leave Our Daughter Alone," printed on page 20 of the *Lexington Post,* 9 August 2003:

. . . I know in my heart I am doing God's will. He holds the power of life and death, and if in His infinite goodness and wisdom He wants us to live we will live, and if He wants us to die we will die. No state and no court can say otherwise. The judge and the doctors are trying to play God, and they are committing a damnable blasphemy. My daughter is willing to die if she must, because she knows there is a better place for her waiting in heaven.

The following is an excerpt from page 67 of the September/October 2003 issue of *American Religion.* It appeared in an article by Mark Signorelli, "A Church-State Battle over Child Custody," printed on pages 65–67:

Interviewed outside court, State's Attorney Dodson said, "Cathy Schillinger's life is in imminent danger, and only this action can save her. If it were her father or any other adult, we would not intervene. But Cathy is a minor, not yet able to make an informed decision about a complicated matter, nor is there evidence that she fully understands the issues involved. It is our policy not to interfere with the parents' raising of their children as they see fit unless the child is abused or in danger. Here the child's right to life takes priority."

This is a letter to the editor of *National News Weekly,* appearing in the 16 August 2003 edition, on page 17:

Dear Editor:

Once again our fundamental American rights and freedoms are being trampled by the very government that was established to protect them. Freedom of religion and the right of parents to raise their children in their own beliefs and values mean nothing to the prosecutors. As a neighbor, I have known the Schillingers for years. They are a loving family, and the parents want Cathy to live. But they and Cathy believe that medical treatment is sinful, and the government must respect that. People must respect the beliefs of others, even if they do not agree with them.

Helen Bridgeman

This is the first sentence from a front-page article in the 17 August 2003 *Essex Herald-Journal*. The headline is "Girl's Death Ends State Attempt at Custody":

> The state's effort to gain custody over 13-year-old Cathy Schillinger was made moot this morning when the girl died of leukemia in her sleep.

No one can read about this case without having an opinion, very likely a strong emotional one. You probably also recognize with the rational part of your brain that the issues here are complicated ones with profound implications and that there is much to be considered on both sides before you can reach a wise decision about their merits.

You can use these sources to write either **subjectively** or **objectively** about the case; that is, you can express your opinion, or you can simply present information to the reader without offering views of your own. As an example of the difference between objective and subjective writing, note that the reporter who was the author of the first source wrote objectively. By reading that article, you cannot tell the reporter's personal feelings about the case. On the other hand, there is nothing objective about Helen Bridgeman's letter to the editor. You know exactly where she stands. She and the reporter were clearly writing for two different purposes.

Often it is wise to write objectively about a controversial matter before expressing an opinion. This ensures that you at least examine the merits of both sides before rushing to a judgment.

In this imaginary paper, let's assume that you have decided first to present the facts from the case objectively and afterward to draw subjective conclusions from what you have found. For this earlier part of the paper, then, you will write a brief objective report on the Schillinger case, informing your readers of the nature of the case and the issues involved.

How do you begin writing an objective report from the five sources that you have discovered? They consist of two tersely written news stories, quotations from some of the principal participants on opposing sides, and an opinion from an outside reader. All of them might offer material you can use. But what do you do with them?

Unlike the summary reports you produced in Chapter 6, you cannot simply summarize each source individually and then present the summaries one after the other. Instead you must interweave your materials. Since you have important statements from participants, you will also want to quote some of their words. You will need, then, to select material from your sources and produce a synthesis. Here is how one student, Keith Pearsall, Jr., wrote a report from these five excerpts:

Keith's paraphrase of a source

> The Schillinger case, another prominent instance of conflicting rights and freedoms, involved a 13-year-old girl with leukemia. On one side of the case stood the girl and her parents, who rejected all medical treatment on religious grounds. On the other stood the state, which sought to force the medical care doctors say she needed to remain alive

("State" 6). Parental and religious rights were in conflict with the right to life itself and with the obligation to protect minors.

> Keith's thesis statement

One question that is raised by the case is the extent to which parents have the right to raise their children in their own religious beliefs and practices. The father of the girl, a minister in the Children of Prophecy church, believed that God alone "holds the power of life and death, . . . and if He wants us to die we will die." The minister also

> Quoting a source directly

believed that in seeking to counteract the divine will, the state was committing a "damnable blasphemy" (Schillinger 20). The daughter, Cathy, subscribed to her parents' beliefs and expressed her willingness to die if necessary rather than undergo treatment they believed to be sinful ("State" 6).

> A note for paraphrased material

According to State's Attorney J. Walker Dodson, on the other hand, the issue was not one of religious freedom but of the state's "first duty . . . to protect its citizens" (qtd. in "State" 6). Dodson argued that the girl was too young to make an informed decision about a matter of vital interest to her and that the state was obliged to protect her right to life (Signorelli 67).

> A note for a quotation

Legal questions in this controversial case have still not been answered, since the girl died before the courts could reach a decision.

> No note for widely available information

Keith has taken five sources and from them has written something that is new and his own. The report is objective, since nowhere are Keith's opinions evident, but he still remains in control throughout. He is aware of the point of the entire report, and he shapes it with several of his own sentences. For example, the last sentence of the first paragraph and the sentence following it are topic sentences, expressing his summary of the main ideas of the passage.

In his handling of sources, Keith avoids three mistakes often made by inexperienced research writers; that is, he observes three important rules:

1. **Don't just quote.**
2. **Don't just quote quotations.**
3. **Don't just note quotations.**

Examples from Keith's report can demonstrate what the rules mean:

Don't Just Quote

Many beginning researchers quote too much, tediously stringing together one quotation after another. Keith avoids that mistake. His three direct quotations all make perfect sense in his report. In addition, he selects only the words from his sources that are most relevant, and he introduces them so that the reader always knows who is being quoted and why. More often than quoting, however, Keith paraphrases his sources. For example, in the first three sentences of his report and the last sentence of his second paragraph, he has rephrased material from his sources into his own words. The result is a clear, readable, effective report.

Don't Just Quote Quotations

Some students quote only material that appeared within quotation marks in their sources. It never occurs to them to quote the sources themselves. Note that Keith does both: The first source contains quotations, and Keith uses them in his report. Although the second source does not quote any other authors, Keith quotes from it as well. This may seem obvious, but many students are unaware of this valuable way researchers can use their sources.

Don't Just Note Quotations

Another mistake made by inexperienced research writers is to give parenthetical notes only for direct quotations. Notice that Keith provides notes not only for sources he has quoted, but also for sources he has paraphrased, such as his citation of the first source in his opening paragraph.

Not every source you use will receive mention in notes. Each of the sources played a role in Keith's writing of the report, but only three of them are noted in parentheses. The fourth source, the neighbor's letter, gave Keith some general ideas, but since it did not provide him with any specific information, he decided not to paraphrase it or quote from it. Therefore, it did not receive a note. Although the fifth source, the mention of Cathy's death in a news story, did contain the information used in Keith's last paragraph, that information is so readily available (found in news accounts throughout the country) that acknowledgment is not necessary.

Because Keith quoted or paraphrased only three of his five sources (and cited them in parenthetical notes), he omitted the two other sources from his list of works cited, which follows:

Works Cited

Schillinger, Paul. "Leave Our Daughter Alone." <u>Lexington Post</u>
    9 Aug. 2003: 20.

Signorelli, Mark. "A Church-State Battle over Child Custody."
    <u>American Religion</u> Sept./Oct. 2003: 65-67.

"State Seeks to Force Cancer Treatment." <u>Essex Herald-Journal</u>
    5 Aug. 2003: 6.

| **Writing an Objective Research Essay** | **EXERCISES** |

Imagine that in writing a paper about how Americans have kept track of time through the years, you discovered the following (purely fictitious) sources. Part of your paper will concern a recent proposal to change our current time zones. Use these sources to write a brief objective report on what you have learned. Acknowledge your sources with parenthetical notes and provide the list of works cited that you would include in your final paper.

1. This news story appeared last year in the May 22 issue of the *Birmingham Star-News* in section B, page 4. Dina Waxman wrote the article under the headline, "Parent Tells Dangers of Time Zone Change."

   Congressional hearings on a proposal to have all the country's clocks tell the same time continued today with testimony from a parents' group opposed to the plan.

   The proposal, put forth by Edna Odom of Muscatine, Iowa, would eliminate the four time zones that now divide the country. She would replace them with a single nationwide zone.

   Testifying against Odom's plan was Floyd Rugoff, president of the Eureka, California, PTA. He argued that it would endanger schoolchildren, who would travel to or from school in darkness.

   Under the proposal, clocks in the Eastern zone would be set back one and a half hours, while Pacific zone clocks would be set ahead by the same period. Central and Mountain zone clocks would receive half-hour adjustments. Alaska and Hawaii would be exempt from the proposal.

   In his testimony Rugoff said, "In December it's already dark in the morning when children leave for school. If we change, California children won't see the sunrise until 8:30, and in New England it will have set by the time children come home from school. We're going to see a big increase in accidents involving children."

2. These excerpts are from Edna Odom's article, "It's About Time," in *Future and Change* magazine. It appeared in last year's January issue on pages 76–78.

   If all of the country operated by the same clock, businesses would reap an enormous advantage. Communication from coast to coast would be simplified. Now, with four time zones, companies operating from nine to five on the two coasts have only five working hours in common, and only three if you remove the two lunch hours. Under my proposal, if an executive in Tucson needs to reach her main office in New York at 4 P.M., she can call and get through. The way it is now, the time in the East would be 7 P.M., and she'd have to wait until Monday morning for the New York office to reopen. Television networks, airlines, and neighboring communities that now straddle time zones would all reap enormous benefits. [page 77]

. . . It isn't as if we were being asked to switch day with night. An hour and a half change isn't that big. The claims of opponents are vastly exaggerated. We already move the clocks an hour twice each year, and everyone adjusts easily. There is nothing that says that the sun has to be overhead at noon. If it's dark at 6 A.M., why can't a farmer milk the cows at 8 instead? Schools could open later or earlier to accord with the sunlight. Why are people so hidebound? If the human race isn't flexible enough to make small adjustments, heaven help us when a major catastrophe strikes. [page 78]

3. "Farmer Ticked by Time Scheme" is the headline for an article that appeared without a byline last May 23 on page 24 of the *Riverside Ledger:*

In his testimony against the OUT (Odom Unified Time) proposal, farmer Duane Wentworth of Millinocket, Maine, argued that the proposal would wreak havoc with livestock producers.

"Animals operate by the sun, not the clock," he said, "and we can't convince them otherwise. If we have to get up at 4 in the morning to tend them, we'll be eating lunch at 9 and going to bed by 8. We'll be out of sync with the rest of the country."

Writing a Brief Subjective Research Essay

Not all writing is objective writing; sometimes your purpose is to express your own opinion in order to convince others. Chapter 14 considers argumentative writing in detail, but here we will take a brief look at how writers can use research sources to support and strengthen an argument. Of course, you are always free to offer an opinion without any outside support at all, but the support of experts can greatly help your case. By taking your facts from sources, you also show your readers that you have gone to the trouble of researching the issue, and you make yourself seem more worthy of their trust. When you quote or paraphrase authorities in support of your opinions, those opinions seem much more impressive than they otherwise would.

For a brief example of how subjective writing can be supported by sources, imagine that you are arguing your own views on the unified time zone plan that was introduced in the exercise above. You can use those sources effectively to support your argument:

Edna Odom's proposal to synchronize all the nation's clocks within a single time zone may seem attractive at first glance, but closer inspection of the scheme reveals serious flaws. Although Odom rightly points out the benefits to TV networks and airlines of eliminating time zone differences, she is too quick to dismiss her plan's opponents as "hidebound" and its problems as "exaggerated" (77–78).

The proposed change would have the most impact on the two coasts, where clocks would be altered by an hour and a half from current settings. While Odom sees this as small, the effects would be considerable for farmers and schoolchildren, to take only two examples. Since livestock regulate their lives by the sun, farmers on the east coast would need to rise as early as 4 A.M. to tend animals at sunrise ("Farmer" 24). And as the president of a California PTA chapter observed in testifying before Congress, it would be dark in winter as western children traveled to school and as eastern children returned home from school. He predicted that the number of auto accidents involving children pedestrians would increase sharply (Waxman 4).

A principal advantage that Odom claims for her scheme is that it would aid communication by standardizing business schedules. But she also recommends that schools and other institutions adjust their opening and closing times to conform with the sun (77–78). She can't have it both ways. If California schools open according to the sun, three hours after New York schools, parents will demand that businesses where they work do likewise, and the uniformity that Odom promises will be lost.

While it would be wonderful if time were the same in all parts of the country—and of the world, for that matter—the fact is that the sun refuses to cooperate. Any proposal that is based on human wishes, without regard for the realities of nature, is doomed to certain failure. Imperfect as our current time system is, it is at least preferable to the alternative.

The list of works cited for this essay would be the same one that you listed for the objective essay in the exercise.

The writer of this essay argues the case against the plan. The sources he uses buttress his arguments and lend it authority. For example, because he has supported it with sources, readers are more likely to accept his claim that the plan would hurt farmers and schoolchildren; the reader can see that this is not just the writer's unfounded speculation.

Notice that the writer has used sources to help make his point. At the same time, he has not been a slave to the sources. While he takes several arguments from sources, much of the language and thought behind the paper is entirely his own. His introduction and conclusion are original, and in the third paragraph he has applied his own logical twist to turn Edna Odom's argument against her.

Sources, in other words, are tools that require the ingenuity of writers to make use of them. There is nothing in the three sources that led inevitably to this paper. In fact, another writer with different views about time zones could use them to write an equally effective paper supporting Edna Odom's proposal.

Writing Subjective Research Essays

EXERCISES

1. Write a subjective essay arguing your views on the Schillinger case. Use the five sources found on pages 430–32 to support your essay. Acknowledge your sources in notes and include a list of works cited.

2. Write a subjective essay that argues in favor of Edna Odom's time zone proposal. Support your position, using the sources in the exercise on pages 435–36.

13 *Writing and Revising the Research Paper*

GETTING ORGANIZED

Once Emily Gould and Justin Stafford had gathered material from their sources and taken notes on index cards, they were ready for the next step: the actual writing of their papers. While writing proved less time-consuming than source-gathering, it was no less important, and, like earlier stages of the research process, it consisted of several substeps. Emily and Justin each received an assignment similar to the following for the first of these substeps:

ASSIGNMENT   **Preparing to Write**

Do the following before our next class meeting in preparation for writing your first draft:

- Complete your note-taking on index cards.
- Formulate a thesis statement; that is, state in a sentence or two your concept of the main idea of your paper.
- Sort your note cards by topic.
- Prepare an updated informal working outline for your first draft.
- Put new topic titles on your note cards as necessary, arrange them in the order suggested by your outline, and put aside (but do not discard) the ones you do not expect to use.

Formulating a Thesis Statement

When Emily began her project, she was afraid she would not have enough to say about her topic. However, halfway through her first source, she had fifteen cards' worth of notes. Aware that she was taking too many notes, Emily concluded that she would need to be more selective. Like almost every other student researcher, she found that a shortage of material would not be a problem for her after all. She sharpened her focus and began to take fewer but more carefully chosen notes. Even so, she ended up taking notes on over a hundred cards, several dozen more than she would end up using.

When Emily began her search for sources, the topic she had in mind was a broad one, issues related to fast-food restaurants. These included health issues, such as the effect of a fast-food diet on America's health; social issues, such as the loss of diversity as national chains replaced local establishments; and employment issues, such as the impact of fast-food jobs on teens. She began to take notes, but before long she saw that her original topic was leading in too many different directions that were far too diverse for one research paper. Her topic, she realized, needed to be more specific, and she soon narrowed it to just work-related issues, a decision made easier by the abundance of sources she found on that topic. Even so, she discovered many different aspects to this topic, and she did not become entirely sure of her paper's thesis or organization until she was well into an early draft of the paper itself. She was then able to formulate a ***thesis statement***, a brief summary of what she expected to be her main focus:

> Thesis: Fast-food restaurants provide many thousands of jobs, but the quality of the jobs is poor and the workers are exploited.

Emily's thesis indicates a point of view, an opinion about fast-food jobs that not everyone would be expected to share. Another writer with less clearly developed opinions might have written about the topic by providing a balanced exposition of two sides of a controversial issue, but Emily's research had led her to a definite opinion, and she made her viewpoint clear from the beginning. She was still learning about her topic, however, and her thesis was, at this point, sufficiently generalized to allow room for her topic to develop.

Student writers are sometimes misled by the advice to *start* a research project with a thesis that is clear, unified, and restricted. Like an outline, a thesis ought to assist the process of searching, thinking, and composing; it should never become a straitjacket. As we have seen, Emily's preliminary research caused her to narrow her focus. Justin, however, was quite certain of his topic, and formulating a thesis statement presented little difficulty. He simply expressed in plain language the goals of his project:

> Thesis: I want to find out if a career in pharmacy fits my abilities, interests, and career objectives and, if so, what I need to do to pursue this career.

As we have seen, premature commitment to a thesis can become a hindrance to thorough, objective inquiry. Nevertheless, many writers prefer to develop a cohesive theme during the early stages of research. They have found that keeping such a theme in view—often in the form of a preliminary thesis statement—can help focus their work. If you have difficulty finding such a focus, try the following procedure:

Tips for Formulating a Thesis Statement

1. **Think about your project in general terms.** In your notebook, write a quick informal paragraph describing what you expect your paper to say and do. It may help to respond to these questions: What main topic have your efforts become focused on? What question(s) have you been trying to answer? What have you learned from your research? Do you now have a point of view about your topic—a conclusion or insight that you want to express in your paper?

2. **Make your general idea specific.** Review the paragraph you have written, and see if you can summarize its main idea in a single sentence.

As you continue your work, you should think often about how each part of your paper supports your focus. Be prepared to eliminate any sections that stray from the main topic. You may, of course, adjust your focus as you proceed with your project. In the final draft of her paper, Emily introduced her readers to her subject with this summary of her thesis:

> Convenience and value have come at a price, however, and many
> believe that benefits to the public are outweighed by the
> costs that this giant industry imposes on its workers.

Sorting Your Note Cards

With an evolving conception of her topic, Emily recorded in her notes material that she thought was usable. While her note cards were a distillation of all she had learned from her reading, they still represented a formidable mass of data. She now had to select and arrange her cards in an order she could use. She read through them and sorted them by topic.

Since Emily had written a topic label at the top of each note card, she was able to group many of her cards together by subject. She found that most of her cards fell into a half-dozen general categories: "background—statistics," "teen employment," "minimum wage," "unionization," and so on. As she sorted, she also set aside many discards—notes it was now clear she could not use. There were also many strays—single cards that did not fit conveniently into categories with any others. Emily had to decide if these belonged in her paper and, if so, how she might use them. In some cases, she would not know for sure until the actual writing.

Even with a good plan and a working outline, the final form of a paper can rarely be predicted in advance. Like Emily, you might follow this procedure:

1. **Read through and sort your note cards.** Sorting your cards into piles on a large table or on the floor can be helpful. Be sure you sort the cards by *topic* (not by any other principle, such as by source). Some piles will contain note cards from several different sources.

2. **When your cards are sorted, think about how they can be used and arranged.** Write about your ideas in your research notebook; think as you write,

using the opportunity to work out ideas for organizing your paper. But do not be dismayed if you encounter loose ends at this stage. You will make many further decisions about your paper's organization as you write it.

3. **Put aside any cards you do not expect to use.** The best way to create an organizational plan for a paper is to think first in terms of the most general categories. The following is one of several excerpts from Emily's research notebook that reveals her thoughts about shaping and organizing her project:

> On the one hand, fast food makes many jobs available for students. On the other the jobs are generally poor ones. Many different aspects to work picture: nonthinking robot work, poor wages, lack of unionization. There are also case histories of workers being cheated out of overtime. . . . There is much about teens but also much about immigrants and poor (disadvantaged groups) who are exploited. How do I ~~make these~~ deal with both of these which have different needs? Teens generally work for spending money, but the poor need to feed their families. Probably put emphasis on teens . . .

Emily did not yet have a clear organization in mind for her paper, but we can see her mind working here—even making decisions as she wrote. She was confident she had good materials to work with, and she had enough ideas for at least a tentative organization that she could try out.

Updating Your Outline

Having thought about the parts of her paper and how she might put those parts together, Emily needed a clearer idea—a diagram of what her paper might look like. That is, she needed an *informal working outline*, an updated plan for organizing her paper.

When you create an outline, the headings you use will correspond, in theory, to the topic labels on your note cards. In reality, though, you will need to make adjustments to both the cards and the outline as a clear conception of the shape of your paper gradually forms in your mind. Try to put your ideas on paper in a handy visual form: A working outline is nothing more than a way of making these ideas visible and concrete.

Checking and rechecking her note cards, Emily developed the parts of an outline and, after several revisions, created an informal scheme, shown in Figure 13.1, to use in writing her first draft. Although some of the details would change in the final version of her paper, Emily found this outline helpful as she wrote, especially in getting started.

During her next class, Emily showed her outline and note cards to the other students in her editing group. She discussed her plans, received suggestions, and—even more valuable—answered questions. Explaining and defending her outline helped Emily notice strengths and weaknesses in her plan. An added

Emily Gould

Thesis and Working Outline

Fast-Food Follies

Thesis: Fast-food restaurants provide many thousands of jobs, but the quality of the jobs is poor and the workers are exploited.

Introduction

    Statistics about usage

    Image of fast food: cheap, friendly, popular

    Reality: not a good workplace (thesis)

Nature of job

    Low pay

    Mindless, decision-free routine

    Unskilled staff: teens, immigrants, others without skills

Legislation

    Protections

        Child-labor laws

        Minimum-wage laws

    Violation of laws

Exploitation

    Overtime not paid

    Workers sent home during slow hours

Conclusion: need for reform

    Union organization of workers

    Respect from employers

Figure 13.1 Emily's thesis and working outline.

benefit of the session was that it familiarized everyone in each editing group with classmates' projects.

◼ WRITING THE FIRST GOOD DRAFT

Having a tentative plan for organizing their papers, Emily and Justin received an assignment like the following from their instructors:

Writing the Paper	ASSIGNMENT

You are now ready to write a careful draft of your paper. Do so, and revise it until you are satisfied that it is as clearly written, well organized, interesting, and informative as you can make it. Be sure to document your sources carefully with parenthetical notes and include an updated list of works cited. You should also consult the guidelines for editing and revising that begin on page 451.

Research Writing: General Guidelines

Emily soon discovered that her outline was only a starting point. In fact, she made changes in her organization from almost the moment she began her actual writing. She encountered difficulties with her opening, and, as her rough drafts would show, she went through at least six versions of the introductory section before she felt ready to move on. Her preliminary outline rapidly became obsolete, but it had served its purpose. It had forced Emily to think about her paper as a whole—about how the individual parts might work together. Once she had made the outline, her concept of what she would accomplish in her writing became considerably less vague.

Although later parts of her draft went more smoothly, Emily discovered there is more to writing a paper than following a plan. Certainly, it is not just a matter of first writing about note 1, then about note 2, and so on throughout the paper. It will help to consider the following guidelines in writing your paper:

1. **Keep your goals in mind.** Novices can easily be overwhelmed by the procedures and details of research writing. Because of the many steps—all the procedures for assembling a list of sources and making note cards, outlines, and parenthetical notes—it is easy to lose sight of what a research paper is really about. The goal of your research is to learn something, to discover truth. In writing your paper, your goal is to present what you have learned so that your readers can also become informed. It follows that your writing should be readable and honest, informative and interesting. Never lose sight of these important goals as you write. Do not be blinded by procedures for their own sake.

2. **Remember that principles of good writing apply to research writing, too.** Like any other type of paper, a research paper should be clear and lively, not

stodgy and pompous. It should be written so it can be read with enjoyment and without difficulty. Quotations and other source material should be neatly integrated into your writing so they are not obtrusive or awkward.

Like any other author, you have a responsibility to make the reader's job easier. Use topic sentences to help the reader know what to expect. Provide paragraph breaks to signal changes in topic or emphasis. Where appropriate, use transitional words and phrases (such as *on the other hand, also, for example,* and *consequently*) to make clear the relationship between successive sentences and paragraphs.

3. **Most of your paper should be you, not your sources.** While your sources may provide you with most of the information that you present, in your paper *you* are the one writing it. Write in your own voice. Your research paper should communicate what you have to say—just like any other paper you write. Remember, too, that your use of sources is simply a means of reaching the goal of informing your readers; it is not an end in itself. Don't let your paper become simply a vehicle for presenting sources. Don't let your sources get in the way of clear writing.

4. **Don't be a slave to your note cards and outline.** Whenever you use a note from one of your cards, think about how it contributes to the point you are making. If a note isn't useful, don't include it. If it isn't clear, explain it. If you realize that your paper would be improved by adding new topics or rearranging your outline, by all means do so.

5. **Don't rely too heavily on one or two sources.** Inevitably, a few of your sources will have proved more helpful than the rest, and you will rely on these more than the others in writing your paper. Remember, however, that it is not your paper's purpose to restate what has already been said by another source or two. A research paper should present something new, a fresh synthesis of information and ideas from many sources. A paper that is largely a summary of only one or two sources fails to do this. A variety of sources should make substantial contributions to your paper. On the other hand, the opposite extreme—where it becomes an end in itself to squeeze in material from every source you find—should also be avoided. Let common sense guide you between these two extremes.

Some Practical Writing Tips

Following are some practical tips on the act of writing itself.

Don't Put Off Your Writing

Although the pressure of an impending deadline may stimulate great energy, it is unwise to begin writing your paper the night before it is due. You will produce a far better paper if you allow time for careful writing and revision. Start writing as soon as possible. Finishing ahead of your deadline will allow you the valuable opportunity to put the paper aside for a day or so, at which time you can take it up again, read it with fresh eyes, and gain new perspectives for improving it further.

Adopt Methods That Work for You

All writers are different. Use your past experience to decide what writing practices give you the best results.

Write in a place you find comfortable. A quiet library setting may free you from distractions and give you ready access to additional sources. On the other hand, you may prefer sitting at your computer keyboard at home. Or perhaps settling into a comfortable easy chair, writing with a pad on your lap and with your note cards on a table by your side, may allow you to do your best work.

Find ways to overcome obstacles. When you get stuck in your writing, perhaps it may help you to pause for a snack or a brief break to recharge your mental batteries—or you may find it best to shift gears, perhaps rereading what you have written or redirecting your attention to another part of the paper.

Adopt Positive Attitudes

Recognize that writing is hard work. Good writers work hard enough to make it *look* easy. Don't be discouraged by the snags that inevitably arise, and be prepared to give your project the time and energy it deserves.

Be persistent in writing. During the hard work of writing, writers are often visited with thoughts of more pleasant things they could be doing. At such times it is tempting to put down the pen or turn off the computer, promising yourself to resume writing later. Such temptations pose stern challenges to one's character and moral fiber. To be a successful writer is to develop self-discipline and to continue when one would rather not. As with any discipline you develop (from quitting smoking to mastering the cello to training for a triathlon), it is important to set realistic goals and to stick with them. At each writing session, set a goal of writing a certain number of pages or working for a certain number of hours—and meet it faithfully. Writing isn't usually fun, although at times it can be. But writing *is* very satisfying, especially when you know you have worked hard and produced a work you are proud of.

Have confidence in yourself. Even if this is your first research project, there is no reason to think you can't achieve admirable results. Remember, there are no secret formulas that others know and you don't. A paper is nothing more complicated than this: You have learned some information and are simply explaining it to readers who are much like yourself. Keep that in mind, tell your story clearly, let your own interest in the topic come through—and you will write a successful paper.

Getting Started

By the time you are ready to write, the hardest work should be behind you. You have plenty to say, as well as a plan for how you want to say it. You have a stack of note cards, arranged in the order in which you expect to use them. Once you are a page or two into your writing, the work should start to flow more smoothly. After students get past the initial unfamiliarity of working with source material, they usually find research writing little different from any other kind. In fact, because they are so well prepared, it is often easier.

Frequently, the most difficult part is simply getting started. In writing her first draft, Emily began by composing her opening section. She decided to establish the pervasive role of fast food in our lives with statistical information. After several drafts, she produced a paragraph that she expected to begin her paper:

An early draft
of Emily's
opening

> In his book <u>Fast-Food Nation</u>, Eric Schlosser provides statistics to illustrate just how much fast food has revolutionized America's eating habits. In 1970, Americans spent $6 billion on fast food. By the year 2000, that figure soared to $110 billion. That is more than the amount Americans spend buying movies, magazines, newspapers, books, videos, and recorded music, combined. Every day, about a quarter of the U.S.'s adult population eats some type of fast food (3).

As she received feedback from other readers and then revised her paper in subsequent drafts, Emily realized that, while certainly intriguing, the numbers didn't give the reader a context in which to consider them. She decided that this statistical information would have more impact if it followed an opening paragraph in which she introduced the paper's theme. Her revised opening can be seen on page 304.

Struggling with an opening is not uncommon. Often it is best to wait until after you have drafted the body of a paper before even attempting to write the beginning. Writers sometimes waste time by overlooking the fact that the parts of a paper do not have to be written in the order in which they are to be read. If you are having difficulty getting started or are unsure about where to begin, start with a section that especially interests you or that seems easiest to write. Once you are successfully under way, composing the rest of the paper may be easier.

Writing the Opening

After you have written a draft of the body of your paper, you are in a better position to see what type of opening is most effective. An introductory section can serve many purposes: to inform readers of what your paper is about and where it is going, to generate interest, and to create a smooth transition into the body of the paper. There are many ways to begin a research paper; the following strategies are among those most frequently used.

Option 1: Begin with a Summary of the Paper's Main Idea

The purpose of beginning with a summary of the main idea is to tell your readers immediately what the paper is about. A version of your thesis statement will figure prominently in the opening, which serves as a summary of the entire paper to come.

This is the way Emily opened the final draft of her paper:

> McDonald's, Burger King, KFC, Wendy's, and other popular chains have brought countless innovations to the restaurant

industry, delivering food fast and at low cost year after
year. Convenience and value have come at a price, however,
and many believe that benefits to the public are outweighed
by the costs that this giant industry imposes on its workers.

While Emily's first sentence introduces the general topic of fast-food restaurants, her second sentence succinctly states the thesis of her paper. The readers' job is made easier because she has given them a clear expectation of what will follow in the paper.

Option 2: Begin with Background

Because your readers may not be well informed about your topic, you can provide them with information that will provide a context for your thesis. For example, Emily might have begun with information to show how widespread teen jobs are in fast-food restaurants:

> One-third of all American workers under the age of 35
> got their first jobs working for restaurants (Yum! Brands),
> and about one-eighth of all workers have, at some point,
> worked for McDonald's (Schlosser 4). Yvonne Zipp of the
> Christian Science Monitor observes that such jobs have become
> "a teen rite of passage as universal as driver's ed." Hiring
> teenagers to prepare and serve us food in a fast-food setting
> has become "so natural, so normal, and so inevitable that
> people . . . think little about it," says Stuart Tannock, a
> lecturer in social and cultural studies at the University of
> California at Berkeley (qtd. in Ayoub A20). The topic is well
> worth considering, however, and we should ask if workers
> benefit or are harmed by work in the fast-food industry.

In this paragraph, the background information leads to a statement of the paper's thesis in the final sentence.

The background you provide may also consist of a history of the topic or a summary of occurrences leading up to the events you describe. For example, if Emily had chosen to focus on the plight of teenage workers, she could have opened her paper with historical background:

> The Fair Labor Standards Act of 1938 set limits on the
> number of hours teens under the age of 16 can work and the
> kinds of work they can do. At 14 or 15, students may work no
> more than three hours on a school day, but when they reach
> 16, all limits on their working hours are removed. At the
> time when our current child-labor laws were passed, most
> teens left school at 16 to become full-time workers earning
> their livelihood. Today, however, 90% of teens graduate from
> high school at 18, and most work primarily for extra spending

money or luxuries such as new cars. Relatively few now work
to help support their families (Zipp 1). Many observers
believe that existing legislation to protect young workers is
no longer suitable to current societal realities.

Option 3: Begin with an Interesting Anecdote

Starting with a specific story not only can capture your readers' interest immediately, but also can be used to lead into your thesis statement. Emily might have begun her paper with a specific story about the dangers of fast-food work:

> On a busy Friday evening, 17-year-old Brittany Krollman
> was working the counter of a fast-food restaurant in West
> Seneca, New York. A few feet away another worker was
> filtering the grease used to cook french fries. Without
> warning, the hot grease exploded, covering Brittany and
> setting her uniform on fire. Her second- and third-degree
> burns on her arms and torso required skin grafts and left
> permanent scars that affect her appearance. The restaurant
> was cited for safety violations and fined $5,000 (Kiger).
> Brittany's story is not an isolated one, as all too many
> teens face dangers in the workplace.

The anecdote not only arrests the readers' attention and emotions, but also leads to a more general statement of theme in the final sentence.

Option 4: Begin by Explaining Your Purpose for Writing

A personal research paper often begins with a section headed "Why I Wrote This Paper" or "What I Wanted to Find Out." Justin began his paper with a statement of his purpose:

> Next to finding the person I will marry, selecting the
> profession that will occupy me for the rest of my life is
> the most important decision I am likely to make. At various
> times as a boy and a teenager, I dreamt about exciting jobs,
> such as being an astronaut, a soldier, a senator, and a rock
> star. Lately, however, my plans have become more practical,
> and for the last year I have given serious thought to a
> career with considerably less sex appeal. Rather than
> piloting the space shuttle or winning a Grammy, I have begun
> to think that I can be successful and happy by becoming a
> pharmacist.
>
> Because the consequences are so great, I do not want to
> make a hasty decision, and this assignment has given me an
> opportunity to learn if pharmacy is the right choice and, if
> so, what I will need to do to pursue this career path.

Many scientific papers also begin by stating specifically what is to come in the rest of the paper. Conventional research papers, however, generally avoid direct statements by the author about purpose. A rule of thumb in writing for the liberal arts is that papers should avoid talking about themselves. That is, they should not contain statements such as "In this paper I will . . ." or "The rest of this paper will examine. . . ." (Note how the other sample beginnings make the theme evident without any such statements.) The personal research paper is an exception to this rule.

Writing the Conclusion

Sometimes, although rarely, a writer explores a topic in a research paper but does not come to any conclusions about it until the end. The writer uses the final section to reveal what is, in effect, the paper's bottom line. Justin's paper, for example, explored the pros and cons of a pharmacy career and only at the end reveals his decision:

> My research into pharmacy has made me enthusiastic about my future. Although several momentous decisions lie before me, I am now increasingly hopeful and confident that this profession offers me the best prescription for my happiness and success.

More often, however, the paper's thesis has already been made clear to the readers, and so the form a concluding passage should take is anything but obvious. After all, once you have said what you have to say, what else remains to be done? Fortunately, it is not as hopeless as that. The principal purpose of a conclusion is not to say something new but to draw the ends of the paper together and to leave the reader with a satisfying sense of closure. Simply put, an ending should feel to the reader like an ending.

One strategy, appropriate for a long paper, is to tie together what you have written by summarizing the paper's content. This may be effective if you can summarize the paper in a fresh and insightful way. A summary serves no purpose, however, if it merely rehashes what has already been made evident to the alert reader.

Emily gave her readers a fresh way of looking at her subject in her final paragraph. The body of her paper was principally devoted to exploring the negative aspects of work for fast-food companies. For her ending, she decided to first remind readers of the positive public image projected by the restaurants in their advertising and then contrast it, in her last two sentences, with a brief summary of her thesis:

> Ads for fast-food companies always show smiling, well-scrubbed, contented workers, and the corporations boast of their employee-friendly policies. Restaurants recruit workers with slogans such as "Everybody's Somebody at Wendy's" (Wendy's) and "A Subway restaurant is a really neat place to work" (Subway). On its Web site, McDonald's

> proclaims, "We're not just a hamburger company serving
> people; we're a people company serving hamburgers," and it
> claims that its goal is "to be the best employer in each
> community around the world" (McDonald's). While many
> thousands of teenagers who annually accept work serving fast
> food find the experience rewarding, many others regard the
> job as anything but friendly. As author Eric Schlosser
> concludes, "The real price [of fast food] never appears
> on the menu" (9).

A word of caution: Strategies such as these are offered as helpful possibilities, not as rules or boundaries. Good writing resists formulas, and good writers continually find original ways of achieving their goals. Adopt whatever strategies work for you, and consider new approaches. That is the best way to extend your range as a writer.

Giving Your Paper a Title

Giving your paper a title may be the final stage of your project. Ideally, your title should both indicate to your readers what your paper is about and arouse their interest. In her first draft, Emily gave her paper the title "Fast-Food Follies." She thought the title reflected her theme of problems in the fast-food workplace, but a classmate who read the draft remarked that from the word "follies" he expected a relation of comic events. He also suggested that her title should reflect her paper's focus on work-related issues. With some regret for the loss of alliteration, Emily gave her final draft the more prosaic but clearer title, "Fast Food Comes at a High Price for Workers." For his paper about his career search, Justin considered the simple title, "Should I Be a Pharmacist?" but finally chose instead the more playful title, "Becoming a Pharmacist: Prescription for Success?"

Arresting, clever, or witty titles are not easy to create—and not always desirable, as there is a fine line between originality and cuteness. Start with a simple, direct title that captures your theme. If later on you are inspired with a better choice, fine, but if not, no one should object to a plain but clear title.

■ EDITING AND REVISING

Writers differ in their work habits. Justin is a constant reviser. Composing, rearranging, and editing at the keyboard of his computer, Justin tends to write a little, pause to read what he has produced, make changes, and then move on. Emily, on the other hand, is more of an all-at-once reviser: She generally writes long passages straight through, forging ahead while ideas are still fresh in her mind. Only after she has written several pages will Emily pause to reread and make changes.

Because of their different work habits, Emily and Justin produced very different kinds of preliminary drafts. Emily wrote several complete drafts, each more polished than the previous one. Justin, on the other hand, emerged with something very close to a final draft after having gradually reached the concluding section of his paper. To call Justin's final paper a single "perfect" draft, however, would be very misleading. Since Justin was constantly rereading, revising, and editing earlier parts of his paper, these parts had actually gone through several drafts by the time he reached his conclusion. His success was due partly to productive work habits and partly to the fact that Justin kept the structure of his paper clearly in view from the outset.

Both writers achieved success by using methods that worked for them. You, too, should feel free to adopt practices that work for you. Basically, though, you can be an effective editor of your own work if you approach it like a reader. Put aside what you have written for a day or more until you can read it with a fresh perspective. Put yourself in your readers' place, trying to anticipate whether they will find it clear, readable, and effective. You may find it helpful to consult the checklist that begins below, considering each question as if you were responding to a paper someone else has written.

Reworking Your Paper

After completing preliminary drafts, both writers put aside what they had written for a while, then came back and reread them with a pencil in hand. Two pages from Emily's early draft in which she made particularly extensive changes appear in Figure 13.2. Although Emily makes handwritten corrections on pages composed at a word processor, other writers prefer working entirely on paper, while still others make all their revisions directly at the computer keyboard.

Checklist for Editing and Revising

Topic, Focus, and Support

- Is it clear what the topic of the paper is? Does the writer provide a thesis statement or otherwise make it evident, early in the paper, what the paper is about? Is any further help needed for the reader to see the paper's point?

- Is the topic adequately narrowed —that is, neither too broad nor too limited for the writer to do it justice in a paper of this length?

- Has the writer kept the promises made by the thesis statement? That is, does the paper remain focused on its thesis? Does it stick to the point?

- Is the thesis supported with a variety of details or evidence?

- Is this support clear and convincing?

- In reading the paper, have you learned what you were expecting to learn from it? What questions remain in your mind? What needs to be developed more? What seems to be missing?

Audience, Style, and Readability

- Is the writing style appropriate for its intended audience? What passages do you have trouble understanding?

Gould 1

Emily Gould

Editing Draft

comes at a High Price for Workers

Fast-Food ~~Follies~~

best-selling *shows*
In his book <u>Fast-Food Nation</u>, Eric Schlosser ~~provides~~

~~statistics to illustrate~~ just how much *such popular chains have* ~~fast food has~~

revolutionized America's eating habits. In 1970, Americans

spent $6 billion on fast food. By ~~the year~~ 2000, that

figure *had* soared to $110 billion. ~~That is more than the~~

~~amount~~ Americans spend " *Schlosser says* *more on fast food than on books, movies,* ~~buying movies~~, magazines,

newspapers, ~~books~~, videos, and recorded music combined . " (3)

Every*day*, about a quarter of the U.S.'s adult population

eats ~~some type of~~ fast food. *in some form. Few, however, give much thought to the* ~~(3)~~. *workers who prepare and deliver their meals.*

Burger King, KFC, Wendy's *popular chains*
McDonald's and other ~~fast-food corporations~~ have

brought countless innovations to the ~~food services~~ *restaurant*

industry, ~~which have~~ deliver*ing* our food faster and *at low cost year after year* ~~cheaper~~

~~over the years.~~ ~~This~~ *C*convenience and value *have* ~~has~~ come at a

price, however, and many ~~who work on the inside of this~~

~~giant industry~~ believe *benefits to the public are outweighed by the costs that this industry* ~~that the consequences far outweigh~~ *imposes on its*

~~the benefits.~~ *workers.*

Hiring ~~Having~~ teenagers *to* prepare ~~and~~ serve us food in the

fast-food setting has become "so natural, so normal, and

so inevitable that people often think little about it , *says Stuart Tannock, a lecturer in social and* *cultural studies at*

(Ayoub A20) *the University of California at Berkeley* ~~While most teenagers do not consider a place~~

~~on a hamburger assembly line to be a fulfilling job, it is~~

~~not only teenagers who are responsible for feeding the~~

Figure 13.2 Emily's editing of a draft.

Gould 2

~~nation. The number of immigrants arriving in the United States is growing, and many of them start life in the United States with a job in fast food.~~ Nevertheless While fast-food workers have become an essential component in the service industry, ~~employment in the~~ a fast-food job ~~industry~~ is usually viewed as an undesirable, a dead-end work job. ~~Most teenagers who work in fast food are only seeking part-time or summer jobs to get extra cash; however, many of the immigrants to the United States depend on these jobs to support themselves and their families. Trends over the past thirty years have indicated that the quality of fast-food jobs is steadily decreasing.~~

One-third of all workers under the age of 35 have gotten their first jobs working for restaurants ^ About one-eighth of all workers in the United States (Yum! Brands), have, at some point, worked for McDonald's (Schlosser 4). and

Yvonne Zipp of the Christian Science Monitor observes that such ~~Fast-food~~ jobs have become ~~such a common occupation for teenagers that they are often considered to be~~ a "teen rite of as universal as driver's ed." passage ~~into the American workforce. Jobs in fast food~~ They are ideal for teenagers because they require no special skills, and many believe that such jobs provide the educational ~~they teach basic, but vital life lessons to~~ benefit of teaching ~~young people, such as~~ responsibility, and good time and money ~~teamwork, and the management.~~ ~~value of a dollar.~~ Studies conducted by the National Academy of Sciences showed that part-time jobs, up to twenty hours a week, were generally a positive experience for teenagers, giving them an increased sense of responsibility and self-esteem. However, Working more than twenty

- Does the paper read smoothly and easily? Does the paper's use of sources and quotations ever become distracting or interrupt the smooth flow of your reading?
- Is the paper free from awkward phrasing, misspellings, typographical errors, and other mechanical flaws?
- Does the paper conform to MLA format (see Chapter C in Part II)?

Organization

- Is the paper organized in a way that makes sense? Can you understand why topics come where they do in the paper? Could any parts be rearranged for greater logic and clarity? Are there passages in different parts of the paper that should be brought together?
- Does the paper begin with a helpful general introduction to the topic? Can you tell from the introduction where the paper is going? Does the paper capture your interest right from the beginning? Could it be made more lively and interesting?
- Does the writer provide smooth and helpful transitions between subjects? Can you always tell how the part you are reading fits into the paper as a whole?
- Does the paper end with a satisfying conclusion?

Use of Sources

- Is the paper based on a variety of sources? Is the use of sources balanced, or is most of the information taken from only one or two sources?
- Is most of the information from sources paraphrased, rather than quoted directly? Are quotations used excessively? When sources are quoted, is there a reason for doing so? (See pages 403–04 for the proper use of quotations.)
- Does the writer avoid "naked quotations"? That is, is each quotation introduced by a phrase or sentence? When sources are referred to in the paper, are they adequately identified in acknowledgment phrases? That is, are you given enough information about them so that you can tell who they are and whether they are experts on the subject? (See pages 404–07)
- Are sources documented? Does the paper credit its sources within parenthetical notes? Does it credit paraphrased material as well as direct quotations? (Consult the Quick Reference Guides on the inside covers of this book.)
- Does the writer avoid overnoting (unnecessary notes for commonly available information) as well as undernoting (paraphrasing a source's ideas without providing a note)?
- Is it clear what each note refers to? That is, can you tell what information goes with what note?
- Are the sources listed in a works-cited page following the paper? Are the number and types of sources adequate for the paper?

- Does each note provide the least amount of information needed to refer you to the works-cited page and to identify the specific pages being referenced by the note?

- Except for longer, indented passages, are the notes placed inside the sentences with the period after, not before, the note?

- Does the punctuation in each note and in each entry in the works-cited page follow the prescribed format exactly? (Check the Quick Reference Guides on the inside covers.) Are items in the works-cited page listed in alphabetical order? Has the writer remembered that in MLA format these items should not be numbered?

Getting Advice from Other Readers

No matter how good a job writers do at editing their own writing, they can always benefit from outside help as well. Writers become so closely involved with their work that they can lose the ability to observe it from the reader's perspective. For that reason, good editing often requires advice from a reader who can point out flaws and possibilities that have escaped the writer's notice.

When she was satisfied with her revisions, Emily brought her printed paper to class for editing. (Students in Justin's class met with partners outside of class time to edit each other's papers.) Emily and her classmates were given the following assignment:

Group Editing ASSIGNMENT

Read the papers written by members of your editing group and offer them the most helpful advice you can give.

Your Role as Editor

- Read each paper with care and interest, as if it were written with you as its intended audience.

- In responding to the paper, think of yourself as a friend trying to help, not as a judge providing a grade or evaluation.

The Editing Procedure

Read each paper at least twice, first for a general impression, then for specific details.

- The first time, read it straight through to gain a general impression. Do not stop to ask questions or write comments. When you have completed your first reading, pause to write a paragraph or two about the paper in general, including the following:

  —State what the paper's main idea seems to be.
  —Describe your general reaction to the paper. What did you learn from it?

—Tell the author how the paper worked for you. Where was the best writing in the draft? Did the paper develop as you expected it to? As you were reading, did questions arise in your mind that the author answered or failed to answer? Did you ever have trouble following it?

—Ask any other questions and make any other general comments about the paper as a whole.

- Now read the paper a second time, paying greater attention to specifics. Pause at any time to write comments, according to the following guidelines:

—Write comments, questions, or ideas in pencil in the margins of the paper. Put checkmarks by passages that you want to talk with the writer about.

—Point out the paper's strengths (note passages you especially like) as well as weaknesses, but be honest. You will not be much help to the author if you say that everything is wonderful when you think the paper might be improved. You are not insulting the writer by offering ideas to improve it. Specific suggestions are much more helpful than vague comments like "?" or "Needs work."

—If you are in doubt about an editing or proofreading matter, consult with your instructor.

- Finally, talk with the paper's author. Explain your comments. Describe your response to the paper, what problems or questions you had while reading it, and what suggestions you have for making it better.

Emily received editing suggestions from the two other students in her editing group. The following pages show the comments of Sean, one of her peers.

Gould 1

Emily Gould

Editing Draft

From your title, I expected some comic stories.

Fast-Food Follies

In his book <u>Fast-Food Nation</u>, Eric Schlosser provides statistics to illustrate just how much fast food has revolutionized America's eating habits. In 1970, Americans spent $6 billion on fast food. By the year 2000, that figure soared to $110 billion. That is more than the amount Americans spend buying movies, magazines, newspapers, books, videos, and recorded music, combined. Everyday, <u>about a quarter of the U.S.'s adult population eats some type of fast food</u> (3). *That's an amazing statistic!*

McDonald's and other fast-food corporations have brought countless innovations to the food services industry, which have delivered our food faster and cheaper over the years. <u>This convenience and value has come at a price, however, and many who work on the inside of this giant industry believe that the consequences far outweigh the benefits.</u>

If this is your thesis, should it go in the first paragraph?

Having teenagers prepare and serve us food in the fast-food setting has become "so natural, so normal, and so inevitable that people often think little about it." (Ayoub A20) While most teenagers do not consider a place on a hamburger assembly line to be a fulfilling job, it is not only teenagers who are responsible for feeding the

Period after the note, right?

Gould 2

nation. The number of immigrants arriving in the United States is growing, and many of them start life in the United States with a job in fast food. While fast-food workers have become an essential component in the service industry, employment in the fast-food industry is viewed as an undesirable, "dead-end" job. Most teenagers who work in fast food are only seeking part-time or summer jobs to get extra cash; however, many of the immigrants to the United States depend on these jobs to support themselves and their families. Trends over the past thirty years have indicated that the quality of fast-food jobs is steadily decreasing.

I'm confused. This sentence doesn't seem to fit with the rest of the paragraph.

About one-eighth of all workers in the United States have, at some point, worked for McDonald's (Schlosser 4).

Another amazing statistic

Fast-food jobs have become such a common occupation for teenagers that they are often considered to be a rite of passage into the American workforce. Jobs in fast food are ideal for teenagers because they require no special skills, and they teach basic, but vital life lessons to young people, such as responsibility, teamwork, and the value of a dollar. Studies conducted by the National Academy of Sciences showed that part-time jobs, up to twenty hours a week, were generally a positive experience for teenagers, giving them an increased sense of responsibility and self-esteem. Working more than twenty hours had nearly the opposite effect. Students who worked

This is balanced.

Gould 3

more than twenty hours a week were more likely to have problems in school, cut classes, drop out, or develop substance abuse problems (Zipp 1).

Child labor laws govern the number of hours teens can work and what kinds of work they can do. Children 14 to 15 years can work up to three hours on a school day and eight hours on non-school days; they may work eighteen hours during a school week, and up to forty hours during a non-school week. They can work during the hours 7/am to 7/pm, *Spaces* except from June 1 to Labor Day, when the hours are extended to 9pm. Children ages 14 to 15 are not allowed to cook and are limited to jobs such as cashier, bagger, or *Teens?* cleanup crew. Children 16 to 17 years are not limited to the number of hours they can work, and while they are allowed to cook in fast food and restaurant kitchens, they are not allowed to use hazardous machinery such as automatic slicers, hamburger patty forming machines, grinders, or choppers (www.dol.gov). *Is this the right format?*

Even though there are laws to protect children in the workplace, many fast-food employers do not abide by these laws. During Schlosser's visit to Colorado Springs, he interviewed many high school students who worked excessive hours, beyond what was permitted by law. In addition, some teenagers that he interviewed claimed that they regularly

Gould 4

This seems to be hearsay, not solid evidence.

used hazardous machinery that, by law, they should not have been using. Schlosser notes, however, that none of these teens were opposed to working long hours or using hazardous materials simply because they enjoyed getting a paycheck (82). With so many young fast-food employees willing to let their employers violate labor laws by keeping them for double shifts or until closing, it seems unwise to refuse to do so, especially when one is easily replaceable.

Do you mean they're afraid they'll be fired?

Fast-food corporations have worked hard to make their employees easily replaceable, so that when a worker quits or is fired, there is little or no interruption in the restaurant's productivity. The fast-food industry seeks out part-time, <u>unskilled workers</u>, who have traditionally been young people, because they are more willing to accept lower pay (Schlosser 68). Today, fast-food restaurants frequently hire disabled persons, elderly persons, and recent immigrants as well, for similar reasons (70).

I'm not sure I see the relationship

Are you saying they make the job simple so they can hire cheap, unskilled people?

Fast-food corporations are steadily moving towards a goal of "zero training" for their employees, by developing more efficient methods and using the most advanced kitchen technology. The fast-food kitchen is like an assembly line in a factory. Food arrives at the restaurant frozen, and its preparation involves very little actual cooking; it is a process performed in the kitchen and is regimented according

Good examples

Gould 5

to a manual, including how the hamburger patties are to be arranged on the grill to the thickness of the fries. Workers are told what to do, and how to do it. They have menus in both English and Spanish in order to spend less time training the more than one-third of the non-native English speakers in the fast-food industry who speak no English at all. All of these factors have contributed to the "deskilled" nature of fast-food jobs, which is in the best interest of the corporations because it increases output, and costs them less in training and in wages (68- *Schlosser?* 72). *He seems to be your main source.*

The lack of skill required to be a fast-food worker has made fast-food jobs one of the worst paying in the United States. The fast food industry pays minimum wage to a higher proportion of its workers than in any other industry. While a minimum wage job is an excellent source of additional income to a teenager still living at home, it is nearly impossible to live off of a minimum wage job, much less support a family. Between the years of 1968 and 1990, during the boom of fast-food restaurants, the "real" value of minimum wage dropped forty percent, and even in the late nineties, despite increases in the federal minimum wage, the value *of the?* minimum wage still remains about 27 percent lower than in 1968. At the same time, the value of restaurant executive earnings has gone up in the past

Gould 6

thirty years (73). The National Restaurant Association is opposed to an increase in minimum wage, however, and some large fast-food chains, such as Wendy's, have backed legislation that would allow states to ignore federal minimum wage laws.

Does this sentence need a note?

Critics of a raise in minimum wage are afraid of what increased labor costs will do to the restaurant industry. In response to a possible federal minimum wage increase in 2001, Scott Vincent, director of government affairs for the National Council of Chain Restaurants feared that the industry would be unable to bear a projected 300 percent increase in minimum wage. According to Vincent, "A lot of chains are franchised, which means they're small businesses with thin profit margins that can't handle more labor costs," which would most likely result in reduced hiring, layoffs, or even closings. The only way to accommodate these higher labor costs would be a price increase, which might result in some unsatisfied customers (Van Houten). Schlosser claims that an increase in the minimum wage by one dollar would hardly have any affect on food prices; a fast-food restaurant would only need to increase the price of a hamburger by two cents to finance the extra labor costs. A spokesperson for the Coalition on Human Needs claims that, based on previous increases in minimum wage, there would be no serious labor problems or

You seem to favor a higher wage, but I'm glad you give two sides.

Gould 7

consequences to the restaurant business. Furthermore, he
claims that benefits from a minimum wage increase would be
seen in low income neighborhoods (Houten).

   This is not the only controversy over wages that has
plagued the fast-food industry. In 1998, a jury in
Washington found Taco Bell guilty of cheating as many as
13,000 workers out of overtime pay (Broydo). According to
federal law, overtime is any time an employee works beyond
the standard forty hours in a week; overtime pay must be
at least one and a half times the normal hourly wage per
hour in overtime (www.dol.gov). In the Taco Bell case, the
jury found that managers had forced workers to wait until
the restaurant got busy to punch in, had them work after
punching out, and failed to correctly record hours worked
by employees. One worker claimed that she regularly worked
70 to 80 hours in a week but was only paid for 40. While
the Taco Bell case is one of the most extreme to date,
there is evidence that Taco Bell is not alone when it
comes to cheating workers out of overtime pay. The
Employment Policy Foundation estimates that employees lose
about $19 billion in wages every year, and some critics of
the fast-food industry claim that this is a conservative
estimate (Broydo).

   Fast-food restaurants use several tactics to avoid
paying extra labor costs associated with overtime. Workers

You give several good, specific examples.

Gould 8

are employed "at will," meaning that they are only employed as needed, so if a restaurant is not busy, a manager can send them home early. Managers try to keep all workers employed for less than thirty hours per week, and try to maintain large crews so that this is possible. Fast-food chains often reward managers who keep labor costs down, and this can lead to abuses such as the ones in the Taco Bell case, such as compensating workers with food instead of money and requiring workers to clean the restaurant on their own time (Schlosser 74-75). In the case that abuses do occur, large fast-food corporations try not to let themselves get involved. For example, the McDonald's corporation has no formal wage policies, so when abuses do occur, the company as a whole can deny involvement.

Does this need a note?

Hourly workers are not the only ones who claim they have been cheated out of overtime pay; managers and other salaried employees of service companies claim that outdated language in wage laws allow them to be cheated out of overtime pay (Star News). Managers and assistant managers in the service industry, which includes fast-food companies, often work up to thirty extra hours a week, and sometimes more. Overtime pay laws state that salaried workers in administrative or professional positions are not included among workers subject to overtime pay;

Gould 9

however, some salaried workers feel as though they are being shortchanged for the work they are putting in. Managers and salaried workers from RadioShack, Wal-Mart, and Eckerd filed lawsuits with their employers claiming overtime payments, and many of them have been successful. RadioShack vice president has called this the issue "du jour," and because of this, one may expect similar lawsuits to crop up among fast-food restaurant managers.

I'm a little confused by this.

In other industries, labor unions have been an effective way for employees to voice concerns and dissatisfaction with company policies and procedures. Union representation at fast-food restaurants has been rare, however. Attempts to unionize McDonald's restaurants have been the most notorious because of the scandal associated with these attempts. The corporation's seemingly anti-union attitude has made unionization difficult; John Cook, the US labor relations chief for McDonald's during the 1970s once said "Unions are inimical to what we stand for and how we operate" (Royle). The company no longer publicizes this sort of anti-union stance, but the continued lack of union success indicated that corporate executives have not changed their opinion. During the 1960s and 70s, there were several attempts to unionize McDonald's restaurants across the country. Corporate executives responded by holding "rap sessions"

with employees so that they could express their
grievances. The company's sudden interest in accommodating
their desires kept many of the unionization attempts from
moving forward, but it has not always worked.

In 1973, during a union drive of a McDonald's in San
Francisco, a group of employees claimed that they had been
threatened with dismissal if they did not agree to take
polygraph tests, and answer questions regarding union
activities. The company was found to be violating state
law by administering lie detector tests, and were ordered
to stop, but the unionization attempt was still
unsuccessful (Schlosser 76).

Labor unions trying to gain representation in fast-
food restaurants have not had much success in the United
States, especially with attempts to unionize McDonald's
restaurants. Unions have turned their attention to Canada
in particular, where unionized workers are more common
with around thirty percent of workers belonging to a
union. In British Columbia, the location of the first
McDonald's to be unionized in recent years, when a
majority of the employees at a business sign union cards,
the remainder of the certification process is completed
without much trouble from the management end.

One of the most notorious unionization attempts in
recent years occurred with a McDonald's in Saint-Hubert,

Gould 11

Quebec, when the restaurant closed with only a short time before a union would gain certification there (<u>Wall Street Journal</u>). In Ohio, the same year, two McDonald's employees claimed that they were fired for trying to organize a union at their restaurant. Even at the McDonald's Squamish, British Columbia, which was successfully unionized in 1998, the management initially tried to combat the certification process by hiring fifty anti-union workers to keep the union from gaining a majority of employees at the restaurant (Hamstra).

The fast-food industry has been more difficult to unionize than other types of labor industries for several reasons. The industry is characterized by a high turnover rate, and it is difficult to cultivate enough support for a union when the majority of the workers are relatively new (Schlosser 184). Fast-food companies have generally hired the more disadvantaged members of society-- teenagers, the elderly, recent immigrants, and the disabled. They are hired because they are a cheap source of labor and less likely to rebel or complain, and often it is difficult for these members of society to find any higher paying jobs with better working conditions; therefore, most of these workers do not want to jeopardize their jobs by expressing their discontent (Schlosser 70).

This repeats what you wrote a few pages back, but I see your point.

Although low wages ~~is~~ *are?* the most notable complaint among fast-food workers, it is not simply higher wages and benefits workers hope to gain by unionizing. Workers trying to unionize, more than anything, want to be treated with more respect and to have a voice in the workplace. Accomplishing this can benefit the company as well as the workers. Studies have shown that the level of service a customer receives is the most important factor in whether they will be a returning customer. According to Jill Cashen, a representative for the United Food and Commercial Workers Union, "When workers are happier, when they have better wages and feel like they have a voice at work, their service is going to be better, and customers are going to come back and that's what helps build a good company." Therefore, keeping labor costs down may not be the best way to maximize profits if customers are unhappy with the service they are getting. Cashen also notes that past experience with large corporations has shown that increased wages for unionized workers has not translated into significantly higher prices for customers. She cites Kroger grocery store as an example; Kroger's workforce is entirely unionized, yet it is still the largest grocery store chain in the country.

Despite recent union successes, unionization is hardly gaining momentum. While not every fast-food

Gould 13

employee is pro-union, and not every employer is corrupt
or greedy, there are plenty that are. Unionization may
solve many of the wage and working condition issues,
however, gaining respect for fast-food employees among the
public is much more difficult.

Since unions are only part of your paper, do you want a conclusion that reflects your entire paper? Both my sisters work at Wendy's, so this paper is very interesting to me. Since you write mostly about the workers, should your title and thesis statement be more about workers? For another source, I'd suggest an interview with a student who works in fast food. This should be a good paper.

-Sean

Gould 14

Works Cited

Ayoub, Nina C. "Nota Bene." Rev. of Youth at Work: The Unionized Fast-Food and Grocery Workplace, by Stuart Tannock. Chronicle of Higher Education 25 May 2001: A20.

Broydo, Leora. "Worked Over." Utne Reader. Jan./Feb. 1999: 20-21.

Cashen, Jill. Personal Interview. 10 Sept. 2002.

Gellar, Adam. "More Workers Challenge Bosses on OT Exemption." Star News Online. 5 Aug. 2002. 29 Sept. 2002. <http://www.wilmingtonstar.com>.

"General Information on the Fair Labor Standards Act (FLSA)." U.S. Dept. of Labor Employment Standards Administration Wage and Hour Division. 29 Sept. 2002 <http://www.dol.gov/esa/regs/compliance/whd/ mwposter.htm>.

Hamstra, Mark. "Unions Seek Momentum from Canadian McD's Certification." Nation's Restaurant News 7 Sept. 1998: 3. MasterFILE Premier. EBSCOhost. 15 Sept. 2002 <http://web3.epnet.com/>.

Houten, Ben Van. "Moving on Up?" Restaurant Business 1 July 2001: 15. MasterFILE Premier. EBSCOhost. 15 Sept. 2002 <http://web3.epnet.com/>.

Royle, Tony. "Underneath the Arches." People Management 28 Sept. 2000: 40.

Gould 15

Schlosser, Eric. Fast-Food Nation: The Dark Side of the
    All-American Meal. Boston: Houghton, 2001.
Wall Street Journal. "Canadian McDonald's First Outlet to
    Join Union." 21 Aug. 1998: B7.   *shouldn't the title come first?*
Zipp, Yvonne. "Virtues of Work vs. Finishing Homework."
    Christian Science Monitor 15 Dec. 1998: 1. MasterFILE
    Premier. EBSCOhost. 15 Sept. 2002
    <http://web3.epnet.com/>.

Emily found Sean's comments valuable because they revealed another reader's response to her paper as well as useful ideas for improving it. Several of Sean's remarks highlight what worked well for him ("You give several good, specific examples"). Others inform Emily about a passage he found unclear ("I'm confused. This sentence doesn't seem to fit with the rest of the paragraph"). Remarks that specify his difficulty are particularly useful ("Do you mean they're afraid they'll be fired?"). In some of his comments Sean responds on a personal level to what Emily is saying ("That's an amazing statistic!"). Sean's longer commentary at the end of Emily's paper includes a personal response ("Both my sisters work at Wendy's, so this paper is very interesting to me"), but it also gives a response to the paper as a whole and makes several helpful suggestions.

Note that Sean's comments are framed in a positive and unintrusive way. When he offers suggestions, he usually does so in the form of questions, making it clear that the paper belongs to Emily and that final editing decisions rest with her ("Since unions are only part of your paper, do you want a conclusion that reflects your entire paper?"). Even when he notes a surface error, he asks rather than tells (Above the verb in Emily's "Although low wages is the most notable complaint . . ." Sean wrote "are?"), and it is clear that Sean's goal is to be as helpful to Emily as possible as she undertakes her revision. His comments are constructive, useful, and confidence-building.

In addition to responding to the valuable suggestions of her classmates and instructor, Emily discovered other ways to improve her paper over the next week. Each time she reread her draft, Emily noticed new possibilities for revising it. She spent many hours rephrasing, clarifying, and even rearranging sections of the paper, until she was ready to submit the polished draft that you read in Chapter 8, which is reprinted, with annotations on the following pages.

Gould 1

Emily Gould

English 12

Professor Katherine Humel

4 October 2002

Fast Food Comes at a High Price for Workers

McDonald's, Burger King, KFC, Wendy's, and other popular chains have brought countless innovations to the restaurant industry, delivering food fast and at low cost year after year. Convenience and value have come at a price, however, and many believe that benefits to the public are outweighed by the costs that this giant industry imposes on its workers.

In his best-selling book Fast-Food Nation, Eric Schlosser shows just how much such popular chains revolutionized America's eating habits. In 1970, Americans spent $6 billion on fast food. By 2000, that figure had soared to $110 billion. Schlosser says Americans "spend more on fast food than on movies, books, magazines, newspapers, videos, and recorded music--combined" (3). Every day about a quarter of the U.S. adult population eats fast food in some form. Few, however, give much thought to the workers who prepare and deliver their meals.

Hiring teenagers to serve us food in a fast-food setting has become "so natural, so normal, and so

> The title is not underlined, italicized, or placed within quotation marks.

> The writer introduces the reader to the paper's topic in her opening paragraph. For other opening strategies, see pages 446-49.

> The writer uses statistics to provide background for her topic.

> The quotation is from page 3 of Schlosser's book.

Gould 2

inevitable that people often think little about it," says Stuart Tannock, a lecturer in social and cultural studies at the University of California at Berkeley (qtd. in Ayoub A20). Nevertheless, while fast-food workers have become an essential component in the service industry, a fast-food job is usually viewed as undesirable, dead-end work.

"Qtd. in" is used when the person quoted is not the author of the source.

One-third of all workers under the age of 35 have gotten their first jobs working for restaurants (Yum! Brands), and about one-eighth of all workers in the United States have, at some point, worked for McDonald's (Schlosser 4). Yvonne Zipp of the Christian Science Monitor observes that such jobs have become "a teen rite of passage as universal as driver's ed" (1). They are ideal for teens because they require no special skills, and many believe that such jobs provide the educational benefit of teaching responsibility and good time and money management. These benefits may be more than offset by costs, however. Zipp cites a study by the National Research Council and the Institute of Medicine in Washington that teens who work more than 20 hours a week are "less likely to get enough sleep and exercise, less likely to go on to higher education, and more likely to use alcohol or drugs." These findings are disturbing, since four-fifths of American teens work at least part-

The writer integrates part of a quotation into her own sentence.

Gould 3

time during the school year, and of these, half work more
than 20 hours weekly (Zipp 1).

Child labor laws offer some protection, governing the
number of hours teens can work and the kinds of work they
can do. Those who are 14 or 15 years of age may work up to
three hours on a school day and up to eight hours on other
days, for a maximum of 18 hours during a school week and
40 hours during a non-school week. They may work only
between the hours of 7 a.m. and 7 p.m., except in the
summer, when the hours extend to 9 p.m. Once they reach
16, however, teens may work an unlimited number of hours
("General").

These boundaries were set by the Fair Labor Standards
Act of 1938, and many believe they are no longer suitable
to current realities. At the beginning of the twentieth
century, most teens left school at 16, and restrictive
laws for children up to 15 years of age were designed to
introduce them to the workforce before becoming full-time
workers at 16. Today, however, 90% of teens graduate from
high school at 18, and most work primarily for extra
spending money or luxuries such as new cars. Relatively
few now work to help support their families (Zipp 1).

Since 2000, Congress has been debating the Young
American Workers' Bill of Rights, a bill that would update
the 1938 labor law. If it is enacted as law, 14- and 15-

Notes are
used for
paraphrased
as well as
quoted
material from
sources.

For a print
source the
note gives
the author's
name and the
specific pages
where the
information
was found.

Gould 4

year-olds could work no more than 15 hours weekly, and
teens 16 and 17 would be limited to a 20-hour work week

Notes for
an Internet
source or
other
sources
without
pages do
not give
page
numbers.

(Kiger). While this bill would only affect work hours,
some critics of teen employment, such as Janine Bempechat,
assistant professor in Harvard's Graduate School of
Education, want to keep teens away from fast-food counters
altogether, claiming that they can get a similar sense of
responsibility and self-esteem from jobs such as peer
tutoring or volunteer work. Others, however, noting that
some teens use their paychecks to save for college, worry
that limiting hours could keep them from earning enough to
pay for tuition (Zipp 1).

Teens are also restricted in the kinds of work they
can do. Workers at 14 or 15 are not allowed to cook and
are limited to jobs such as cashier, bagger, or member of
the cleanup crew. More options are available to 16- and
17-year-olds, who can cook but cannot use hazardous
machinery such as automatic slicers, grinders, choppers,
or machines that form hamburger patties ("Prohibited").

A note
identifies an
anonymous
source by the
first word or
two from
the title.

Even though such regulations are intended to ensure safety
in the workplace, many employers are either not obeying
the laws or not doing enough to protect young workers. A
teen gets injured on the job every 40 seconds, and one
dies from a work-related injury every five days. Responding
to these alarming statistics, the U.S. Department of Labor

Gould 5

has tried to crack down on violations of child labor laws with heavy fines (Kiger). Funding for these efforts has increased, with money going toward inspection of workplaces, investigations, and occasional sweeps of industries suspected of serious violations. The Department can impose fines of up to $10,000 on employers who willfully break labor laws and can sentence individuals to six-month jail terms for each employee working in violation of the law. One of the largest fines was incurred by a fast-food company in Ohio, when a 15-year-old cut her finger while using a meat slicer, a piece of equipment that should have been off-limits to her according to federal law. The company was ordered to pay $333,450 after it was found to have 32 other unauthorized employees using similar equipment, including one under the age of 14 (Pass and Spector).

In recent years, reported cases of employer misconduct have declined, but the injury rate among teens at work has not seen a similar drop. Although fines for violators are steep, critics worry that the Labor Department is not doing enough to reduce violations. Only a thousand inspectors are responsible for the safety of all 100 million workers in the nation. As a result, most employers are not fined until someone is injured. Under the proposed Young American Workers' Bill of Rights, an employer who

Notes for sources with multiple authors list all the last names that appear in the Works Cited listing.

Gould 6

willfully ignores child labor laws could be sentenced to as long as five years in prison for each teen who is seriously injured on the job and up to ten if a teen dies as a result of the employer's neglect. Regardless, however, of whether stricter child labor legislation is passed, companies and young workers alike have a strong economic incentive to break whatever laws are on the books. U.S. businesses save an estimated $155 million each year by employing teens, and the economic gains that result from hiring them to do jobs meant for older, more experienced workers often outweigh the consequences of getting caught (Kiger). Furthermore, teens are unlikely to refuse an illegal assignment and risk losing the only job they are qualified to hold.

The absence of a note indicates that the writer is expressing her own observations.

Because most fast-food jobs require little skill, they are among the worst paying in the United States. The fast-food industry pays minimum wage to a higher proportion of its workers than any other sector of employment. While a minimum-wage job may be a good source of spending money for a teenager living at home, it is nearly impossible for an adult to live off such wages, much less support a family. Between 1968 and 1990, the boom years for fast-food restaurants, the purchasing power of the minimum wage dropped 40 percent, and even now, despite increases mandated by federal law, it still purchases about 27

Gould 7

percent less than it did in 1968. At the same time, the
earnings of restaurant executives have risen dramatically.
Nevertheless, the National Restaurant Association opposes
any further increase in the minimum wage, and some large
fast-food chains, such as Wendy's and Jack in the Box,
have backed legislation that would allow states to exempt
certain employers from federal minimum-wage regulations
(Schlosser 73).

Schlosser is the source for all the information in this paragraph.

Critics of a higher minimum wage fear the effects of
increased labor costs on the restaurant industry. Scott
Vincent, director of government affairs for the National
Council of Chain Restaurants, says, "A lot of chains are
franchised, which means they're small businesses with thin
profit margins that can't handle more labor costs" (qtd.
in Van Houten). Higher wages, he maintains, would result
in reduced hiring, layoffs, or even closings. The only way
to compensate would be price increases, which would lessen
the appeal of fast food to customers with limited means
and therefore reduce business.

Acknowledgment phrases identify sources not familiar to the reader and establish their authority.

The writer presents opinions from both sides of a controversy.

A spokesperson for the Coalition on Human Needs
expresses a contrary view, asserting that the effects of
previous increases in the minimum wage suggest that no
serious consequences to the restaurant business would
result, while low-income neighborhoods would derive
the greatest benefits from a minimum-wage increase

Gould 8

Since the writer identifies the interview source, no note is needed following the quotation.

(Van Houten). Author Eric Schlosser calculates that an increase of one dollar in wages would cause the price of a hamburger to increase only two cents (73). Furthermore, Jill Cashen, a representative of the United Food and Commercial Workers Union, argues that better wages and working conditions for workers would actually benefit the consumer:

Longer quotaions are indented one inch. No quotations marks are used.

> The service that customers get when going to shop is one of the main reasons why they'll come back and be repeat customers. . . . When workers are happier--when they have better wages and feel like they have a voice at work--their service is going to be better, and customers are going to come back, and that's what helps build a good company.

The ellipsis signifies that the author has omitted some of the sources' words.

Without a minimum-wage increase, however, the pay that fast-food workers receive is unlikely to rise because they have so little bargaining power. The industry recruits part-time, unskilled workers, especially young people, because they are more willing to accept lower pay. Today, fast-food restaurants also hire disabled persons, elderly persons, and recent immigrants, for similar reasons (Schlosser 68, 70). When such employees grow dissatisfied, they are replaced quickly and easily, with little disruption of the restaurant's operations.

The note indicates that the information came from two discontinuous pages.

Gould 9

Fast-food restaurants see an annual turnover rate in employees of over 75% (White). To accommodate easy replacement of workers, companies are steadily reaching a goal of "zero training" for employees by developing more efficient methods and adopting the most advanced kitchen technology. The fast-food kitchen is like an assembly line. Food arrives at the restaurant frozen, and preparation, which involves little actual cooking, is regimented by a manual, which includes such details as how hamburger patties are to be arranged on the grill and the thickness of the fries (Schlosser 68-72). One college student who worked at Wendy's said, "You don't even think when doing work, and you never make any decisions. You're always told what to do. When you make hamburgers there are even diagrams about where the ketchup goes" (Williams). All these factors have contributed to the "de-skilled" nature of fast-food jobs, which corporations believe to be in their best interest because it increases output and reduces the cost of training and wages.

A note is needed when an interview source is not identified in the paper by name.

Others, however, claim that the high turnover in fast-food jobs costs employers more than they save through low wages. Fast-food restaurants lose at least $500 for each employee who has to be replaced. Managers are forced to spend time in recruiting, hiring, and training new employees, and additional staff is often needed to help

Gould 10

process applications. Current employees are also burdened with extra responsibilities when they pick up the tasks of replaced workers (White).

Other controversies involving wages have plagued the fast-food industry. In 1998, a Washington state jury found Taco Bell guilty of cheating as many as 13,000 workers out of overtime pay (Broydo 20), which, according to federal law, must be paid whenever an employee works more than 40 hours in a week and must be at least one and a half times the normal hourly wage ("General"). In the Taco Bell case, the jury found that managers had forced workers to wait until the restaurant got busy to punch in, had them work after punching out, and failed to record hours correctly. One worker claimed that she regularly worked 70 to 80 hours a week but was paid for only 40. While these are among the worst violations, there is evidence that many other companies deprive workers of earned overtime pay. The Employment Policy Foundation estimates that employees lose $19 billion in unpaid overtime wages every year (Broydo 20).

The writer uses transition words to provide continuity and coherence.

Fast-food restaurants adopt several other tactics as well to lower costs. Workers are employed "at will," meaning that they are employed only as needed, so if a restaurant is not busy, a manager can send them home early. Managers also avoid the cost of benefits for full-time

Gould 11

employees by hiring large crews and keeping all workers employed for less than 30 hours per week. Fast-food chains often reward managers who keep labor costs down, leading to such abuses as compensating workers with food instead of money and requiring them to clean the restaurant on their own time. When such abuses do occur, corporations try to distance themselves from responsibility. For example, the McDonald's corporation has no formal wage policies, so it accepts no blame for the abuses of its franchisees (Schlosser 74-75).

In various industries, dissatisfied workers have turned to labor unions to gain a voice in the workplace and to secure better wages and working conditions. At fast-food restaurants, however, union representation is rare. Organizers attribute their failed attempts to unionize McDonald's restaurants during the 1960s and 70s to the high turnover of workers and the corporation's opposition to unions. John Cook, U.S. labor-relations chief for McDonald's during the 1970s, said, "Unions are inimical to what we stand for and how we operate" (qtd. in Royle 40).

While the company no longer publicizes its anti-union stance, its efforts to forestall unions have continued. In 1998, two McDonald's employees in Ohio claimed that they were fired for trying to organize a union (Hamstra). In

Gould 12

1973, during a union drive at a McDonald's in San Francisco, a group of employees claimed that they had been threatened with dismissal if they did not agree to take polygraph tests and answer questions about their involvement in union activities. The company was found in violation of state law and was ordered to stop; nevertheless, the attempt to unionize was unsuccessful (Schlosser 76).

Having established various problems at fast-food restaurants, the writer begins her conclusion by reminding readers of the public image they project.

Ads for fast-food companies always show smiling, well-scrubbed, contented workers, and the corporations boast of their employee-friendly policies. Restaurants recruit workers with slogans such as "Everybody's Somebody at Wendy's" (Wendy's) and "A Subway restaurant is a really neat place to work" (Subway). On its website, McDonald's proclaims, "We're not just a hamburger company serving people; we're a people company serving hamburgers," and it claims that its goal is "to be the best employer in each community around the world" (McDonald's). While many thousands of teenagers who annually accept work serving fast food find the experience rewarding, many others regard the job as anything but friendly. As author Eric Schlosser concludes, "The real price [of fast food] never appears on the menu" (9).

The writer then concludes with a succinct statement of her theme.

Gould 13

Works Cited

Ayoub, Nina C. "Nota Bene." Rev. of <u>Youth at Work: The</u>

<u>Unionized Fast-Food and Grocery Workplace</u>, by Stuart

Tannock. <u>Chronicle of Higher Education</u> 25 May 2001:

A20.

Broydo, Leora. "Worked Over." <u>Utne Reader</u> Jan./Feb. 1999:

20-21.

Cashen, Jill. Personal Interview. 10 Sept. 2002.

"General Information on the Fair Labor Standards Act

(FLSA)." U.S. Dept. of Labor Employment Standards

Administration Wage and Hour Division. 29 Sept. 2002

<http://www.dol.gov/esa/regs/compliance/whd/

mwposter.htm>.

Hamstra, Mark. "Unions Seek Momentum from Canadian McD's

Certification." <u>Nation's Restaurant News</u> 7 Sept.

1998: 3. <u>MasterFILE Premier</u>. EBSCOhost. 15 Sept. 2002

<http://web3.epnet.com/>.

Kiger, Patrick. "Risky Business." <u>Good Housekeeping</u> Apr.

2002: 114. <u>MasterFILE Premier</u>. EBSCOhost. 15 Sept.

2002 <http://web3.epnet.com/>.

McDonald's USA. "Why McDonald's Has a People Promise and a

People Vision." 22 Sept. 2002.

<http://www.mcdonalds.com/corporate/promise/>.

Pass, Caryn G., and Jeffrey A. Spector. "Protecting

Teens." <u>HR Magazine</u> Feb. 2000: 139. <u>MasterFILE</u>

Sources are listed in alphabetical order.

Sources are not numbered.

Give the date when you consulted an electronic source.

For a source with multiple authors, only the first is listed with first and last names inverted.

Gould 14

Premier. EBSCOhost. 15 Sept. 2002 <http://
    web3.epnet.com/>.

"Prohibited Occupations for Non-Agricultural Employees."
    U.S. Dept. of Labor. Elaws--Fair Labor Standards Act
    Advisor. 29 Sept. 2002 <http://www.dol.gov/elaws/esa/
    flsa/docs/haznonag.asp>.

Royle, Tony. "Underneath the Arches." People Management 28
    Sept. 2000: 40.

Schlosser, Eric. Fast Food Nation: The Dark Side of the
    All-American Meal. Boston: Houghton, 2001.

Subway Restaurants. "Subway Job Opportunities." 22 Sept.
    2002 <http://www.subway.com/>.

Van Houten, Ben. "Moving on Up?" Restaurant Business 1
    July 2001: 15. MasterFILE Premier. EBSCOhost. 15
    Sept. 2002 <http://web3.epnet.com/>.

Wendy's International. "Welcome to Wendy's Career Center."
    22 Sept. 2002. <http://www.wendys.com/w-5-0.shtml>.

White, Gerald L. "Employee Turnover: The Hidden Drain on
    Profits." HR Focus Jan. 1995: 15. InfoTrac OneFile.
    21 Sept. 2002 <http://infotrac.galegroup.com/>.

Williams, Tamicah. Personal interview. 24 Sept. 2002.

Yum! Brands. "Great Jobs." 22 Sept. 2002. <http://
    www.yumjobs.com/>.

Zipp, Yvonne. "Virtues of Work vs. Finishing Homework."
    Christian Science Monitor 15 Dec. 1998: 1. MasterFILE

When a corporation's Web site is cited, list the corporation as "author."

Give the online location of electronic databases.

Premier. EBSCOhost. 15 Sept. 2002 <http://
web3.epnet.com/>.

TYPING AND PROOFREADING YOUR POLISHED DRAFT

Emily and Justin benefited from the comments and suggestions they received from classmates in their editing groups and from their instructors. They made further revisions in their papers and submitted them in polished form, in accordance with the assignment they had been given, which follows.

ASSIGNMENT   **Submitting Your Portfolio**

Submit the following items in your folder:

- Your typed polished draft
- All earlier drafts and outlines
- Your note cards in two packets:
  —those you used in your paper, in the order you used them
  —those you wrote but did not use
- Your research notebook

When you prepare your final draft, be sure that you observe formatting conventions described in Chapter C of Part II, along with any others your instructor may specify. Before you submit your paper, read it through several times, slowly and carefully, looking for errors. Look for typing mistakes, misspellings, missing words, punctuation problems, and any other surface errors that may have escaped your notice in earlier readings. It is especially useful to have a friend proofread the paper as well, because by now you have become so familiar with what you have written that you may have difficulty noticing surface details.

Neatly cross out a minor error with a single line and write the correction above it. Never erase, and do not use correction fluid for making handwritten changes. Any page with a major error or numerous minor errors should be reprinted.

After proofreading their final drafts, Emily and Justin brought them to class, where their instructors gave them one final assignment:

ASSIGNMENT   **Final Proofreading**

Read the final drafts of the other students in your editing group. Do not mark on their papers, but if you find an error, point it out to the author so that it can be corrected.

At last, Emily and Justin submitted their final drafts. For both, the project had been difficult but rewarding work. Like their classmates, they had struggled with the previously unfamiliar process of research and research writing. They had uncovered and managed a large body of research materials. From these sources, they had created essays that had substance, form, and interest—essays they were proud of. They had also learned a great deal, not only about their particular topics, but also about research, about college scholarship, and even about the meaning of an education itself. It is likely that after the hard work of your own research project is completed, you too, like Emily, Justin, and many thousands of other students before you, will feel a well-deserved sense of satisfaction with what you have accomplished.

14 Argument: Reading, Writing, and Research

You don't have to be hostile or arrogant to argue effectively. You don't even have to be an expert or have firsthand experience with your topic. In fact, in writing a college-level argument, you should avoid sounding overconfident, too sure you have found the truth. You are expected to be reasonable, fair-minded, and logical. In a way, that may be a relief, since you don't face the pressure of needing to win at any cost. Unlike a debater, to whom winning is everything, a writer engaged in a serious argument should be above mere victory. The goal is more important—an honest search for truth in a world where we must acknowledge and respect competing representations of reality. Of course, you always want to make your case convincing enough to have an impact on an audience, but you "win" in argumentative writing when you are fair, thorough, and clear. The challenge of argument is to place ideas in a public forum to see if they stand up under scrutiny. College students construct arguments not to trick or outmaneuver others, but to test the validity of ideas. This is the intellectual excitement and ethical challenge of argument.

Of course, not every form of persuasion adheres to these ideals. Most advertisements, for example, are designed to stimulate purchases rather than to discover truth. And, in some cases, fairness and ethics have little to do with how advertisers influence consumers.

If you visualize argument as a horizontal line or continuum, at one end you would place the rigorous logic and impersonal language of the physical sciences—for example, a geologist's efforts to demonstrate to professional colleagues that her experimental findings challenge accepted theories of beach erosion. At the other end of the spectrum, you might place a richly colored photograph of a vacation fantasy that tries to persuade us to book reservations at an exclusive beach resort. The two extremes of this continuum would look like this:

Logical reasoning ⟵————————⟶ *Emotional appeal*

EMOTIONAL PERSUASION

Although emotional appeals are not the primary concern of this chapter, we begin by examining the tactics of advertisement. At times, these tactics seem obvious. But even though we understand that ads are designed to manipulate consumers, most of us are influenced by them. They succeed because most people observe ads casually, if not subconsciously, on billboards and in magazines; rarely do we analyze them systematically. In their appropriate context, ads are evidently effective, since people spend billions of dollars on products and services that are not necessities.

When we study advertising techniques, we discover how ads and other forms of emotional persuasion can motivate people to behave and believe in accordance with the desires of others. Awareness is the best defense against manipulation.

The advertisement in Figure 14.1 (page 492) illustrates this type of persuasion. Like most other magazines ads, it is concerned more with stimulating desires than with explaining the features of a product or service. In fact, the advertisement illustrates a formula developed by Hugh Rank, a prominent analyst of advertising and propaganda. First comes *attention-getting*. When readers first encounter this ad, they are likely to notice the pristine mountain landscape and close-up image of a bear, which evoke a unique and intimate encounter with nature and its wildlife. Second comes *confidence-building*. Traveling to this region in the small ships of Cruise West is bound to get readers "close enough to see bears on a shoreline, and the barnacles on a humpback's tail." Presumably, it is truly an "up-close, casual, and personal" experience. Third comes *desire-stimulating*. The advertisement speaks of "the magic" of traveling from "the outermost reaches of Alaska to the wildlife-rich jungles of Costa Rica and Panama." Fourth comes *urgency-stressing*. Since this could be the only "travel experience [that] can bring you closer to a region's wildlife, culture, and natural history," failing to contact Cruise West to make a booking may lead to regret. Finally comes *response-seeking*. Readers are encouraged to call the number provided or visit the Web site for brochures and availability before it is too late.

Few ads illustrate Rank's formula quite so clearly as the one in Figure 14.1. However, many ads maximize the emotional appeal of products without providing specific information about ingredients, specifications, or cost. Ads are subject to constant testing and research to make sure that the emotions and desires they evoke actually motivate consumers. As you study the following ads, try to decide whether you are among the audience that their creators have targeted.

Emotional Persuasion

EXERCISE

After carefully examining the advertisements on the following pages (Figures 14.2 and 14.3), freewrite for five to ten minutes about each of them. What audience do the advertisers have in mind, and what responses do they hope to stimulate? How does the advertiser expect people to be persuaded by the appeal? Is one ad more logical than the other? Is emotional appeal a component of either or both ads? Now try to envision ads that seek the same results without resorting to emotional appeals. How would they differ from the ads pictured here? Would they be more or less effective in furthering the advertisers' goals?

Figure 14.1 Ad illustrating the Hugh Rank formula.

Figure 14.2 **Ad using emotional persuasion.**

Peace of mind.

All professionally installed with Home Depot At-Home Services.
Our trusted network of licensed installation and service professionals can tackle a wide range of projects. So visit your local Home Depot or www.homedepot.com for installation and maintenance services you can trust. And the next time you don't feel like doing a project yourself, let us do it for you.

Figure 14.3 Ad using emotional persuasion.

◼ LOGICAL ARGUMENT

In contrast to emotional persuasion, formal argument relies primarily on facts and logic. Some arguments, like the following passage from a book by a noted biologist and conservationist, adhere to a tightly organized pattern:

> For species on the brink, from birds to fungi, the end can come in two ways. Many, like the Moorean tree snails, are taken out by the metaphorical equivalent of a rifle shot—they are erased, but the ecosystem from which they are removed is left intact. Others are destroyed by a holocaust, in which the entire ecosystem perishes.
>
> The distinction between rifle shots and holocausts has special merit in considering the case of the spotted owl *(Strix occidentalis)* of the United States, an endangered form that has been the object of intense national controversy since 1988. Each pair of owls requires about three to eight kilometers of coniferous forest more than 250 years old. Only this habitat can provide the birds with both enough large hollow trees for nesting and an expanse of open understory for the effective hunting of mice and other small mammals. Within the range of the spotted owl in western Oregon and Washington, the suitable habitat is largely confined to twelve national forests. The controversy was first engaged within the U.S. Forest Service and then the public at large. It was ultimately between loggers, who wanted to continue cutting the primeval forest, and environmentalists determined to protect an endangered species. The major local industry around the owl's range was affected, the financial stakes were high, and the confrontation was emotional. Said the loggers: "Are we really expected to sacrifice thousands of jobs for a handful of birds?" Said the environmentalists: "Must we deprive future generations of a race of birds for a few more years of timber yield?"
>
> Overlooked in the clamor was the fate of an entire habitat, the old-growth coniferous forest, with thousands of other species of plants, animals, and microorganisms, the great majority unstudied and unclassified. Among them are three rare amphibian species, the tailed frog and the Del Norte and Olympic salamanders. Also present is the western yew, *Taxus brevifolia*, source of taxol, one of the most potent anticancer substances ever found. The debate should be framed another way: what else awaits discovery in the old-growth forests of the Pacific Northwest?
>
> This cutting of primeval forest and other disasters, fueled by the demands of growing human populations, are the overriding threat to biological diversity everywhere. But even the data that led to this conclusion, coming as they do mainly from vertebrates and plants, understate the case. The large, conspicuous organisms are the ones most susceptible to rifle shots, to overkill and the introduction of competing organisms. They are of the greatest immediate importance to man and receive the greater part of his malign attention. People hunt deer and pigeons rather than sowbugs and spiders. They cut roads into a forest to harvest Douglas fir, not mosses and fungi.
>
> Not many habitats in the world covering a kilometer contain fewer than a thousand species of plants and animals. Patches of rain forest and coral reef harbor tens of thousands of species, even after they have declined to a remnant of the original wilderness. But when the *entire* habitat is destroyed, almost all of the species are destroyed. Not just eagles and pandas disappear but also the smallest, still uncensused invertebrates, algae, and fungi, the invisible players that make

up the foundation of the ecosystem. Conservationists now generally recognize the difference between rifle shots and holocausts. They place emphasis on the preservation of entire habitats and not only the charismatic species within them. They are uncomfortably aware that the last surviving herd of Javan rhinoceros cannot be saved if the remnant woodland in which they live is cleared, that harpy eagles require every scrap of rain forest around them that can be spared from the chain saw. The relationship is reciprocal: when star species like rhinoceros and eagles are protected, they serve as umbrellas for all the life around them.

—Edward O. Wilson, *The Diversity of Life*

The Structure of Logical Argument: Claims, Evidence, and Values

Although environmental issues often arouse an emotional reaction, Edward O. Wilson appeals to reason by adopting the techniques and strategies of formal argument. He advances a central point, an ***argumentative assertion*** or ***claim***: that environmental debates oversimplify or ignore transcendent issues when they focus on the fate of one or two "charismatic species." Wilson supports this claim with various types of ***evidence:*** demonstrable ***facts*** (e.g., "patches of rain forest and coral reef harbor tens of thousands of species"), opinions or ***inferences*** derived from facts ("the cutting of primeval forests and other disasters, fueled by the demands of growing human populations, are the overriding threat to biological diversity everywhere"), and ***judgments*** based on ethical values or political views (e.g., "the debate should be framed another way"). Because his argument seems logical and his tone is calm and confident, many readers may conclude that Wilson has authority and reason on his side.

Presented in the abstract, the rules of argument seem straightforward and unambiguous. However, anyone who has witnessed a vigorous discussion among friends, colleagues, or family members who hold contradictory views can testify to the difficulty of distinguishing facts from opinions or claims from truth. Nevertheless, a few basic guidelines should serve your needs as a reader and writer of arguments in college. First, a valid argument is one that advances a claim about which reasonable, educated adults can disagree. You cannot base a worthwhile argument on an assertion of fact (e.g., *The Adventures of Huckleberry Finn* reveals Mark Twain's disapproval of slavery) or an expression of individual taste (e.g., *The Adventures of Huckleberry Finn* is the greatest American novel).

An effective argument does not, however, evade or ignore individual ***values.*** On the contrary, responsible writers acknowledge their own attitudes and predispositions as they appeal to those of a particular audience. E. V. Kontorovich, for example, appeals to the values of a conservative audience, readers of the *National Review,* by defending the exclusion of atheists and homosexuals from the Boy Scouts of America (pages 326–28) on the grounds of a "First Amendment right of free association—the right to fraternize with whomever one wants, a crucial underpinning of civil society." On the other hand, Barbara Dority appeals to the values of a more liberal audience, readers of the *Humanist* (pages 228–31), by reminding them that the Boy Scouts is "a national organization with wide-ranging government support that continues to discriminate against persons on the basis of sexual orientation and religion." Although they may not change many minds, both writers resist irresponsible claims. Kontorovich, for example, does not condemn atheists as un-American and therefore unfit to affiliate themselves with the Scouts. Dority, likewise, does not try to blame the Scouts for hate crimes committed against gay teenagers.

Varieties of Evidence

Perhaps the most common obstacle to productive argument is disputed or misleading evidence. Writers undermine their credibility when they insist on the authority of their claims, belittle or ignore competing claims, or misrepresent evidence. On the other hand, uncritical readers can be misled by careless inferences or hasty judgments when they are asserted as self-evident truth.

Facts

Facts, though they offer convincing proof, are sometimes hard to come by. Few arguments can be supported entirely with indisputable facts: for example, alcohol acts as a depressant. Other facts, though not universally acknowledged throughout history, are nonetheless authoritative: for example, motorists are more likely to cause accidents when they drive under the influence of alcohol. Still other facts require proof: for example, Festerhagen was intoxicated when he swerved to miss the neighbor's cat and collided with a police car. This last fact demands verification (visual evidence based on the testimony of witnesses, the results of a breathalyzer test, or a blood-alcohol reading) that may hinge on legal definitions that vary from one state to another.

One impediment to fair, logical argument is confusing facts with inferences: for example, since Festerhagen was intoxicated, he caused the accident that injured Officer Reilly. Although this is a reasonably persuasive inference—an opinion based on the fact that Festerhagen was legally under the influence of alcohol—a competing fact to consider is that drunk drivers are sometimes involved in accidents caused by others. Likewise, writers often err by mistaking correlations for causes. For example, there is a well-known correlation between the incidence of Down syndrome and the age of a mother during pregnancy. However, it has yet to be proved that a mother's age is a direct *cause* of Down syndrome. Moreover, the fact that an overwhelming majority of babies born to women over the age of thirty-five do not have birth defects, along with the fact that many children who have Down syndrome are born to women under that age, seems to weaken a causal argument.

Inferences

Important as they are in validating claims, facts usually are not the crux of an argument. More often, people argue issues of interpretation—inferences or conclusions drawn from factual evidence. Chapter 4 introduced **inductive** and **deductive** reasoning as organizational patterns. These terms apply also to formal argument.

An inductive argument arrives at an inference or judgment after weighing specific facts. For example:

- **Fact.** Professor Fangle permitted Bushrod to enroll in his American literature class after the published deadline for adding courses—with the strict understanding that he would make up the work that other students had already completed.

- **Fact.** By the end of September, Bushrod still had not submitted any of this work.

- **Fact.** At the urging of his instructor, Bushrod scheduled an office conference to discuss the assignments and to agree on a reasonable deadline for submitting them. However, he did not keep his appointment.

- **Fact.** By fall break, Bushrod had accumulated six more absences and failed three daily quizzes.

- **Fact.** Explaining that his return flight from Bermuda had been delayed, Bushrod was absent from class the day after fall break and therefore missed an opportunity to review material covered on the midterm examination, which he subsequently failed.

- **Fact.** At this point, Professor Fangle offered Bushrod the option of withdrawing from the course without failing, but he rejected the offer indignantly.

- **Fact.** Although Bushrod submitted the two essays assigned during the second half of the semester, both were late. One of them dealt with an eighteenth-century French play, and the other plagiarized an article about Edgar Allan Poe published in a well-known literary journal.

- **Fact.** Confronted with this evidence, Bushrod became verbally abusive and threatened to assault his instructor physically. He refused to leave Professor Fangle's office and was escorted away by the campus police.

- **Inference.** Bushrod has no legitimate basis for appealing his grade in Professor Fangle's class.

Unlike a deductively organized paragraph, a deductive argument does not necessarily open with a summarizing assertion or conclusion. Instead, it is distinguished by the logical relationship between two statements (both facts, or a fact and an inference) that support an argumentative claim. The preceding argument about Festerhagen's accident, for example, is actually based on deductive reasoning:

- **Fact.** A motorist is more likely to cause an accident while driving under the influence of alcohol.

- **Fact.** According to the results of an on-site breathalizer test, Festerhagen was legally intoxicated when he swerved to miss the neighbor's cat and collided with a police car.

- **Claim.** Festerhagen bears responsibility for the accident that injured Officer Reilly.

Presented fairly, as a logical conclusion, the claim that Festerhagen bears responsibility for the accident is more persuasive and ethical than it would be if it were presented as fact.

Analogy

An argument based on *analogy* makes a comparison. The following condensation of Edward Wilson's argument (pages 495–96) provides an illustration:

> For species on the brink, from birds to fungi, the end can come in two ways. Many, like the Moorean tree snails, are taken out by the metaphorical equivalent of a rifle shot—they are erased, but the ecosystem from which they are removed is left intact. Others are destroyed by a holocaust, in which the entire ecosystem perishes.
>
> The distinction between rifle shots and holocausts has special merit in considering the case of the spotted owl (*Strix occidentalis*) of the United States, an endangered form that has been the object of intense national controversy since 1988. . . .
>
> Overlooked in the clamor was the fate of an entire habitat, the old-growth coniferous forest, with thousands of other species of plants, animals, and microorganisms, the great majority unstudied and unclassified. . . .
>
> The large, conspicuous organisms are the ones most susceptible to rifle shots, to overkill and the introduction of competing organisms. They are of the greatest immediate importance to man and receive the greater part of his malign attention. . . .
>
> But when the entire habitat is destroyed, almost all of the species are destroyed. Not just eagles and pandas disappear but also the smallest, still uncensused invertebrates, algae, and fungi, the invisible players that make up the foundation of the ecosystem. Conservationists now generally recognize the difference between rifle shots and holocausts. They place emphasis on the preservation of entire habitats and not only the charismatic species within them.

Because most people regard genocide as a more heinous crime than homicide, many readers will accept Wilson's argument that preserving entire ecosystems is a more urgent priority than protecting any one individual plant or animal species.

Testimony

Writers often support their arguments with the *testimony* of acknowledged experts. As we noted in Chapter 3, the most persuasive, reliable sources for research writing are persons with recognized authority in an appropriate field. Notice how James Surowiecki uses testimony in the following passage from his article "The Financial Page: The Talking Cure" (pages 276–77):

> This outbreak of straight talk is Wall Street's way of addressing the collapse of its credibility. Everyone agrees that conflicts of interest riddle the securities and accounting industries—research analysts touting dubious companies to win their business, auditors signing off on dubious numbers to keep it—and that something must be done, so Wall Street has decided to adopt the talking cure. The problem with the conflicts of interest, the argument goes, is that no one knows about them. Fess up, and the problem goes away.
>
> It's a nice thought, but the diagnosis is facile, and the remedy won't work. Start with the central tenet: that during the boom the conflicts of interest were kept secret. The truth is, people knew more than they like to admit. Back in 1998 a *Business Week* cover story called "Wall Street's Spin Game" put the matter succinctly: "The analyst today is an investment banker in sheep's clothing." When Merrill Lynch hired Henry Blodget as an Internet analyst in 1999, the media explained the decision by saying that Blodget, with his rosy predictions, would

help the firm bring in more investment-banking business. Jack Grubman, the former Salomon Smith Barney analyst, bragged of his intimate relationship with the companies he was supposed to be evaluating objectively. And the problems in the accounting industry were even more obvious. Though the firms maintained their game face, it was no secret, by the late 1990s, that the game itself was rigged. Most investors accepted this state of affairs with the genial tolerance of pro-wrestling fans.

Why? One reason, clearly, was the boom itself—people didn't care why an analyst recommended a stock, as long as it went up. But there was something else: it turns out that people think conflicts of interest don't much matter. "If you disclose a conflict of interest, people in general don't know how to use that information," George Lowenstein, an economics professor at Carnegie Mellon, says. "And, to the extent that they do anything at all, they actually tend to underestimate the severity of these conflicts."

Usually, conflicts of interest lead not to corruption but, rather, to unconscious biases. Most analysts try to do good work, but the quid-pro-quo arrangements that govern their business seep into their analyses and warp their judgments. . . . "People have a pretty good handle on overt corruption, but they don't have a handle on just how powerful these unconscious biases are," Lowenstein says.

Ethical and Emotional Appeals

Earlier in this chapter we contrasted the emotional appeals of advertisements with the logical evidence presented in formal argument. This, like many other distinctions, can be oversimplified and exaggerated. The fact is that while writers who argue effectively rely on sound reasoning (sometimes called *logos*), they also recognize that the minds of readers are not impassively mechanistic. Classical rhetoricians understood that effective argument also appeals to the emotions of an audience (*pathos*) and rests on the character (*ethos*) projected by a speaker or writer, often referred to as a *persona.*

Ethos

Writers use *ethical appeals* to project a credible, trustworthy persona. Credibility and trust are earned through careful research, clear writing, and humility. Notice how historian Lawrence Stone creates such a persona in the following passage from "A Short History of Love" (pages 48–51):

Historians and anthropologists are in general agreement that romantic love— that usually brief but intensely felt and all-consuming attraction toward another person—is culturally conditioned. Love has a history. It is common only in certain societies at certain times, or even in certain social groups within those societies, usually the elite, which have the leisure to cultivate such feelings. Scholars are, however, less certain whether romantic love is merely a culturally induced psychological overlay on top of the biological drive for sex, or whether it has biochemical roots that operate quite independently from the libido. Would anyone in fact "fall in love" if they had not read about it or heard it talked about? Did poetry invent love, or love poetry?

Some things can be said with certainty about the history of the phenomenon. The first is that cases of romantic love can be found in all times and places and have often been the subject of powerful poetic expression, from the Song of Solomon to Shakespeare. On the other hand, as anthropologists have discovered, neither social approbation nor the actual experience of romantic love is common to all societies. Second, historical evidence for romantic love before the age of printing is largely confined to elite groups, which of course does not mean that it may not have occurred lower on the social scale. As a socially approved cultural artifact, romantic love began in Europe in the southern French aristocratic courts of the twelfth century, and was made fashionable by a group of poets, the troubadours. In this case the culture dictated that it should occur between an unmarried male and a married woman, and that it either should go sexually unconsummated or should be adulterous.

By the sixteenth and seventeenth centuries, our evidence becomes quite extensive, thanks to the spread of literacy and the printing press. We now have love poems, such as Shakespeare's sonnets, love letters, and autobiographies by women concerned primarily with their love lives. The courts of Europe were evidently hotbeds of passionate intrigues and liaisons, some romantic, some sexual. The printing press also began to spread pornography to a wider public, thus stimulating the libido, while the plays of Shakespeare indicate that romantic love was a concept familiar to society at large, which composed his audience.

Whether this romantic love was approved of, however, is another question. We simply do not know how Shakespearean audiences reacted to *Romeo and Juliet*. Did they, like us (and as Shakespeare clearly intended), fully identify with the young lovers? Or, when they left the theater, did they continue to act like the Montague and Capulet parents, who were trying to stop these irresponsible adolescents from allowing an ephemeral and irrational passion to interfere with the serious business of politics and patronage?

Stone projects authority by explaining historical facts and trends, summarizing scholarly research, and alluding to literary texts. Yet he concedes the limits of his knowledge by posing questions at various points. Another impressive ethical appeal is the clarity and careful organization of Stone's writing.

Similarly, Edward O. Wilson tries to project objectivity in the following paragraph from his book *The Diversity of Life* (page 495):

The controversy [surrounding the spotted owl] was first engaged within the U.S. Forest Service and then the public at large. It was ultimately between loggers, who wanted to continue cutting the primeval forest, and environmentalists determined to protect an endangered species. The major local industry around the owl's range was affected, the financial stakes were high, and the confrontation was emotional. Said the loggers: "Are we really expected to sacrifice thousands of jobs for a handful of birds?" Said the environmentalists: "Must we deprive future generations of a race of birds for a few more years of timber yield?"

Wilson establishes credibility by summarizing two conflicting arguments without endorsing either. Rejecting both arguments as extreme and simplistic, he projects a cautious, deliberate persona.

Stone and Wilson each adopt a persona that is effective in specific ***rhetorical situations***. Molly Ivins, on the other hand, projects a very different persona in the following passage from "'Ernie's Nuns' Are Pointing the Way" (pages 280–81):

Middle-aged activists who waste time bemoaning apathy on campus could help by getting off their duffs and helping spread word about the USAS boycotts.

Lest you think hideous working conditions are found only in the Third World, consider the case of Big Chicken, the poultry industry in America.

Workers in chicken factories endure conditions that would shame Guatemala or Honduras. Many stand for hours on end in sheds that reek of manure, or chop chickens all day in cold, dark plants, or are constantly scratched by live chickens that have to be crammed into cages by the thousands. . . .

The wages are so low, workers often qualify for welfare. And as Texans know from our experience with Big Chicken in East Texas, these plants are often notorious polluters as well, fouling both air and water.

Ivins presents herself as a morally outraged citizen. She invokes stark contrasts—right and wrong, heroes and villains. She tries to goad people into immediate action and is prepared to shame them if necessary. Individual readers may disagree about whether a more deliberate, objective persona would have been more effective in this rhetorical situation. However, the fact that Ivins's syndicated column appears in daily newspapers throughout the United States indicates that many readers respect or at least enjoy her persona. Whether Ivins alters the opinions of readers is, of course, not so clear.

Pathos

Individual readers will not agree about the appropriateness of emotional appeals in specific rhetorical situations. For example, some may argue that the word *holocaust* conjures up such dreadful associations that Edward O. Wilson's use of the term (page 495) is unwarranted or irresponsible. Others may feel that it is a uniquely effective means of arousing the attention of apathetic readers who do not fully recognize what is at stake.

E. V. Kontorovich goes a step further when he assails a court decision prohibiting discriminatory practices by the Boy Scouts (pages 227–28):

Recently, a New Jersey appellate court forced the Boy Scouts to give a scoutmaster post to James Dale, a gay activist and editor at *Poz*, a magazine for HIV-positive people. . . .

The wave of litigation against the Scouts is not ultimately about the rights of gays, or atheists, or females. It is a challenge to the BSA's right to exist in its present form. Such an attack should not be surprising; if anything, it's odd that the Boy Scouts have hung on for so long. . . .

The existence of the Scouts irritates the ideologues of modernity—and so hordes of litigators, the antibodies of a dissolute culture, have responded by attacking the foreign body. If the courts find in favor of the plaintiffs in the undecided cases, the meaning of the Boy Scouts will be greatly eroded. The organization will become the Gay Godless Girl/Boy Scouts of America. It is only the right to restrict membership and insist that members follow rules that can give a civic group definition.

For example, the Scout's oath has a clause about "keeping myself . . . morally straight," a provision the BSA says is on its face incompatible with homosexual activity. "There is nothing in [the Scout's oath] about homosexuality," says Timothy Curran, the California gay seeking reinstatement as a scoutmaster. "It says you must be 'morally straight,' but you can define that any way you want." Which is precisely what New Jersey's jurisprudes chose to do.

Kontorovich engages in name-calling—comparing plaintiffs' attorneys to microbes and implying that his opponents are "dissolute." Likewise, his reference to judges as "jurisprudes" (a word that Kontorovich has apparently coined) slyly invokes another label—*prude,* a self-righteous person who tries to control the manners and behaviors of other people.

Dubious emotional appeals appear in arguments from every point along the ideological spectrum. (Barbara Dority, for her part, calls the Boy Scouts "bigoted" and accuses them of "doggedly . . . loathing" atheists and homosexuals.) The prevalence of such appeals has led some commentators to deplore the "declining civility" of contemporary discourse. Reviewing the political rhetoric of past eras indicates that these expressions of alarm lack perspective. But whether or not reckless emotional appeals are effective is a different question, and they are clearly out of bounds in most of the arguments you read and write as a college student.

▪ AN INFORMAL ANALYSIS OF ARGUMENTS

Having considered the elements and techniques of argument, you should now be prepared to examine an argumentative text by analyzing its components. Most arguments can be assessed in terms of the following five elements:

- **Purpose.** What audience does the writer seem to have in mind; that is, whom does he intend to influence? What attitudes do his readers (or listeners) probably share? How and why does the writer want to influence this audience? What does the writer want them to do in response to his message?

- **Thesis** (also called the **assertion, claim,** or **proposition**). What main point or idea is the writer trying to persuade readers to accept or act on? Is this point clearly and explicitly stated? Does the writer present it as the only reasonable view of the issue at hand?

- **Evidence.** What kinds of evidence does the writer use to support the thesis? facts? inferences? analogies? expert testimony? Is the evidence appropriate, credible, and sufficient? Is the argument based on logic, emotion, or both? How is the evidence arranged or organized?

- **Refutation.** Are opposing views presented fairly? Would opponents feel that their opinions have been stated accurately? Does the writer effectively show that opposing views are inadequate or invalid? Does the writer overlook any opposing arguments?

- **Persona.** How would you characterize the writer's attitude and credibility? Does the writer seem hostile? conciliatory? reasonable? sarcastic? Is the writer obviously biased or bound by a narrow perspective? Does the language sound reasonable? conciliatory? pedantic? aggressive? Do you trust the writer to argue fairly and objectively?

These questions can be applied to any persuasive text, providing a valuable way to analyze argumentative techniques and to assess their effectiveness.

To observe the processes of informal analysis, start by reading the following editorial published in *The Nation*, a magazine of opinion with a liberal slant. The author, Roger W. Bowen, is president of the State University of New York (SUNY), New Paltz.

PRACTICE READING

The Price of Democracy

Roger W. Bowen

A 1998 ruling by the U.S. Court of Appeals for the Seventh Circuit, if it is not reversed by the Supreme Court this autumn, will undermine democratic student government and seriously harm the already fragile sense of community in public institutions of higher education across the nation. The case, *Board of Regents v. Southworth*, involves a suit against the University of Wisconsin by several self-described conservative students who are unhappy because a portion of their mandated student fees is being used to support eighteen student groups whose activities run counter to the plaintiffs' ideological, political, or religious beliefs. Among the groups are Amnesty International; the Lesbian, Gay, Bisexual, and Transgender Campus Center; and the Campus Women's Center. The Court of Appeals struck down the university's fee policy as violating the plaintiffs' First Amendment rights.

At first blush the principle informing *Southworth*, taxpayer choice, is an appealing one. The conservative Wisconsin plaintiffs have argued that whoever pays the piper should get to call the tune. By this logic, whether mandated student fees or government taxes are at issue, the payer should have the right to determine how his or her money will be spent by the governing authority.

Many years ago I argued in a *New York Times* Op-Ed that taxpayers should have the right to determine how their total tax payment is distributed to the various levels of government. I advocated paying to my village that which I owed to the federal government. My motivation for wanting a change in the rules was simple: I had lost confidence in the federal government's ability to use my hard-earned tax dollars wisely; I felt that my local government was, if not wiser, then at least more accessible and therefore potentially more receptive to my views.

The similarity between that view and *Southworth* is deceptive. Despite the apparent agreement on the principle of taxpayer sovereignty, the conservative Wisconsin students' position involves the right not to subsidize any organization espousing principles they dislike. I was not seeking a tax reduction; the conservative Wisconsin students are; they want to fight to reduce their fees and hence their overall support for a university they voluntarily attend. A comparable approach, if applied to my scheme, would be a taxpayer's right to deduct monies from any government function not meeting with the taxpayer's approval—a line-item veto.

Choice is one thing, veto power something else entirely. Democratically elected governments, including student governments, are disinclined to relinquish such powers to individual members of the community. To do so would destroy state sovereignty in the name of libertarianism. Government would not just cease to be effective, it might cease to be.

Equally destructive is the damage inflicted on the sense of community. Universities and nation-states are something more than their constituent parts. They are communities whose members accept some loss of freedom in exchange for certain benefits—some tangible, some not—and who appreciate that the common good is best advanced if all members' differences are respected. If a community is to work, pluralism in all its crazy messiness must be accepted, even celebrated.

The Wisconsin litigants, like many on the fight in today's culture wars, do not, it seems, so much want membership in a community as they want ownership. Ownership for them is the right to retain control over some portion of the dues that signify community membership and which, if paid in their entirety, would make them full members. Partial membership is what *Southworth* makes possible.

The academy has always been racy, unconventional, and intellectually daring, all traits inimical to conservative values. Paradoxically, this means that conservatives may feel out of place in the academy, but it does not change the fact that their voice is central to the academy's intellectual vibrancy. Without conservatives as full members, yin lacks yang, conversation becomes sterile, debate can become monotonal, and learning may be reduced to mindless absorption of orthodoxy. The academy needs—indeed, depends upon—thinking conservatives who courageously challenge the dominant liberal ethos. This happens occasionally in ways that create stronger community. A recent example is the 1995 University of Virginia case *Rosenberger v. University of Virginia*, in which a group of conservative religious students successfully challenged the university's refusal to provide funding for a Christian student publication.

In that case the conservative Virginia students, unlike those in Wisconsin, did not say that they wanted to opt out of paying mandated fees for student organizations whose values they disliked; rather, they only wanted university funding for their own activity, a religious newspaper, to be equitably (not equally) provided from these same mandated student fees. Virginia's Christian students sought full membership in a pluralistic community. Wisconsin student conservatives seek exactly the opposite by arguing that they are under no obligation to support "speech with which they disagree," in the words of the court ruling. This argument is dangerous. In matriculating at Wisconsin, all students, whether they know this or not, enter into a moral compact defined in terms of the university's charter or mission statement. If Wisconsin's resembles SUNY, New Paltz's, and I suspect it does, then it includes a statement of principles reflective of democracy's values, chief of which is the right of free expression as central to the academic enterprise.

Regrettably, the Wisconsin conservative students lack democratic dispositions; they ask not for a fair distribution of the community's wealth to advance their own interests but instead wish to deny other groups their fair share. This profoundly negative act will, I hope, be seen by the Supreme Court as weakening democracy, the community, and the academy, and for those reasons be overturned. If the Court decides otherwise, will it be only a matter of time before conservatives request a partial tuition refund, calculated on the basis of the number of objectionable words and/or ideas uttered by liberal faculty members in the classroom? Or, writ large, will I be permitted in the future to withhold that portion of my federal taxes going to the Pentagon?

The following brief extemporaneous notes demonstrate how the questions on page 503 might be used to analyze Bowen's argument:

<u>Purpose</u>: Bowen appeals to readers who share his political
values and convictions. He disputes the ostensibly logical
argument that people shouldn't have to subsidize an

organization committed to an agenda to which they are strongly opposed. He wants to reassure readers with liberal views that supporting the "establishment" in this particular case is not incompatible with democratic principles, including respect for diversity and individualism. As a university president, Bowen probably has a vested interest in the debate, since the current court ruling could cause a bureaucratic nightmare for public institutions like SUNY, New Paltz.

Thesis: Bowen opens by stating his position and an assessing what's at stake. In other parts of the essay, however, Bowen acknowledges the logical appeal of contrary points of view-- at least on the surface--before he tries to refute them.

Evidence: In his introduction, Bowen demonstrates his knowledge of the Southworth case. But in following paragraphs, he relies more on abstract logic and reasoning, until paragraph 8, where he refers to another court decision. In his last three paragraphs, Bowen calls on his authority as a university administrator to offer pronouncements about the guiding principles of an academic community. The last two sentences of the essay introduce an emotional appeal: if the Southworth ruling is sustained, the ideals of academic life will be compromised. Bowen's prediction that students may ask for refunds based on their exposure to liberal views is probably facetious.

Refutation: In paragraphs 2-3, Bowen concedes that the court ruling may seem reasonable, acknowledging that he himself once adopted an ostensibly similar position regarding federal taxes. But in paragraphs 4-5 he distinguishes his former position (in favor of redirecting tax payments) from the argument presented in the Southworth case (in favor of avoiding an assessment). The distinction, he claims, is one of choice vs. veto power. Since an appeals court has ruled in favor of the conservative students, their case must have some merit; so Bowen tries to show that he has considered this before rejecting their position. He also anticipates that some people may accuse him of inconsistency, if not hypocrisy. So he tries to deflect those charges by asserting the value of conservative dissent within the academy and by referring to the Rosenberger case, in which conservative students adopted another position, which he considers stronger and more principled.

Persona: Though he opens with a tone of urgency, presenting the Southworth ruling as a threat to the ideals of a university, Bowen is at pains to avoid a combative stance.

Acknowledging the logic of the students' argument and his own
vulnerability to charges of inconsistency, Bowen appeals to
the better instincts of his readers--a shared commitment to
rational, fair-minded inquiry and debate. He also makes
prominent use of the word community, a term with positive
connotations of cooperation and equality. He tries to
approach this as an inclusive discussion rather than a
contentious debate.

Informal Analysis of Argument

EXERCISES

1. Two differing approaches to argument are named *Aristotelian* and *Rogerian* (for the ancient philosopher Aristotle and the modern psychologist Carl Rogers). Adopting an Aristotelian approach, you try to influence readers by citing authorities and presenting overwhelming evidence to support your views. You silence the opposition by building an irrefutable case. Projecting confidence in your views, you assume that all reasonable people will agree with you. You win; the opposition loses. Adopting a Rogerian approach, you listen to opponents, trying to understand their values and assumptions. According to this view, neither side is all wrong; there are various reasonable positions. Therefore, you try to paraphrase your opponents' opinions in a way they can accept. You try to engage in dialogue, seeking a partial solution. You enlist mutual respect and find common goals rather than seeking victory.

    a. What elements of each appeal do you find in Bowen's essay?

    b. What might you change in Bowen's essay to make it more Rogerian or more Aristotelian?

2. You are now ready to analyze an argument. Keeping in mind the previous example, read the following editorial published in the *Washington Post* by Bill McKibben, a scholar in residence at Middlebury College. Before you begin, it may help to know that Rael is the leader of a religious organization, the Raelian Movement, and founder of a company supposedly involved in cloning humans. After reading the editorial, respond to the questions on page 503.

A Threat to Our Coherent Human Future

Bill McKibben

As the world waits for scientific confirmation or debunking of claims by the Raelians that they have cloned a human being, much attention has been paid to just how odd the group is. And rightly so. I interviewed Rael at UFOland, his Quebec headquarters, last summer, and it was among the strangest days of my life: a cordial chat with a former sportswriter wearing a white jumpsuit that looked like something from a *Star Trek* prop closet, just down the hall from a mock-up of the spacecraft where "the Elohim" first revealed themselves to him.

But the weirdness of the Raelians should not be allowed to obscure the wider mission they share with other self-proclaimed pioneers on the human genetic frontier—people who, though cloaked in science instead of sectarianism, foresee remaking human beings in ways that make the genesis of [the allegedly cloned] baby Eve seem almost innocent.

Robert Lanza, for instance, a vice president at Advanced Cell Technology, called the Raelian announcement "appalling," "irresponsible" and "a sad day for science." Yet Lanza, two years ago, predicted that soon we would not just be cloning children but genetically souping them up: "We're close to being able to add twenty or thirty IQ points, and an equivalent boost of their muscle mass" to embryos, he said, adding "Who among us wouldn't say 'yes'?"

His boss at Advanced Cell Technology, Michael West, recently met with Senate majority leader Bill Frist to promote his firm's cloning work. In the past, West has complained bitterly about Rael, asking, "Why is Congress debating this by talking to someone who says he flies around in flying saucers?" And yet this same Michael West has acknowledged to many interviewers that his real goal is physical immortality. We can imagine, he says, "body components one by one each made young by cloning. Then our body would be made young again segmentally, like an antique car is restored by exchanging failing components." Should this lead to planetary overcrowding, well, "The answer is clearly to limit new entrants to the human race, not to promote the death of those enjoying the gift of life today."

And they are not isolated examples. Even James Watson, who will celebrate the fiftieth anniversary of his co-discovery of the double helix this spring, has advocated genetic manipulation to ensure that people aren't born "stupid" or "ugly" or "cold fish."

Understanding this kind of genetic grandiosity is key to making sensible political decisions in the months ahead. As a practical matter, cloning would be a necessary step toward the genetic manipulation of embryos—toward adding IQ or muscle mass or, as other researchers have speculated, a host of behavioral and emotional traits. Similar work already has been carried out on a range of other animals. The threat posed by such work to the human species and to our societies is far greater even than the possibility that Rael or his competitors may have damaged the particular children they set out to clone.

Some researchers, like Lanza and West, now say they seek not to clone children but merely to harvest stem cells from cloned embryos for use in treating Parkinson's and other diseases. If so, they should fall in behind a moratorium proposal from a presidential commission that is designed to allow enough time to write legislation guaranteeing that such stem-cell work does not inadvertently ease the work of baby cloners or of those who would "enhance" human embryos by altering their minds, bodies, or personalities. Such legislation is being backed not only by right-to-lifers and religious conservatives but by feminists, environmentalists, human and civil rights advocates, and others who understand the threat these new technologies pose to a coherent human future.

As important as such legislation is, however, it's even more crucial that the scientific community take the opportunity offered by these events to repudiate the pernicious notion that we should "improve" the species through genetic tinkering. Rael may be a kook—but his rhetoric, and his vision, resemble all too closely a spreading idea of a post-human world.

A CRITIQUE OF AN ARGUMENT

As you probably noticed in the previous section, analyzing another writer's argument is an effective way to understand how persuasive texts are constructed. But it can also help you analyze and clarify your own positions and provide the motivation and ideas to compose arguments of your own. Good writers of arguments are good *readers* of arguments.

Before composing an argument, it may be useful to engage in another kind of reading analysis—*critique.* A critique is more formal and objective than the type of analysis described and illustrated in the previous section, though it too expresses opinions. You begin composing a critique by addressing the same questions, but you try to move beyond personal responses and to become more detached and analytical. After expressing your initial reaction to the argument you wish to critique, try to stand back and examine more deliberately the writer's claims and evidence. Above all, try to judge fairly.

To critique is not to find fault. It involves weighing strengths and weaknesses in order to reach a balanced assessment. Of course, it may turn out that, in your judgment, a particular argument is not very sound. That's fine. All you can do is make a sincere effort to analyze its strengths and weaknesses. Your purpose is first to search for the truth and then to write a clearly organized evaluation of the entire argument. Not only does critiquing an argument help you see more clearly what a writer is saying; it also prepares you to write capable, cogent arguments yourself.

The following procedure can be used to critique an argument. Notice how the developing dialogue between you and the writer can lead naturally to a written critique.

GUIDELINES for Writing a Critique of an Argument

Preparation

1. Read the text twice. The second time, read with a pencil, underlining important ideas and writing comments in the margins.

2. Respond to the text subjectively. Freewrite for five minutes, recording any personal responses: agreement, anger, bewilderment, engagement, or any other reaction.

3. Write a brief objective summary of the text without inserting your own ideas.

Analysis

Responding to the questions on page 503, consider each of the following five elements:

- Purpose
- Thesis
- Evidence

- Refutation
- Persona

Writing the Critique

1. Begin with a brief objective summary of the argument and a thesis statement that presents your judgment of the text.

2. Support your thesis by analyzing the evidence presented in the text.

3. Comment on any of the five elements that you consider noteworthy.

Revision

Reread and edit your critique. Ask others to read it. Consider their suggestions as you revise. Prepare your polished draft and proofread it with care.

To observe how this procedure can lead to an effective critique, read the following article by Michelle Cottle, published in the *New Republic*, a magazine of opinion. Cottle disputes the perception that violence in the workplace is a growing menace in the United States. After reading the article, observe how one writer uses the recommended sequence to critique Cottle's argument.

PRACTICE READING

Workplace Worrywarts
The Rise of the "Going Postal" Industry

Michelle Cottle

Look over at the colleague toiling in the next cubicle. Is he a white man in his thirties or forties? Does he seem stressed out? Does he suffer from low self-esteem? Do people suspect he's experiencing personal problems—tiffs with the wife, attitude from the kids? If so, you should start being really, really nice to this guy, because he fits the profile of someone at risk to go berserk one day soon and start blowing away his coworkers like a character in a Tarantino flick.

Don't take my word for it: I learned these tips from a new newsletter called *Workplace Violence Briefings: News You Need to Know*. For $195 a year, you too can receive a monthly dose of anxiety-inducing stats, headlines, and snippets such as "Routine HR Activities Can Trigger Violence" and "Why the Risk of Workplace Violence Will Increase." Also included are quickie articles on prevention: "Watch for These Subtle Warning Signs of Impending Violence," "Similarities in the Backgrounds of Those Who Erupt in Violence," "How to Say 'No' Diplomatically." Most valuable of all, the newsletter provides contact info for myriad experts in the now white-hot field of workplace violence prevention.

It was bound to happen. In response to growing fear of high-profile workplace tragedies—the most sensational recent example being [the] Atlanta massacre, in which day trader Mark Barton went on a shooting spree that left nine dead and thirteen wounded—a cottage industry of consultants has sprung up, pledging to protect your organization from a similar fate. While such rampages may seem frighteningly random, consultants insist they are able to employ a variety of tools to identify and defuse potentially bloody situations: employee background checks, profiles to screen out unbalanced job applicants, manager training to help spot on-the-edge employees, security systems to keep out angry people with weapons, and so on. Costs vary depending on what you want and how many employees will participate: basic training videos are a few hundred dollars, while comprehensive programs and security systems can easily hit six figures.

Companies of every size and flavor are signing on: Mazda, CalTrans, the city of San Francisco, the state of New Jersey—even the U.S. Air Force. Some clients want help addressing an existing "situation"—a disgruntled ex-employee or friction among coworkers. Others simply hope to guard against the chaos they're seeing on television; most consultants say that in the wake of media events such as Columbine and Atlanta, demand for their services rises dramatically.

Such a response is understandable—but unfortunate. Many prevention programs are a monumental waste. Sure, there's a chance your organization can reduce—though never eliminate—the risk of "an incident." But, for the vast majority of businesses, the additional margin of safety will not be worth the necessary investment of time, money, and emotional energy. And that doesn't even factor in the intangible social cost of promoting the idea that employers are somehow responsible for shielding us against not only foreseeable hazards such as shoddy equipment or toxic substances but also the most irrational, unpredictable tendencies of our fellow man.

Forget what you think you know from the media. There is no epidemic of deadly workplace violence; in fact, fatalities are down almost twenty percent from 1992. Last year, the Bureau of Labor Statistics put the total number of workplace homicides at 709—just seven more than the number of workers killed by falling from a roof, scaffold, or other lofty perch. Still, if that figure makes you nervous, there are basic steps you can take to safeguard your person. Number one: Don't drive a taxi. Cabbies have long endured the highest death rate of any occupation: between 1990 and 1992, forty-one of every 100,000 were killed on the job. You should also steer clear of jobs at liquor stores or gas stations. More than seventy-five percent of workplace homicides in this country occur during the commission of another crime, such as robbery. Referred to as Type I violence, these attacks are perpetrated by strangers seeking money, not coworkers seeking vengeance.

Other employees at increased risk of violence are police officers, prison guards, security guards, and health care workers. They face what the state of California calls Type II violence, "an assault by someone who is either the recipient or the object of a service provided by the affected workplace or the victim" (e.g., getting injured or killed while trying to restrain a violent convict or mental patient).

Obviously, we don't want to downplay these dangers. There are concrete precautions that employers can and should take to improve worker safety in high-risk fields: installing security cameras, additional lighting, bulletproof partitions, lock-drop safes, and panic buttons. Similarly, the Occupational Safety and Health Administration (OSHA) has violence-prevention guidelines for the health-care industry.

More and more, however, what companies are angsting about—and what consultants are focusing on—is Type III violence, which consists not only of coworker rampages but also of instances in which domestic discord spills over into the workplace, and a crazed husband storms into the office itching to teach his woman (and anyone else who crosses his path) a brutal lesson. "Companies are looking to prevent the sensational stuff," says Richard Fascia, president of Jeopardy Management Group in Cranston, Rhode Island.

For consultants, the advantages of specializing in Type III violence prevention are clear. Although Type III episodes occur far less frequently than do other types, their random nature means that essentially any organization is a candidate for prevention counseling. ("Everyone needs it—absolutely," says Dana Picore, a Los Angeles cop-turned-consultant.) Moreover, while the owner of the corner liquor store might be loath to drop big bucks on violence prevention, the management of a large accounting firm might not even blink at the cost. Thus, instead of targeting the industries hardest hit by violence, the market is becoming saturated with employment attorneys, clinical psychologists, and retired law-enforcement agents clamoring to advise you on how to keep the Mark Bartons at bay. There has been "an explosion of training, an explosion of consultants," says Joseph A. Kinney, president of the National Safe Workplace Institute, a consulting firm in Charlotte, North Carolina.

So why should we care if some hysterical human-resources managers fall for the latest consulting craze? Put aside the practical matter that there are almost certainly better ways to spend corporate (or government) resources. In a broader sense, this trend just isn't healthy: bringing in a high-paid consultant to talk at length about what to do if a colleague decides to try a little target shooting in the executive washroom is just as likely to exacerbate our collective fears as to alleviate them. "If we have big programs to counter a danger, then the danger must be large—or so our reasoning goes," says Barry Glassner, a professor of sociology at the University of Southern California and the author of *The Culture of Fear*. "The more programs we have and the bigger they get, the bigger the problem seems. . . . In fact, we're living in about the safest time in human history."

Consultants counter that they're concerned with preventing not only homicides but also the more common eruptions of low-level violence: shouting matches in the boardroom, abusive language, fistfights on the loading dock. But it's clearly the sensational killings they want employers to think of. The Web site of one Sacramento consultant features graphics depicting bullet holes and exploding bombs and cautions: "We often hire the person that kills us. It is the killer in our ranks that we must address. . . ." Another firm's ad sucks you in with the words "HE'S GOT A GUN!" in bold red letters.

Then, of course, there are the two words guaranteed to make any manager's blood run cold: *legal liability*. Consultants note that, while they cannot guarantee you a violence-free work environment, they can protect you from lawsuits if something does occur. They are quick to cite the "general duty" clause of the Occupational Safety and Health Act, which requires employers to guard against "recognized hazards" in the workplace. All Safety Training's Web site shrieks, "If you have employees, you have a Workplace Violence problem! Because you are required to provide a safe workplace, you can be held liable, and your costs can run into the MILLIONS of dollars!"

But this threat, too, is wildly overstated. OSHA has no specific guidelines on the Type III violence most companies fear. The agency has issued safety recommendations for high-risk workplaces, such as late-night retail establishments, but it is exceedingly vague about what it expects from, say, brokerage firms. "It's very rare that workers are able to sue employers for workplace violence," says Charles Craver, a professor of employment law at George Washington University. Because of the broad immunity workers'-comp laws provide employers, "in most assault-type cases, the recourse against an employer is solely workers' compensation," he explains. There are rare exceptions—if, for example, there's proof that an employer deliberately injured workers or that the company negligently brought someone on board whom they knew, or suspected, to be prone to violent behavior. But the burden of proof is high. As long as a company behaved with "reasonable care," says Craver, the suit will likely go nowhere.

This is not to imply that consultants are preying on our fear simply to make a fast buck. Many of them got into the field after years in law enforcement and are painfully aware of the dark side of human nature. They speak movingly of the tragedies they have witnessed on the job and of lives shattered by violence. But do we really want to adopt their understandably paranoid perspective in our workplaces? This seems an unreasonably high price to pay to combat what is, in reality, a blessedly marginal danger.

Here is a freewritten response to Cottle's article:

> Cottle pooh-poohs the popular belief that workplace violence has reached epidemic proportions. Writers for magazines like the <u>New Republic</u> often display skepticism of widely held views and disdain for conventional wisdom. I kind of admire that stance because, in this case, a writer who scoffs at our fears of violence or questions the reactions of people who have been affected by violence will be suspected of insensitivity. So I see Cottle as kind of gutsy. However, I find myself irritated by her heavy sarcasm and mocking tone. I resist her assertion that safety carries a self-evident price tag—her confidence that a cool-headed reckoning of costs and benefits can lead us to a fair, cheap, and easy solution to the problem. She belittles her opposition, dismissing their fears as hysterical. Frankly, I'm even inclined to mistrust her use of statistics and expert opinion. Near the end of her article, she seems concerned mainly with the bottom line for employers: Don't worry, you won't get sued.

Freewritten response

This freewriting explores an initial, subjective response. The following objective summary provides perspective:

> Michelle Cottle argues that experts in the field of violence prevention are exaggerating the dangers posed by employees who carry personal stress into the workplace. Cottle suggests that consulting firms exploit fears aroused by the Columbine massacre and the shooting spree in an Atlanta office building. She also implies that these firms offer false hope that random, irrational acts of violence can be anticipated and prevented. Cottle distinguishes violence that occurs in dangerous working environments, like liquor stores and prisons, from violence caused by stress and other factors affecting the personal lives of mentally unstable employees. She claims that some consultants have used scare tactics to persuade companies to waste time and money on services of dubious value.

Objective summary

An informal analysis of the article helps prepare the writer to draft a formal critique:

Informal
analysis

Purpose: Cottle tries to persuade employers that irrational violence is, by its very nature, random and unpredictable. She urges them not to overestimate the likelihood that this type of violence will erupt in any given workplace and warns of the scare tactics that consulting agencies use to market their services as an effective deterrent to violence. She argues that the advertising claims of consultants are misleading, that the costs of their services exceed any plausible benefit, and that they deliberately exaggerate dangers in hopes of gaining clients. She ridicules the fear of violence, characterizing it as the "hysterical" response of "worrywarts" influenced by a current "craze." However, Cottle is so derisive of both the fear of violence and the methods of consultants that it is not completely clear whether she is more committed to persuading readers than she is to winning an argument by belittling her opponents.

Thesis: Cottle states her thesis in paragraph 5: "Many prevention programs are a monumental waste," adding that "for the vast majority of businesses, the additional margin of safety will not be worth the investment of time, money, and emotional energy."

Evidence: Cottle quotes the newsletters and advertising literature of consulting agencies, comparing their exaggerated claims to data provided by the U.S. Bureau of Labor Statistics (from which she also derives the classifications of violence discussed in paragraphs 6-10). Is this fair? Advertising, in general, appeals to the emotions and rarely provides thorough, objective facts about products or services. For example, does anyone expect TV ads for children's cereal to offer detailed, reliable information about nutrition or preservatives? (Perhaps Cottle would argue that consultants, many of whom are former police officers, ought to uphold a higher standard of ethics.) She seeks to buttress her criticism of consultants by quoting two university professors (Glassner and Craver), though the first of these sounds like it may have been taken out of context. However, she undermines the appearance of fairness and objectivity by introducing one quotation from a consulting firm's brochure with the word <u>shrieks</u>.

<u>Refutation</u>: Cottle seems more concerned with destroying the arguments of her opponents than with affirming her own point of view. The first instance of refutation appears in paragraph 5 when she concedes that fear of violence is "understandable--but unfortunate." She also acknowledges that organizations <u>can</u> reduce safety risks, though she adds that the possibility of violence is never eliminated. But she dismisses these reservations by arguing that the cost of any "additional margin of safety" far outweighs the benefits. In her next paragraph, Cottle anticipates and refutes the argument that news reports offer proof of a rise in workplace violence: "Forget what you think you know from the media." (A familiar ploy: "the media" are constantly blamed for exaggerating problems while overlooking the "real" story.) In paragraph 8, Cottle deflects accusations of insensitivity by saying, "Obviously, we don't want to downplay" the risk of Types I and II violence. But she cleverly uses this concession to trivialize Type III violence, the kind that "companies are <u>angsting</u> about" (another derisive phrase). In paragraph 11, Cottle addresses the why-should-we-care argument. In this case, her tactic is to pass over or "put aside" a supposedly stronger argument in support of her position (there are better

ways to spend money than to hire consultants) in favor of a simpler, presumably irrefutable assertion (validating fears of violence "isn't healthy"). It's as if she's saying, "Let me save time here." Also, any skeptics inclined to quibble are served warning that she's holding more powerful ammunition in reserve. Cottle then refutes the claim that consultants may alleviate less ominous types of workplace stress by citing the emotional appeals found in some of their advertisements. (But does this really prove that consultants <u>can't</u> help companies reduce the likelihood of verbal abuse and fistfights?) Concluding her argument, Cottle adopts the "I'm-not-saying-that . . ." strategy: "This is not to imply that consultants are preying on our fear simply to make a fast buck." Though she seems to acknowledge the sincerity of "many" consultants, Cottle asks readers whether "we really want to adopt their understandable paranoid perspective." (Are "paranoid" views <u>ever</u> understandable? Isn't this another instance of loaded diction?)

<u>Persona</u>: Cottle relies on some of the emotional appeals that she imputes to consultants. Her language is inflated. "Hysterical" personnel managers are falling prey to a momentary "craze"; advertisements for consulting services "shriek"; former law enforcement officers are "paranoid"; attorneys and clinical psychologists "clamor" to offer their services. She tries to belittle consultants, portraying them as hucksters who hope to "suck you in" with "quickie" answers and describing their services as a new "cottage industry" in "the now white-hot field of workplace violence prevention." On the other hand, when Cottle refers to acts of violence, she uses understatement and euphemism--words like "situation" and "incident," placed in quotation marks as if to distance herself from popular jargon. In paragraph 6, she adopts a

condescending tone: among the "basic steps you can take to safeguard your person" is not to drive a taxi. In other words, causes and remedies are so self-evident that no one needs to hire a consultant to recognize what they are.

Having developed some ideas, the writer is ready to draft her critique. Notice that she begins objectively with a summary and explanation of Cottle's argument, then examines its persuasiveness, and finally expresses reservations and disagreement.

A Critique of Michelle Cottle's "Workplace Worrywarts"

Michelle Cottle, writing for the New Republic, argues that news reports often sensationalize the menace of the deranged office employee and thereby exaggerate the danger of workplace violence. Fears aroused by these reports play into the hands of consultants who offer programs aimed at minimizing the risk of violence perpetrated by stressed-out workers. Cottle believes that hiring these consultants wastes money and jeopardizes employee morale by propagating the mistaken belief that workplace violence has reached epidemic proportions. While Cottle may be correct in claiming that violence is sensationalized, she weakens her argument by adopting a contentious stance, ridiculing the fears of employers and attributing greedy opportunism to consultants.

To show how consulting agencies exploit fears of workplace violence, Cottle cites ominous headlines from a trade publication that she derides as "a monthly dose of anxiety-inducing stats, headlines, and snippets." She acknowledges, however, that these scare tactics fuel a demand for programs, often expensive, that are supposed to anticipate and prevent seemingly random acts of violence. Cottle finds this demand "understandable--but unfortunate" because it causes companies to waste money and encourages workers to blame employers for hazards that no one can foresee. She also contends that the fear-mongering of consultants has obscured a statistical decline in workplace violence and diverted attention from the more preventable hazards of truly dangerous work like driving a taxi or working in a liquor store or a prison. Cottle distinguishes between reasonable efforts to enhance the security of workers who are logical targets of crime and futile attempts to avoid violence brought on by stress or mental illness. She concludes that consultants exaggerate the danger of these random, unpredictable events and mislead employers about their responsibility to prevent them. Cottle is most persuasive when she supports her case with data provided by the Bureau of Labor Statistics. However, the fact that 709 homicides occurred on the job last year is not reassuring, even though it is "just" seven more deaths than were caused by falling. Cottle responds to this objection glibly: persons troubled by the statistic should consider the risks of driving a cab or working in a liquor store--as if concern for personal safety were unjustified so long as anyone else has to face greater danger. Police officers, prison wardens, security guards, and others who perform hazardous work usually enter their careers conscious of the risks; persons who choose other fields of work cannot be blamed for wanting to avoid comparable, or even lesser, dangers.

More troublesome are the logical fallacies in Cottle's argument. Having argued that office work is safer than many other types of employment, Cottle sets up a false dilemma: "instead of targeting the industries hardest hit by crime," consultants are exploiting a "market saturated with employment attorneys, clinical psychologists, and retired law enforcement agents clamoring to advise" companies about the less urgent needs of office workers. Shouldn't we find ways to improve everyone's security? A similar fallacy appears in Cottle's quotation from Barry Glassner's book <u>The Culture of Fear</u>, which blames programs designed to remedy problems for magnifying public perceptions of problems. Assuring modern workers that they live "in about the safest time in human history" is hardly different from telling coal miners and factory workers of the nineteenth century that, compared to the Middle Ages, they lived during a time of extraordinary comfort, security, and opportunity.

Another weakness in Cottle's argument is the assumption that we can calculate the value of safety. When Cottle says that any "additional margin of safety will not be worth the necessary investment of time, money, and emotional energy," she speaks for employers; workers might hold a different view. Later, disputing claims that safety programs reduce the risk of liability, Cottle offers reassurance in Professor Craver's statement that employees are not likely to win lawsuits involving workplace violence. If the danger has been so irresponsibly exaggerated, why does Cottle go to such pains to show how companies are not liable?

Finally, Cottle seems too intent on overwhelming opponents in a debate that need not end with a triumphant victor and a silenced loser. She alienates uncommitted readers by denigrating the field of consulting as a "craze" or "a cottage industry" in a "white-hot field," consultants as opportunists who "clamor" and "shriek," managers of human resources as "hysterical," and much of the public as "worrywarts." Readers who come to the article with little prior knowledge are offered a polarized view in which the author concedes only that her opponents are "understandably paranoid." Most fair-minded readers will recognize that few issues are quite so clearcut.

You may not agree with this critique. Although the writer attempts to weigh the strengths and weaknesses of "Workplace Worrywarts," she is influenced by what she considers an unfair presentation of opposing arguments and is alienated by Cottle's combative, Aristotelian approach to argument. Note that her critique acknowledges these subjective responses (biases, perhaps) yet strives to be fair and logical. Note also that some of the writer's irritation, expressed in the informal analysis, is removed or modulated in the critique. Any analysis of an argument should be rigorous and balanced, but in writing a critique, you should be clear about your own views. An issue worth debating has more than one side, and not everyone can be brought to the same position. Another reader might find Cottle's argument valid and therefore view this critique as unduly harsh. A critique of an argument balances objective and subjective judgments. You may want to try writing your own critique of Cottle's essay.

EXERCISES | ## Critique of an Argument

1. How successful is this critique of Michelle Cottle's argument? Has the writer been fair in her judgments? Are her arguments reasonable? Did she miss something that you would have commented on? Which writer do you find more convincing, Cottle or the author of the critique? Is there a part of each writer's opinion that makes sense to you? How might each be made more persuasive?

2. Now it is your turn. Use the procedures presented in this section to compose a polished written critique of the following essay by Michael Shermer, a political columnist and publisher of *Skeptic* magazine. Use your own ideas to evaluate the author's arguments. Remember that a critique is not necessarily an attack on another person's argument; you may find yourself agreeing with someone whose writing you critique. Your critique should address whatever successes and flaws you find in the text you analyze.

Why Not Allow Human Cloning?

Michael Shermer

Ever since scientists in the 1970s first began cloning experiments on simple organisms, ethicists and lawmakers have been wringing their hands in Ludditean fear and existential angst over what to do when cloning technology approaches the human barrier.

Last week, Brigitte Biosselier, the scientific director of Clonaid—associated with the Raelians, a group that believes that life was seeded on Earth by aliens from other worlds—announced that her team had done just that with a thirty-one-year-old American woman who, they claim, gave birth to the world's first human clone, nicknamed, appropriately, Eve.

Whether the Raelians succeeded is irrelevant. It is clear that someone, somewhere, sometime soon is going to generate a human clone. And once that happens, others will be quick to follow through the door, and we will learn whether medical complications make cloning impractical as a form of fertility enhancement.

What I find disturbing is not cloning per se but three fundamental myths about it: the Identical-Personhood Myth, the Playing-God Myth, and the Human-Rights- and Dignity-Myth.

The Identical-Personhood Myth is perpetuated by those who say: "It's a horrendous crime to make a copy of someone." But what they should be saying is: "Clone all you like; you'll never produce another you because environment matters as much as heredity."

The best scientific evidence to date indicates that roughly half the variance between humans is accounted for by genetics; the balance is by environment. Because it is impossible to duplicate the near-infinite number of environmental permutations that go into producing an individual human being, cloning is no threat to unique personhood.

The Playing-God Myth has numerous promoters, the latest being Stanley M. Hauerwas, a professor of theological ethics at Duke University who responded to the Clonaid announcement with this unequivocal denunciation: "The very attempt to clone a human being is evil. The assumption that we must do what we can do is fueled by the Promethean desire to be our own creators."

He is not alone in his belief. A 1997 *Time*/CNN poll, conducted on the heels of the news that a cloned sheep, Dolly, had been born, revealed that seventy-four percent of Americans said it was "against God's will" to clone human beings.

But cloning scientists don't want to play God any more than fertility doctors do. What's godly about in vitro fertilization, embryo transfer, and other fully sanctioned birth-enhancement technologies? Absolutely nothing. Yet we cheerfully accept these advances because we are accustomed to them.

The Human-Rights- and Dignity-Myth is embodied in the Roman Catholic Church's official statement against cloning, based on the belief that it denies "the dignity of human procreation and of the conjugal union."

The same sentiment is also found in a Sunni Muslim cleric's demand that "science must be regulated by firm laws to preserve humanity and its dignity."

The reality is that clones will be no more alike than twins raised in separate environments, and no one is suggesting that twins do not have rights or dignity or that twinning should be banned.

In the interest of assuaging these and other fears, I propose the Three Laws of Cloning.

A human clone is a human being no less unique in his or her personhood than an identical twin.

A human clone is a human being with all the rights and privileges that accompany this legal and moral status.

A human clone is a human being to be accorded the dignity and respect due any member of our species.

Instead of restricting or banning cloning, I propose that we adopt the Three Laws of Cloning.

The soul of science is found in courageous thought and creative experiment, not in restrictive fear and prohibitions. For science to progress it must be given the opportunity to succeed or fail.

Let's run the cloning experiment and see what happens.

■ AN ARGUMENTATIVE RESEARCH ESSAY

In writing a critique, you respond to another writer's argument. You express agreement or disagreement—or some of each. In any case, you cannot avoid an argumentative approach. Still, you are responding to an argument rather than making one. This section will prepare you to write an argument of your own, perhaps one that others will want to critique. In particular, we will focus on writing an argumentative essay that is also a research paper—that is, one that uses sources to inform and support its argument, thereby gaining authority and credibility.

Dozens of books are devoted exclusively to the complexities of argumentative writing. The subject has a long scholarly tradition that goes all the way back to Aristotle's *Rhetoric,* a study of argument still used as a text to teach theories and tactics for persuading audiences.

Arguments take so many forms—writers can find so many different ways to persuade readers—that there is no easy formula for argumentative writing. We can offer suggestions, however. Like other types of academic writing, an argumentative research paper can seem intimidating if you have had little experience in composing one before. With practice, however, you can learn to argue effectively and persuasively. As you did when you critiqued the arguments of others, you need to pay attention to the principal elements that constitute an argument. The following sections discuss important ideas to consider whenever you write an argument.

Purpose

The best advice is to have a genuine reason to persuade others and to keep that reason in mind as you write. Argue about a topic you care about and believe in. Argue because you feel it is important for others to learn the truth. Argue to make the world a better place. Without commitment, argument becomes an empty exercise, offering little prospect for success or satisfaction. But when you pursue an objective you care about, argument can be an exciting, fulfilling activity—and one at which you are likely to succeed.

Although commitment is important, it is also wise to keep an open mind, willing to be persuaded yourself when better ideas and new information present themselves. The purpose of college writing, as we have suggested, is not to win a contest or wield power; rather, it is to test ideas in a sincere search for truth. To that end, you must be honest and fair, while upholding your duty to present the views you believe in as effectively as possible.

Thesis

Although writers of arguments may feel at times that they can be more effective by disguising actual objectives, college writers should make their aims clear to readers. State your thesis in a sentence or two, early in your paper.

Not every thesis is worth arguing. The thesis you write about should meet the following criteria:

- It should be *controversial.* You should argue a claim about which reasonable people can disagree. Instead of claiming that pollution is dangerous (a point that few people would dispute), you could argue for or against restricting the production of vehicles with internal-combustion engines.

- It should be *arguable.* Argue a thesis that is open to objective analysis. Instead of arguing that racquetball is more fun than tennis (a matter of personal taste), you could argue that racquetball promotes cardiovascular health more effectively than tennis does. Research can examine this claim, evidence can be collected, and readers can draw conclusions based on objective criteria.

- It should be *clearly defined.* Words and phrases like *freedom, law and order, murder,* and *obscenity* may seem perfectly clear to you, but friendships and even lives have been lost over differing interpretations of "obvious" terms. You can argue for removing pornography from television, but if you do, you must make very clear what you mean by pornography and propose some reasonable method of testing whether a show is pornographic.

Audience

Construct your argument with a particular audience in mind. Whom do you want to persuade? Who will be reading your argument? What do your readers expect from you and you from them? Why might they ignore you, and what can you do to avoid that? The tone of your writing, the language you use, and the sophistication of your evidence must all be adjusted to the interests, values, and education of your readers. What appeals to first-year college students may fail miserably with students in either junior high or graduate school. Arguments must be tailored to specific audiences.

It is not dishonest to write in different ways for different readers. Sometimes it is important to withhold a belief that you know will offend or alienate readers. Mature people know not to utter every thought that comes to mind. If diplomats at the United Nations said exactly what they thought of each other, there would be few civil discussions. You cannot get people even to listen to your argument if you threaten them or make them feel defensive. If you are addressing readers who disagree with you, try to understand their point of view, to view reality from their perspective. Not only will this allow you to explore issues more thoroughly; it will also help you present your own argument more effectively.

Persona

When you write an argument, you should be acutely aware of how you sound to your audience. You want to project an image appropriate to the situation at hand. You may adopt the role of a concerned environmentalist, a crusading member of the student senate, or a frustrated commuter campaigning for additional parking places. Each of these personas can be adopted sincerely at various times by the same writer. Being yourself means being flexible as well as honest.

Regardless of how well researched and carefully constructed your arguments are, you must sound trustworthy in order to appear credible. To establish trust, you must maintain a reasonable tone. Extreme statements and emotional rhetoric work fine at pep rallies or in sermons to the already converted, but they can repel the undecided as well as those who disagree with you. You should resist the temptation to belittle your opponents or to engage in name-calling. Shocking an audience may make you feel better, but rarely does it help you appear balanced and fair. Readers need to feel rapport with a writer before they will alter their opinions.

Evidence

In supporting your thesis, you can make emotional appeals, as advertising does, or you can present facts and logical inferences, as participants in scientific debates strive to do. Argumentative writing often presents both kinds of support. What you should avoid, however, is the kind of emotional appeal that aims only at the fears and insecurities of readers. On the other hand, you should avoid a persona so coldly impersonal that your essay may as well have been written by a computer.

Since the ideas you present in an argumentative essay reflect your thinking and personality, your own voice should come through. On the other hand, it is important to win your readers' trust through the authority of your evidence. Research can help. Sources lend support to your thesis, but they also provide evidence, convincing readers that you have studied your topic carefully enough to be trusted. Library research may be most appropriate when you are arguing about a controversy that has received public attention, such as gun control or drunk-driving laws. Observation, interviews, or questionnaires may be appropriate in researching a local issue or original proposal, such as a plan to improve food services on your campus.

Opposition

Remember that any point worth arguing will arouse opposing points of view. You must acknowledge this in your essay. And you must do so in a way that is fair to those with whom you disagree. People do not usually cooperate or alter their beliefs when they feel threatened; instead, they become defensive and rigid. You increase your credibility when you admit that those who differ with you are reasonable. You should also realize that since alert readers will think of counterarguments, it is wise to anticipate any objections and try to refute them. Experienced writers do this briefly, realizing that they don't need to devastate their opponents. Let readers see that you understand the complexity of an issue; then give a reasonable, brief response to opposing arguments. You will seem more trustworthy if you acknowledge other points of view as well as defending your own.

Organization

You can organize your essay in various ways, but you may find the following arrangement helpful, particularly in a first attempt at argumentative writing:

1. *Introduction.* Provide background information so that your readers are informed about the controversy; then state your thesis.

2. *Evidence.* Support your thesis. (This will be the longest part of your essay.)

3. *Opposition.* Acknowledge and refute opposing points of view.

4. *Conclusion.* Draw conclusions from the evidence so as to reaffirm your thesis.

You are now ready to research and write an argumentative essay.

Writing an Argumentative Research Paper   A S S I G N M E N T

Write an argumentative essay in support of a thesis that you believe in. It can be about a national controversy, a local issue, or a proposal. Support your thesis with evidence from research as well as your own reasoning. You can invent a purpose and an audience for your essay if you choose. For example, you can write it in the form of a letter to your college board of trustees, petitioning greater support for the women's intramural program. Acknowledge your sources with parenthetical notes and provide a list of works cited.

A SAMPLE ARGUMENTATIVE ESSAY

Following is an argumentative research essay written by a first-year college student named Ellie Stephens. Ellie wrote on the topic of Title IX, a milestone in gender equity. You may not agree with Ellie's conclusions, but notice how she has used research to explore ideas and bolster her opinions. The result is a paper with great credibility. As readers, we cannot dismiss Ellie's opinions as uninformed; instead, we note the care she has used to research the topic, and we are obliged to treat her presentation with respect.

Stephens 1

Ellie Stephens

English 201

Professor Kathleen Hallmark

14 March 2003

Title IX: Leveling the Playing Fields

The signing of Title IX on June 23, 1972, is now regarded as a milestone in gender equity. At the time of its adoption, few people anticipated the impact that this federal law would have on sports and recreation in the United States. But in the years that followed, thousands of female athletes enjoyed opportunities unavailable to their mothers. Today, Title IX is under attack, accused of promoting the very thing it was intended to prohibit: discrimination based on gender. As unfair and exaggerated as these accusations are, the best strategy for preserving the benefits of Title IX is to support proposed modifications aimed at appeasing its most vocal critics. Suitably amended, Title IX can still carry out its fundamental purpose of leveling the playing field for men and women. Its repeal would be a severe setback.

Critics of Title IX often overlook the discriminatory conditions that the law was designed to remedy. George Bryjak, Professor of Sociology at the University of San Diego, details some of those conditions:

Stephens 2

In 1961, nine states prohibited interscholastic sports for females. On the eve of Title IX in 1971, a mere 7.5% of the almost 4,000,000 high-school student-athletes were girls. . . . Prior to Title IX, women comprised 15% of college athletes, but received 2% of the total athletic budget. While male teams often traveled via first-class accommodations paid for by the athletic department, women's teams were forced to make expenses by way of bake sales, car washes, and raffles.

Since they cannot dispute the historical record, critics of Title IX focus their attacks on the use of "proportionality" as a measure of compliance. One provision of the law stipulates that the ratio of male to female athletes should correspond (within one to three percent) with the proportion of men and women enrolled in the institution. Critics stigmatize this provision of Title IX as an imposition of mandatory quotas. Such quotas, they claim, ignore relative levels of interest among men and women and thus promote gender equity at the expense of popular, well-established programs for men. They cite, for example, curtailed funding for male wrestling and gymnastics teams in some colleges.

This, admittedly, has been an unfortunate consequence of Title IX, but it results from voluntary choices by athletic directors in response to the law's mandates, rather than from any directives contained in the law itself. Title IX does not require colleges to reduce their support for men's teams. Instead, says Peg Bradley-Doppes, president of the National Association of Collegiate Women Athletic Directors: "Institutions have made such decisions based on a number of factors. . . . Athletics departments could provide more money to preserve opportunities for men, but some of them have spent excessively on a few sports--namely football and basketball--to the detriment of others" (qtd. in Robinson et al. B7).

The cost of football, in fact, is a particularly sensitive issue in the controversy. While many of Title IX's supporters regard the elimination of excellent men's programs in gymnastics, wrestling, and soccer as a mistake, they blame college administrators for squandering resources on football programs, which consume the largest part of the athletic budgets of most colleges and universities (Young). For example, the University of Southern California, which recently dropped men's swimming and gymnastics for an annual saving of $250,000, spends $5.5 million on football (Boyce 6). The elimination of two nationally distinguished athletic programs at USC is

Stephens 4

something to lament, but to attribute it to Title IX is to ignore alternatives available to the athletics department.

A weaker argument advanced by critics of Title IX is that relatively few women are "really interested" in sports. Granting, for the sake of argument, the validity of this dubious claim, one must still consider the influence of cultural conditioning in a society that has often discouraged, if not stigmatized, most forms of athletic achievement and competition among women. The best way to perpetuate any supposed lack of interest is to tell women athletes that gender equity shouldn't apply to them because they are too small a minority. As law professor Robert Farrell has observed, "It is hard to have a high level of interest in a sports program that does not exist" (qtd. In Bryjak). It is a curious irony that sports enthusiasts who eagerly embrace the popular notion that "if you build it they will come" rarely apply it to women's athletics.

Although critics of Title IX have not always argued logically or fairly, provisions of the law can be improved. Definitions of proportionality, in particular, bear review. One proposed amendment is to allow a variance of seven percent. Thus, a college that enrolls an equal number of men and women would remain in compliance so long as forty-three percent (or more) of its athletes were

Stephens 5

female. Another proposal would treat opportunities for team membership as equivalent to actual participation. If, for instance, a men's and a women's soccer team each provided thirty opportunities for membership, but only twenty women tried out while walk-ons increased the men's roster to forty, both teams could claim thirty participants (Brady). Either of these "close-is-good-enough" policies would facilitate compliance with Title IX, encouraging colleges to serve the interests of prospective athletes without being forced to recruit equal numbers of men and women.

Other recommendations also deserve consideration. Some have suggested that colleges conduct surveys to determine relative levels of interest in athletics. The results of these surveys would determine thresholds of compliance. Some have suggested that nontraditional-age students, many of whom are older women with less interest in athletics, should be excluded from calculations of proportionality (Davis 22).

Title IX, whatever its flaws, has been too successful to warrant repeal. The year it was enacted, only 32,000 women participated in intercollegiate sports; today the number exceeds 163,000 (Schneider 40). Criticism of Title IX is often uninformed, specious, or downright sexist. Nevertheless, the best strategy for advocates of gender

Stephens 6

equity is to acknowledge the problems surrounding strict
quotas and to support the proposed amendments currently
before Congress. After all, the purpose of this law is not
just to increase women's participation in athletics but
also to dispel negative beliefs about the role of women in
sports. Supported by a majority of the American public, an
amended Title IX can keep the playing field level.

Stephens 7

Works Cited

Boyce, B. Ann. "Title IX: What Now?" Journal of Physical
    Education, Recreation, and Dance 73.7 (2002): 6-7.

Brady, Erik. "Proposal to Revamp Title IX Focuses on
    'Proportionality.'" USA Today 5 Dec. 2002: 1C.
    MasterFILE Premier. EBSCOhost. 6 Mar. 2003
    <http://web3.epnet.com>.

Bryjak, George J. "The Ongoing Controversy over Title IX."
    USA Today July 2000: 62-63. Lexis-Nexis. 2 Mar. 2003
    <http://www.lexisnexis.com>.

Davis, Michelle. "Title IX Panel Contemplates Easing
    'Proportionality' Test." Education Week 11 Dec. 2002:
    22.

Robinson, J., et al. "Gender Equity in College Sports: Six
    Views." Chronicle of Higher Education 6 Dec. 2002:
    B7-10.

Schneider, Jodi. "A Face-Off over Title IX." U.S. News and
    World Report 27 Jan. 2003: 40.

Young, Cathy. "Good Sports?" Reason Nov. 2001: 22-24.
    MasterFILE Premier. EBSCOhost. 6 Mar. 2003
    <http://web3.epnet.com>.

Critiquing an Argumentative Essay

Using the procedure outlined on pages 509–10, critique Ellie Stephens's essay "Title IX: Leveling the Playing Fields." In particular, consider the following: Ellie resists an opinion that many people hold. Are her arguments sufficient to make others consider her position? If you did not begin the essay in agreement with Ellie, were your views altered as you read her arguments? What kinds of arguments and evidence does she use to make her case? Does she give a fair presentation of opposing arguments? Does she seem interested in fair play? Does she use her research effectively? What kind of persona does she project? Does her style contribute to the effectiveness of her argument?

PART II

Research Paper
Reference Handbook

List of Works Cited (MLA Format)

A **list of works cited,** placed at the end of a research paper, identifies all the sources you have quoted, paraphrased, or referred to. A **working bibliography** is a list of possible sources that you draw up as you begin your research and that you revise and update throughout your research project. You should provide your readers with citations of your sources to give the authors rightful credit for their contributions to your work and to allow your readers the opportunity to consult your sources directly. Consequently, it is important that you cite sources with care.

BIBLIOGRAPHIC FORMATS

A list of works cited is expected to conform to a certain **bibliographic format**—a prescribed method of listing source information. Every academic field, such as English, sociology, or mathematics, has a preferred format that dictates not only what information about sources should be in the list of works cited but also how it should be arranged and even punctuated.

Unfortunately, each format has its own quirks and peculiarities. Which one you use will depend on the academic discipline in which you are working. If you are writing a paper for a psychology course, for example, you may be required to use a different format than you would use in a chemistry paper. The research papers in Part I follow the **Modern Language Association (MLA) format,** which is widely used in humanities courses (courses in such fields as literature, history, philosophy, theology, languages, and the arts), and it is frequently accepted for use in other courses as well. Two other formats widely used in the social and applied sciences—that of the **American Psychological Association (APA)** and the **numbered references** system—are presented in Chapters E and F. Fortunately, you do not need to memorize the details of these various formats. However, it is important that you know they exist, that you know how to find and use them, and that you follow whatever format you use with care. These chapters can serve as a reference guide to the various bibliographic formats you may encounter throughout your college career.

■ GENERAL GUIDELINES—MLA FORMAT

The following general guidelines apply to MLA-style bibliographies. Notice how Emily Gould followed the format in her working bibliography on page 384 and in her list of works cited on pages 316–18.

1. What to include? Emily's working bibliography listed the sources she had discovered during the preliminary stages of her project. She had not yet examined all of them, and some she would not use in her paper. Later, in her list of works cited, she would include only the sources she used in writing the paper. You should include a source in your list of works cited if you have quoted or paraphrased from it or if you have made reference to it. Do not list a work if you consulted it but did not make use of it in writing the paper.

2. In what order? Sources are presented in alphabetical order, *not* in the order in which they are used in the paper. Do not number the items in your list.

3. What word first? Each entry begins with the author's last name. When a work is anonymous—that is, when no author's name is given—the title is listed first. If the first word is *a, an,* or *the,* put that word first, but use the next word of the entry to determine its place within alphabetical order.

4. What format for titles? In typed or handwritten papers, titles of longer works, such as books and magazines, are *italicized* or <u>underlined</u>. Do not underline the period that follows a title. Titles of shorter works, such as articles and book chapters (which are published as subparts of longer works), are printed within quotation marks (" "). Thus in Figure A.1 we observe that the article "Worked Over" was published in the magazine *Utne Reader*.

5. What format for publishers? Publishers' names are shortened in MLA style. If a publishing firm is named after several persons, only the first is used (e.g., *Houghton* instead of *Houghton Mifflin Co.*). Omit first names (write *Knopf* instead of *Alfred A. Knopf, Inc.*), and omit words such as *Books, Press,* and *Publishers.* Use the abbreviation *UP* to represent *University Press* (e.g., *Indiana UP, U of Michigan P,* and *UP of Virginia*). When questions arise, use your judgment about identifying a publisher accurately. For example, you may write *Banner Books* to distinguish it from *Banner Press.*

6. What margins? The first line of each entry begins at the left margin (one inch from the left edge of the page). The second and all following lines are indented one-half inch. In other words, each entry is "*out*dented" (also called a *hanging indent*), the reverse of the way paragraphs are *in*dented. The purpose is to make it easy for readers to find the first word of the entry so they can quickly locate individual items from a long list.

7. What spacing? Double-space throughout, both within and between entries. Do not skip extra lines between entries.

Gould 13

Works Cited

Ayoub, Nina C. "Nota Bene." Rev. of <u>Youth at Work: The</u>
        <u>Unionized Fast-Food and Grocery Workplace</u>, by Stuart
        Tannock. <u>Chronicle of Higher Education</u> 25 May 2001:
        A20.

Broydo, Leora. "Worked Over." <u>Utne Reader</u> Jan./Feb. 1999:
        20-21.

Cashen, Jill. Personal Interview. 10 Sept. 2002.

"General Information on the Fair Labor Standards Act
        (FLSA)." U.S. Dept. of Labor Employment Standards
        Administration Wage and Hour Division. 29 Sept. 2002
        <http://www.dol.gov/esa/regs/compliance/whd/
        mwposter.htm>.

Hamstra, Mark. "Unions Seek Momentum from Canadian McD's
        Certification." <u>Nation's Restaurant News</u> 7 Sept.
        1998: 3. <u>MasterFILE Premier</u>. EBSCOhost. 15 Sept. 2002
        <http://web3.epnet.com/>.

Figure A.1 Sample works cited page.

8. **What punctuation?** Punctuation conventions, however inexplicable they may seem, should be observed with care. Follow the models in this book whenever you create a list of works cited, paying close attention to periods, commas, parentheses, underlining, quotation marks, and spaces. In MLA style, most entries have three principal components, each one followed by a period: the author, the title, and the publication information. The most common oversight is to omit the period at the end of each entry.

9. **What heading?** Informal bibliographies do not require any special heading. A formal list of works cited, except in short papers with few sources, should begin on a separate page at the end of your paper. Center the heading:

Works Cited

(or *Bibliography,* if you prefer) and double-space (skip one line within and between entries). Do not skip an extra line between the heading and the first entry.

Citing Electronic Sources

Not many years ago, students who wrote research papers encountered almost all of their written sources in print form. Today, many research sources are likely to be gathered electronically. These might include a newspaper article retrieved from an online database, an entry from an encyclopedia on a CD-ROM, a Web page on the Internet, even a play by Shakespeare stored on some distant computer. As with other sources, you are expected to cite electronic sources so as to give credit to their authors and to allow your readers to retrieve and consult them directly.

A problem peculiar to electronic sources, particularly online sources, is that many of them are subject to being updated without notice or moved to another electronic address or even withdrawn altogether, so that someone seeking to consult a source next week may not find it in exactly the same form as another person who consulted it last week—or perhaps may not find it at all. In contrast, a printed work, such as a book, can be cited in the certainty that others who consult it will be able to find exactly the same text that you encountered. Although thousands of copies may be printed, all of them have the same words on the same pages. A book may be updated (e.g., the book you are now reading has been updated five times since its initial publication), but each update is identified with a new edition number. (This is the sixth edition of *Writing, Reading, and Research.*)

Being able to identify electronic sources accurately is not a great problem with **portable electronic sources** such as software programs on CD-ROM or diskette, which, like books, are identified with edition or version numbers. **Online sources** such as World Wide Web pages and some databases, however, are subject to frequent updating and revision. For such sources, it may not be possible to provide a citation that will allow others to consult the source in exactly the same form it took when you consulted it. In your citation of such sources, you should give information that is as adequate as possible, as well as the date when you consulted the source. Consult the models that follow for citing both portable and online electronic sources.

■ MODEL ENTRIES—MLA FORMAT

You are likely to encounter many different kinds of sources in your research. When you compile a list of works cited using MLA style, you should find the appropriate model for each source from the samples that follow and copy its format with care. If you still have questions about a source you wish to list, consult the *MLA Handbook for Writers of Research Papers,* sixth edition, which can be found in the reference section of most college libraries, or ask your instructor for assistance.

Examine the following model entries and read the explanatory notes. For quick reference later on, you can consult the model MLA citations printed on the inside front and back covers.

Sources in Books

Citations for books have three main divisions:

```
Author's name. The title of the book. Publication information.
```

For the ***author's name,*** list the last name first, followed by a comma, followed by the author's other names. Abbreviations such as *PhD* and titles such as *The Rev.* are omitted from citations. The ***book title*** is underlined. List the full title, including any subtitle. When there is a subtitle, place a colon immediately following the main title and then list the subtitle. ***Publication information*** is cited in this format:

```
City of publication: publisher, year of publication.
```

You can find this information on the book's title page and its copyright page (usually the page following the title page). Use the shortened version of the ***publisher's name.*** If the ***year of publication*** is not recorded on the title page, use the most recent year on the copyright page. If more than one ***city of publication*** is listed, give the first. If the city is not widely known, you can also list the state (using standard post office abbreviations—two capital letters, no periods) or foreign country.

Books

Following are sample entries for books (accessed in print form). For online books, see Internet and Electronic Sources on pages 554–55.

A Book with One Author

```
Macdonald, James. A Free Nation Deep in Debt: The Financial
      Roots of Democracy. New York: Farrar, 2003.
Wheelock, Arthur K., Jr. Vermeer and the Art of Painting. New
      Haven: Yale UP, 1995.
```

In the first example, a colon is placed between the book's title and its ***subtitle.*** Publishers' names are abbreviated: *Farrar* is short for the publishing company Farrar, Straus and Giroux. *UP* is the standard abbreviation for University Press, as in *Yale UP*. However, you may give the publisher's name in a more complete form, particularly if you are in doubt (*Hill and Wang* rather than *Hill,* to avoid confusion with Ernest Hill Publishing or Lawrence Hill Books).

A Book with Two or Three Authors

Dingman, Robert L., and John D. Weaver. <u>Days in the Lives of</u>
     <u>Counselors</u>. Boston: Allyn, 2003.

Reid, Jo Anne, Peter Forrestal, and Jonathan Cook. <u>Small Group</u>
     <u>Learning in the Classroom</u>. Portsmouth, NH: Heinemann,
     1990.

The first book is written by Robert L. Dingman and John D. Weaver. Note that only Dingman's name is inverted (last name first), since only the first author's last name is used to determine the work's alphabetized placement in the list of sources. In the second book, the three authors' names are not listed alphabetically; they are listed in the order in which their names appear on the title page. You may use the state abbreviation when you consider it helpful in identifying a city of publication that is not well known, such as *Portsmouth, NH.*

A Book with More Than Three Authors

Courtois, Stéphane, et al. <u>The Black Book of Communism: Crimes,</u>
     <u>Terror, Repression</u>. Cambridge, MA: Harvard UP, 1999.

Courtois is one of six authors of this book. The term *et al.* is a Latin abbreviation meaning "and others." It is not italicized or underlined in lists of works cited. You may also list all the authors, if you consider it desirable to acknowledge them by name.

Two or More Works by the Same Author

Asimov, Isaac. <u>Adding a Dimension</u>. New York: Discus, 1975.

---. "Fifty Years of Astronomy." <u>Natural History</u> Oct. 1985:
     4+.

---. <u>The New Intelligent Man's Guide to Science</u>. New York:
     Basic, 1965.

Asimov, Isaac, and John Ciardi. <u>A Grossery of Limericks</u>. New
     York: Norton, 1981.

The first three works (two books and a magazine article) are written by the same author, Isaac Asimov. The fourth work is written by Asimov and another author. When you have used more than one work by the same author, your works-cited list should arrange the works alphabetically by title. (In our example *Adding* comes before *Fifty,* which comes before *New.*) Replace the author's name for all but the first work with three hyphens followed by a period. The reader can then see at a glance that the author is represented more than once and is alerted not to confuse one work with another. Use hyphens only when works have identical authors; notice that Asimov's name is not replaced for the fourth work, since its authors (Asimov and Ciardi) are not identical with the author of the first three works (Asimov alone).

A Book with No Author Listed

Addison Wesley Longman Author's Guide. New York: Longman, 1998.

In the works-cited list, give the book alphabetically according to the first main word of the title.

A Book with a Corporate or Group Author

Sotheby's. Nineteenth Century European Paintings, Drawings and
    Watercolours. London: Sotheby's, 1995.

U of North Carolina at Wilmington. 2002-2003 Code of Student
    Life. [Wilmington, NC]: n.p., [2002].

Cite the group as author, even if it is also the publisher. Publication information that can be inferred but is not printed in the publication is placed in brackets. If publication information is not known, use *n.p.* for "no place" or "no publisher," and use *n.d.* for "no date." Note that these abbreviations do not require italics or underlining.

A Book by a Government Agency

United States. Dept. of Health and Human Services. Substance
    Abuse and Mental Health Services Admin. Center for Mental
    Health Services. What You Need to Know about Youth Violence
    Prevention. Rockville, MD: GPO, 2002.

For a work produced by a government, first state the name of the government (e.g., *United States*), followed by the agency (and subgroup, if any) authoring the work. *GPO* stands for the Government Printing Office.

A Book with a Translator

> Ramos, Julio. Divergent Modernities: Culture and Politics in
>
> Nineteenth-Century Latin America. Trans. John D. Blanco.
>
> Durham: Duke UP, 1999.

Ramos's book was translated into English by Blanco. Note that *translator* is capitalized and abbreviated as *Trans.*

A Book with an Author and an Editor

> Shakespeare, William. Henry V. Ed. T. W. Craik. New York:
>
> Routledge, 1995.

Shakespeare is the author of the play, which is published in an edition edited by Craik. Note that *edited by* is capitalized and abbreviated as *Ed.*

A Book with an Editor

> Stimpson, Catherine R., and Ethel Spector Person, eds. Women:
>
> Sex and Sexuality. Chicago: U of Chicago P, 1980.

Stimpson and Person edited this book, an **anthology** of essays by various writers. Note that *editors* is lowercased and abbreviated as *eds.* It should be noted that occasions when you refer to such a collection *as a whole* in your research will be relatively rare. More frequently, you will use material from a selection in the collection, and you will cite that specific work (rather than the collection as a whole) in your list of works cited. See "A Selection from an Anthology" on page 546.

A Book in a Later Edition

> Skinner, Ellen. Women and the National Experience. 2nd ed. New
>
> York: Longman, 2003.

Skinner's book is in its second edition. Use *3rd, 4th,* and so on for subsequent editions. Abbreviate *edition* as ed.

A Book in a Series

> Matthee, Rudolph P. The Politics of Trade in Safavid Iran: Silk
>
> for Silver, 1600-1730. Cambridge Studies in Islamic
>
> Civilization. New York: Cambridge UP, 2000.

Matthee's book is one of several books published by Cambridge University Press in a series entitled Cambridge Studies in Islamic Civilization. Note that the series title follows the book title and is neither italicized or placed within quotation marks.

A Multivolume Book

When an author gives different titles to individual volumes of a work, list a specific volume this way:

> Brinton, Crane, John B. Christopher, and Robert Lee Wolff.
>
>   Prehistory to 1715. Vol. 1 of A History of Civilization.
>
>   6th ed. 2 vols. Englewood Cliffs, NJ: Prentice, 1984.

When individual volumes do not have separate titles, cite the book this way:

> Messenger, Charles. For Love of Regiment: A History of British
>
>   Infantry, 1660-1993. 2 vols. Philadelphia: Trans-Atlantic,
>
>   1995.

If you use only one of these volumes, cite it this way:

> Messenger, Charles. For Love of Regiment: A History of British
>
>   Infantry, 1660-1993. Vol. 1. Philadelphia: Trans-Atlantic,
>
>   1995.

Note that when citing a specific volume, *volume* is capitalized and abbreviated to *Vol.* When citing the number of volumes that exist, *volumes* is lowercased and abbreviated to *vols.*

A Book Published before 1900

> Nightingale, Florence. Notes on Nursing: What It Is, and What It
>
>   Is Not. New York, 1860.

The publisher's name may be omitted for works published before 1900. Note that a comma, instead of a colon, follows the place of publication.

A Paperback or Other Reprinted Book

> Horwitz, Tony. Confederates in the Attic: Dispatches from the
>
>   Unfinished Civil War. 1998. New York: Vintage, 1999.

The book was originally published (in hardcover, by a different publisher) in 1998. Note that the copyright year of the original publication follows immediately after the book title and is punctuated with a period.

Selections from Books

A Selection from an Anthology

> Leifer, Myra. "Pregnancy." <u>Women: Sex and Sexuality</u>. Ed.
>
> Catherine R. Stimpson and Ethel Spector Person. Chicago:
>
> U of Chicago P, 1980. 212-23.
>
> Lichtheim, George. "The Birth of a Philosopher." <u>Collected</u>
>
> <u>Essays</u>. New York: Viking, 1973. 103-10.
>
> Rushdie, Salman. "A Pen Against the Sword: In Good Faith."
>
> <u>Newsweek</u> 12 Feb. 1990: 52+. Rpt. in <u>One World, Many</u>
>
> <u>Cultures</u>. Ed. Stuart Hirschberg. New York: Macmillan, 1992.
>
> 480-96.

Leifer's article "Pregnancy" is one of the essays in the collection *Women: Sex and Sexuality* edited by Stimpson and Person. Leifer's essay appeared on pages 212 to 213 of the book. (See the "Page Numbers" box on page 549 for information on how to list pages.) The Lichtheim book in the example does not have an editor; he is the author of all the essays in the book. Rushdie's article originally appeared in *Newsweek;* the person who wrote this listing found it in Hirschberg's book, where it had been **reprinted** (*rpt.*).

Several Selections from the Same Anthology

If several essays are cited from the same collection, you can save space by using **cross-references.** First, include the entire collection as one of the items in your list of works cited, as follows:

> Stimpson, Catherine R., and Ethel Spector Person, eds. <u>Women:</u>
>
> <u>Sex and Sexuality</u>. Chicago: U of Chicago P, 1980.

Then you are free to list each article you refer to in your paper, followed by an abbreviated reference to the collection—just the last names of the editors and the pages on which the articles appear, as follows:

> Baker, Susan W. "Biological Influences on Human Sex and Gender."
>
> Stimson and Person 175-91.

Diamond, Irene. "Pornography and Repression: A Reconsideration."

  Stimson and Person 129-23.

Leifer, Myra. "Pregnancy." Stimson and Person 212-23.

An Article in an Encyclopedia or Other Reference Work

Harmon, Mamie. "Folk Arts." The New Encyclopaedia Britannica:

  Macropaedia. 15th ed. 2002.

"Morrison, Toni." Who's Who in America. 57th ed. 2003.

"Yodel." The Shorter Oxford English Dictionary. 1973.

The *Britannica* is a printed encyclopedia. Pages need not be listed for reference works whose entries are arranged alphabetically (and can therefore easily be found). In many reference works, such as *Who's Who in America,* no authors are named for individual entries. Publishers need not be cited for well-known reference books. Provide publisher information for *lesser-known reference works:*

Hames, Raymond. "Yanomamö." South America. Vol. 7 of

  Encyclopedia of World Cultures. Boston: Hall, 1994.

For a reference work that you have accessed on the Internet, see Internet and Electronic Sources on page 556.

A Preface, Introduction, Foreword, or Afterword

Bradford, Barbara Taylor. Foreword. Forever Amber. By Kathleen

  Winsor. 1944. Chicago: Chicago Review, 2000.

The entry begins with the author of the preface, introduction, foreword, or afterword. The book's author follows the title (preceded by the word *by*).

Sources in Periodicals and Newspapers

Following are entries for a periodical and newspaper (when accessed in print form). Periodical entries are also summarized in Figure A.2. For articles accessed online, see Internet and Electronic Sources on pages 555–57.

An Article in a Magazine

Block, Toddi Gutner. "Riding the Waves." Forbes 11 Sept. 1995:

  182+.

```
Jellinek, George. "Record Collecting: Hobby or Obsession?" Opera
    News Feb. 2003: 85.
Van Zile, Susan. "Grammar That'll Move You!" Instructor
    Jan./Feb. 2003: 32-34.
```

This format is used for all weekly, biweekly, monthly, or bimonthly periodicals, except for scholarly journals. The Van Zile article appears on pages 32 through 34. The Block article is not printed on continuous pages; it begins on page 182 and is continued further back in the magazine. For such articles, only the first page is listed, immediately followed by a plus sign (+). Although some magazines may show a volume or issue number on the cover, these are not needed in the entry.

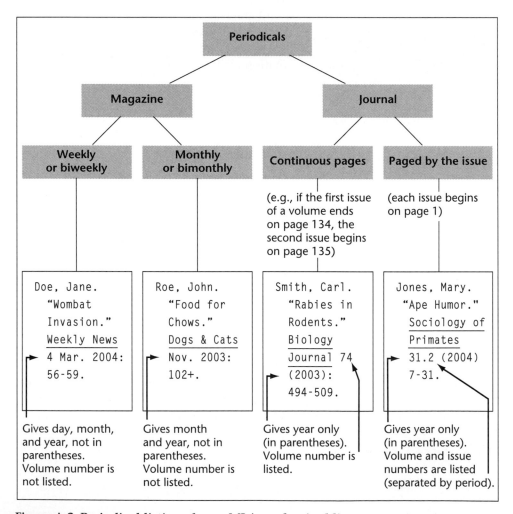

Figure A.2 Periodical listings for an MLA works cited list.

> **Page Numbers**
>
> **Book.** Do not give page numbers when citing a book in a works-cited list.
>
> **An article or a selection from a book.** Give the page numbers on which an essay or article appears within a larger work, such as a book or periodical. List the pages for the *entire* selection, not just pages cited in your paper.
>
> **Page number style.** In listing page numbers, omit all but the last two digits of the final page number, unless they are different from those of the first page. *Examples:*
> **5-7**
> **377-79** (not -9 or -379)
> **195-208**
> **1006-07** (not -7 or -1007)
> **986-1011**
>
> **Noncontinuous pages.** For articles that are continued on pages further back in the publication, list only the first page and a plus sign. For example, for an article that appears on pages 45 to 47 and continues on pages 123–130, list the following:
> **45+**

Names of months, except for May, June, and July, are abbreviated. Note that there is no punctuation between the periodical's name and the publication date. For a magazine article that you have accessed on the Internet, see various entries under Internet and Electronic Sources on pages 555–57

An Article in a Journal

Larter, Raima. "Understanding Complexity in Biophysical

     Chemistry." Journal of Physical Chemistry 107 (2003): 415-29.

Journals are usually scholarly publications and are typically published three or four times yearly. Each year begins a new volume. The volume number (107 in this case) is included in the entry for a journal article. It is not necessary to include the seasonal designation (Winter, Spring, etc.). Pages in many journals are numbered according to the volume, not the issue. For example, if the Winter issue of volume 107 of *Journal of Physical Chemistry* ended on page 110, the Spring issue would begin on page 111. The paging of the next volume (108) would begin again with page 1. Some journals, however, begin each issue on page 1; for these, add a period and the issue number following the volume number, as follows:

Mitchell, W. J. T. "The Surplus Value of Images." Mosaic 35.3

     (2002): 1-23.

The number 35.3 tells you that the article appeared in volume 35, issue 3, of *Mosaic*. Periodical listings are also shown in the chart on page 548. For a journal article that you have accessed on the Internet, see various entries under Internet and Electronic Sources on pages 555–57.

An Article in a Newspaper

> Argetsinger, Amy. "Lobbying Gets Old College Try." Washington
>   Post 13 Jan. 2003: B2.
> Leonhardt, David. "Defining the Rich in the World's Wealthiest
>   Nation." New York Times 12 Jan. 2003, natl. ed.: sec. 4: 1+.
> Ranii, David. "New AIDS Drug Is Step Closer to Approval." News
>   and Observer [Raleigh] 7 Nov. 1995: 1D+.

The article *The* is omitted from citations of newspapers such as the *Washington Post*. When the newspaper's name does not include the city (e.g., *News and Observer*), provide the city name in brackets; however, do not give a city for national newspapers like the *Wall Street Journal* and *USA Today*. Number pages as they appear in your source. The number on the page of the newspaper where the Argetsinger article appears is B2 (i.e., page 2 of section B), while the newspaper where the Ranii article appeared has the section and page numbers reversed (it begins on page 1D). When both the section and pages are numbered, present them as in the second example (*sec. 4: 1+*). Because the *New York Times* publishes two different editions (called the late and the national editions), it is necessary to specify which edition you used. For a newspaper article that you have accessed on the Internet, see various entries under Internet and Electronic Sources on pages 555–57.

An Editorial

> "Six Sigma Schools." Editorial. Wall Street Journal 15 Jan.
>   2003: A10.

A Letter to the Editor

> Rothschild, Michelle. Letter. Kiplinger's Jan. 2003: 14.

A Review

> Flanagan, Caitlin. "Get a Job." Rev. of What Should I Do with My
>   Life?, by Po Bronson. New York Times Book Review 12 Jan.
>   2003: 4.

Glenn, Kenny. Rev. of Man on the Moon [film]. Premiere Jan. 2000: 20.

Rev. of Going to the Territory, by Ralph Ellison. Atlantic Aug.
    1986: 91.

Stearns, David Patrick. Rev. of The Well-Tempered Clavier, by J. S.
    Bach [CD]. Angela Hewitt, piano. Stereophile Dec. 1999: 173+.

The first and third reviews are of books; the second is of a film; the fourth is of a music recording on CD. Information in review listings appears in this order: the reviewer's name; the title of the review; the work reviewed; its author; performers and performance information, if applicable; and the publication information. Notice that only the first review was published under a title. In the third review, Ralph Ellison is the author of the book reviewed; the review itself is published anonymously. If the medium of the reviewed work is not obvious, it can be added in brackets after the name of the work (e.g., *[CD]*).

Other Sources

An Audio Recording

Dickinson, Dee. Creating the Future: Perspectives on Educational
    Change. Audiocassette. Minneapolis: Accelerated Learning
    Systems, 1991.

Mahler, Gustav. Symphony No. 7. Michael Tilson Thomas, cond.
    London Symphony Orch. CD. RCA Victor, 1999.

Shuster, George N. Jacket notes. The Poetry of Gerard Manley
    Hopkins. LP. Caedmon, n.d.

Audio recordings vary greatly in type and purpose, so do not hesitate to exercise judgment about what information is important. In general, label each recording by medium (CD, audiocassette, LP, etc.), although the label is optional for compact discs, which are assumed to be the standard audio medium. For a musical recording, list first the name of the composer or performer or conductor, depending on what aspect of the recording you are emphasizing. Recordings are produced by print-media publishers as well as traditional record companies, with the line separating them increasingly blurred; list either the manufacturer and year (as in the second example) or city, publisher, and year (as in the first example). Cite jacket or liner notes as in the third example. When a date is unavailable, as in the last example, use *n.d.* for "no date." For a multidisc publication, follow the medium with either the total number of discs included or the specific disc number being cited.

A Film, DVD, or Video Recording

25th Hour. Dir. Spike Lee. Screenplay by David Benioff.

    Touchstone, 2003.

For a film, give the title, the director, the distributor, and the year of release. You may include other information you consider pertinent, such as the screenwriter and principal performers. For a film viewed on videocassette, DVD, or videodisc, provide that same information, but also identify the medium, the distributor, and the video release date:

All about Eve. Dir. Joseph L. Mankiewicz. Perf. Bette Davis,

    Anne Baxter, and George Sanders. Fox, 1950. DVD. Studio

    Classics, 2003.

Cite a nontheatrical video as follows:

The Classical Hollywood Style. Program 1 of The American Cinema.

    Prod. New York Center for Visual History. Videocassette.

    Annenberg/CPB, 1995.

A Government Document

See "A Book by a Government Agency" on page 543.

A Lecture

Granetta, Stephanie. Class lecture. English 315. Richardson

    College. 7 Apr. 2003.

Kamenish, Eleanor. "A Tale of Two Countries: Mores in France and

    Scotland." Public lecture. Friends of the Public Library.

    Louisville, 16 Apr. 2003.

A Pamphlet

Golden Retriever Club of America. Prevention of Heartworm. n.p.:

    GRCA, 2004.

Who Are the Amish? Aylmer, Ont.: Pathway, n.d.

Pamphlets are treated like books. Use these abbreviations for unknown informa-tion: *n.p.* for both "no place" or "no publisher," *n.d.* for "no date," and *n. pag.* for "no pagination" (when the source lacks page numbers). Because pamphlets vary widely, you should exercise judgment to make your listing clear.

An Interview

Barefoot, Blake. Personal interview. 18 Sept. 2002.

Spacey, Kevin. Interview with Terry Gross. <u>Fresh Air</u>. Natl.

      Public Radio. WHOR, Wilmington, NC. 21 Jan. 2003.

Trump, Donald. "Trump Speaks." Interview with Aravind Adiga.

      <u>Money</u> Feb. 2003: 28.

All interviews begin with the name of the person being interviewed, not the in-terviewer. Label an interview that you conduct as *Personal interview*. Label a broad-cast or print interview as *Interview with [interviewer]*. Only those print interviews that are presented in a question-and answer format are listed in this way; other print sources in which a person is quoted are listed in a standard format (author's name first).

A Television or Radio Program

<u>The Crossing</u>. Dir. Robert Harmon. Screenplay by Sherry Jones and

      Peter Jennings. History Channel. 1 Jan. 2000.

Stone, Susan. Report on Japanese comic books. <u>All Things</u>

      <u>Considered</u>. Natl. Public Radio. 9 Jan. 2003.

An Unpublished Essay

Gould, Emily. "Fast Food Comes at a High Price for Workers."

      Essay written for Prof. Katherine Humel's English 12 class.

      Fall semester 2002.

An Unpublished Letter

Cilano, Cara. Letter to author. 5 Mar. 2003.

See also "E-Mail" on page 558.

An Unpublished Questionnaire

```
Questionnaire conducted by Prof. Barbara Waxman's English 103

    class. Feb. 2003.
```

A citation for a project or paper written for a college class needs be no more formal than this. An essay meant for wider circulation, however, would need to include the title of the course and the name of the college. Common sense is your best guide in these matters.

Internet and Electronic Sources

A basic principle for citing a print source found online is to provide the information one would supply for the print source, followed by information about the online source. Unlike citations for books that have three major divisions, a citation for an electronic publication may have up to five:

```
Author's name. "Title of document." Information about print

    publication. Information about electronic publication.

    Access information.
```

Access information include the date of access and the URL. Following are examples of both print and nonprint sources found online.

An Online Book

```
Irving, David. Hitler's War. New York: Viking, 1977. 19 Jan.

    2003 <http://www.fpp.co.uk/books/Hitler/>.

Richards, Hank. The Sacrifice. 1996. 3 Mar. 2003

    <http://www.geocities.com/Area51/Vault/8101/>.

Wollstonecraft, Mary. Vindication of the Rights of Women. 1792.

    Bartleby.com, 1999. 13 Feb. 2003 <http://www.bartleby.com/144/>.
```

For an online book that first appeared in print, such as the first and third examples, provide standard information for the print source of the reproduced text, if available. Then provide the name of the online "publisher" and the date of the online publication (not known in the first example; *Bartleby.com, 1999* in the third). Finally, give the date you consulted the online work, immediately followed (no period) by the online address within angle brackets. If an online address cannot fit completely on one line, you can break it following a slash (/), but do not use a hyphen to show the break. Richards's book did not first appear in print and is available on a personal Web page. Because electronic sources vary widely, you may need to use your judgment about how best to identify your source.

A Part of an Online Book

Coyle, Edward R. Spies and Their Work. <u>Ambulancing on the French
Front</u>. 1918. 30 Apr. 2003 <http://www.ku.edu/carrie/
specoll/medical/Coyle/Coyle04.htm#18>.

Note that if the selection is a standard part of the book such as a chapter, preface, or introduction, the title does not need to be placed within quotation marks. However, when the selection is a poem or essay, then quotation marks are needed. Also note that the URL should indicate the specific location of the part of the book you are citing.

A Print Periodical (Newspaper, Magazine, or Journal) Accessed on the Publication's Web Site

The following works appeared in print but were accessed on the Web sites of the publications. See also "A Work Accessed in an Online Database" below.

Falsani, Cathleen. "Did Respect for Religion Cloud 'Clone'
Coverage?" <u>Chicago Sun-Times</u> 10 Jan. 2003. 19 Jan. 2003
<http://www.suntimes.com/output/falsani/cst-nws-fals10.html>.

Fineman, Howard, and Tamara Lipper. "Spinning Race." <u>Newsweek</u> 27
Jan. 2003. 19 Jan. 2003 <http://www.msnbc.com/news/
861383 .asp?>.

Young, A. J., A. S. Wilson, and C. G. Mundell. "Chandra Imaging
of the X-Ray Core of the Virgo Cluster." <u>Astrophysical
Journal</u> 579.2 (2002): 560-70. 19 Jan. 2003 <http://
www.journals.uchicago.edu/ApJ/journal/issues/ApJ/
v579n2/54935/54935.html>.

For online periodical articles that also appeared in print, first provide the same information as for the print article, including the publication, the date of print publication, and the articles' pages, if available. Finally, give the date you consulted the online work, immediately followed (no period) by the online address, within angle brackets.

A Nonprint Periodical Accessed on the Publication's Web Site

```
Clinton, Bill. "The Path to Peace." 10 Sept. 2002. Salon.com 20
     Jan. 2003 <http://www.salon.com/news/feature/2002/09/10/
     clinton/>.
```

The essay was published in the exclusively online magazine *Salon.com*.

A Work Accessed in an Online Database

Use the following format when you access a work in an online database such as EBSCOhost, InfoTrac, LexisNexis, ProQuest, or WilsonWeb.

```
Jovanovic, Rozalia. "Snowmobilers Tied to Rules of the Road."
     National Law Journal Aug. 5, 2002: B1. InfoTrac OneFile. 20
     Jan. 2003 <http://infotrac.galegroup.com/>.
Parks, Noreen. "Dolphins in Danger." Science Now 17 Dec. 2002:
     2-3. Academic Search Elite. EBSCOhost. 20 Jan. 2003
     <http://web3.epnet.com/>.
"Political Inclination of the States." Associated Press 9 Jan.
     2003. LexisNexis Academic Universe. 20 Jan 2003
     <http://web.lexis-nexis.com/universe>.
```

Provide the standard publication information, including the pages of the original publication, if available. Include the name of the database and underline it (in the first example, InfoTrac OneFile) and the name of the database family if not included in the database name (in the second example, EBSCOhost). Because the Internet address of an individual citation is often a very long temporary address that cannot be used on later occasions, give only the general address of the database or of the library where you accessed the database.

An Online Encyclopedia Article

```
"Humpback Whale." Encyclopaedia Britannica 2003. Encyclopaedia
     Britannica Online. 28 Jan. 2003 <http://
     0-search.eb.com .uncclc.coast.uncwil.edu/eb/>.
```

An Online Review

```
Ebert, Roger. Rev. of Identity, dir. James Mangold. Chicago Sun-
     Times Online 25 Apr. 2003. 29 May 2003 <http://
     www.suntimes.com/output/ebert1/wkp-news-identity25f.html>.
```

Eprile, Tony. "'Red Dust': Settling Scores in South Africa."

    Rev. of <u>Red Dust</u>, by Gillian Slovo. <u>New York Times Online</u>

    28 Apr. 2003. 29 May 2003

    <http://nytimes.com/2002/04/28/books/review/

    28EPRILET.html?ex=1051761600&en=0f435a46a2f839eb&ei=5070>.

In Ebert's movie review, the director's name (preceded by *dir.*) follows the movie's title. In Eprile's book review, the name of the book's author (preceded by the word "by") follows the book title.

An Organization's Web Site

<u>The Coral Reef Alliance</u>. "Coral Friendly Guidelines." 21 Jan.

    2003 <http://www.coralreefalliance.org/parks/

    guidelines.html>.

Note that the name of the site is <u>underlined</u>. And, if available, the editor (*Ed.*) of the site immediately follows it.

A Course Web Page

Reilly, Colleen. English 204: Introduction to Technical Writing.

    Course home page. U of North Carolina at Wilmington.

    Spring 2003. 29 Apr. 2003 <http://people.uncw.edu/

    reillyc/204/>.

The course title is not underlined or placed within quotation marks.

An Academic Department Page

Dept. of English home page. U of North Carolina at Wilmington.

    10 Mar. 2003 <http://www.uncwil.edu/english/>.

A Personal Web Page

Hemming, Sally. Home page. 4 Feb. 2003 <http://

    www.sallyhemming.com>.

If the page has a title, it is <u>underlined</u> and placed before the word Home page.

Khan, Genghis. <u>Latest Conquests</u>. Home page. . . .

E-Mail

```
Wilkes, Paul. E-mail to author. 29 Dec. 2002.
```

Computer Software

```
Atoms, Symbols and Equations. Vers. 3.0. Software. 2002 <http://
        ourworld.compuserve.com/homepages/RayLec/atoms.htm>.
Twain's World. CD-ROM. Parsippany, NJ: Bureau Development,
        1993.
```

The first example is of software downloaded from the Internet; the second is software published on a CD-ROM. The boundary between pure software and a book or other work that is published in an electronic medium is not a distinct one. See also "A Work on CD-ROM or Diskette" above.

EXERCISE | ## A List of Works Cited

This exercise practices many types of bibliographic entries. Imagine that (in a temporary lapse from sanity) you have written a paper called "The Shoelace in History" and you have made use of the following sources. Compile your list of works cited, paying close attention to proper MLA format.

As a first step, circle the word in each of the following items that would begin the listing. Second, order the entries alphabetically. Third, put each listing in proper MLA form. (*Warning:* Some listings contain irrelevant information that you will not use in your works-cited list.) Finally, prepare the finished list.

1. The book *Sandals in Greece and Rome* was written by Sally Parish and published in 1997 by Wapiti Press in Omaha.
2. You found Walter Kelly's article "Shoelaces" on page 36 of volume 12 of the 1994 edition of *Encyclopedia of Haberdashery,* published in New York by the Buster Green Company.
3. During World War II, Fiona Quinn wrote *Knit Your Own Shoelaces* as part of the Self-Reliance Series printed in Modesto, California, in 1942 by Victory Press.
4. On page 36 of its July 23, 1977, edition, *Time* magazine published "Earth Shoes Unearthed in Inca Ruins." No author is given.
5. Two days ago, using the Internet, you consulted an online book by Imelda Markoz, *Never Too Many Shoes.* Two years ago, it had appeared in print, published by Converse Press in Wichita. You found the book at the address http://www.shoebooks.umanila.edu.
6. Constance Jowett translated a book by Max Philador and Elisaveta Krutsch, *Shoelaces in Africa and the Far East 1800–1914.* It was published in 1999 by Vanitas Publishers, Inc. Cities listed on the title page for Vanitas are Fort Worth, Texas; Chicago; Amsterdam; and Sydney, Australia.

7. On January 5 of this year Louise K. Frobisher wrote you a letter about her father's shoelace research.

8. You found volume 3 of Fiona Quinn's six-volume work of 1950: *The Shoe in the English-Speaking World,* published by S. T. Bruin & Sons of Boston.

9. On pages 711 and 712 of volume 17 of the *Indiana Journal of Podiatry* (November 1974) appears an essay, "Solving the Loose Shoe Problem" by Earl Q. Butz.

10. Leon Frobisher, Werner Festschrift, Ella Fitsky, and Ian McCrimmer published the twelfth edition of *Shoemaking with a Purpose* in 1996. The publisher, Hooton-Muffin of Boston, has published editions of the book since 1939.

11. The Society of Legwear Manufacturers wrote a book, *Laces, Gaiters, and Spats,* in 1901. Provolone-Liederkranz Publishers, Ltd., of Toronto reprinted it in 1955.

12. Mr. O. Fecteau and Ms. Mary Facenda edited a 1993 anthology, *An Ethnography of Footwear,* published in New Orleans by Big Muddy Publications. You found an article on pages 70–81, "Footloose and Sandal-Free," by J. R. R. Frodobaggins.

13. Norman Zimmer thoroughly explores "The Shoelace Motif in Finno-Latvian Sonnet Sequences" in the Fall 1993 edition (volume 43), pages 202 through 295, of a scholarly journal called *PMLA.*

14. Theodore and Louisa Mae Quinn edited a book written by their mother, Fiona Quinn, shortly before her death. The book, *Old Laces and Arsenic,* is published by Capra Press of Los Angeles. Copyright dates given are 1947, 1952, and 1953.

15. In the February 4, 1968, *Hibbing Herald* newspaper, the article "Lace, Lady, Lace" appeared under Robert Dylan's byline. A week ago today, you printed out a copy of the article online in the MasterFile Premier database by using the EBSCOhost search engine. EBSCOhost's homepage is http://www.epnet.dome/chost/.

16. You draw on information from a television exposé, "The Shoelace Coverup," which appeared last Sunday on the CBS show *60 Minutes.* Leslie Stahl is the narrator.

17. *Dog's Life* is a monthly magazine published in Atlanta. In volume 16, number 3, of that publication (whose date is August 2000), Walter Kelly's article "Little Laces for Little People" appeared. It began on pages 32 to 37 and continued on pages 188 and 189. You found it using the ProQuest reference service (homepage: http://www.bellhowell.infolearning.com/proquest/).

18. You used the World Wide Web to read an article, "Tasteless Laces" by M. R. Blackwell. It appeared this year in the January issue of *Cyberlace,* which calls itself "the e-zine for the well shod." The address of the article is http://www.knotco.edu/cyberlace/notaste.html.

Congratulations. Having completed this exercise, you are now prepared for almost any situation that you may face as you prepare lists of sources in the future.

Remember, for quick reference, consult the summary of MLA bibliographic models on the inside front covers.

Parenthetical Notes (MLA Format)

B

Research writing has two principal devices for giving detailed information about sources: lists of works cited and notes. The former is a *general,* alphabetized list of all the sources you used in your writing. A *note,* in contrast, acknowledges the *specific location* within a source of a *specific quotation* or bit of information in your paper. For example, if you quoted this very sentence in a paper you were writing, you would include the sixth edition of *Writing, Reading, and Research* in your list of works cited. A note, however, would also be needed with the quotation to tell your readers that it came from page 560 of this book.

◼ TYPES OF NOTES

Notes are of three principal kinds: parenthetical notes, footnotes, and endnotes. Parenthetical notes are by far the simplest kind of notes to use, and they are the standard method for documenting sources in MLA style. Footnotes and endnotes, however, are sometimes used by scholars in such fields as history, theology, and the fine arts. The following case illustrates the differences among these three types of notes.

Imagine that you included the following source in your list of works cited:

A works-cited listing

    Sternberg, Robert J., and Todd I. Lubart. Defying the Crowd:
        Cultivating Creativity in a Culture of Conformity. New
        York: Free, 1995.

Suppose you made use of the following passage about the invention of Post-it® Notes, which appeared on page 4 of that book:

A passage from that source

Consider, for example, the Post-its on which many people jot reminders of things they need to get done. These "stick-ums" were created when an engineer at the 3M Company ended up doing the opposite of what he was supposed to. He created a weak adhesive, rather than the strong one that was the goal of his working division. But instead of throwing out the weak adhesive, he redefined the problem he was trying to solve: namely, to find the best use for a very weak adhesive. . . . Some of the greatest discoveries and inventions happen when people do just the opposite of what they have been told to do!

Assume you paraphrased material from this passage in your paper as follows:

```
Creativity consists in seeing possibilities where others see
only dead ends. For example, the discovery of a weak adhesive
by an engineer who was actually looking for a strong adhesive
led to the invention of Post-it® Notes.
```

Your
paraphrase
of the source

It is your obligation to identify the specific source you used in writing this paraphrase. Here it is done with a *parenthetical note:*

```
Creativity consists in seeing possibilities where others see
only dead ends. For example, the discovery of a weak adhesive
by an engineer who was actually looking for a strong adhesive
led to the invention of Post-it® Notes (Sternberg and Lubart
4).
```

A parenthetical
note

The note tells your readers that you discovered this information on page 4 of the Sternberg and Lubart book, the complete citation for which can be found in your list of works cited.

By contrast, if you use the footnote or endnote system, you mark your paraphrase with a raised number:

```
Creativity consists in seeing possibilities where others see
only dead ends. For example, the discovery of a weak adhesive
by an engineer who was actually looking for a strong adhesive
led to the invention of Post-it® Notes.[1]
```

Reference to a
footnote or
endnote

The raised number refers the reader to the following note:

```
[1] Robert J. Sternberg and Todd I. Lubart, Defying the
Crowd: Cultivating Creativity in a Culture of Conformity (New
York: Free, 1995), 4.
```

A footnote or
endnote

As a *footnote,* it would be typed at the bottom of the page on which the reference appeared. As an *endnote,* it would be typed in a list of notes at the end of the paper.

Unless you are using a word processor that automatically formats and arranges your footnotes for you, you will find endnotes easier to type than footnotes. Both, however, involve redundancy; notice that the sample footnote repeats all the information already found in the works-cited listing. In contrast, parenthetical notes are far simpler and more economical than either footnotes or endnotes. In this chapter, we will focus on the MLA parenthetical style, but a full discussion of footnotes and endnotes can be found in Chapter D, and still other styles of notation are explained in Chapters E and F.

▪ PARENTHETICAL NOTES

The rationale for parenthetical notes is that a note should give the least amount of information needed to identify a source—and give it within the paper itself; readers who want to know more can consult the list of works cited for further information. Different academic fields use slightly different formats for parenthetical notes. We consider here one general-purpose format, but you should be aware that papers written for other classes may require some adjustment in their note form. Always ask your instructor for format information if you are in doubt.

In the style used here as a model—the MLA style—a note is placed in the paper at the point where it is needed to identify a source. A typical note consists of two bits of information, in this format: (author pages). That is, the author's last name and the pages from which the information is taken are placed in parentheses. Here is an example of how a parenthetical note is used with a quotation:

```
One textbook defines false arrest as "an intentional,

unlawful, and unprivileged restraint of a person's liberty,

either in prison or elsewhere, whereby harm is caused to the

person so confined" (Wells 237).
```

Observe that the note follows the quotation and that the period is placed *after* the parentheses, not at the end of the quotation. In other words, the note is treated as a part of the sentence. If a quotation ends with a question mark or exclamation point, add a period after the note, as follows:

Period follows the note

```
Schwitzer taped a quotation from Thoreau to the wall above

his desk: "I have never yet met a man who was quite awake.

How could I have looked him in the face?" (Johnson 65).
```

If the author's name already appears in your sentence, it can be omitted from the note. For example:

```
Wells writes that "a false arrest or false imprisonment is an

intentional, unlawful, and unprivileged restraint of a

person's liberty, either in prison or elsewhere, whereby harm

is caused to the person so confined" (237).
```

For a longer, indented quotation, the note can be placed immediately following the acknowledgment phrase, as follows:

> Historians of the last century maintained a firm belief in
> human progress, according to British historian Edward Hallett
> Carr (324):
>> The liberal nineteenth-century view of history had a
>> close affinity with the economic doctrine of laissez-
>> faire--also the product of a serene and self-confident
>> outlook on the world. Let everyone get on with his
>> particular job, and the hidden hand would take care of
>> the universal harmony.

Alternatively, the note can be placed at the quotation's end, as in this example:

> Although the earth is a small planet in a remote corner of a
> minor galaxy, there are reasons for arguing its importance:
>> One should not be impressed too much by mere quantity;
>> great dimensions and heavy mass have no merit by
>> themselves; they cannot compare in value with
>> immaterial things, such as thoughts, emotions, and
>> other expressions of the soul. To us the earth is the
>> most important of all celestial bodies, because it has
>> become the cradle and seat of our spiritual values.
>> (Öpik 9)

Period precedes the note in an indented quotation

Notice one oddity of the parenthetical style: When a note is placed after an indented quotation, it follows the final period. (In the other cases we have seen, the period follows the parenthetical note.)

Many students mistakenly assume that notes are used only for quotations, but they are used for paraphrased ideas and information as well. For example:

> John Huston's first movie, The Maltese Falcon, is a faithful
> adaptation of Dashiell Hammett's novel (Fell 242).

Note for paraphrased material

Fell's book is the source of the information, but the sentence is not a direct quotation. This point is important and needs to be stressed: *Use notes whenever you make use of a source's ideas and information, whether you quote the source's words directly or paraphrase them.* Since your research paper will contain more paraphrasing than direct quotation, most of your parenthetical notes will follow information written in your own phrasing.

The beauty of parenthetical notes is their simplicity: They provide the *least* amount of information needed to identify a source from the list of works cited, and the same form is used whether the source is a book, a periodical, or a newspaper. Only a few special cases require any variation from this standard form.

Some Special Cases

Notes should be as unobtrusive as possible; therefore, they should contain the least information needed to identify the source. In the following special cases, you will have to include additional information in your notes.

An Anonymous Work (Unidentified Author)

For works where no author is given, substitute the title (the item that comes first in the entry for that work in the list of works cited; remember that the point of notes is to refer your readers to the list of works cited if further information is needed). For example, consider a note for an anonymous article listed like this:

> "An Infant's Cries May Signal Physiological Defects." <u>Psychology
> Today</u> June 1974: 21-24.

A parenthetical note referring to this article might look like this:

> ("An Infant's" 22)

Notice that when a title is long, only the first word or two should be given in the note, with no ellipsis dots. Also notice another difference: The list of works cited locates the complete text of the article, pages 21 through 24, whereas the note lists only page 22. The reason is that a list of works cited gives *all the pages* on which an article appears, whereas a note refers to the *specific page* or *pages* from which a quotation or piece of information is taken.

Works with Two or More Authors

Notes for works with multiple authors list their names just as they appear in your list of works cited. (You can find the works-cited entries for these two sources on page 542.)

> (Reid, Forrestal, and Cook 52-54)
>
> (Courtois et al. 112)

Two or More Works by the Same Author

When two or more works by the same author appear in your list of works cited, add the first word or two from the title to your note to distinguish one work from another. For example, if your paper uses both a book by Isaac Asimov, *Adding a Dimension,* and a magazine article by him, "Happy Accidents," notes for those two sources might look like this:

(Asimov, Adding 240-43)

(Asimov, "Happy" 68)

Two Authors with the Same Last Name

When two authors with the same last name are cited in a paper, include their first names in notes so as to distinguish between them. For example:

(George Eliot 459)

(T. S. Eliot 44)

A Multivolume Work

If you are citing a book published in more than one volume, you do not need to list the volume number in the note if it is shown in the list of works cited.

Take, for example, the following entry:

Agus, Jacob Bernard. The Meaning of Jewish History. 2 vols.

London: Abelard, 1963. Vol. 2.

Since your list of works cited shows that only this one volume is used in your paper, your notes should not list the volume number. For example:

(Agus 59)

If, on the other hand, your paper uses more than one volume of a work, each note needs to specify the volume as well, as in these examples:

(Agus 1: 120)

(Agus 2: 59)

A Reference to an Entire Work

When you refer to a work as a whole, rather than to a specific passage, no page numbers are needed, as in this example, which refers readers to three different sources found in the list of works cited:

At least three full-length biographies of Philbin have

been written since his death (Brickle; Baskin;

Tillinghast).

More often, when a work as a whole is referred to, the author's name is mentioned in the paper itself, so no note is needed. For example:

Fermin's book on wine-making is sold only by mail-order.

A Reference to More Than One Work

Sometimes a note needs to refer to more than one work. You can list multiple sources in a note, separated by semicolons:

Broadwell's controversial theory about the intelligence of

lizards has been disputed by eminent herpetologists

(Matsumoto 33; Vanderhooten 7; Crambury 450).

A Reference to Discontinuous Pages

When you have taken source material from discontinuous pages of a work, list the pages, separated by commas:

(Witanowski 47, 103)

An Interview or Other Source without Pages

Many sources, such as recordings, television programs, and interviews, have no pages. For example, suppose you have conducted an interview for your paper and have this entry in your list of works cited:

Philcox, Arthur C. Personal interview. 17 Oct. 2003.

Information from the interview can be cited simply with the interviewee's name:

During World War II, children in Hadleyville played at being

civil defense spotters on the levee, searching the skies for

German aircraft (Philcox).

If the interviewee's name appears in the passage, no note at all is needed, as shown here:

```
Retired teacher Arthur Philcox says that ballpoint pens did

not replace fountain pens in Hadleyville's grade schools

until the mid-1950s.
```

References with Other Forms of Page Numbering

Page references in parenthetical notes should use the same numbering system as in the text being referred to. For example, a reference to pages with Roman numbering would look like this:

```
(Bullock iv-viii)
```

Reference to a newspaper article uses the system employed by that newspaper:

```
(Carlton B17-B18)
```

An Electronic Source

Some electronic texts look much like their printed versions, and the text appears on numbered pages. An example is David Irving's book *Hitler's War,* which you would list on a works-cited page like this:

```
Irving, David. Hitler's War. New York: Viking, 1977.

    20 Jan. 2000 <http://www.focal.org/books/hitler/

    HW.pdf>.
```

Because page numbers are visible on screen, you would cite a reference to this book as you would to any other—for example:

```
(Irving 166)
```

Some works, however, display no page numbers on screen, such as Kenneth Robinson's online book *Beyond the Wilderness.* Consequently, a parenthetical note referring to that work as a whole or to any part of the work would simply be:

```
(Robinson)
```

The same is true for periodical articles that you have not consulted in their original print forms but only as reproductions, without page numbers, in an electronic database. For example, the newspaper article in the following works-cited listing was consulted online through the Newspaper Source database, where it was reproduced without page numbers:

```
Yue, Lorene. "Economists Expect Federal Reserve to Leave

     Rates Unchanged." Detroit Free Press 20 Dec. 1999.

     Newspaper Source. EBSCOhost. 14 Jan. 2000 <http://

     www.epnet.com>.
```

Since it was consulted online and not in its original print form, a parenthetical note would not list page references:

```
(Yue)
```

One Source Cited in Another

Sometimes you wish to quote a source whom you have found quoted in *another* source. In such a case, your note should cite the actual source from which you take the material you are using. Imagine, for example, that in reading a book by an author named Robinson, you encounter a quotation from an article by another author named Amoros. Robinson provided a note (*Amoros 16*), to cite the quotation's location in Amoros's article. However, unless you actually then go to Amoros's article to look up the quotation, you would list Robinson as your source, preceded by *qtd. in* (an abbreviation for "quoted in"):

Quoting a print source found in another source

```
Amoros writes that "successful politicians, like successful

     actors and teachers, always stay in character" (qtd. in

     Robinson 199).
```

Also use *qtd. in* for notes when the person being quoted was an interview source. For example, if Robinson had interviewed and then quoted someone named Reese, you would give Robinson as your source for the Reese quotation:

Quoting an interview source found in another source

```
Reese said, "The secret to life is learning how to write off

     your losses" (qtd. in Robinson 208).
```

However, if you paraphrased Reese, you would omit *qtd. in:*

Paraphrasing one source found in another source

```
Reese believes that people should not dwell on past setbacks

     (Robinson 208).
```

Once you have practiced citing sources in your own research writing, you will quickly become familiar with the techniques involved. Observe the way notes are used in the works that you read, as in Emily's and Justin's papers on pages 304–35. In writing your own research papers, refer to the Quick Reference Guide on the inside back covers of this book as needed, and use this chapter for fuller explanations. When unusual situations arise and you are uncertain how to cite a source, the wisest course may be to improvise, guided by your common sense. Always keep in mind that the purpose of notes is to acknowledge your sources in a clear, brief, consistent, and unobtrusive way.

Using Parenthetical Notes

Assume that the following passages are all taken from the same research paper. Parenthetical notes have been omitted, but information about their sources is given in brackets following each passage. First, write the list of works cited that would appear at the end of the paper (assuming that these are the paper's only sources). Second, insert parenthetical notes in the passages.

1. The world's most advanced bicycle was invented in 1977 by Swiss inventor Ugo Zwingli.

[You discovered this information on page 33 of Vilma Mayer's book, *101 Offbeat Ideas,* published by the Phantom Company of Chicago in 1994.]

2. When he first encountered Zwingli's invention, cyclist Freddie Mercxx exclaimed: "This will either revolutionize road racing or set it back a hundred years!"

[Mercxx wrote this on page 44 of his column, "New Products," which appeared on pages 44 and 45 of the November 1978 *Cyclist's World.*]

3. According to Rupert Brindel, president of the International Bicycle Federation, "The cycling world was in a tizzy about the Zwingli frame. Supporters called it 'the bike of the future,' while detractors said it removed the sport from the sport of cycling."

[You found this in Melba Zweiback's book, *Two Wheels,* on page 202. She is quoting from Brindel's article, "The Zwingli Fiasco," which appeared on page 22 of the *Sporting Times* newspaper, April 13, 1993. *Two Wheels* was published in Montreal by Singleday in 2000.]

4. Zwingli had discovered a revolutionary way to reinforce tissue paper. The result was a frame so lightweight that it would actually gain speed while coasting uphill.

[This too was taken from Mayer's book, page 36.]

5. In his <u>Memoirs</u>, Zwingli wrote, "I was overjoyed by how strong the tissue-paper frame was. The first prototype held up well under every test--until the first rainstorm."

[He wrote *Memoirs* in 1988; the quotation is from the bottom of page 63 and the top of page 64. Zigurat Press of Zurich published it.]

6. Zwingli's bicycle was a mere curiosity until the following year, when he made his second brilliant discovery: waterproof tissue paper.

[You paraphrased this from "And Now: Non-Absorbent T.P.," an anonymous brief article on page 416 of the July 1978 *Applied Chemistry Bulletin* (volume 28), a journal with continuous paging.]

7. The twin brother of Freddie Mercxx, also a world-class cyclist, wrote:

> With all other bicycles, the strongest and
> fittest cyclist wins the race. With the Zwingli
> bike, the lightest racer wins. I'm tired of
> being wiped off the track by skinny guys on tissue
> paper.

[Otto Mercxx wrote this in a letter to his brother dated 28 January 1980.]

8. The fate of the Zwingli bicycle was sealed in 1985 when it was outlawed for competition by a vote of 70 to 3 of the International Bicycle Federation.

[You found this information on page 54 of Melba Zweiback's magazine article, "IBF Disposes of Tissue Paper 10-Speed," published on pages 54, 55, and 56 of the August 1985 *Newsmonth*.]

9. Although the following week's Tour de Finland race was marred by protests from newly unemployed lightweight riders, the cycling world soon returned to normal.

[This information appeared on page C17 of the *New York Times-News-Post* newspaper dated August 22, 1980, in an article by Greg LeMoon under the headline "Featherweight Furor in Finland." You read the article last Tuesday in the AllSports-News online database, using the BOSCOworld online reference service at http://www .BOSCO.com.]

When Are Notes Needed?

It is your privilege as a scholar to make use of the scholarship of other people in your writing. It is your obligation as a scholar to make it clear to your readers which words and ideas in your writing are your own and which ones came from your sources. The general rule for when notes are needed is this: *Provide notes for all quotations; provide notes for all paraphrased information that is not commonly available knowledge.* The examples that follow illustrate this rule.

A frequent mistake made by beginning scholars is to give notes only for quotations. Remember that you need to acknowledge your debts to your sources, whether you quote their exact words or only borrow their ideas. You should give a note for information you have used, even if you have phrased it in words entirely your own. For example, assume you are writing an article on the Black Death, the plague that devastated medieval Europe, and one of your sources is Barbara Tuchman's book *A Distant Mirror.* Imagine that you found this passage on page 94:

> . . . Although the mortality rate was erratic, ranging from one fifth in some places to nine tenths or almost total elimination in others, the overall estimate of modern demographers has settled—for the area extending from India to Iceland—around the same figure expressed in Froissart's casual words: "a third of the world died." His estimate, the common one at the time, was not an inspired guess but a borrowing of St. John's figure for mortality from plague in Revelation, the favorite guide to human affairs in the Middle Ages.
>
> A third of Europe would have meant about 20 million deaths. No one knows how many died. Contemporary reports were an awed impression, not an accurate count.

If you wrote any of the following sentences based on this passage, you would need to give credit to Tuchman in a note.

It is widely accepted that about one third of Europe's population died from the Black Death (Tuchman 94).

Although a mortality of 20 million Europeans is usually accepted for the Black Death, no accurate figures exist to confirm this estimate (Tuchman 94).

Even if the usual mortality estimate of one third of Europe (Tuchman 94) is not accepted, the Black Death still exacted a horrendous toll of the population.

None of these passages is a direct quotation, but since they are based on your source, they require notes. In the first two examples, by placing the note at the end of the sentence, you signal that all the information is from Tuchman's book. In the third example, by placing the note in the middle of the sentence, you indicate that only the material preceding the note is from that source.

You do not need to note information from a source if it is widely available and generally accepted. For example, you might have learned this information in an encyclopedia or almanac: *Oklahoma became a state in 1907*. Although you did not know this fact before you looked it up, it is such common information that it is in effect public property, and you need not acknowledge a source in a note. The facts on the Black Death in Tuchman's article, on the other hand, represent her own research findings, and she deserves full acknowledgment when her ideas are used.

The distinction being drawn here may not always be an obvious one. As is often the case with research writing, your best practice is to let common sense be your guide. You can usually tell when information is public property and when a source deserves credit for it in a note. But when you are in doubt, the safest course is to provide the note.

How Many Notes Are Enough?

In writing a research paper, you are creating something new, even if almost all the ideas and information in it are from your sources. At the very least, your contribution is to synthesize this information and to present it in a fresh way. For this reason your research paper will be based on a variety of sources. A long paper based on only one or two sources serves little purpose since it does nothing new. Consequently, your research papers are likely to have a number of notes, indicating the contributions of your various sources.

Sometimes you will have to use many notes to acknowledge a complex passage that is developed, quite legitimately, from several different sources. For example:

```
Herbal folk remedies have been imported to the West with
mixed results. An East African tea seems to be effective
against cholera ("Nature's" 6), while moxibustion, a
Chinese remedy for diarrhea, is still largely untested
("Burning" 25). A Chinese arthritis medicine called "Chuifong
Toukuwan," on the other hand, is a positive danger to health
(Hunter 8).
```

The second sentence requires two notes because it is based on two separate sources.

On the other hand, there can be a danger in overloading your paper with notes. One reason the format of notes is so brief is to keep them from getting in the way of what you are saying in the paper. When a paper is filled with note after note, even brief notes call attention to themselves, and they distract and annoy readers. With notes—as with quotations, brackets, and ellipsis dots—there can be too much of a good thing. Avoid passages like this in your writing:

```
In 1948, Isaac Stork ran for president (McCall 80) on the

Anti-Vice ticket (Sullivan 42). His platform included a

prohibition on all sweetened or alcoholic beverages (McCall

80), fines for wearing brightly colored outfits (Stokes 124),

and the clothing of naked cats, dogs, and horses (McCall 81).
```

Bad (too many notes)

The notes here are annoying, not only because they interrupt the passage so often but also because they are unnecessary. It is evident that the writer has done some research and is eager to show off. The writer is deliberately juggling three sources, all of which contain the same information. The first sentence would seem to state commonly available information that does not require acknowledgment. Information in the second sentence might also be considered public property, but to be safe, the writer might provide a single joint note after the final sentence like this:

```
. . . cats, dogs, and horses (McCall 80-81; Stokes 124).
```

Judging When Notes Are Needed

EXERCISE

Imagine that it is some time in the near future and that you are writing a brief research report. Imagine too that, having found the following six passages in your research, you have then written the report that follows them. What remains for you to do is to supply notes for the report.

1. Horseradish (*Armoracia lapathifolia*), a plant of the mustard family, is grown for its pungent, white fleshy root. [*Source:* Elizabeth Silverman's book, *Common Plants of North America,* page 208.]

2. I first met Mr. Finnahey when I stopped by his farm to get forms filled out for his medical benefits. When I asked him his age, he said, "I forget the exact year I was born. It was the same year the Brooklyn Bridge was built." Naturally I didn't believe him since he didn't look a day over 40, and his wife, Becky, was 26. Imagine my surprise when he brought out his birth certificate. [*Source:* social worker Marlys Davenport, quoted on page 35 of a newspaper article written by Lester Grady.]

3. The Brooklyn Bridge was built in 1883. [*Source:* an anonymous article in *Encyclopedia Galactica,* volume 4, page 73.]

4. When I arrived to examine Julius Finnahey, he was eating a lunch of peanut butter and horseradish sandwiches. "Best thing for you," he said. "I eat 'em every day—always have." This was my first clue to the cause of his longevity. My research into his diet led to a discovery that may provide humans of the future with lifetimes lasting perhaps two centuries. [*Source:* Chester Vinneman writing on page 19 of his article, "Radish-Legume Combination Slows the Aging Process," in the *New England Medical Report.*]

5. Chester Vinneman discovered that the combination of the trace element *vin-nemanium,* which occurs in the common horseradish root, with amino acids in the common peanut retards the decay of the cell wall lining in human tissue. To Vinne-

man, the increased longevity which his discovery will provide is a mixed blessing: "I find the prospect both thrilling and frightening. The questions and problems that it raises stagger the mind." [*Source:* an unsigned article, "Life Everlasting Now a Reality?" in *Timely* magazine, page 78, continued on page 80.]

6. Chester Vinneman won the Nobel Prize for medicine for his discovery of the miracle age retardant. He is a professor of biochemistry at the University of Manitoba. [*Source: Who's Who,* page 993.]

Here is a section of your report, which is based on the preceding list of sources. Supply the appropriate parenthetical notes.

Important discoveries are often the result of chance occurrences. If it had not been for a routine inquiry by social worker Marlys Davenport, Chester Vinneman might never have won the Nobel Prize for medicine. It was Davenport who confirmed Julius Finnahey's amazing statement that he was born in 1883, "the year the Brooklyn Bridge was built."

Professor Vinneman made the connection between Finnahey's extraordinary youthfulness and his diet of peanut butter and horseradish sandwiches. Horseradish (Armoracia lapathifolia) was not previously thought to have benefits beyond the flavor of its pungent root. Through extensive tests, however, Vinneman discovered a previously unreported trace element in horseradish, which he named vinnemanium. This element, when combined with amino acids such as those found in peanuts, prevents human cell walls from decaying.

Vinneman predicts that as the result of his discovery, human lifetimes may extend in the future to as many as two centuries. He finds the prospect of such longevity "both thrilling and frightening. The questions and problems that it raises stagger the mind." It remains to be seen how wisely humankind will cope with greatly extended lives.

Finally, explain why you placed notes where you did and why you provided notes for some statements and not others.

How Much Material Can One Note Cover?

A parenthetical note comes after borrowed material, but how can a writer make clear *how much* of the preceding material is referred to by the note? The following passage illustrates the problem:

> Haagendazs was considered one of Denmark's premier eccentrics. He continually wore the same heavy woolen sweater, regardless of the occasion or season. Former colleagues attest that he worked in near darkness, and he reportedly kept exotic spiders and beetles as pets (Noland 18).

The extent of the reference is not clear. Is Noland the source for all three examples of Haagendazs's eccentricities or just the latter two (or the last one)? The ambiguity could be avoided, perhaps, by placing a note after each paraphrased sentence. But the paper would then be overloaded with notes, and readers would find it annoying to meet with identical notes sentence after sentence.

A somewhat clearer way to define a long borrowed passage is to mark its beginning with an acknowledgment phrase. For example:

> Noland reports that Haagendazs was considered one of Denmark's premier eccentrics. He continually wore the same heavy woolen sweater, regardless of the occasion or season. Former colleagues attest that he worked in near darkness, and he reportedly kept exotic spiders and beetles as pets (18).

The acknowledgment phrase marks the beginning of the borrowed passage

The note marks the end of the passage

Here it is clear that the entire passage is taken from page 18 of a work by Noland. However, acknowledgment phrases are not commonly used with factual information, and an excess of acknowledgment phrases can be as distracting to readers as an excess of parenthetical notes. Alas, some ambiguity in the scope of your references is probably unavoidable. Rely on your judgment about whether a borrowed passage is adequately marked, but if you are in doubt, supply the acknowledgment phrase. You may also ask your instructor for advice.

Judging When Borrowed Material Is Adequately Marked

EXERCISE

Examine the parenthetical notes in the research papers by Emily and Justin on pages 304–35. For each parenthetical note, is it clear how much material is borrowed from the source? If not, can you suggest a way to make it clearer?

■ INFORMATION FOOTNOTES

Even when you use parenthetical notes to acknowledge sources, you can still use footnotes to supply information that you feel does not belong in the text of your paper. To mark an *information footnote,* place a raised asterisk (*) in the place where you invite the reader to consult the note, like this:

```
. . . domesticated animals such as dogs, cats,* and . . .
```

At the bottom of the same page, type ten underline bars and present your footnote on the next line, beginning with a raised asterisk, like this:

```
          * Witherspoon does not classify the common house cat as

a "domesticated" animal but as a "wild" animal that merely

"coexists" with humans (16).
```

Typing footnotes can be cumbersome. Fortunately, most word-processing programs can place footnotes automatically at the bottom of the proper page.

If you use a second information footnote on the same page, mark it with a double asterisk (**) or dagger (†). You should, however, use information footnotes rarely. Almost always when you have something to tell your readers, it is better to say it within the paper itself. This is in line with the general rule that anything which interrupts the reader or makes reading more difficult should be avoided.

C Research Paper Format (MLA Style)

FORMAT FOR YOUR POLISHED DRAFT

The polished draft of your paper should be printed (using word processing software on a computer). A neatly handwritten paper may be allowed in rare cases, but only a printed paper presents a professional appearance. When you are communicating with others, appearance counts. Although the paper's appearance does not alter the content of your writing, it most certainly does affect the way your writing is received. Instructors try to be as objective as possible in judging student work, but they are still swayed, like all other humans, by appearances. Computer-printed papers give the impression of more serious, careful work, and they are certainly more inviting and easier to read. In the professional world, reports and correspondence are always computer-printed; anything less would be unthinkable. There is no reason to treat your college writing with any less respect.

Computer word processing offers the greatest benefits for composing, revising, copyediting, and printing your paper. With a word processor, you can make additions, deletions, corrections, and rearrangements of passages easily and at any time. The spell-check feature can identify errors in spelling and typing that you might otherwise miss. And, of course, the finished product has a polished, professional appearance.

When you compose your paper, follow the format exemplified by one of the sample papers shown in Chapter 8. In particular, pay attention to the following conventions.

Format for Computer-Printed Papers

The following are standard format guidelines for research papers. Individual instructors may wish to modify some of them according to their preferences. Check with your instructor if you have questions about the required format.

Paper

For computer printing, use plain white, heavyweight, 8½ × 11-inch paper. Print on one side of the paper only.

Ink

Use only black ink. Replace the cartridge in your printer if it no longer produces a dark copy.

Type Font

A high-quality printer, such as a laser or inkjet printer, produces the most readable, professional-looking papers. If your software allows a choice of fonts, choose Times Roman, a proportional-space font, or a monospaced font such as Letter Gothic or Courier. You can also use a sans-serif font such as Arial if your instructor approves. Never use a fancy font such as script. Use italics for book titles (*Moby Dick*) and foreign words, although underlining is also acceptable (<u>Moby Dick</u>). Do not use boldface (**bold**) for titles or section headings or for emphasis.

Standard Fonts for Research Papers
Times Roman   (a proportional font)
Letter Gothic   (a monospaced font)
Arial   (a sans-serif font)

Nonstandard and Usually Unacceptable Fonts
Any script font
Any other fancy font

Spacing

Double-space (leave every other line blank) throughout the paper. This includes indented quotations and the list of works cited, which are also double-spaced. Do not skip additional lines between paragraphs, although it is acceptable to skip extra lines before a new section with a heading. Notice how Justin Stafford skipped extra lines before the "What I Found" section of his paper on page 324. Either one or two spaces is permitted after final periods or question marks, as long as you are consistent throughout.

Margins and Alignment

Set your margins at one inch at the top, bottom, right, and left of your paper. Choose "left" alignment for your text, not "full" alignment. Research papers differ from books such as this one, where the text is aligned with the right margin. Do not have the computer divide words with hyphens to achieve a straighter right margin.

Your computer may allow you to avoid a ***widow line*** or an ***orphan line***—the typesetting terms for stranded lines. An orphan is the first line of a new paragraph printed as the last line of a page. A widow is the final line of a paragraph printed as the first line of a page. Notice how Emily Gould avoided a widow at the top of page 306.

Indenting

Indent each new paragraph one-half inch from the left margin. Indent long quotations one inch from the left margin only; do not indent from the right margin. (For additional directions, see pages 410–11.) Figure C.1 shows an excerpt from a research paper demonstrating how margins and indentations should be handled.

One-inch margin

moderately better by 14 months and substantially better at age two (White, Kaban, and Attanucci 130). ← Period follows parenthetical note in the text.

Indent paragraph one-half inch.

Second, Zajonc believes that older children enjoy a significant advantage by having to assume the role of "teacher." He explains the advantage as follows:

Indent one inch for a long quotation.

Approximately one-inch margin

One who has to explain something will see from the other's reactions whether the explanation was well understood, and be prompted to improve the explanation, with the consequence that his or her own understanding of the matter is improved. (231)

Do not indent quotations from the right margin.

Double-space throughout.

Period precedes parenthetical note for an indented quotation.

In fact, the only firstborns who do not achieve substantially better in these areas are those who have done little teaching of their siblings (Smith 352).

Section headings are optional.

Skip 3 lines (double-space twice) before a section heading.

Middle Children

Psychologist Kevin Leman, a frequent talk-show guest, describes a popular view of middle children in The Birth Order Book: "They were born too late to get the privileges and special treatment the first born

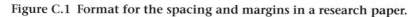

Figure C.1 Format for the spacing and margins in a research paper.

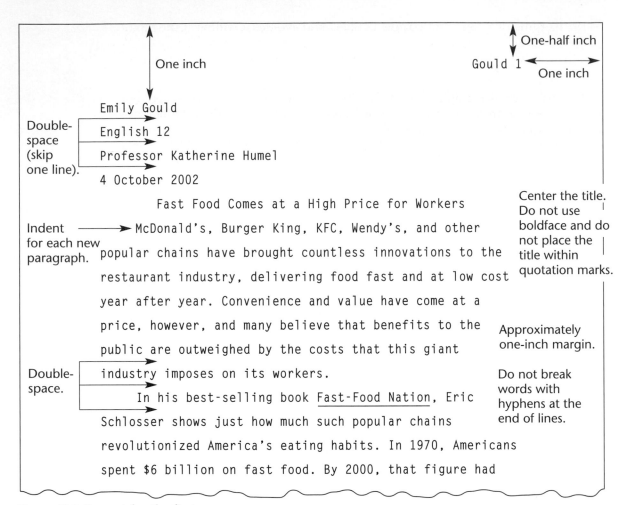

Figure C.2 Format for the first page.

The First Page

The format of your first page should resemble that of Emily's paper in Figure C.2.

- **Page identification.** Your last name and the page number go at the top of the first page and each subsequent page. If you are using a standard word-processing program with a "header" feature, you can have it automatically put this header at the upper right of each page. Number the first page of the paper as page 1, even if you use a cover page. Do not precede the page number with *p.* or *page.*

- **Author information.** Type your full name, course information, and the date in the upper-left corner of the first page, about one inch from the top of the page. If you use an automatic header for the page identification, the author information goes on the first line of the paper itself, immediately below the header. A separate title page is needed only for lengthy reports (see page 585).

- **Title.** The title follows immediately under the author information. Writers have the option of whether or not to skip additional lines before and after the title. Only the first letter of each important word in the title should be capitalized; do not capitalize a word such as *the* (article), *and* (conjunction), or *of* (preposition) unless it is the first word of the title or the first word following a colon. Do not use underlining, italics, or bold for the title and do not enclose it in quotation marks. Of course, you should use standard punctuating conventions for titles of works that you include within your own title. For example:

The Depiction of Old Age in <u>King Lear</u>

and in "The Love Song of J. Alfred Prufrock"

- **Body.** Indent the first line of each new paragraph and double-space throughout. Do not skip additional lines between paragraphs.

Subsequent Pages

The format of subsequent pages is shown in Figure C.3. If you use an automatic header, have the computer automatically place your last name and page number at the top right of each page. If not, type this information at the top right, and then double-space twice (skip three lines); the first line of text should begin one inch from the top of the page.

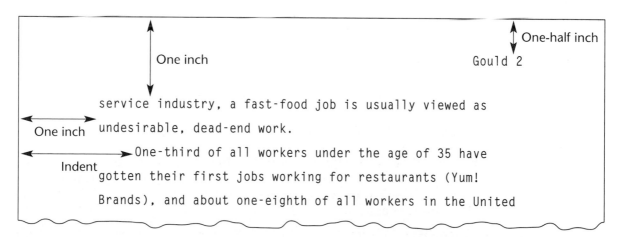

Figure C.3 Format for subsequent pages.

Reagan 8

Other statistics show that although the number of
medical students in their thirties and forties is
increasing, one's chances of being admitted to medical
school decrease with age, as Table 1 demonstrates:

The table is referred to within the paper.

Each table or figure is given a number and a label.

Table 1

Percentages of Men and Women Accepted by Medical Schools
(1989)[a]

Quadruple-space before and after each table or figure.

Raised lower-case letters are used for footnotes within tables and figures.

Age	Men	Women
21-23	73	67
24-27	58	55
28-31	49	53
32-34	46	51
35-37	41	46
38 and over	27	34

Each line of a table begins at the left margin (it is not centered).

Double-space throughout the table.

Source: Plantz, Lorenzo, and Cole 115

[a] The chart is based on data gathered by the American
Medical Association.

The table ends with the source and footnotes (if any).

I have learned that there are many criteria other
than age that medical schools consider when reviewing
applications.

The paper resumes following the table.

Figure C.4 Sample page with table.

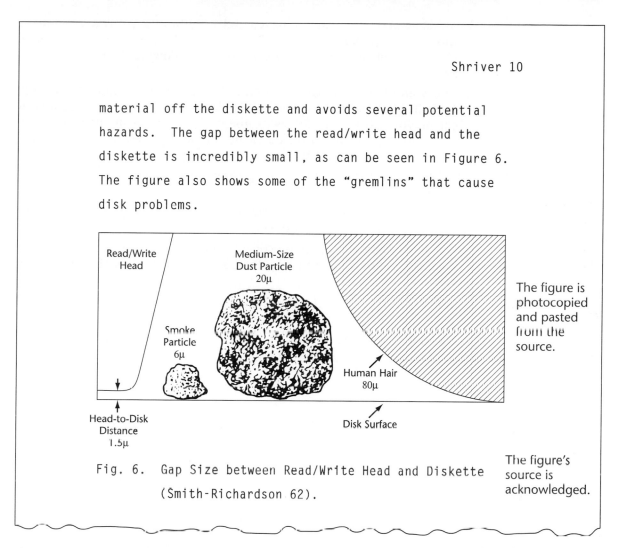

Figure C.5 **Sample page with a figure.**

Tables and Figures

You can include *tables*—the presentation of data in columns—and *figures*—drawings, graphs, photographs, or other inserts—in your paper. Tables and figures can be either of your own creation or copied from a source (and duly acknowledged). A sample page from a research paper that includes a table is illustrated in Figure C.4. Figure C.5 shows a figure that the writer photocopied from a source he acknowledged.

Observe the following guidelines when you include tables and figures:

1. All tables and figures should be referred to within the paper (e.g., "Table 1 shows the variation among . . .," ". . . as can be seen in Figure 6," etc.). Place the table or figure as close as possible following its mention in the paper.

2. Tables and figures should be numbered consecutively (Table 1, Table 2, Table 3, . . . ; Figure 1, Figure 2, . . .). Each table should be given a clear explanatory label on the following line, and each figure should have an explanatory caption typed on the same line and placed below the figure. Each line begins at the left margin; it is not centered.

3. Double-space throughout, but skip three lines (double-space twice) both before and after a table or figure.

4. Lines may be drawn across the page (as in Figure C.4, e.g.) to set a table or figure apart from the rest of the paper.

5. A table or figure may be photocopied from a source and pasted onto your page (see Figure C.5). You may then wish to photocopy the entire page again.

6. If the table or figure is taken from a source, acknowledge the source on a line following the table or figure.

7. If you use footnotes (as in Figure C.4), assign them raised lowercase letters (a, b, c, etc.) and place the notes below the table or figure (and source citation, if given).

Indent second subsequent lines of each entry one-half inch.

Three hyphens followed by a period indicate a second work by the same author.

Stafford 12

Works Cited

American Association of Colleges of Pharmacy. "Career
    Options." 16 Sept. 2002 <http://www.aacp.org/>.

Double-space throughout.

---. "Hospital and Institutional Practice." 16 Sept. 2002
    <http://www.aacp.org/>.

Barefoot, Blake. Personal interview. 18 Sept. 2002.

"The Career Interests Game." U of Missouri Career Center.
    14 Sept. 2002 <http://success.missour.edu/career/>.

Figure C.6 Sample works cited page.

List of Works Cited

Begin the list of works cited on a new page. (The exception is a very brief list, which you can begin after skipping three lines from the end of the text.)

- **Title.** Center the title *Works Cited* (or *Bibliography*) about one inch from the top of the page; that is, skip three lines following the page number.
- **Spacing.** Double-space between the title and the first entry and throughout the list. Do not skip additional lines between entries.
- **Entries.** Follow the guidelines in Chapter A. Remember to "outdent" each entry; that is, begin each entry at the left margin and indent the second and subsequent lines one-half inch (five spaces). List items in alphabetical order. Do not number your entries. The list of works cited should include only works that you quoted or paraphrased in writing the paper, not works you consulted but did not use.

Refer to Figure C.6 for a sample works-cited page.

Fastening the Paper

Fasten your paper with a paper clip in the upper left-hand corner. Do not staple or rivet pages together or place your paper in a cover unless you are requested to do so by your instructor.

Title Page

A title page is standard only for a book-length report, a paper with multiple chapters, or a paper with preliminary material such as a formal outline or preface. If you use a title page, it should follow the format shown in Figure C.7.

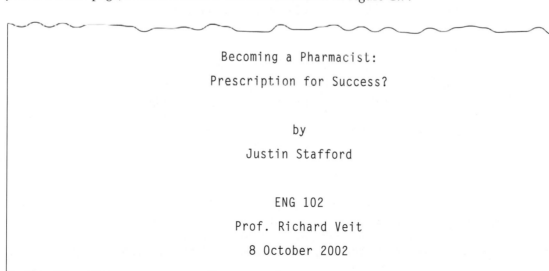

Becoming a Pharmacist:
Prescription for Success?

by
Justin Stafford

ENG 102
Prof. Richard Veit
8 October 2002

Figure C.7 Sample title page.

Title-page information is typed in the center of the page. Center each line, and leave equal space above and below the typed material. Most word-processing programs can automatically center material on a page from top to bottom.

Errors

Use the spell-check feature of your word-processing program and proofread to make your paper as error-free as possible before you print your final draft. For errors discovered during proofreading, neatly cross out a minor error with a single line, and write the correction above it. Never erase, and do not use correction fluid for making handwritten changes. Any page with a major error or numerous minor errors should be corrected on the computer and reprinted.

Format for Handwritten Papers

Most of the guidelines for computer-generated papers also apply to handwritten papers, with the following adjustments. Consult your instructor to determine if handwritten papers are acceptable.

Paper

Use lined, non-see-through 8½ × 11-inch loose-leaf paper. Never use sheets torn or cut from a spiral notebook. Paper should be college ruled (3½ lines per inch) and have a left margin line. Write on only one side of each sheet of paper.

Pen

Use a fine-point pen with dark blue or black ink. Never use a pen that smudges or that leaves small ink blotches when touched to the page.

Handwriting

Write in a neat, clear hand. Hard-to-read, distractingly fancy, or slovenly handwriting detracts from the effectiveness of your presentation. If you have difficulty with your handwriting, you would be wise to have your paper typed. Do not make your writing excessively large or leave excessive space between words. Handwritten papers with only a few words on each line are unpleasant to read because they demand constant eye movement.

Margins

Leave about a one-inch margin from the top and from the left of each page. That is, begin each page on the second line, and begin each line at the red margin line. Do not leave space for right and bottom margins, unless requested to do so by your instructor. The title and page numbers are placed as in typed papers.

Spacing

Single-space your paper unless you are requested by your instructor to double-space.

Errors

Handwritten papers should be error-free. Neatly cross out a minor error with a single line, and write the correction above it. Never erase or use correction fluid to make corrections. Any page with a major error or numerous minor errors should be recopied.

Excerpts from a handwritten paper are shown in Figures C.8 and C.9.

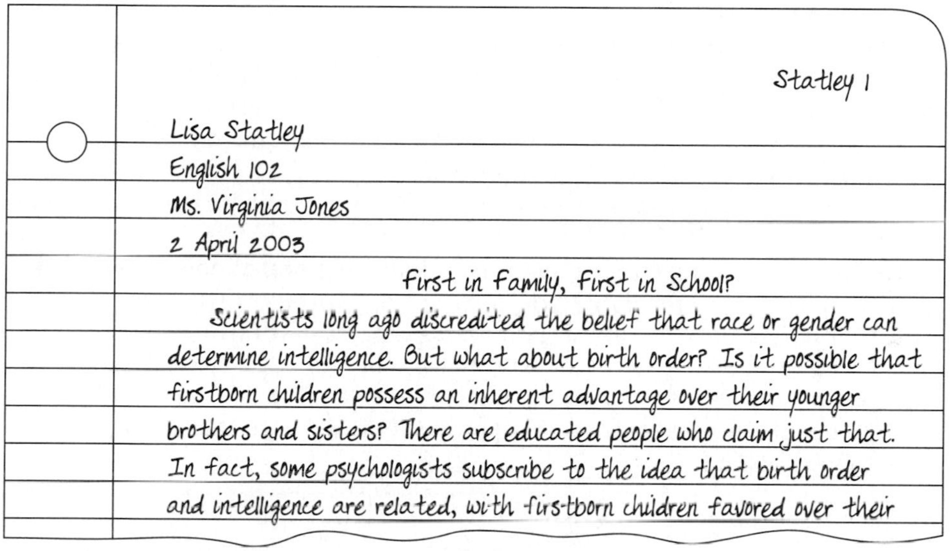

> Statley 1
>
> Lisa Statley
>
> English 102
>
> Ms. Virginia Jones
>
> 2 April 2003
>
> First in Family, First in School?
>
> Scientists long ago discredited the belief that race or gender can determine intelligence. But what about birth order? Is it possible that firstborn children possess an inherent advantage over their younger brothers and sisters? There are educated people who claim just that. In fact, some psychologists subscribe to the idea that birth order and intelligence are related, with firstborn children favored over their

Figure C.8 Sample first page of a handwritten paper.

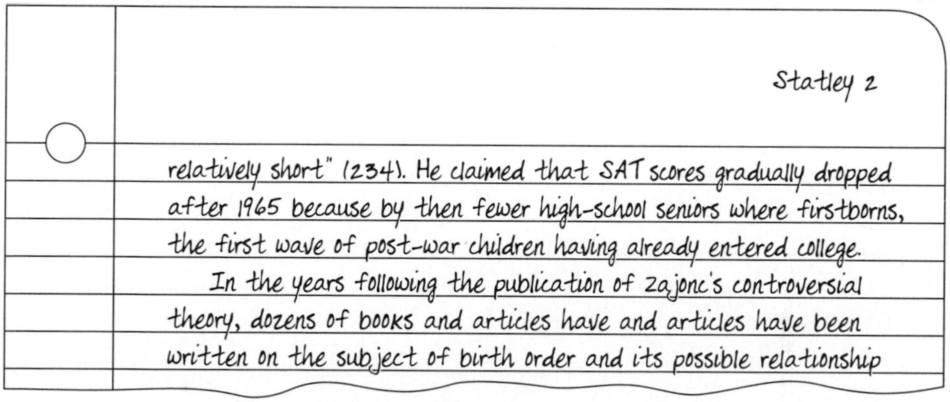

> Statley 2
>
> relatively short" (234). He claimed that SAT scores gradually dropped after 1965 because by then fewer high-school seniors where firstborns, the first wave of post-war children having already entered college.
>
> In the years following the publication of Zajonc's controversial theory, dozens of books and articles have and articles have been written on the subject of birth order and its possible relationship

Figure C.9 Subsequent page from a handwritten paper.

■ A FORMAL OUTLINE

The general, *informal outlines* that Emily Gould used in writing her early drafts (see pages 392 and 442) helped her organize her research materials. The length and complexity of a research paper require writers to have a plan for arranging it—one that is general and flexible enough so that they can develop and alter it as they discover new ideas.

Informal outlines are valuable, but most writers—both beginners and professionals alike—find it difficult and limiting to create a detailed, formal outline *before* they write. As you have now read many times in this book, writing is a learning process. Writers rarely know exactly how a paper will turn out before they write it. Even the best-prepared writers are usually surprised by the final form their writing takes. This occurs because our minds are actively at work when we write, and writing stimulates new thoughts that can take our writing in unforeseen directions.

Although a *formal outline* is limited in usefulness when it is prepared before you begin writing, it *can* be useful as part of the revision process—when it is written *after* you have completed a preliminary draft. As a scaled-down map of your paper, the formal outline allows you to see its organization with clarity. It can point out the flaws of your arrangement and suggest new possibilities. Some instructors require that a printed, formal outline be included as a part of the research paper to make sure that their students have considered organization carefully. The detailed formal outline that Emily submitted with her paper is printed on the following page.

Fast Food Comes at a High Price for Workers

I. Introduction
    A. Thesis: Benefits outweighed by cost to workers
    B. Background information about fast-food use
    C. Benefits and costs of teen employment

II. Workplace issues
    A. Hours worked
        1. Current government regulations
        2. Proposals for new regulations
    B. Safety issues
        1. Restrictions on permissible jobs for young
            workers
            a. Teens endangered by lax enforcement
            b. Proposals for better enforcement
        2. Economic incentives for employers to violate
            laws
    C. Wages paid
        1. Minimum wage
            a. Decline in purchasing power
            b. Proposals for increase
                (1) Opposition from restaurants
                (2) Support from unions
        2. Lack of bargaining power by workers
            a. Unskilled work--duties highly mechanical
            b. High turnover
    D. Instances of unfair practice
        1. Overtime not paid
        2. Other abuses
    E. Unsuccessful efforts to unionize

III. Conclusion
    A. Benign public image created by restaurants
    B. Reality: high price paid by fast-food workers

An outline can be as detailed—or as general—as you wish. Emily's outline is reasonably complete, but she could have made it either shorter or longer if she wished. Compare it to this excerpt from a less detailed version of Emily's outline:

I. Introduction: Benefits of fast-food employment come at a price
II. Workplace issues
   A. Hours worked
   B. Safety issues
      1. Restrictions on permissible jobs for young workers
      2. Economic incentives for employers to violate laws
   C. Wages paid
      1. Minimum wage
      2. Lack of bargaining power by workers
   D. Unfair practices
   E. Unsuccessful efforts to unionize
III. Conclusion: high price paid by fast-food workers

On the other hand, Emily could also create a far more detailed outline of her paper. For example, she could expand Section II-C of her outline as follows:

C. Wages paid
   1. Minimum wage
      a. Decline in purchasing power
         (1) Adequate for many teens
         (2) Inadequate for supporting a family
      b. Proposals for increase
         (1) Opposition from restaurants
            (a) Support for exemptions from minimum wage
            (b) Arguments against wage increase
               i) Loss of jobs
               ii) Increased prices
         (2) Support from unions
            (a) Benefits to low-income neighborhoods
            (b) No harm to companies
               i) Minimal increase in prices
               ii) Happier workers
   2. Lack of bargaining power by workers . . .

When you are revising your paper, a detailed outline can help you see how each part fits into the whole. When you have difficulty in creating an outline, the cause is often a problem with the organization of your paper. Your attempts to create a logical outline can often suggest a workable rearrangement of material within your paper. For example, before Emily created her formal outline, she had placed a long quotation from a union representative about wages with her final section on unions. Only when she created her outline did she decide that it belonged more logically in her earlier section on the minimum wage.

On the other hand, a writer should not be a slave to a rigidly symmetrical outline. In the final analysis, the nature of your material and not form-for-form's sake should determine your outline.

Standard Numbering System

Formal outlines usually follow the format that Emily used. Notice that each major part of Emily's outline is divided into subparts. These subparts are indented and marked with numbers and letters, following this *standard system:*

Paper Title

     I. First major part of the paper
        A. First subpart of I
        B. Second subpart of I
            1. First subpart of B
            2. Second subpart of B
    II. Second major part
        A. First subpart of II
            1. First subpart of A
            2. Second subpart of A
        B. Second subpart of II
            1. First subpart of B
            2. Second subpart of B
   III. Third major part
        A. First subpart of III
            1. First subpart of A
            2. Second subpart of A
            3. Third subpart of A
        B. Second subpart of III
            1. First subpart of B
            2. Second subpart of B
                a. First subpart of 2
                b. Second subpart of 2
                c. Third subpart of 2
            3. Third subpart of B

Decimal System

The *decimal system* is also widely used for outlines, particularly for scientific papers.

    1. First major part
    2. Second major part
       2.1 First subpart of 2
       2.2 Second subpart of 2
           2.2.1 First subpart of 2.2
           2.2.2 Second subpart of 2.2
               2.2.2.1 . . .
               2.2.2.2 . . .
  3. . . .
     3.1 . . .
     3.2 . . .
     3.3 . . .

Some instructors who assign formal outlines require, in the interest of symmetry, that whenever a part is to have subparts, there must be at least two of them; that is, they prefer that there not be a part 1 without at least a part 2, and so on. For example, they would find level A1a in the following to be faulty because it is the only entry on its level (there is no A1b):

A. Hours worked
   1. Current government regulations
      a. Child labor laws
   2. Proposals for new regulations

It should be stressed that not everyone objects to lone subparts. For those who do, the preceding can be adjusted easily by incorporating the subpart into the part above it:

A. Hours worked
   1. Current government regulations: child labor laws
   2. Proposals for new regulations

EXERCISES | **Formal Outlines**

1. Following are the parts of an outline for an argumentative paper. They appear in the proper order, but they have not been numbered or indented. Number them according to the *standard system* for outlining.

The Case against Saturday Morning Cartoons

Introduction
Background: description of current situation
Thesis: harm to children by Saturday morning cartoon shows
Counterarguments (those favoring these shows)
Positive-benefit arguments
Benefit to parents: babysitting
Benefits to children
Cartoon violence a harmless outlet for children's aggression
Children taught about life from cartoons
Free-market arguments
Programming determined by ratings, sponsors
Children's viewing up to parents, not networks
Censorship dangerous to our way of life
Refutation of counterarguments
Refutation of positive-benefit arguments
Damage to parents: deprived of interaction with their children
Damage to children
Shown only violent solutions to problems
Shown only the worst aspects of life
Refutation of free-market arguments

Morality, not only profits, a responsibility of networks
Parents unable to judge and screen all programming
Voluntary controls, not censorship, requested
Additional argument: danger to society of children's viewing
A nation of antisocial zombies
A nation of viewers, not doers
Conclusion: a call for reform

2. Renumber the preceding outline entries using the decimal system.

Topic and Sentence Outlines

The preceding formal outlines are examples of *topic outlines,* in which all the parts consist of phrases rather than complete sentences. In a *sentence outline,* the parts consist of complete sentences. For example:

> II. Various issues in the workplace affect employees.
>   A. Limits on the hours teens can work are not always effective.
>   1. Child-labor laws offer some but not complete protection.
>   2. New laws have been proposed to update protections.
>   B. Legislation is not always effective in keeping young workers safe.
>   1. Laws seek to limit the kinds of jobs available to young workers.
>   A. Teens are endangered by lax enforcement.
>   B. Better enforcement has been proposed.
>   2. Employers have economic incentives to violate safety laws. . . .

You can use either the topic or sentence outline method, but whichever you choose, be certain that you follow it consistently.

Like some of the other steps in research writing, the details of outline-writing may strike you as complicated—as undoubtedly they are—but they do serve a purpose. Use your informal and formal outlines to help you organize, write, and revise your paper. But remember that an outline is a tool to help you produce a better paper and not an end in itself. It is important at all times to remember the central goal of your research writing: to communicate what you have discovered in an effective way. Like all parts of the research process, the outline will work best and be of most help to you if you approach it with common sense.

Sentence Outlines   EXERCISES

1. Continue revising Emily Gould's outline on page 589 to make it a sentence outline.

2. Rewrite the outline in the preceding exercise beginning on the previous page to make it a sentence outline. Each line of the outline should be a complete sentence.

D Footnotes and Endnotes

Scholars in the fields of art, dance, history, music, religion, and theater often use footnotes and endnotes, instead of parenthetical notes, to document sources. Although it should not be necessary for you to memorize the details of the format, you should know how to use this chapter as a reference guide whenever you need to write footnotes or endnotes. When you do, consult it carefully and be certain to follow the format exactly, paying special attention to the mechanics of arrangement and punctuation.

Figures D.1 and D.2 show how a portion of Emily Gould's research paper would have looked if she had used footnotes instead of parenthetical notes. (Compare them with her use of parenthetical notes on pages 311–12.) The excerpt in Figure D.3 shows what her "Notes" page would have looked like if she had used endnotes.

Footnotes and endnotes serve the same purpose as parenthetical notes—to identify and give credit to your sources for their specific contributions to your paper. In the same place in your paper where you would put a parenthetical note, put a raised number to refer your readers to the note. Number your notes consecutively throughout the paper, starting with number 1. For footnotes, type each note at the bottom of the same page where the reference occurs. For endnotes, type all notes, in numerical order, on a separate page following the paper but preceding the list of works cited.

■ SAMPLE FOOTNOTES AND ENDNOTES

The models in this chapter show the footnote/endnote format for works cited in Chapter A. Note that complete information about a source is required only the first time it is cited in a note. Subsequent notes use an abbreviated format. (See sample footnote 21 in Figure D.1.)

Gould 8

for similar reasons.[19] When such employees grow
dissatisfied, they are replaced quickly and easily, with
little disruption of the restaurant's operations.

Fast-food restaurants see an annual turnover rate in
employees of over 75%.[20] To accommodate easy replacement of
workers, companies are steadily reaching a goal of "zero
training" for employees by developing more efficient
methods and adopting the most advanced kitchen technology.
The fast-food kitchen is like an assembly line. Food
arrives at the restaurant frozen, and preparation, which
involves little actual cooking, is regimented by a manual,
which includes such details as how hamburger patties are
to be arranged on the grill and the thickness of the
fries.[21] One college student who worked at Wendy's said,
"You don't even think when doing work, and you never make

[19] Eric Schlosser, Fast-Food Nation: The Dark Side of
the All-American Meal (Boston: Houghton, 2001) 68, 70.

[20] Gerald L. White, "Employee Turnover: The Hidden
Drain on Profits," HR Focus Jan. 1995: 15, InfoTrac OneFile,
21 Sept. 2002 <http://infotrac.galegroup.com/>.

[21] Schlosser 68-72.

Notes are numbered consecutively throughout the paper. The numbers are superscripts (raised slightly above the line).

Double-space twice (skip 3 lines).

After the first reference to a souce (see footnote 19), the abbreviated form is used (see footnote 21).

Double-space within and between footnotes.

Figure D.1 A sample page from a paper that uses footnotes.

little disruption of the restaurant's operations.

Fast-food restaurants see an annual turnover rate in employees of over 75%.[20] To accommodate easy replacement of workers, companies are steadily reaching a goal of "zero

---

[18] Cashen, Jill. Personal Interview. 10 Sept. 2002.

[19] Eric Schlosser, Fast-Food Nation: The Dark Side of the All-American Meal (Boston: Houghton, 2001) 68, 70.

[20] Gerald L White, "Employee Turnover: The Hidden Drain on

Footnote 20 must be continued on the following page.

---

and training new employees, and additional staff is often needed to help process applications. Current employees are also burdened with extra responsibilities when they pick

---

Profits," HR Focus Jan. 1995: 15, InfoTrac OneFile, 21 Sept. 2002 <http://infotrac.galegroup.com/>.

[21] Schlosser 68-72.

[22] Tamicah Williams, personal interview, 24 Sept. 2002.

A line drawn on the page signals that the first footnote beneath it is continued from the previous page.

Figure D.2 Format for a footnote continued on the following page.

Gould 10

Notes

[1] Eric Schlosser, Fast-Food Nation: The Dark Side of the All-American Meal (Boston: Houghton, 2001) 3.

[2] Qtd. in Nina C. Ayoub, "Nota Bene," rev. of Youth at Work: The Unionized Fast-Food and Grocery Workplace, by Stuart Tannock, Chronicle of Higher Education 25 May 2001: A20.

[3] Yum! Brands, "Great Jobs," 22 Sept. 2002 <http://www.yumjobs.com/>.

[4] Schlosser 4.

[5] Yvonne Zipp, "Virtues of Work vs. Finishing Homework," Christian Science Monitor 15 Dec. 1998: 1, MasterFILE Premier, EBSCOhost, 15 Sept. 2002 <http://web3.epnet.com/> 1.

[6] "General Information on the Fair Labor Standards Act (FLSA)," U.S. Dept. of Labor Employment Standards Administration Wage and Hour Division, 29 Sept. 2002 <http://www.dol.gov/esa/regs/compliance/whd/mwposter.htm>.

[7] Zipp 1.

[8] Patrick Kiger, "Risky Business," Good Housekeeping Apr. 2002: 114, MasterFILE Premier, EBSCOhost, 15 Sept. 2002 <http://web3.epnet.com/>.

[9] Zipp 1.

[10] "Prohibited Occupations for Non-Agricultural Employees," U.S. Dept. of Labor, Elaws--Fair Labor Standards

Figure D.3 Sample notes page from a paper that uses endnotes.

Books

Following are sample entries for books (accessed in print form). For online books, see Internet and Electronic Sources on page 604.

A Book with One Author

> [1] James Macdonald, <u>A Free Nation Deep in Debt: The Financial Roots of Democracy</u> (New York: Farrar, 2003), 123-26.

Footnotes/endnotes differ from works cited entries in several particulars. The first line of each footnote/endnote is indented; the author's first (not last) name comes first; the publisher and date are enclosed in parentheses; and commas (not periods) separate major items. Also, unlike works cited entries (but like parenthetical notes), footnotes/endnotes give the specific page or pages from which the cited information is taken.

Second and Subsequent References—All Sources

After a work has been cited in one note, you do not need to repeat all the same information in subsequent notes that refer to that same source. For second and subsequent references to a source, footnotes/endnotes should contain the least amount of information needed to identify the source (usually the author and page number).

> [2] Macdonald 45.

A Book with Two or Three Authors

> [3] Robert L. Dingman and John D. Weaver, <u>Days in the Lives of Counselors</u> (Boston: Allyn, 2003) 88-103.

> [4] Jo Anne Reid, Peter Forrestal, and Jonathan Cook, <u>Small Group Learning in the Classroom</u> (Portsmouth, NH: Heinemann, 1990) 110.

A Book with More Than Three Authors

> [5] Stéphane Courtois, et al., <u>The Black Book of Communism: Crimes, Terror, Repression</u> (Cambridge, MA: Harvard UP, 1999) 248-49.

A Book with No Author Listed

> [6] <u>Addison Wesley Longman Author's Guide</u> (New York: Longman, 1998) 11.

A Book with a Corporate or Group Author

[7] Sotheby's, <u>Nineteenth Century European Paintings,
Drawings and Watercolours</u> (London: Sotheby's, 1995) 306.

[8] U of North Carolina at Wilmington, <u>2002-2003 Code of
Student Life</u> ([Wilmington, NC]: n.p., [2002]) 23-31.

A Book by a Government Agency

[9] United States, Dept. of Health and Human Services,
Substance Abuse and Mental Health Services Admin., Center for
Mental Health Services, <u>What You Need to Know about Youth
Violence Prevention</u> (Rockville, MD: GPO, 2002) 3-4.

A Book with a Translator

[10] Julio Ramos, <u>Divergent Modernities: Culture and
Politics in Nineteenth-Century Latin America</u>, trans. John D.
Blanco (Durham: Duke UP, 1999) 97-99.

A Book with an Author and Editor

[11] William Shakespeare, <u>Henry V</u>, ed. T. W. Craik (New
York: Routledge, 1995) 88.

A Book with an Editor

[12] Catherine R. Stimpson and Ethel Spector Person, eds.,
<u>Women: Sex and Sexuality</u> (Chicago: U of Chicago P, 1980), 11.

A Book in a Later Edition

[13] Ellen Skinner, <u>Women and the National Experience</u>, 2nd
ed. (New York: Longman, 2003) 206-21.

A Book in a Series

[14] Rudolph P. Matthee, <u>The Politics of Trade in Safavid
Iran: Silk for Silver, 1600-1730</u>, Cambridge Studies in
Islamic Civilization (New York: Cambridge UP, 2000) 368.

A Multivolume Book
Volumes individually titled:

[15] Crane Brinton, John B. Christopher, and Robert Lee Wolff, Prehistory to 1715, vol. 1 of A History of Civilization, 6th ed., 2 vols. (Englewood Cliffs, NJ: Prentice, 1984) 303.

Volumes not individually titled:

[16] Charles Messenger, For Love of Regiment: A History of British Infantry, 1660-1993, vol. 1 (Philadelphia: Trans-Atlantic, 1995), 388.

A Book Published before 1900

[17] Florence Nightingale, Notes on Nursing: What It Is, and What It Is Not (New York, 1860) 27.

A Paperback or Other Reprinted Book

[18] Tony Horwitz, Confederates in the Attic: Dispatches from the Unfinished Civil War (1998; New York: Vintage, 1999) 177.

Selections from Books

A Selection from an Anthology

[19] Myra Leifer, "Pregnancy," Women: Sex and Sexuality, ed. Catherine R. Stimpson and Ethel Spector Person (Chicago: U of Chicago P, 1980) 215.

[20] George Lichtheim, "The Birth of a Philosopher," Collected Essays (New York: Viking, 1973) 109.

[21] Salman Rushdie, "A Pen Against the Sword: In Good Faith," Newsweek 12 Feb. 1990: 52+, rpt. in One World, Many Cultures, ed. Stuart Hirschberg (New York: Macmillan, 1992) 487-88.

An Article in an Encyclopedia or Other Reference

[22] Mamie Harmon, "Folk Arts," The New Encyclopaedia Britannica: Macropaedia, 15th ed., 2002.

[23] "Morrison, Toni," Who's Who in America, 57th ed., 2003.

[24] "Yodel," The Shorter Oxford English Dictionary, 1973.

[25] Raymond Hames, "Yanomamö," South America, vol. 7 of Encyclopedia of World Cultures (Boston: Hall, 1994).

A Preface, Introduction, Foreword, or Afterword

[26] Barbara Taylor Bradford, foreword, Forever Amber, by Kathleen Winsor, 1944 (Chicago: Chicago Review, 2000) iv-viii.

Sources in Periodicals and Newspapers

For articles accessed online, see Internet and Electronic Sources on pages 605–07.

An Article in a Magazine

[27] Toddi Gutner Block, "Riding the Waves," Forbes 11 Sept. 1995: 182.

[28] George Jellinek, "Record Collecting: Hobby or Obsession?" Opera News Feb. 2003: 85.

[29] Susan Van Zile, "Grammar That'll Move You!" Instructor Jan./Feb. 2003: 33.

An Article in a Journal

Pages numbered continuously throughout a volume:

[30] Raima Larter, "Understanding Complexity in Biophysical Chemistry," Journal of Physical Chemistry 107 (2003): 417-19.

Each issue begins on page 1:

[31] W. J. T. Mitchell, "The Surplus Value of Images," Mosaic 35.3 (2002): 11.

An Article in a Newspaper

[32] Amy Argetsinger, "Lobbying Gets Old College Try," Washington Post 13 Jan. 2003: B2.

[33] David Leonhardt, "Defining the Rich in the World's Wealthiest Nation," New York Times 12 Jan. 2003, natl. ed.: sec. 4: 1.

[34] David Ranii, "New AIDS Drug Is Step Closer to Approval," News and Observer [Raleigh] 7 Nov. 1995: 1D.

An Editorial

[35] "Six Sigma Schools," editorial, Wall Street Journal 15 Jan. 2003: A10.

A Letter to the Editor

[36] Michelle Rothschild, letter, Kiplinger's Jan. 2003: 14.

A Review

[37] Caitlin Flanagan, "Get a Job," rev. of What Should I Do with My Life?, by Po Bronson, New York Times Book Review 12 Jan. 2003: 4.

[38] Kenny Glenn, rev. of Man on the Moon [film], Premiere Jan. 2000: 20.

[39] Rev. of Going to the Territory, by Ralph Ellison, Atlantic Aug. 1986: 91.

[40] David Patrick Stearns, rev. of The Well-Tempered Clavier, by J. S. Bach [CD], Angela Hewitt, piano, Stereophile Dec. 1999: 185.

Other Sources

An Audio Recording

[41] Dee Dickinson, Creating the Future: Perspectives on Educational Change, audiocassette (Minneapolis: Accelerated Learning Systems, 1991).

42 Gustav Mahler, Symphony No. 7, Michael Tilson Thomas, cond., London Symphony Orch., CD, RCA Victor, 1999.

43 George N. Shuster, jacket notes, The Poetry of Gerard Manley Hopkins, LP, Caedmon, n.d.

A Film, DVD, or Video Recording

44 25th Hour, dir. Spike Lee, screenplay by David Benioff, Touchstone, 2003.

45 All about Eve, dir. Joseph L. Mankiewicz, perf. Bette Davis, Anne Baxter, and George Sanders, Fox, 1950, DVD, Studio Classics, 2003.

46 The Classical Hollywood Style, program 1 of The American Cinema, prod. New York Center for Visual History, videocassette, Annenberg/CPB, 1995.

A Government Document

See "A Book by a Government Agency" on page 599.

A Lecture

47 Stephanie Granetta, class lecture, English 315, Richardson College, 7 Apr. 2003.

48 Eleanor Kamenish, "A Tale of Two Countries: Mores in France and Scotland," public lecture, Friends of the Public Library, Louisville, 16 Apr. 2003.

A Pamphlet

49 Golden Retriever Club of America, Prevention of Heartworm (n.p.: GRCA, 2004) 4.

50 Who Are the Amish? (Aylmer, Ont,: Pathway, n.d).

An Interview

51 Blake Barefoot, personal interview, 18 Sept. 2002.

52 Kevin Spacey, Interview with Terry Gross, Fresh Air, Natl. Public Radio, WHQR, Wilmington, NC, 21 Jan. 2003.

[53] Donald Trump, "Trump Speaks," interview with Aravind Adiga, _Money_ Feb. 2003: 28.

A Television or Radio Program

[54] _The Crossing_, dir. Robert Harmon, screenplay by Sherry Jones and Peter Jennings, History Channel, 1 Jan. 2000.

[55] Susan Stone, report on Japanese comic books, _All Things Considered_, National Public Radio, 9 Jan. 2003.

An Unpublished Essay

[56] Emily Gould, "Fast Food Comes at a High Price for Workers," essay written for Prof. Katherine Humel's English 12 class, Fall semester 2002.

An Unpublished Letter

[57] Cara Cilano, letter to author, 5 Mar. 2003.

An Unpublished Questionnaire

[58] Questionnaire conducted by Prof. Barbara Waxman's English 103 class, Feb. 2003.

Internet and Electronic Sources

An Online Book

[59] David Irving, _Hitler's War_, New York: Viking, 1977, 19 Jan. 2003 <http://www.fpp.co.uk/books/Hitler/> 177.

[60] Hank Richards, _The Sacrifice_, 1996, 3 Mar. 2003 <http://www.geocities.com/Area51/Vault/8101/>.

[61] Mary Wollstonecraft, _Vindication of the Rights of Women_, 1792, Bartleby.com, 1999, 13 Feb. 2003 <http://www.bartleby.com/144/4.html> ch. 4, para. 14.

Part of an Online Book

[62] Edward R. Coyle, Spies and Their Work, <u>Ambulancing on the French Front</u>, 1918, 30 Apr. 2003 <http://www.ku.edu/carrie/specoll/medical/Coyle/Coyle04.htm#18>.

A Print Periodical (Newspaper, Magazine, or Journal) Accessed on the Publication's Web Site

[63] Cathleen Falsani, "Did Respect for Religion Cloud 'Clone' Coverage?" <u>Chicago Sun-Times</u> 10 Jan. 2003, 19 Jan. 2003 <http://www.suntimes.com/output/falsani/cst-nws-fals10.html>.

[64] Howard Fineman and Tamara Lipper, "Spinning Race," <u>Newsweek</u> 27 Jan. 2003, 19 Jan. 2003 <http://www.msnbc.com/news/861383.asp?>

[65] A. J. Young, A. S. Wilson, and C. G. Mundell, "Chandra Imaging of the X-Ray Core of the Virgo Cluster," <u>Astrophysical Journal</u> 579.2 (2002): 560-570, 19 Jan. 2003 <http://www.journals.uchicago.edu/ApJ/journal/issues/ApJ/v579n2/54935/54935.html>.

A Nonprint Periodical Accessed on the Publication's Web Site

[66] Bill Clinton, "The Path to Peace," 10 Sept. 2002, <u>Salon.com</u> 20 Jan. 2003 <http://www.salon.com/news/feature/2002/09/10/clinton/>.

A Work Accessed in an Online Database

[67] Rozalia Jovanovic, "Snowmobilers Tied to Rules of the Road," <u>National Law Journal</u> Aug. 5, 2002: B1, <u>InfoTrac OneFile</u>, 20 Jan. 2003 <http://infotrac.galegroup.com/>.

[68] Noreen Parks, "Dolphins in Danger," <u>Science Now</u>, 17 Dec. 2002: 2-3, <u>Academic Search Elite</u>, EBSCOhost, 20 Jan. 2003 <http://web3.epnet.com/>.

[69] "Political Inclination of the States," Associated Press, 9 Jan. 2003, LexisNexis Academic Universe, 20 Jan. 2003 <http://web.lexis-nexis.com/universe>.

An Online Encyclopedia Article

[70] "Humpback Whale," Encyclopaedia Britannica 2003, Encyclopaedia Britannica Online, 28 Jan, 2003 <http://0-search.eb.com.uncclc.coast.uncwil.edu/eb/>.

An Online Review

[71] Roger Ebert, rev. of Identity, dir. James Mangold, Chicago Sun-Times Online 25 Apr. 2003, 29 May 2003. <http://www.suntimes.com/output/ebert1/wkp-news-identity25f .html>.

[72] Tony Eprile, "'Red Dust': Settling Scores in South Africa," rev. of. Red Dust by Gillian Slovo, New York Times Online 28 Apr. 2003, 29 May 2003 <http://www.nytimes.com/2002/04/28/books/review/28EPRILET.html?ex=1051761600&en=0f435a46a2f839eb&ei=5070>.

An Organization's Web Site

[73] The Coral Reef Alliance, "Coral Friendly Guidelines," 21 Jan. 2003 <http://www.coralreefalliance.org/parks/guidelines.html>.

A Personal Web Page

[74] Sally Hemming, home page, 21 Jan. 2003 <http://www.sallyhemming.com/>.

E-Mail

[75] Paul Wilkes, e-mail to author, 29 Dec. 2002.

Computer Software

76 <u>Atoms, Symbols and Equations</u>, vers. 3.0, software, 2002 <http://ourworld.compuserve.com/homepages/RayLec/atoms.htm>.

77 <u>Twain's World</u>, CD-ROM (Parsippany, NJ: Bureau Development, 1993).

E APA Format

FORMATS OTHER THAN MLA

Although you will use the MLA parenthetical or footnote/endnote format to acknowledge sources in papers that you write for humanities courses (such as research papers in a composition class), other disciplines may require you to use different formats. Since many journals establish their own conventions for documenting sources, you are also likely to encounter various other formats when you conduct library research. A glance through scholarly journals in your college library will show you that dozens of different formats are in use—usually varying only in minor ways from MLA format or the formats described in this chapter.

Although it is not practical to describe all the different formats here, you should be familiar with the most commonly used formats for citing sources. It is probably unnecessary for you to memorize the details of any of them, but when you use a particular format, you should be prepared to model your own references carefully on sample entries, such as those in this chapter. Note the ways in which these formats differ from MLA format and pay close attention to the information that is presented in each entry, the order in which it is presented, and the punctuation used to denote and separate items.

Two principal formats, besides the MLA, are in wide use among scholars. The APA format (described in this chapter) gives special prominence to the source's publication date in all citations. In the numbered references format (described in the following chapter), each source is assigned a number in the list of works cited; each note in the paper refers to a source by its assigned number.

APA STYLE

Next to the MLA style, the most common format for documenting sources is that of the American Psychological Association—*APA style.* This format (or a variation of it) is widely used for course papers and journal articles in psychology but also in many other disciplines in both the social and natural sciences. Although APA format differs in many particulars from MLA format, the main difference is the prominence its citations give to the source's publication date. In fields where new theories and discoveries are constantly challenging past assumptions, readers must know if a writer's sources are up-to-date. Note how the date is featured in the following sample APA citations. Parenthetical notes in APA style always include the date, as in the following:

```
. . . tendency of creative people to be organized (Sternberg

& Lubart, 1995, p. 246).
```

Following is the listing for that same source, as it appears in the references page (list of works cited). Notice that the date is given in parentheses immediately following the author's name.

```
Sternberg, R. J., & Lubart, T. I. (1995). Defying the crowd:

    Cultivating creativity in a culture of conformity. New

    York: Free Press.
```

The particulars of APA reference style are explained in the following sections.

APA Bibliographic Citations (Reference List)

At the end of the paper, all sources are listed on a separate page, under the title *References* (not *Works Cited*). Like the MLA format, the APA also arranges works alphabetically, according to the first word in each item. See, for example, Figure E.1 on page 610.

In addition to the prominence given to publication dates, bibliographic citations in APA style differ from MLA listings in three principal ways:

1. In APA style, only the author's last name is given in full. Initials are used for first and middle names. Thus, an author who would be listed in MLA style as *Sternberg, Robert J.* is listed as *Sternberg, R. J.* in APA style.

2. Except for proper names, only the first word of the work's title (and, if there is a subtitle, the first word following the colon) is capitalized. Thus, a book title that would be listed in MLA style as *Defying the Crowd: Cultivating Creativity in a Culture of Conformity* is listed in APA style as *Defying the crowd: Cultivating creativity in a culture of conformity.*

3. Titles of periodical articles (and other works shorter than book-length) are not enclosed in quotation marks as they are in MLA style.

Other differences can be seen in the following sample entries.

Model Entries

Punctuation following italicized text is also italicized in APA style.

Fast Food 13

References

Ayoub, N. C. (May 25, 2001). Nota bene. [Review of the

Author's last names and first initials are given.

book *Youth at work: The unionized fast-food and grocery workplace*]. *Chronicle of Higher Education*, p. A20.

Article titles are not placed in quotation marks.

Broydo, L. (1999, January/February). Worked over. *Utne Reader, 16,* 20-21.

General information on the fair labor standards act (FLSA). (n.d.). U.S. Department of Labor Employment

Online sources are cited in this format.

Standards Administration Wage and Hour Division. Retrieved September 29, 2002, from http://www.dol.gov/ esa/regs/compliance/whd/mwposter.htm

Hamstra, M. (1998, September 7). Unions seek momentum from Canadian McD's certification. *Nation's Restaurant News, 32:* 3. Retrieved September 15, 2002, from MasterFILE Premier database (Item 1099749).

Titles are capitalized according to the rules for sentence capitalization.

Figure E.1 Sample APA references page.

Books

Following are sample APA entries for books (accessed in print form). For online books, see Internet and Electronic Sources on page 617.

A Book with One Author

Macdonald, J. (2003). *A free nation deep in debt: The financial roots of democracy.* New York: Farrar, Straus and Giroux.

Wheelock, A. K., Jr. (1995). *Vermeer and the art of painting.* New Haven, CT: Yale University Press.

The complete names of publishers are given. Words like *University* and *Press* are not abbreviated.

A Book with Two to Six Authors

```
Reid, J. A., Forrestal, P., & Cook, J. (1990). Small group
     learning in the classroom. Portsmouth, NH: Heinemann.
```

All authors, not just the first, are listed last name first, followed by initials. An ampersand (&) is used before the name of the last author.

A Book with More Than Six Authors

```
Martin, S., Smith, L., Forehand, M. R., Mobbs, R., Lynch, T. F.,
     Renfrew, E. J., et al. (2003). Migratory waterfowl.
     Lincoln, NE: Wendell Press.
```

List only the first six authors, followed by *et al.*

Two or More Works by the Same Author, Different Years

```
Irwin, E. (2000). New . . .
Irwin, E. (2003). Lessons . . .
```

When two or more works have the same author(s), arrange the works chronologically, not alphabetically by title.

Two or More Works by the Same Author, Same Year

```
Bushman, D. E. (2003a). Development . . .
Bushman, D. E. (2003b). Lessons . . .
```

When the author(s) has two or more works in the same year, arrange the works alphabetically by title, and place lowercase letters (*a, b, c,* etc.) immediately after the year.

A Book with No Author Listed

```
Addison Wesley Longman author's guide. (1998). New York: Longman.
```

A Book with a Corporate or Group Author

```
Sotheby's. (1995). Nineteenth century European paintings,
     drawings and watercolours. London: Author.
```

A Book by a Government Agency

U.S. Department of Health and Human Services. Substance Abuse and Mental Health Services Administration. Center for Mental Health Services. (2002). *What you need to know about youth violence prevention.* Rockville, MD: Government Printing Office.

A Book with a Translator

Ramos, J. (1999). *Divergent modernities: Culture and politics in nineteenth-century Latin America* (J. D. Blanco, Trans.). Durham, NC: Duke University Press.

A Book with an Author and Editor

Shakespeare, W. (1591). *Henry V* (T. W. Craik, Ed.). New York: Routledge. (Edition published 1995)

A Book with an Editor

Stimpson, C. R., & Person, E. S. (Eds.). (1980). *Women: Sex and sexuality.* Chicago: University of Chicago Press.

A Book in a Later Edition

Skinner, E. (2003). *Women and the national experience* (2nd ed.). New York: Longman.

A Book in a Series

Matthee, R. P. (2000). *The Politics of trade in Safavid Iran: Silk for silver, 1600-1730.* Cambridge Studies in Islamic Civilization. New York: Cambridge University Press.

A Multivolume Book

Messenger, C. (1995). *For love of regiment: A history of British infantry, 1660-1993* (Vol. 1). Philadelphia: Trans-Atlantic Publications.

List all volumes of the work that you cite; for example, *(Vols. 2-3).*

A Paperback or Other Reprinted Book

Horwitz, T. (1999). *Confederates in the attic: Dispatches from the unfinished Civil War.* New York: Vintage. (Original work published 1998)

Selections from Books

A Selection from an Anthology

Baker, S. W. (1980). Biological influences on human sex and gender. In C. R. Stimpson & E. S. Person (Eds.), *Women: Sex and sexuality* (pp. 212-223). Chicago: University of Chicago Press.

Rushdie, S. (1992). A pen against the sword: In good faith. In Hirschberg, S. (Ed.), *One world, many cultures* (pp. 480-496). New York: Macmillan. (Reprinted from *Newsweek, 115,* February 12, 1990: 52-57)

An Article in an Encyclopedia or Other Reference

Harmon, M. (2002). Folk arts. In *The new encyclopaedia Britannica: Macropaedia* (15th ed., Vol. 19, pp. 306-338). Chicago: Britannica.

Morrison, T. (2003). In *Who's who in America* (57th ed.). Chicago: Marquis.

Hames, R. (1994). Yanomamö. In *South America. Encyclopedia of world cultures* (Vol. 7, pp. 374-377). Boston: G. K. Hall.

A Preface, Introduction, Foreword, or Afterword

Bradford, B. T. (2000). Foreword. In K. Winsor, *Forever amber* (pp. iii-xi). Chicago: Chicago Review.

Periodicals and Newspapers

Following are APA entries for periodicals and newspapers (when accessed in print form). For articles accessed online, see Internet and Electronic Sources on pages 617-18.

An Article in a Magazine

> Block, T. G. (1995, September 11). Riding the waves. *Forbes,*
>   *156,* 182, 184.
>
> Jellinek, G. (2003, February). Record collecting: Hobby or
>   obsession? *Opera News, 67,* 85.
>
> Van Zile, S. (2003, January/February). Grammar that'll move you!
>   *Instructor,* 32-34.

The date of a periodical is given (year first) immediately following the author's name. Months are not abbreviated. Neither quotation marks nor italics are used for article titles. All important words in a periodical's title are capitalized (*Opera News*). The volume number of a periodical is italicized and follows the name of the periodical (*Forbes, 156*). All page numbers are given immediately afterward. For magazine and journal articles (unlike newspaper articles), neither *p.* nor *pp.* is used. The Block article appeared on pages 182 and 184.

An Article in a Journal

A journal whose pages are numbered continuously throughout a volume:

> Larter, R. (2003). Understanding complexity in biophysical
>   chemistry. *Journal of Physical Chemistry, 107,*
>   415-429.

A journal, every issue of which begins on page 1:

> Mitchell, W. J. (2002). The surplus value of images. *Mosaic*
>   *35*(3), 1-23.

The number *35*(3) tells you that the article appeared in volume 35, issue 3, of *Mosaic*. Only the volume number is italicized. Page numbers are not shortened, as they are in MLA style; pages in the Larter article are written 415–429 (not 415–29).

An Article in a Newspaper

> Argetsinger, A. (2003, January 13). Lobbying gets old college
>   try. *Washington Post,* p. B2.
>
> Leonhardt, D. (2003, January 12). Defining the rich in the
>   world's wealthiest nation. *New York Times,* national
>   edition, section 4, pp. 1, 8.

An Editorial

Six sigma schools. (2003, January 15). [Editorial]. *Wall Street Journal*, p. A10.

A Letter to the Editor

Rothschild, M. (2003, January). [Letter to the editor]. *Kiplinger's*, p. 14.

A Review

Flanagan, C. (2003, January 12). Get a job. [Review of the book *What should I do with my life?*]. *New York Times Book Review*, p. 4.

Glenn, K. (2000, January). [Review of the film *Man on the moon*]. *Premiere*, *13*, 20.

[Review of the book *Going to the territory*]. (1986, August). *Atlantic*, *120*, 91.

Stearns, D. P. (1999, December). [Review of the CD *The well-tempered clavier*]. *Stereophile*, *10*, 173, 175.

Other Sources

An Audio Recording

Dickinson, D. (Speaker). (1991). *Creating the future: Perspectives on educational change* [Audiocassette]. Minneapolis, MN: Accelerated Learning Systems.

Mahler, G. (1999). Symphony No. 7 [CD]. United States: RCA Victor.

A Film, DVD, or Video Recording

Lee, S. (Director). (2003). *25th hour* [Film]. United States: Touchstone.

Mankiewicz, J. L. (Scriptwriter and director). (2003). *All about Eve*. [DVD]. Hollywood, CA: Studio Classics. (Film produced 1950).

The classical Hollywood style [Videocassette]. (1995). Program 1
of *The American cinema*. Washington, DC: Annenberg/CPB.

A Lecture

A source that cannot be retrieved by your readers, such as a classroom or public
lecture which is not available in print or on recording, is not listed among your
paper's references. However, it is cited in the paper in a parenthetical note: (*S.
Granetta, classroom lecture, April 7, 2003*).

A Personal Interview

A personal interview that you conduct cannot be retrieved by your readers, so it is
not listed among your paper's references. However, it is cited in the paper in a
parenthetical note: (*B. Barefoot, personal communication, September 18, 2002*).

A Broadcast or Published Interview

Gross, T. (2003, January 21). [Interview with Kevin Spacey]. In
Fresh air. National Public Radio. Wilmington, NC: WHQR.

Adiga, A. (2003, February). Trump speaks. [Interview with Donald
Trump]. *Money, 32*, 28.

A Television or Radio Program

Harmon, R. (Director). (2000, January 1). The crossing
[Television program]. Stamford, CT: History Channel.

Stone, S. (Reporter). (2003, January 9). [Report on Japanese
comic books.] In *All things considered*. Washington, DC:
National Public Radio.

An Unpublished Essay

Gould, E. (2002). Fast food comes at a high price for workers.
Unpublished essay for Prof. Katherine Humel's English 12
class, University of North Carolina, Chapel Hill.

An Unpublished Letter or E-Mail

Unpublished correspondence cannot be retrieved by your readers, so it is not
listed among your paper's references. However, it is cited in the paper in a parenthetical note: (*C. Cilano, personal communication, March 5, 2003*).

An Unpublished Questionnaire

```
Doe, J. (2003). [Survey of student attitudes on dating].
     Unpublished raw data.
```

Internet and Electronic Sources

An Online Book

```
Irving, D. Hitler's war. (1977). New York: Viking. Retrieved
     January 19, 2003, from http://www.fpp.co.uk/books/Hitler/
```

A Print Periodical Accessed Online

```
Clinton, B. (2002, September 10). The path to peace. Salon.com.
     Retrieved January 20, 2003, from http://www.salon.com/news/
     feature/2002/09/10/clinton/
Falsani, C. (2003, January 10). Did respect for religion cloud
     'clone' coverage? Chicago Sun-Times. Retrieved January 19,
     2003, from http://www.suntimes.com/output/falsani/
     cst-nws-fals.html
Fineman, H., & Lipper, T. (2003, January 27). Spinning race.
     Newsweek. Retrieved January 19, 2003, from http://
     www.msnbc.com/news/861383.asp?
Young, A. J., Wilson, A. S., & Mundell, C. G. (2002). Chandra
     imaging of the x-ray core of the Virgo cluster.
     Astrophysical Journal 579(2), 560-570. Retrieved January
     19, 2003, from http://www.journals.uchicago.edu/ApJ/
     journal/issues/ApJ/v579n2/54935/54935.html
```

A Work Accessed in an Online Database

Use the following format when you access a work in an online database such as EBSCOhost, InfoTrac, LexisNexis, ProQuest, or WilsonWeb.

```
Jovanovic, R. (2002, August 5). Snowmobilers tied to rules of
     the road. National Law Journal, 24, B1. Retrieved January
     20, 2003, from InfoTrac OneFile database (Item A91884653).
```

> Associated Press. (2003, January 9). Political inclination of
>   the states. Retrieved January 20, 2003 from LexisNexis
>   Academic Universe database.

Include an item number for the article, if available.

An Online Encyclopedia Article

> Humpback whale. (2003). Encyclopaedia Britannica 2003.
>   Retrieved January 28, 2003, from Encyclopaedia Britannica
>   Online.

An Organization's or Individual's Web Site

> The Coral Reef Alliance. (n.d.). Coral friendly guidelines.
>   Retrieved January 21, 2003, from http://
>   www.coralreefalliance.org/parks/guidelines.html
> Hemming, S. (n.d.). [Home page]. Retrieved January 21, 2003,
>   from http://www.sallyhemming.com/

Use (*n.d.*) for "no date."

Treatment of other sources, as well as detailed information about APA format, can be found by consulting the latest edition of the *Publication Manual of the American Psychological Association*. You can find the book in the reference section of most college libraries.

Notes in APA Style

Parenthetical notes in APA format are handled similarly to the MLA method, but with three notable differences:

1. The year of publication is included in the note.
2. All items are separated by commas.
3. Page numbers are preceded by the abbreviation *p.* or *pp.*

When a work is referred to as a whole, no page numbers are needed:

> In a study of reaction times (Sanders, 2003), . . .

Only the year is needed when the author's name appears in the sentence:

> Sanders (2003) studied reaction times . . .

Include pages when the source can be located more specifically:

> ". . . not necessary" (Galizio, 1999, p. 9).

Give the first word or two from the title when the author's name is unknown. Book titles are italicized; periodical titles in notes (unlike in the reference list) are enclosed in quotation marks; all important words are capitalized (also like reference-list citations):

> . . . the book (*Culture*, 2002).

> . . . the article ("US policy," 1999).

Only the year, not the complete date, is given in notes referring to periodical articles.

For a work with six or fewer authors, the note lists all authors' last names:

> (Andrulis, Beers, Bentley, & Gage, 2001)

However, only the first author's name is given for a work with more than six authors:

> (Sabella et al., 2003)

When the reference list cites two or more works written by the same author in the same year, use lowercase letters to differentiate them, as in reference-list citations:

> (Bushman, 2003a)

> (Bushman, 2003b)

These two notes cite different works by Bushman, both written in 2003.

When a note refers to more than one work, list the references alphabetically and separate them with a semicolon:

> (Earle & Reeves, 1999; Kowal, 2002)

Sample Pages in APA Style

Any paper written using MLA format can also be written in APA format. For example, Emily Gould could have used APA style for her paper on fast food.

A cover page is typically used for APA papers. The cover page is numbered as page 1, and a shortened version of the title precedes the page number on each page, as in Figure E.2.

The title is repeated on the opening page of the paper, numbered as page 2. Compare Figures E.3 and E.4 with pages from Emily's MLA-style paper on pages 304–18. Compare Figure E.1 with Emily's list of works cited on page 316.

Fast Food 1

Running head: FAST FOOD

Fast Food Comes at a High Price for Workers

Emily Gould

University of North Carolina at Chapel Hill

Professor Katherine Humel

English 12

Section 16

October 4, 2002

Figure E.2 Sample APA cover page.

Fast Food 1

Fast Food Comes at a High Price for Workers

McDonald's, Burger King, KFC, Wendy's, and other
fast-food chains have brought countless innovations to the
food services industry, delivering our food faster and
cheaper over the years. Convenience and value have come at
a price, however, and many believe that benefits to the
public are outweighed by the costs that this giant
industry imposes on its workers.

In his book *Fast-Food Nation*, Eric Schlosser (2001)
shows just how much fast food has revolutionized America's
eating habits. In 1970, Americans spent $6 billion on fast

Figure E.3 Sample APA opening page.

Fast Food 2

Having teenagers prepare and serve us food in the
fast-food setting has become "so natural, so normal, and
so inevitable that people often think little about it,"
according to Stuart Tannock, a lecturer in social and
cultural studies at the University of California at
Berkeley (Ayoub, 2001). While fast-food workers have
become an essential component in the service industry, a
fast-food job is viewed as undesirable, dead-end work.

One-third of all workers under 35 got their first job
working for a restaurant (Yum! Brands, n.d.), and about
one-eighth of all workers in the United States have, at
some point, worked for McDonald's (Schlosser, 2001, p. 4).
Fast-food jobs have become such a common occupation for
teenagers that they become what Yvonne Zipp (1998) of the
Christian Science Monitor calls "a rite of passage" into
the American workforce. They are ideal for teens because

APA parenthetical
notes include the
publication date.
No page is given
for a one-page
source.

Citation of a
source without
author, date,
or pages.

Citation of a
source with
a page
reference.

Citation of
a source
following
author's name.

Figure E.4 Sample APA notes.

F Format Featuring Numbered References

Another common bibliographic format uses **numbered references** to identify sources. Variations on this format are used most widely in fields such as mathematics, computer science, finance, and other areas in the applied sciences.

Sources are assigned a number in the references page (list of works cited) and are referred to in the paper by that number rather than by the author's name. Items in the references list can be arranged either in alphabetical order or in the order in which references occur within the paper. Figure F.1 shows how the references list at the end of Emily Gould paper might have looked if she had used this style. In this case, the references are numbered in the order in which they first appear in the paper.

Here is how the first three sentences with notes in Emily's paper would have appeared if she had used the numbered-references style:

<table>
<tr>
<td>The paper's first note is numbered 1.</td>
<td>Schlosser says Americans "spend more on fast food than on movies, books, magazines, newspapers, videos, and recorded music--combined" [1, p. 3].</td>
<td></td>
</tr>
<tr>
<td>The page reference follows the note number.</td>
<td>Having teenagers prepare and serve us food in the fast-food setting has become "so natural, so normal, and so inevitable that people often think little about it," according to Stuart Tannock, a lecturer in social and cultural studies at the University of California at Berkeley [2, p. A20].</td>
<td></td>
</tr>
<tr>
<td>A later reference to a source cited earlier in the paper.</td>
<td>One-third of all workers under 35 got their first job working for a restaurant [3], and about one-eighth of all workers in the United States have, at some point, worked for McDonald's [1, p. 4]. Fast-food jobs have become such a</td>
<td>Note for a source without pages.</td>
</tr>
</table>

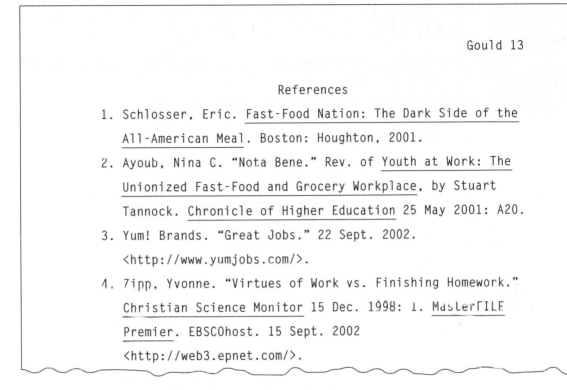

Gould 13

References

1. Schlosser, Eric. Fast-Food Nation: The Dark Side of the All-American Meal. Boston: Houghton, 2001.

2. Ayoub, Nina C. "Nota Bene." Rev. of Youth at Work: The Unionized Fast-Food and Grocery Workplace, by Stuart Tannock. Chronicle of Higher Education 25 May 2001: A20.

3. Yum! Brands. "Great Jobs." 22 Sept. 2002. <http://www.yumjobs.com/>.

4. Zipp, Yvonne. "Virtues of Work vs. Finishing Homework." Christian Science Monitor 15 Dec. 1998: 1. MasterFILE Premier. EBSCOhost. 15 Sept. 2002 <http://web3.epnet.com/>.

Figure F.1 Sample list with numbered references.

common occupation for teenagers that they become what Yvonne Zipp of the Christian Science Monitor calls "a rite of passage" into the American workforce [4, p. 1].

Apart from the use of reference numbers, there is no uniform style for citing bibliographic sources in this format. Individual items in the bibliography could follow the principles of MLA format, APA format, or yet some other format. If you are required to use numbered references for a course paper, be sure to check with your instructor for specific format details.

Another characteristic of papers using this format is that citation of page references is far less common than in either MLA or APA style. Usually, sources are referred to in the paper solely by their reference numbers, which are usually written within brackets:

Smith and Gurganus [6] showed that . . .

Often even the authors' names are omitted:

```
Other examples of this approach are [1, 4, 5]. In 1996, [3]
analyzed . . .
```

Instead of brackets, alternative formats that use numbered references place them either within parentheses:

```
Fort (7) disputes the findings of Byington (3) . . .
```

or as raised numbers:

```
It has been demonstrated¹ that artifacts that occur . . .
```

The raised number *1* in the preceding example refers not to a footnote or endnote but directly to the first source in the references list.

Credits

TEXT

Page 5   From "I Stand Here Writing" by Nancy Sommers in *College English*, Vol. 55, No. 4, April 1993. Copyright © 1993 by the National Council of Teachers of English. Reprinted with permission.

Pages 40–41   From "Reading and Revelation" by Wendy Lesser in the *Chronicle of Higher Education*, April 19, 2002. Reprinted by permission of the author.

Page 42   From "Serialism as a Museum Piece" by Greg Sandow in the *Chronicle of Higher Education*, June 14, 2002. Reprinted by permission of the author.

Page 43   From "American Visionary" by Allan Ulrich in the *San Francisco Examiner*, September 5, 1999. Reprinted with permission.

Pages 46–47   From "Metropolitan Diary" by Enid Nemy in the *New York Times*, April 22, 2002. Copyright © 2002 by the *New York Times*. Reprinted by permission.

Pages 48–51   "A Short History of Love" by Lawrence Stone from *Passionate Attachments. Thinking About Love* edited by Willard Gaylin and Ethel Person. Copyright © 1988 by Friends of Columbia Psychoanalytic Center, Inc. Reprinted with the permission of the Free Press, a Division of Simon & Schuster Adult Publishing Group.

Page 58   Excerpt from "I'm Not Sick, I'm Just in Love" by Katherine Davis in *Newsweek*, July 24, 1995. All rights reserved. Reprinted by permission.

Pages 59–63   From *Reading Don't Fix No Chevy* by Michael W. Smith and Jeffrey D. Wilhelm. Copyright © 2002 by Heinemann. Reproduced with permission of Greenwood Publishing Group, Inc., Westport, CT.

Pages 65–67   From *Word Freak* by Stefan Fatsis. Copyright © 2001 by Stefan Fatsis. Used by permission of Houghton Mifflin Company. All rights reserved.

Pages 68–69   "Fairy Tales as a Learning Tool for Young Offenders" by Richard Rothstein from the *New York Times*, July 24, 2002. Copyright © 2002 by the *New York Times*. Reprinted by permission.

Pages 69–71   "Just Showing Off: Complaints Lead to Closer Police Scrutiny of Social Gatherings" by Millard K. Ives from *Sunday Star-News*, July 28, 2002. Reprinted by permission of Wilmington Star News.

Pages 71–75   "The Holly Pageant" by Lavonne Adams from *Critical Issues in Contemporary Culture*. Ed. Christopher Gould and Ele Byington. Copyright © 1997 by Allyn and Bacon. Reprinted with permission.

Page 83   "Pay Your Own Way! (Then Thank Mom)" by Audrey Rock-Richardson from *Newsweek*, September 11, 2000. All rights reserved. Reprinted by permission.

Page 89   Excerpt from "Free at Last!: The Burgeoning 'Copyleft' Movement Is Reshaping the Idea of Intellectual Property" by Leif Utne in *Utne Reader*, May-June, 2002. Reprinted with permission from *Utne Reader*.

Page 89   Excerpt from "Baffled by Math? Wait 'til I Tell You About Benford's Law" by Kevin Maney in *USA Today*. Copyright © 2000 by *USA Today*.

Pages 90–92   From *Human Development*, 7th Edition, by Diane E. Papalia, Sally Wendkos Olds, and Ruth Duskin Felman. Copyright © 2001 by the McGraw Hill Companies. Reprinted by permission.

Pages 94–95   "Keeping Parents Off Campus" by Judith Shapiro from the *New York Times*, August 22, 2002. Copyright © 2002, the *New York Times*. Reprinted by permission.

Pages 95–96   From *The Sound of Mountain Water* by Wallace Stegner. Copyright © 1969 by Wallace Stegner. Used by permission of Doubleday, a division of Random House, Inc.

Pages 98–99   "Not a Drop to Drink" a review by Timothy Egan of *What You See in Clear Water* by Geoffrey O'Gara in the *New York Times Book Review*, January 21, 2001. Copyright © 2001 by the *New York Times*. Reprinted by permission.

Page 100   Excerpt from *Zen and the Art of Motorcycle Maintenance* by Robert Pirsig. Copyright © 1974 by Robert M. Pirsig. Reprinted by permission of HarperCollins Publishers, Inc.

Pages 104–06   "Learning How to Learn" by Glenn C. Altschuler in the *New York Times*, November 12, 2002. Copyright © 2002 by the *New York Times*. Reprinted by permission.

Pages 106–08   "Adapting to College Life in an Era of Heightened Stress" by Glenn C. Altschuler in the *New York Times*, August 6, 2000. Copyright © 2000 by the *New York Times*. Reprinted by permission.

Pages 110–15   "The Challenge of First-Generation College Students" by Roland Merullo in the *Chronicle of Higher Education*, June 14, 2002. Reprinted by permission of the author.

Pages 115–121   "Class Struggle: Poor, Black and Smart, An Inner-City Teen Tries to Survive at MIT" by Ron Suskind from the *Wall Street Journal*, September 22, 1994. Reprinted by permission from Copyright Clearance Center, Inc.

Pages 121–23   "When a Dad Says Goodbye to His Daughter" by Roger H. Martin in the *New York Times*, August 6, 2002. Reprinted by permission of the author.

Pages 124–26   "Take Your Parents to Work? No Way, Says Adam Markey: His Mom Started a Day for It in Chicago That Causes Joy and Cold Sweats" by Jeffrey Zaslow from the *Wall Street Journal*, June 18, 2002. Reprinted by permission from Copyright Clearance Center, Inc.

Pages 137–39   "Postal System Input Buffer Device" by Joe Robertson and Gil Osborne in *Datamation*, September-October, 1960.

Pages 139–143   "The Etiology and Treatment of Childhood" by Jordan W. Smoller from *Oral Sadism and the Vegetarian Personality*, Ed. Glenn C. Ellenbogen. Copyright © 1986 by Brunner-Routledge. Reprinted by permission of Routledge/Taylor & Francis Books, Inc.

Page 145   Excerpt from a Letter to the Editor by Jeffrey Geibel in the *New York Times Magazine*, April 21, 2002. Reprinted by permission of the author.

Page 145   Excerpt from "Rejected by College of Choice? Relax" by Walter Shapiro in *USA Today*, April 11, 2001. Copyright © 2001 by *USA Today*.

Page 148   Excerpt from "A Destruction Site: The Demolition of an Important Neutra House Kicks Up a Desert Storm" by Brad Dunning in the *New York Times Magazine*, April 21, 2002. Copyright © 2002 by Brad Dunning. Reprinted by permission.

Pages 149–151   "Another Day, Another Indignity" by Barbara Ehrenreich from the *New York Times*, June 30, 2002. Copyright © 2002, the *New York Times*. Reprinted by permission.

Pages 153–54   "Get a Job" a review by Jonathan Miles of *A Working Stiff's Manifesto* by Iain Levison in the *New York Times Book Review*, April 21, 2002. Copyright © 2002 by the *New York Times*. Reprinted by permission.

Pages 154–55   "Before College, Start with a Side Order" by Lisa Black from *Chicago Tribune*, June 20, 2001. Copyright © 2001, Chicago Tribune Company. All rights reserved. Used with permission.

Pages 155–56   "Revisiting the Lessons of Youth Thirty Years Later" by Peter H. King from *Los Angeles Times*, June 28, 2001. Used with permission.

Pages 160–61   Excerpt from "Style: Baltimore Babylon" by Bob Morris in the *New York Times Magazine*, August 6, 2000. Copyright © 2000 by Bob Morris. Reprinted by permission.

Page 161   "Lying in a Hammock at William Duffy's Farm in Pine Island, Minnesota," from *Above the River: The Complete Poems* by James Wright. Copyright © 1990 by Wesleyan University Press. Reprinted by permission.

Page 163   Excerpt from "Advice from the Clueless" by Bob Morris in the *New York Times*, June 30, 2002. Copyright © 2002 by the *New York Times*. Reprinted by permission.

Page 163   Excerpt from "Out of Kilter" a review by George Johnson of *Lucifer's Legacy* by Frank Close in the *New York Times Book Review*, August 6, 2000. Copyright © 2000 by the *New York Times*. Reprinted by permission.

Page 166   Excerpt from "Still Obsessive After All These Years" by Roger Rosenblatt in *Time*, May 20, 2002. Copyright © 2002 by TIME, INC. Reprinted by permission.

Page 166   Excerpt from "Within the Style of No-Style" by Ellis Weiner in the *New York Times*, April 21, 2002. Copyright © 2002 by the *New York Times*. Reprinted by permission.

Page 166   Excerpt from "Ubiquitous Ads Devalue All Messages" by Daniel Akst in the *New York Times*, June 2, 2002. Copyright © 2002 by the *New York Times*. Reprinted by permission.

Pages 171–75   Excerpts from "Girls Just Want to Be Mean: It's Not Just Boys Who Can Bully" by Margaret Talbot from the *New York Times Magazine*, February 24, 2002. Copyright © 2002 by Margaret Talbot.

Pages 177–78   Excerpt from *Real Boys: Rescuing Our Sons from the Myths of Boyhood* by William Pollack. Copyright © 1998 by William Pollack. Used by permission of Random House, Inc.

Pages 179–180   "Vengeance Destroys Faces, and Souls, in Cambodia" by Seth Mydans in the *New York Times*, July 22, 2001. Copyright © 2001 by the *New York Times*. Reprinted by permission.

Pages 181–82   "Murder of Teen Resembles Case That Became Movie 'Boys Don't Cry'" by Yomi S. Wronge and Putsata Reang from *San Jose Mercury News*, October 18, 2002. Used with permission.

Pages 187–88   Excerpt from *Telling It Like It Isn't: Language Misuse and Malpractice and What We Can Do About It* by J. Dan Rothwell. Copyright © 1982, Prentice Hall. Reprinted by permission.

Pages 190–91 "The King of Cool Celebrates a Century" by James Bone in *The Times*, London, July 18, 2002. Copyright © 2002 by Times Newspapers Limited. Reprinted by permission.

Pages 191–92 Excerpt from "On Language: The Concealment of Sex" by William Safire from the *New York Times Magazine*, January 1, 1995. Copyright © 1995 by William Safire. Reprinted by permission.

Pages 192–93 Excerpt from "A Polyandry Solution" by William Safire in the *New York Times*, May 21, 2001. Copyright © 2001 by the *New York Times*. Reprinted by permission.

Page 193 Excerpt from "A Threnody for Street Kids: The Youngest Homeless" by David Levi Strauss in *The Nation*, June 1, 1992. Reprinted with permission from the June 1, 1992 issue of *The Nation*.

Page 195 Excerpt from "The Debates Over Placing Limits on Racist Speech Must Not Ignore the Damage It Does to Its Victims" by Charles R. Lawrence III in the *Chronicle of Higher Education*, October 25, 1989. Reprinted by permission of the author.

Page 197 Excerpt from "Grade Conflation: A Question of Credibility" by Richard Kamber and Mary Biggs in the *Chronicle of Higher Education*, April 12, 2002. Reprinted by permission of the authors.

Pages 198–202 From "America's Secret Culture" by Roland Merullo in *Chronicle of Higher Education*, March 1, 2002. Reprinted by permission of the author.

Page 204 From Elements of Tragedy by Colson Whitehead, et al., from the *New York Times Magazine*, September 23, 2001. Copyright © 2001 by Colson Whitehead. Reprinted by permission.

Pages 210–13 From *Sweet Freedom's Song: 'My Country 'Tis of Thee' and Democracy in America* by Robert James Branham and Stephen J. Hartnett. Copyright © 2002 by Oxford University Press, Inc. Used by permission of Oxford University Press, Inc.

Pages 214–16 "The Anglophile Angle" by Terry Lefton from *Brandweek*, June 6, 1999. Reprinted by permission of VNU Business Media Inc.

Pages 216–18 "Brand Builders: Open for Business" by Gerry Khermouch from *Brandweek*, October 5, 1998. Reprinted by permission of VNU Business Media Inc.

Pages 218–19 "Endangered Species" by Leigh Gallagher from *Forbes*, May 31, 1999. Reprinted by permission of Forbes Magazine, copyright © 2003 Forbes, Inc.

Pages 223–24 "Corporate Ties Squeeze the Life Out of Sports" by Joe Cappo from *Crain's Chicago Business*, April 12, 1999. Reprinted by permission of Reprint Management Services.

Page 224 "Deconstruct This: Thomas Kinkade Paintings" from the *Chronicle of Higher Education*, February 22, 2002. Copyright © 2002, the Chronicle of Higher Education. Reprinted with permission.

Pages 226–28 "Scout's Honor" by E. V. Kontorovich from *National Review*, April 6, 1998. Copyright © 1998 by National Review, Inc., 215 Lexington Avenue, New York, NY 10016. Reprinted by permission.

Pages 228–231 "The Bigoted Scouts of America" by Barbara Dority from *Humanist*, July-August 1998. Reprinted with permission of the author.

Pages 239–246 Excerpt from *Mosquito: The Natural History of Our Most Persistent and Deadly Foe* by Andrew Spielman. Copyright © 2001 by Andrew Spielman. Reprinted by permission of Hyperion.

Pages 248–256 From "Midgley: Saint or Serpent?" by George B. Kauffman in *Chemtech*, December 1989. Reprinted by permission.

Page 259 Excerpt from "Freshman Disorientation" by David Sachs and Peter Thiel in *National Review*, September 25, 1995. Copyright © 1995 by National Review, Inc., 215 Lexington Avenue, New York, NY 10016. Reprinted by permission.

Pages 260–61 "Department of Commitment: Unmarital Bliss" by Rebecca Mead from the *New Yorker*, December 9, 2002. Copyright © 2002 by the New Yorker. Reprinted by permission of The Condé Nast Publications.

Pages 261–62 "Control and Choice: You're in Charge When You Research and Book Your Travel Online" by Leo Mullin in *Sky*, July 2002. Reprinted by permission of Delta Air Lines, Inc.

Page 263 "Maron-1: Robo Helper" from *Weekly Reader*, Edition 4, November 29, 2002. Copyright © 2002 by Weekly Reader Corp. All rights reserved. Reprinted by permission.

Page 263 From "ISS Gyro Fails as Astronauts Bolster Canadian Robotics" by Craig Covault in *Aviation Week and Space Technology*, Vol.156, Issue 24, June 17, 2002.

Pages 265–66 Excerpt from "A Common Syndrome Seldom Discussed" by Jane E. Brody in the *New York Times*, August 8, 2000. Copyright © 2000 by the *New York Times*. Reprinted by permission.

Page 266 "Irritable Bowel Syndrome Linked to Emotional Abuse" from *Tufts University Health and Nutrition Newsletter*, Vol. 18, No. 2, 2000. February 22, 2002. Reprinted with permission, Tufts University Health and Nutrition Letter, tel: 1-800-274-7581 or <www.healthletter.tufts.edu.>

Pages 266–270 "Who Cares, as Long as It's Natural?" by Daniel Akst in the *New York Times*, August 6, 2000. Copyright © 2000 by the *New York Times*. Reprinted by permission.

Pages 271–72 Excerpt from "In Good Company" by Kostya Kennedy in *US Airways Attaché*, February 2001. Reprinted by permission of the author.

Pages 273–74 Excerpt from "In the Dough" by Rebecca Gray in *US Airways Attaché*, February 2001. Reprinted by permission of the author.

Pages 276–77 "The Financial Page: The Talking Cure" by James Surowiecki from the *New Yorker*, December 9, 2002. Copyright © 2002 by the New Yorker. Reprinted by permission of The Condé Nast Publications.

Pages 277–79 "Retailers' Siren Song" by Elizabeth Razzi in *Kiplinger's Personal Finance*, November 2000. Reprinted by permission of PARS International Corp.

Pages 280–81 "'Ernie's Nuns' Are Pointing the Way" by Molly Ivins from *Fort Worth Star-Telegram*, October 21, 1999. Reprinted by permission of the author.

Pages 285–87 "Opening Ourselves to Unconditional Love in Our Relationships with Students" by Sara Hopkins-Powell in the *Chronicle of Higher Education*, June 28, 2002. Reprinted by permission of the author.

Pages 289–91 "Crossing the Fine Line Between Teacher and Therapist" by M. Garrett Bauman from the *Chronicle of Higher Education*, July 12, 2002. Reprinted by permission of the author.

Pages 292–95 "Hollywood Goes to School: Recognizing the Super-Teacher Myth in Film" by Adam Farhi from *Clearing House*, Vol. 72, No. 3, pp. 157–59, 1999. Reprinted with permission of the Helen Dwight Reid Educational Foundation. Published by Heldref Publications, 1319 Eighteenth St. NW, Washington, DC 20036-1802. Copyright © 1999.

Page 353, Fig. 9.1 From the University of North Carolina Coastal Library Consortium catalog, used with permission of the University of North Carolina at Wilmington.

Page 353, Fig. 9.2 From the University of North Carolina Coastal Library Consortium catalog, used with the permission of the University of North Carolina at Wilmington.

Page 359, Fig. 9.3 Used with permission of EBSCO.

Page 360, Fig. 9.4 Used with permission of EBSCO.

Page 361, Fig. 9.5 Used with permission of EBSCO.

Page 363, Fig. 9.7 Used with permission of EBSCO.

Page 364, Fig. 9.8 Used with permission of EBSCO.

Page 365, Fig. 9.9 Used with permission of THE GALE GROUP.

Page 366, Fig. 9.10 Reprinted with the permission of LexisNexis.

Page 367, Fig. 9.11 Netscape website © 2002 Netscape Communications Corporation. Screenshot used with permission.

Page 369, Fig. 9.12 Used with permission of Google.

Page 370, Fig. 9.13 Used with permission of Google.

Pages 371, Fig. 9.14 Used with permission of Google.

Page 501 Excerpt from *The Diversity of Life* by Edward O. Wilson. Copyright © 1992 by Edward O. Wilson. Reprinted by permission of the Belknap Press of Harvard University Press.

Pages 504–05 "The Price of Democracy" by Roger W. Bowen from *The Nation*, September 27, 1999. Reprinted with permission from the September 27, 1999 issue of *The Nation*.

Pages 507–08 "Clones Threaten Human Future" by Bill McKibben from *Wilmington Morning Star*, January 10, 2003. Reprinted by permission of the author.

Pages 510–13 "Workplace Worrywarts" by Michelle Cottle from *New Republic*, October 25, 1999. Reprinted with permission.

Pages 520–21 "Why Not Human Cloning?" by Michael Shermer from *Wilmington Morning Star*, January 10, 2003. Reprinted by permission of the author.

PHOTOS

Page 83 Danny La

Page 492 Courtesy of Cruise West

Page 493 Courtesy of Save America's Forests, <www.SaveAmericasForests.org>

Page 494 Courtesy of The Home Depot

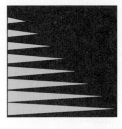

Index

Parenthetical Notes (MLA Style): Quick Reference Guide

Detailed information on parenthetical notes can be found on pages 560–575.

PURPOSE

Use a note to identify the specific source location for a specific idea, piece of information, or quotation in your paper.

FORMAT

Give the specific page reference, preceded by the *least* amount of information needed to identify the source in your list of works cited.

PLACEMENT

Place the note following the passage.

MODEL ENTRIES

Standard Reference

Give the author and page(s):

    A fear of thunder is common among dogs (Digby 237).

Author Identified in the Passage

Omit the author's name in the note:

    Digby noted that dogs are often terrified of thunder (237).

An Anonymous Work (Unidentified Author)

Use the first word or two from the title:

    ("An Infant's" 22)

A Work with Two or Three Authors

    (Reid, Forrestal, and Cook 48-49)

A Work with More Than Three Authors

    (Courtois et al. 112)

Two or More Works by the Same Author

Add the first word(s) from the title:

    (Asimov, Adding 240-43)
    (Asimov, "Happy" 68)

Two Authors with the Same Last Name

Include the authors' first names:

    (George Eliot 459)
    (T. S. Eliot 44)

A Multivolume Work

The volume number precedes the page number(s):

    (Agus 2: 59)

Exception: Omit the volume number if only one volume is identified in your list of works cited:

    (Agus 59)